Kinishba Lost and Found: Mid-Century Excavations and Contemporary Perspectives

Edited by
John R. Welch

With Contributions by:
Mark T. Altaha, Richard Ciolek-Torello, T. J. Ferguson,
Carl D. Halbirt, Nicholas C. Laluk, Patrick D. Lyons,
J. Jefferson Reid, Charles R. Riggs, James B. Shaeffer,
Margaret M. Shaeffer, Daniela Triadan, John R. Welch

Arizona State Museum
THE UNIVERSITY OF ARIZONA.

Arizona State Museum Archaeological Series 206

Arizona State Museum
The University of Arizona
Tucson, Arizona 85721-0026
Copyright © 2013 by the Arizona Board of Regents
All rights reserved.
Printed in the United States of America

ISBN (paper): 978-1-889747-92-7
Library of Congress Control Number: 2013939206

ARIZONA STATE MUSEUM ARCHAEOLOGICAL SERIES

General Editor: Richard C. Lange
Technical Editors: Alicia M. Vega

The *Archaeological Series* of the Arizona State Museum, The University of Arizona, publishes the results of research in archaeology and related disciplines conducted in the Greater Southwest. Original, monograph-length manuscripts are considered for publication, provided they deal with appropriate subject matter. Information regarding procedures or manuscript submission and review is given under Research Publications on the Arizona State Museum website: *www.statemuseum.arizona.edu/research/pubs*. Information may be also obtained from the General Editor, *Archaeological Series*, Arizona State Museum, P.O. Box 210026, The University of Arizona, Tucson, Arizona, 85721-0026; Email: langer@email.arizona.edu. Electronic publications and previous volumes in the Arizona State Museum Library or available from the University of Arizona Press are listed on the website noted above. Print-on-demand versions of the latest Arizona State Museum Archaeological Series may be obtained from several booksellers on-line.

The Arizona State Museum *Archaeological Series* is grateful to the many donors and supporters who continue to make this publication possible.

Covers: Front: View of Kinishba reconstructed, 1941. Tad Nichols photographer (cropped from original), courtesy Arizona State Museum.   Back: Figure 3.3 from this volume.

Editor's Dedication

To

David A. Gregory (1949-2010),
a generous friend and exceptional archaeologist,

and to

Arthur Alchesay Guenther (1923-2012),
who worked with Dean Cummings at Kinishba
and conveyed Cummings's flame of enthusiasm to so many.

Contents

Contents	v
List of Figures	ix
List of Tables	xi
Acknowledgments	xii
Chapter 1: Un-Silencing Kinishba *by John R. Welch*	1
Volume Purposes	3
Personal Commitments and Professional Ethics in Knowledge Creation	4
Editing the Shaeffer Reports	7
Volume Scope and Content	10
Chapter 2: Episodes in Kinishba's Cultural and Management Histories *by John R. Welch*	13
Regional Cultural History and Local Periods of Rapid Change	13
Preceramic Traditions	13
Ceramic Traditions	15
Kinishba on the Cusp of History	18
Cummings and Kinishba	19
The Shaeffers at Kinishba	20
Site Preservation and Museum Management	21
Post-1939 Excavations and Resulting Collections	23
Notes on Kinishba Collections and Management Following the Shaeffers	26
Chapter 3: The Excavation of Group VI, Ruins of a Small House Unit	
by James B. Shaeffer and Margaret M. Shaeffer	31
Environment	31
Culture and Research History	32
Plan of the Site	33
The Plan and Building Phases of Group VI	34
Material Culture	38
Fireboxes	38
Flagged (Paved with Flagstone) Areas	38
Mealing Bins	40
Covers	40
Stone Axes	40
Choppers	40
Flints (chipped stone bifaces)	41
Hammerstones	41
Handstones	41
Two-Handed Manos	41
Metates	41
Polishing Stones	42
Arrow Shaft Polishers/Straighteners	42
Rubbing Stones	43
Deer Bone Awls	43
Shell	43
Paint	43
Turqoise	43
Fetishes and Other Exotics	44
Painted Deer Jaw Bone	44
Quartz Crystals	44

Stalagmite	44
Stone Ball	44
Colored Stones	44
Ceramics	44
Summary and Conclusions	46

Chapter 4: The Excavation of the Group I Great Kiva *by James B. Shaeffer and Margaret M. Shaeffer* — 51

The Great Kiva	56
The Smaller Earthen Kivas	69
Kiva A	71
Kiva B	74
Kiva C	75
Kiva D	77
Kiva E	78
Ceramic Stratigraphy	79
Age of the Kivas	83
Factual Summary	83
Interpretation	85
Acknowledgments	89

Chapter 5: Before Kinishba: Two Late Pit House Period Settlements Near Fort Apache *by Richard Ciolek-Torello and Carl D. Halbirt* — 91

Background	91
The Project	92
Buh bi laá Village	94
Architecture, Mortuary, and Extramural Features	94
House Type 1	95
House Type 2	99
House Type 3	99
Site Structure	104
Tree-Ring Dates	105
Ceramics and Other Artifacts	107
Botanical and Faunal Remains	109
East Fork Village	109
Summary and Conclusions	114
Regional Interaction	114
Primary Cremations in Central Arizona	115
Hohokam Expansion from the Desert to the Mountains	117
Final Thoughts on the Hohokam Connection	119
Acknowledgments	121

Chapter 6: A Grasshopper Architectural Perspective on Kinishba *by Charles R. Riggs* — 123

The Importance of Architecture	124
Comparative Description	125
Grasshopper Pueblo	126
Community Layout	129
Core vs. Outliers	130
Domestic Architecture and Room Use	132
Early Abandoned Rooms	133
The Two- or Three-Story Room Problem and its Implications for Room Function	133
Room Size and Community Size	134
Room Function and Households	136

Ceremonial Architecture	138
The Great Kiva	140
Conclusion	141
Chapter 7: "By their fruits ye shall know them" The Pottery of Kinishba Revisited	
by Patrick D. Lyons	145
Previous Research on the Kinishba Ceramic Assemblage	145
Research During the 1930s	146
Research from 1960 to 1970	149
Research During the 1990s and the Early 2000s	150
Reanalysis of Kinishba Ceramics	152
Results of the Reanalysis	153
Roosevelt Red Ware	153
Recently Defined Types	154
Roosevelt Red Ware Seriation	154
Assigning an Absolute Date Range	158
Dating Post-Cliff Polychrome Types	159
The Roosevelt Red Ware Whole Vessel Assemblage	160
The Roosevelt Red Ware Sherd Assemblage	160
White Mountain Red Ware	161
The White Mountain Red Ware Sherd Assemblage	164
Cibola White Ware	165
The Cibola White Ware Sherd Assemblage	165
Mogollon Brown Ware Painted Types	165
Indeterminate Decorated	165
White-on-red	166
Maverick Mountain Series	168
The Maverick Mountain Series Whole Vessel Assemblage	170
The Maverick Mountain Series Sherd Assemblage	170
Tusayan White Ware	170
The Tusayan White Ware Sherd Collection	173
Zuni Glaze Ware	174
Jeddito Yellow Ware	174
Red Ware	174
Kinishba Red	174
Other Red Ware Types	175
Brown Ware	175
Corrugated Pottery	178
Mogollon Brown Ware Utility Pottery	178
Wares and Types Represented in the Sherd Assemblage Only	179
Chronology	179
Conclusion: Knishba Pottery in Regional Conext	180
The Kayenta Diaspora	181
Salado as the Kayenta in Diaspora	182
The Salado Feasting Tradition	183
Roosevelt Red Ware Bowl Size	183
Roosevelt Red Ware Bowl Shape	184
Decorative Field and Decorative Focus	184
Why Feasting?	184
Comparing Feasting Traditions	185
Future Research	185
Acknowledgments	188

Chapter 8: Compositional and Distributional Analyses of Some Fourteenth Century Ceramics from Kinishba Pueblo: Implications for Pottery Production and Migration
    by Daniela Triadan   209
        Previous Research   210
        The Whole Vessel Assemblage   211
            White Mountain Red Ware   213
            Kinishba Polychrome   214
            Kinishba Red   215
        Distributions of Whole and Reconstructible Vessels   217
            Distribution of Vessels from Room Floors and Roofs   217
            Distribution of Vessels in Burials   220
            On-site Pottery Manufacture at Kinishba   225
        Compositional Analyses of Kinishba Ceramics   226
            Instrumental Neutron Activation Analysis   226
            Petrography   228
        Conclusions   230
        Acknowledgments   234

Chapter 9: The Kinishba Boundary Survey *by John R. Welch, Nicholas C. Laluk, and Mark T. Altaha*   243
    Grasshopper Settlement   245
    Kinishba Settlement   248
    Sites Within a One-mile Perimeter of Grasshopper and Kinishba   249
    Sites with 25 or More Rooms   252
    Discussion and Conclusion   253
        Site Visibility and Agricultural Intensification   253
        National Historic Landmark Boundary Validity   254
        Social Centrality and Agricultural Sustainability   255
        Interrregional Tensions   258
    Research and Management Recommendations   258

Chapter 10: Apache, Hopi and Zuni Perspectives on Kinishba History and Stewardship
    by John R. Welch and T. J. Ferguson   261
    White Mountain Apache Tribe Heritage Stewardship and Repatriation   263
    NAGPRA Mandates and Repatriation Realities   266
    Putting Patria Back into Repatriation: Project Methods   268
    Hopi Cultural Affiliation wth Kinishba   269
    Zuni Cultural Affiliation with Kinishba   274
    Apache Perspectives on Kinishba Cultural Affiliation   277
    Translating Wisdom into Policy and Practice   283
        General Stewardship Recommendations   283
        Repatriation Policy and Action Recommendations   285
        Kinishba Stewardship Recommendations   286
    Conclusion: Reclaiming Kinishba   287
    Acknowledgments   287

Chapter 11: Encounters with Kinishba: A Grasshopper Perspective *by J. Jefferson Reid*   289
    Kinishba: Classroom and Showroom   289
    A Framework For Future Critiques   292
    Archaeology and the White Mountain Apache   293

References Cited   295

Figures

1.1.	The Mogollon Rim region and the locations of sites and regions discussed in this volume	2
2.1.	Kinishba Ruins, showing major room groups	17
2.2.	Byron Cummings at Kinishba, circa 1940	21
2.3.	The remains of the Kinishba Museum and curator's quarters, 2003	25
2.4.	James B. "Jack" Shaeffer at the Stuhr Museum of the Prairie Pioneer, circa 1969	27
3.1.	Plan view map of Ruins Group VI	34
3.2.	Tad Nichols and other members of Cummings' excavation crew clearing Group I masonry walls at Kinishba, circa 1936	36
3.3.	Some sources of ceramic design styles found at Kinishba	48
4.1.	Oblique southerly aerial view of Group I excavations and rebuilding, circa 1936	52
4.2.	The Great Kiva plan map showing features and posts	55
4.3.	Cross-section of Patio A and Patio B, Group I	56
4.4.	Courtyard, showing depths of foundations for walls of rooms surrounding Patio A and Patio B	57
4.5.	Southerly view along the west side of the courtyard during Patio A clearing, circa 1934	59
4.6.	Pole-masonry kiva in Patio B during rebuilding, circa 1936	59
4.7.	Great Kiva roof support system	61
4.8.	Rendition of the southern portion of the Great Kiva	61
4.9.	Southerly view of Patio A, with the Great Kiva's south pillar base or shrine, circa 1932	63
4.10.	Great Kiva north pillar base (F2), 1948	64
4.11.	Post hole and charred Juniper remnant of Post 12 (P12)	65
4.12.	Post 10 post hole (P10) with ash removed	65
4.13.	Reinforced base of remnant of Post 9 (P9)	66
4.14.	Artifacts associated with Post 6 (P6) at floor level of the Great Kiva	67
4.15.	Sub-floor caches and holes in southeast portion of Great Kiva	69
4.16.	Remains of a possible stone-lined cache (F4)	70
4.17.	Northerly view of five structures found below the Great Kiva, Group I	70
4.18.	Kiva A	71
4.19.	Kiva B ventilator (two sides)	73
4.20.	Kiva B	75
4.21.	Kiva C	76
4.22.	Kiva D	77
4.23.	Plan view of Patio A subsurface features	80
4.24.	General view of Kiva E	80
4.25.	Rectangular cover and unshaped slab from ventilator, Kiva E	81
4.26.	Triangular slab and circular stone cover from ventilator, Kiva E	81
5.1.	Plan view of Buh bi laá Village	97
5.2.	Plan view and cross-sections of House 14a, House Cluster B, Buh bi laá Village	98
5.3.	Plan view and cross-sections of House 7asu, House Cluster B, Buh bi laá Village	100
5.4.	Remains of a possible jacal structure and nearby cremation pits and extramural features	103
5.5.	Plan view of excavated portion of East Fork Village	110
5.6.	Plan view and cross-sections of House 1, East Fork Village	110
5.7.	House 2 at East Fork Village, view north	111
5.8.	Plan view and cross-sections of House 3, East Fork Village	112
5.9.	House 3 at East Fork Village, view northeast	112
5.10.	House 4 at East Fork Village, view southeast	113
5.11.	Map of east central Arizona and west central New Mexico showing locations of sites and archaeological regions mentioned in text	116
6.1.	Comparative layout of three Pueblo IV Period village sites in east-central Arizona	127
6.2.	Plan view map of Kinishba room Groups I and II	131

7.1.	Late Roosevelt Red Ware types	155
7.2.	Map showing locations of places mentioned in the text and the spatial distributions of Gila and Tonto Polychrome	156
7.3.	Map showing the spatial distributions of Gila and Tonto Polychrome	157
7.4.	A Showlow Glaze-on-white jar from Kinishba	162
7.5.	The type specimens of Kinishba Polychrome	163
7.6.	Kinishba White-on-red bowl from Kinishba	167
7.7.	Kinishba White-on-red jar bearing decoration reminiscent of Kechipawan Polychrome	167
7.8.	Maverick Mountain Series vessels from Kinishba: Maverick Mountain Polychrome jars	171
7.9.	Tusayan White Ware jars from Kinishba	172
7.10.	Babe-in-cradle effigy fragments from Kinishba	173
7.11.	Unusual Kinishba Red vessel forms	176
7.12.	Perforated plate fragments from Kinishba	177
7.13.	Distribution of sites that have yielded perforated plates	178
8.1.	Light-paste Fourmile Polychrome bowl, ASM A-33,397	213
8.2.	Kinishba Polychrome bowl, ASM A-33,530	214
8.3.	Exterior (left) and interior (right) views of a sherd from a Kinishba Polychrome/Fourmile Polychrome hybrid bowl	215
8.4.	Kinishba Red bowl, ASM A-33,386	216
8.5.	Quantity of vessels on room floors by ware or type	220
8.6.	Quantity of vessels in burials by ware or type	222
8.7.	Bivariate plot of principal component scores, showing principal components 1 and 2 of the four light-paste White Mountain Red Ware groups	227
8.8.	Bivariate plot of principal component scores, showing principal components 1 and 3 of the four light-paste White Mountain Red Ware groups	228
8.9.	Bivariate plot of principal component scores, showing principal components 1 and 2 of the three large light-paste White Mountain Red Ware groups and groups of ceramics produced locally at Grasshopper, Point of Pines and Kinishba	229
9.1.	The Kinishba and Grasshopper regions, including schematic locations for all large Pueblo sites located within about 10 miles of Grasshopper and Kinishba	247
9.2.	Sites in the Kinishba vicinity	250
10.1.	White Mountain Apache, San Carlos Apache, Hopi, and Zuni tribal lands in eastern Arizona	262
10.2.	Locations for fieldwork completed for the cultural affiliation project, White Mountain Apache Tribe lands	264
10.3.	Hopi research team stands around the remains of the shrine in the Kinishba plaza	272
10.4.	Leigh Kuwanwisiwma and John Welch discuss Muntsotsokpi, as Lee Wayne Lomayestewa and Ramon Riley inspect the dry waterfall	272
10.5.	Mongtsomo (Owl Point) on the horizon west of Kinishba	273
10.6.	White Mountain Apache tribal lands superimposed on the distribution of Western Apache groups and bands circa 1850	279
10.7.	Traditional migrations of Apache clans	282

Tables

2.1.	Concordance of Archaeological Chronologies for the Eastern Arizona Uplands	14
3.1.	Selections from J.B. Shaeffer's Group VI Excavation Notes	35
3.2.	Items in Group VI Rooms	39
3.3.	Shaft Straighteners in Group VI Rooms	42
3.4.	Rubbing Stones in Group VI Rooms	43
3.5.	Summary of Element and Trait Occurrences in Group VI Rooms	45
3.6.	Ceramic Ware Occurrence in the Aggregated Group VI Assemblage	45
3.7.	Comparison of Element and Trait Occurrences in Group VI and Group I	47
4.1.	Post, Post Hole, Pillar Base, and Cache Features Identified in the Great Kiva Excavations	53
4.2.	Features Identified in the Earthen Wall Kiva Excavations	62
5.1.	Summary of Pit House Characteristics	96
5.2.	Tree-Ring Dates From Bu Bi Laá and East Fork Villages	106
5.3.	Frequencies of Hohokam Plainware and Hohokam Buffware from Selected Mogollon Pit House Villages with Hohokam Ceramics	108
6.1.	Architectural Characteristics and Behavioral Correlates	125
6.2.	Comparison of Grasshopper's East and West Villages	128
6.3.	Estimated Number of Rooms for Kinishba's Seven Mapped Room Blocks	135
6.4.	Summary of Key Architectural Characteristics and Suggestions for Future Research	143
7.1.	White Mountain Red Ware Vessels from Kinishba	189
7.2.	Roosevelt Red Ware Vessels from Kinishba	190
7.3.	Cibicue Polychrome Vessels from Kinishba	190
7.4.	Roosevelt Red Ware Vessels from Kinishba	190
7.5.	Pinedale Black-on-white Vessels from Kinishba	190
7.6.	Whole or Reconstructible Vessels from Kinishba	191
7.7.	The Kinishba Whole and Reconstructible Vessel Assemblage	195
7.8.	Roosevelt Red Ware Types, Dates, Summary Descriptions, and References	199
7.9.	Vessel Forms Exhibited by the Kinishba Whole and Reconstructible Vessels	201
7.10.	Dates Assigned to Pottery Types Represented in the Kinishba Vessel or Sherd Assemblages	205
7.11.	Sources of Wares and Types Recovered from Kinishba	208
7.12.	Mean Maximum Diameter of Roosevelt Red Ware Bowls by Type	208
8.1.	Vessels from Kinishba in Arizona State Museum Collections	212
8.2.	Kinishba Polychrome Sherds Identified in Surface Collections	216
8.3.	Rooms Excavated at Kinishba Pueblo	217
8.4.	Reconstructible and Partial Vessels on Room Floors and Roofs	219
8.5.	Kinishba Burials	222
8.6.	Vessels in Burials	223
8.7.	Burials with Vessels	224
8.8.	Kinishba Ceramic Samples Analyzed by INAA and Petrography	236
9.1.	Sites within One Mile of Grasshopper Ruins	246
9.2.	Sites within One Mile of Kinishba Ruins	247
9.3.	Pueblos with 25 or More Rooms in the Grasshopper Region	249
9.4.	Pueblos with 25 or More Rooms in the Kinishba Region	257
10.1.	Western Apache groups	280

Volume Acknowledgments

I am gratified and grateful for assistance and support received from numerous elders, colleagues and students. Arthur Guenther, Alexander Lindsay, William Neil Smith, Raymond Thompson, and Antony Cooley deserve particular recognition for sharing their memories and insights concerning the places, people, and contexts involved in the Shaeffers' work. Alan Ferg collaborated in the transfer of the source documents from the National Park Service Western Archaeological and Conservation Center to the University of Arizona's Arizona State Museum Archives and lent generous and expert assistance to the work in many other ways. Copies or originals of all primary source documents referred to in this volume are available in the Arizona State Museum Archives. Sarah Baldry, Ryan Dickie, Robyn Ewing, Jami Macarty, Ian Song and Dan Todd assisted in the conversion of typescript texts and tables into digital files. Richard Ciolek-Torrello, Patrick Lyons, Jeff Reid, Chuck Riggs, Daniela Triadan and Stephanie Whittlesey responded favorably to preliminary requests to contribute to the volume. Dave Gregory, Barbara Mills, and Dave Wilcox provided good advice for employing the project to catalyze complementary contributions to our regional knowledge. Joe Watkins worked with personnel at the University of Oklahoma and the Southern Plains Indian Museum in a search, ultimately unsuccessful, for documents, photographs, and artifacts relating to the Shaeffers' work at Kinishba. Jessica Waite at the Stuhr Museum of the Prairie Pioneer provided information on the Shaeffers' post-Kinishba careers and gave permission to use the photograph of Jim Shaeffer in Chapter 2. Beth Grindell, Rich Lange, Chuck Adams, Patrick Lyons, John McClelland, Michael Jacobs, Michael Brescia and other ASM colleagues supported the project in important ways. Chuck Riggs, Craig Rust, and Allen Denoyer updated and customized several of the figures used here. I am especially indebted to the venerable Roy Carlson and the two anonymous peer reviewers, whose thoughtful critiques made this a better volume. Finally, and most emphatically, I thank those official representatives and members of the White Mountain Apache Tribe, the Hopi Tribe, and Zuni Pueblo who have so graciously supported and assisted research, preservation, and rehabilitation efforts at lovely Kinishba.

Chapter 1
Un-Silencing Kinishba

John R. Welch

This volume gives voice to both new and long-muffled perspectives on Kinishba. Known in Hopi oral traditions as *Ma'öp'ovi* ("High Place of Snakeweed") and by Apaches as *kį dałbaa* ("brown house"), Kinishba Ruins National Historic Landmark is the sprawling remains of a plaza-focused village occupied from about A.D. 1200 into the 1400s. Located just west of Fort Apache and Whiteriver, on White Mountain Apache Tribe lands in the Mogollon Rim region of east-central Arizona, the site sits in a grassy, conifer-fringed valley that drains into the White River (Figure 1.1). Beginning in 1931, Byron Cummings adopted an anglicized version of the Apache place name and dedicated most of the last two decades of his long academic career to the site (Bostwick 2006). He supervised students and local Apache workers in excavating about 240 of Kinishba's approximately 600 rooms, in rebuilding about half of those excavated, and in launching a site museum that ultimately withered and foundered (Welch 2007a,b,c). Withdrawal in the 1950s of archaeologists, museum professionals, and the Bureau of Indian Affairs left Kinishba's protection and management to the White Mountain Apache Tribe. In the 1990s the tribal council directed its Historic Preservation Office and the non-profit Fort Apache Heritage Foundation to work with local Apache elders and with the Hopi Tribe and Zuni Pueblo. Tribal leaders were determined to provide culturally appropriate site stewardship and to facilitate Kinishba's preservation in conjunction with the preservation and redevelopment of the Fort Apache and Theodore Roosevelt School historic district (Welch 2000, 2007a; Welch and Ferguson 2007, Chapter 10; Welch and Brauchli 2010).

Beyond this basic historical outline, Kinishba is the site nobody really knows. The ruin ranks among the most extensively excavated, rebuilt and visited, yet least analyzed or published sites in the American Southwest. Neither personal and institutional memories nor accessible documentation are available to guide inquiries into what archaeologists did at Kinishba, why they did it, or precisely what they found. Many archaeologists and thousands of visitors have paused and pondered the rubble of Cummings's swan song as it falls again into ruin (see Kingsolver 1990). But no archaeologist alive in the twenty-first century has conducted on-site research beyond preservation planning, surface mapping, and inventory surveying within a one mile radius of the site (Laluk and Altaha 2004; Mills et al 2008; Welch 2007a; Welch et al., Chapter 9). Most archaeologists with interests linked to Kinishba have accepted the notion that Cummings's thin monograph and progress reports (Cummings 1931, 1932, 1933, 1934, 1935a, 1935b, 1935c, 1938, 1940), along with a cluster of student reports and theses (e.g., Baldwin 1934, 1935a, 1935b, 1937, 1938a, 1938b, 1939, 1941; Jones 1935; Mott 1936) are all that is available or likely to become available to learn about what happened in and around Kinishba during times

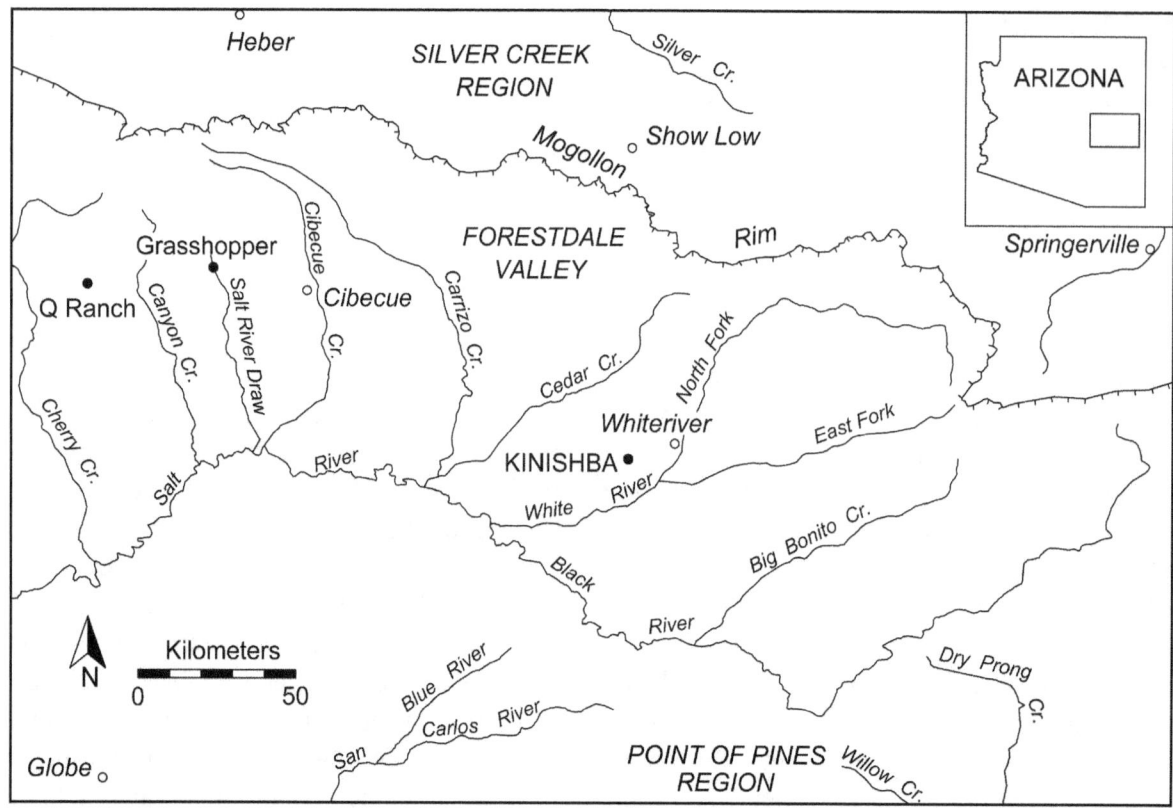

Figure 1.1. The Mogollon Rim region and the locations of sites and regions discussed in this volume (Charles R. Riggs).

beyond memory. It seems most archaeologists assumed that additional knowledge concerning Kinishba's archaeological record would have to await scholars possessing tenacities and industries sufficient to create knowledge from the incomplete and chaotic excavation records and collections scattered in the wake of Cummings's quixotic Kinishba quest. This volume is a step in that direction. The chapters assembled here report modest progress toward bringing Kinishba back into discussions concerning Southwestern archaeology and White Mountain Apache cultural heritage stewardship.

Recent archival studies (Bostwick 2006; Welch 2007a,b,c; see also Reid and Whittlesey 1989; Thompson 2005) have laid foundations for understanding what happened at Kinishba in the twentieth century. It is now clear that Cummings envisioned Kinishba as a living museum and eventual U.S. National Park Service monument. We now know Cummings vigorously pursued these visions well in to his eighties, laboring to create a special place that would inspire youthful imaginations, boost visitor appreciation for American Indians and archaeology, and catalyze regional growth in what we today refer to as heritage tourism (Bostwick 2006; Reid and Whittlesey 2005; Welch 2007a,b,c).

Documentary research in the archives of the Arizona State Museum, where most of the unpublished records referenced in this volume are stored, have also debunked common assumptions about Kinishba. First, contrary to widespread notions that Cummings somehow pulled the project together without substantial and sustained financial assistance or major partners, it turns out that Kinishba's management history includes significant administrative and financial contributions to investigation, administration, and preservation from the U.S. Bureau of Indian Affairs (Welch 2007a). Second, and of greater importance here, neither research nor facility maintenance came to an end when Cummings faded from the Kinishba scene in the mid-1940s (see also Baxter et al. 1997).

The new facts and perspectives relating to Kinishba's ancient and twentieth century histories center on James Ball Shaeffer and Margaret Whiting Murry Shaeffer. Correspondence and government documents demonstrate that, in 1946, the Bureau of Indian Affairs, with Cummings's blessing, hired the Shaeffers to serve as Cummings's successors. In addition to a series of noteworthy photographs made at and around Kinishba by another husband-and-wife team, Esther Henderson and Chuck Abbott (Welch 2007b), the documentary research turned up clear evidence for major excavations and architectural preservation treatments conducted by the Shaeffers at Kinishba.

Jim and Margaret Shaeffer have been previously known to Arizona archaeologists primarily on the basis of Margaret's masters thesis on Kinishba ceramics (Murry 1937), Jim's seldom-cited Columbia University dissertation (Shaeffer 1954), and their Kinishba visitor guide (Shaeffer and Shaeffer 1956). Shortly before Margaret and Jim passed away in 2004 (*Pueblo Chieftain* 2004), however, they made a final contribution. Believing that Cummings's most ardent wish had come true—that Kinishba had become a national monument under the protection of the U.S. National Park Service—Jim sent a package of vintage Kinishba documents and ephemera to the Park Service. Now curated at Arizona State Museum, the documents substantiate the Shaeffers' extensive and complex involvement with Kinishba's archaeology, architecture, and museum management. Most notably, the records include multiple drafts and supporting materials relating to two major excavations that Jim directed beginning in 1947 and continuing into at least early 1949. The documents also confirm that Margaret was a full partner in all of the Shaeffers' Kinishba efforts, including the excavation projects.

VOLUME PURPOSES

Employing the Shaeffers' two excavation reports as centerpieces and catalysts, this volume serves several related purposes. Persistent gaps between what we know about Kinishba and what we would like to know, together with the lack of current plans for additional field studies at Kinishba and a vague interest in making the Shaeffer reports available, grew gradually into a sense of responsibility. Accordingly, the volume's first purpose is to provide for the long-delayed reporting of the Shaeffers' substantial excavations in the Great Kiva (1949; Chapter 3) and Group VI room block (1951; Chapter 4). The volume thus offers the only systematic presentations of excavation findings at this important site. Although the two manuscripts fall well short of twenty-first century reporting standards, they nonetheless complement previously published works on Kinishba. More specifically, the reports and the chapters presented here add substance and depth to Cummings's (1940) breezy synthetic monograph and boost our abilities to understand Kinishba's archaeological record and cultural history in relation to neighboring sites in the Forestdale, Grasshopper, and Q Ranch regions (see Chapters 5–11).

The second purpose, pursued in Chapter 2, is to place the Shaeffers' excavations in the context of developments in Kinishba's use and management during the twentieth century. Archaeologists continue to come to terms with personal, historical, and institutional factors affecting what, where, how and with whom we work, as well as the consequences—beneficial and otherwise—of our studies (e.g., Reid and Whittlesey 2010; Welch et al. 2011). It is thus important to examine the admittedly limited evidence available regarding the circumstances associated with the Shaeffers' excavations and how their work was received.

The volume's third and final intended purpose—to optimize the values of the Shaeffer reports and use them as pretext and point of comparative departure for related studies and management initiatives—took shape through conversations with many colleagues. These discussions centered on a constructive sense of opportunity to add breadth and context to the Shaeffers' nearly lost work. My exhortative notes to prospective contributors referred to this collaboration as making do with limited data qualities and quantities by "squeezing the Kinishba lemon." The project team's intentions ultimately became fixed on employing the Shaeffers' "orphaned" reports as a foundation for research to create and mobilize new knowledge and perspectives relating to Kinishba. The "salvage archival archaeology" represented here should facilitate the expansion of ongoing stewardship partnerships and engender additional study, outreach, preservation work, and publication, at Kinishba and related sites. The volume contributors have gone well beyond basic obligations, admirably crafting and integrating diverse knowledge while highlighting new perspectives on Kinishba's various values and the Shaeffers' energetic efforts.

The three broad purposes guiding this volume are particularly worthy in light of the disconnection between, on the one hand, Kinishba's undeniable importance in understanding what happened along the eastern Mogollon Rim from about A.D. 1200 to about 1400 and, on the other, the small amount known about the site's archaeological record. With this issue at the fore, this introduction now considers intellectual and ethical mandates to publish the results of archaeological investigations, especially excavations and other forms of destructive analysis. Following the discussion of ethical mandates to carry forward and share knowledge from the past—in this case by assuring the wide availability of archaeological studies—I review editorial decisions made in presenting the work and briefly describe each of the volume's chapters.

Personal Commitments and Professional Ethics in Knowledge Creation

Perhaps because I worked for many years as a preservation archaeologist on and around White Mountain Apache lands, I feel a weighty sense of responsibility generally linked to archaeology and specifically tied to sites on White Mountain Apache lands. I have benefitted personally and professionally from a long association with the region's archaeology and archaeologists and have a particular sense of opportunity and duty to add to knowledge of Kinishba. During two decades spent, among other things, planning and leading preservation treatments, conducting innumerable site tours, and listening to people with very different understandings and interests linked to Kinishba, I developed a natural affection for the place and the people who care about it.

Commitments to making Kinishba accessible, presentable, and useful to Hopi and Zuni descendants, to Apache stewards, and to fellow archaeologists motivated my efforts to maximize the benefits of work done at Kinishba by my professional forbears and benefactors (Welch in Nicholas et al. 2007). Pursuing these commitments is based in part on individual obligations to create full and impartial records of the past, the ultimate rationale for publishing this volume. Setting personal motivations aside, both professional mandates and disciplinary desiderata guide archaeologists' obligations. In *Silencing the Past: Power and the Production of History*, Michel-Rolph Trouillot (1995) examines history creation, the often complicated link between what happened in the past and what knowledge we have of what happened. Trouillot points out that we alternately silence or amplify elements of the past as we use or ignore, save or discard, and modify, declaim or dispense with knowledge, items, places and institutions that convey ideas and traditions across generations. The cumulative effects of such silencing and amplifying choices, although proximally individual, ultimately define and determine history, both in the sense of that which actually happened and that for which we have evidence (Trouillot 1995; Welch et al. 2011).

Trouillot's identification of the various types of "silencing" that commonly intervene in efforts to learn about and report what happened are at least as relevant to archaeologists as they are to historians and other heritage professionals. At a minimum, silencing can and does occur in or through the following processes:

> Fact Creation—which events get described, recorded, or remembered in a manner that allows them to transcend the time of their occurrence?
>
> Fact Compilation—what choices are made, accidents occur, and priorities change in the establishment and management of archives and other fact storehouses?
>
> Fact Retrieval—how, why, and when do narrators select facts for consideration and use?
>
> Fact Publication—how and why do some narratives persist while others are forgotten or lost?

The corpus of the recorded or remembered past will, of course, vary substantially for historians, critical readers, general public, indigenous communities, and other interested parties. As archaeologists well know, only a very small subset of what happened becomes part of the final story of what is said to have happened. Only a fraction of human behavior is registered in the archaeological record; only a fraction of that record has been or ever will be systematically studied; and only a fraction of those studies will result in inferences about the past that are plausible, published, and, last but not least, read. Possibly because of the tremendous odds against the archaeological retrieval and mobilization of any one fact about the past, archaeologists understand, perhaps more profoundly than historians, that clear windows into the past are rare indeed. The unique, fragmentary, and often disturbed storehouses that are our data sources—archaeological records—can typically be consulted but once in their entirety. Unlike other historical and social modes of inquiry, archaeology in its most widely recognized form of digging is an emphatically extractive and consumptive pursuit. This truth distinguishes archaeology not only from history, but also from laboratory and other experimental sciences, where replication is a foundation for confidence in making inferences and inspiring follow-up research.

For all of these reasons, excavators assume particularly ponderous intellectual and ethical burdens when we remove and study elements of the archaeological record. Archaeologists have not always met our professional obligations. Among archaeology's "claims to shame" is the truth that, until recently, common sense mandates relating to both careful excavations and scrupulous record keeping and reporting were not taken seriously by many professionals (Fagan 1995). I would wager that, as of 2013, the practicing professional archaeologists who have thoroughly recorded and adequately interpreted and published every element of every archaeological record they have "consumed" are in the minority. On the other hand, I am confident that this minority is growing and will soon be in the majority. The antiquarian fascination with exploration and collection has yet to be reconciled with the sobering reality that in many regions, especially metropolitan areas, we are running out of the high integrity archaeological sites that are "our" primary data sources. These are, obviously, often the same places held dear, even sacred by descendant communities, groups of people archaeologists generally both admire and rely upon as collaborators in research and preservation projects (Zimmerman 2006).

Our collective disciplinary history of voracious consumption (and incomplete analytic and interpretive digestion) is now generally counterbalanced by special ethical obligations. These are reinforced and institutionalized in professional codes requiring competent uses of the archaeological record and the compilation, preservation, and disposition of documentary and graphic records and reports on all extractive and consumptive analyses, especially excavations (see Lynott and Wylie 1995; Vitelli and Colwell-Chanthaphonh 2006).

Sobering notions regarding archaeologists' obligations at personal and disciplinary levels, admittedly more complex than I have presented them here, have straightforward implications that distill to what Lipe (1974) has referred to as the "conservation model." Most archaeologists unhesitatingly support expanding protections for archaeological records and limiting consumptive access to those who understand and act in accord with ethical mandates to conserve, curate and publish. Most also support rewarding those who give voice to and provide stewardship for our archaeological inheritance, including judicious pursuit of both educational opportunities and, where necessary, administrative, civil and criminal sanctions against those who silence or misappropriate the past. These are elementary and often-offered recommendations, to be sure. However, in light of the ongoing, profit-driven decimation of irreplaceable and little-studied regional records, neither the threats nor the need for counter-action can be overstated. This is particularly true in relation to the wholesale removal of Native American heritage in areas now densely settled by non-natives. I urge archaeologists to be prepared to explain our roles in this removal. I suggest that being able to point to careful, continuous, and balanced consultations and publications is the best justification available. With this in mind, I encourage reconsideration of attitudes toward archive and artifact collections and the creation of research and publication opportunities linked to these collections (Voss 2012).

Stepping off the soapbox and returning to Kinishba and the goals of this volume, it is particularly imperative that we make the best and fullest use of un- and under-published records pertaining to previous extractive studies. Doing so affirms and fulfills our ethical commitments while also enhancing discipline-wide reconciliation between the conservation ethic and professional practice, both past and present. Although Kinishba itself is not under imminent threat by either looters or urban sprawl, the probability that additional research excavations will occur there in the near future is low. The White Mountain Apache Tribe maintains culturally grounded commitments to site preservation and typically welcomes only non-invasive research proposals (Welch 2000; Welch et al. 2009). This reality makes me particularly grateful for generous responses from my esteemed colleagues, the volume contributors who have dedicated their fine minds and precious time to squeezing the best and most useful information out of Kinishba. Like weekend scavengers of historical mines seeking precious remnants in abandoned spoil heaps, we have labored to extract, connect, make meaningful, and carry forward nuggets of knowledge otherwise forsaken. The gleanings offered here are data points and interpretations that break a long and debilitating silence.

Despite the intelligence and imagination evident in the volume's individual chapters, Kinishba's "unsilencing" has barely begun. No clear path has yet emerged among the scattered, incomplete and incompletely organized notes and collections that might allow the Shaeffers' work to be placed in even fuller and more useful context. If we apply today's standards for data recovery, analysis and publication, the Shaeffers, Cummings and their closest collaborators failed to adequately represent both Kinishba and the excavated contexts. We cannot yet know—on the basis of the Shaeffer reports and the other materials available here and accessible in the holdings of the Arizona State Museum—all we want to about Kinishba's Group VI room block or the features the Shaeffers unearthed below the Group I Plaza surface. These contexts need and deserve to be understood in relation to one another, to other regional site records, and to site- and region-level events, processes and dynamics.

Despite such uncertainties and the challenges inevitably faced in knowing more about Kinishba, we owe it to the place, to the communities of descendants and stewards, and to our imperfect professional forebears, to squeeze, steadily and smoothly, all we can out of the sources available to us. This is archaeologists' debt to the ancient places and peoples that are our fascinations and meal tickets, as well as to the women and men who paved the way to making archaeology a viable and compelling intellectual and professional pursuit. The Shaeffers may not have fully appreciated the ethical burdens of their excavations. We do. And we must not shirk these burdens or bequeath them to our successors. To the maturation of our discipline, as well as to the posterity that will be one arbitrator of the worthiness of our lives and works, we owe respectful and full disclosure of investigations at sites we excavate and samples we destroy. A latently silent archaeological record is appropriate, but once that record has been exhumed it is imperative that its messages be decoded, made legible and amplified. I take this key tenet of archaeology's conservation model (Lipe 1974) seriously. I encourage others to do the same and note that publishing others' work becomes more and more difficult as time passes, memories fade, and collections disperse. Salvage archival archaeology is an apt means for improving intergenerational professional communications, for enhancing regional interpretive contexts, and for refreshing collegial awareness of how ideas and institutional arrangements got to be the way they are, as well as for meeting ethical mandates. The best time for such research is now.

Editing the Shaeffer Reports

This section describes steps taken and processes used in transforming rough drafts of the Shaeffers' excavation reports (Shaeffer 1949, 1951) into Chapter 3 and Chapter 4. Like the Kinishba excavations they undertook, the Shaeffers' analytic and writing efforts seem to have taken place in fits and starts. There are few clear historiographic clues relating to the two reports, but it appears that the Shaeffers first approached the digs as the basis for Jim's initial doctoral thesis (Shaeffer 1954). Several decisions—for Jim to broaden his dissertation topic into a review of Mogollon prehistory, for Jim to return to active military duty during the Korean conflict, and for Jim to pursue employment in Oklahoma following his overseas duty—likely prompted the Shaeffers to de-prioritize completion of the draft reports.

Numerous versions of each report were included in the parcel Jim sent to the Park Service in 2004. Although the most recent of these typescripts contain citations to scholarly works as late as 1960, I used the dates on the report title pages to assign "original" years to the Great Kiva and Group VI reports, respectively, of 1949 and 1951. A form of "horizontal" stratigraphic analysis, one familiar to those who research previously edited documents, was required to determine the most recent versions of the two manuscripts and their constituent subsections. The analysis entailed comparing and sequencing typescript versions by identifying instances in which penciled-in editorial comments and alterations had been incorporated in typescripts. This exercise, coupled with attempts to decode sometimes cryptic notations and changes in handwriting, suggest that years, even decades elapsed between episodes of work on the reports. Margaret almost certainly participated in writing editing and typing, and Margaret, Jim, or both of them made marginal notes as recently as the late 1990s or early 2000s.

It is at least equally clear that the Shaeffers were more interested in and committed to the publication of the Great Kiva report (Chapter 4) than they were to the report on the Group VI excavations (Chapter 3). The chapter addressing Group VI is a basic description of what the Shaeffers did and found, with minimal graphic support or interpretation. As presented here, the Great Kiva report includes brief critical reviews of comparable work as well as all of the known photographs made during the excavations and some line drawings. In terms of tone, organization, content and line drawings, both chapters appear to be loosely modeled on reports prepared by Paul S. Martin and his colleagues (Martin 1940, 1943; Martin and Rinaldo 1947, 1950; Martin et al. 1949, 1950). It also appears, on the basis of correspondence and comparisons with other work (see Murry 1937; Shaeffer and Shaeffer 1956), that all or most of the illustrations were prepared by Margaret. For these reasons, and as partial remedy to her unexplained exclusion from and demotion in authorship elsewhere, Margaret is listed here as the second author of both chapters. There is no doubt that Margaret's work made the draft reports possible.

In addition to the various versions of the typescript reports on the work at Group VI, Shaeffer sent to the Park Service 11 pages of informal handwritten notes, field number lists, and sketch maps relating to the project (again, all materials are now archived at Arizona State Museum). The notes include brief and sporadic journal entries relating to the Group VI excavations, beginning September 28 and concluding October 19, 1947. The sketches consist of a single profile ("Room # 1 x section looking West") and three unscaled plan maps: a view of Group VI apparently delineating the areas excavated each day, a post-excavation depiction of the Group VI room configuration, and an interpretation of Kinishba's construction sequence showing five stages. Although difficult to read and interpret, the notes seem not to include references to project personnel, individual rooms, or comparisons of the processes or results of the work within individual rooms.

The editing undertaken to prepare the reports for this volume entailed deciphering and attempting to comprehend all of the materials from the Shaeffers' perspectives. After settling on matters of voice and focus, I proceeded to make—as correctly, unobtrusively and consistently as possible—the thousands of minor and less minor changes to each report, as required to make as clear and compelling as possible the Shaeffers' methods and findings. Most of the original prose and presentation style are retained, but the versions provided here bear only substantive resemblances to the typescript drafts now curated in the Arizona State Museum Archives. Once I identified the most recent versions of the two reports and many of the various report sections and amendments, I edited each to comport with early twenty first century professional reporting conventions. This work entailed clarifying and regularizing each footnote, parenthetical remark, penciled-in annotation, and informal list. I then incorporated these and the small number of coherent sketches I found scattered through the various typescript versions into the body of the text or formal tables. I also edited the Shaeffers' sundry photographs, line drawings, tables and appendices, ultimately integrating these into a single system for enumeration and presentation. None of these supplements to the texts were either copy-ready or adequately referenced in the Shaeffers' typescripts. Because no reliable plan view map or sketch of the Group VI rooms was available, I hastily mapped the eight rooms on a cold afternoon in January 2012. Due to the simple, lamentable truth that the whereabouts of the Shaeffers' collections remain unknown, it was not possible to reconcile the ceramic type and tool descriptions included in the typescripts with twenty-first century identification and publication conventions. We must trust, at least for now, the Shaeffers' skills in ceramic typology.

I worked through the typescript reports by seeking to eliminate or reconcile obvious redundancies, inaccuracies (e.g., replacing "malapai" with "basalt"), and inconsistencies. I addressed a common conflation in references to social and archaeological contexts (e.g., village vs. site; tool vs. artifact). I added metric equivalents, where appropriate and possible, for dimensional measurements the Shaeffers set forth in the English system. Because neither of the reports included appropriate references to relevant published works, I added citations wherever I could identify a valid source for a comparative point of evidence or interpretation. In order to boost the context for interpreting the excavation results, citations were added without regard to whether the Shaeffers would have had access to the work. When urges to offer historical commentary or critical clarification proved irresistible, I added a sentence or two. Finally, as a means for sharpening discourse and softening the boundaries between archaeological knowledge and Puebloan oral traditions, I replaced the Shaeffers' occasional uses of "abandonment" and "prehistoric" with more specific and less divisive referents. I hope these are both more precise and less objectionable to members of Kinishba's descendant, steward, and research communities. Despite innumerable changes, the two chapters retain most of the original reports' structures, subheadings and voice.

It bears mention that much of the Shaeffers' general approach in the Great Kiva work and report, as well as in many specific presentational decisions, seem to have been intended to highlight differences between what the Shaeffers and Byron Cummings found and interpreted at Kinishba, and what Terah Smiley and Emil Haury were finding and interpreting in their work on kivas at Point of Pines (Smiley 1952). The Shaeffers tend, generally speaking, to blunt and blur critical remarks regarding Cummings's work; they tend to sharpen distinctions between the four subsurface nonresidential structures that Smiley excavated in 1947 and those that occupied the Shaeffer team's time that same summer. Although Haury's 23 October 1986 letter to Richard Woodbury declined the invitation to assist personally in publishing the Shaeffers' Great Kiva report, Haury sagely noted that great kivas are, "an aspect of Pueblo, Anasazi, and Mogollon complexes that cannot be ignored" (Haury 1986). I agree, obviously, and hope readers will do more than concur by pursuing additional research along these lines.

VOLUME SCOPE AND CONTENT

Once the Shaeffers' edited manuscripts were generally presentable, I circulated the texts and some draft introductory notes as an "open call" to the potent cluster of about 20 colleagues sharing interests in the ancient history of the eastern Mogollon Rim. The initial distribution included invitations to contribute to this volume and to reach out to other scholars who might be interested in doing so. In recognition of the limited opportunities for new studies relating to Kinishba, as well as to the small number of sites and contexts available for close comparisons, I left the format of the contributions open. The seven chapters that follow the presentation of the Shaeffers' reports are the gratifying response to this invitation. The chapters use the Shaeffers' works (Chapters 3 and 4) as points of departure for presenting unpublished or under-published data and interpretations on Kinishba and regional culture histories, ancient community processes and ongoing community connections.

Chapter 5, by Richard Ciolek-Torello and Carl Halbirt, anchors Kinishba's thirteenth and fourteenth century developments in regional culture history. They do this by reporting the most important findings from excavations conducted in 1983 and 1984 of two pit house villages located fewer than ten kilometers south and southeast of Kinishba. As is true for the volume as a whole, this chapter redeems through publication some of the professional debts incurred through excavations. There have been few contributions to our understanding of developments prior to surface pueblos in the eastern Mogollon Rim region since Haury's (1940, 1985) work in the Forestdale Valley, and these new data are significant and useful, particularly in the ongoing quest to understand relationships among archaeological and living cultures (see Gregory and Wilcox 2007; Reid and Whittlesey 2010).

The next five chapters present an impressive range of analyses and findings made on the basis of existing excavations and surveys. Chapter 6, by Charles Riggs, uses high-resolution architectural data available from sites adjacent to the Kinishba region (especially Grasshopper Ruins), to draw a series of compelling hypotheses and inferences concerning Kinishba's structural, developmental, and community organization. In the first of two data-rich chapters on ceramics from Kinishba, Patrick Lyons (Chapter 7) takes a fresh look at the whole and nearly whole vessels from Kinishba curated at the Arizona State Museum. In Chapter 8, a compositional study aimed at the movement of pots and people in to and out of Kinishba, Daniella Triadan demonstrates, among many other things, that at least some of the documentation from Cummings's excavations can be harnessed in fruitful analyses. Chapter 9—contributed by Nicholas Laluk, Mark Altaha, and me—reports findings from a pedestrian inventory of the terrain within one mile of Kinishba. Chapter 10 concludes the data-based chapters with a discussion, authored by me and T. J. Ferguson, of relevant results from a cultural affiliation study of White Mountain Apache Tribe lands. In the Chapter 11 conclusion, Jefferson Reid offers sage perspectives on Kinishba and the other chapters, seasoned by his career commitment to understanding regional archaeology and research history and by his close intellectual associations with principal volume themes of culture histories, affinities, and dynamics.

The volume is by no means the final word on Kinishba. At best it is, we hope, the icebreaker for a necessary discussion after a pronounced and unfortunate silence. The chapters show that we still have much to learn and indicate promising methods and directions for follow-up investigations. The volume makes clear the great potential that remains for additional study and use of Kinishba and of the diverse cultural, scientific, historical, social, and management values it embodies and perpetuates. The approaches taken in the chapters are but a few of the many possible avenues for learning more about and from the site. I hope others will pursue better models and foster more productive networks for supporting students and colleagues willing to give voice to those archaeological records silenced by the whims of history and the caprices of personal and professional priorities.

Chapter 2
Episodes in Kinishba's Cultural and Management Histories

John R. Welch

Kinishba is quiet these days, a good perch for contemplating ruins both ancient and twentieth century, along with the wisdom they embody about time's fleet arrow and the impermanence of most human initiatives. But the place has not always been quiet. Even a quick look at the site and region in archaeological and historical context reveals multiple pulses of intense and doubtlessly complicated interactions among peoples and places. The available evidence also highlights gaps in current knowledge and underscores the range of cultural, scientific, tourism and management values embedded in the site.

This chapter summarizes Kinishba's cultural and management histories, giving particular attention to what happened at Kinishba in the aftermath of Byron Cummings's 1946 retirement and departure. The goal is to describe aspects of the archaeological, historical and social contexts for the Shaeffers' excavations reported on in the next two chapters. Tracing the outlines of what we know about the people who lived in and around Kinishba and what their lives were like underscores the rapid changes that occurred during certain episodes and the relative calm at other times. Background information also helps to frame questions of potential interest to archaeologists and historians, as well as planners interested in boosting community development in particular and heritage conservation and tourism more generally.

REGIONAL CULTURAL HISTORY AND LOCAL PERIODS OF RAPID CHANGE

On the basis of many decades of research focused on the eastern Mogollon Rim region, most of which was conducted by archaeological field schools under the auspices of the University of Arizona's Department of Anthropology and Arizona State Museum, investigators have developed various frameworks to define and discuss the region's occupational sequence (Haury 1989; Reid and Whittlesey 2005) (Table 2.1). The following culture history summary is abstracted from authoritative reviews offered in Hoffman (1992), Reid and Whittlesey (1997, 2005), and Roos (2008), sources to which interested readers should turn for additional details and references. The summary is offered to highlight the twin truths that a lot was going on in the region prior to the thirteenth and fourteenth century establishment of large, plaza-focused farming communities and, also importantly, that the size of the villages we know as Kinishba, Grasshopper, etc., as well as the scale of their interregional relations, were unprecedented.

Preceramic Traditions

Few indications of the small groups of hunters who exploited the area during the Paleo-Indian period (ca. 12,000–6,000 B.C.) at the end of the Pleistocene have survived. The period is

Table 2.1. Concordance of Archaeological Chronologies for the Eastern Arizona Uplands

Dates (AD)	Hohokam Periods / Phases	Generic Regional	Grasshopper (Reid 1989)	Forestdale (Haury 1985)	Point of Pines (Gifford 1980)	Plateau-Pecos (Kidder 1927)
1500	O'odham / Yavapai Depopulation	Apache Depopulation	Abandonment	Skidi Phase (Apache)	Apache Abandonment	Pueblo V
	- - -		Mogollon Pueblo	Hiatus	Point of Pines Phase	Pueblo IV
1400		- - -		- - -	------	
	Late Classic / Civano Phase	Late Mogollon Pueblo / Western Pueblo	Aggregation ∨ ∨ ∨ *Dispersion*	Canyon Creek Phase	Canyon Creek Phase	
1300	------		*Expansion*	------	Pinedale Phase	------
	Early Classic / Soho Phase		*Establishment* ∧ ∧ ∧ Mogollon Pueblo Reorganization	Pinedale Phase	*Maverick Mountain*	Pueblo III
1200		------		------	Tularosa Phase	
	------	Early Mogollon Pueblo (small, cobble-jacal pueblos)		Linden Phase	------	------
1100			- - -	------	Reserve Phase	Pueblo II
	Sedentary / Sacaton Phase		Mogollon Expansion and Differentiation	Carrizo Phase		
1000		------		------	------	
	------	Late Pithouse Period		Dry Valley Phase		
900	Late Colonial / Santa Cruz Phase			------	Nantack Phase	------
	------			Corduroy Phase	------	Pueblo I
800	Early Colonial / Gila Butte Phase			------	Dry Lake Phase	
				Forestdale Phase	------	
700	------				Stove Canyon Phase	
600	Pioneer / Snake-town Phase	- - -			------	------
500	- - - Pioneer / Sweetwater Phase	Early Pithouse Period	- - - Mogollon Initiation	Cottonwood Phase	------	Basketmaker III
400				------ Hilltop Phase	Late Circle Prairie Phase - - - Early Circle Prairie Phase	------ Basketmaker II
	Early Ceramic Horizon					

known in the Mogollon Rim region only from finds of a few distinctive spear points (Mabry 1998). Although Paleoindian groups may have used the Mogollon Rim region, the area's high energy stream channels and other dynamic depositional environments suggest a low probability of identifying truly ancient materials in stratigraphic context.

During the Archaic period (6,000 B.C.–A.D. 1) the Mogollon Rim region was occupied by mobile groups of hunter-gatherers who seem to have incorporated limited agricultural pursuits into their economy late in the period (Mabry 1998). No Archaic period sites in Kinishba's immediate vicinity have been documented, much less excavated, but the Fort Apache Indian Reservation site files (FAIRsite) include three nearby sites that fit the Archaic profile: surface scatters of ground stone and chipped stone artifacts that lack ceramic fragments, historical period items, and other traces of both Mogollon Pueblo and Apache occupation and use. One of these three sites, located on a ridge line about three kilometers west of Kinishba, includes at least one small hand stone similar to others thought to date to the Archaic period.

Groups living in the Kinishba region and along the Mogollon Rim prior to A.D. 1 appear to have moved frequently, presumably in accord with the area's ever-shifting patchwork of seasonally available plant foods, as well as the game animals that similarly targeted grasses, fruits and nuts. Welch's (1996) review of elevational and interannual variation in the availability of wild plant foods in the Grasshopper region, located about 60 km west of Kinishba, provides one basis for understanding the diversity of foods within reach of people living around Kinishba.

The beginning of the end of the Archaic period, in the Mogollon Rim region and elsewhere, is signaled by the first cultivation of domesticated plants (Geib and Huckell 1994).

Around Kinishba the Archaic is represented only by a few artifact scatters, none of which have been carefully investigated. The closest detailed and well-dated information is from the Cibecue valley, about 45 km west of Kinishba. Even excavations have yet to yield answers to obvious questions in regional culture history. For example, it is not known whether the Mogollon Rim region's residents obtained corn, beans and other domesticated seed stocks through down-the-line exchange, direct procurement, or visitors. In any case, toward the end of the Archaic period many but not all groups using the Mogollon Rim region appear to have been planting crops along creeks while maintaining a flexible schedule of seasonal movements to exploit food resources widely distributed across regions and seasons (Geib and Huckell 1994).

Ceramic Traditions

Plain brown pottery marks the close of the Archaic and the beginning of the Early Pithouse period (A.D. 1–600) and the development along the Mogollon Rim of cultural traditions ancestral to modern Pueblo groups. Large pit structures, called great kivas, suggest ceremonies contributed to the solidarity of these communities (Haury and Sayles 1947). During the Late Pithouse period (A.D. 600–1150) the region's forager-farmers tended to locate their villages on valley floors (Haury 1985). The number of villages, their overall size, and the size and complexity of storage facilities and communal structures suggests a steadily growing regional population and level of reliance on cultivated foods. Where farming is likely to have been more productive, larger populations and villages were possible. In mountainous areas a more equally balanced forager-farmer lifestyle probably persisted. The Shaeffers' excavations below the floor of Kinishba's Group I Plaza (Chapter 4) may have revealed evidence of an earlier, pit house-based occupation at the site. This evidence, together with the presentation in Chapter 5 of findings from two pit house sites in the Kinishba vicinity, is relevant to understanding the geographical and cultural sources of Kinishba region populations, as well as the locations and configurations of settlements prior to the thirteenth century colonization of the eastern Mogollon Rim region and the transition to predominantly above-ground residential architecture, which began around 1100.

The Mogollon Pueblo period (A.D. 1150–1450) is our focus in this volume. The period is marked by the emergence of distinctive architectural and community forms across the Mogollon Rim. On the basis of investigations focused in the Silver Creek drainage just north of the Rim, Barbara Mills and her colleagues have built a case for the arrival in the region, from the north and the east, of significant populations and cultural influences beginning shortly after A.D. 1000 and continuing for about two centuries (Herr 2001; Mills 1998, 1999b, 2011; Mills, Herr and Van Keuren 1999). Herr (2001) suggests that great kivas and the ceremonial systems they reflect were part of the region's "pull" on immigrants. Regardless, by A.D. 1150, multi-household pit house and masonry pueblo settlements occur in many locations across the region's forests and woodlands. "Push" factors linked to the dissolution of the Chaco system and, by the last decades of the A.D. 1200s, variable and generally meagre precipitation and other conditions limiting agricultural success on the Colorado Plateau may have prolonged or intensified the migration trends. Reid (1989) thinks that, prior to about A.D. 1250, the sub-Mogollon Rim portion of the region with the exception of the Forestdale area, was occupied by communities having substantial reliance on farming, large communal structures, and no more than about 20 residential spaces. Site surveys conducted on White Mountain Apache lands in the wake of the 2002 Rodeo-Chediski Fire have, however, documented several much larger sites dating to the A.D. 1200s on the eastern flanks of the Grasshopper Region (David Gregory, personal communication 2010; see Mills, Herr, Kaldahl, Newcomb, Riggs, and Van Dyke 1999).

Although perceived patterns for pre-A.D. 1200 settlement forms and associations are likely to shift as new data emerge, the post-1200 shifts to larger, aggregated, plaza-focused villages like Kinishba remains undeniable (Figure 2.1). The dissected uplands below the Mogollon Rim, where surface water is always available and game populations enjoy abundant cover and habitat diversity, attracted additional colonists throughout the A.D. 1200s. The arrivals may have come in large numbers, including groups from specific sites in the modern Four Corners region (Lyons, Chapter 7; Triadan, Chapter 8; see Ezzo 1992, 1993; Ezzo and Price 2002; McClelland 2003; Price et al 1994). The ancestral Hopi and Zuni villages known as Point of Pines, Kinishba, Grasshopper, Bailey, and Q Ranch attained their greatest size as people dry-farmed parklands surrounding reliable domestic water sources. Increased reliance on farming, decreased seasonal movements, and the filling in of unoccupied landscape niches apparently accompanied growth in both the size of individual communities and the density of regional populations (Reid 1989; Welch et al., Chapter 9; Mills, Van Keuren, Stinson, Graves, Kaldahl, and Newcomb 1999).

This transition was not always peaceful. The rise and development of the big pueblos and their settlement systems was accompanied in most regions by evidence of dietary stress, uncertainty, and possibly violence (Ezzo 1994; Haury 1958; Triadan and Zedeño 2004; Tuggle and Reid 2001; Welch and Bostwick 2001; Welch 2001). Although few clear indications of similar inter-group tensions have been identified for Kinishba, questions concerning the co-residence of distinctive social groups, variation

2: Episodes in Kinishba's Cultural and Management Histories   17

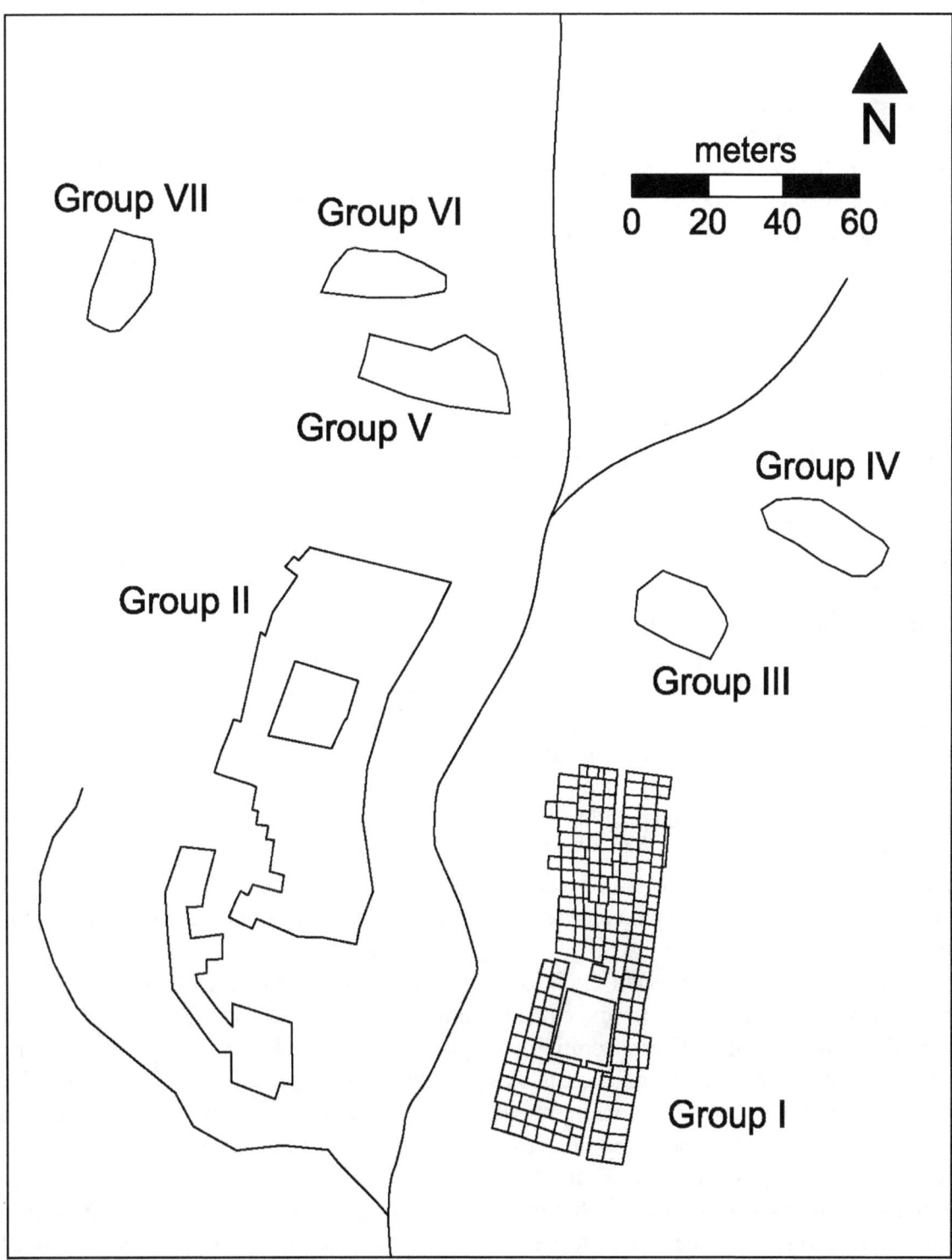

Figure 2.1. Kinishba Ruins, showing major room groups (Charles R. Riggs).

in agricultural productivity and health status, and how conflicts arose and were managed at and around Kinishba are all topics that deserve future research attention. Perhaps the most obvious gap in our regional knowledge pertains to the chronological and cultural affinities of the many large pueblos located in the basaltic, conifer-clad uplands east of Kinishba (Welch et al., Chapter 9).

Kinishba on the Cusp of History

As we await opportunities to pursue such studies, it is worth reflecting on that which we do know from archaeological data and how this knowledge comports with oral traditions and perspectives from the Hopi and Zuni descendants of Kinishba's occupants and from the ruin's Apache stewards. According to Hopi traditions, Kinishba Ruins was once known as the village of *Ma'öp'ovi* ("High Place of Snakeweed"). The village was made of sandstone masonry, mud mortar and juniper and ponderosa pine timbers from nearby stream terraces. As the largest of the nearly 20 large (150 or more rooms), plaza-focused pueblos linked to the colonization of the eastern Mogollon Rim region, *Ma'öp'ovi* was also made of people—their stories, families, hopes and memories (see Welch and Ferguson, Chapter 10).

Kinishba's original occupants' choices—where to live, what kinds of houses and villages to build, what sorts of utilitarian crafts and sacred arts to pursue—all signal unmistakable interest in the soils, rains and communal institutions necessary to sustain their agricultural lifeway in a region of uncertain and fast-changing environmental conditions. But much of the information and perspective presented in this volume shows that people were interested not only in corn farming and deer hunting, but in regional and interregional politics. The latter may well have been conceived of in terms of the geographical and spiritual or cultural affinities of specific groups or entire settlements. Triadan (Chapter 8) offers new data on ceramic manufacture and exchange that show significant variation in the type and level of participation in the development of ceramic styles by people at Kinishba and Grasshopper. Families, and possibly lineages, came and went from Kinishba. There were undoubtedly conflicts over the appropriate use of village spaces, over allocations of farmland, and over specific decisions as well as decision-making processes themselves. Household, lineage and community leaders kept an eye on opportunities and threats presented or promised by developments in the village's natural and social environs.

Some of these opportunities and threats were likely at the heart of the reason or reasons the village did not endure. The people may have been pushed out, driven from their homes by crop failures or other factors. Alternatively, they may have been pulled, beckoned by prophesy or other divine mandate to pursue their destiny elsewhere. In any case, the ancient people moved on, leaving "footprints"—masonry and petroglyphs, pottery forms, diverse household and ritual items, and their ancestors' and family members' burials (Welch and Ferguson 2007, this volume). They took with them stories and feelings that persist as meaningful links between people and place. Patrick Lyons (Chapter 7) demonstrates that Kinishba was among the last places in the region that Pueblo people migrated away from. By 1400 or shortly thereafter, the mountains south of the Mogollon Rim quieted once more, no longer the hosts for large farming villages.

The exact dates at which ancestors of the Western Apache (Ndee) moved into Arizona or established their dominion over Ndee Dawada Bi Ni', the Western Apache homeland, are not known (Herr et al. 2009). By the late 1600s Spanish priests were well aware of the Ndee presence, and Ndee held unchallenged control of the area stretching south from the Mogollon

Rim to the Gila River and from the Verde River eastward, beyond what would become the New Mexico state line and to the San Francisco River. The adoption of horses and the raiding of Mexican settlements enabled Ndee and other Apache groups to increase their geographical range, and it appears that they gradually shifted toward greater emphasis on farming without forsaking seasonal movements or capacities to plunder distant settlements. Ndee kept their options open. By the mid 1800s, at the latest, about sixty interrelated Apache bands were closely associated with both social clusters of clans and shifting territories (Goodwin 1942). Ancestral Apaches developed profound affinities with their territories (Basso 1996). For many Ndee households, hunting and plant gathering remained important elements of their subsistence strategy until the mid 1900s (Buskirk 1986; Watt and Basso 2004).

Conflicts between Ndee and Anglo Americans resulted in the designation, beginning in the early 1870s, of four areas as Apache reservations. The federal government reserved one of these four tracts, the White Mountain Indian Reservation (later divided into the Fort Apache and San Carlos reservations), for the bands of Cibecue and White Mountain Ndee living along the southern slopes of the Mogollon Rim, from the Sierra Ancha and Cherry Creek watershed on the west to the White Mountains and the Black River on the east. Following establishment of the reservations, the federal government's primary strategies for assimilating Apaches into Euro-American society involved stimulation of market economies, conversion to Christianity and youth attendance at boarding or day schools (Welch 2010). The strategy met with mixed success, and Ndee today retain many elements of pre-reservation society. These elements are integrated into contemporary social patterns that maintain important links to cultural and geographical birthrights while using reservation lands as economic foundations.

Kinishba's history did not end when its ancestral Hopi and Zuni occupants left *Ma'öp'ovi*, but the lack of evidence for the site's use appears to archaeologists as a silence that endured for a half millennium, from the 1400s until the later 1800s. The site's Ndee stewards followed their elders' advice and left the place alone (Welch et al. 2009). More silence. Then, for the first time, with the 1870 establishment of the U.S. Army outpost that would become Fort Apache, the Mogollon Rim region gradually came under non-Indian control. Groups of soldiers began looting the ancient village as a pastime. The place, sacred in the minds and memories of Apaches as well as the Hopi and Zuni descendent communities, became known as the Fort Apache Ruin. The site attracted observant visitors, including Bandelier (1890–92), Barnes (1941), Hough (1907), Spier (1919), Reagan (1930), and Gila Pueblo surveyors (Baldwin 1941; Welch 2007c).

Cummings and Kinishba

Alternating silences and sprees of treasure-hunting persisted until 1931, when "Dean" Byron Cummings, decided it was time to make some new kinds of noise at the site. The venerable and vivacious founder of the University of Arizona Department of Archaeology (later Department and currently School of Anthropology) and Director of the Arizona State Museum, Cummings turned his 30-something mind and 70-year-old body to giving something back to archaeology and the Native people who had hosted and otherwise helped him with the many projects that had comprised his long career. Cummings set out to break the silence with sounds of constructive additions, not just extractions. Over the next few years, Cummings's notions settled upon a quest, essentially unprecedented in the U.S., to integrate, simultaneously, four distinct pursuits: (1) archaeological research and training, (2) Native American community engagement, (3) collaborative, interagency historic preservation, and (4) museum and tourism enterprise development (Bostwick 2006; Welch 2007a,b,c).

Ever-attuned to prospective new "markets" for innovative educational and tourist products, Cummings wanted the new sounds being made at Kinishba to be romantic and tribal. Accordingly, Cummings championed archaeological field schools, Depression-era works programs, funding from the Bureau of Indian Affairs, and a singular quest to establish a national monument at the site. During the next 16 years Cummings and his crews of students and Apaches excavated about 240 rooms, rebuilt about 140 of those, erected a visitor and interpretive center, and otherwise pioneered the creation of what we today recognize as a "living museum" (Welch 2007a,b,c).

In the later 1930s, as University of Arizona support for Cummings's Kinishba project waned, the Bureau of Indian Affairs and the White Mountain Apache Tribe took up the slack (Welch 2007a). BIA support expanded through modest federal appropriations sponsored by Arizona's long-lived senator, Carl Hayden. Cummings, who had labored for several years at Kinishba with only his University pension to support him, worked with BIA and Hayden to fund a curator salary for the Kinishba Museum he had opened on a shoestring budget in 1941.

In the silence (at least in the Arizona uplands) of World War II, Cummings's once-superior vitality, vision, and hearing finally began to wane. The time had come to find a new champion for Kinishba. Cummings reached in to his vast network of students and supporters, pulling James and Margaret (Murry) Shaeffer out of his pith helmet (Figure 2.2). The couple returned to Kinishba in 1946, a decade after working with Cummings for several seasons there as students, for a joint appointment with the Bureau of Indian Affairs as curators. They were charged with continuing the pursuit of Cummings's compelling vision for Kinishba and set out to create a life for themselves and their three children.

The *Holbrook Tribune News* commemorated the changing of the guard at Kinishba with a front page story on October 18, 1946. The paper's parting tribute states, in part: Cummings's "birthright of keen mental powers and great physical stamina, that defies even the encroaching four score and six years, has been given freely to the service of his fellow men, to the study of their prehistoric efforts and the restoration and preservation for posterity of their crumbling dwellings and buried culture." The article continues, "He has now stepped into the background offering to younger hands and keener eyes the distinguished position as the curator of the greatest potential archaeological museum of its size in America." To make room for the Shaeffers, Cummings vacated his cherished quarters in the Museum building he had finished building a few years earlier. He moved his personal items into a "suite" of rebuilt pueblo rooms in the northwestern corner of Group I before retreating southward from Kinishba for the winter. Cummings returned to Kinishba to assist the Shaeffers in the spring of 1947, but seems to have felt in the way. He "left with regret," apparently never to return (Cummings and Cummings n.d.:209). Later that same year, shortly after his eighty-seventh birthday, Cummings married Ann Chatham, a long-time friend, and turned his still-impressive energies to building their retirement home and writing two books (Cummings 1952, 1953).

THE SHAEFFERS AT KINISHBA

The Shaeffers arrived at Kinishba with their own histories and aspirations. Jim Shaeffer

Figure 2.2. Byron Cummings at Kinishba, circa 1940 (courtesy White Mountain Apache Tribe Heritage Program).

was among the host of WWII veterans resuming participation in civilian life and eager for opportunity. The Shaeffers were well acquainted with Cummings and his work at Kinishba and had learned first-hand of Cummings's original and persistent vision for the site as an "outdoor museum." This vision centered on the conceptually innovative though practically challenging intention to present and interpret the site to visitors using four distinct contexts: unexcavated, excavated and rebuilt portions of the ancient ruin, as well as indoor museum displays of more precious artifact types (Cummings 1940). The following description of the Shaeffers' work at Kinishba offers a summary of their site management and excavation activities. I conclude this chapter with a few educated guesses concerning what they excavated and what became of the products from the digs.

Site Preservation and Museum Management

Correspondence copied from the Kinishba files at the White Mountain Apache Tribe Historic Preservation Office includes detailed communications between the Shaeffers and their

Washington-based boss, Bureau of Indian Affairs Director of Education, Dr. Willard Beatty. Both parties earnestly wanted to make the most of the unique situation. Jim's January 11, 1947 letter report to Beatty highlights some of the preservation and interpretation challenges stemming from 16 years of excavation, reconstruction, and new building under Cummings:

> [Y]ou outlined in general terms the plans you had in mind covering (1) more effective preservation of the ruin, (2) more effective display of the museum materials, (3) making the ruin and museum of easier access, and (4) calling attention of the general public.... [T]he roofs of the reconstruction.... are eroded, some are warped, and one is completely washed through....this problem should be the object of a special study...if the reconstruction is to be economically maintained and the safety of the public is to be considered....[W]ork in the museum has consisted of segregating the archaeological material from the ethnological.... entirely new exhibits should be arranged.... Should this [ethnological] exhibit be devoted exclusively to the Apache or should other tribes be included?....[T]here should not be too much publicity until a coordinated program for the outdoors is worked out....I am hampered by a lack of familiarity with your other museums and with general objectives.

Beatty's February 7 response reflects his interests in Kinishba's success coupled with concerns about the viability of Cummings's rebuilt structures. Beatty informs the Shaeffers that a BIA facilities supervisor will consult on providing "for adequate roofing for these structures without violating the archaeological or artistic side." The letter further recommends "a selective presentation of material which will assist the observer to understand the people who occupied the ruin and their culture." Beatty concludes with an invitation for Jim to visit "our museum at Browning, Montana, and...the new Indian displays at the Chicago Museum of Natural History," suggesting that the ethnological collections at Kinishba be used "to display the story of the Apache and omit Pueblo and other miscellaneous material." With concerns about operating funds coming to the fore, Shaeffer's February 24 memo to Beatty proposes "three feasible ways to augment our income: (1) establishment of an entrance fee, (2) the formation of a non-profit museum association similar to those cooperating with the majority of National Park museums, and (3) the procurement of substantial contributions from private donors."

The Beatty-Shaeffer correspondence offers rare insights into a little-studied federal museums program administered by the Bureau of Indian Affairs in collaboration with local governments. In a rare, post-WWII application of New Deal institutional development models, Beatty oversaw federal responsibility for four museums: Kinishba; the Sioux Indian Museum, South Dakota; the Museum of the (Northern) Plains Indian, Montana; and the Southern Plains Indian Museum, Oklahoma. Beatty established a loose network for interpreting their respective regional "culture areas" to visitors and for promoting tourism-related economic development. Taking cues from his founding membership on the U.S. Indian Arts and Crafts Board, Beatty prioritized investments in facilities and programs that encouraged crafts production as a means for boosting household incomes, intergenerational education, and intertribal and intercultural communications (Schrader 1983:260-261). Beatty was apparently grooming Kinishba for service as the Bureau of Indian Affairs' regional center for interpreting the Southwest's Native American cultures and for stimulating and satisfying arts and crafts markets.

But, for at least four overlapping reasons, Kinishba was ultimately excluded from Beatty's ambitious program. First, structural problems both chronic and acute plagued the Kinishba Museum's operations and budgets. Federal money was tight, and some particularly wet winters in the later 1940s damaged many of the rebuilt pueblo rooms beyond easy repair. The annual Bureau of Indian Affairs budget allocation for repairs in 1948 ($450) was no match for the $15,000 estimate for a new roof for the rebuilt pueblo (Welch 2007a:34-35).

Second, even aside from financial considerations, there seemed no way to justify Bureau investment in Kinishba. Although visitation to Kinishba was growing—711, 986, 1516, and 1793 registered visitors in 1946, 1947, 1948, and 1949, respectively—these numbers were still too small to drive the underdeveloped market for Apache crafts to new level. Kinishba was not the only Bureau of Indian Affairs museum on reservation land (the Museum of the Plains Indian is on Blackfeet land), but it was the only one of the four located so far away from urban populations, major transportation corridors, and well established tourist destinations. No clear, cost-effective plan for drawing distant markets to Kinishba emerged at that time, and none has since.

Third, Kinishba was the only Bureau museum irrevocably linked to an archaeological site and the only one of the four interpreting a twentieth century tribe (i.e., White Mountain Apache) as well as a distinct and ancient cultural tradition. Cummings sought to cultivate and interpret this linkage and set the Kinishba Museum up to display an admixture of archaeological materials from his excavations as well as Apache artifacts acquired from friends, workers and local artisans.

Beatty, and perhaps the Shaeffers, had concerns about linking Apache and Pueblo heritage. Beatty seems also to have worried about associating the Bureau with archaeological work. Tensions stemming from archaeologists' growing dominance in interpreting Native American heritage were established by the 1940s, especially in the U.S. National Park Service (Colwell-Chanthaphonh 2005). Beatty and the Indian Arts and Crafts Board may have wanted to distance their missions and operations from National Park Service approaches and goals. From this perspective, limiting associations with archaeological collections and interpretations would have been appealing.

Fourth, the Shaeffers' talents and energies were not focused exclusively on site preservation and museum development. The Shaeffers juggled many responsibilities while at Kinishba. In addition to parental, doctoral student, and museum curator duties, the Shaeffers installed an elaborate subsurface drainage system. Margaret supervised the re-roofing of 40–70 rooms, assisted by Apache crew leaders Huge Massey and Chester Holden. A tree-ring study that examined primary beams in Kinishba's rebuilt rooms identified 19 dates clustered at 1950, confirming that all or most of the more than 100 trees that yielded the beams were harvested by the Shaeffers and their helpers (Baxter et al.1997). And there was still more. Trained as an archaeologist, interested in doctoral studies, and encouraged by Cummings to excavate rather than administer, Jim dug. Like his mentor, Jim dug a lot, administered some, and wrote a little.

Post-1939 Excavations and Resulting Collections

Cummings, too, excavated at Kinishba following the November 1939 "Pow-Wow" that celebrated the completion of the Group I excavation and rebuilding reported in Cummings's monograph (1940). Correspondence records and the Kinishba Museum catalog cards on file in the Arizona State Museum Registrar's office, indicate substantial excavations from 1941 until 1944, when catalog card entries cease. The cards are divided into those that received ASM accession numbers and those that did not. Only a small number of the cards include useful collection descriptions or precise provenience information, but the dates and names on the cards do help outline a chronology of 1940s excavations. Cummings and Turner Thompson excavated parts of Group VIII: room 3 in 1940, room 4 in 1941–1942, and room 14 (?) in 1942. Cummings and James Thompson and Turner Thompson excavated Group IV (rooms 7 and 12, as well as fill south of room 10) from 1942 to 1944, making substantial collections. Cummings's 1940 site report does not address excavations in Group III, but both the building stone and the original foundations of this room block were reused in constructing, circa 1945, guest quarters, storage rooms, and workshops for the Kinishba Museum (Figure 2.3).

The Shaeffers took up where Cummings left off. A two-page *Arizona Republic* article (Sunday, July 9, 1950) article states:

> When Dr. Cummings left Jim became curator, continuing the work of probing the ancient pueblo.... His major undertaking was the excavation of the huge courtyard, which Dr. Cummings suspected might open doors to new knowledge....He went east to complete work at Columbia University for his doctor's degree, and Margaret became curator, remaining at Kinishba with their children, Peter, Murray [sic] and Sarah. Jim is still on leave, writing the thesis for his degree, and it is Margaret who officially is supervising the work....Kinishba today is preserved with its rich index to prehistory as an Indian Service museum.

Regrettably, the archival records found thus far do not specify precisely where excavations did (and did not) occur, who participated, what was found, or the disposition of the collected materials. The Shaeffers approached the excavations as part of their official duties as Bureau of Indian Affairs curators, and there is no record of Antiquities Act permit issuance, permission from or consultation with the White Mountain Apache Tribe or other entities, or specific reporting or curatorial requirements. Albert Schroeder's field notes from his November 16, 1955 inspection of Kinishba on behalf of the National Park Service state, "Fire pits and bins in rooms in fairly good shape....Some digging in mound on W. side, but old. Probably Schaffer's [sic]."

Reports and correspondence do point up some basic facts about the excavations. In the summer of 1947 Jim led an effort to find and dig all of the features that both his work and Cummings's earlier trenching identified in the Group I plaza. The Shaeffers' findings support the conclusion that all or most of the main plaza area in Group I was roofed and then un-roofed beginning after A.D. 1230 (Shaeffer 1949; Chapter 4). The excavations also contribute rare data to the regional corpus of information bearing on the morphology and use of subsurface structures. Later in 1947, Jim Shaeffer and Holden, perhaps with assistance from other Apache men, dug all eight rooms comprising Group VI, along with scattered and apparently unreported excavations on Kinishba's west side (Chapter 3). Lastly, we know from letters Shaeffer exchanged with Terah Smiley—and from Schroeder's above-noted 1955 field observation—that the Shaeffers explored widely, and possibly also deeply—in the Group II plaza and room areas on the west side of the stream channel that bisects Kinishba.

Because the documentary records of these excavations are sparse, virtually every shred is presented in this volume. The Group VI dig-

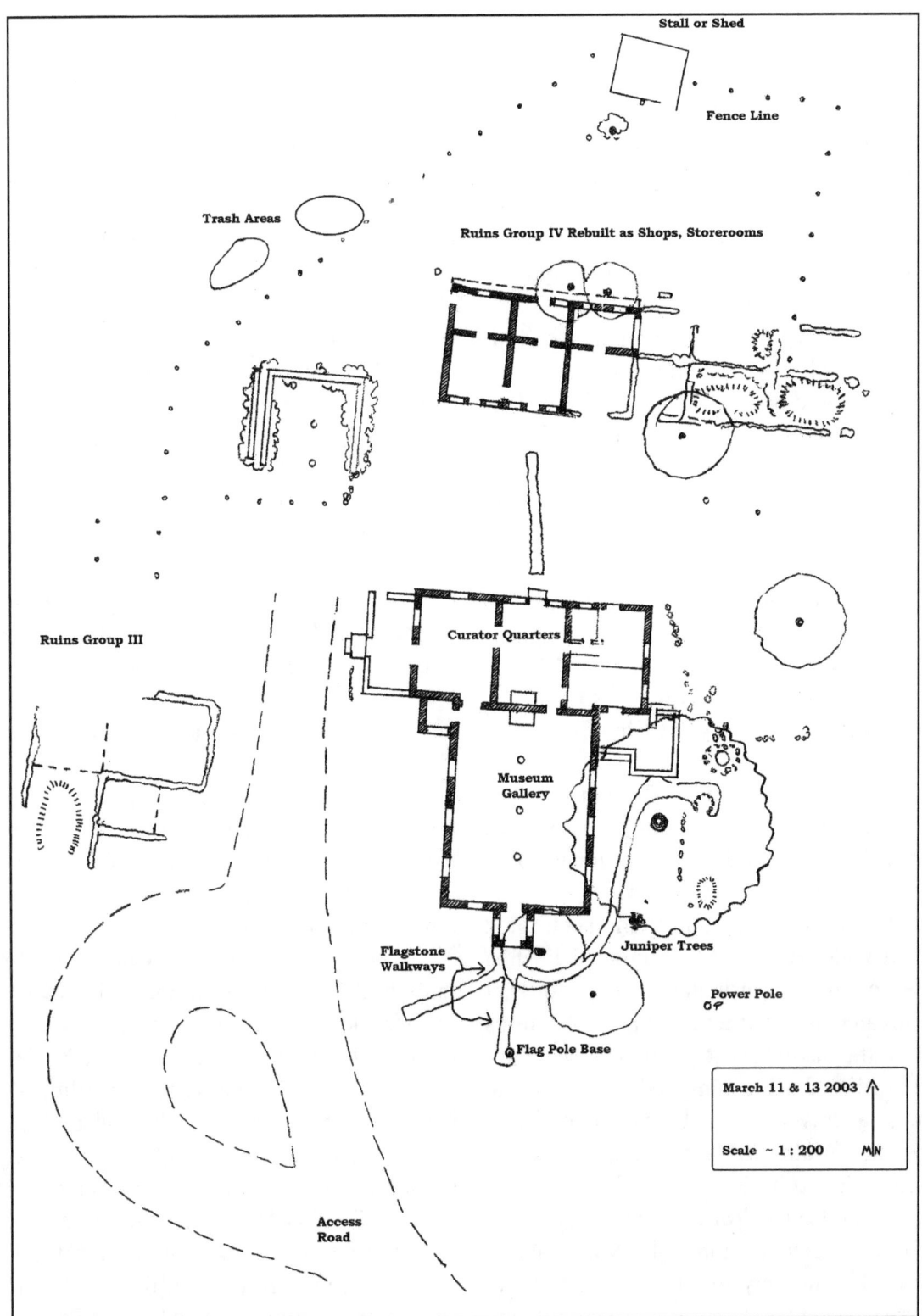

Figure 2.3. The remains of the Kinishba Museum and curator's quarters, 2003 (David A. Gregory, courtesy White Mountain Apache Tribe Historic Preservation Office).

ging is documented in a report (Chapter 3) that remains rudimentary despite developmental editing. Documentation for the Great Kiva excavations is more extensive, and the report more complete in its data presentation and interpretation (Chapter 4). In neither case have collections, full field notes or other primary excavation materials been found to substantiate or expand the Shaeffers' typescript descriptions. There is no original graphic documentation of the Group VI work beyond a rough sketch of the room block configuration and some pages of unsystematic notes. More troubling still is that documentation has yet to surface for the Shaeffers' excavations in Group II. Diligent attention to the possibility of disturbance by the Shaeffers and other undocumented excavators will be required accompaniments to any future Kinishba excavations or damage assessments.

Notes on Kinishba Collections and Management Following the Shaeffers

The materials recovered and recorded during the Shaeffers' excavations have not been located. In an effort to find additional documentation relating to the Shaeffers' excavations and to locate the artifact collections, I consulted far and wide. Beyond the original Kinishba Museum catalog cards and other records, I investigated archival and artifact collections at all of the institutions that Jim and Margaret were affiliated with: University of Arizona, Columbia University, the University of Oklahoma, the Southern Plains Indian Museum, Nebraska's Stuhr Museum of the Prairie Pioneer, and New York's Franklin County Historical Society (Figure 2.4) (Note that Jim was most commonly referred to as "Jack" in later years and that efforts to find a photograph of Margaret were, lamentably, unsuccessful). Nothing linked to Kinishba or the Shaeffers was catalogued or otherwise recorded at these museums. Nor is there any indication that the Shaeffers' collections somehow became embedded in and "swamped" by materials collected in the course of Cummings's digging.

What the limited documentary evidence does suggest is a complex history for the Kinishba Museum collections. Per the terms of the U.S. Antiquities Act permits that Cummings secured for each excavation season, 1931–1939, Cummings's excavation collections were transferred to Arizona State Museum for curation and interpretation. In 1940, when the newly completed Kinishba Museum's exhibit cases were ready for use, Cummings approached Arizona State Museum in his capacity as the Bureau of Indian Affairs' museum curator, asking Haury to borrow back a selection of Kinishba artifacts. An October 3, 1940 letter from Haury to the Fort Apache Agency Bureau of Indian Affairs Superintendent authorized a loan of 17 ceramic vessels and an array of ornaments from the site. Additional loans of items excavated from the site and curated at Arizona State Museum took place during the next few years (Welch 2007a:23). Both Cummings and the Shaeffers also acquired items for the Kinishba Museum through the purchase of ethnographic and archaeological objects throughout the 1940s.

The Kinishba Museum bumped along through the mid-1950s. In the spring of 1952, the Marine Corps reactivated Jim for duty in Korea. Margaret and the kids left Kinishba in June. Lack of success in propelling Kinishba into the currents of federal budgeting condemned the site to a perpetual struggle for solvent and sustainable management. The Bureau of Indian Affairs kept the museum open that summer, using local staff from the Fort Apache Agency. Reports of theft and vandalism at the museum circulated at the 1953 Pecos conference. In 1954, when the Indian Arts and Crafts Board absorbed the meager annual funding ($66,000) for all four Bureau of Indian

Figure 2.4. James B. "Jack" Shaeffer at the Stuhr Museum of the Prairie Pioneer, circa 1969 (courtesy Stuhr Museum of the Prairie Pioneer).

Affairs museums, Kinishba's entire budget was transferred to the Board, but responsibilities for managing and preserving Kinishba were not. The Bureau's Fort Apache Agency was left with a crumbling reconstructed pueblo and a museum desperate for professional management, but bereft of budget. The Shaeffers moved to Oklahoma following Jim's tour of duty. When Cummings died in May of 1954, Kinishba's future was uncertain, to say the least.

A May 1956 field trip by the White Mountain Apache Tribal Council to review the site's condition and prospects left the Council unimpressed with both the Bureau's management of Kinishba and the prospect of assuming site responsibilities. What the Council was willing to do, however, was to let the Bureau off the hook. Following the visit, the Council voted to support transferring site administration to the National Park Service, bringing an end to the Bureau's specific responsibility for Kinishba.

The Council decision spelled the end of the active, hands-on management required, with or without sustained institutional sponsorship, to foster Cummings's vision for Kinishba. Episodic spurts of correspondence among federal, tribal, and state officials continued through the 1960s. A small cluster of Cummings's most dedicated students—the Shaeffers, Emil Haury, Eric Reed, and Albert Schroeder—soldiered on as Kinishba preservation advocates (see, for example, Reed (1942, 1946). But as was the case with the fabled Humpty Dumpty, all the king's men, could not put Kinishba together again. Welch (2007a) chronicles the bureaucratic intrigues that brought Kinishba to the brink of designation as a national monument, followed by eventual adoption by the White Mountain Apache Tribe and the Fort Apache Heritage Foundation (see also Hoerig 2010; Welch 2000, 2009; Welch and Ferguson 2007, Chapter 10). Stewart Udall's 1964 declaration of Kinishba as a National Historical Landmark retired all but the faintest hopes for an emphatic response to the siren song of a 'monument to Native American civilization' that summoned Cummings to Kinishba and wed him to the place for the last best years of his long life.

What happened with and to the Kinishba Museum collections after the Shaeffers departed is known only on the basis of a few recorded transactions. On July 24, 1956, Bob Baker, Jim Gifford, and Bill Wasley arrived from Arizona State Museum to remove all collections, records, and Cummings's personal library from the Kinishba Museum. That fall, presumably after inspecting the recently arrived materials, Haury culled dozens, and possibly hundreds of items deemed not to be artifacts or to otherwise possess scientific value, apparently discarding these. In late 1958 or 1959, when Kinishba's incorporation into the National Park Service system seemed imminent, Haury authorized the transfer of the Kinishba Museum collections to the National Park Service Southwest Archaeological Center in Globe (later the Western Archaeological Conservation Center in Tucson). It seems likely, based on records indicating continuous custody of the ethnographic collections from the Kinishba Museum, that only the archaeological collections were transferred to the Park Service. In late 1968 or early 1969, when it became clear that Kinishba would not become a national monument, Dave Tuggle, Bion Griffin and others moved the archaeological collections back to Arizona State Museum from Park Service facilities in Globe.

There are at least three plausible scenarios for the disposition of the collections from the Shaeffers' excavations that cannot be ruled out on the basis of the available evidence: one, the Shaeffers took the collections with them when they moved and their location is unknown; two, the collections were stolen, misappropriated, or otherwise dispersed before the 1956 transfer to Arizona State Museum; three, the collections were culled or otherwise dispersed following the 1956 transfer.

Despite persistent rumors that much of the Kinishba Museum collection was pilfered in the wake of the Shaeffers' departure, the most valuable and marketable elements of Cummings's Kinishba collections remain at Arizona State Museum, suggesting that the collections were largely intact when initially moved there. If Haury did cull the Shaeffers' collections after 1956, it may be presumed Haury's decisions were based in part on the lack of documentation required to place the collections in curatorial context. The quest to understand the scope and contents of the Kinishba's archaeological collections in general and to locate the materials gathered in the course of the Shaeffers' excavations in particular, brings to mind the old quip, "three moves is the same as a fire" (Mike Jacobs 2009, personal communication).

As a final note on the collections, it bears mention that the White Mountain Apache Tribe claims all materials removed from Kinishba as tribal property and consistently requests participation in decisions relating to collections use and management. An Interior Department Solicitor opinion (Horn 1988) suggests that collections made from tribal trust lands under the authority of Antiquities Act permits are U.S. government property. The opinion seems not to consider either the facts specific to the Tribe's ownership claims or the U.S. Constitution's Fifth Amendment prohibition against taking private property (including tribal property) without just compensation (see Welch and Ferguson 2007, Chapter 10).

And so, after the 1953 museum closure, silence resumed at Kinishba, punctuated mainly by the intermittent clatter and rumble of walls and roofs collapsing. During the 1960s, 70s and 80s, the Cummings-Shaeffer restoration succumbed to the universal architectural solvents of weather and gravity. The same period witnessed the dissolution, in baths of postmodern rationality, of colonial models for tribal relations. The White Mountain Apache Tribe responded strongly to calls for cultural heritage stewardship. But cries for preserving Kinishba (which one: ruin? rebuilt pueblo? both?) were drowned out by appeals to salvage Apache culture and language. Apaches focused their cultural heritage revitalization efforts at the veritable source of their subjugation—Fort Apache (Welch 2008, 2010; Welch and Brauchli 2010). The Tribe's Cultural Center at Fort Apache has shepherded investments in developing local capacity in the documentation of oral traditions, the development of heritage tourism markets, and the balancing of Euroamerican accounts of local history and culture with perspectives derived from Apache and Pueblo knowledge and experience.

By the 1990s, shared interests in re-establishing respect for ancestral sites became the basis for inter-tribal collaborations. Efforts to stabilize Kinishba's architecture and to repatriate human remains and funerary objects removed during excavations are grounded in the combination of, on the one hand, Ndee ties to their lands and admiration for the builders and occupants of the region's pueblos and, on the other, enduring Zuni and Hopi concern for their ancestral homes and extended families (Welch and Ferguson 2007, Chapter 10).

As for the Shaeffers, only snippets of their post-Kinishba careers have surfaced. By 1956, Jim Shaeffer had assumed the directorship of the Southern Plains Indian Museum in Anadarko, Oklahoma. He went on to work at the University of Oklahoma's Archaeological Salvage Project (Shaeffer 1960) and later, with Margaret, at the Stuhr Museum of the Prairie Pioneer in Nebraska (Shaeffer 1963) and the Jefferson County Historical Society in New York, where Margaret became the director from 1972 through 1986 (*Pueblo Chieftain* 2004). In his letter of July 25, 2003 to the National Park Service Jim acknowledges that Kinishba's first and most complete visitor guide (Shaeffer and Shaeffer 1956) "was written by Margaret ... for the Bureau of Indian Affairs... They paid for the salaries and operating costs of running the Pueblo for tourists and our meager excavational [sic.] costs."

The visitor guide seems to have been the Shaeffers' final rescue attempt, but was probably printed too late to create benefits or even have on-site distribution. Efforts to establish communications with the Shaeffers to discuss their time at Kinishba led to a retirement home in upstate New York. The manager informed me that Jim had passed away within a few weeks of Margaret's death in 2004 (*Pueblo Chieftain* 2004). The individual was confident that the Shaeffers would have been pleased to know that work continued toward Kinishba's respectful study and visitation. My faltering communications with the Shaeffers' three children and their colleagues at the Jefferson County Historical Society failed to yield additional information or a photograph of the couple. The quest to find the materals excavated by the Shaeffers and place these in the context of the family's experience dead-ended.

Although it is not possible to know with full certainty that this volume carries forward the best and most important knowledge of the Shaeffers' excavations at Kinishba, it seems safe to claim that the publication of the Shaeffers' works offers significant testimony that came perilously close to being forever silenced. Colleagues and readers are encouraged to not only continue the quest to un-silence Kinishba, but to heed the cautionary tales embedded in the history of Cummings's and the Shaeffers' quests to extract, interpret, and perpetuate the cultural, scientific, management, and economic development values embedded in Kinishba and similar places. These lessons might be summed up, simply and with apology to Samuel Johnson, as 'the road to ruins is paved with good intentions.' Without the promise of sturdy institutional support, the seductive lures of excavation and architectural interpretation focused on serving the interests of small communities are usually no match for fiscal and climatic vicissitudes operating on generational scales.

Chapter 3

The Excavation of Group VI, Ruins of a Small House Unit

James B. Shaeffer
Margaret M. Shaeffer

Kinishba Ruins is a large Pueblo III–IV ruin of some 500 ground floor rooms, located north and west of the White River (Figure 2.1). The site was first noted in archaeological literature by Bandelier (1890–92) and excavated by Dr. Byron Cummings during the summers 1931–1939 (Cummings 1940; see also Baldwin 1934, 1941). The site is situated toward the northern or upper end, and on the western side, of a large valley about 4 km wide. This broad valley slopes southward toward the White River. This is the largest valley in the immediate area and the only one subsidiary to the White River suitable for extensive agriculture. Kinishba is the largest agriculturally oriented settlement on the Fort Apache reservation; the second largest such settlement, Grasshopper, is located in the second largest expanse of land suitable for dry farming, about 60 km west of Kinishba (see Welch 1996; also Reid and Whittlesey 1999, 2005; Riggs 2005).

In plan view, the ruins of Kinishba consist of two main groups on either side of an arroyo, with each group consisting of over 200 ground floor rooms (Figure 2.1). Scattered north of these main groups are six smaller groups ranging from five to twenty rooms. Seventy-six tree ring dates range between the years A.D. 1233 and 1307 (Baldwin 1935a, 1935b), but correspondence with the Laboratory of Tree-Ring Research at the University of Arizona and other evidence suggests that the site may have been occupied both earlier and later than these dates (Smiley 1951; see Lyons, Chapter 7). At least some of Kinishba's small room groups are thought to have been occupied at roughly the same time, A.D. 1200 to 1400, as the larger blocks of rooms (Group I and II), while others may have only been built late in the sequence (Chapter 3).

Environment

At the present time the floor of the Kinishba valley, which varies in elevation from about 1500–1700 m (4900–5600 feet) above sea level, is dotted with clusters of piñon and juniper. These trees are recent invaders from the surrounding hills and their profusion stems from or has been encouraged by the introduction of cattle and the suppression of rangeland fires. Local old-timers say the conifers have taken over the flat ground only since about 1930. Ponderosa pines are scattered along the bases and crests of hills, outliers of the main belt of western yellow pine beginning some 16 km to the north and about 300 m higher in elevation than in the Kinishba valley. The hills which surround the valley floor still hold remnants of the wildlife which formerly must have abounded here: mountain lion, black bear, deer, elk, coyote, rabbit, squirrel, turkey, and hawks, mountain lion, porcupine, rabbit, ringtail or cacomistle, skunk, squirrel, crow, eagle, hawk, owl and turkey. Upon the higher mesas and mountains, and in the river valleys, there are in addition beaver, elk, javelina (arrival following Kinishba's depopulation), fox, muskrat, otter, wolf, prairie dog, raccoon, duck, geese and grouse.

The variation of climate today is probably much as it was when the site was occupied, being little given to extremes at any season (U.S. Department of Agriculture 1941:763, 772). In summer the daily temperature rises as high as 105 °F but in the main averages 72.6 °F; the winter average is 36.6 °F, with occasional dips to zero and below. Snow rarely remains on the ground for a long period. Average precipitation amounts to 17.83 in a year, falling mainly in July and the first part of August and again from December through March. While this is sufficient for dry farming in most years, it is to be noted that Kinishba is now located some five miles from the nearest reliable surface water, the White River. For a settlement the size of Kinishba, this is quite a distance. There is not much overt evidence for believing that a source of water existed in the arroyo which bisects the site during the pueblo's occupation, but some non-Indians claim to recall a sluggish flow there around 1920. Apaches who have lived in this vicinity say there has not been running water in the arroyo within the memory of the old men. Tom Friday (see Kessell 1974), who has visited Kinishba several times recently, insists that the arroyo has not flowed except after storms since at least around 1900. Of course, the topography and climate may have changed sufficiently to have made the spring water retreat underground, but there is no way to prove this. Altogether, it is probable a source of water once existed in the arroyo that divides the site.

Culture and Research History

The site is located near the heart of what has been called the Western Pueblo complex (Reed 1948). This was a main area of reconcentration following the depopulation of the Four Corners area beginning toward the close of the A.D. 1100s. Here, south of the Little Colorado River between the present towns of Holbrook and Globe, extending to the New Mexico border in the east and to the Verde River in the west, is a mountainous belt forested with piñon and juniper and, at higher altitudes, ponderosa pines. During the extreme drought in the latter A.D. 1200s—an apparent cause of population dispersion in the greater Four Corners area—this mountain region evidently continued to be sufficiently watered to support large communities which sprang up at favorable points along the Mogollon Rim. Among the more prominent ones mentioned in the literature are the sites of Pinedale (Haury 1931), Point of Pines to the south (Haury 1989), and Grasshopper to the west (Reid and Whittlesey 1999, 2005). The Point of Pines sites are more extensive and appear to have been occupied for a greater time span. In any case, all of the largest sites in this broad region feature concentrated blocks of rooms built around central courts of what were once covered aboveground kivas (Shaeffer 1954, Chapter 4). There are still many sites of considerable size in the Mogollon Rim region that have yet to be fully recorded or reported in publications (see Reagan 1930; Welch et al., Chapter 9).

Early accounts of Kinishba Ruins (Bandelier 1890–92; Spier 1919) describe the surface aspects of the site. The first organized digging at Kinishba was initiated in 1931 by Dr. Byron Cummings, then head of the Department of Archaeology, University of Arizona, and Director of the Arizona State Museum. Cummings continued digging each summer until 1939.

Excavation was carried out mainly by students attending Cummings's archeological field school, but supplementary funds and Apache labor were supplied by the Indian Division of the Civilian Conservation Corps, administered by the United States Indian Service (later known as the Bureau of Indian Affairs). Most published work has addressed the two largest units, especially Group I, which dominate the site and face each other from either side of a deep arroyo (Cummings 1940; Baldwin 1941).

In addition to these large units, seven smaller groups surround or are adjacent to the main room blocks (Figure 2.1). Less investigative attention has been given to these smaller units. On the east bank of the arroyo, on the outskirts of Group I, are the three small units identified as Group III, Group IV, and Group VIII, each of which comprises from four to eight rooms. On the west bank are the three small satellite units of Group II: Group V, Group VI, and Group VII. This report deals with the excavation of Group VI and attempts to place it temporally in relation to the other groups (Figure 3.1).

The excavation took place during the fall and winter of 1947, when Jim and Margaret Shaeffer were curators in charge of the ruins and museum, at that time under the jurisdiction of the Division of Education, U.S. Indian Bureau. Table 3.1 provides a transcription of the most legible and pertinent portions of the only field notes thus far found from the excavations at Group VI. Assistance in the excavation was given by the museum caretaker, Chester Holden. Analysis of the material was completed during the summer of 1948, prior to Jim Shaeffer's departure for graduate work at Columbia University. A draft of the excavation report was completed in 1949. A dissertation (Shaeffer 1954), the Korean War, changes of residence from Arizona to Oklahoma, and work in other fields caused the manuscript to be put aside. The present report lacks photographic coverage due to loss of negatives and dispersion of the material. It nevertheless adds to the records of excavation at Kinishba, the largest and possibly the most important center of population south of the Mogollon Rim and north of the Salt River during the latter Pueblo III period and earlier Pueblo IV period (circa A.D. 1200–1400; see Table 2.1).

Plan of the Site

Kinishba's two main ruins groups are bisected by the arroyo running north–south through the site (see Figure 2.2). Each group consists of the remains of large apartment house surrounding a central court and three much smaller outlying room blocks. Each of the large units contain approximately 200–240 ground floor rooms; the largest of the smaller groups contains 16 rooms and the smallest 6, making in all a conservatively estimated total of more than 500 ground floor rooms.

On the east bank of the arroyo is Group I, the large apartment house completely excavated and partially restored under Cummings. Of the three smaller eastern units, Group III and Group IV have been completely excavated. Cummings and his helpers partially excavated Group VIII in the early 1940s. On the west bank considerably less excavation and no reconstruction work has been done. Group II has only been sampled. The three outlying room groups west of the arroyo—V, VI, and VII—were, until the present work was begun, practically untouched.

The project reported on here sought to address the relative lack of work done on Kinishba's western side and to gather additional data to explain to the public the probable relationships among the small outlying groups and between the clusters of groups on either side of the arroyo. Group VI was small enough to

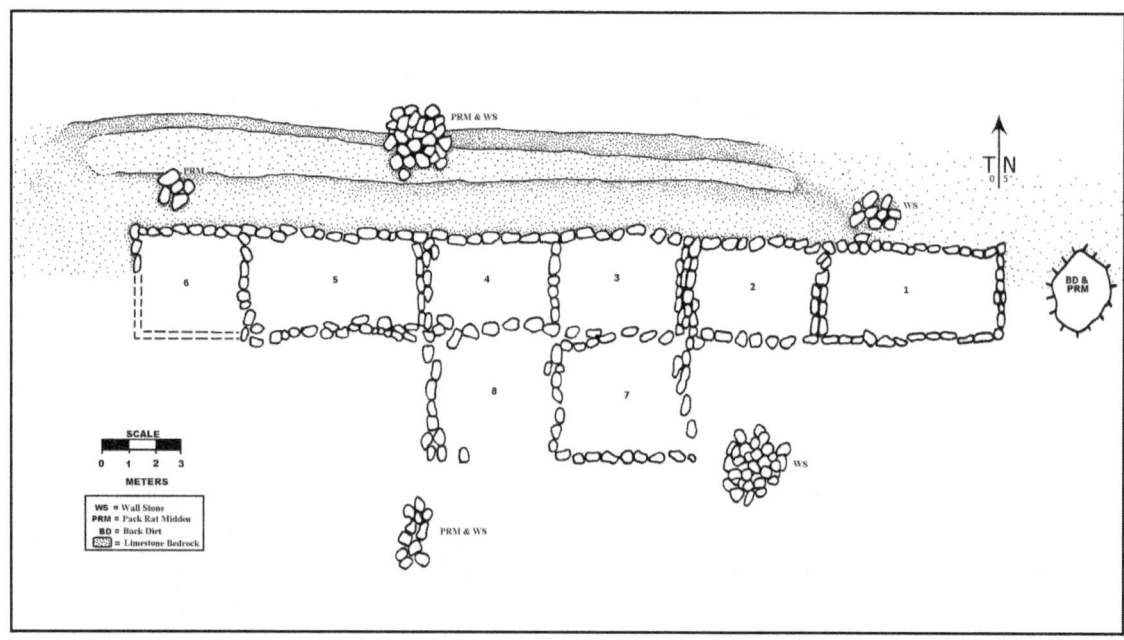

Figure 3.1. Plan view map of Ruins Group VI (John R. Welch, courtesy White Mountain Apache Tribe Historic Preservation Office).

insure its complete excavation in a relatively short time and was therefore selected with the idea of using it as a means for gathering the information required to assist with public interpretation.

THE PLAN AND BUILDING PHASES OF GROUP VI

Group VI is located on the west bank of the arroyo, north of Group II and slightly beyond Group V, but set back farther from the arroyo edge than the latter (see Figure 2.1). Because of the proximity of groups II, V, and VI, it seems likely that they may prove to be contemporaneous and that the occupants used the two open areas between them in common, perhaps as a plaza. However, this possibility has yet to be assessed, and doing so would require additional excavations.

Group VI was built on a slight slope at the base of a hill, with the land behind it rising to the north (Figure 3.1). This resulted in run-off water being directed over Group VI, and the walls are broken down more completely than those that comprised the larger adjacent groups. In fact, the western and southern walls of Room 6 in Group VI have been almost totally swept away. The highest walls found in Group VI were those of Room 3, which stood about 75 cm in height upon excavation. The walls of the other rooms became progressively lower to the east and west, so that the southern portion of Room 1 was only 30 cm high, while that of Room 6 at the western end was a mere foundation, 15–20 cm high.

Prior to the excavations it was estimated that the group consisted of six rooms. But subsequent work revealed Rooms 5 and 6 below the present ground level. This made a row of six rooms on an east–west axis with two large, additional rooms projecting southward from the middle of this line of rooms. At first it was

Table 3.1. Selections from J.B. Shaeffer's Group VI Excavation Notes

Sept 28
Cleared off yucca, thorn bushes, junipers from east end of Group VI, exposing probably two rooms on east end . . . small enough to complete this winter . . . . [will] try to correlate this and Groups I & II   Flank front of Group 5 or courtyard with kiva between. Worked after dinner to dark.

Sept 29
Established E, N & S walls at east end. Found two smaller walls . . . opposite each other on N & S walls. From sherds possibly later surface occupation. East end robbed of stones.

Sept 30
Moved our equipment south, two tables of sawhorses, water jars, sherd cleaning equipment, ladders and drawing equipment. Afternoon started flattening throughout . . . floor 8.

Oct 2
Morning widened trench N. wall. . . . part of olla found. Afternoon worked on east wall trench . . . Found first whole pot, part ¾ groove ax. Evening uncovered a wall only partly there.

Oct 3
Completed east side exposing wall, also south wall as far as initial exposure out 13' from SE corner. About 6 stones in E wall . . . stone 11 cut in mark in stone facing as (++++++) . . . .
More pottery N side; little on south. Little stone N west South side. . . . Possibly standing wall collapsed outward while other roofs occupied . . . . Some evidence of fire just under filler walls.

Oct 4
Worked S. wall to . . . wall of room jutting out to South.

Oct 5
Cleaned out all of #12 rocks & walls up to 3' at W end.
Little sherds some stone influents rubble of wall not very defined floor.

Oct 6
Corner of joint out to east end so far.   used as outdoor fireplace . . . . Marked stones out

Oct 7
Possible . . . cover indicates 2 story. . . .

Oct 17
Wall material flattening out at 1' level
2nd floor or 1st floor roof about 1' level
Pots resting on top of scattered small pieces of charcoal
Small rock on top of this level sandstone . . . .
This wall stood a while before toppling

Oct 18
10' x 17' room   Long narrow not like Group 1 which are about 10 x 12.
More Like ULC [Upper Little Colorado] pueblos. Puerco ruins.

thought that the construction resulted from the partitioning of a parallel row of walls with the later addition of two larger rooms on the front. However, more careful analysis of the masonry showed a different story.

The masonry of Group VI is of the same general type as that found elsewhere at Kinishba, namely ashlar exterior walls of large, evenly coursed blocks of sandstone separated by courses of smaller spalls, or "chinks" (Figure 3.2). The individual stones in the large courses of the rooms comprising Group VI are not so often separated by spalls as they are in parts of Group I. The interior portion of these double walls is of coursed rubble set in mud. This is in definite contrast to the random setting of the rubble so often encountered in Group I. The ashlar part of this type of wall acts as the supporting unit; the rubble serves as the stabilizing unit.

The apparent consistency in the use of ashlar masonry in exterior wall construction permits retracing of the structural development of Group VI. The rubble face, being more susceptible to weathering, was of necessity intended to serve as the more protected interior

Figure 3.2. Tad Nichols and other members of Cummings' excavation crew clearing Group I masonry walls at Kinishba, circa 1936 (Tad Nichols, Tad Nichols Collection, Box 1, Folder 5, courtesy Arizona State Museum).

surface. Using this assumption as a premise, it is possible to establish the following construction phase sequence for Group VI.

Examination of the Group VI building plan reveals that only Room 6 has four interior walls of rubble. This suggests that Room 6 was built first. It is possible to keep the ashlar (weather-side, or exterior) wall on the outside only if construction then proceeded from west to east. Had construction progressed from the east, a rubble face would have been on the exterior. A similar situation would occur in regards to the rubble walls were it to be assumed that Rooms 7 and 8 had been constructed first.

Examination of the north and south walls of Room 6 revealed, however, that they were laid in an unbroken line as far as the east wall of Room 3 and, consequently, that Rooms 4, 5 and 6 formed one unit, which had been closed at both ends and partitioned. Thus, the original unit appears to have consisted of two living rooms with fireplaces and a storage room having a lateral entrance. The remaining walls of the other rooms were so low that lateral entrances, if they did exist, could not be identified. Roof entrance is the more common practice across Kinishba's other excavated groups, and reported exclusively so for Group III (see Cummings 1940:41-42).

With the initial building unit identified, the next step was to determine whether the additional rooms were added first to the east or to the south. The unbroken east wall common to Rooms 3 and 7 shows that these were added at the same time. This finding raises the question of priority between these two rooms and Room 8. If Rooms 3 and 7 had been built first, the west wall of Room 7 would have had rubble on the exterior. If Room 8 was built first then ashlar exteriors would have been maintained on all walls. Rooms 3 and 4 could then have been added as a single construction phase, followed by Rooms 1 and 2, each added separately. In summation, the building phases consist of the following rooms added in apparently discrete construction episodes: 4, 5 and 6; then 8; then 3 and 7; then 2; and lastly 1—a total of five construction phases for this group.

The fact that this small group was expanded one or two rooms at a time underscores the gradual manner of much pueblo growth, at least in portions of Kinishba. Building materials may have had to be carried here a mile or more, not counting other labor, all of which took time off from the routine of livelihood. The most probable source of the majority of stone used in Kinishba's construction is a subsurface stratum of sandstone on the east side of the arroyo. Little of this stratum remains, and the stone exposed in the arroyo today is very friable and is found only occasionally as a component of the rubble facing of the walls. Because this friable type lies beneath the hardier stratum, it is clear the arroyo was not as deep at the time of occupation as it is at present. Indeed, the quarrying and removal of the building stone likely contributed to arroyo entrenchment.

The substantial labor investments alone may have been sufficient reason to put off the addition of new rooms as long as possible. It is not difficult, therefore, to imagine the time involved in the construction of large groups such as Group I and Group II, where perhaps one half of the total mass of rooms would have been added by slow accretion after construction of the original nucleus. Roberts (1931) provides another example of structural analysis as the basis for understanding pueblo growth and aspects of demographics. A more careful study of Kinishba construction phases across the room groups might result in a clearer conception of the rate and manner of pueblo growth, as well as a firmer basis for comparing the groups and estimating Kinishba's changing population.

Material Culture

The following pages list and describe the types of material culture found in the Group VI rooms. The findings are grouped by general type to facilitate understanding of the range of local variability and as a complement to item-by-item documentation. The report first describes the various types of architectural features, including slab-lined hearths (Table 3.2a), paved areas (Table 3.2b), and mealing bins (Table 3.2c). This discussion is followed by an enumeration of the stone implements (Tables 3.2e-3.2k, 3.3 and 3.4) and ceramic wares (Table 3.6). The simple statistical tabulations for each type of material culture are followed by summaries that aggregate and synthesize the data to facilitate comparisons of element and trait distributions within Group VI (Table 3.5) and between Group I and Group VI (Table 3.7).

Fireboxes

Fireboxes, or slab-lined hearths occurred in all but two of the rooms in Group VI (Table 3.2a). The difference between variants 1 and 2 likely may signify nothing more than individual or family preference. The variation is not an indication of a trend within the community since the deeper rectangular variant apparently occurs in rooms built both before and after the construction of rooms containing the shallower squarish variant.

One peculiar arrangement found alongside four of the fireboxes was the placing of an upended mano on one side of the fireplace so that it projected at an angle some four or five inches above the stone side of the firebox. The exact purpose is not certain but, in Room 5, a large, oval-shaped stone cover was found alongside the firebox. Examination of the cover's underside revealed a burned area and ash similar in color and texture to that found in the firebox. In this particular instance, it seemed to show that the mano was used to support this cover in a tipped position, which would allow the fire to continue to burn. Such an arrangement could have served either as a damper or as some sort of a cooking surface, though for the latter purpose the surface of the cover was very irregular and somewhat convex.

Flagged (Paved with Flagstone) Areas

Among the unusual features of Group VI is the presence of flagged areas in all but two of the rooms (Table 3.2b). Flagging occurred in rooms either as a rectangular area in one corner or as a four-foot strip across the entire length of one end of the room. The flagging consisted of irregular sandstone slabs laid within two or three inches of each other but in no definite pattern. The paved surfaces were invariably found buckled rather than even or smooth. The edging was in all cases fairly regularly aligned. Artifacts were found on all these areas. Flagging of this sort, extent, and consistency has not been encountered before at Kinishba, either in Group I or in any of the smaller groups excavated.

Just what function the flagged areas might have served is uncertain. They seem too uneven and irregular to have served as a base for bedding. Their position at the ends and corners of rooms seems to preclude them being areas under overhead entrances since these were usually more centrally located. It is possible the pavements could have been set aside for ceremonial use or that they afforded extra protection for food storage areas sequestered from the room spaces by wattle and daub partitions not discerned in the excavations. If the paving reflects a specific use of paved space then the flagged areas may have served as workshops of some sort.

Table 3.2. Items in Group VI Rooms

Variants	Occurrences	Diagnostic	Average Dimensions
		a. Fireboxes	
1	4	rectangular, deeper	13 ¾ x 11 ¼ x 7 ½
2	2	squarish, shallower	16 ½ x 14 ½ x 6
		b. Flagstone Pavements	
1	2	located in room corner	45" x 50"
2	6	located across end of room	50" x 100"
		c. Mealing Bins	
1	2	single bin	45" x 50"
2	1	double bin	50" x 100"
		d. Covers	
1	7	rectangular shape	17 x 15 x 1¼
2	5	oval shape	15 x 10 x 1¼
		e. Stone Axes	
1	5	round headed - short bitted	4½ x 2½ x 1½
2	2	round headed - long bitted	5½ x 2¼ x 1¾
3	2	flat headed - short bitted	3½ x 2¼ x 1¾
4	1	round headed - center hafted	5½ x 2¼ x 1½
		f. Choppers	
1	4	curved chopping edge	5¼ x 4 x 2
2	3	straight chopping edge	5½ x 3½ x 1½
		g. Bifaces	
1	4	curved cutting edge	variable
2	4	straight cutting edge	variable
		h. Handstones	
1	7	sandstone	5¼ x 3½ x 1¾
2	3	same but basalt	4½ x 3 x 1¾
		i. Two-Hand Manos	
1	18	medium length, basalt	9 x 4 x 1¼
2	5	longer, basalt	11 x 4 x 1¼
3	6	medium length. sandstone	8 ¾ x 4¼ x 1¼
		j. Metates	
1	7	slab	12¾ x 9½ x 2½
2	2	trough	18 x 11½ x 5
3	1	slab with enclosing rim	11 x 7½ x 2½
		k. Polishing Stones	
1	14	oval or egg-shaped	6¾ x 3½ x 2
2	8	flattish, circular	4½ x 1½
		l. Deer Bone Awls	
1	3	split bone	5 ½ x ¼ x ¼
2	3	polished splinters	5 ¼ x ¼ x ¼
3	2	whole cannon bone	8 ½ x 2 ¾ x ½

Mealing Bins

The mealing bins in Group VI are constructed of four pieces of flat sandstone partially shaped into a roughly rectangular form (Table 3.2c). These slabs were embedded in the dirt to form and open box and left projecting four to six inches above the floor.

Each of the three bins found in Group VI contained a basalt metate of variable size set at an angle in mud. Below the end of the metates was a drop of several inches to a partly flagged surface composed of small flat pieces of sandstone. In one instance the scraping out and removal of the meal was further facilitated by the emplacement of a large ceramic bowl fragment to one side at the end of the metate.

Covers

A surprising abundance of so-called hatch or entry covers were recovered (Table 3.2d). Comparative data, such as exists for other groups, indicate that the frequency of the number of covers in Group VI was much higher than encountered in the previously excavated room groups.

Cover variant 1 was formed from slabs of sandstone and limestone evidently selected because of their natural rectangular shape. Only one occurrence had all four sides shaped and worked, but the corners were rounded on every rectangular cover. The common presence of the covers—two or three to the room—suggests that not all of these slabs were hatch covers. Several of the rectangular covers showed traces of paint and others were stained, leading to the hypothesis that they may have been associated with ceremonial paraphernalia or activities. However, it is to be noted that the surfaces were in most cases irregular.

Variant 2 was made of volcanic material and possibly does not represent variations of the same artifact. The possible use of these items as dampers or stove lids was discussed in the section on fireboxes.

Stone Axes

The Group VI excavations yielded four closely related stone axe variants, all made from a granite or diorite running from a grey to a light greenish color (Table 3.2e). These are all roughly polished, three-quarter grooved axes with the exception of variant 4, in which the top part of the full groove is very shallow and the surface is more highly polished.

Choppers

Variant 1 consists of a relatively thick, semi-circular piece of stone in which the edge was used as a sort of chopper (Table 3.2f). The edges show signs of battering as if they have been used to smash. It is probable that this so-called variant is not a formal, intentionally manufactured tool, but rather an implement that resulted from the utilization of broken halves of polishing stones. This is quite likely since so few were found; at the same time, the shape of the items is generally uniform and distinctive.

Variant 2 seems less likely to have resulted from utilizations of cast-off tools. Instead, a naturally formed river cobble of a roughly rectangular shape was selected in which one side was thicker and the other tapered off to a natural edge. This edge was then roughly but definitely chipped and became more so with use. Whatever the source of the chopper variation, utilization seems to have been only occasional, as the use did not appear to have been prolonged or consistently demanded enough to have resulted in the creation of a definite or abundant tool type.

Flints (chipped stone bifaces)

Variant 1 is distinguished by a very thin blade and was probably used as a side scraper; Variant 2 is an end-scraper somewhat thicker at its edge and not so expertly chipped (Table 3.2g).

In addition to these blades, the Group VI excavations recovered about a dozen unworked chips of various sizes (mostly of black diorite), the tip of a long thin flint awl or arrow point of chalcedony, and a lone fragment of obsidian.

Hammerstones

These consist of small, heavy river stones of diorite or granite. A number showed flat grinding planes at one end and were evidently also used as crushers or polishers.

Handstones

Also known as one-handed manos, these are smaller versions of the larger, two-handed manos described below (Table 3.2h). They reflect similar patters of variation and were probably used for purposes other than corn grinding and on smaller metates. Because of the more restricted motion, these implements were inclined to be more regular in shape.

It deserves mention that the percentage of sandstone to basalt as a material is higher in this type than in the two-handed manos, possibly because different products, including mineral pigments and other non-foodstuffs, were milled. This tool seems to have a lower occurrence in Group VI than in Group I.

Two-Handed Manos

About 80 percent of the manos found in Group VI were made of basalt and 20 percent were sandstone (Table 3.2i). This contrasts somewhat with the near absence of sandstone metates, which seems rather unusual in light of common conceptions that grinding and mill stones are most compatible when made of the same material. This apparent discontinuity may indicate either that the objects recovered are a poor reflection of the implements used by the occupants of Group VI, that mano and metate did not wear down at the same rates, or some combination. Comparably detailed information from Kinishba's other room groups is unavailable; however, the relative lack of sandstone manos might be a useful diagnostic should this pattern prove to be more widespread.

At first glance there seems to be a great variability in mano morphology. The usual mano form at Kinishba is a rectangular block of stone with parallel sides and squarish ends of either a long or a medium length and of either sandstone or vesicular basalt. Variations from this pattern that do occur represent not so much divergence of original shaping as they represent the same tool type in various stages of use. For example, the occurrence of narrow, beveled-edge manos in both sandstone and basalt seems to have resulted from deliberate attempts to prolong the life of the tool, possibly because of particularly abrasive texture or for less rational reasons. The beveled edge form seems to have been the final stage in the mano's use life, not a special-function implement.

Metates

The outstanding characteristic of the Group VI metates is the almost exclusive use of basalt as a material (Table 3.2j). There was only one other instance of the use of another material—porphyritic granitic. No sedimentary metates were observed in conjunction with the excavation of Group VI. While there has been as yet no isolation of early P II or early P III traits at Kinishba, the almost exclusive use of basalt as a metate material probably indicates a very definite trend away from the use of sedimentary rock. Limestone, sandstone and granite metates comprised as much as 25–30 percent of those found during the Group I excavations. This dominance of basalt metates in Group VI is in all probability another indication of a late trend.

In shape, too, there is remarkable conformity. Eight large slab metates were found in bins at floor level and nine slab metate fragments were found adjacent to the exterior walls. Fourteen of these 17 had parallel sides, ends well rounded, bottoms convex and the grinding showing a slight 1" – 7/8" concavity.

The trough variant was represented by one specimen found almost at the surface level of Room 4 and may thus not be truly associated with the original or main occupants of Group VI. The trough metate is somewhat larger and heavier, but differed mainly in the grinding surface being depressed about half an inch below parallel rims on either side, forming a shallow but distinct trough.

The remaining three metates are of the type often referred to as "paint metates." There is also one small-sized metate completely enclosed by a rim.

Polishing Stones

So called polishing stones are made for the most part of grey granite, the surface of which has been worked smooth, in some cases to a vitreous finish (Table 3.2k). The occupants apparently selected stream stones in two characteristic shapes, a flat circular form and a thick oval or egg shape.

These artifacts have been termed polishers but no doubt the name refers as much to their surface polish as to the function for which they were intended. Quite a number of those found, especially the flat variant, have traces of paint still on them and almost all of them bore marks at one point or another of having been used to crush or hammer. Also, where grinding surfaces do occur they are rather small indicating a restricted milling motion such as might result when applied weight was doing most of the action. It is likely that one of their primary functions must have been use in the preparation of paints and other finely milled products and materials.

Arrow Shaft Polishers/Straighteners

Most single-groove shaft polishers appear to be informal, consisting of naturally shaped, oblong stones (Table 3.3). One instance features a definite attempt to form a tubular slot. The material used was a hard, homogenous granite with little abrasive power. While it is generally said that these tools were used to finish or polish wood, especially arrows, it seems doubtful whether they would have produced either the secondary marks found in the bottom of the large groove or the striations visible on all the sides. In addition, the almost black color and greasy feel of this implement suggests an additional, if not primary, use in the polishing and working of bone implements, perhaps awls.

The multi-grooved variant, in this case three grooves, had been worked into a definite rectangular shape. The specimen was made of a soft stone, probably steatite from the area west of Grasshopper, which when applied to bone, stone, or wood tends to give them a dull, wax-like luster. Applied to arrows, steatite would have made them slippery.

Table 3.3. Shaft Straighteners in Group VI Rooms

Variant	Occurences	Diagnostic
1	6	single-groove
2	1	multi-groove

Rubbing Stones

Normally such indefinite items as rubbing stones are ignored. Because these items aggregate as the most common item of stonework in the Group VI rooms, however, their occurrence deserves consideration (Table 3.4). Generally speaking the material composing these stones are rough types of conglomerates and granites, with sedimentary rocks being in the minority. In shape they vary from flat to round to oblong. Many have been partially or completely pecked. A number have been used as hammers or mauls. Some are stained. Because the stones occur in all shapes and sizes, they undoubtedly represent a variety of functions.

A common denominator for these unformed implements is that all have been occasionally used as abraders. An interesting possibility exists that abrading stones may represent a sector of technology which has persisted almost unchanged throughout the history of the Southwest, from early, preceramic Cochise up into the late Pueblo periods. More formal, specialized tools seem to have augmented these primitive forms but never replaced them. Also, there is the possibility that the common occurrence of these items throughout the cultural sequence is an indication of the persistence and importance of the gathering aspect of Pueblo economy, an idea seldom stressed in the literature.

Table 3.4. Rubbing Stones in Group VI Rooms

Occurrences	Size Class
6	1 – 2½"
20	3 – 4"
31	4½ – 5½"
15	6½ – 7½"
5	8½ – 10½"

Deer Bone Awls

Awls fall into three variants common across most of the Pueblo Southwest: those made by grinding the whole bone to a point; those made by splitting it lengthwise; and those made by polishing the splinters. No turkey, rabbit or bear bones were found in Group VI (Table 3.21).

Awls made from the ulna or upper foreleg of the deer, although quite common in Group I, have not been observed in Group VI. It is impossible to say whether this represents imperfect sampling, but because a number of other variants were found it suggests that the apparent reduction in the occurrence of such implements may be another late phase diagnostic.

Shell

The only example of shell work, almost certainly imported rather than locally crafted, was a worked *Conus* shell found about a foot above the floor in the southwest corner of Room 1. The shell had been ground flat at its larger end. Part of the spiral had been cut off, and a notch put at the small end of the cone. It was evidently part of a necklace.

Paint

Scattered in Rooms 1, 3 and 4 were about a dozen small deposits of paint, red being the most common color. In addition, white (kaolin), yellow (limonite) and a brilliant light blue (azurite) were found.

Turquoise

Only one item, a very small but well-shaped pendant fragment was found. Again, this was located relatively high above the floor and so may have been intrusive.

Fetishes and Other Exotics

Listed here are those items of unusual shape, finish or material which because of these properties were possibly part of medicine kits or a suite of ceremonial paraphernalia.

Painted Deer Jaw Bone

This large fragment was found outside of Room 8 in a partially burned condition but with sufficient stain remaining to identify the half-inch wide strips of alternating red and black which decorated its lower end. This jaw is similar to a number of others found in Groups I and III (Cummings 1940:Plate XXXV).

Quartz Crystals

Several of these, one to two inches long, were found in a floor cache in the southwest corner of Room 3. They are quite similar to finds from Group I.

Stalagmite

Cone-shaped and measuring about ¾" long and 2½" at the base, it was found on the floor in Room 1, closely associated with the remains of red and yellow paint.

Stone Ball

¾" in diameter, well-worked and smoothed, of volcanic rock. Whether part of a fetish, toy, game or weapon is not certain. A considerable number of various sizes in Group I have been found.

Colored Stones

Light pink in color, small and smoothed from handling, lacking grinding planes, from upper levels of Room 5.

Table 3.5 provides a summary of the various types of material culture and their occurrence in Group VI.

Ceramics

In all some 45 pottery vessels, complete but mostly smashed, were found on the floors of Group VI rooms (Table 3.6). Rooms 5 and 6 were bare except for sherds. Of these pieces, 29 are ollas, 15 are bowls, and one is a seed jar.

In the decorated wares, the outstanding fact is the presence of Gila Polychromes and the absence of Little Colorado Polychromes, black-on-white wares and black-on-red wares. The two phases established by earlier work at this site for the Pueblo III Period feature a main phase, with Little Colorado Polychromes developing and dominating and a shorter late phase with Gila polychrome and an increasing abundance of redware. Accordingly, it seems that the profile of decorated ware at Group VI places the rooms in the late phase.

The redware situation at Group VI also differs from the series encountered in the Little Colorado Phases of Group I. The dominant type in Group VI is the so-called "onion skin," where the surface appearance seems to result from horizontal strokes with a round stone. The next most common type is a redware having a very flat slip with granular temper showing through in places. Mica is apparent in some of these pieces. An unusual introduction is the appearance of four bowls having a definitely yellow temper apparently not well fired and very friable, especially when first uncovered. All these types only weakly represented, even in the late phase in Group I.

The plain ware differs in that while the interiors are smudged they are not polished, being flat and unslipped on both the interior and exterior. In the earlier phases of Group I, this type was polished inside and out, but the

Table 3.5. Summary of Element and Trait Occurrences in Group VI Rooms*

	Room 1	Room 2	Room 3	Room 4	Room 7	Room 8
Mealing Bins	1	1			1	
Fire Pits	1	1			1	1
Covers	1	2		3		3
Manos—Basalt	14	5	5	1	2	8
Manos—Sedimentary			3	2	5	1
Metates	2	1	1	1	3	1
Rubbing-Polishing-Hammer Stones	18	10	14	9	8	8
Arrow Shaft Smoothers	1				3	2
Axes	4			2		2
Flakes	1		1	1		
Choppers	2			1		
Cores	2		2			
Scrapers			3			
Knives	1		2	2		1
Points		1		1		
Fetishes	1	1	3	4		2
Pendants	1			1		
Awls	5	2	1	2	1	3

*Note: Rooms 5 and 6 contained no significant artifacts or features.

Table 3.6. Ceramic Ware Occurrence in the Aggregated Group VI Assemblage

Ware	Percentage
Gila Polychrome (Roosevelt Redware?)	5
Red Ware (White Mountain Redware?)	27
Plain Ware (Brownware?)	11
Utility Ware (Obliterated Corrugated?)	51
Unknown	6

higher levels feature unslipped interior surfaces for this type. This trend seems to have been carried further here. The exterior treatment suggests a thin and somewhat granular wash applied before firing.

As a group, the utility ware shows considerable change through time. Most pieces feature the partial obliteration of the primary indented corrugated pattern. Types with definite finger indentations are very rare, and all types of indented design are covered with the same rather granular wash mentioned above. This seems to complete the trend toward the obliteration of the indentations begun in Group I in early Pueblo III.

Very few sherds were found in the fill above the room floors. The exception to this rule is at Room 3, where a second story is believed to have existed. A few Little Colorado black-on-red sherds and one black-on-white sherd were encountered a little above floor levels. These finds likely represent redeposition from the slope to the north, especially as there were no corresponding indications of large shards or whole vessels. However, these might indicate that construction was as early as the end of the Little Colorado Polychrome phase, with occupancy continuing into the Gila phase and until the room occupants moved out.

Summary and Conclusions

Group VI seems to have been built late in Kinishba's occupancy, perhaps a little before the middle of the fourteenth century. The room block was probably occupied until the inhabitants moved out around the time of the village's general depopulation. The arrangement of the artifacts in some of the rooms, especially the grouping of the pottery around the mealing bins, may indicate the grinding of large amounts of grain as last acts before an exodus.

A comparison of artifacts from Group VI with those from Group I suggests certain trends, but the interpretive significance of these changes depends largely on the size of the groups compared and other sampling considerations (Table 3.7). Nonetheless, differences do exist and further research should be pursued to evaluate these trends.

As regards the relative position of Group VI in Kinishba's developmental sequence, this too remains uncertain. A comparative study of the contents of other small house groups which have been excavated—Groups III, IV and V—based upon the overall inventory of artifacts, reveals few if any significant differences in material culture. This impression is augmented by the lack of discernible difference between the masonry type in any of these buildings. This would seem to be another indication that all the small buildings uncovered so far were constructed and occupied contemporaneously during the late history of this site, probably sometime late in Pueblo III and continuing into the early Pueblo IV.

However, within the relatively stable architectural period a comparison of the pottery does reveal certain differences. In general, the pottery shows a pronounced southern or Middle Gila influence, particularly in the presence and dominance of Gila Polychrome and Red Ware and in the frequency of mica temper and "onion skin" surfacing. Modest variations in the comparative abundance of the pottery wares make it possible to tentatively assign each group to a relative position in Kinishba's developmental sequence. In light of the small amount of material under consideration, it is essential to note that such assignments are not conclusive and may be products of analytic process rather than reflections of true history.

Based on the ceramic evidence, Group VI appears to be occupied later than Group III or Group II. This conclusion is based on the fact that Gila Polychrome is the only decorated ware found in Group VI. Gila Polychrome

Table 3.7. Comparison of Element and Trait Occurrences in Group VI and Group I

Element or Trait	Group I	Group VI
Ashlar Spalling	+	-
Coursed Rubble	-	+
Firebox Manos	-	+
Flagged Areas	-	+
Bin Flagging	-	+
3/4 Groove Axe, Short Bit	-	+
3/4 Groove Axe, Long Bit	+	-
Full Groove Axe	+	-
Choppers	=	=
Rectilinear & Curvilinear Covers	-	+
Flint—Scrapers	=	=
Flint—Points	+	-
Flint—Diorite Material	-	+
Flint—Other Material	+	-
One-Handed Manos	+	-
Two-Handed Manos—Basalt	-	+
Two-Handed Manos—Sedimentary	+	-
Metate—Basalt	-	+
Metate—Sedimentary	+	-
Metate—Granite	+	-
Hammer, Polishing & Rubbing Stones	=	=
Arrow Shaft Tool—Triangular	-	+
Arrow Shaft Tool—Round	=	=
Arrow Shaft Tool—Multi-groove	+	-
Bone Awl—Ulna	+	0
Bone Awl—Other Types	=	=
Painted Mandibles	+	-
Quartz Crystals	=	=
Stalagmites	=	=
Stone Balls	+	-
Colored Stones	=	=
Shell	+	-
Paints	=	=
Turquoise	-	+
Burials Under Room Floors	+	0
Pottery—Gila Polychromes	-	+
Pottery—Little Colorado Poly.	+	0
Pottery—Black-on-Reds	+	0
Pottery—Black-on-Whites	+	0
Pottery—Redware	-	+
Pottery—Obliterated Corrugated	-	+
Pottery—Indented Corrugated	+	-

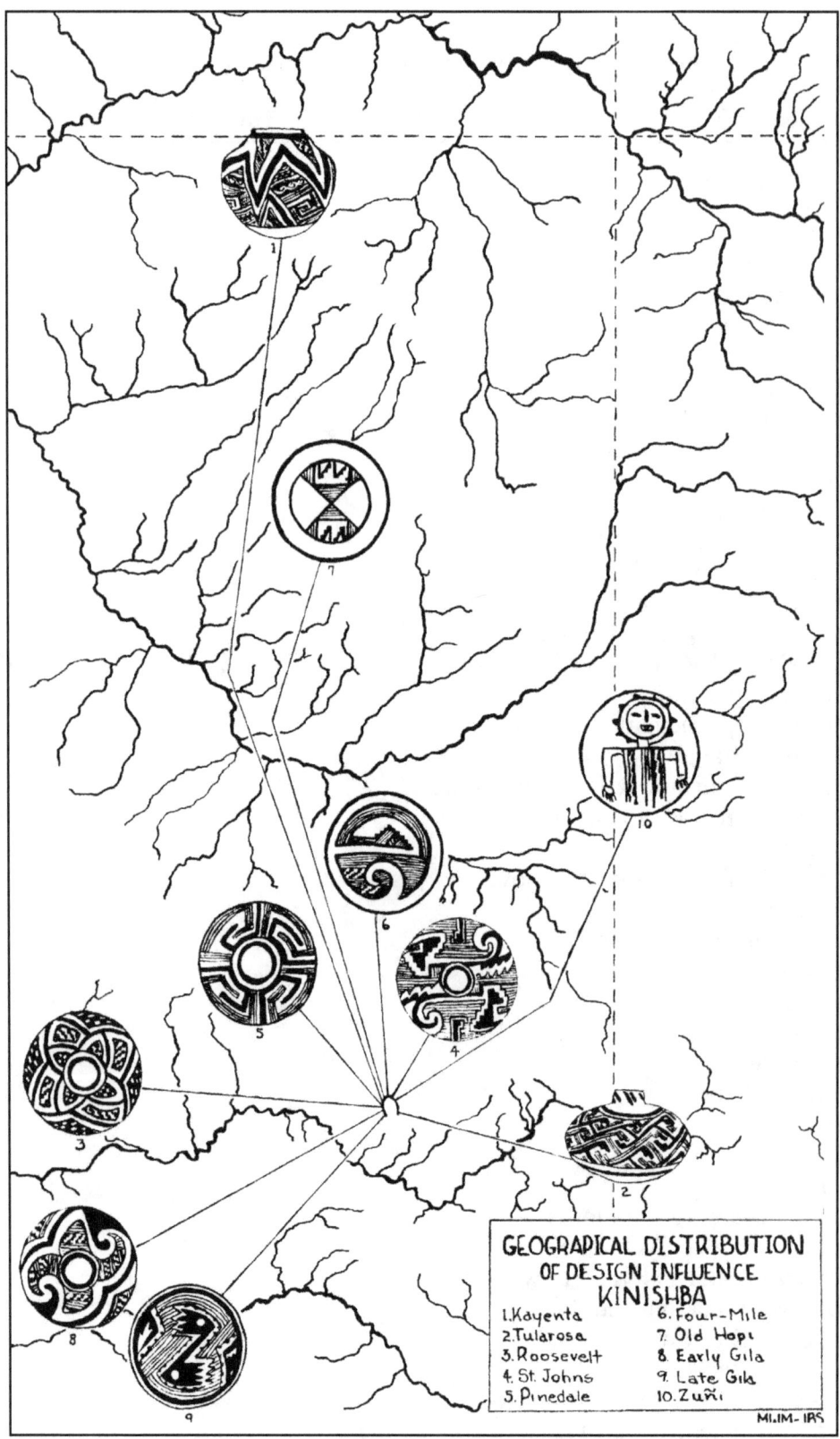

Figure 3.3. Some sources of ceramic design styles found at Kinishba (after Murry 1937).

seems to be the latest pottery type present in abundance at Kinishba. Although a considerable amount of Gila Polychrome has been found elsewhere on the site, especially in Group I, Group VI seems to be the only room block where it occurs in a pure horizon. The upper levels of stratigraphy established for the courtyard of Group I were less than ideally preserved, but Gila Polychrome did follow the Four Mile Series there (see Figure 3.3; Shaeffer and Shaeffer Chapter 4).

Again relying on the exclusive presence of ceramic evidence of Gila Polychrome at Group VI, the room block appears to be occupied later than either Group IV or Group II.

As to the relative positions in the sequence of Group III and IV, the ceramics suggest that the latter is the more recent, containing Gila Polychrome, Four Mile, and an earlier Little Colorado type, while Group III contains only Four Mile and Little Colorado black-on-white sherds. On the basis of this very thin evidence it is suggested that the general sequence of the small building groups at Kinishba are as follows—III, IV, VI—the last being the latest.

Comparable data are not available to assign relative chronological positions to the small room groups in relation to the larger room block of Group I and Group II. Although there are ceramic indications of sequencing, no clear architectural changes present themselves. It has been observed in Group I that black-on-white pottery is most heavily concentrated in the northern or earlier part of this group. It therefore seems likely that the outlying room groups may date to the middle or final phases of Kinishba's occupancy. Important questions concerning the relationship between developments on the opposite banks of the arroyo are not settled by this one small dig; however, the work suggests that the latest occupation of Kinishba occurred on the west side, in the small room block excavated in 1947.

Chapter 4
The Excavation of the Group I Great Kiva

James B. Shaeffer
Margaret M. Shaeffer

The excavations described in this chapter came about as the result of requests from Kinishba visitors for detailed information about the Group I courtyard or plaza, the southern extent of which Cummings designated "Patio A." On the basis of Dean Cummings's preliminary test excavations in Group II on the west bank of the arroyo, and in consideration of truck access and other logistical issues, Cummings decided to concentrate his excavations at Group I, the large unit of ruins on the east bank, as well as the three smaller, outlying ruin groups (Cummings 1940; Figure 4.1).

Digging and rebuilding around the central plaza or courtyard of Group I became a focus for Cummings's initiatives in research, training and interpretation. Cummings describes the Group I courtyard as an imperfect rectangle unevenly divided into a large southern "Patio A" and a smaller "Patio B." He notes that Patio A is "completely surrounded by a low bench 1' 8" high, varying in width from 3 to 4 feet . . . faced with a fairly good wall . . . and filled in with stone and clay" (Cummings 1940:16; Figure 4.5). Cummings observes that Patio A was the primary open space in Group I: "As the pueblo grew the homes clustered about this court to the west, to the east, and to the south until it was largely surrounded and the homes formed a large village" (Cummings 1940:7).

Cummings dug four trenches across Patio A, each 1.2 m wide. His "trenching on the south side of the patio revealed three surface levels that had formd [sic] floors of this patio at different stages of its occupation. In the surface or the last floor level, 6½' from the south wall and 4½' from the west wall stands a good fireplace 2' square....This evidently was a place for outdoor cooking, as is also evidenced by numerous burnt cobble stones found on the two lower levels" (Cummings 1940:19).

Cummings also investigated and rebuilt "Patio B," the northern extension of the Group I courtyard. Situated slightly higher (approximately 1 m) than Patio A, Patio B also contains evidence of successive refuse deposition, leveling, and construction episodes. A subterranean room, interpreted by Cummings as a subterranean, pole-masonry type kiva, occupies the southeastern portion of Patio B. Cummings uncovered a slab-lined hearth or "firebox" near the southwestern corner of Patio B (Figure 4.5).

Cummings's discovery of occupation surfaces and fireplaces well below the 1930s surfaces of Patio A and Patio B, together with his identification of segments of walls and remains of roof supports beneath the foundations of rooms adjacent to Patio A, suggest a complex construction and reconstruction sequence (Cummings 1940:7-9). Cummings concludes, "there was once a pueblo of considerable size which fell in to ruins, was partially covered. Then the location was leveled off and a new and larger village grew" (Cummings 1940:13).

But Cummings stopped short of a full

Figure 4.1. Oblique southerly aerial view of Group I excavations and rebuilding, circa 1936. The entry corridor to Patio A runs north from the west edge of the rebuilt rooms at the southeast corner of Group I. The Patio A bench is exposed but not rebuilt. Patio B (east of the north-most rebuilt room) is excavated and harbors backdirt that obscures the pole-masonry kiva. Cummings' field camp (upper right) and kitchen (lower right) are in the trees along arroyo bottom (Tad Nichols, Tad Nichols Collection, Box 1, Folder 7, courtesy Arizona State Museum).

investigation of the structural remains and features beneath the courtyard's last occupation surfaces. In particular, the limited understanding of Patio A precursors prompted the excavations described here. In the summer of 1948, as part of an attempt to relocate the fireplace Cummings found in the earlier excavations, a trench was begun at one of the posts whose top showed along the side of the Patio A bench on the west side (Post 2; Table 4.1 lists this and other architectural features uncovered in Patio A). In extending the trench, the stone surrounding the top of Post 7 was uncovered. Because Post 7 lined up with Post 15, which was also visible next to the bench on the east side of the patio, and because excavation at a similar distance to the north resulted in exposing the top of Post 6, it was realized that Patio A represented, at least during one period in its history, large covered communal room, a Great Kiva. Subsequent stripping in the vicinity of the low wall or "altar" at the southern end of Patio A revealed

Table 4.1. Post, Post Hole, Pillar Base, and Cache Features Identified in the Great Kiva Excavations and Depicted in Figure 4.2

Feature	Description	Diameter (cm)	Base Depth from Surface (cm)	Length (cm)	Width (cm)	Height (cm)
	Juniper post	31.6	90.0	-	-	
P2	Juniper post	29.1	110.0	-	-	n/a
P3		33.0	110.0	-	-	n/a
P4	Juniper post	26.6	80.0	-	-	n/a
P5	Post hole	43.1	120.0	-	-	n/a
P6	Oval post hole	81 x 56	120.0	-	-	n/a
P7	Oval post hole	38 x 66	110.0	-	-	n/a
P8	Juniper post	43.1	150.0	-	-	n/a
P9	Juniper post	38.1	140.0	-	-	n/a
P10	Post hole	55.8	80.0	-	-	n/a
P11	n/a	n/a	n/a	-	-	n/a
P12	Juniper post	45.7	90.0	-	-	n/a
P13	Juniper post	31.6	50.0	-	-	n/a
P14	Juniper post	35.5	90.0	-	-	n/a
P15	Juniper post	30.4	100.0	-	-	n/a
P16	Juniper post	40.6	90.0	-	-	n/a
P17	Post hole	60.9	40.0	-	-	n/a
P18	Oval post hole	46 x 53	50.0	-	-	n/a
P19	Post hole	60.9	20.0	-	-	n/a
P20	Post hole	50.8	20.0	-	-	n/a
P21	Post hole	50.8	20.0	-	-	n/a
P22	Post hole	43.1	10.0	-	-	n/a
P23	Oval post hole	48 x 38	20.0	-	-	n/a
P24	Oval post hole	28 x 25	10.0	-	-	n/a
P25	Post hole	45.7	20.0	-	-	n/a
F1	Pillar base remnant	-	n/a	150.0	40.0	60
F2	Pillar base	-	n/a	90.0	60.0	43
F3	See Table 4.2	n/a	n/a	n/a..	n/a	n/a
F4	Sub-floor cache	45.7	12.7	-	-	n/a
F5	Sub-floor cache	-	27.9	76.2	60.9	n/a
F6	Sub-floor cache	-	45.7	152.4	116.8	n/a
F7	Sub-floor cache	35.6	10.2	-	-	n/a
F8	Sub-floor cache	-	15.2	55.9	45.9	n/a
F9	Sub-floor cache	76.2	35.6	-	-	n/a
F10	Sub-floor cache	-	35.6	76.2	55.9	n/a
F11	Sub-floor cache	43.2	17.8	-	-	n/a
F12	Sub-floor cache	-	33.0	152.4	139.7	n/a
F13	Sub-floor cache	45.7	5.1	-	-	n/a
F14	Sub-floor cache	55.9	22.9	-	-	n/a
F15	Sub-floor cache	38.1	20.3	-	-	n/a

a line of stones. Further testing showed this to be the south wall of what was then designated as "Kiva A." The designation was made in accord with Roberts' (1929:74) definition: "Kiva, a chamber specially constructed for ceremonial purposes" (see also Martin et al 1961). Other subterranean structures were later found, excavated, and designated in alphabetical order. Throughout this discussion the term "courtyard" applies to the open area defined by Kinishba's Group I surface structures both before and after Great Kiva construction (and following Cummings's rebuilding). The term "patio" refers to the subdivisions of the courtyard, and "Great Kiva" refers to that portion of the courtyard (Patio A) that was roofed over (Figure 4.2).

These excavations have added a chapter to Kinishba's history and substantiated the presence there of a great kiva, a type of ceremonial architecture defined for Puebloan culture on the basis of archaeological rather than ethnographic observations. Great kivas are more widely known and intensively researched in the northern Southwest (see, for example, Adler and Wilshusen 1990; Roberts 1929, 1932), but also played roles in culture history and settlement system organization in the Mogollon Rim region (Haury 1950; Herr 2001; Herr et al. 1999; Reid and Whittlesey 1997, 1999). The 1948 excavations show that the Group I plaza was used in late Pueblo III times for a series of five rather small, earthen wall dirt kivas (four rectangular and one "D" shaped). Thereafter, during a latter part of Pueblo III and early Pueblo IV, the same area was used again. This time the five subterranean rooms were filled in and leveled off. The courtyard was modified and the area roofed over, thus forming a new, large rectangular, above-ground room referred to here as the Great Kiva. Cummings supervised the architectural clearing and trenching of the Group I courtyard and notes that features embedded in Patio A include,

"eight posts, four on the east and four on the west side. The stubs of two on the east and three on the west are still discernible, and the northernmost one on the west side still stands at a height of 4' 7" above the surface. The others seem to have been burned off at the surface as though the patio had been partially destroyed by fire. These posts...may have served as supports for stringers upon which rested the ends of timbers that extended into the walls of the building and formed the rafters of the roof of a portico that covered the benches on these two sides and served as a front porch for the second story rooms on the east and west sides of the court. We have not attempted to rebuild a porch on these two sides of the patio because we were not sure that this was the form of the original construction…. Within the court were found the stubs of two other posts….The one near the north wall rested on the floor of the older patio or court" (Cummings 1940:17-18).

The 1948 excavations substantiate a still incompletely understood type of great kiva ceremonial room recognized south of the Mogollon Rim in work done at Point of Pines, 65 km southeast of Kinishba (M. Gerald 1957; Haury 1989). Shortly after the conclusion of World War II, Haury established a summer archaeological field school at Point of Pines and began excavations in an extensive series of sites. During the summer of 1947, Haury and his students uncovered a courtyard containing a large number of irregularly placed stone concentrations. Haury postulated from their arrangement and size that they represented stone bases for wooden post supports which had since disappeared. Inasmuch as no rooms of this size or kind had been recognized previously in the greater Mogollon Rim region, there was some

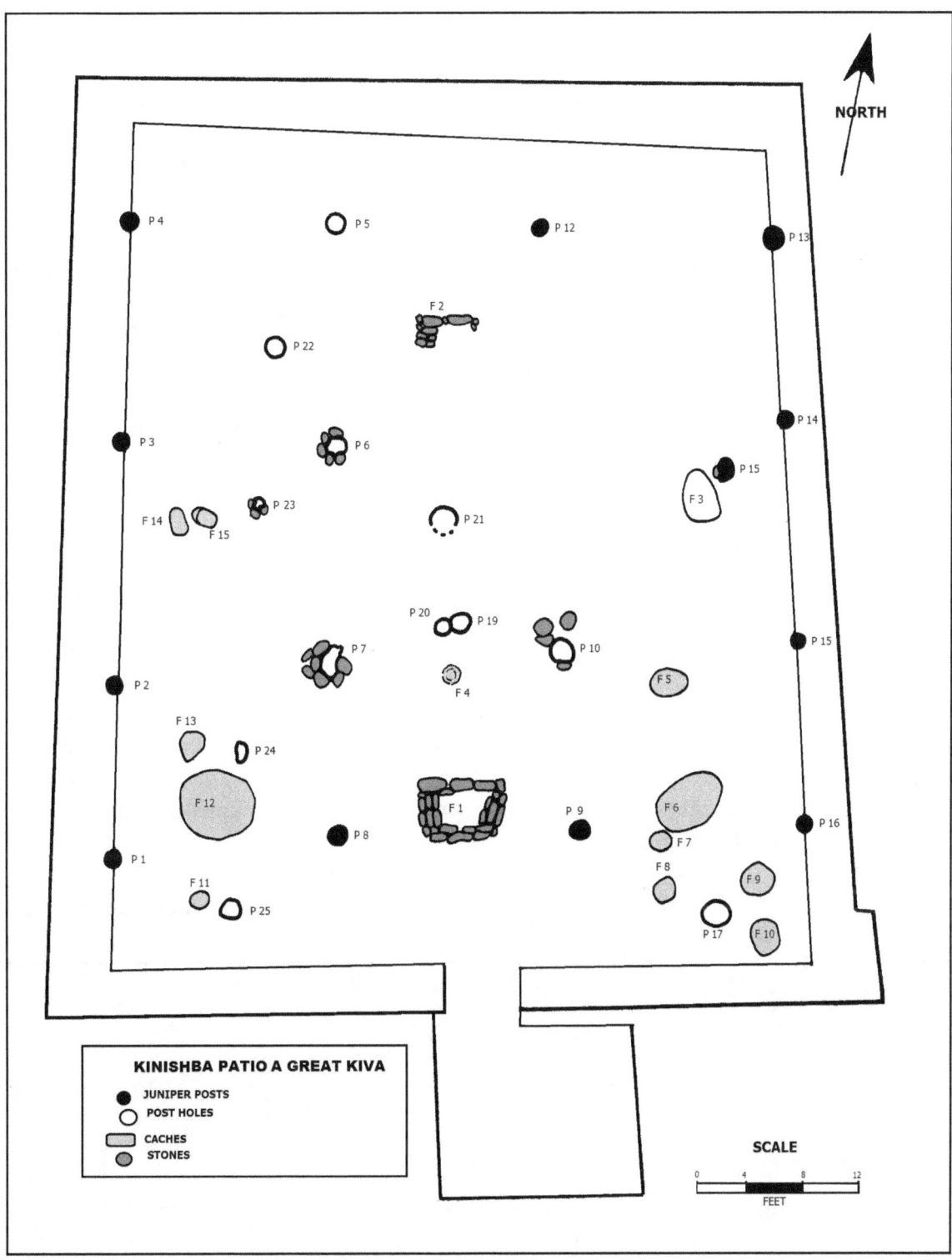

Figure 4.2. The Great Kiva plan map showing features and posts (M. M. Shaeffer, courtesy Arizona State Museum).

question as to this interpretation. Kinishba's Group I Patio A offered the opportunity to excavate, within the same geographical area, a courtyard comparable in size but with actual post-butts in place, thus providing a means to evaluate and expand upon Haury's original theory (see Reid and Whittlesey 1999).

The next section describes the characteristics of the Group I Great Kiva at Kinishba, those of the five smaller subterranean kivas found beneath it, and their probable relationships as evidenced by the ceramic stratigraphy contained in the fills of these structures. The chapter concludes with a discussion of the origins and development of the Kinishba kivas.

THE GREAT KIVA

As noted above, the Group I Great Kiva temporarily occupied an intramural open area about 51 feet wide and 63 feet long (15.5 x 19.2 m) bordered by a low, masonry-faced earthen bench. To the south is a large room or antechamber connecting with a long covered passageway linking the courtyard with extramural areas (Figure 4.1). Architectural analysis of the foundations of the rooms surrounding the courtyard indicate that the construction of the five kivas below the Great Kiva was not completed during a single building period, but rather resulted from gradual development or accretion that defined and reaffirmed the courtyard.

In general, three foundation levels can be observed (Figures 4.2 and 4.3). Most rooms have relatively deep foundations of 20.3 to 30.5 cm; second in frequency of occurrence are foundations 10.2 to 15.2 cm in depth; the remaining foundations are superficial—5 cm or less. It is probable that the differences in depth represent inequalities in the substrate, as many variations are found within single rooms and other small areas. This would seem to mean different surface levels over a period of building time rather than inequalities of a single original ground surface.

Using this reconstruction as a premise, the general picture of development is that, while the courtyard was an open space during most of Kinishba's occupation, its size and shape varied. The deepest foundations indicate that Patio A and Patio B (Figure 4.4) originally formed a large courtyard which was not completely surrounded or defined by masonry rooms. The early courtyard was apparently open in the northeast and northwest corners, while the rooms along the west side

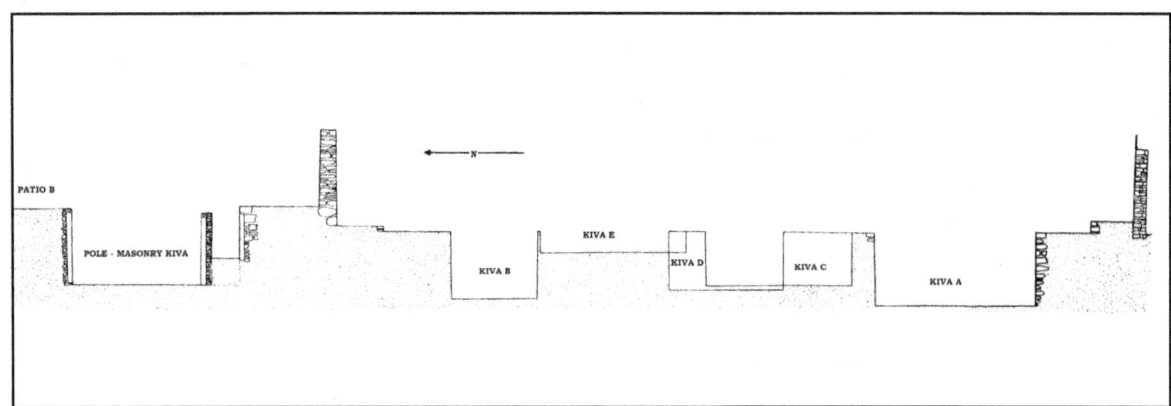

Figure 4.3. Cross-section of Patio A and Patio B, Group I, showing positions of Kivas A, B, C, D, and E (M. M. Shaeffer, courtesy Arizona State Museum).

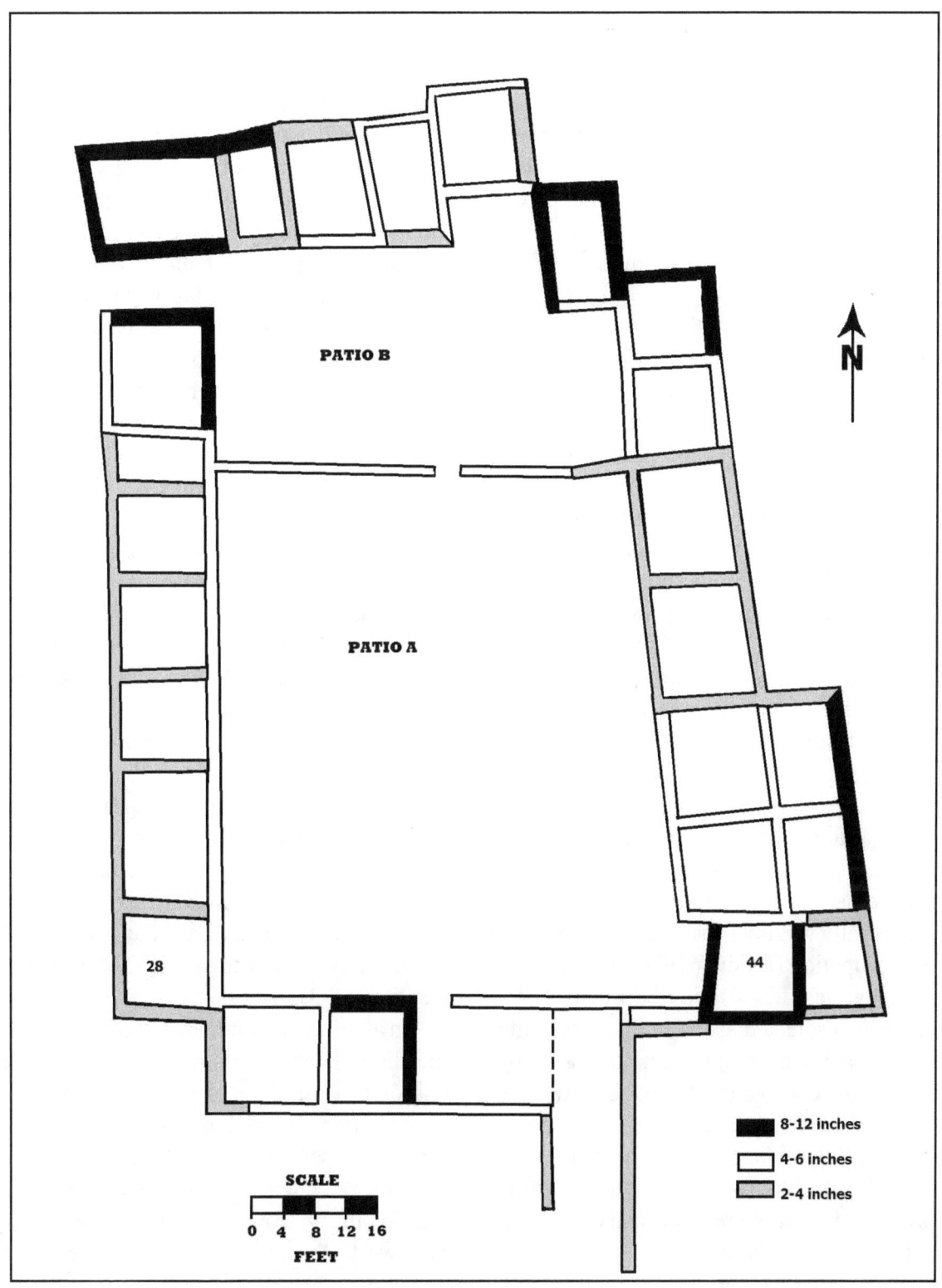

Figure 4.4. Courtyard, showing depths of foundations for walls of rooms surrounding Patio A and Patio B (M. M. Shaeffer, courtesy Arizona State Museum).

and the central part of the east side must have extended farther toward the center, making the courtyard narrower and longer at the south than it is today. In the earlier period of earth-walled subterranean room spaces, the courtyard was probably U-shaped with some few rooms along the arroyo on the west, another small group on the eastern side, and the greatest and most coherent concentrations of rooms to the north and south.

The construction of the Great Kiva seems to have begun at or shortly after this time. The west rooms, which apparently were out of line, were pushed back (westerly) and a single straight wall was erected in front of the remaining rooms. On the east side, less alteration was necessary to produce a straight side for the Great Kiva. Perhaps only one room in the northwest corner of Patio A was demolished. At any rate, a lengthy but shallow extension seems to have been added here to the deeper wall of what may have been a room. This extension runs across the northern third of the courtyard, dividing it into two sections and forming the northern wall of the Great Kiva. During the original excavation of this area, evidence of a narrow doorway between the two patios was found about midway in the wall. But this entrance had been filled in with large stones, and evidently was not in use during the pueblo's later occupation (Baldwin 1934:41-42).

Why was this division between Patio A and Patio B selected as the northern terminus of the Great Kiva instead of employing the full length of the courtyard? One plausible answer is that the community was not large enough to require such a large, special purpose room (see Adler and Wilshusen 1990). Another possibility is that the pole-masonry kiva at its northern end, in Patio B, may have been in use as sacred space and thus inviolate. This subterranean room is roughly square (3.35 m on each side) and about 1.5 m deep, with a central fireplace lined with four stone slabs set on edge. The dirt walls were faced with upright posts, between which builders packed stone laid in clay mortar. On the south side, running the width of the room was a distinct narrow chamber about 75 cm above the floor of the latter. It is entered by two steps and a low doorway. Cummings (1940:7-12) thought it likely this partitioned closet served as storage for ceremonial paraphernalia.

Although the pole-masonry kiva in Patio B was undoubtedly roofed, no posts or other clear indications that Patio B had been entirely roofed over were found. The stone firebox or slab-lined hearth in the southwest corner, and the reported wall stub to the north (Cummings 1940:19; Figure 4.5), indicate an additional row of two rooms at the eastern end of this courtyard. Because this small space had never been completely turned into living quarters, and the masonry walls of the small kiva came almost to the ground surface, it is probable that the masonry kiva continued in use for some time (Figure 4.6). This theory is supported by evidence found in the exploratory trenches dug by Cummings, who notes the presence of polychrome pottery in all stratigraphic levels with increasing frequencies in upper layers (Cummings 1940:12-13). Therefore, there is little evidence that Patio B formed a northern alcove of the Great Kiva, or that it was otherwise directly related to Great Kiva functions (see Figure 4.3).

In altering the southern end of Patio A, the inner line of rooms was made straight by the addition of wall sections and the construction of a wall across a portion of the southern end. The eastern section of this latter wall blocks the former southern entrance to the courtyard, diverting traffic from the covered passageway to the west. Because it would have been much simpler to allow a direct opening into the Great Kiva from the passageway, it is probable that it was intentionally blocked, perhaps with the idea of obliging a more central entrance into

Figure 4.5. Southerly view along the west side of the courtyard during Patio A clearing, circa 1934. Note the slab-lined hearth in the southwest corner of Patio B, the remnant of Post 4 (P4 in Figure 4.2, here used as a coat rack), and the broad bench along the west wall in Patio A (Tad Nichols, Tad Nichols Collection, Box 1, Folder 5, courtesy Arizona State Museum).

Figure 4.6. Pole-masonry kiva in Patio B during rebuilding, circa 1936. Note "cyclopean" style masonry (large, irregular boulders surrounded by numerous chinking stones) in stub wall shown in upper center (Tad Nichols, Tad Nichols Collection, Box 1, Folder 5, courtesy Arizona State Museum).

the kiva. It is likely that this southern passageway afforded the only extramural entrance into patio A and, later, the sole access route into the Great Kiva, via the antechamber, into the kiva proper. Baldwin (1934:28) reports that, at the time of initial excavation, the entrance into the courtyard at the south was "4 feet in width and about 6 feet in height." "On either side were the remains of a post set close to the wall, as if to support the lintel and floor of the second story." The fact that there were no features in this antechamber—no lateral doorways in the walls, very few sherds, and no items except a painted jaw bone—further suggest that it was used primarily or exclusively as an entrance chamber (Baldwin 1934:28-29).

In general, the Great Kiva roof seems to have been an elaboration of the type widely used in the construction of smaller rectangular kivas—i.e., a main supporting beam with evenly spaced cross beams coming in at right angles from each side to rest on a central beam. In the case of the Great Kiva, the central support probably consisted of two beams lashed side by side. These were likely sustained at the north end by the wall separating Patio A from Patio B, and otherwise by two buttresses, described below. Between these primary supports were pairs of heavy juniper posts. On each side of these paired pillars and posts were two rows of fairly evenly spaced and aligned juniper posts. The outside rows on the east and west of the kiva were set along the edge of the bench. Figure 4.7 is a structural schematic of the roof; Figure 4.8 is a graphic reconstruction of the Great Kiva. Tables 4.1 and 4.2, respectively, list features associated with the Great Kiva and the earthen-wall spaces excavated below the Great Kiva.

Before the present excavation was begun, a masonry structure or low platform had been found at the south end (Figure 4.9). This feature may have served as an altar or shrine (Cummings 1940:18) or a combination fireplace-deflector, as is sometimes found in the northern reaches of Puebloan territory (Baldwin 1934:40-41). However, the finding of a poorly preserved structure and otherwise similar concentration of stone rubble at the north end (Figure 4.10), and the occurrence of the several posts between the two structures, suggests that at least some of these features functioned as masonry roof supports, perhaps in concert with upright juniper posts. Excavation within the two structures revealed, in both cases, a very hard, packed clay mass 30 cm thick and containing sherds and charcoal. The space enclosed between the sides of the foundation could have allowed for the insertion of two posts, each about 38 cm in diameter. These could have rested on or been slightly embedded within this hard packed base. No ash is reported to have been found around the southern pillar, but a considerable amount of grey ash several inches thick was found at the level of the northern pillar foundation.

Judging from the condition of the remaining uprights, it seems possible the period of Great Kiva use ended with a fire and the removal of the burned debris. No charred crossbeams were found and none were reported by Cummings. A single piece of oxidized roofing clay was found associated with a small pile of charred, coarse grass near cache F-4 (see below). These finds probably do not represent a fragment from the Great Kiva roof, but one from that of Kiva A, as a considerable amount of similar roofing clay was found in the northwest corner of that room near the floor.

The absence of roof debris suggests that the Great Kiva was stripped of its superstructure by (1) the aforementioned fire, (2) later occupants of the pueblo, (3) neighbors following the primary residential use of Group I, (4) users of the Great Kiva who turned it into a courtyard when religious practices changed to emphasize use of smaller, above-ground ceremonial rooms, or (5) some combination.

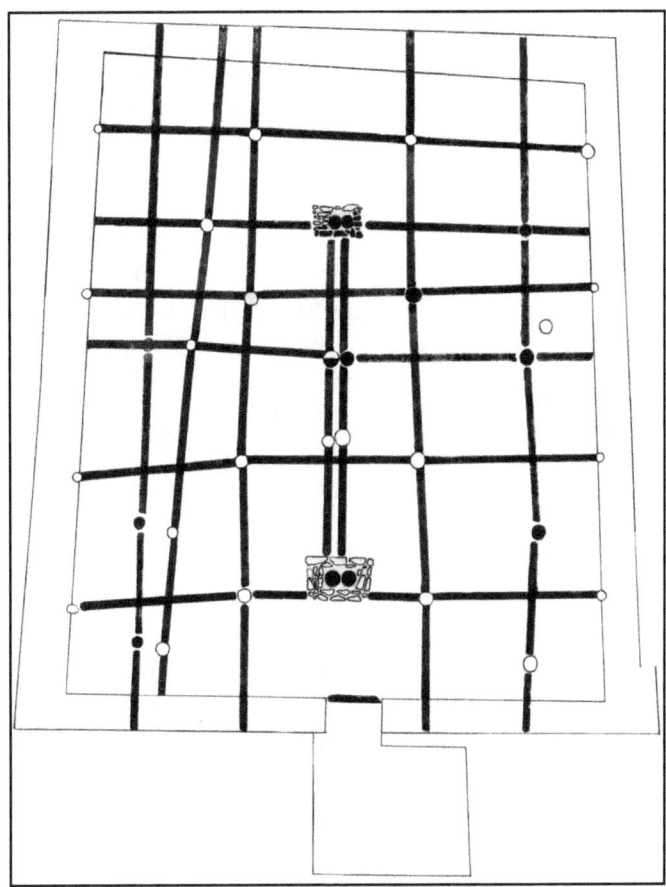

Figure 4.7. Great Kiva roof support system, as inferred from post holes and structural remains (M. M. Shaeffer or J. B Shaeffer, courtesy Arizona State Museum).

Figure 4.8. Rendition of the southern portion of the Great Kiva, showing likely roof construction details (M. M. Shaeffer, courtesy Arizona State Museum).

Table 4.2. Features Identified in the Earthen Wall Kiva Excavations

Kiva	Description	Length (cm)	Width (cm)	Height from Floor (cm)	Base Depth from Surface (cm)	Diameter (cm)
A	North wall		n/a	160	n/a	-
A	South wall		n/a	170	n/a	-
A	East wall		n/a	160	n/a	-
A	West wall		n/a	100	n/a	-
A	East entry ramp		40	100 – 140	n/a	-
A	Vent shaft in S wall		90	30 – ?	n/a	-
A	Central hearth		n/a	-	13.9	61 x 48
A	NE corner floor cache		40	n/a	12.7	-
A	SW corner floor cache		40	n/a	13.9	-
A	SE corner metate rest		40	n/a	12.7	-
A	Central hole		-	-	10.2	25.4
A	North-central hole		-	-	10.2	10.2
A	Loom socket in SE quad.		n/a	-	7.6	10.2
A	Central post in W wall		n/a	n/a	n/a	17.8
A	Central post in N wall		n/a	n/a	n/a	16.5
A	Central post in E wall		n/a	n/a	n/a	17.8
A	Central post hole, S wall		n/a	n/a	n/a	20.3
B	North wall		n/a	150	n/a	n/a
B	South wall		n/a	150	n/a	-
B	East wall		n/a	150	n/a	-
B	West wall		n/a	150	n/a	-
B	Katchina niche		10	40	n/a	23 deep
B	E-W beam		n/a	110	n/a	n/a
B	N wall post hole		n/a	n/a	n/a	12.7
B	Center post hole		n/a	n/a	n/a	12.7
B	S wall post hole		n/a	n/a	n/a	7.6
C	North wall		n/a	n/a	134.6	-
C	South wall		n/a	n/a	127	-
C	East wall		n/a	n/a	132	-
C	West wall		n/a	n/a	129.5	-
C	Firebox		50	n/a	12.7	63.5
C	SW corner cache		n/a	-	12.7	10.2
D	North wall		n/a	n/a	127	-
D	South wall		n/a	n/a	121.9	-
D	East wall		n/a	n/a	124.4	-
D	West wall		n/a	n/a	124.4	-
D	Central firepit		-	-	17.8	48.3
D	NE corner entry		90	30	76.2	-
D	NE corner niche		120	10	91.4	-
D	NW corner basin metate		50	-	12.7	-
D	SE corner basin metate	60	50	-	17.8	-

Table 4.2 Features Identified in the Earthen Wall Kiva Excavations, cont'd

Kiva	Description	Length (cm)	Width (cm)	Height from floor (cm)	Base Depth from Surface (cm)	Diameter (cm)
D	SW corner wall cache	90	60	n/a	n/a	-
D	NW corner wall cache	38	24	38	n/a	-
D	E corner pot (olla) rest	-	-	-	20.3	35.6
D	NW corner metate	35	23	-	2.5	-
D	NW corner mano	10	9	-	10.2	n/a
D	N central wall post	n/a	n/a	-	n/a	20.3
E	West wall (segment)	n/a	n/a	n/a	91.4	3.1(?)
E	Central hearth	48	40	-	n/a	-
F	S post hole	n/a	n/a	n/a	40.6	60.9
E	N post hole	n/a	n/a	n/a	40.6	33
E	Post hole 1 along W wall	n/a	n/a	n/a	86.4	20.3
E	Post hole 2 along W wall	n/a	n/a	n/a	86.4	7.6
E	Post hole 3 along W wall	n/a	n/a	n/a	81.3	15.2
E	Post hole 4 along W wall	n/a	n/a	n/a	50.8	10.2
E	Post hole 5 along W wall	n/a	n/a	n/a	50.8	10.2
E	Post hole 6 along W wall	n/a	n/a	n/a	83.8	17.8
E	E vent or subfloor cache	210	40	-	109.7	82.3

Figure 4.9. Southerly view of Patio A, with the Great Kiva's south pillar base or shrine (F1) in right foreground, circa 1932 (probably Byron Cummings, courtesy Arizona State Museum).

Figure 4.10. Great Kiva north pillar base (F2), 1948 (M. M. Shaeffer or J. B Shaeffer, courtesy Arizona State Museum).

Evidence from Room 27, found along the western side of the Great Kiva, suggests the Great Kiva was not the only ceremonial space in contemporary use. Although it appears that Room 27 was built prior to the Great Kiva, subsequent remodeling for ceremonial use is suggested by the addition of a ventilator that penetrated the Great Kiva bench. It is thus probable that Room 27 represents a ceremonial room employed during a later period of Great Kiva use.

All identified post remnants are either charred at the top (Posts 1, 2, 3, 4, 8, 9, 1.5, 16) or have been reduced to ash or charcoal (Posts 5, 6, 7, 10, 21) (see Table 4.1) All post remnants are juniper, the region's most weather-resistant and abundant timber, if not the straightest or the longest. The posts along the bench seem to have ranged from 23 to 30 cm in diameter; those in the interior rooms from 30 to about 35 cm in diameter (Figures 4.11 and 4.12). The posts were sunk from one to five feet, apparently depending primarily on the condition of the substrate, as the post holes were generally dug to a point where the soil was hard. The posts were usually placed on a flat stone or in a V-shaped basin of rocks, presumably to improve both stability and drainage. Post holes along the bench were set deepest; the depth of the central post holes varied with the depth of the floors of the antecedent structures and the hardness of the earth. All of the post holes excavated in 1948 contained ash, charcoal, or both.

Posts holes dug into the fill of the older kivas had been reinforced, without exception, by large pieces of broken rock placed in the holes before they were filled with dirt. Posts

Figure 4.11. Post hole and charred Juniper remnant of Post 12 (P12) (M. M. Shaeffer or J. B Shaeffer, courtesy Arizona State Museum).

Figure 4.12. Post 10 post hole (P10) with ash removed (M. M. Shaeffer or J. B. Shaeffer, courtesy Arizona State Museum).

elsewhere had no more than a few rocks around them, and typically none. Only Posts 6, 7, and 9 (Figure 4.13; see Figure 4.2) had an inordinate amount of stone around them, and these were all posts placed in the fill of the smaller kivas. Post 9 had been carefully set on the narrow entrance ramp, and large rocks had been placed around and under the post's base, giving the appearance of being cast into the hole as fill rather than deliberately employed as masonry support. Post 7 was somewhat similar, but more stones were used from the surface down to the older kiva floor level. The stones only occurred from the surface down to the old floor level. Where the post continued beyond the floor level, it was in hard ground; buttressing was unnecessary.

Post 6 was the only post supported by masonry, which was well constructed and of an unusual type. The masonry post support consisted of a carefully coursed lower base and a loosely constructed upper half. The lower half rose from the floor of Kiva E more than 60 cm, and the upper section was about as high, bringing it to within 15 cm of the 1930s ground surface. The lower portion consisted of a roughly circular basalt boulder upon which the post rested and around which was erected an enclosing wall, 51 cm in diameter and formed of basalt cobbles laid in

Figure 4.13. Reinforced base of remnant of Post 9 (P9), resting upon Kiva A entry ramp and showing use of puddled mud and stone (M. M. Shaeffer or J. B. Shaeffer, courtesy Arizona State Museum).

fairly even courses. This lower masonry was then sheathed in hard-packed clay with a base wider than the top, giving it the appearance of a truncated cone. Both the masonry and the sheath extended 23 cm beneath the floor level of Kiva E and part way under the fireplace of the same structure. The top half consisted of several courses of large, flat stones standing on edge and in a rather tumble-down condition. Four flat pieces of wood about 15 cm long were found in the south side, just below the topmost stone of the lower section. This suggests that there may have been a fence-like arrangement of very small poles or sticks thrust in around the upper part of the base to form a support for keeping the exposed stones in place above the floor level.

Whatever the exact arrangement, Post 6 evidently had some special significance in the symbolism or use of the Great Kiva because a small, well-formed Roosevelt olla was found at approximately the Great Kiva floor level. It contained a miniature indented bowl and was covered by two stone covers, between which there seems to have been at one time some sort of perishable material. On top of the covers was a small circular polishing stone. Nearby was found some green malachite paint, and below the paint, at the floor level of Kiva 3, some reddish ochre. East of this same post, at the floor level of Kiva E, was a small, thin sandstone plaque (Figure 4.14). Only faintly visible in the photograph, the painting on one side of the plaque appears to represent some sort of insect with green body and legs outlined in black. The only other post offering occurred

Figure 4.14. Artifacts associated with Post 6 (P6) at floor level of the Great Kiva, diameters of stone covers probably less than 10 cm (M. M. Shaeffer or J. B. Shaeffer, courtesy Arizona State Museum).

at the southwest side of Post 10. There, a small circular piece of black-on-white pottery had been placed to hold three thin, rectangular pendants and a bead, all of turquoise.

In addition to the 16 main beam supports, there was a secondary system of supports. Two supplementary rows of four posts each cut the distance between the outer rows of the main posts in half. The central beam system described above served the same purpose between the two central rows of main posts. These secondary posts probably carried stringers, thus cutting the distance between supports to between 2 m and 2.3 m. Of the eight posts predicted to occur along the sides, six were found. In all cases, they had been standing on the floor or slightly below it. Four of those identified had burned (Posts 17, 18, 25, 27), and two had stones around the base (Posts 23, 24).

The only other features of the Great Kiva were the surrounding bench, already mentioned, and a series of sub-floor caches. Shortly after Patio A was excavated, Baldwin (1934:40) noted that the

> "banquette that surrounded the patio was not constructed of stone like the coursed walls behind it, but was made of hard-packed earth and clay, with a facing of stone along the outer edge. The rocks were irregular, with only one side having been worked, and were set on edge along the front of the bench, often not coming clear to the top of the clay. This bench was rather wide, varying from 3 feet at the northern end to 3 feet 11 inches on the eastern side. It was more regular in height, measuring about 1 foot 8 inches on the average."

Regarding sub-floor caches and holes, these were located at the southern end of the Great Kiva along both the east and west sides (Figure 4.15; Table 4.1). There were six in all; two large and oval-shaped, and four smaller and rounder. The oval-shaped caches were aligned rather evenly on the opposite sides of the room on a roughly east–west axis. The loose fill of both was almost identical. Fill contents included a number of small stones—somewhat burned but not thermally fractured—as well as a considerable number of sherds and parts of an animal skeleton.

No clear pattern was evident in the arrangement of the stones found in the caches. There did not seem to be enough of them to have lined the sides of the pits, but there was a sufficient number to form possible rims. The eastern cache differed from the western in that it was divided into two chambers by a thin, rubble-type partition of undetermined height. The presence of charcoal mixed with the fill may indicate that the caches were covered, thereby explaining the absence of finished sides.

The other type of cache—smaller and rounder—seemed to be associated with the secondary post system flanking both sides of the Great Kiva. The fill and contents were similar to those found in the larger caches, but contained many more stones in proportion to the size of the holes, suggesting a rubble lining for the walls. Fewer bones and sherds were found in the rounder type of cache. A yellow organic substance, possibly pollen or corn meal, was found in all these caches. Although distributed to several institutional laboratories, the substance could not be identified. It is quite possible that this substance was stored there in bowls, because large fragments of pottery vessels were present. One burned corn cob was found.

In addition to these more formal caches, indications of various holes were found on both sides of the southern section of the Great Kiva (See Figure 4.2). Feature f-7 represents a shallow hole which may have been an olla stand; f-8 had small stones around the rim but was devoid of contents. Hole f-10, in the southeast

Figure 4.15. Sub-floor caches and holes in southeast portion of Great Kiva. Top of reconstructed wall in left foreground (M. M. Shaeffer or J. B. Shaeffer, courtesy Arizona State Museum).

corner, suggests by the slope of its floor that it was used to hold a metate. Both corn and paint residues were found in association with f-10.

One small, stone-lined cache (f-4) was found in the center of the room. This consisted of a roughly circular stone 25 cm in diameter, 30 cm below the surface and surrounded by small, thin stones set on edge around, and resting on this stone base (Figure 4.16). The first impression was that it was a post hole. However, there was no ash, no charcoal and no signs of burning on the stone itself—an important point given that all of the other posts in this part of the room had been charred or burned completely out. It is possible that it was the base of a support for a sagging beam; however, it is more likely that it was a small, stone-lined, sub-floor cache lacking an identifiable cover.

THE SMALLER EARTHEN KIVAS

Five small, subterranean, dirt-walled rooms were found beneath the floor of the Great Kiva (Figures 4.3, 4.17). These rooms have been designated as kivas or underground ceremonial rooms for reasons which will be discussed following descriptions of each structure.

Figure 4.16. Remains of a possible stone-lined cache (F4) (M. M. Shaeffer or J. B. Shaeffer, courtesy Arizona State Museum).

Figure 4.17. Northerly view of five structures found below the Great Kiva, Group I; Clockwise from bottom left: Kiva D, Kiva E, Kiva B, Kiva C, and Kiva A (M. M. Shaeffer or J. B. Shaeffer, courtesy Arizona State Museum).

Kiva A

This is the largest and deepest of Patio A's five rectangular dirt kivas (Figure 4.18). Its main features are:

1. An irregular and fragmentary stone cap or rim around the top of the kiva walls;

2. A V-shaped ventilator in the middle of the south wall;

3. Five posts—a central post hole and one in the middle of each wall;

4. An interior entrance ramp;

5. A well-made circular, clay firepit;

6. Two shallow storage pits, one of which has a stone floor;

7. Several miscellaneous smaller holes of undetermined use.

Discussion of each of these Kiva A features follows. The masonry cap of the walls in all probability surrounded the dirt room completely during use, varying in depth from 30 to 61 cm. Only fragments remained when exposed during excavations. The best preserved section tops the west wall, which is divided into two separate sections by the roof support post

Figure 4.18. Kiva A, showing east wall and ramp, with foundation and remnant of juniper post from Great Kiva, with small juniper post in foreground. Note ash marks of burned reed "wicker-work" wattle along base of the east wall below the ramp (probably photographed by BIA photographer J. Lee or C. Longenbaugh, courtesy White Mountain Apache Tribe Heritage Program).

extending upward from the floor. The southern section consists of three uneven courses of large boulders set in mud, with some smaller, flattish river stones separating the main courses in a haphazard way. The northern section of this west wall consists of a single course of boulders set at an angle toward the floor. Meeting this at right angles is the rim of the north wall, made of smaller, uncoursed river stone about 45 cm deep and extending about half way across the room. The east rim consists of a single row of three stones in the northeast corner, with several isolated boulders above it. On the south wall there is no rim, except for a 45 cm stub at right angles from the west wall. This is made of four courses of irregular, flat sandstone with some river boulders on top.

The other stone architectural feature in Kiva A is a V-shaped masonry ventilator in the middle of the south wall (Figure 4.19, left and right). This extends from the ground level to within 25.5 cm of the floor. It is made of river boulders and squared sandstone laid in uneven courses and crudely chinked at various places with smaller flat and round spalls. The sides of the V taper gradually, then terminate at a flat slab, 2.5 cm thick, that serves as a lintel for the opening into the flue (Figure 4.19, left).

Excavation along the outside of the south wall revealed the ventilator flue. The roof of this flue, which met the wall of the ventilator in the kiva about halfway down, consisted of horizontally-laid river boulders about 18 inches long, placed side by side. Although partially filled in with sediments, the flue's stone roof had been so well-fitted and chinked that a hollow passage remained for discovery through excavation. It is likely that the flue for the ventilator was made by digging a narrow, horizontal or slightly inclined trench in the center of the south wall. The placement of the flue's stone roof began at the outside opening of the shaft and worked northward, toward the interior space. The stone section in the kiva wall was the last feature completed, its V-shaped outline hinting as to the shape of the trench and suggesting an efficient and stable means for maintaining an opening. The flue roof extended about 90 cm south from the kiva wall and was initially covered with sediment. At its end was a rectangular outer opening fashioned of stone and rising about 30 cm above the roof of the flue (Figure 4.19 left, right).

In front of the ventilator opening in the interior of the kiva was a post hole 18 cm in diameter (Figure 4.19, left). Directly opposite, in the north wall, a similar post had been set into the wall. Hard, sandy clay had filled the post hole but this material was easy to distinguish from the surrounding sediment by its texture and color. At its base, the burned semi-circle where the post had rested was readily visible on the floor. This same type of hard, sandy clay fill was observed in the middle of the east wall just above the ramp. Here, fortunately, the clay had formed a cast of the lower part of the original post showing the outline, knots and even the worm-workings. Opposite this cast in the west wall were the actual remains of a rotted juniper post. Only 2.5 to 5 cm of the original 15 to 18 cm diameter post remained, but there was sufficient to trace it from floor level to within 12 inches 30 cm of the surface. This post was flanked on both sides by small, flat pieces of sandstone. In the center of the room was a hole which lined up directly with the north–south post holes and suggested a north–south primary beam supported in three places by upright posts and a perpendicular cross beam having two post supports. A similar situation was found later in Kiva B. It is possible that this so-called center post hole may actually have been the "sipapu" or symbolic entrance to Spirit World (Martin et al. 1947:135), but there were no distinguishing signs to mark it as such.

The most interesting feature of this kiva was the narrow bench or "walkway" extending along the length of the east wall. It consists of

Figure 4.19. Left: Stone ventilator from inside Kiva B (M. M. Shaeffer or J. B. Shaeffer, courtesy Arizona State Museum); Right: Kiva B ventilator, showing shaft and flue underneath south entry to Great Kiva. Note south pillar base for Great Kiva (F1) in upper left; south wall of Great Kiva at right corner (M. M. Shaeffer or J. B. Shaeffer; courtesy Arizona State Museum).

two flat levels of equal length, the southern half being lower. These two levels were connected by two steps which made obtuse angles of about 60° with the east wall. If there had ever been a further extension of the bench northward beyond the room, it was not discernible.

Along the base of the ramp, with the exception of a blank space at either end, was a series of over 100 separate ash marks 2.5–18 cm high and 2.5–5 cm above the floor level. It is believed these represent ash remains of sticks which apparently formed a banister or low, wattle-and-daub wall bordering the bench or narrow walkway. It was possible to establish the existence of this latter feature due to a light burning or sooting of the entire lower part of the room. This sooting even made possible accurate tracing of the depressions in the steps (see right foreground, Figure 4.18).

As for the floor of the room itself, the principal feature was the firepit in the center of the south half of the room, directly opposite the ventilator. This firepit was slightly oval in shape, with clay sides rising abruptly from a flat hard bottom to form a narrow ridge around the rim. When it was uncovered, the firepit was full of a very hard, white ash.

In the northwest corner was a shallow, rectangular storage cache with rounded corners, the bottom of which was paved with small, flat stones. There was some indication that the sides had been stone-lined as well. A similarly shaped, but unlined, cache occurred in the southwest corner. The only other depression, located adjacent to the south end of the entrance ramp, had an inclined floor and is thought to have been used as a metate rest. In addition to these major features there were several small holes of undetermined use in the eastern portion of the room between the ramp and the firepit. Two of these holes, containing small flat stones set on edge to define a hollow triangle, likely served as loom anchors.

Kiva B

This well-constructed, dirt-walled kiva was the smallest investigated. The dirt walls seem never to have been capped or rimmed with stone, as encountered at Kiva A. Nonetheless, the condition of the plastered walls was excellent. Great care had been exercised in construction; the walls were smooth and straight, the corners regular and well-balanced. Additional features included the post hole arrangements and a small "kachina niche" in the center of the northern wall (Figure 4.20).

The arrangement of the post holes is similar to that seen in Kiva A, the only other largely undisturbed kiva. The primary crossbeam, which was discovered lying horizontally, on an east–west axis apparently very close to where it had served its structural function, was probably 15–20 cm in diameter originally, but the wood had rotted to a diameter of 7.5–10 cm when found. Further investigation revealed traces of this beam near the tops of the east and west walls. The indication was that the beam had rested on the ground surface above the Kiva B walls and been supported as well by a central vertical post. On the west wall, several small rectangular stones suggested use to keep the beam in place.

Evidence of three other posts aligned on an approximately north–south axis was uncovered in the floor of Kiva B. The first, a post hole in the middle of the room, was followed down to within a few inches of the floor. In the middle of the north wall, about 15 cm south of it, was another small post hole. The third, a stump, was found flush against the middle of the south wall. The other feature of interest in the room is a small, rectangular, stone-lined niche near the center of the north wall. The niche was a well-crafted box of sandstone slabs—four separate overlapping pieces forming the top, with a single slab making up the sides and rear wall (Figure 4.20). A quarter

Figure 4.20. Kiva B, showing a small, slab-lined "kachina niche" in north wall (M. M. Shaeffer or J. B. Shaeffer, courtesy Arizona State Museum).

of a black-on-white ladle and a small black-on-red sherd were found inside the feature. The ladle fragment had no handle, and a chip had been knocked off the bottom, apparently so it would sit level without rolling. One of its edges had been worn down as if to form a scoop or scraping edge. The northern position and careful construction of this wall niche suggests it was used like similarly located and built features in the northern Pueblo area (see also Riggs 2001:76). Designated by archaeologists as "kachina niches" in keeping with similar features in Hopi homes, these features seem to have been variously used as shrines, as repositories for ritual paraphernalia and as altars—an opening into which supplication to certain deities might be addressed (Roberts 1932:p. 12(b); pp. 60-61, 78, 82, 84; Roberts 1939:125, 212).

We found some charcoal at the floor level in the southeast corner of Kiva B, but there was no evidence of a firepit. There was an absence of storage holes in the floor, little evidence of burning in the fill and none along the walls.

Kiva C

Because two of Cummings's trenches had previously passed through this kiva, one slightly below floor level, complete identification of the features in this structure was impossible. However, an attempt was made to establish the position of the slab-lined hearth excavated by Cummings's crew in relation to the probable walls of the original structure (see Figure 4.21). The fill of both trenches was readily distinguished from the native earth through which they had been cut, and it was possible to establish definitely the north wall and some of the west wall. The east wall was identified within 15–20 cm of its original position by following fragments of burned flooring. However, the location of the south wall is approximate because the burning could not be followed due to disturbance not only by Cummings's trench, but by the sinking of Post 10 of the Great Kiva.

The presence of a circular subfloor cache in the southwest corner of the room, together with the close proximity of the wall of Kiva A, would seem to indicate that the location of the south wall is within 30–60 cm of its original position. This cache contained a few corrugated sherds, a bone awl, a worked piece of deer bone with three encircling incisions or rings, and several unusual fragments of animal bone. At the north end of the cache was a deeper and smaller hole, evidently for the storage of smaller objects.

The only other feature in Kiva C was the rectangular, slab-lined hearth formed by setting four stones on edge. Several small holes about pencil size were found in the northwest corner of the room, and there seem to have been some small post holes in the northwest corner. However, the disturbed condition of the floor

Figure 4.21. Kiva C (M. M. Shaeffer or J. B. Shaeffer, courtesy Arizona State Museum).

made the pattern uncertain. Except for these features, little evidence of the original structure could be found. Nothing found during the digging suggested the presence of a deflector or a sipapu.

Kiva D

This kiva, the second largest of the group uncovered in the courtyard, is similar in many respects to Kiva A (Figure 4.22). The main features consist of a clay-lined firepit, two shallow rectangular floor bins with sloping floors, two wall caches, a circular depression (probably an olla rest), and a semi-circular entrance vestibule .

The firepit included a bowl-shaped floor but no encircling rim or lip. It was not well-finished, and when found contained 12.7–15.2 cm of fine white ash and two large stone fragments, presumably used as pot rests. The rectangular bins located in the southeast and northwest corners of the room appear to have been made to hold metates. The bin in the southeast corner of Kiva D had a steeply inclined floor sloping to the north and was lined with flat stones, but no metate was found. At the north end of this depression is a well-formed, circular depression in the floor having a distinct, 5 cm rim, possibly used as an olla holder in connection with the grinding process. The floor of the bin in the northwest corner is not as steeply inclined as that of the other bin. At the bottom of this second bin was found a slightly curved piece of unworked sandstone. Its surface was too rough to have been used for grinding and, inasmuch as the remains of a number of black walnuts were found with a battered oval polishing stone worn down by use on all edges and both sides, it is presumed

Figure 4.22. Kiva D, view probably southeasterly, showing Great Kiva Post 7 in the southern (right) section (M. M. Shaeffer or J. B. Shaeffer, courtesy Arizona State Museum).

this stone was used in shelling and preparing of nuts. An interesting detail of the bins is the presence of a small, arched depression 25 cm high and 25 cm deep immediately behind the metate bin at floor level in the north wall. At first it was thought that this might have been a kachina niche but, because of its position, it was more likely dug in so that the legs of the grinder might be accommodated between the wall and the edge of the bin.

In the southwest corner there had been a rectangular wall cache. The floor of the storage space was slightly below that of the rest of the room. Just how high it had been could not be determined, as the earlier trench had entered the room at this point. On the floor of the cache we found the articulated skeletal remains of a deer leg, a small rectangular handstone, an arrow polisher with one groove, and a mano fragment—all the stone implements being of basalt.

The single wall post, found in the middle of the north wall, was well-rotted and extended about 36 cm above the floor. However, the sandy clay that had filled the cavity above the stub could be traced to within 30 cm of the present surface. The post, its original diameter perhaps 20 cm, rested on the floor. Immediately in front of the post and embedded in the floor was a flat stone.

Perhaps the most questionable feature of Kiva D is what appears to have been an entrance vestibule in the northeast corner. A large river boulder was found in the face of the wall after the room was cleared. This proved to be a level which could be traced to establish a semi-circular occupation surface. Because no difference could be noted in the fill above the ash layer which was level with the boulder, it was assumed that it was not a cache dug into the wall. Further, because similar entrance forms are not widely known, the question of its original function is left open. Side entry ways are characteristic of pit houses in this area, and from this fact it might be inferred that this and other similar subterranean rooms were in pit houses rather than kivas or ceremonial rooms. However, the lateness of the pottery, the stylistic origins of the pottery outside the Mogollon region, and the arrangement of the subsurface structures within the courtyard, makes this unlikely. More work needs to be done in the White Mountain area before the question of ceremonial room identity can be definitely stated, especially for the period from A.D. 800 to 1200 (Haury 1936, 1940; Roberts 1931; Ciolek-Torello and Halbirt, Chapter 5). A small, rectangular wall cache was found in the northwest corner below the vestibule area. In the niche there was a small amount of sea-green paint.

It might be noted, in regard to the general subject of entranceways, that a side entrance has been definitely established only in Kiva A. In considering Kiva C, nothing definite could be determined. Because Kiva A had a side entrance, it is possible that the "storage room" at the south end of the masonry kiva in Patio B corresponded in function with the entrance in Kiva A. What little evidence we have seems to indicate that some sort of side entrance was present in some of Kinishba's small, rectangular, dirt kivas.

Kiva E

As can be seen in the Great Kiva floor plan (Figure 4.23), various features were sunk into or in close proximity to Kiva E. resulting in considerable disturbance. In consequence, it was possible to identify a wall only for the western half of this structure. The fill consisted of a very fine, grey ash beginning 30 cm or so below the surface and gradually thinning out as it reached sterile soil. The structure was identified by exposing this floor of native soil until the firebox and the wall were encountered. The room's curvilinear outline, shallow depth, irregularly distributed post holes, and two other large floor holes distinguish this kiva from the other, deeper, rectilinear structures.

In as much as the east wall could not be found, the unusual trench in the east part of the structure (F-3) may be either a ventilator for Kiva E or a sub-floor vault of the Great Kiva. Oriented on an east–west axis and located 1.2–1.5 m in front of Pillar 2, this narrow trench expands at its west end into a circular depression directly in the center of the Great Kiva (Figures 4.23 and 4.24). The northern side of this circular area had been strengthened and at the same time flattened by the erection of a short masonry wall. The inside of this wall seems to have been plastered, but the walls of the trench were not so carefully prepared.

While there is no question that the circular end extended up to the floor of the Great Kiva, the same cannot be definitely said of the walls of the trench. If the latter did extend up to the floor of the Great Kiva, then this trench must have been dug into the east wall, and fill of Kiva E for the sides could not be identified until the native earth was encountered at the kiva's floor level. At the western end of the trench, 15–20 cm above the floor, we found a well-shaped, rectangular cover next to a wider and heavier slab of unaltered stone. These were lying side by side on an east–west axis (Figure 4.25).

At the southwest side of the circular wall, at the eastern end of the trench, 23 cm below the present surface, we found the remnant of a small juniper pole 5–7.5 cm in diameter. It apparently had rested on or just above the stone wall on the other side. Immediately below this we found a large circular stone cover tipped at a decided angle. Directly below this, with its base resting on the floor and leaning against the south side, was a triangular-shaped piece of limestone 91 cm in length. Its two sides were chipped on both surfaces like an oversize arrow, which it resembled in outline. The other end was broken in a straight line across the base; in the center of this break was a hole, 5 cm in diameter. Nearby, against the east side and just off the floor, was a small carefully-shaped and smoothed circular stone 15 cm in diameter (Figure 4.26).

Finding these items in close proximity suggests the possibility of a stone cover supported on poles across the top of the circular opening. At any rate, the thickness of the covers and slabs indicate that this particular trench, if it was a part of the Great Kiva, did not serve as part of a foot drum. More likely, this feature represents the remains of the ventilator for Kiva E, with the possibility that the latter originally was D-shaped (J. O. Brew, personal communication with J. Shaeffer, probably during a visit to Kinishba made with Emil Haury in the summer of 1947; see Welch 2007a:41).

Ceramic Stratigraphy

The sherds scattered from the top to the bottom in the small kivas, together with those from the Great Kiva, represent the first vertical stratigraphy of any extent which has been documented at Kinishba. It was hoped, therefore, that correlation of the stratigraphic sections would offer the means for establishing a definite ceramic sequence, at least for Group I. Unfortunately, because of prior disturbance—in conjunction with both ancient remodeling and Cummings's 1930s digging and rebuilding—this was only partially possible. Disturbed fill dominated in Kiva C. Similar conditions prevailed in Kiva D, which had been disturbed through the installation of Post 7 for the Great Kiva, and Kiva E, which was also intruded into by ancient construction activities. In Kiva A there had been some digging around the base of Pillar 1. These facts substantially impeded the establishment of a clear-cut pattern across the nine stratigraphic profiles exposed in the Patio A excavations. It must be acknowledged that

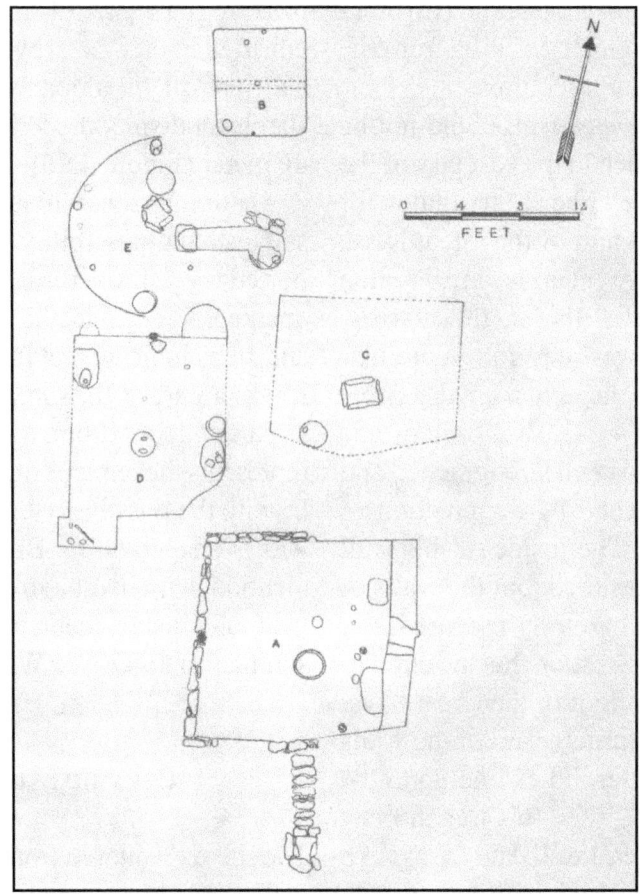

Figure 4.23. Plan view of Patio A subsurface features (M. M. Shaeffer, courtesy Arizona State Museum).

Figure 4.24. General view of Kiva E, showing Great Kiva Post 6 resting on the floor to the left of the room fireplace. Note "dedicatory stones" at Great Kiva floor level (M. M. Shaeffer or J. B. Shaeffer, courtesy Arizona State Museum).

Figure 4.25. Rectangular cover and unshaped slab from ventilator, Kiva E (M. M. Shaeffer or J. B. Shaeffer, courtesy Arizona State Museum).

Figure 4.26. Triangular slab and circular stone cover from ventilator, Kiva E (M. M. Shaeffer or J. B. Shaeffer, courtesy Arizona State Museum).

much of the record examined in the course of this project has been blurred by so much living in such a small area by such a large number of people.

Although critical subtleties of the stratigraphic pattern are lacking, some major features are clearly evident. The discovery in Kiva B of the undisturbed east–west primary beam, together with the form of the central upright beneath it, indicates that Kiva B, alone, contained undisturbed fill. Stratigraphically, the outstanding feature is the superposition of a polychrome series, principally of Four Mile types, over a lower level from which they were absent. The break between these two levels occurred in all of the kivas at 61–68.5 cm below the pre-excavation surface. Because the bichrome types which occurred in the lower levels continued up through the upper levels and there seemed to be no break in typology and no sterile layers in any of the kivas, both site occupation and ceramic development appear to have been continuous.

Stratigraphically, the bichrome series progressed in stages from (1) developed types of black-on-red, one a flat black-on-red of Tusayan appearance, the other a black-on-yellowish brown or light orange slip, to (2) undeveloped black-on-reds of deep red and dark paste (possibly St. John's?), to (3) Pinedale black-on-red. These earlier types of Stage 1 seem to show northern and northeastern affiliations in color range, apparently to the Wingate or Marsh Pass Series (Colton and Hargrave 1937). Invariably associated with these types is an over-fired decorated ware, the original slip color of which is undeterminable. St. John's polychrome comes in about Stage 2, together with the beginning of undeveloped Four Mile polychromes having a dark, slightly granular paste. This development is closely followed by the appearance in Stage 3 of the typical Pueblo III Four Mile polychrome series with its characteristic panel design, bright orange slip, fine temper, and whitish paste.

The upper or Four Mile polychrome series is accompanied by some Gila polychromes, which occur within 15–38 cm of the surface. Because this level may represent secondary filling or leveling in conjunction with Cummings's rebuilding, the association might be spurious. However, except for one Gila-like sherd found in Kiva B below the Four Mile series, the former are confined to the topmost levels. The occurrence of this sherd at a good depth in an undisturbed fill does suggest the possibility of early, undeveloped Gila and Four Mile types coming in almost contemporaneously, but with Gila polychrome at best weakly represented until the very late period of Kinishba's occupation.

The preceding description of the ceramic sequence is based principally upon analysis of the fill of Kiva B, since it contained the only undisturbed stratigraphy. In looking over these sherds for intrusive types from other localities, almost all the specimens appear to be of the local White Mountain series. The only intrusive noted was a black-on-white sherd with carbon paint identified on the basis of a single sherd as Flagstaff Black-on-White. Unfortunately, except for the original definition of the Four Mile series and a sketch of the pottery series at Kinishba, little has been published on the ceramic typology of this area (see Baldwin 1937, 1938b; Haury 1930, 1931). For that reason, the ceramic interpretation lacks both geographical breadth and local specificity.

This problem aside, Kinishba's prevailing stratigraphic pattern allows a restricted definition of the local ceramic series. The characteristic type of the decorated wares, running from top to bottom, was the black-on-yellowish brown or light orange slip previously mentioned in Stage 1. In paste and color range it is almost identical with Klagetoh black-on-yellow, differing only in being somewhat darker in surface color and slightly less polished (Colton and Hargrave 1937:123). Haury has designated an apparently related type found at Point of Pines as Pinto black-on-red and has designated types referred to here as related to Tusayan black-on-red as Gila black-on-red. These types appear to be parts of a single series. Nomenclature used here implies relationship of local types to a northern source; Haury's nomenclature suggests relationship to a southern source. (Note that because the Shaeffers' collections are not available for comparison with type specimens and other diagnostics, it is not possible to confirm or modify these type designations. For full discussions of Kinishba's ceramics and related issues, see Lyons, Chapter 7 and Triadan, Chapter 8).

Kinishba's black-on-whites are of the general "Tularosa type." In reference to the Museum of Northern Arizona type collection, Showlow black-on-white or Whipple black-on-white are probably indicated. The black-on-reds are of the Pinedale and Showlow series. Polychromes are of the Four Mile series—St. John's Polychrome, Pinedale Polychrome and Four Mile Polychrome. Pending more conclusive study, redwares may be lumped together as parts of the White Mountain Redware series. In general, there seems to be a continuous development of ceramic types, and surprisingly little evidence of intrusive vessels.

AGE OF THE KIVAS

Despite the number of large posts uncovered in the course of the Great Kiva investigation, all were juniper. No tree-ring dates were obtained. Nonetheless, estimates can be made on the basis of the ceramic sequence and stratigraphic associations of the dirt kivas in relation to the Great Kiva. The bi-chrome pottery types occurring in the fills of the small kivas appear to resemble what has been designated at Point of Pines as the Willow Creek phase, A.D. 1100–1200 (Haury and Sayles 1947).

In arriving at a date for the construction of the Great Kiva, two sets of tree-ring dates for rooms immediately adjacent to the courtyard can be referenced. According to the previous analysis of room foundations surrounding the Great Kiva (Baldwin 1934:105), Room 44 in the southeast corner (dated 1284–1301) represents the latest building period, with four walls all of shallow depth. In the Great Kiva's opposite (southwest) corner, Room 28 (tree-ring dated to 1232–1233) shows three walls belonging to the oldest building period and a wall of lesser depth later built across its front. It thus remains uncertain whether 1232 represents the approximate date for the construction of the original room or the approximate date for Room 28 modifications undertaken as part of the Great Kiva construction. If the former, the modification would fall 1230–1300, and probably around 1260, as the two other dated rooms in the southwest section of Group I show corresponding building activity at that time. In addition, that date would correspond roughly with the middle position of the greater part of the Great Kiva wall in regard to the depth of its foundation. However, if 1232 represents the modification date, then construction would be at that time. Therefore, from the evidence on hand, the construction date of the Great Kiva can be conjectured as being between A.D. 1230 and 1260.

FACTUAL SUMMARY

Excavations in the Group I courtyard at Kinishba indicate two, or possibly three, phases of ceremonial use. The earliest evidence of the courtyard's ceremonial use is seen in the series of six subterranean rooms—five dirt structures in Patio A and one masonry kiva in Patio B—in a long, narrow courtyard. The five dirt kivas were then filled in, the courtyard was divided, and the larger, southern portion (Patio A) utilized as a single large ceremonial room—a Great Kiva. Finally, it appears that the Great Kiva was dismantled and ceremonies held partly in specialized rooms within the pueblo room groups and partly in the courtyard which was reestablished through the removal of the Great Kiva roof.

In phase one, the five ceremonial rooms consisted of four rectangular structures (Kivas A, B, C, D) and one D-shaped or circular room (Kiva E), all of them having earthen walls. Kivas A and B were about 1.5 m deep; Kivas C and D about 1.2 m deep, and Kiva E about 90 cm deep. On the basis of sherds found in the fill of these structures, differences in depth may also represent differences in construction dates, with the deeper rooms being older.

It has not escaped our notice that few formal or specialized ceremonial features are associated with these rooms, the exceptions being the carefully constructed stone ventilator of Kiva A and the stone-lined wall or kachina niche of Kiva B. No artifacts were found on the occupation surfaces of any of the rooms with the exception of Kiva B, where a few stone tools were encountered. Except for the ladle fragment found in the wall niche in Kiva B, no complete or large sections of pottery vessels were found during the excavations. The kivas were crowded together as closely as possible and this, together with changes in the surrounding walls of the courtyard, suggests that the kivas were constructed at a time when the courtyard was narrower than during its use as a Great Kiva or as rebuilt by Cummings.

Following this initial occupation and use, a second phase began with the construction of the large rectangular, above-ground room measuring 15.5 m x 19.2 m. This Great Kiva had a southern antechamber which connects at its eastern side with a long entrance passageway through the southern room cluster of Group I. Patio B, the smaller adjoining open space north of the Great Kiva, contained a small, masonry-walled kiva, and seems to have been separated, structurally as well as functionally, from the Great Kiva at the time of this remodeling. Great Kiva construction entailed leveling and enlarging Patio A, erecting a series of dual posts to support the central primary beams, and placing 16 large juniper posts to serve as principal roof supports. These posts were 45–60 cm in diameter and arranged in four rows of four posts each. Because of the apparently keen intention on the part of the builders to reach undisturbed soil, the posts were set at varying depths, and those posts which had to be placed in the fill of the earlier kivas were buttressed by loose rock or by rock and clay bases. It thus appears that the Great Kiva's builders were either aware of the older structures, understood the superior structural support properties of the native soils, or both. In addition to the primary posts, a system of secondary supports was installed between the larger posts. These uprights appear to have been erected upon shallow rock bases set just below the Great Kiva floor level.

The Great Kiva roof is thought to have consisted of a series of north–south oriented primary beams supported by pairs of upright posts. The posts at each end of the primary beams rested slightly below the Great Kiva floor on platforms of rock and hard-packed clay. These posts were further supported by rectangular masonry buttresses extending about a meter above the floor. Between these buttresses were at least two other sets of substantial secondary posts set only slightly into the floor. Altogether, including central supports, other main supports, and the secondary support, a "forest" of some 28 or more posts supported the Great Kiva roof. The other features of the Great Kiva consisted of a low bench at the base of each of the four walls and a series of floor caches. Although all post remnants identified as part of this excavation showed signs of burning, either partial or total, the discovery of only a single specimen of burned roofing debris is taken to indicate that the Great Kiva was deliberately dismantled either before or after the fire, at a time when a substantial portion of the pueblo was occupied. The fire may have been either intentional, due to change in religious custom or in conjunction with the removal of construction timbers—i.e., "post-robbing" for use elsewhere or in later building episodes.

Ceramic evidence suggests that the small kivas were in use by the late 1100's or early 1200's. On the basis of the tree-ring dated rooms in the southeast and southwest corners of the Great Kiva (rooms 28 and 44, see Figure 4.4), the Great Kiva was likely constructed between A.D. 1230 and 1260.

It is possible that, during the final period of the occupation of the pueblo, the area of the Great Kiva was a courtyard, as it is today. In other words, sometime after perhaps 1280 A.D., Kinishba's occupants seem to have dismantled the Great Kiva and either held their ceremonies in the open air of Patio A (Cummings 1940:31) or in smaller interior spaces, perhaps in the smaller, above-ground ceremonial rooms which have been found at Kinishba and other regional sites (for example, Cummings 1940:36-38; Lowell 1991; Reid and Whittlesey 1999:122-124). These specialized rooms seem analogous to the fraternity rooms found today among the Hopi and Zuni (Roberts 1932:158-161). In this case, the posts of the Great Kiva seem to have been intentionally burned off, the debris removed, the northern masonry post buttresses leveled, and one of the southern buttresses rebuilt to serve as an altar similar to those found in early twentieth century Hopi courtyards. Such speculation cannot be critically evaluated at this point except through further investigation of the sequence of late ceremonial architecture in the White Mountain region (see Gerald 1957; Haury 1950; Herr 2001; Smiley 1952).

INTERPRETATION

Kinishba's Great Kiva represents an important example of a large, rectangular, above-ground ceremonial room in the central Southwest. The development of both curvilinear and rectilinear ceremonial rooms has been previously discussed in terms of parallel changes in small and "great" structures. Small kiva development, closely associated with changes in domestic pit houses, has involved dirt-walled subterranean or semi-subterranean structures generally followed by masonry walled kivas. The masonry structures also occur as subterranean or semi-subterranean, followed in general regional terms by the occurrence of above-ground specialized rooms. The developmental trajectory of the "Great Kiva" phenomenon has similarly followed the pattern of dirt-walled subterranean or semi-subterranean structures succeeded by masonry-walled constructions, also mostly subterranean or semi-subterranean (see Herr 2001; Herr et al. 1999). In terms of broad regional distribution, the curvilinear structures are generally concentrated in the northern Southwest. There, the developmental sequence started with the small, dirt-walled kiva and ended with the very large masonry Great Kiva. Invariably rare in the northern Southwest until after 1300 A.D., rectilinear ceremonial rooms persist among the Hopi in northeastern Arizona and the Zuni of west-central New Mexico (Smiley 1952).

To the south, in the belt of Mogollon uplands that marks the Sonoran Desert's northern boundary, ceremonial architecture develops along a somewhat different sequence. The earliest manifestations of the Mogollon cultural tradition feature ceremonial structures much larger than the domiciliary structures, an opposite trend from that found early in the north (Haury and Sayles 1947). The earliest structure of this sort was found about 32 km northwest of Kinishba at the Bluff Site in the Forestdale

Valley, dated around A.D. 300 (Haury 1950). Some of the large, curvilinear, subterranean structures at the Bluff Site have dirt walls and lack specialized features, but all are considerably larger in size than the associated domiciliary pit houses. A hiatus of some 300 years or more occurs before the next known type of ceremonial structure appears, around A.D. 650, in the Forestdale Valley (Haury 1940:7). This type, documented at the Bear Ruin, is about 10.7 m in diameter and dirt-walled. The structure includes additional specialized architectural features consisting of four recesses oriented to the cardinal points of the compass, a central hearth, and a floor framework for a possible loom. Another hiatus of 300 years or more in knowledge of local ceremonial room development exists until around 1000 A.D. when a circular, dirt-walled kiva is reported, also for the Forestdale Valley (Haury 1950:31). Another example of this same general type follows around A.D. 1200–1300.

This series of circular Great Kivas, the only ones so far described for the White Mountain region surrounding Kinishba, hardly seems to fill the ancestral qualifications needed for the later, larger, rectangular, above-ground room found at Kinishba. In fact, there is nothing in the literature of the immediate area which connects with or assists in the explanation of Kinishba's Great Kiva in a developmental sense. There are no transitional forms so far reported in the Forestdale area which link the early large, circular, subterranean or semi-subterranean kivas with the later rectangular, above-ground form. In view of the lack of transitional forms of ceremonial structures, the overall impression is one of diffusion into the area of a new form developed elsewhere.

At the present time the only possible transitional forms occur directly to the east, in the San Francisco River drainage of central New Mexico. There, around A.D. 900–1000, during what is known as the Late Pithouse period of that region's Mogollon development (see Table 2.1), large circular ceremonial structures were succeeded by rectangular, subterranean and semi-subterranean rooms which were partially or wholly masonry lined (Haury 1936:89). These rooms contained almost no specialized features. Because the general trend in this area was for the floor of the associated rectangular domiciliary houses to rise, it is logical to evaluate whether this trend is evidenced as additional ceremonial rooms are excavated. At the present time, however, no such developments have been reported for the San Francisco drainage. Additional work will be required to replace absence of evidence with affirmative evidence of absence.

Certainly the enclosed plan of some of the later large pueblos suggests the Kinishba type of Great Kiva. At the Swartz Ruin Cosgrove (1932:23) reports raised platforms on the courtyard floor, interpreting these as rests for posts. These may represent a variation of the stone concentrations found at Point of Pines. It is probable that such surface support for posts, rather than the excavation of large post holes such as occurred at Kinishba, will prove to be the general rule. The later method was probably a special solution due to the problem of the preexisting small kivas underneath the floor area which made for a soft fill and consequently an unstable sort of base for supporting heavy, weight-bearing uprights.

Altogether, because of the lack of the necessary transitional forms, the possibilities at present do not seem to favor the Forestdale branch of the Mogollon as the developmental center for the rectangular, above-ground Great Kiva. On the other hand, in the San Francisco–Mimbres area this transitional form is present in the large subterranean, rectangular structures of the Three Circle phase (the final phase, A.D. 900–1100) of that region's Late Pithouse period. It is therefore probable that the Kinishba type of Great Kiva developed in the San Francisco–Mimbres area and diffused westward at a later date.

One other suggestion as to the possible origin of this type of structure seems appropriate. The rectangular great kiva may be a collateral development of the subterranean kivas rather than a continuous development out of it. It might be that the ancestor of the rectangular, above-ground great kiva is to be found in ramada type structures. These flat-roofed, temporary shelters supported by uprights and sometimes branch-walled, apparently occur in Mogollon culture in association with underground rooms from earliest times (Haury 1940:51; Hough 1923:5; Martin 1940:32, 1943:168). Today among the Apache, who have derived a considerable amount of their basic religious practices from ancient sources, the ramada or dazdo is the favored spot for certain ceremonies, especially those related to curing, since it is outside the house. This is an insurance against contamination or having to burn down a house in case a patient dies. It might be that this type of structure had some use in ancient times for certain kinds of ceremonies as well.

Regarding the smaller underground structures found beneath the Great Kiva at Kinishba, the question arises whether they represent domiciliary or ceremonial rooms. As previously stated, the evidence suggests their function was ceremonial and that they were contemporaneous with the then smaller, above-ground stone pueblo. The reasons for this interpretation include:

1. Their circumscribed and central location under the floor of the Great Kiva;

2. The occurrence in some cases of specialized Anasazi kiva features;

3. The absence of pottery vessels and dearth of other artifacts in the rooms;

4. The lack of analogous house types in those Mogollon sub-areas where the architectural sequence has been worked out in some detail.

This, however, is but one opinion. Work at Point of Pines by the University of Arizona has convinced workers there that such structures were late pit houses, and therefore they argue that the same applies at Kinishba (personal communications with Emil Haury and E.B. Sayles, 1948; see also Smiley 1952). Regarding the relative position of the subterranean rooms, a comparison of the general layout of the pit house villages in the Forestdale Valley or the San Francisco–Mimbres area shows that most or all such sites are more spread out than Kinishba (Haury and Sayles 1947:13; Haury 1940:18; Martin 1940: Map 3, 1943: Map 14; Martin and Rinaldo 1947: Map 25; Nesbitt 1938:51). Satisfactory explanations for this crowding have yet to be produced. The subterranean rooms in the Kinishba courtyard are so close together that they seem impractically located for living purposes. Kiva D seems to have been placed so close to Kiva A that it was necessary to eliminate the construction of the southwest corner to fit it into the available space. The only reason that comes to mind for this is that the available building space was restricted, and the structures were therefore crowded into the center. So far as is known at the present time, no other deep pit houses are located under the southern half of Group I.

Another bit of evidence as to the ceremonial nature of these rooms is the occurrence of some architectural features which are generally associated in the Anasazi area with kivas. In particular, the ventilators in Kivas A and E, the well-constructed wall niche in Kiva B, the possible loom holes in the floor of Kiva A and possibly the D-shape of Kiva E suggest ceremonial functions. Above all, if these structures were primarily residential, it seems implausible that so little occupational debris and so few of the typical pit house features would be present. Not a single whole vessel was found either in the fill or on the floor contexts of these structures. The only rooms which showed some signs of food preparation—the presence of the two metates, several polishers, and a deer foreleg—was Kiva D, but here too, there was no pottery. If these were living rooms, the only explanation for such a dearth of artifacts is that the rooms were completely cleared before being abandoned, not only a rare practice in the Southwest, but a situation which would suggest a movement of but a short distance. In view of these facts, the need for substantiating proof of the domiciliary nature of these structures is at least as strong as is further evidence supporting their ceremonial function.

From the standpoint of architectural typology in the Mogollon area, the prospects for acquiring such evidence seem dim. The courtyard structures at Kinishba are not closely analogous to any rectangular pit houses thus far described for this area or any of the other Mogollon branches. In the Forestdale area, the pit house sequence at the present time stops around A.D. 800 and is succeeded by masonry surface structures (Haury and Sayles 1947:85). Therefore, the identification of a pit house village dating to A.D. 1100 or 1200, as is indicated by the ceramics and stratigraphy of the five structures discussed here, would indicate either a significant gap in our current understanding of regional settlement history and the existence of an unknown number of developmental phases which have yet to be fitted in before the side-entered pit houses of the Forestdale phase evolved into the Kinishba types. While this is a possibility, it seems more likely that the idea of the small kiva was probably associated with the northern Anasazi idea of stone pueblos and diffused into the White Mountain area along with it.

Were this the case, then the Forestdale type of domiciliary pit house might have survived as a centrally located subterranean ceremonial room, as did the old domiciliary house of the Anasazi. In this circumstance, there would be an apparent analogy with the Mogollon pit houses, even though that level of culture had long since died out as a habitation pattern. The hypothesis of both Anasazi and Mogollon kiva types representing the final stage of pit house development would account for the predominance of round kivas in the north part of the Puebloan Southwest and of rectangular ones to the south. That the small rectangular kiva came to dominate in the north after A.D. 1300 provides another indication of the reversal of culture flow which followed the break-up of the large pueblo pattern in the north due to the Great Drought at the end of the thirteenth century. It bears mention that this theory is consistent with the correlation between the unspecialized nature of the Mogollon kiva and domiciliary pit house in comparison with the more specialized nature of the Anasazi kiva and architectural elaboration of the northern pit house.

Of course, what is apparent in all this discussion of origins and development of the rectangular ceremonial structures in the Forestdale branch of the Mogollon is that interpretation cannot yet be grounded in facts. A considerable amount of digging remains to be done before any of the hypotheses concerning origins can either be substantiated or rejected. Evidence for the origin of the Great Kiva requires the identification of clear transitional forms either in the Forestdale branch or the San Francisco–Mimbres branch. To establish the validity of the small rectangular subterranean rooms as kivas, either the same pattern must be found in the courtyards of other large pueblos, or isolated examples of this type must be found in proximity to small early pueblos in this area. An aid in the reconstruction of this sequence of ceremonial structures would be the proper temporal placing of the large specialized, above-ground room, such as has been found at Kinishba, in order to determine whether it preceded or followed the Kinishba type of Great Kiva, the assumption being that above-ground ceremonial rooms are a later development leading to the fraternity rooms of the modern Hopi and Zuni villages. However, in conjunction with excavation, what is required is a review the present definition of ceremonial structures as they apply to the Mogollon area.

As a result of the application of Anasazi definitions of ceremonial features to Mogollon architecture, a dichotomy of ceremonial structures has been built up. The earliest group of Mogollon structures were identified as ceremonial on the basis of size, while for later times the criteria have been changed so that only those rooms which have Anasazi ceremonial features such as ventilator, recess, deflector, bench, etc. fall into the ceremonial category (see Smiley 1952). It would seem that in approaching the problem this way, two different sets of criteria are being applied to what is essentially a single cultural tradition. The Mogollon religious complex, like other aspects of this tradition, is distinguished by simplicity, and this characteristic persists through to the final stage of the large pueblos in this area. Where specialized features do occur, rather than consider them as the sole criteria of ceremonial structures, it might be well to regard them as intrusive from the Anasazi area—features which were individually accepted into an established religious complex that was not only less elaborated, but which possibly was altogether different in ideology. Where recognizable Anasazi kivas occur—e.g., at Showlow Ruin or Point of Pines—one might suspect actual migrations of Anasazi groups (Haury 1931). A great deal of excavation and analysis remain to be done before a satisfactory answer is found to the problem of the development of ceremonialism and religious architecture not only at Kinishba, but in the Mogollon area generally. However, more progress can be made if southwestern religious practices are interpreted in terms other than that of the single pattern found in the Anasazi area. To my mind, the unelaborated ceremonial structures at Kinishba not only mean it was peripheral to the Anasazi area in terms of material culture, but that ideologically the people who built them were the inheritors, along with the rest of the carriers of Mogollon culture, of a more archaic religious tradition. Therefore, at a time when the intrusive pottery concretely shows the White Mountain area to be in direct contact with that of the Anasazi, the religious structures remained unelaborated. This would appear to reflect a continuity in the greater simplicity of their religious beliefs.

Acknowledgments

We thank Dr. Frank H.H. Roberts, Jr., Smithsonian Institution, for reading the original manuscript and for his editorial suggestions; Dr. Harold S. Colton, Museum of Northern Arizona, for the identification of a number of sherd specimens and for the use of his institution's type collections; Dr. William Duncan Strong, Columbia University; Dr. Henry A. Shapiro, American Museum of Natural History, and Dr. J. O. Brew, Harvard University for advice and aid. On-the-scene assistance was generously provided by Mr. John W. Lee and Mr. Clay Longenbaugh of Whiteriver, who took some of the better photographic shots. Chester Holden, a trusted tribal member who worked at Kinishba for many years, did the other half of the shoveling.

Chapter 5

Before Kinishba: Two Late Pithouse Period Settlements Near Fort Apache

Richard Ciolek-Torello
Carl D. Halbirt

This chapter presents the results of excavations by the Museum of Northern Arizona (MNA) between 1983 and 1984 at two Mogollon pit house villages in the vicinity of Kinishba and Fort Apache, Arizona. Buh bi laá (NA17,903) and East Fork Villages (NA17,962) were inhabited during the transition between the Forestdale and Corduroy phases (Table 2.1). Three distinct periods of occupation are represented dating from A.D. 750 to A.D. 875. Investigations at these sites presented the first opportunity since the 1940s to investigate Mogollon pit house villages in the Forestdale region and to apply modern analytic techniques to the study of early Mogollon culture. Data recovered from these two villages provide insights into early cultural development in east-central Arizona, especially the important roles Hohokam and Anasazi influences played in the development of the Mogollon archaeological tradition.

BACKGROUND

In the introduction to his report on Kinishba, Cummings (1940:1-2) briefly characterizes cultural history in the Kinishba region. He divides the development sequence into three "great epochs that may be designated as Archaic, Pithouse, and Great Pueblo," the latter culminating in towns like Kinishba. According to Cummings (1940:2), "the Archaic extended from some unknown time B.C. to the beginning of the Christian era, whereas the Pithouse epoch extended from the "beginning of the Christian era to approximately 900 A.D." Cummings noted evidence for pit houses in three locations near the vicinity of Kinishba, but did not investigate them.

For the first deliberate efforts to understand Kinishba's predecessors, we must turn to Emil Haury's investigations in the nearby Forestdale Valley (located about 30 km north of Kinishba). In the same year that Cummings completed his book on Kinishba, Haury was completing excavations at the Bear Ruin, a village of approximately 15 pithouses and a "proto" Great Kiva in the Forestdale Valley. A year later, in 1941, Haury finished excavation of the Tla Kii Ruin, a small pueblo and kiva built over four earlier pit houses. At about the same time, Haury began excavation of the Bluff Site, a Forestdale Valley pit house village that predated the Bear Ruin. The excavations of these three small sites formed the basis for the definition of the Forestdale Branch of Mogollon culture (Haury 1940, 1985; Haury and Sayles 1947; Wheat 1955). The Bluff Site provided evidence for the establishment of the Hilltop and Cottonwood phases, which represented the Early Pithouse period occupation; excavations of the pit houses at the Bear and Tla Kii Ruins established the Forestdale and Corduroy phases of the Late Pithouse period (Haury 1985:15). Excavations at Tla Kii Ruin were also the basis for the definition of the Dry Valley and Carrizo phases, the initial phases of Pueblo period occupations (Table 2.1).

The impetus for much of Haury's work in the Forestdale Valley was to gather information to support the concept of Mogollon as an archaeological tradition distinct from the Anasazi, a contemporary archaeological culture defined in part by pit house residences and similar agricultural practices (Haury 1985:xvii). Haury demonstrated that subtle differences between the Mogollon and Anasazi were due to more than living in different environments—the mountains versus the high elevation deserts of the Colorado Plateau. The Forestdale evidence suggested Mogollon emergence as a culture distinct from Anasazi and other Southwest cultures during the Hilltop phase. In fact, Haury argued that at this early date, the Mogollon interacted more with their southern neighbors, the Hohokam, who resided in the lower elevation desert regions of central Arizona, than they did with the Anasazi. Nevertheless, Haury (1985:367) claimed that the Anasazi influence on the Mogollon distinguished the succeeding Cottonwood phase from the earlier Hilltop phase, and "with each succeeding phase in the local prehistory, Anasazi cultural elements were in the ascendency." Haury (1985:385-386) thought the appearance of black-on-white ceramics in the Corduroy phase represented the adoption of Anasazi ceramic technology, whereas the transition to above-ground masonry architecture in the Dry Valley phase as "a further step in the 'Anasazization' of the Mogollon people."

Many of Haury's conclusions regarding early Mogollon culture were supported by contemporary research carried out by Paul S. Martin and the Field Museum in the Pine Lawn Valley of west-central New Mexico and, later, in the upper reaches of the Little Colorado River watershed just north of the Fort Apache Reservation (Martin 1940, 1943; Martin and Rinaldo 1947, 1950; Martin et al. 1947, 1949, 1967). Little subsequent work was carried out in east-central Arizona to evaluate Haury's conclusions, and what little research was conducted did not involve the Mogollon Late Pithouse period (Hammack 1969; Stafford and Rice 1980). Thus, MNA's excavations at Buh bi laá and East Fork villages were the first in several decades to bring new information to bear and shed new light on the issue of Mogollon origins and development. As we describe in this chapter, these excavations suggest Hohokam culture had a much more important influence on early Mogollon development than did the Anasazi, at least in the Kinishba area. Haury (1985:383) recognized interaction between the early Mogollon and Hohokam largely in the form of intrusive ceramics. Excavations in the Kinishba area reveal that these interactions went beyond exchange of ceramics and extended to pit house architecture and mortuary patterns.

THE PROJECT

In 1980, the White Mountain Apache Tribe endorsed plans to construct a wastewater treatment system that would upgrade and improve existing service to the Whiteriver, East Fork, Fort Apache, and Canyon Day communities. The treatment plant was to be constructed at Canyon Day Flat so that the treated water could be used to irrigate newly developed fields in the area, thereby increasing agricultural productivity and providing additional sources of income for the members of these communities. Funds for the project were made available through the Arizona Department of Health Services, representing the Environmental Protection Agency.

In consultation with the State Historic Preservation Office (SHPO), the Tribal Development Office (TDO) determined that an evaluation of the effects of the proposed construction on cultural resources in the area should be made prior to the start of construction. As a result, the Office of Cultural Resource Management at Arizona State University (ASU) was contracted to conduct a survey of the wastewater facility and associated sewer trunk lines. This survey identified nine ancient sites in the vicinity, including AZ V:4:6 (ASU) (McKenna and Rice 1980), later called Buh bi laá Village (NA17,903). In December 1980, ASU was again contracted to conduct an archaeological testing program at Buh bi laá for the purpose of evaluating the nature, extent, and National Register eligibility of the site. ASU conducted a backhoe trenching program in conjunction with a remote sensing magnetometer survey and systematic surface collection. The ASU crews found five pit house depressions and 19 pits. Based on the area investigated and the number of trenches (22) excavated, the site was projected to contain over 20 pit houses and as many as 200 other features (Halbirt and Dosh 1986).

The results of ASU's testing program led to a determination by the TDO and SHPO that a data recovery program should be implemented at Buh bi laá and AZ V:4:5 (ASU), a single room masonry structure identified in ASU's original survey. MNA submitted a proposal that was eventually accepted, and a contract for data recovery was negotiated between MNA and International Engineering Company, Inc. (IEC) on behalf of the White Mountain Apache Tribe (Ciolek-Torrello and Halbirt 1982). The data recovery program was designed to maximize participation of tribal members and use of tribal facilities, as well as to minimize costs. It was anticipated that 40 percent of project funds would be returned to the tribe in the form of salaries and benefits to laborers, payments for the use of tribal equipment and facilities, and purchases of supplies from local businesses. In addition, on-the-job training was to be provided and structured towards developing a labor pool of sufficiently trained technicians that could be employed for similar archaeological projects in the future.

Data recovery was initiated in December of 1983, at which time AZ V:4:5 (ASU) was excavated and surface collections and additional trenching were begun at Buh bi laá (Halbirt 1984; Halbirt and Ciolek-Torrello 1985; Halbirt and Dosh 1986). Trenching and excavation of pit houses and extramural features at Buh bi laá continued until February, 1984. During this time, MNA was requested by IEC to conduct an archaeological survey along a realignment of the sewer trunk line between East Fork and Fort Apache. One archaeological site, NA17,962 (soon to become known as East Fork Village), was recorded during this survey (Keller 1984). It was initially thought that rerouting the sewer line around the site could be done without impacting what appeared to be the main part of the site. Monitoring was recommended and construction trenching began in March 1984. This work was halted when a pit house was exposed in the sewer trench. A smaller exploratory trench was then excavated within the easement to determine if any other features might be present. The discovery of five additional features, including four pit houses, led to the development of a data recovery program for this site as well (Halbirt 1983). Finally, during the monitoring of the sewer trench at East Fork Village, three human burials were exposed along another segment of the sewer line adjacent to a large ruin, Hough Site 133 – Spier Site 228, that had been previously tested by Hough (Hough 1907:81; Spier 1919:377). These burials were excavated and recorded by MNA personnel, then immediately reinterred at a nearby safe location. Based on nine ceramic vessels associated with the three graves, the burials were interred between A.D. 1300 to A.D. 1350 or during the Canyon Creek Phase, when Kinishba was in use. Identified vessels include a Cedar Creek Polychrome bowl, a Pinedale Polychrome bowl and a Black-on-red pitcher, a Heshota Polychrome bowl, and a Showlow Polychrome jar (Halbirt 1984). The following summarizes salient aspects of Buh bi laá and East Fork villages and their contributions toward understanding Mogollon prehistory.

Buh bi laá Village

Buh bi laá Village was located 2 km southerly of Kinishba Ruins, near the community of Canyon Day, on the White Mountain Apache Reservation. The site is situated at an elevation of 1491 m at the edge of an escarpment overlooking the White River. The escarpment is part of a broad flat that caps basalt strata dissected by the White River. A large petroglyph site is located just over the edge of this escarpment adjacent to Bu bi laá. The site itself was located in a plains grassland biotic community (Lowe 1964:43-44), with a piñon-juniper community on adjacent uplands.

The aims of the data recovery project were to recover, through a systematic program, as much material as possible before the site was destroyed. Emphasis was placed on an intensive backhoe testing phase and subsequent excavation of pit houses considered to have a high probability for containing datable wood as well as archaeobotanical remains. A total of 38 additional trenches were excavated (in addition to the 22 excavated by ASU), and the remainder of the site was surface collected. The testing phase revealed that the pit houses were arranged in four clusters labeled A-D. It was decided to excavate at least one house from each cluster. In addition, areas found to contain a high density of pits were sampled in order to determine the kinds of activities that occurred outside pit houses.

A total of 18 pit houses were identified during data recovery. One additional house was found during grading activities related to construction of the sewer pond in the summer of 1984. Time constraints and weather conditions did not permit the excavation of all burned pit houses (15 were recorded) or all activity areas. Nine burned pit houses were excavated either partially or entirely, and three unburned pit houses were partially stripped of overburden to obtain information related to their shape, size and orientation. Feature definition was facilitated by the fact that most of the structures and extramural pits had been cut into the cultural sterile subsoil, an orange clay with scattered cobbles and caliche deposits.

The final phase of fieldwork consisted of manual stripping of overburden from areas suspected on the basis of testing results to contain extramural features. Three such areas were investigated, and each proved to be different in terms of features and materials recovered. These consisted of a ceremonial/mortuary locus, two activity areas identified as ramadas based on charred wooden beams around and atop artifacts, and a possible mortuary area associated with the courtyard of House Cluster B. In addition, four human burials in scattered locations—unearthed during the backhoe testing phase—also were investigated. The results of these excavations provide a significant database for determining the structure of Mogollon pit house communities and concomitant social organization, subsistence activities and relationships with Hohokam and Anasazi groups.

Architecture, Mortuary, and Extramural Features

A total of 18 pit houses, two ramadas, scattered

burials, and a jacal (wattle-and-daub) structure were identified at Buh bi laá (Table 5.1, Figure 5.1). These houses could be divided into three distinct house types on the basis of roof construction, depth of pit, and shape.

House Type 1

House Type 1 was the most common and consisted of deep, squarish structures with a four-post roof support pattern. These houses were highly variable in size, ranging from 11.4 m² to 20.2 m² (average size 16.2 m²) and a depth below ground surface ranging from 1.0 to 1.6 m. That portion of the wall in contact with the sterile subsoil was essentially vertical with a prepared clay surface, which had been preserved when the structure was burned. Both prepared and packed earth floor surfaces were evident in this category. Five houses could be placed in this category (1asu, 2asu, 14a, 8, and 38a) and as many as seven other houses fit either House Type 1 or 2, based on the depths of the house pits. These houses could be entered either from the roof or a side entry, although the entryway to one of the structures (House 8) may have also incorporated a tunnel adjacent to the east corner. Three of the four Type 1 structures contained clay-lined hearths and in situ floor artifact assemblages consisting of a few ceramic vessels, milling equipment or both.

House 14a, which was the largest structure documented at Bu bi laá, was distinguished from the other Type 1 houses by the presence of a large number of jars, suggesting a primary storage function. An estimated 24 vessels including 17 Alma Plain jars, a Gila Butte Red-on-buff plate, a Hoot Owl Plain jar, 2 Forestdale Plain jars, and about 3 Alma Plain and Forestdale Red seed jars were found on the floor of this structure (Figure 5.2). Hoot Owl Plain is a tufaceous temper, brown paste type that has its origins near the Point of Pines area (Dr. Emil W. Haury, personal communication in Halbirt and Ciolek-Torrello 1985). Other items found on the floor included 14 manos, a mortar and pestle, 2 grinding slabs, a slate palette, 4 hammerstones, a comal (stone griddle), a polishing stone, and several large flat unworked sandstone and basalt slabs. House 14a did not contain a hearth and was apparently entered from the roof. The roof of this house was supported by four posts set within the floor of the structure with additional smaller posts embedded in the floor and in the walls. Both the walls and the floor exhibited evidence of plastering. House 14a was centrally located between three of the four house clusters identified at Buh bi laá Village. These were clusters A, C, and D (see below).

Feature 8, a smaller house in House Cluster B, was another notable Type 1 house. Measuring only 12.3 m², it was characterized by vertical pit walls with plaster evident on the southwest wall around what appeared to be a ventilator opening. It was apparently entered from the roof. The floor was not plastered and the only interior features were a hearth and area of consolidated ash. The roof was supported by four posts placed within the floor of the structure. The house had apparently been filled with trash after abandonment, although four manos, a trough metate, a core, and a small number of flakes and sherds were associated with the floor. A poorly preserved skeleton of an adult male was found sprawled on his back on top of the hearth. Burned roof beams resting on top of the lower portion of the body had charred several bones, indicated that this individual probably died during or immediately before the burning and collapse of this structure.

House 1asu may also be classified as a Type 1 house. Although it was completely excavated, no internal postholes were documented to indicate the roof-support system. Based on its depth and size (11.4 m²), it is comparable to House 8—a Type 1 structure. Around the hearth the floor exhibits plastering,

Table 5.1. Summary of Pit House Characteristics

House	Type	Shape	Area (m²)	Depth (m)	Entry	Roof Support	Floor Features	Comments
Bu Bi Laá Cluster A								
1asu	1	square	11.4	1.4	roof?	-	hearth, storage pit	Burned with adult female on floor
2asu	1	square	19.8	1.0	side	4-post	-	Burned
3asu	1/2	-	~12	1.4	-	-	-	Burned
3	1/2	-	-	1.1	-	-	-	May not be a house
4	3	-	~9	0.7	-	-	-	Burned
Bu Bi Laá Cluster B								
14a	1	square	20.2	1.1	roof	4-post	none	Numerous vessels and food processing tools
14b	1/2	square	~12	1.0	-	-	-	Partially stripped, unburned
9	1/2	rectangular	~12	1.0	-	-	-	
7asu	2	rectangular	16.1	1.4	ramp	2-post	hearth, ash pit	Burned
8	1	square	13.3	1.6	roof	4-post	hearth	Burned with adult on floor
Bu Bi Laá Cluster C								
25	3	oval	7.4	0.7	side	4-post	firepit	Burned
11asu	1/2	-	~12	1.2	-	-	-	Burned
22a	1/2	-	~12	1.3	-	-	-	Burned
22b	1/2	-	~12	1.0	-	-	-	Burned
Bu Bi Laá Cluster D								
31	3	square	9.0	0.7	-	4-post	firepit	Burned
34	3	square	12.2	0.7	roof?	-	-	Burned, stripped
38a	2	rectangular	13.9	1.2	ramp	-	none	Burned with bench
38b	1	square	16.8	1.5	roof?	4-post	hearth, ash & storage pits	Burned
East Fork Village								
1		rectangular	10.4	0.4	ramp?	6-post	hearth	Burned
2		square	10.6	0.5	ramp	6-post	hearth	Burned
3		square	20.6	0.2	side	4-post	firepit	
4		rectangular	18.4	0.15	ramp	-	ash stain	Burned, 2 cremations, numerous food preparation tools
5		subrectangular	24.0	0.1	-	4-post?	fire & trash pits	Burned, numerous food preparation tools

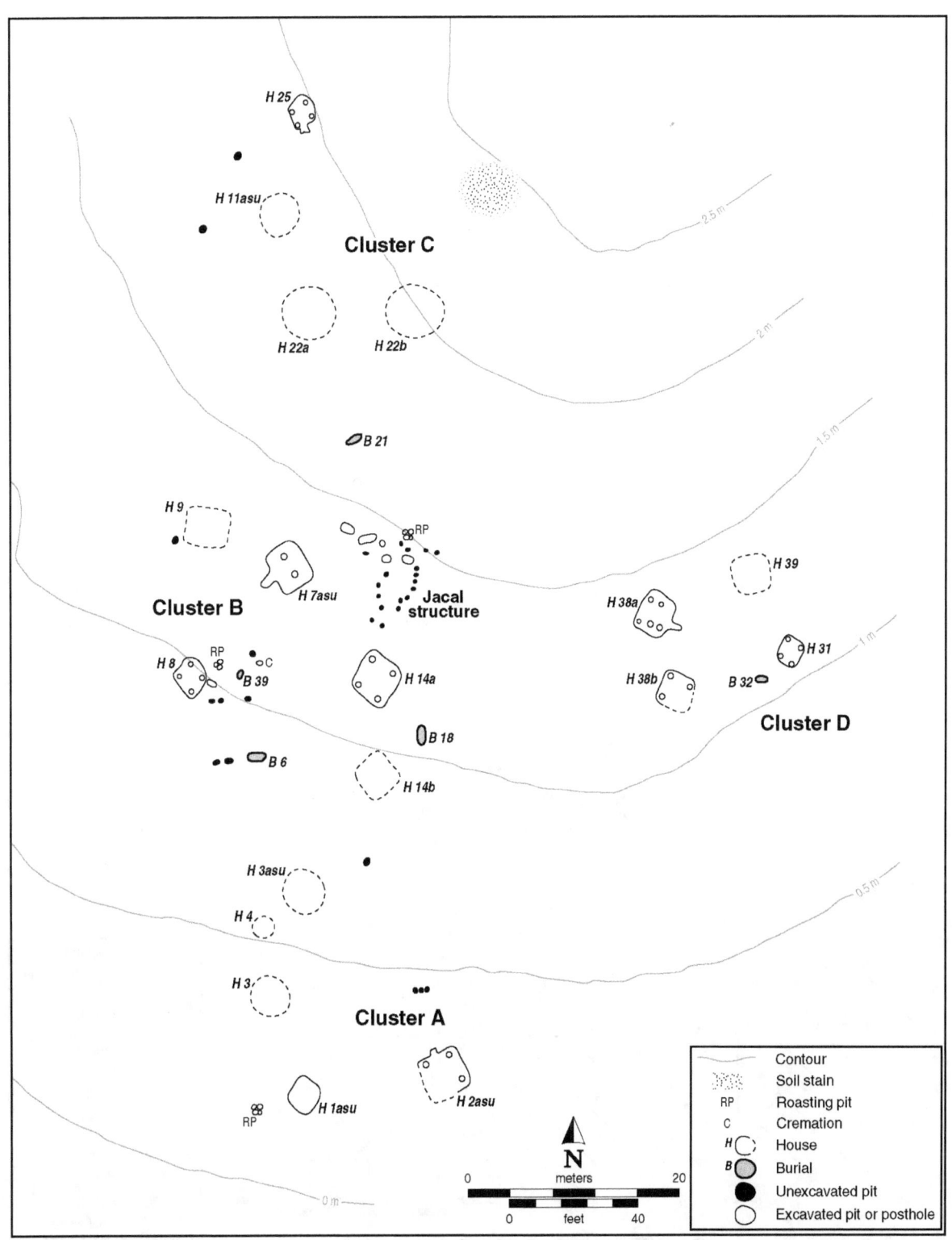

Figure 5.1. Plan view of Buh bi laá Village.

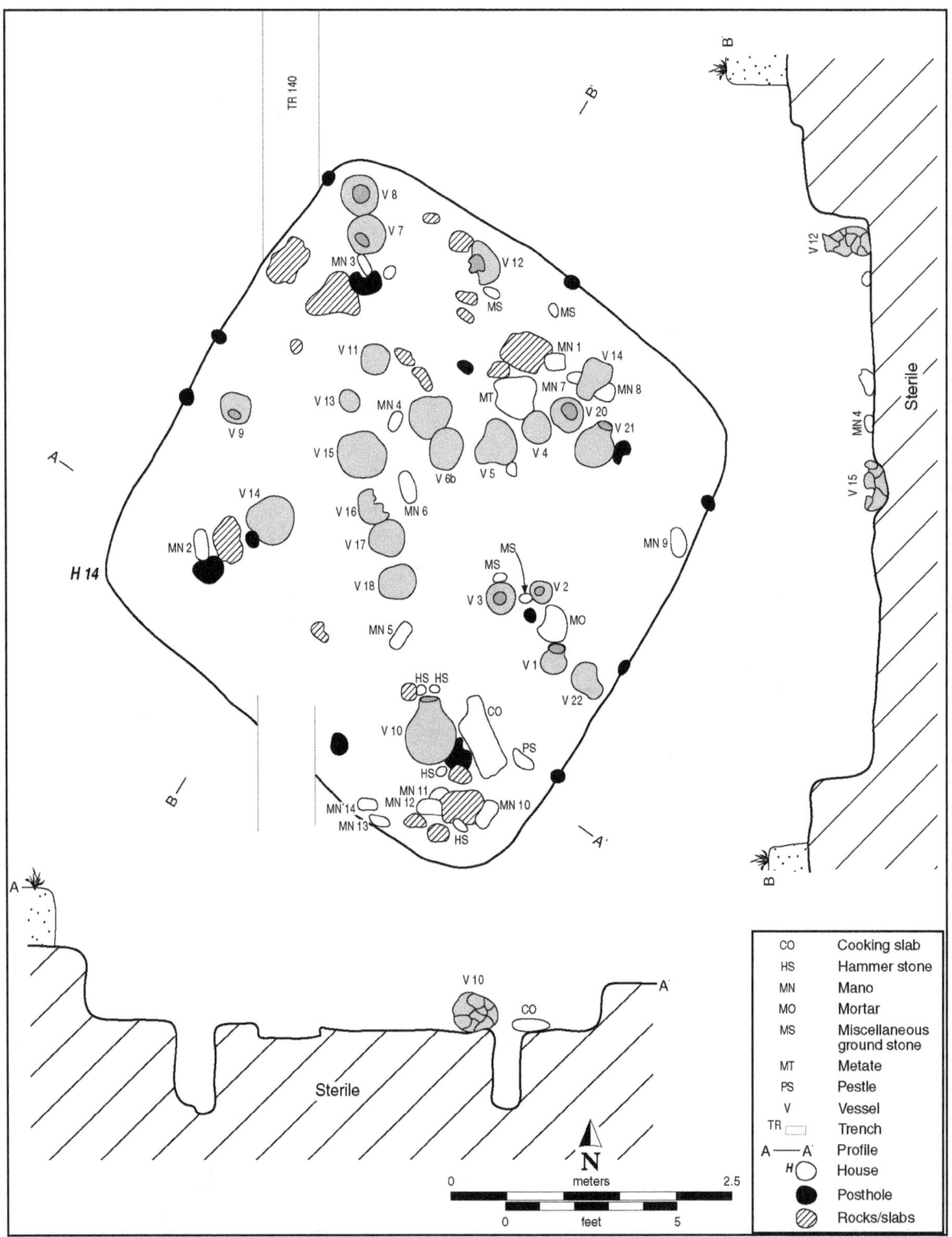

Figure 5.2. Plan view and cross-sections of House 14a, House Cluster B, Buh bi laá Village.

with the rest of the structure having been damaged by burrowing animals. Artifacts found on the floor included two manos, a partial ceramic bowl, and a fossil. An interesting parallel with House 8 is that House 1asu also contained the remains of an adult, probably a female, on the floor near the hearth. The individual was prone, extended with charred logs across her back and legs. The position of the skeleton suggested the individual's last act was an attempt to push away from the floor and escape the burden of the collapsed roof members.

House Type 2

House Type 2 is represented by rectangular structures with either two- or six-post roof supports, which are considered to be representative of a gabled roof (Bullard 1962). In his analysis of pit house architecture at the Stove Canyon and Lunt sites, which date to the same time period as Buh bi laá Village, Neely (1974:311) suggests two- and six-post patterns are variations on the same roof construction theme. Two houses at Buh bi laá (Houses 7asu and 38a) fit this category (Figure 5.3). Both houses share similar characteristics, yet they exhibit differences. They are similar in size (14 and 16 m^2), with deep vertical walls, were accessed via ramped entryways, and contained hearths. Differences between the two structures are reflected in the ramp entryway construction and orientation, other interior floor features, and architectural elements. House 7asu, also located in Cluster B, was built with vertical walls within a 1.5 m deep pit. The primary roof supports were two main posts, centrally located in each half of the house. Additional smaller posts were embedded in the east and west walls. The house was accessed by a long, southwest-facing, stepped entry ramp lined with vertical slabs. A slot trench (53 cm by 17 cm by 7 cm in depth) was located behind the hearth. Floor artifacts included two manos, a grinding slab, a hammerstone, a shell bracelet fragment, sherds and debitage. House 38a (a 6-post structure) had postholes at the beginning of an east facing ramp, a bench along the back wall and an ash pit.

The seven houses that can be classified as either Type 1 or 2 include Houses 3, 3asu, 9, 11asu, 14b, 22, and 22B. Houses 9 and 14b were outlined during stripping operations, whereas the others were documented during backhoe trenching. We tentatively place these houses into either Type 1 or 2 based on the outlines of the house pits exposed in plan view or length and depth exposed in profile, respectively.

House Type 3

House Type 3 is characterized by small, shallow houses with a four-post roof support pattern. They differ from House Type 1 in their much smaller size (7.4 to 12.2 m^2), shallower depth, and either square or pentagonal shape. Type 3 houses extended roughly 70 cm into the subsoil, whereas Type 1 and 2 houses were excavated a meter or more into the subsoil. Given their shallowness, access may have been through side entryways, but a roof entry cannot be ruled out. The small size, irregular construction, shallow depth, and lack of a well-defined hearth suggest that Type 3 houses are temporary or summer habitations, whereas the presence of a hearth and deeper pit suggests that the majority of the Type 1 and 2 houses are more permanent winter habitations. Two houses, Houses 25 and 31, represent House Type 3; Houses 4 and 34, may also be classified as Type 3.

House 25, located in House Cluster C, is the smallest (7.4 m^2) documented house at Buh bi laá. It was eccentric in shape and built within a 75-cm-deep pit. The walls were both vertical and sloping, with a bulbous, stepped entry opening in the south wall. Posts were

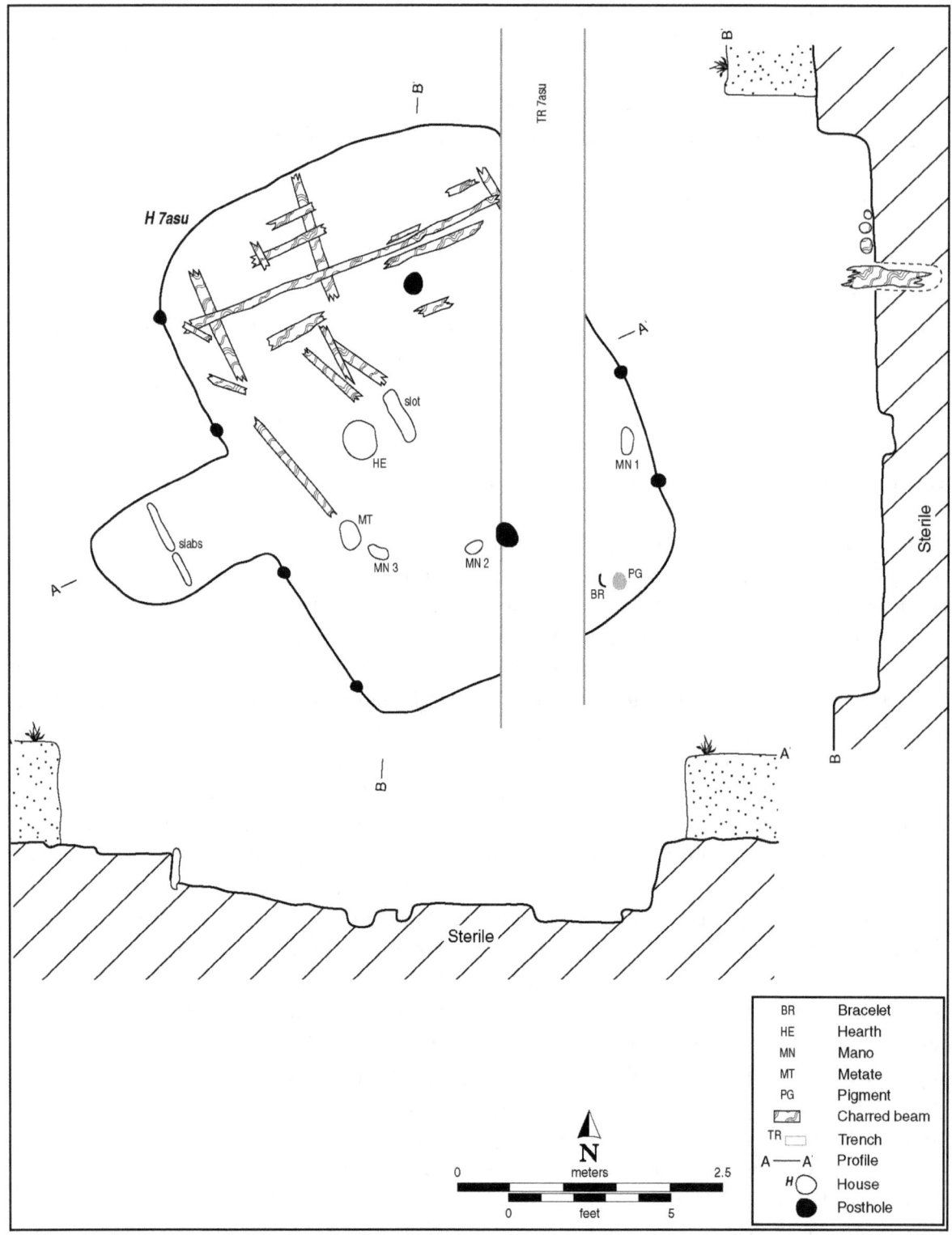

Figure 5.3. Plan view and cross-sections of House 7asu, House Cluster B, Buh bi laá Village.

located on either side of the entry. The floor was of packed earth and a poorly defined fire pit was found near the center of the house and a cluster of fire-affected rock was found in the northeast corner. The floor assemblage included two slab metates, two manos, a pestle, a core, and a small quantity of debitage and sherds. A cluster of fire-affected rock was found in the northeast corner.

House 31 was square and measured 9.0 m². Both the walls and floor appeared to have been plastered. No entry was documented; however, possible vestiges of an entry were found along the west wall, suggesting it may have been removed during backhoe trenching. As such, it may have shared a courtyard area with House 38a. Artifacts were minimal and consisted of a small quantity of debitage and sherds.

The outline of House 34 was documented during stripping of overburden. The square shape of this house suggests it may be a Type 1 house although its size (12.2m²) is at the lower range of Type 1 houses. The shallow depth (0.7 m) of this house, as evidenced in the backhoe trench, however, places it into the Type 3 category. House 4 was exposed in a backhoe trench; its small size and shallow depth are consistent with Type 3 houses.

In addition to these houses, two ramadas were identified at Buh bi laá. One small ramada, about 6 m² in size, was found adjacent to House 2asu in House Cluster A. A metate with 132 charred juniper seeds atop its grinding surface and four manos were recovered from this structure, suggesting use as a milling station. A much larger ramada (21 m²) was found atop House 14a in House Cluster B. It contained two metates, eight manos, a pestle, three cores, eleven flakes, a shell bracelet fragment, and eight ceramic vessels (4 jars, 3 bowls, and a sherd scoop). A partially clay-lined hearth and rock-filled pit were also present.

The different types of houses appear to be distributed among House Clusters A, C, and D, but not House Cluster B (see Table 5.1). Cluster A contains five houses: two Type 1 (Houses 1asu and 2asu), one Type 3 (House 4), and two Type 1 or 2 (Houses 3 and 3 asu), as well as a ramada. House 2asu is large (19.8 m²). The size of House 3 is unknown. The other three houses are small to medium sized (9 to 12 m²). House Cluster C contains at least three Type 1 or 2 houses and one Type 3 house, all of which are relatively small (7.4 to 12 m²). House 25, a Type 3 house, was the only one of these houses that was excavated. House Cluster D contains four houses: one Type 1 house (House 38b), one Type 2 house (House 38a), and two Type 3 houses (Houses 31 and 34). House 38b is large, whereas the others are small to medium in size (9 to 13.9 m²).

This distribution of house types within Clusters A, C, and D suggests that each represents the tangible remains of an extended household group (cf. Ciolek-Torrello 1996, 2009; Ciolek-Torrello et al. 2000; Huntington 1986; Klucas et al. 1998). The similarity of floor features and assemblages in each cluster suggests a focus on residence and food preparation. It is also possible that the presence of Type 1 and 2 houses versus Type 3 houses in each cluster represents seasonal movement of the household residents from winter to summer homes within the same location, assuming contemporaneity between the houses occupied in each cluster. Based on ceramic frequencies and similarity in tree-ring dates for Houses 1asu and 2asu in Cluster A (see below), this is a tangible hypothesis. The small size, irregular construction, shallow depth, and lack of a well-defined hearth suggest that Type 3 houses may have been used during temperate climatic conditions (such as summer, when temperatures average 33 °C for highs in July [91.5 °F] and 15 °C [59 °F] for lows [Sellers and Hill 1974:550]). By contrast, the presence of a hearth and deeper pit suggests that the majority of the Type 1 and 2 houses are more permanent winter habitations, providing shelter when temperatures average from a daily high of 12 °C (53 °F) to a low 6 °C (2 °F) in January.

House Cluster B is distinct in that it contains only Type 1 or Type 2 houses, all of which are medium to large in size (12 to 20.2 m^2). Furthermore, the other three house clusters date to the early construction episode (see below); whereas, House Cluster B is multi-component. The seven structures that comprise this cluster (5 houses, a ramada, and a ceremonial and mortuary area) need to be considered according to the period of use. The earliest use is represented by House 14a—a large Type 1 structure used for storage that dates to the early construction episode at the site and is unique to Cluster B. The other two excavated pit houses in Cluster B (House 7asu and House 8) date to a later construction episode and represent a large Type 2 house and a moderate-sized Type 1 house, respectively. House 9, exposed in a backhoe trench, also is considered to be associated with this later construction episode. It is uncertain how House 14b fits within Cluster B in terms of time.

The ramada was situated atop the fill of House 14a and measured approximately 21 m^2 in area based on the distribution of artifacts and charred beams. This work area contained two metates, eight manos, a pestle, three cores, eleven flakes, a shell bracelet fragment, and eight ceramic vessels (4 jars, 3 bowls, and a sherd scoop). A partially clay-lined hearth and rock-filled pit were also present. Ceramic types and frequencies found associated with the ramada were similar to the post-occupational fill deposits above Houses 7asu and 8, suggesting that the ramada postdates the late construction episode (see below). A similar work area, exposed over the fill of House 8, contained 6 metates (four fragments), three manos, a grooved maul fragment, a grinding slab, and a secondary cremation placed inside two Alma Plain bowls—one inverted over the other. A Forestdale Red pitcher was adjacent to the cremation. Also recovered from the fill above House 7asu and the area above House 8 were some Kiatuthlanna Black-on-white sherds, which have a date range from A.D. 825 to 950 (Oppelt 2008:21).

The ceremonial/mortuary area located in House Cluster B contained a possible jacal structure evidenced by 18 postholes and three or four rectangular, clay-lined primary cremation pits in an area measuring roughly 10 m^2 (Figure 5.4). In addition, three isolated human burials and four secondary cremations were found scattered in the area identified as Cluster B.

Most of postholes representing the jacal structure are spaced 50 to 100 cm apart and arrayed in an ellipse measuring 7 m by 3 m (21 m^2). A few postholes were found at either end of this structure; however, their association is unclear. Postholes varied from 10 to 20 cm in diameter and 25 to 50 cm in depth. The soil matrix between Trenches 19 and 20 contained an abundance of small pebbles and cobbles that could have formed part of a jacal wall anchored by posts. This soil matrix was not found in the cremation area. No floor surface could be identified in the area encompassed by the postholes.

In the corners of two of the primary cremation pits, Features 2 and 7, were wooden posts, each surrounded by a thick, clay coping that appeared to have been exposed to fire or intense heat. All three pits ranged in size from 1.4 to 1.6 m in length, 0.40 to 0.50 m in width, and 0.45 to 0.60 m in depth. Feature 2 contained a clay pipe placed within an Alma Plain bowl and traces of charred human bone, representing a young adult. Feature 7 contained a Forestdale Plain bowl, a Forestdale Red or Smudged bowl, and two small Alma Plain bowls that were associated with charred human bone fragments. All the vessels were

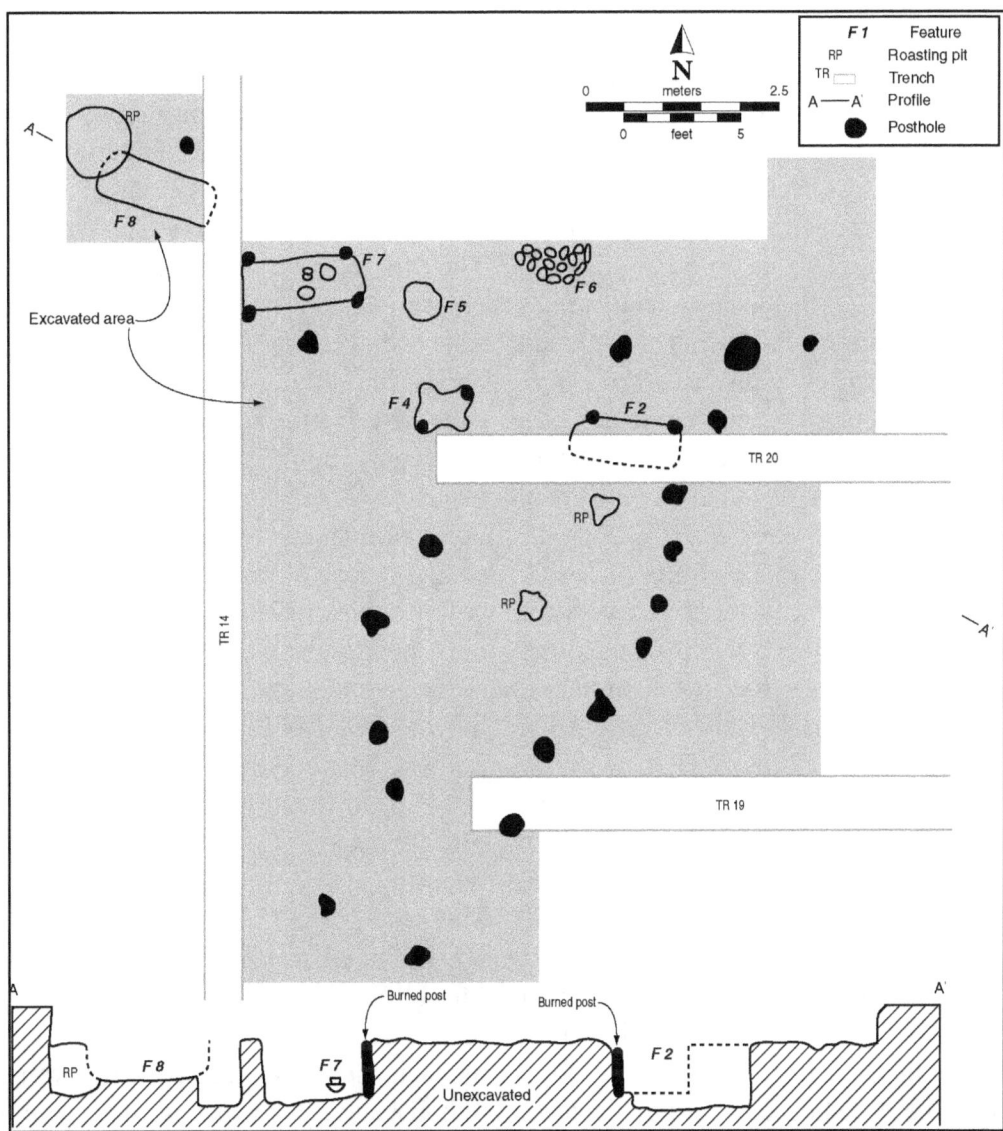

Figure 5.4. Remains of a possible jacal structure and nearby cremation pits and extramural features, Buh bi laá Village.

severely heat altered; the two small bowls had melted and the larger vessels were deformed. Several large sherds exhibited bubbling on both surfaces, and a small amount of charcoal was found near the bottom of the pit. Feature 8 did not contain any posts, vessels, or human remains. Features 2 and 7 appear to represent the locations of primary cremations in which bodies and associated funerary items were placed on platforms built above rectangular pits. Feature 8 appears to have been prepared for this purpose, but never used. Feature 4 is a much smaller pit measuring 0.75 by 0.35 m and only 25 cm deep. It contained two corner posts, but no evidence of clay-lining, burning, or human remains. A broken grayware ladle was the only artifact recovered from this feature. Feature 4 may have been prepared for a child or infant cremation.

Whether the jacal structure and cremation pits were contemporaneous is questionable. Feature 2 intersects the outline of the jacal structure. Likewise, Feature 4 is adjacent to the outline. As such, this special purpose area could have been used throughout the occupation of Buh bi laá Village. A tree-ring date of 727, obtained from one of the posts in Feature 2, as well as the cremation vessels from this pit and Feature 7, are consistent with the early occupation episode. By contrast, ceramic frequencies from soil deposits and pit fill are similar to those found in Houses 7asu and 8, which date to the later occupation episode.

Twelve other extramural pits and rock clusters were found in Cluster B, at least three of which contained burials. None of the other house clusters had more than three extramural pits and only two burials were found outside of Cluster B. House Cluster B is centrally located within Buh bi laá with Clusters A, D, and C located to the south, east, and north. In the absence of a Great Kiva, which is typical of small Mogollon villages of this time period, Cluster B may represent the ceremonial and storage center for this settlement. Each of the other clusters, which presumably represent residential loci, are approximately 20 m away from the store house or ceremonial area, indicating a planned settlement with a central household integrating three surrounding household groups.

A total of nine human burials were identified at Buh bi laá: five were inhumations and four were cremations, including the two primary cremations found in Features 2 and 7. In addition to the formal burials, two other individuals were found sprawled on the floors of burned houses, suggesting they had been killed when the houses burned and collapsed or prior to the fires. One was found in House 1asu in Cluster A and the other in House 8 in Cluster B. Inhumations were found in shallow pits and most lacked grave goods. The exception was an infant burial, Burial 39, which was associated with Kiatuthlanna Black-on-white and Forestdale Black-on-red bowls. Burial 39 was found in House Cluster B along with Burials 6 and 18, whereas Burial 21 was located midway between House Clusters B and C. The fifth inhumation, Burial 32, was found in House Cluster D. The final two burials consisted of secondary cremations placed within bowls. Burial 8.1, found within a refuse deposit overlying House 8, consisted of the remains of a young adult, possibly a male, deposited inside an Alma Plain bowl, with a second bowl inverted over the top. A short distance to the east of House 8 was another cremation placed within two Alma Plain bowls. Thus, seven of the nine burials, including all the primary and secondary cremations at Buh bi laá, were found in House Cluster B, and one other was located midway between this and House Cluster C.

Site Structure

The arrangement of house clusters at Buh bi laá distinguishes this site from similar sized Mogollon pit house villages. One generally recognized attribute of early Mogollon settlements is the lack of a plan for the arrangement of house; houses seem to have been built wherever it was convenient, with little regard for village organization (Bullard 1962:109; Wheat 1955:35). Two common features, however, suggest that some kind of plan was present. First, a standard feature of most Mogollon settlements was the presence of a single, large and architecturally distinct pit house that apparently was used for communal or ceremonial purposes (Anyon and LeBlanc 1980; Bullard 1962:109; Wheat 1955:35). At the SU site, one such "communal house" was located in each of the two large clusters of houses that were present. Often the communal house was located at the center of the settlement. A second feature of early Mogollon settlements is the parallel and generally eastward orientation of most houses (Wheat 1955:42), which may reflect a culturally specified norm, rather than the arrangement of household activities (Gregory 1995). These patterns continued into the Late Mogollon Pithouse period, as is evident at the Bear Ruin in the Forestdale Valley, although a Great Kiva apparently replaced the "communal house" there (Haury 1985:150).

Based largely on his work at the Duncan site, Kent Lightfoot (1984:109-111) suggests that some early Mogollon villages may have exhibited a loose, circular arrangement of between 5 and 11 houses. These houses surrounded an open plaza area, which Lightfoot interpreted as a communal work area. Distances between houses at the Duncan site were quite large, ranging from 10 to 30 m. The plaza area was about 30–60 m in diameter.

In contrast to these Mogollon house arrangements, the house clusters at Buh bi laá Village more closely resemble Hohokam courtyard groups, in which houses are arranged in smaller and tighter clusters of two to four houses separated by 5 to 10 m and surrounding a courtyard measuring only 10–20 m across (Wilcox et al. 1981; Howard 1985). These courtyard groups appear to represent the domains of a single, extended family household. This is in contrast to the larger Mogollon house clusters, which appear to represent groups of many independent nuclear households (Ciolek-Torrello 1998b; Gregory 1995). Houses in these groups do not have common orientations; rather, their entryways open onto the common courtyard area. In addition, burial areas and communal food processing facilities are placed on the periphery of the courtyard. The number of houses and size of the four house clusters at Buh bi laá fit the Hohokam courtyard pattern more than the looser arrangements of Mogollon house clusters. Furthermore, the five houses at Buh bi laá with side entryways do not exhibit a common easterly orientation; rather, four of these houses (Houses 25, 7asu, 2asu, and 38a) open onto the presumed courtyard areas in their respective house clusters. Only House 8 is oriented away from the other houses in Cluster B. Communal houses were common in Hohokam settlements in the Pioneer period (Ciolek-Torrello 1998b, 2009; Haury 1976). These then disappeared in the Colonial period, when the courtyard arrangement prevailed in Hohokam settlements. Thus, the large, central storage house, House 14a in House Cluster B at Buh bi laá, is more suggestive of communal houses in Late Mogollon Pithouse period villages. Communal houses, however, resembled large habitation structures that may have been inhabited by the leader of the settlement, not storage rooms like House 14a.

Tree-Ring Dates

Six of the nine excavated pit houses at Buh bi laá and one of the cremations yielded 17 tree-ring dates (Table 5.2). Although most are "vv" dates, which provide only poor date estimates (Bannister et al. 1966:4-5), the series of dates generally falls into two temporal groups, which we characterize as early and late construction episodes. The early construction episode dates to the Forestdale phase, between A.D. 708 and A.D. 786 (cf. Haury and Sayles 1947:Figure 34, Table 1), and includes Houses 1asu and 2asu in House Cluster A, House 14a, and the Feature 2 primary cremation in House Cluster B, and House 38a in House Cluster D. A gap of at least 40 years appears to exist between the two construction episodes. The second construction episode dates to the Corduroy phase (between A.D. 827 and A.D. 864) and includes House 7asu and 8 in House Cluster B. A single cutting date for House 7asu suggests it was built or repaired around A.D. 864. A cutting date from House 8 indicates that the sampled wood was cut around A.D. 831; however, a "vv" date from

Table 5.2. Tree-Ring Dates From Bu Bi Laá and East Fork Villages

Feature	Context	Date
Bu bi laá Early Episode		
House 1asu	Roof fall	739+vv
	Floor fill	756vv
House 2asu	Floor fill	745+vv, 784vv
House 14a	Floor fill	706vv, 733vv, 743+vv, 748+vv
	House fill	763vv
	Ramada*	755vv, 779+vv
House 38a	Roof fall	786vv
Unit 20	Cremation pit	727vv
Bu bi laá Late Episode		
House 7asu	Floor fill	827vv, 864+r
House 8	Floor fill	831r, 850vv
East Fork		
House 1	Roof fall	827vv, 832r
	Fill	835vv
House 2	Roof fall	838vv, 846vv
	Fill	850+vv
	Floor	840vv

*The ramada was found atop the pit house fill, however, the two tree-ring dates are thought to be associated with the pit house.

this same house places construction after A.D. 850. The latter date probably represents a date close to the final construction or modification of this house, as wood much older than 25 years probably was not used in the same house. In all probability, the pit house occupation began sometime during the mid to late A.D. 700s and ceased sometime during the mid A.D. 800s.

This small sample of dates suggests that the early construction episode was the most intensive. Four of the six pit houses and one of the primary cremation pits date to this time. The village layout during the early construction episode appears to have consisted of a large, centrally located storage and ceremonial/mortuary area in House Cluster B, surrounded by at least two of the outlying House Clusters (A and D). No dates were obtained from features in House Cluster C, but given the layout of the site, it is reasonable to conclude that this group was also established during the first episode. House 14a, the only house in House Cluster B, appears to have been a specialized storage structure and exhibits no evidence of ever having been used as a habitation.

Following the second construction episode, the center of the site was used as a seasonal campsite. This campsite area consisted of burials, extramural pits, and rock cluster features that were superimposed over the fill of Houses 7asu, 8, and 14b and may have extended into the ceremonial/mortuary area in House Cluster B. The encampment represented by these features may have been associated with mortuary activities that started in this area of the site during the early construction episode and continued throughout the occupation of the site.

Ceramics and Other Artifacts

Artifacts recovered from Buh bi laá Village are similar to most Mogollon pit house assemblages. Represented are numerous ground stone items as well as a preponderance of plainware ceramics; we typed 73.4 percent of all sherds as Alma Plain. Flaked stone implements were present, although their quantity was low in comparison with other artifact classes. Buh bi laá Village, however, contrasted markedly with other contemporary Mogollon villages in terms of the high frequency of nonlocal ceramics (Table 5.3). We recovered a high percentage of Hohokam wares, especially Gila Plain, which accounted for 14.1 percent of all sherds.

Decorated ceramics were minimal, however; only 17 decorated sherds and three painted vessels were recovered. Gila Butte Red-on-buff, which was found in low frequencies throughout the site, was the most common decorated type found at Buh bi laá. Most notable was the presence of a shallow, reconstructible Gila Butte Red-on-buff bowl on the floor of the large storage structure (House 14a) dated to the mid to late eighth century. A single Santa Cruz Red-on-buff sherd was found on the floor of House 38b. A smaller number of Corduroy Black-on-white and Forestdale Black-on-red sherds were recovered from Houses 7asu and 8, which represented the later construction episode. A Kiatuthlanna Black-on-white bowl recovered from Burial 39, as well as a few sherds from the possible work area atop House 8, represented the later seasonal reoccupation of the site.

In addition to the relatively high frequency of Hohokam plain and buff wares at Buh bi laá, the slate palette found on the floor of House 14a and the *Glycymeris* shell bracelet fragments recovered from several other houses and the site surface are noteworthy. These artifacts, together with the secondary cremations and architectural influences point to intensive interaction with contemporary Hohokam populations to the southwest or, perhaps, even a Hohokam enclave at the site. Although there appears to have been interaction with both the Hohokam and Anasazi during

Table 5.3. Frequencies of Hohokam Plainware and Hohokam Buffware from Selected Mogollon Pit House Villages with Hohokam Ceramics

	Bu bi laá	East Fork	Bear Ruin (Haury 1940:79)	Bluff Site (Haury & Sayles 1947:56)	Tla Kii (Haury 1985:81)	Crooked Ridge (Wheat 1954:92-3)	Nantack (Breternitz 1959:Table 3)	Duncan Site (Lightfoot 1984:39)
Vahki Plain						19		
Gila Plain	825	50	36	7	17	3	87	
Sweetwater Red-on-grey						10		
Snaketown Red-on-buff						9		
Gila Butte Red-on-buff	6	1	6		1			
Santa Cruz Red-on-buff	1	15				4		
Sacaton Red-on-buff							50	
Sacaton Red-on-buff, Safford variety						271		
Casa Grande Red-on-buff								1
Unknown Buffware	1	3	3				62	
Total Ceramics	6347	2472	22000+	2900	4000+	35209	50768	3020

the early occupation of Bu bi laá, interaction with the Hohokam appears to have been most intensive during the ninth century. These associations appear to have been replaced by more intensive Anasazi interaction by the end of the occupation, when the site probably became a seasonal encampment.

Botanical and Faunal Remains

Biocultural remains collected at the site indicate the presence of cultigens as well as native plants and animals in the diet. Edible plants recovered include corn, squash, Cheno-ams, purslane, sunflower, grasses, prickly pear, yucca seed and leaf fragments, buckwheat, walnut and juniper. Of particular interest is the high incidence of charred juniper seeds recovered from many proveniences, which is uncommon for prehistoric Southwest samples (Robert E. Gasser, personal communication 1984). Juniper berries are known to have been regularly collected in late Fall by Western Apaches (Goodwin 1942:157). When ubiquity values for flotation samples are compared for the various plant taxa, weeds and juniper berries clearly predominate. Corn is a distant third. However, corn pollen was encountered in most of the features sampled. For some structures corn pollen counts exceeded five percent of the total pollen count (e.g., in Houses 8, 14a, and 31) suggesting that corn processing or storage may have taken place within these houses. Animal remains recovered at the site include of large amounts of Artiodactyl fragments (of which only mule deer was securely identified) and smaller frequencies of jackrabbit, cottontail rabbit, dog or wolf, pocket gopher and mouse remains.

An analysis of the dental pathologies for the 10 individuals studied during excavations indicated that the inhabitants of Buh bi laá Village were not heavily dependent on high-carbohydrate, stone-ground plant foods such as corn. Instead, game and wild plant produce constituted a major part of their diet (Hartman 1986). Thus, subsistence patterns suggested by botanical and faunal data are supported by the dental data. Furthermore, there do not appear to be significant differences in plant ubiquity values between either of the construction episodes or between the earlier, residential occupation and the later, seasonal campsite.

EAST FORK VILLAGE

East Fork Village (NA17,962) is located at an elevation of 1544 m on the first bench of the East Fork of the White River, near its confluence with the North Fork and 1 km east of Fort Apache. The site is situated within a Great Basin Conifer Woodland biotic community (Brown and Lowe 1980), with a plains grassland community just to the east. In addition to juniper and piñon pine, the woodland is characterized by scattered oak, Ponderosa pine, and Douglas fir. A well-developed riparian community thrives along the channel of the East Fork of White River, located 300 m north of the site.

Excavation at East Fork Village focused on six features, including five houses that were exposed in an exploratory trench along the sewer line (Figure 5.5). All five houses and a pit of unknown function were excavated. These houses appear to represent two types that differed in size, shape, floor features and assemblages, and period of occupation (see Table 5.1). Two small houses, Houses 1 and 2, about 10.5 m^2 in interior area, were built in pits 40 to 50 cm deep, with clay-lined hearths, associated pot rests, and a small domestic tool kit consisting of a ceramic vessel, metate, and a few manos and hammerstones (Figures 5.6 and 5.7). These houses had entry ramps, a few perimeter postholes, and additional interior roof supports. They were subrectangular to

110 Ciolek-Torello and Halbirt

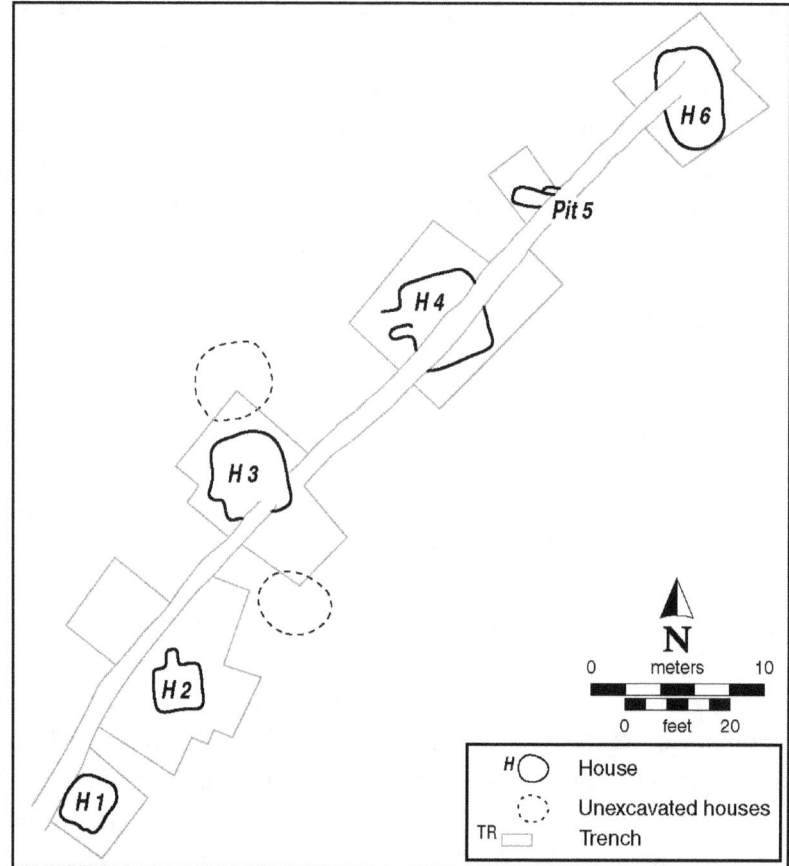

Figure 5.5. Plan view of excavated portion of East Fork Village.

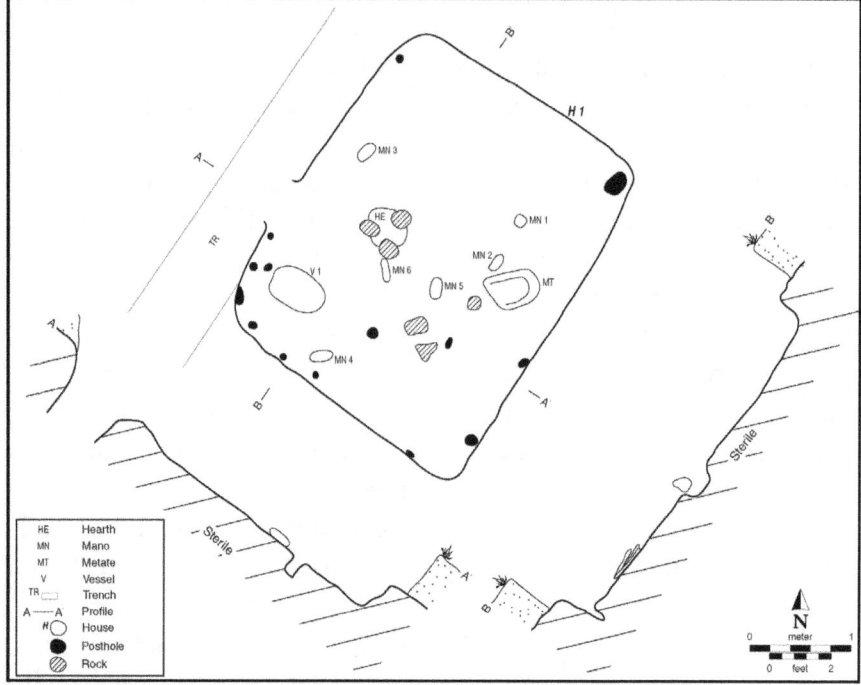

Figure 5.6. Plan view and cross-sections of House 1, East Fork Village.

Figure 5.7. House 2 at East Fork Village, view north (Richard Ciolek-Torello).

squarish in shape and had plastered walls and floors. The three other houses were much larger structures, ranging in size from 18.4 to 24.0 m² in interior area. All three houses were built in shallow pits 10 to 20 cm deep with perimeter roof support post holes suggestive of Hohokam houses-in-pits. These houses were squarish to oval in shape. In addition, four interior roof support postholes were identified in Houses 3 and 5 (Figures 5.8 and 5.9). These two houses contained informal firepits and large quantities of food processing artifacts that covered the entire floor area. House 3 had an ash-stained area and large quantities of lithic manufacturing tools and debris covering the floor area. House 4 had a west-facing entry ramp and House 3 had a large west-facing bulbous side entry (Figure 5.10). The entryway of House 5 could not be determined.

Tree-ring dates were obtained only from Houses 1 and 2 at East Fork Village. The dates suggest these structures were roughly contemporary with Houses 7asu and 8 in Cluster B that represented the later ninth century occupation episode at Buh bi laá (see Table 5.2). Archaeomagnetic samples were also obtained from the hearths in these two houses and support a ninth century date for both. The other three houses appear to post-date the occupation at Buh bi laá based on associated ceramics. Houses 1 and 2 are similar in size to the small seasonal houses (Type 3) at Buh bi laá but are more similar in construction to the larger Type 2 houses. Houses 3, 4, and 5 at East Fork Village are more similar in size to the largest Type 1 houses at Buh bi laá, but their shallow pits and perimeter postholes are more similar to Type 3 houses at Buh bi laá. These characteristics are suggestive

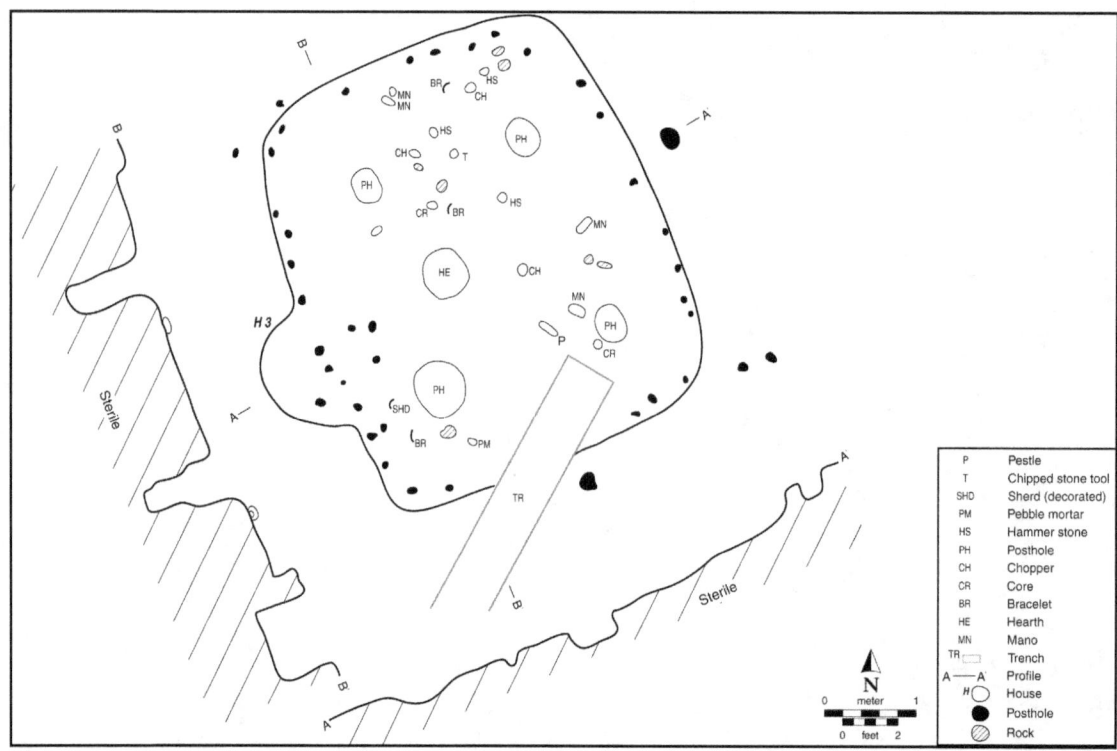

Figure 5.8. Plan view and cross-sections of House 3, East Fork Village.

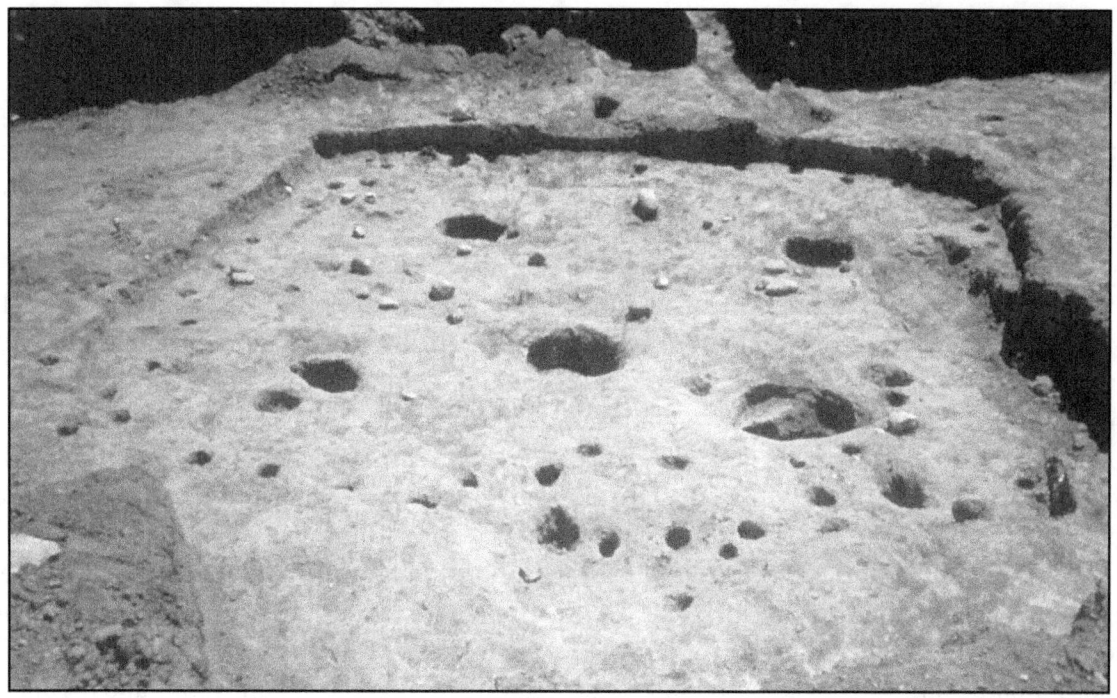

Figure 5.9. House 3 at East Fork Village, view northeast (Richard Ciolek-Torello).

Figure 5.10. House 4 at East Fork Village, view southeast (Richard Ciolek-Torello).

of Hohokam architectural influences, although they lacked the floor groove and subrectangular shape of contemporary Hohokam houses (cf. Wheat 1955; Haury 1976). Two secondary cremations found in House 4 provide additional evidence for Hohokam influence. One of the cremated individuals, the remains of an adult female, was buried under the entry ramp, probably emplaced there during the occupation of the house. This cremation was associated with an Alma Neck-banded jar, two Alma Plain bowls, and a small Santa Cruz Red-on-buff jar. The second cremation pit intruded the north wall of the house and entry ramp. A broken Alma Plain bowl and a small, broken Santa Cruz Red-on-buff jar were found in this individual's cremation pit. No primary cremations were found.

The ceramic collection from East Fork Village consisted primarily of local ceramics such as Alma Plain, which comprised 86 percent of the collection. Other local types included Alma Textured, Alma Neck-banded, Forestdale Plain, Forestdale Red, Forestdale Smudged, and San Francisco Red, with each comprising three percent or less of the collection. Thirteen partially reconstructible vessels were recovered from house floors: 1 Alma Plain jar from House 1; 4 Alma Plain jars, 1 Alma Textured jar, and 1 Alma Neck-banded jar from House 4; and 3 Alma Plain jars and one bowl, 1 Alma Neck-banded jar, and 1 Forestdale Smudged jar from House 6. The collection also included low quantities of nonlocal decorated types (such as Corduroy Black-on-white, Gila Plain, Gila Butte Red-on-buff, and Santa Cruz Red-on-buff). Gila Plain constituted about two percent of the collection, whereas Hohokam

Buff Ware constituted less than one percent. Santa Cruz Red-on-buff was by far the most abundant identifiable type. Of particular note is the difference in the frequencies of Hohokam Buff Ware between Buh bi laá and East Fork villages (see Table 5.3). Gila Butte Red-on-buff was more common at Buh bi laá Village during the early construction period; Santa Cruz Red-on-buff was more common at East Fork Village during the occupation postdating Houses 1 and 2. This pattern suggests that the transition between these two types may have occurred sometime between A.D. 800 and 850, although there may have been some lag in the appearance of Santa Cruz Red-on-buff in this region. Finally, the presence of Lino Gray, Kiatuthlanna and Snowflake Black-on-white suggests increasing interaction with the Upper Little Colorado area and other populations north of the Mogollon Rim, although these types were much less common than the Hohokam ceramics. Together, these ceramic types and the tree-ring dates from East Fork Village suggest that the occupation of this site occurred primarily in the Corduroy phase (Haury and Sayles 1947:Figure 34, Table 1).

Based on the limited excavation at East Fork Village, additional conclusions about the structure of this settlement or other attributes are difficult to reach. Like Buh bi laá Village, however, the houses appear to have been clustered. Four of the five excavated houses had side entryways or ramps that indicate their orientation. No entryway was evident in House 6, and it may have been entered from the roof. Like Buh bi laá, and in contrast to other pit house settlements in the Forestdale and Point of Pines regions, no clear spatial orientation is evident at East Fork Village. The four houses are oriented to the west (Houses 3 and 4), northwest (House 1), and north (House 2). Houses 2 and 4 are about 10 m apart and their entryways are oriented toward a common area, clearly reminiscent of Hohokam-style courtyard groups. These houses, however, reflect different architectural types and are probably not contemporary.

Summary and Conclusions

Buh bi laá and East Fork Villages were occupied during the late eighth and ninth centuries, a time which corresponds with the late Forestdale and Corduroy phases of the Late Mogollon Pit House period and the Gila Butte and early Santa Cruz phases of the Colonial period in the Hohokam sequence. Both villages were agrarian in their economy and located near arable land along the main stem of the White River and its East Fork, respectively. Wild plant and animal foods were important components of the subsistence base, although the most important foods appear to have been corn, juniper berries, cheno-ams, wild grasses, and deer and rabbits.

Evidence from Buh bi laá Village indicates that this small settlement consisted of three or four groups of largely independent extended families living in small clusters of pit houses. These houses were arranged around a common area, where food was stored and the deceased were cremated and buried. East Fork Village appears to have been of similar size and may have been organized in a similar fashion, although no evidence of a common area was identified in the limited excavations at this site.

Regional Interaction

Perhaps the most striking aspect of these two small settlements is the extensive evidence for interaction with Hohokam Colonial period populations. Gila Plain and Hohokam Buff Ware sherds were common at both sites. The unusual occurrence of a Gila Butte vessel found on the floor of one house at Buh bi laá Village, along with two small Santa Cruz Red-on-buff jars in cremations at East Fork Village, suggest Hohokam influence was more than incidental. The presence of cremations at both settlements further indicates that relations with neighbors well to the west and southwest extended beyond material exchanges. Finally, indications of Hohokam architectural influences, such as shallow house-in-pit structures and the arrangement of houses within small courtyard groups, reveal strong Hohokam influences on domestic arrangements.

In these respects, Buh bi laá and East Fork Villages stand in stark contrast to Mogollon settlements in the nearby Forestdale Valley. For example, architecture at the Bear Ruin, which was similar in size and occupied in the early Forestdale phase (Haury 1940), consisted of typical Late Pit House period Mogollon circular and squarish pit houses built in deep pits, with long narrow entry ramps (Haury 1936; Martin 1943; Wheat 1955). Although these houses were distributed in several clusters, courtyard groups were not evident. All the entryways at Bear Ruin face eastwards. Great Kivas were also common in Mogollon settlements of the Late Pithouse period, and one was present at Bear Ruin. Significantly, none were identified at either Buh bi laá or East Fork villages.

Haury did identify Hohokam pottery in the Forestdale Valley, but intrusive sherds from regions to the west and southwest occurred in lower frequencies than in the Kinishba area and were usually outnumbered by sherds from Anasazi pottery made well to the north. Gila Plain (n = 7) and a single Hohokam buffware sherd were identified at the Bluff Site, which dates to the Hilltop and Cottonwood phases of the Early Mogollon Pithouse period (Haury and Sayles 1947) (see Table 5.3). Gila Plain (n = 36) and Gila Butte Red-on-buff (n = 6) sherds were also recovered at the Bear Ruin (Haury 1940:79). Anasazi ceramics, however, were about ten times more abundant than the Hohokam ceramics at the Bear Ruin and included two Lino Gray vessels. The Corduroy phase occupation of the Tla Kii ruin produced two whole Gila Plain vessels, 15 Gila Plain sherds, and a single Gila Butte Red-on-buff sherd (Haury 1985:81). Hohokam pottery, however, disappeared from the Forestdale Valley in succeeding phases. None has been found in Dry Valley phase contexts and only a single sherd of Gila Plain was recovered from Carrizo phase contexts, whereas Anasazi pottery increased in frequency over time (Haury 1985:91, 103).

Perhaps the most striking difference between the Kinishba and Forestdale Valley areas during the Late Pithouse period was the presence of primary and secondary cremations in the Forestdale and Corduroy phase occupations in the Kinishba area. Inhumation was the only mortuary treatment found throughout the occupational sequence of the Forestdale Valley.

Primary Cremations in Central Arizona

The type of primary cremation found at Buh bi laá has figured prominently in studies of ancient ethnicity in central Arizona. For example, Elson (1992) argues that these primary cremations represent a mortuary ritual associated with indigenous early Formative period populations that were distinct from contemporary Hohokam and Mogollon populations.

Although not common, similar examples of these primary cremations have been documented at other sites in central and southern Arizona during the ninth and tenth centuries. Primary cremation pits with corner posts that may have supported a platform have been documented at Deer Creek Village (Elson 1992) and the Ushklish Ruin (Haas 1971) in the upper Tonto Basin; at the JR Site in the Wheatfields area (Berg et al. 2003); at the Picacho Pass site in southern Arizona (Greenwald and Ciolek-Torrello 1987); at the Mescal Wash site in southeastern Arizona (Garraty et al. 2010); and in the Mimbres Valley in New Mexico (Creel 1989) (Figure 5.11). In each of these areas, the features represent an unusual variant of the cremation ritual. Many of the pits from these sites contained human remains and offerings, whereas others appear to have been cleaned out. All of the datable examples indicate occupations between the eighth and tenth centuries.

Although secondary cremations were the dominant mortuary custom in the Phoenix Basin, primary cremations found in rectangular pits nonetheless occur with greater frequency in the Phoenix Basin than in other regions prior to the Classic period. At Snaketown, Haury (1976:166) reports four, shallow, elongated cremation pits; three of similar size to those at Buh bi laá and a larger one with remains of multiple individuals. Haury dated two of the pits to the Pioneer period (including the large pit), one to the Colonial, and one to the Sedentary period. The three primary cremation pits found at Los Hornos dated to the Snaketown and Gila Butte phases (Motsinger 1993:223-225). These contained no vessels and little to no bone, but featured shell bracelets and other likely grave offerings. Corner posts, like those found at Buh bi laá and elsewhere, are not mentioned by either Haury or Motsinger, suggesting that platforms were not built over these Hohokam pits.

Many primary cremations were found at Pueblo Grande. These, however, date primarily to the Sedentary period, with a minority dating

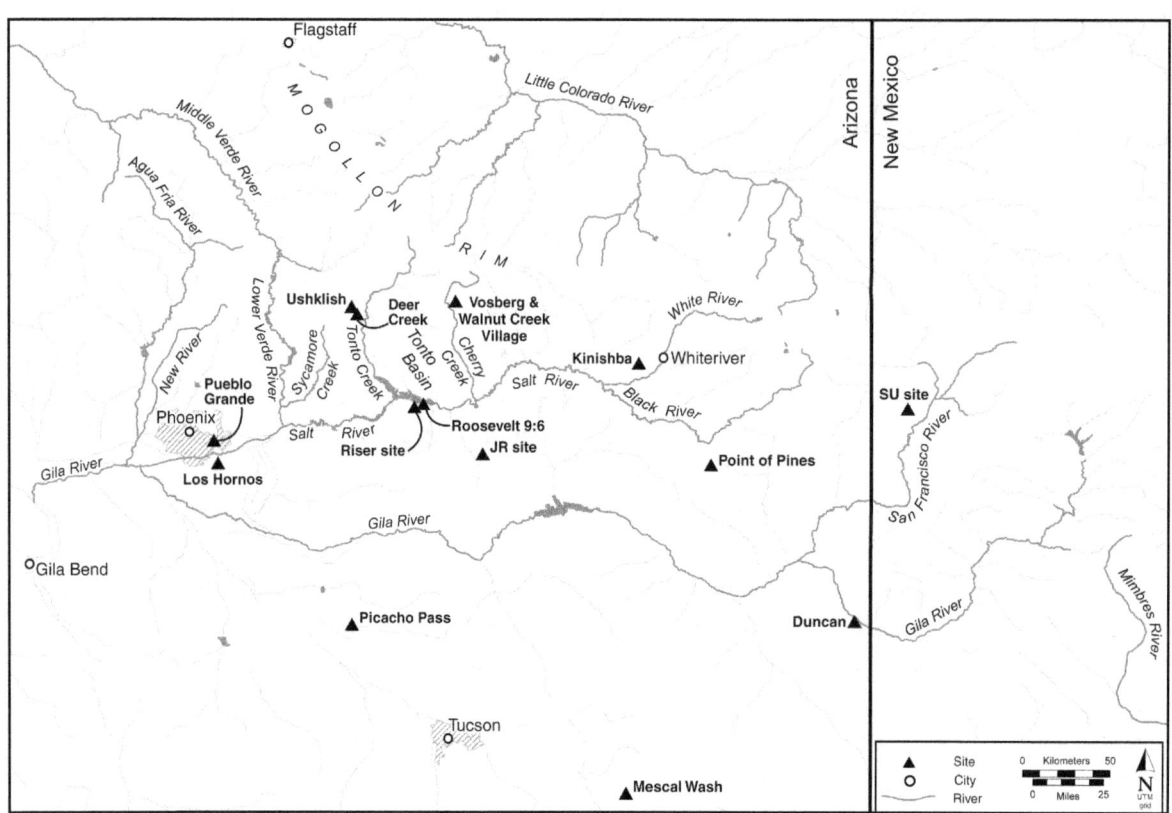

Figure 5.11. Map of east central Arizona and west central New Mexico showing locations of sites and archaeological regions mentioned in text.

to the Classic period (Mitchell et al. 1994:207-209). At Pueblo Grande, primary cremations were identified in shallow (20 cm deep), oval to subrectangular pits with basin-shaped cross-sections (Mitchell et al. 1994:143-147). Most of these features contained a smaller pit at one end, and almost all of these pits contained an urn. Cremated human remains were found in these pits or the urns. None of these features produced identifiable bone from more than one individual, indicating that each was used for a single cremation. Although they contained cremated remains, only 11 of the 26 primary cremation pits at Pueblo Grande exhibited evidence of burning. Mitchell et al. (1994:145-146) suggest that the lack of intensive burning means the actual cremations "were raised above ground and that the fires attained a suitable temperature in a short amount of time." No evidence of supporting posts, like those found at Buh bi laá and Deer Creek Village, are noted, however.

Taken together, this evidence suggests that the primary cremations at Pueblo Grande are not contemporary with those in surrounding areas. Although it may have started as early as the Pioneer period, this form of mortuary ritual was most common in the Phoenix Basin in the Sedentary period and persisted into the Classic period, when it was no longer practiced in surrounding areas. Furthermore, the lack of corner posts and the association with urns in the Phoenix Basin examples suggest a different form of cremation behavior. Thus, the primary cremation pits with platforms, like those found at Buh bi laá, appear to be restricted largely to areas outside of the Phoenix Basin proper and may not constitute a Hohokam trait.

This evidence is consistent with Elson's (1992:150) assertion that primary cremation pits with platforms are not a Hohokam trait. These features, however, extend well beyond the boundaries of Tonto Basin and Central Arizona into southern Arizona and at least as far as the Mimbres Valley in New Mexico. Thus, contrary to Elson's (1992:151) conclusions, they cannot be considered a marker of an indigenous Central Arizona population. Rather, these features occur over a vast region in which the Hohokam interacted with Mogollon populations.

Hohokam Expansion from the Desert to the Mountains

Apart from the primary cremations, does our evidence suggest the Kinishba area was colonized, or simply occupied by Hohokam during the Forestdale and Corduroy phases? Beginning at the end of the Pioneer period and increasing in the Gila Butte and Santa Cruz phases, Hohokam traits began to expand well beyond the confines of the Phoenix Basin (Fish et al. 1980; Gladwin and Gladwin 1935; Haury 1932, 1976). Within the Phoenix Basin itself, the Colonial period witnessed dramatic changes, including an increase in the number and size of settlements, innovations in ceremonial architecture, the spread of new material culture elements and an elaborate mortuary ritual, and the development of new patterns in settlement and domestic organization (Ciolek-Torrello et al. 1999:32; Doyel 1991). These changes in the Hohokam heartland were associated with the spread of Hohokam culture out of the Gila River area and the development of a Hohokam regional system that encompassed much of southern and central Arizona from about A.D. 750 to 1100 (Doyel 1991; Wilcox 1979). A system of ballcourts, the focal point of this regional system, spread throughout most of Arizona, from the Tucson Basin in the south as far north as the Flagstaff area and west to the Gila Bend area. The spread of ballcourts was itself associated with the spread of Hohokam architectural characteristics—most notably, the distinctive house-in-a-pit form of construction—as well as Gila Plain and Hohokam

Buffware ceramics and a mortuary ritual involving secondary cremation, palettes, and censers. Many of these elements spread eastward into Tonto Basin (Haury 1932), although they were not accompanied by ballcourts in that region (Ciolek-Torrello 1998a; Elson 1992:151). Small Hohokam settlements largely indistinguishable from those in the Phoenix Basin were established in the lower Verde Valley (Ciolek-Torrello 1998a), Sycamore Creek (Ciolek-Torrello et al. 2009; Vanderpot et al. 1999), and Tonto Basin areas (Elson and Lindeman 1994; Haury 1932). Roosevelt 9:6 (located in Tonto Basin), in fact, was defined as the type site for the Hohokam Colonial period (Haury 1932). It is important to recognize that in each of these areas, Hohokam culture was distinguished by the presence of house-in-a-pit construction, Hohokam ceramics, and the suite of characteristics found in Hohokam mortuary ritual—secondary cremation (in pits or Hohokam vessels) with palettes and censers.

More common in the upland regions surrounding the Phoenix Basin to the north and east, however, were settlements exhibiting a mixture of Hohokam, Mogollon, and sometimes Anasazi characteristics. The earliest archaeological investigations of the middle Verde Valley interpreted the area as peripheral to the major culture areas, a zone of contact among the major cultural traditions of the ancient Southwest (Fish and Fish 1977, 1984). Based on similarities in ceramic plain wares, house-in-pit construction, cremations, and other aspects of material culture, a predominantly Hohokam influence has generally been recognized for the middle Verde Valley during the Hohokam Colonial and Sedentary periods (that is, about 800–1125). During this time, settlement and subsistence patterns were similar to those of the northern Phoenix Basin. Villages were common along streamside terraces (Breternitz 1960; McGuire 1977). Ballcourts at the larger sites are most strongly identified with the Hohokam (Fish and Fish 1984; Pilles 1976). Numerous canals date to this period. Soil and water conservation systems related to dry farming were also present. The villages of the middle Verde Valley, however, lack the structure of pre-Classic period Hohokam villages. There is no obvious plan or order and houses are randomly oriented and spaced (Fish and Fish 1984).

Anasazi ceramics and cultural materials are just as widespread in the Verde valley, suggesting admixtures of cultural influences, exchange, ethnic co-residence, or some combination. Most investigators have proposed some degree of Hohokam colonization in the region. Schroeder (1953, 1957, 1960), however, posits the presence of an indigenous culture with whom Hohokam immigrants resided. By contrast, Breternitz (1960) proposed a "trading post" type of relationship between the Hohokam and indigenous people, who lived side by side in houses-in-pits and deep pit houses, respectively.

Contemporary settlements in Tonto Basin—such as Deer Creek Village (Swartz 1992), the Riser Site (Vanderpot et al. 1994) and Ushklish Ruin (Haas 1971)—exhibit an admixture of Hohokam, Mogollon, and Anasazi characteristics. In a pattern similar to the Buh bi laá and East Fork villages, these sites contain both Hohokam-style houses-in-pits and Mogollon-style pit houses, Hohokam and Mogollon ceramic types, and cremations as well as inhumations. Primary cremations similar to those at Buh bi laá Village are also present at the Deer Creek site and Ushklish Ruin. In most of these other areas, however, houses are oriented in a parallel fashion and face eastward in a pattern more typical of early Mogollon settlement structure. One of the house clusters at Deer Creek Village, however, reflects the Hohokam courtyard group arrangement (Swartz 1992). Significantly, no ballcourts have been found in Tonto Basin, which sets it apart from most of the areas that are considered part of the pre-Classic period Hohokam regional system. Their absence suggests that early residents of Tonto Basin interacted differently with the Hohokam than did the residents of the Tucson Basin, Gila Bend, Verde Valley and Flagstaff areas. The absence of ballcourts in the Kinishba area suggests a relationship with the Hohokam similar to that evident in Tonto Basin.

Settlements similar to the Buh bi laá and East Fork villages are also found in the Vosberg area, located east of the Sierra Ancha, near Q Ranch and approximately midway between Tonto Basin and Kinishba. The earliest Vosberg area settlements are contemporary with the Hohokam Colonial and Sedentary periods and contained five to eight pit houses located in the better-watered woodland settings, with low relief and deep alluvium. At Walnut Creek Village, the houses in the earliest phase of occupation were oval to subrectangular in shape with parallel, east-facing entryways, reflecting the early Mogollon settlement structure. Later houses were found in two distinct forms: Hohokam-style houses-in-pits with floor grooves and peripheral posts; and deeper, Mogollon-style pit houses with earthen or clay-lined walls and up to six interior roof supports (Morris 1970). Morris (1970) labelled one deep pit house a kiva, a designation based on its round shape, lack of lateral entry, and the presence of a sipapu, foot-drum, and possible loom holes. Cross-dated ceramics indicated that both styles of pit house were occupied contemporaneously. The predominant burial treatment appears to have been extended inhumation. Local indigenous Vosberg Plain was the dominant pottery type, but a locally made variety of Hohokam Buff Ware and early Anasazi white wares dominate the small decorated ceramic collection (Chenhall 1972).

These sites in the middle Verde Valley, Tonto Basin and Vosberg areas suggest that Hohokam influence was widespread, but highly variable during the Colonial and Sedentary periods. The evidence for Hohokam in the Kinishba area during the contemporary Forestdale and Corduroy phase is not surprising. What is striking, however, is the apparent lack of a distance decay factor in this influence. In many respects, Buh bi laá and East Fork Villages exhibit more Hohokam characteristics than Walnut Creek Village and some Tonto Basin and middle Verde Valley settlements located much closer to the Phoenix Basin.

Final Thoughts on the Hohokam Connection

We cannot explain with certainty the Hohokam influence in the Kinishba area. Hohokam immigrated into the Agua Fria, New River, and lower and middle Verde areas where they could practice irrigation and floodwater farming, collect agave, and hunt deer (Ciolek-Torrello 1998a; Ciolek-Torrello et al. 2009). By contrast, Lange (1982) suggests that the Hohokam were attracted to the higher elevation woodlands in the Vosberg area because of the presence of steatite and serpentine minerals used to make stone beads, as well as palettes and censers important in pre-Classic period cremation ritual. Opportunities for floodwater farming and big-game hunting are present in the Kinishba area, but it is unknown whether these or other factors attracted Hohokam.

Although the precise nature of Hohokam influence on and residence in the Kinishba area is not known, some form of Hohokam co-residence with local Mogollon populations probably occurred in the Kinishba area during the late Forestdale and Corduroy phases. Whether this involved colonists or "resident traders" cannot be discerned. The equation of material culture traits and ethnicity is fraught with problems. The mere presence of Hohokam sherds and vessels at Buh bi laá and

East Fork villages is not unassailable evidence of co-residence, as these artifacts could have been obtained from down-the-line exchange. Goldstein (2001:251) states, "mortuary ritual is extremely conservative and represents critical social and symbolic aspects of societies." Thus, the presence of secondary cremations might be considered among the strongest evidence of Hohokam occupation at East Fork and Buh bi laá villages. The presence of Hohokam vessels in association with secondary cremations strengthens this evidence. Domestic architecture and household arrangements can also be considered as culturally conservative; thus, the presence of houses-in-pits and courtyard groups also merits consideration as evidence for Hohokam co-residence at these two settlements.

The significance of the primary cremation pits with platforms is debatable. These unusual features occur in areas of Hohokam and Mogollon interaction, but their origin is unclear. Do they represent a specific Hohokam or Mogollon mortuary ritual or a ritual derived from interaction between the two cultures in upland areas?

The use of both Mogollon and Hohokam vessels in the cremations also weakens the co-residence argument. Hohokam plainware and decorated vessels were available to the residents of the site, raising questions about why Hohokam vessels were not used exclusively in these cremations, especially if they represent the remains of Hohokam residents. It may be equally important that no censors or palettes—items commonly associated with Hohokam cremations in upland regions—were found in association with the cremations or elsewhere at Buh bi laá and East Fork villages. Thus, although Hohokam influence was apparently strong and probably involved the presence of Hohokam settlers at these sites, it remains unclear whether these were individuals, who may have established temporary residence, individuals who intermarried with local residents, or an enclave of immigrant Hohokam families.

Although the nature of Hohokam residence in the Kinishba area is not precisely understood from excavations at these two small settlements, Hohokam influence seems to have disappeared from the Kinishba area and other upland regions by the end of the Hohokam Sedentary period, when the Phoenix Basin turned inwardly upon itself and became largely isolated from surrounding areas (Ciolek-Torrello 1998a, 2009, 2012; Doyel and Crary 1996; Wilcox et al. 2001a). This period corresponds with the Carrizo phase in the Forestdale sequence, when Anasazi culture became the primary external influence on both the Forestdale and Kinishba areas. At this time, groups of Anasazi settlers immigrated into the highlands of central Arizona and established pueblos in the region (Haury 1985; Reid 1989; Whittlesey et al. 2000). Initially, these were small unit-type pueblos, like the Tla Kii Ruin in the Forestdale Valley (Haury 1985). By the mid-thirteenth century, much larger pueblos, like Kinishba, emerged from the coalescence of populations from smaller pueblos and new immigrants from above the Mogollon Rim (Longacre 1975; Reid 1989).

Finally, we cannot discern at present what lasting influence the Hohokam had on subsequent events in the Kinishba area. Clearly, the Western Pueblo tradition represented by the Kinishba Ruin was heavily influenced by Anasazi culture. Haury (1940, 1985:110), however, suggests that the Hohokam had much more than a passing influence on the Mogollon of the Forestdale Valley. Haury (1940:85) suggests that interaction between the Mogollon and Hohokam explains "the strong Hohokam flavor in the designs of the first indigenous black-on-white [pottery] of the area," which appeared in the Corduroy phase. The evidence for greater Hohokam-Mogollon interaction in the Kinishba area during the Late Pithouse period suggests that the Hohokam also may have had an important influence on the development of the later Western Pueblo expression at Kinishba. Additional research is needed to address this issue and systematically assess the indicators of Hohokam influence in the Kinishba area in comparison with other upland areas with similar subsistence and mineral opportunities.

Acknowledgments

The information regarding Buh bi laá and East Fork Villages presented in this chapter was obtained primarily from an unpublished manuscript prepared by Carl Halbirt and Steven Dosh. The authors acknowledge the efforts of Mr. Dosh, Mr. Donald Keller, Mr. Kurt Dongoske, who served as the project crew chiefs, and the members of the White Mountain Apache Tribe, who served as the excavation crew. Dr. Donald E. Weaver, Jr. served as the project principal investigator. We also wish to thank the Tribe for the opportunity to undertake this important study, and the community of Whiteriver for their hospitality to the field team. Finally, we wish to thank Dr. David R. Wilcox, of the Museum of Northern Arizona, for his help in obtaining original field records, and Statistical Research, Inc. for providing the lead author with time to prepare portions of this chapter and the services of Mr. Luke Wisner in preparing the illustrations.

Chapter 6
A Grasshopper Architectural Perspective on Kinishba

Charles R. Riggs

Approaching Kinishba's rebuilt eastern room block (Group I) from the small parking area, the visitor gets a first glimpse of the now crumbling walls of Cummings's rebuilding. As a scholar devoted to studying ruined pueblo architecture, I am simultaneously both thankful to and somewhat annoyed at Cummings for his work at this important Puebloan ruin. To see a late prehistoric pueblo rise up out of its ruins and to be manifest once again is in one sense inspiring, as Cummings clearly intended it to be (Bostwick 2006:278). Furthermore, to be able to watch the pueblo succumb to the ravages of time and weather offers insights into decay processes that have unfolded at other large pueblos as they to fell into ruins beginning in the latter part of the A.D. 1400s, a result surely not anticipated by Cummings (Welch 2007a).

As a researcher interested in architecture, it has always seemed a shame to me that so much was excavated at Kinishba, and yet we know so little about it. This is as much a result of archaeological practice in the 1930s as it is of Cummings's preferences and activities. Cummings has been taken to task for his lack of attention to detail (Martin 1941). This further limited the already inadequate architectural recording standards of the time. Furthermore, much of what Cummings rebuilt at Kinishba was not based on careful observations of wall fall debris, but rather on speculation about how Kinishba should look. Thus, many excavation data points critical to understanding Kinishba, not as a ruin, but as a living community were either not collected or were forsaken in Cummings's drive to build his impressive monument. His records were seldom complete and not all of the observations he documented have been preserved. Simply put, a detailed architectural study of Kinishba is not possible based on the archival data currently available to us.

In lieu of renewed excavations at Kinishba, if we wish to make inferences regarding some of these details we must examine better documented and better reported analogs like Grasshopper Pueblo. In the pages that follow, I primarily use Grasshopper, but also rely on other analogs to fill in certain details about Kinishba as a community and I also attempt to correct some of Cummings's misconceptions about the ruins at Kinishba. To do this, I employ three documents produced by Cummings and his staff. First, his 1940 publication on Kinishba, though sparse in descriptive detail, provides a detailed map of the excavated spaces in Group I. From this map I was able to identify numbers and sizes of rooms and to count floor features, particularly hearths and mealing bins. This work is augmented by the Shaeffers' two reports (Chapters 3 and 4). To these limited data, I apply the massive Grasshopper architectural database, which has been collected and refined over a now 50-year period. I divide the discussion that follows into three parts; these are: overall community layout, domestic architecture and room function, and ceremonial architecture. For each of these categories I compare Kinishba to Grasshopper and other roughly contemporary pueblos where appropriate. Kinishba, Grasshopper, Turkey Creek Pueblo, and several other large Ancestral Puebloan communities of the late thirteenth and early fourteenth centuries, are part of the Mogollon Pueblo Tradition. This term describes the archaeological manifestation of pre-contact Puebloan architecture of the central Arizona uplands (Gifford 1980; Reid 2001; Riggs 2005; Rinaldo 1964; Wheat 1955). As such, these villages are likely the best comparative analogs for Kinishba.

The Importance of Architecture

The study of pre-Columbian architecture in the American Southwest continues to lag behind studies of ceramics and other artifact categories. There are numerous challenges to applying consistent methods and techniques to large architectural samples. On one hand, it is difficult to "collect" a large and representative sample of architectural remains. For a pueblo of 600 to 800 rooms like Kinishba, even a modest 10 percent sample represents an enormous amount of labor and expense. Architecture is also complicated by the fact that buildings are remodeled over periods of time, and the original function of one or more spaces may be lost or altered during the process. Thus we have to be mindful of possible differences between rooms' originally intended use and their last use (Riggs 2007). The many decisions that go into determining architectural forms are also problematic. For example, the use of a particular species of tree or type of stone for construction may reflect personal preference, cultural norms, restricted access to resources, resource depletion, or some combination of these factors (Riggs 2001).

This list of potential issues goes on and on, but despite these challenges, architecture remains a powerful indicator of human behavior in the Southwest and elsewhere (Kent 1990; Rapoport 1969, 1982). Its non-portability ensures that the behavioral decisions it reflects are those of the local inhabitants rather than distant trading partners. Whether one focuses on technological style (Lemonnier 1993), proxemics (Hall 1968), structuration theory (Giddens 1979), space syntax (Hillier and Hanson 1984; Ferguson 1996) or any number of other approaches, architectural remains reflect a wide variety of human behavioral decisions and are hence an important material class for understanding social organization, migration, settlement history, human ecology and land-use practices in particular communities, including the one that occupied Kinishba Ruins.

I have applied many of the aforementioned perspectives to the architecture of Grasshopper Pueblo in order to better understand its social structure and migration history (Riggs 2001, 2005, 2007). Based on community layout, room construction rates, comparative presence and absence of wall features, the size of wall features, the use of different types of wood and building stone, and the size and shape of rooms, Kinishba's largest close neighbor, Grasshopper Pueblo, contained at least two and perhaps three large social groups. Many of the members of these groups moved into the area from elsewhere (Ezzo and Price 2002; Reid and Whittlesey 1999; Riggs 2001, 2007). These architectural characteristics expressed learned patterns or frameworks of construction behavior that reflected subtle variations indicative of different group identities (Table 6.1; cf. Clark 2001; Lemonnier 1986; Sackett 1990). The differences in these social groups were marked overtly in the layout of the Grasshopper Com-

Table 6.1. Architectural Characteristics and Behavioral Correlates

Architectural Characteristic	Behavioral Correlate(s)
Community layout	Overt display of identity (Ethnicity)
Room construction and community growth patterns	Intra-site settlement patterns Migration rates
Wall features	Culturally specific construction practices/ learned building styles
Building stone	Cultural preferences Community rules regarding access to resources
Wood use	Cultural preferences Community rules regarding access to resources Room function
Room size	Culturally specific notions of space Availability of, and access to, resources Room function
Room shape and orientation	Culturally specific notions of space Culturally specific construction practices
Room function	Culturally specific notions of space Culturally specific construction practices Culturally specific belief systems/worldview Access to resources

munity on either side of Salt River Draw, much like Kinishba's layout. Given striking similarities in community layout between Grasshopper and Kinishba, it is likely that Kinishba's more subtle architectural characteristics likewise reflect subtle indications of group identity.

Comparative Description

As noted, a detailed, records-based architectural study is not possible for Kinishba. Not only were many of the records lost, but these records were not up to today's recording standards to begin with. Furthermore Cummings's rebuilding of much of Group I, while leaving the ruins open for future study, likely damaged the original masonry work and other architectural characteristics in unknown ways. Aside from a close analysis of Kinishba's excavation photographs, which would be fruitful for capturing some architectural details, the best that can be done is to make inferences about aspects of Kinishba on the basis of Grasshopper Pueblo's architectural remains. There are many inherent dangers in conducting such a study, not the least of which is the problem of external validity (Bernard 2006:113), which is an assessment of how far one can generalize from one experiment, or in this case, one pueblo ruin to another. In the case of Kinishba and Grasshopper, it is important that we assess how appropriate of an analog Grasshopper Pueblo is for those elements of Kinishba's architecture for which we lack specific information. External validity can be increased through more intensive and randomized sampling. Grasshopper's excavated sample is representative of overall community architectural variability in numerous ways (Riggs 2001:25-33). Although I cannot state with absolute certainty that what holds for Grasshopper will be true for Kinishba, I can affirm with confidence that, because of the quality of the Grasshopper sample, Grasshopper Pueblo is the best available analog for understanding the architecture of Kinishba.

At least three facts support my confidence. First, in the 30 years of field study at Grasshopper, the University of Arizona field school produced a 24 percent sample of its 447 room spaces (Reid and Whittlesey 2005; Riggs 2001). Second, the two sites are not only within 60 km (37.4 air miles) of one another, but are strikingly similar in their layout. Both consist of two core large architectural units and a scattered suite of smaller outlying blocks of rooms arrayed on either side of a stream channel (Riggs 2005:330). Furthermore, although Kinishba was occupied for a longer period, the two pueblos were largely contemporaneous and were likely both constructed through a similar process of local and non-local population aggregation (Lyons, Chapter 7; Triadan, Chapter 8; Triadan et al. 2002; Welch 2007a). Thus, in overall layout, construction sequence and temporal placement the two sites are similar in shape and size and likely were constructed by means of similar processes. These processes reflect common behaviors as large-scale population aggregations began to take place in the region. Below I describe some of these behaviors as they were expressed at Grasshopper and how they might have been expressed by Kinishba's builders. Before proceeding to the comparative discussion of architectural details, it is first necessary to provide some background on Grasshopper Pueblo.

Grasshopper Pueblo

Grasshopper Pueblo, like Kinishba, is comprised of two large groups of rooms situated on either side of a perennial stream (Figure 6.1). Also like Kinishba, the inhabitants of Grasshopper constructed smaller room blocks around the main architectural units (Cummings 1940; Reid 1973; Reid and Shimada 1982; Riggs 2001; Thompson and Longacre 1966; Shaeffer and Shaeffer, Chapters 3,4). At Grasshopper Pueblo, we know that these smaller units were not only constructed later in the community's history but contained larger rooms on average and consisted of low-walled masonry with brush or *jacal* superstructures (Riggs 2001:90-93). Rooms in Grasshopper's central core room blocks, also known as the "Main Pueblo," consisted of both one- and two-story masonry rooms arrayed around three central plaza areas. One of these, Plaza 3, was converted into a great kiva sometime between A.D. 1320 and 1338, and most likely around A.D. 1330 (Riggs 2001:134).

Rooms in Grasshopper's Main Pueblo exhibit a number of architectural characteristics that accord well with evidence for community subgroups obtained from the human remains interred under Grasshopper room floors. Analyses of cranial and post-cranial continuous and discrete traits suggest biological differences among individuals associated with the eastern and western room blocks (Birkby 1973, 1982; Shipman 1982). These differences are reinforced by dietary stress markers and the spatial distributions of individuals with local and non-local dietary signatures, which also correspond to individuals buried under and around the room blocks on either side of Salt River Draw (Ezzo 1993; Ezzo et al. 1997; Ezzo

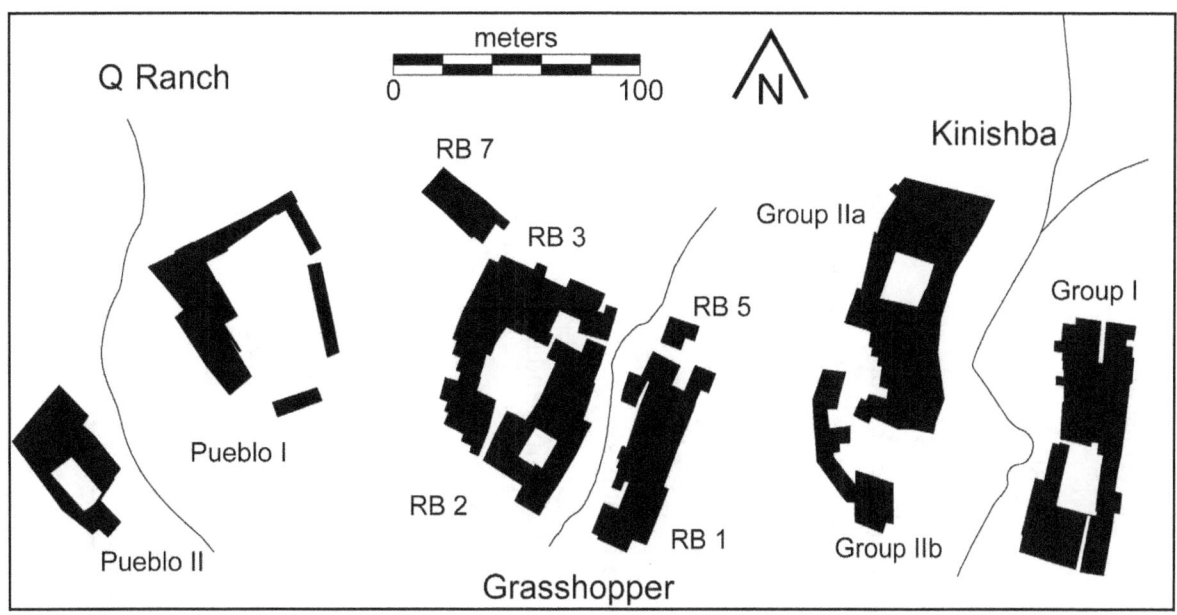

Figure 6.1. Comparative layout of three Pueblo IV Period village sites in east-central Arizona.

and Price 2002; Hinkes 1983). This suggests the presence of diverse populations, apparently derived from both immigrants and local people having slightly different construction practices and other cultural attributes (Reid and Whittlesey 1982).

Because this matter has been discussed in detail elsewhere (Riggs 2001, 2005), I simply summarize the differences here in order to establish expectations for behaviors and architectural reflections at Kinishba. Table 6.2 summarizes the architectural characteristics that differentiate the East and West Villages at Grasshopper (Figure 6.1). The architectural units on the west side of Salt River Draw, collectively also known as the "West Village," seem to have been constructed by local people (Room Block 2) and a group of immigrants (Room Block 3) from a population elsewhere in the Mogollon region (Reid and Whittlesey 1999; Riggs 2001). As Table 6.2 demonstrates, the builders of the east unit (or East Village), consistently built larger rooms with a preference for a north-south orientation in these rectangular spaces. They never constructed crawlways. They built shorter and fewer doors and were less likely to build other wall features like vents and niches. When they did install these, they were usually smaller than those constructed on the west side of Salt River Draw. East Village builders more frequently made use of juniper and piñon pine relative to ponderosa pine. They never constructed large storage bins but used double mealing bins on occasion (these were not documented in the West Village). They did not incorporate the higher quality sandstone in construction as frequently, built no kivas (only ceremonial rooms) and constructed no formal plaza areas (Riggs 2001:165, 2005:337).

Overall, detailed analyses of Grasshopper provide evidence for distinctive construction practices among the builders of the two large architectural units. The architectural characteristics outlined above reflect learned building styles that probably indicate different cultural traditions. The inhabitants of these two large buildings expressed their learned architectural knowledge as they collected stone for building,

Table 6.2. Comparison of Grasshopper's East and West Villages Based on Architectural Characteristics (after Riggs 2001:Table 5.10)

Architectural Characteristic	East Village (Room Block 1)	West Village (Room Blocks 2 and 3)
Community layout	East of Salt River Draw Includes no formal public spaces Spatial isolation	West of Salt River Draw Includes 2 plazas and a great kiva Room blocks connected by roofed corridors
Room construction and community growth patterns	Last founded Slow growth (13 construction phases)	First founded (RB2) with rapid growth (7 construction phases) Slow growth in RB 3 (14 construction phases)
Wall features	Few per room Smaller doorways Smaller vents and niches No crawlways	More per room Larger doorways Larger vents and niches Crawlways
Building stone	Low frequency of quality sandstone	High frequency of quality sandstone
Wood use	More juniper relative to other species	Less juniper relative to other species
Room size	Larger rooms	Smaller rooms (RB 2) Variable (larger) rooms (RB 3)
Room shape and orientation	North-south oriented Rectangular rooms	East-west oriented (or square) rooms (RB 2) Randomly oriented rooms (RB3)
Room function	Double mealing bins No large storage bins Ceremonial rooms but no kivas	No double mealing bins Large storage bins Ceremonial rooms and kivas

as they harvested trees for roof construction, as they laid out the foot-prints of their room spaces, and as they constructed doorways and other wall features. Although masonry styles at Kinishba are distinct from those at Grasshopper and likely reflect yet another set of learned behaviors, the extent to which more subtle differences can ever be observed within the architectural units at Kinishba is, unfortunately, limited by the quality of the data that Cummings and his associates left for us.

The Grasshopper data demonstrate that photographs are a highly useful tool for examining wall-faces and bond-abut relationships. These relationships were instrumental in both delineating construction sequences (Riggs 2001) and in understanding the sizes of the various social groups that built and occupied Grasshopper (Riggs 2007). The extent to which this record is complete and representative of Cummings's Kinishba excavations will partially determine the extent that photographs can be useful. The same can be said of detailed field drawings. Given that Cummings was criticized at the time for his shortfalls in reporting on details (Martin 1941), it is unlikely that these records ever existed with sufficient detail to conduct a high- or even moderate-resolution study. It would be possible, however, to conduct a new study of wall corners and wall faces in the open rebuilt rooms. Initial observation suggests that it is not particularly difficult to distinguish between Cummings's rebuilt upper walls and the original walls that were uncovered during excavation and subsequently added to by the Apache crews who did the rebuilding. Though time-consuming, I think this approach would be fruitful.

The goal of performing a new architectural analysis, of course, would be to assess the strength of the analogy with Grasshopper and, possibly, to identify and assess architectural variation present at Kinishba and not at Grasshopper. If we can, for example, demonstrate that the east unit at Kinishba was assembled in a manner similar to one or more of the large room blocks at Grasshopper, we can further improve the external validity of the Grasshopper sample as it specifically relates to Kinishba's architecture. This in turn would result in higher confidence that the similarities I discuss below represent similar behaviors. The likenesses in community layout, room function, and the use of open space already compel us to think of these two sites as similar in many ways, as I now demonstrate.

Community Layout

The most striking similarity between Kinishba and other contemporary sites in the east-central Arizona highlands is in overall community layout (Figures 2.1, 6.1). Kinishba is one of three large, contemporary pueblos laid out on either side of a stream channel draining the south-facing slope of the Mogollon Rim. The third site, Q Ranch Pueblo located to the west of Grasshopper, between Canyon Creek and Cherry Creek, has two large room blocks that together comprise approximately 230 rooms and are located on either side of Ellison Creek (Britton n.d.; Hohmann 2004; Reid et al. 1982). Despite the fact that the site has been partially excavated by the Arizona Archaeological Society, no detailed report has been published. Hence, Q Ranch provides little in the way of comparative data for Kinishba, apart from general layout characteristics.

From Grasshopper we know that this dual community division had social significance. In fact, it separated the community into a local population on the west and a non-local population on the east (Reid and Whittlesey 1999; Riggs 2001, 2007). This overt community division was not a result of geographic convenience or spatial circumscription. Kinishba, Grasshopper and Q Ranch Pueblos were all built in locales with plenty of adjacent open space suitable for construction. Therefore the location of the pueblos' principal structures on either side of stream channels represent an intentional division of people into two social groups rather than a practical necessity dictated by topography. From the discussion above, it is clear that this overt spatial division was reinforced by more subtle architectural decisions. These decisions reflect different learned styles for the builders of the two large units (cf. Lemonnier 1986) and it is likely that the same holds for Kinishba and Q Ranch.

This seemingly consistent layout pattern invites further speculation about social organization. At Grasshopper duality is a means of accommodating a diverse population (Riggs 2001, 2005, 2007). As immigrants and locals settled into Kinishba, Grasshopper, and Q Ranch, they likely settled in the part of the village that clan and community leaders specified based on ethnic identity and kinship affinities (cf. C. Mindeleff 1900). Through time, as villagers participated in non kin-based sodality groups (Reid and Whittlesey 1999) and as they intermarried, these distinctions probably became blurred. The longer a community was occupied, the less marked the spatial divisions became. In central Arizona communities like Point of Pines Pueblo and Turkey Creek Pueblo in the Point of Pines Region, and like Tundastusa in the Forestdale Valley, the initial immigration streams arrived before the Pueblo III–Pueblo IV transition that shaped the architecture of Grasshopper, Kinishba, and Q Ranch. In the former cases we find that the spatial duality, though present in the form of spatially discrete room blocks, is not overtly marked with reference to an intervening stream channel (Riggs 2005).

What this means for Kinishba is that we can infer that that the dual architectural division of the community likely reflects a dual social division. Although we cannot know if it represents a local vs. non-local population, as has been inferred for Grasshopper, it is interesting to think about Kinishba's inhabitants negotiating community membership as the village grew over time. I would anticipate, based on the fact that great kivas are a Mogollon characteristic (Anyon and LeBlanc 1980; Riggs 2005), that the east-west division at Kinishba may not reflect an identical local-nonlocal division to that at Grasshopper. Grasshopper's East and West Villages (see above) reflect a dual social division wherein a Mogollon group settled on the west side and an Anasazi group settled to the east (Reid and Whittlesey 1999). The association of the Great Kiva with the Mogollon West Village is an important overt marker of group identity.

The great kiva documented in Chapter 4 is on the east side of the intervening drainage, whereas at Grasshopper it is on the west side. However, because the limited excavations in Kinishba's western unit were not carefully documented or reported, it is possible that the large open space in the north end of the western unit could represent a second great kiva (Figure 6.2). If so, the separation would likely reflect two Mogollon groups, in which case the entire social organization at Kinishba would have been markedly different than that at Grasshopper. The fact that Kinishba is larger than Grasshopper (for example, Group I at Kinishba is more than twice the size as Room Block 1 at Grasshopper in terms of total number of rooms) implies that it could have supported a second great kiva. Unfortunately, this question can only be answered by means of renewed excavations in Group II. Until then, inferences must be based on measured comparison and reasoned speculation.

Core vs. Outliers

Grasshopper and Kinishba are also similar in layout in the sense that the large central room

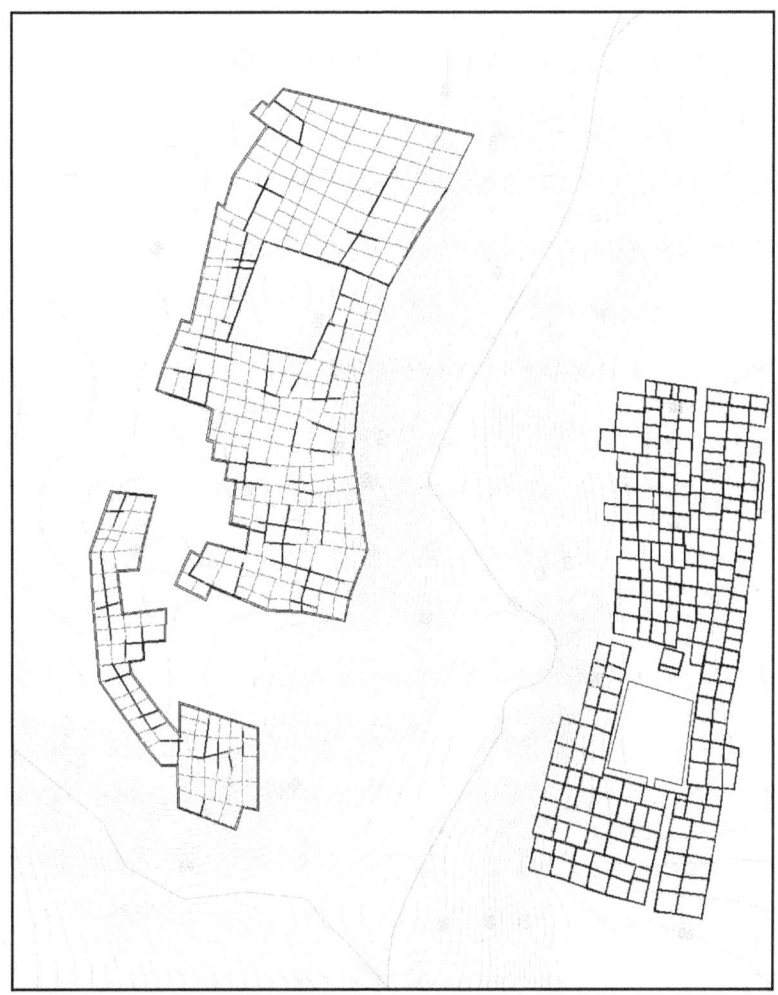

Figure 6.2. Plan view map of Kinishba room Groups I and II (Charles R. Riggs).

blocks are surrounded by a number of smaller room blocks. At Grasshopper, these are referred to as the Outliers and are different from the core room groups in important ways. First, they are chronologically later than the core room blocks. Much of the core architecture contained in Room Blocks 1, 2 and 3 was in place prior to A.D. 1330. Many of the outliers were built later, during what Grasshopper researchers refer to as the Dispersion Phase, which began around A.D. 1330 (Reid 1973; Reid and Whittlesey 1999; Riggs 2001). These rooms are also larger on average, and tend to incorporate a more diverse set of activities (Reid and Whittlesey 1982). Perhaps most distinctively, the Outliers were not constructed as full-standing masonry rooms like the one- and two-story spaces in the Main Pueblo. Instead, Grasshopper's outliers had low masonry walls with brush or *jacal* upper walls and roofs (Riggs 2001:90- 93).

In addition to his extensive excavations in Group I at Kinishba, Cummings and his staff also excavated at least two of these outlying units (Cummings 1940:114; Shaeffer and Shaeffer, Chapter 3; Figure 2.1). Although the Shaeffers' description does not provide extensive details about Group VI, there seem to be some intriguing similarities with Grasshopper's outliers, which further strengthen the analogy. First, as is true for Grasshopper's outliers,

Group VI seems to have been constructed late in the pueblo's history (Shaeffer and Shaeffer, this volume, Chapter 3). Perhaps even more intriguing is the fact that Group VI was apparently constructed with the same low-walled technique as the outliers at Grasshopper. Although the Shaeffers attribute the fact that "the *highest* walls in Group VI were those of Room 3, which were about 2 ½ feet in height" (Shaeffer and Shaeffer, this volume, Chapter 3, emphasis added), due at least in part to post abandonment erosion, it is highly probable that Group VI, like the Grasshopper outliers, never had full-standing masonry walls. Cummings's (1940:114-115) own brief mention of the condition of Group III as where he found "no indications of side entrances in the walls, although there is only a *little of the outer walls still standing* high enough to show the presence of side doorways" (emphasis added) further supports this interpretation. Furthermore, in Grasshopper's outliers, doorways of any kind were rare. Room spaces in the Main Pueblo averaged 1.5 doorways per room, whereas the Outliers average 0.8 doorways per room. This is likely as much a result of the low-walled construction style as anything else. It is interesting to think that Kinishba's outliers may represent similar construction practices, an inference further reinforced by the similar sizes of Kinishba's outlying room blocks and their similar pattern of distribution around the core architecture.

Elsewhere, others and I have suggested that the outliers at Grasshopper represent a return to construction practices as they existed prior to the large-scale aggregation in the region (Reid and Whittlesey 1999; Riggs 2001, 2005). Although the builders of these pre-aggregation settlements tended to focus their rooms around courtyards, plazas or even great kivas, it was unnecessary to do this at post-A.D. 1330 Grasshopper, where plazas already existed. At Grasshopper, this trend also correlates with the conversion of Plaza 3 into the Great Kiva sometime around A.D. 1330 (see also below). At Grasshopper, Kinishba, and other large pueblos it may be that the construction of great kivas and older structural forms—like the low-walled rooms just described—could represent a "reification of the past" (Riggs 2005:340) wherein the inhabitants sought to return to old ways before finally giving up and moving on to other areas. Given that Kinishba's great kiva seems also to be a later construction, that it was also built in former plaza area, and that it might correlate with the construction of an older form of architecture, the similarities with Grasshopper are, once again, striking.

Domestic Architecture and Room Use

Parallels in overall community layout suggest that other similarities may also be present. At Grasshopper, the core room blocks were assembled largely over a 30-year period (A.D. 1300–1330), as locals and immigrants from other parts of the Mountain Transition Zone and from the southern Colorado Plateau moved into the region and built rooms next to people with whom they shared cultural affinities (Ezzo and Price 2002; Reid and Whittlesey 2005; Riggs 2001, 2007). The overall distribution of rooms at Kinshba suggests that a similar settlement history may have been present. Grasshopper researchers were able, through bond-abut and wall-face analysis (Reid 1973; Reid and Shimada 1982; Riggs 2001), to reconstruct this process in detail. At Kinishba, these types of detailed data were not collected during the excavations of the eastern room block. On the other hand, Cummings (1940:16) notes that "the pueblo grew toward the south," thus indicating his awareness of how Group I was constructed.

Given the general disregard for detailed architectural information during the 1930s and

1940s, it is not surprising that Cummings and his students did not record the data necessary to develop a detailed growth sequence. As noted above, however, it would be possible to complete a detailed wall-face and bond-abut study of the portions of Kinishba where it is possible to differentiate between original masonry and Cummings's rebuilding. Such a study remains, for now, a task for the future. In the meantime, data from Grasshopper suggest hypotheses and support inferences regarding room use and household structure at Kinishba.

Early Abandoned Rooms

Large pueblos like Kinishba are products of long sequences of separate construction decisions. One category of such decisions relates to the choice to abandon a room space. At Grasshopper, early abandoned rooms are recognizable because they are filled with trash and lack de-facto refuse on the floors (Montgomery 1993). By calculating the ratio of artifacts found in the fill to those found on the floor, a room abandonment measure can be generated. In the Main Pueblo at Grasshopper we have found that 21 percent of the excavated rooms were abandoned during occupation (Riggs 2001).

Applying the Grasshopper ratio to Kinishba's Eastern room block suggests that approximately 42 rooms (21 percent of 202 rooms) would have been abandoned and likely used for trash disposal by people still residing in the pueblo. Calculating the number of rooms that had fallen into disuse before final community abandonment is important because it has implications for our ability to accurately count the number of resident households. Based on ceramics (Triadan, Chapter 8) and tree-ring dates (Bannister and Robinson 1971:28-31), Kinishba appears to have been occupied slightly longer than Grasshopper, suggesting the number of early abandoned rooms at Kinishba may be even larger. Without detailed excavation data, however, this cannot be verified.

The Two- or Three-Story Room Problem and its Implications for Room Function

The number of stories contained in a room space also has implications for estimating the number of abandoned rooms and assessing room function. Apart from some obvious exceptions, like cliff dwellings and the great houses in Chaco Canyon, buildings of three stories are rare in the precontact Southwest, and even two-story buildings were probably not common until after A.D. 1300. Furthermore, Puebloan people today and in the past, made extensive use of roof surfaces for all sorts of activities, from grinding corn to cooking (Adams 1983; Cameron 1999; V. Mindeleff 1891; Reid and Whittlesey 1982, 1999). This practice can complicate archaeological assessments of the number of stories in ruined pueblos (Riggs 2001). One of the issues with Cummings's rebuilding has been his interpretation that the east unit was primarily two stories, but in some places was as many as three stories in height (Cummings 1940:20). Cummings (1940:23) mentions that second-story hearths were found in a number of rooms. He apparently does not, however, consider the possibility that many roof surfaces likely included hearths, as is common at other pueblo sites in the Southwest (Adams 1983; Reid and Whittlesey 1982; Riggs 2001). In other words, Cummings likely did not attempt to separate what he referred to as second-story hearths from hearths that were located on the roofs of single-story rooms.

At Grasshopper there are few two-story rooms in the Main Pueblo and none in the Outliers. Based on a study of the standing wall height of excavated rooms and their relationships to surrounding architecture, 68 of the 287 (24 percent) room spaces in Grasshopper's

Main Pueblo were two-story rooms. When this ratio is applied to Kinishba's east unit, we can estimate that approximately 50 (48 percent) of the East Unit's 202 rooms were likely to have been two stories. Furthermore, based on Grasshopper, we can expect that these two-story rooms were primarily in the center of the room block, were likely not surrounding the Great Kiva, and were most likely built on top of the oldest rooms. These oldest rooms were likely circumscribed by later room additions, necessitating vertical expansion of resident households rather than horizontal expansion. Regardless of room placement, however, the Grasshopper data suggest that Cummings seriously overestimated the number of two story rooms at Kinishba. Contrary to Cummings's assertions regarding three-story rooms, the Grasshopper example also strongly suggests that there were no three-story rooms at Kinishba.

The discussion of the number of stories also has important implications for determining the number of households in residence. At Grasshopper, as at most multi-story pueblos in the Southwest, it is common for the habitation rooms to be located on the second story of two-story household suites (Adams 1983; Riggs 2001). At Grasshopper we have found that the lower floor in two-room suites was almost always remodeled to serve a new, limited activity function, like storage, or was abandoned and used for refuse disposal (Riggs 2001:174-178). For Kinishba then, we would expect to be able to reduce the total number of habitation rooms regardless of the presence of rectangular hearths. It is possible that some of the hearths depicted on Cummings's map represent hearths from earlier floors that were subsequently covered over to serve new functions. If we could figure out which of these spaces contained a second story and were likely to have been remodeled to serve a new function, we could eliminate some of the rooms with hearths from the habitation category, thus arriving at a more reliable estimate of the number of habitation rooms than an estimate based on a simple count of rooms with hearths.

At Grasshopper, 13 excavated rooms were two stories and had rectangular slab-lined hearths on one or more of their original ground floors. Of these, only one space remained a habitation room (8 percent), seven rooms changed function from habitation rooms to something else (54 percent), and five were simply abandoned and filled with trash (38 percent). Because we do not know which rooms at Kinishba were actually two-story spaces, we can determine neither which of the rooms with rectangular hearths had two stories, nor which ones without these features were two stories. Therefore, any attempts to apply the Grasshopper ratios just discussed would be largely meaningless. Instead, it is probably best to simply acknowledge that a number of the rooms depicted on Cummings's map that contain rectangular hearths are likely to have been two stories and hence served some limited-activity types of functions.

Room Size and Community Size

Room size can be an indicator of not only function as it is often described in the Southwest, but more importantly, of culturally specific notions of adequate space (cf. Hall 1968). Using Cumming's map, I was able to estimate that the average room size in Group I at Kinishba (n = 202 rooms) is 11.68 m^2 with a standard deviation of 4.09 m^2. At Grasshopper, the average room size for the Main Pueblo (n = 287 rooms) is 15.42 m^2, with a standard deviation of 4.14 m^2. Based on these numbers we can conclude that, whereas the overall variability in room size is similar at these two sites, Kinishba's core buildings contain smaller rooms than Grasshopper's core buildings. This could mean one of at least two things. It could simply be that the closely available stands of ponderosa pine and Douglas fir at Grasshopper allowed for the construction of larger rooms, whereas the environment around Kinishba limited the use of these species. On the other hand, it could also suggest that the inhabitants of Kinishba represented different groups of people than the builders of Grasshopper, groups who may have had different concepts of the necessary amount of space for daily habitation, storage and ritual needs. One way to address this question would be to examine the tree-ring collection from Kinishba to determine the wood species used in construction.

Apart from individual room size, we can use the average room size from Kinishba and combine it with our estimated two-story room counts to help more accurately predict the number of total rooms (Table 6.3). Based on the re-mapping of Kinishba I directed as part of the University of Arizona field school in 2004 (Mills et al. 2008), we have a much more accurate map of Group II. The new map suggests that Group II may be two separate room blocks, which I designate Group II north and south in Table 6.3. Because I am confident that the new map represents as precise of an outline of Group II as can be obtained without additional excavation, I simply divided the total areas of Group II south and Group II north by the average room size calculated for Group I. This yields a total of approximately 314 ground floor rooms. Based on my own perceptions of the western mound I would not expect any of Group II south to contain 2-story rooms, so I only applied the Grasshopper ratio to Groups I and II north. Together these suggest a total of about 110 second-story spaces.

The outliers were calculated a bit differently because these areas were not remapped by the University of Arizona as part of the 2004 project. Based on the sizes of the polygons depicted on Cummings's original site map, it is clear that the room block outlines depict the extent of the rubble mounds and not the true edges of the buildings. To more accurately calculate the number of rooms in the outliers, I used the numbers of rooms provided in the reports for the two excavated outliers Groups III (Cummings 1940) and VI (Shaeffer and Shaeffer, Chapter 3) and calculated a ratio of

Table 6.3. Estimated Number of Rooms for Kinishba's Seven Mapped Room Blocks

Group	Ground Floor	Second-Story	Total
I	202	50	252
II North*	251	60	311
II South	63	0	63
III	12	0	12
IV	11	0	11
V	16	0	16
VI	8	0	8
VII	9	0	9
Total	572	110	682

*Note: several rooms in Group II have eroded away

the number of rooms per square meter of rubble mound. I then applied this ratio to the remaining rubble mounds. I am fairly confident that this technique is accurate to within one or two rooms per unit. Putting all of this together, I estimate that there were approximately 700 rooms at Kinishba. This reasoned speculation is based on the total room count provided in Table 6.3, plus an estimated 20 rooms lost to erosion along the eastern side of Group II, plus the fact that Kinishba was occupied longer than Grasshopper and may have indeed had more second-story rooms.

Room Function and Households

In any society, past or present, simple or complex, the household is the primary social unit (Steadman 1996; Wilk and Rathje 1982). The ability to identify households archaeologically is often, though not exclusively, predicated on our ability to delineate the function of various types of buildings. The tried and true method of accomplishing this in Southwestern archaeology has been to identify spaces with a habitation function. There are many ways of doing this, but the simplest generally involves focusing attention on the presence of cooking features.

As already discussed, research at Grasshopper was able to not only determine the number of two-story rooms, but also establish that approximately 21 percent of the rooms in the core buildings were abandoned and used for refuse disposal during the life of the pueblo. Thus, when we calculate the overall number of rooms with habitation functions, we find that 24 percent of ground floor rooms in the Main Pueblo were used as habitation rooms and approximately 33 percent of all rooms at Grasshopper were habitation rooms, representing households of various sizes (Reid and Whittlesey 1982; Riggs 2001, 2007). This latter number is probably a better approximation of the overall total primarily because excavations in Room Block 2 at Grasshopper were clustered around the Great Kiva. Excavations showed these rooms to be specialized spaces likely associated with Great Kiva function (Riggs 2001:181-¬183). Hence, the bias at Grasshopper is probably toward a slightly lower overall percentage of habitation rooms than were actually constructed.

Turning to Kinishba, and being mindful of the two-story room problem, we can make some rough calculations to estimate the number of households as reflected in the ground-floor architecture. These can then be compared to the numbers derived for Grasshopper. First, Cummings's map of the Group I depicts 202 room spaces. Of these, 105 contained rectangular slab-lined hearths, which are the hallmark of a habitation room at Grasshopper and at other sites in the Mogollon Rim Region (Ciolek-Torrello and Reid 1974; Hill 1970; Martin et al. 1961; Martin et al. 1967; Reid and Whittlesey 1982; Riggs 2001, 2007). If we calculate the ratio of rooms with one or more rectangular hearths to rooms without rectangular hearths in Group I at Kinishba, we find that 52 percent of the rooms potentially served a habitation function. We expect, however, that many of these rooms were likely abandoned and filled with trash or changed function with the addition of a second story. If we use Grasshopper's 21 percent room abandonment figure we can subtract 42 rooms from the 202 in Group I and then multiply this by the 52 percent habitation ratio above to estimate that 41 percent (83 rooms) of Group I's remaining rooms may have been used for habitation. This, of course, does not account for two-story rooms, where we know that the lower floor, based on Grasshopper and other pueblos (Adams 1983; Cameron 1999; V. Mindeleff 1891), did not typically serve a habitation function.

Thus, we also know that an important reason for abandoning a room is as a response to the addition of a second story. The fact that we cannot reliably identify and eliminate all two story-rooms plus an additional subset of other abandoned rooms limits this approach. To simplify matters, I contend that eliminating an estimated number of two story rooms is probably a more accurate calculation than the 41 percent that is predicted simply through the elimination of early abandoned rooms. If we eliminate two-story rooms from the mix, we find that 39 percent of the rooms in Kinishba's east unit were likely habitation rooms, a number more in line with expectations from Grasshopper. Again, further adjustments to the number of abandoned rooms might need to be made to account for the longer occupation span at Kinishba.

Although this latter ratio is closer to the Grasshopper example, it does, however, suggest that room construction practices and household make-up at Kinishba may have been slightly different than at Grasshopper. Grasshopper households came in two types, single-room and multi-room households (Reid and Whittlesey 1982:694). The latter type of household ranged in size from two rooms to as many as three rooms and their associated roof surfaces. Finally, it is also probable that related households may have shared storage or limited-activity rooms (Riggs 2007), much like they shared ceremonial rooms and kivas (Reid and Whittlesey 1982). The higher ratio of habitation rooms to other rooms at Kinishba suggests that there were more households relative to total community size, and that Kinishba's households may have been smaller. In other words, there may have been more single-room households at Kinishba than at Grasshopper. Turkey Creek Pueblo, a thirteenth century site located in the Point of Pines Region, represents the earliest local aggregated pueblo community in the region. There, Lowell (1991: Table 4.10) found that rooms with rectangular hearths comprised 35 percent of the total sample of excavated rooms. This figure, too, is in line with estimates from both Grasshopper and Kinishba, indicating that habitation rooms in general make up slightly more than one third of the total room sample in late Mogollon Pueblos. As with the early abandoned rooms mentioned above, the longer span of occupation at Kinishba relative to that at Grasshopper might necessitate adjusting the estimated number of two story rooms upward. This, with similar adjustments to the number of early abandoned rooms, would serve to decrease the number of ground floor habitation rooms, perhaps bringing it more in line with Grasshopper and Turkey Creek.

One obvious issue with this approach is the argument that the upper floor of all two-story rooms probably had a habitation function. In this case, we could simply count each two-story room as a habitation room regardless of lower-story function. Doing this would substantially raise our estimate of the number of habitation rooms at Grasshopper and Kinishba. There is, however, insufficient research on multi-story, open-air pueblos (non-cliffdwellings) to support this assertion. Furthermore, if we look at villages like Turkey Creek Pueblo, which was entirely single story, we find, once again, that 35 percent of the rooms had a habitation function.

Finally, it is necessary to briefly discuss mealing bins. Because these tend to indicate activities related to food-processing and other core household functions, they are indicators of habitation. At Grasshopper, mealing bins are common features in both generalized and specialized habitation rooms and are commonly found in roof contexts (Reid and Whittlesey 1982; Riggs 2001). In fact, of Grasshopper's 33 habitation rooms, 18 (55 percent) contained mealing bins on the floor or on the roof. Overall, because of the problem of distinguishing mealing bin stones from entryway elements and other wall fall debris, the number of mealing bins recorded from roof fall contexts is probably underestimated at Grasshopper. Based on Cummings map of Group I, it is readily apparent that mealing bins at Kinishba may reflect an entirely different pattern with regard to habitation function. In fact, only six of the spaces on Cummings's map (three percent of the excavated rooms) contained mealing bins. This may indicate that the practice at Kinishba was to locate mealing bins on roofs and in second story rooms, rather than on roofs and in ground floor rooms, as at Grasshopper.

CEREMONIAL ARCHITECTURE

At Grasshopper, as at other Mogollon Pueblos, the inhabitants constructed large public spaces for ritual, including plazas and great kivas, as well as smaller and more private spaces for household or larger social group use. At Grasshopper, these latter spaces are divided into two types, kivas and ceremonial rooms (Reid and Whittlesey 1982). Both types of room spaces were incorporated into room block architecture, and cannot be differentiated from other room types without excavation. Kivas at Grasshopper contain a masonry bench, a ventilator and a circular stone-lined hearth, whereas ceremonial rooms have a circular stone-lined hearth and a small, slab-lined ash box (Reid and Whittlesey 1982, 1999). At Grasshopper, ceremonial rooms seem to have been shared by approximately three households, whereas as many as six households likely shared a kiva (Reid and Whittlesey 1982:698).

Although Grasshopper's ceremonial spaces (kivas and ceremonial rooms) are partially distinguished by the presence of circular, stone-lined hearths, less formal circular fire pits occur in many non-ceremonial rooms. In all, the excavated rooms in Grasshopper's core room blocks yielded seven spaces with ceremonial functions, which equates to 10 percent of the excavated sample. If we assume all of the circular hearths depicted on Cummings's map for Group I represent formal circular hearths, and if we further assume that these also represent ceremonial spaces, we can estimate on the basis of the Grasshopper practice of building circular hearths in ceremonial rooms that only six percent of the rooms in Group I served ceremonial functions. This number is not consistent with Kinishba's estimated number of households from the discussion above.

Using circular hearths is likely not an accurate means of identifying rooms with ceremonial functions at Kinishba for two reasons. First, the sparse descriptions available for the circular hearths imply that they are not the formal, stone-lined firepits found at Grasshopper, but rather are more like the circular, clay-lined firepits often associated with limited-activity rooms at Grasshopper. Second, the one formal kiva described by Cummings is outfitted with a rectangular slab-lined hearth (Cummings 1940:9). Although this practice is not unheard of at Grasshopper (for example, Room 341 in Room Block 7; Riggs 2001:228), it is not the normal pattern for ceremonial spaces. On the other hand, the Shaeffers' (Chapter 4) description of the earlier kivas underlying Patio A (Great Kiva) notes that both circular and rectangular hearths were used in these spaces. The fact that these likely predate the large-scale population aggregation at Kinishba, are fragmentary in their preservation, and seem to represent a range of kiva types, complicates their use as the basis of extrapolation.

By looking at the roughly contemporary nearby sites represented by accessible site reports, it is clear that there is a great deal of variability in the use of rectangular and circular hearths for rooms with ceremonial functions. Haury and Hargrave (1931:47-52) describe a kiva from the Pinedale Ruin, which is located northeast of Grasshopper, above the Mogollon Rim. Like Grasshopper, the Pinedale kiva was located within a room block and was outfitted with a circular hearth. Moving farther afield, closer to the Zuni region, the kivas Haury and Hargrave (1931:81-94) describe at Kin Tiel are like those from Grasshopper, but with rectangular hearths, rather than circular ones. At Hooper Ranch Pueblo in the Vernon-Springerville area, Martin et al. (1961:42-53) describe kivas with rectangular hearths. In contrast, at Broken K Pueblo, near Snowflake, Arizona, there appear to have been both room kivas, like those at Grasshopper, and subterranean kivas, like the one in Kinishba's Patio B. These are outfitted with a variety of different types of hearths, including circular, rectangular and one D-shaped hearth (Martin et al. 1967).

Finally, at Canyon Creek cliff dwelling (Haury 1934), which has severed as an analog for Grasshopper in numerous ways (Riggs 2001), there is only a single recorded "ceremonial room." Like all rooms at Canyon Creek, this room (Room 22B) had a shallow, circular, informal hearth and was only differentiated from other rooms by the presence of a ventilator, deflector and an "altar slab, on which were found several unusual items (Haury 1934: 52-54)."

All of this suggests that there is no consistent correlation between hearth shape and ceremonial room function. The only pattern that can be gleaned from this brief discussion is that there does seem to be a west-to-east gradient in hearth shape, with circular hearths being more common to the west (Grasshopper/Pinedale) and rectangular hearths being representative of ceremonial spaces to the east (Hooper Ranch/Kin Tiel). Kinishba's location east of Grasshopper (and south of Broken K, where both rectangular and circular hearths are present) may suggest that it is located in an area where rectangular hearths were more common. Future work on this subject may clarify this relationship, perhaps making it easier to delineate room function based on hearth shape.

All of this suggests that the pattern for ceremonial room features may not have been the same at Grasshopper and Kinishba. The construction of stone-lined, circular firepits in ceremonial rooms does not seem to have been part of the construction practices for people at Kinishba; at least not in Group I. It is likely, given this information, that counting rectangular hearths could overestimate the number of habitation rooms. It may be better to assume that all of the rooms at Kinishba with rectangular hearths could have potentially been used for ceremonial or habitation purposes, allowing for the use of a ratio to estimate room function.

Looking at Grasshopper, we find that 45 of the excavated rooms were classified as either habitation or ceremonial spaces. All of these would have been outfitted with a formal hearth (either circular or rectangular depending on room function). Of rooms with any type of formal hearth, 27 percent (12 rooms) were ceremonial spaces (3 kivas and 9 ceremonial rooms). This yields a ratio of 1:3.75 for ceremonial to habitation rooms. Applying this number only to rooms with rectangular hearths (given that circular firepits at Kinishba have already been eliminated as the informal type), suggests that 28 of Kinishba's rooms were ceremonial in function. This leaves 77 spaces as habitation rooms, 38 percent of the rooms in Group I. I have not attempted to further refine this number based on one- and two-story rooms or abandoned rooms for two reasons. First, because it is not uncommon to find ground floor ceremonial rooms at Grasshopper, making use of any single equation to estimate both two-story rooms and ceremonial rooms highly suspect. Second, if we try to account for the possibility that some of the rooms with rectangular hearths could have been ceremonial in function, this approach suggests approximately 1/3 of the rooms in Group I were habitation rooms.

Adding support to the idea that ceremonial activities at Kinishba might have been organized differently than those at Grasshopper is the presence of the subterranean kiva, which is located just north of the Great Kiva in Group I's enclosed plaza area (Patio B, Cummings 1940:7-12). Its subterranean construction and detached location alone make it different than the kivas at Grasshopper, which are always above ground and always incorporated into room blocks (Reid and Whittlesey 1999; Riggs 2001). Furthermore, the kiva at Kinishba was outfitted with a rectangular, slab-lined hearth rather than the circular, stone-lined hearths characteristic of the ceremonial rooms at Grasshopper. As Cummings (1940:8-9) implies, these characteristics make Kinishba's kiva more similar in its location and, at least to some extent its features, to traditional Hopi kivas than to the kivas at Grasshopper. Unfortunately, however, the extant excavation records do not shed light on the stratigraphic relationship between the subterranean kiva and the Great Kiva, so we do not know which was constructed and used first.

The Great Kiva

Although it has proven difficult to distinguish rooms with ceremonial functions from rooms with habitation functions, the Great Kiva at Kinishba is another issue entirely. It shares many similarities with the Great Kiva at Grasshopper and with excavated great kivas at other excavated Mogollon pueblos (Riggs 2005). The following discussion offers a practical assessment of the architectural evidence and how it relates to not only room construction, but also to construction decisions. The details of the Great Kiva provided by the Shaeffers (Chapter 4) likewise need not be repeated here. Instead, I augment their discussion based on Grasshopper's Great Kiva. The goal is to highlight some parallels as a means of further understanding Kinishba and its place among large aggregated pueblos in the Arizona uplands.

The most striking similarity between these two structures is their location. Both are enclosed within the southern portion of a large block of masonry rooms, and both were constructed in a former plaza area (see also Reid and Whittlesey 1999; Riggs 2001, 2005). Furthermore, the overall construction is remarkably similar to that for the Great Kiva at Grasshopper with respect to the use of and placement of wooden support posts and primary beams (cf. Riggs 2001:107-111). The two rectilinear spaces are similar in shape, with their long axes running north-south, rather than east to west. The Kinishba Great Kiva (18.85 m by 16.54 m) is more irregularly shaped than Grasshopper's (14.88 m by 12.22 m), but both have similar length to width ratios of 1.14:1 and 1.22:1 respectively, making Kinishba's great kiva slightly squarer than Grasshopper's. Both spaces contained an entryway consisting of a room with a doorway that opened into the Great Kiva. At Grasshopper, this entryway was located on the eastern wall in the southeast corner of the structure, a location that is common in Mogollon great kivas. At Kinishba, this entry vestibule was to the south, a position also common in Mogollon kivas and great kivas (Anyon 1984; Anyon and LeBlanc 1980; Riggs 2005; Wheat 1955).

As the Shaeffers report (Chapter 4), it was necessary for the builders of Kinishba's great kiva to modify existing rooms to make the space fit the proper dimensions. At Grasshopper, the Great Kiva was constructed, not by modifying rooms, but by adding a set of rooms to the east and west sides of Plaza 3 in order to create a smaller rectangle and have walls on which to anchor the kiva roof, which minimized the span of the *vigas* (Riggs 2001:111). The only reconstruction that might have taken place at Grasshopper would have been wall modifications on the north and south sides of the kiva to facilitate anchoring of the *latillas* and other secondary roofing elements. The excavators made no mention of this, perhaps because post-occupation/pre-excavation wall collapse destroyed this evidence.

The structures are also similar in the type and placement of floor features. These similarities in construction and use are supported by similarities in the timing of construction. As noted above, the construction of the Great Kiva and outliers at Grasshopper marks the beginning of what Grasshopper researchers call the "Dispersion Phase" in reference to the onset of diminishing occupation intensity at Grasshopper beginning around A.D. 1330 (Reid 1973; Reid and Shimada 1982). Based on similar timing, form and construction practices, Kinishba's Great Kiva may represent a similar change in occupation intensity. The primary difference between the two great kivas relates to the necessity of manipulating standing walls at Kinishba versus the need to construct new ones at Grasshopper. Because walls to the east and west did not exist prior to the Great Kiva's construction at Grasshopper, they were added to make the structure. At Kinishba, where existing room walls circumscribed the intended location of the Great Kiva, it was necessary to modify existing walls. In both cases, the goal was a Great Kiva. Although the particular construction circumstances slightly differed, the decision to construct a Great Kiva in both cases seems to have occurred as the Mogollon core population tried to reassert traditional religious practice, which included the use of a great kiva in late stages of community development and prior to depopulation.

CONCLUSIONS

In this chapter I have attempted to enhance our understanding of Kinishba by drawing on other excavated Mogollon pueblos, particularly Grasshopper Pueblo. Although often speculative because of the limited information available regarding Kinishba, the discussion highlights some apparently significant similarities between these two communities, as well as a few important differences.

The two communities are almost identical with respect to their layout. Based on the Grasshopper example it is likely that the spatial division of the Kinishba community by a stream channel reflects a social division that was intentionally maintained by the community. The apparent timing and similar construction techniques in the outlying room blocks of both communities is also interesting. At Grasshopper, the outlying room blocks were constructed later in the occupation and were built using the low-walled construction techniques indicative of occupation in the region prior to aggregation. This return to traditional construction practices at Grasshopper has been interpreted to represent a return to a less intensive occupation of the area just prior to more momentous regional depopulation. The seemingly similar construction techniques in Kinishba's outliers suggest intriguing similarities in behavior. Most notably, that the builders may have been anticipating a shift to a more seasonal use of the locale and were investing less time and energy by building more impermanent structures. Future work around this question will need to look more closely at regional architectural practices prior to aggregation at Kinishba and will perhaps have to delve more deeply into the extant records for excavations at Kinishba's outliers.

The picture regarding room function is not quite as straightforward as that of community layout. Overall, there is compelling evidence to suggest that slightly more than one-third of Kinishba's rooms could have served habitation functions. In this regard it appears it would have been similar to not only Grasshopper Pueblo, but also to Turkey Creek Pueblo in the Point of Pines Region. Some of the issues identified at Kinishba regarding an accurate count of habitation rooms revolve around the number of rooms that were abandoned during community occupation, the number of two-story rooms and the nature of rectangular versus circular hearths. As it currently stands it is probably safe to say that Kinishba housed a proportionally similar number of households when compared to Grasshopper and Turkey Creek, although the perhaps slightly larger number of rooms with rectangular hearths suggests that multi-room households may have been less frequent at Kinishba. On the other hand, it may simply be that the environmental differences between the two areas dictated that the inhabitants of Kinishba could spend more time outdoors during the cooler times of the year. Heavier snowfall and lower temperatures at Grasshopper may have necessitated more time indoors and thus larger rooms, while the more moderate climate at Kinishba may have allowed for generally more time spent outdoors and less demand on interior spaces.

Regarding ceremony, the picture for Kinishba as it compares to Grasshopper is less clear. Focusing specifically on the great kivas suggests that there are some clear and important similarities in the timing of construction, the nature of construction and the overall use of the spaces. Both of these large spaces came late in the occupation and both were built using similar roof support systems and with similar floor features. Both structures were also built on the traditional Mogollon pattern, with separate entry vestibules located to the south (Kinishba) or east (Grasshopper). The situation with other ceremonial spaces is considerably less clear. Ceremonial rooms and kivas at Kinishba do not seem to exhibit the same construction style as those at Grasshopper. First, they do not seem to have been outfitted with circular hearths and second, they were found both to be room kivas and subterranean kivas, more similar to modern Hopi kivas. In this way they more closely match the pattern at places like Kin Tiel, Hooper Ranch or possibly even Broken K, than they do to sites like Grasshopper and Pinedale, which are located farther to the west. The evidential basis for the pattern suggested by this small sample, however, should be expanded to pursue more definitive assessments than those made here.

In the end, this exercise has generated at least as many questions as answers. Table 6.4 summarizes what we know about Kinishba as a result of this study and provides a series of recommendations for future research. Many of the questions posed in Table 6.4 can be answered through analyses of artifacts recovered from the floors. This would provide additional evidence regarding room function at abandonment. Many extant ancient walls, those basal courses for Cummings's rebuilding, are still visible and could provide valuable information about learned construction behaviors, room-set additions and overall room block growth. A reanalysis of the recovered tree-ring material with an eye toward species identification will be useful in relating room size to wood use, and perhaps to cultural preferences for the use of different species. An analysis of stone used in the various room blocks could shed light on preferences in stone selection and construction techniques, as well as whether the supply of raw materials affected these preferences.

The original records from the Kinishba excavations are sparse, incomplete, and often difficult to locate and use. Furthermore, Cummings rebuilt Group I based on an incomplete understanding of how many multistory rooms it originally had. Despite the fact that the building has since fallen again into ruins, the outdoor laboratory at Kinishba is available for renewed scientific study. The original walls are still exposed in many places, awaiting renewed documentation and measurement. The original floor features are still intact, though buried under a thin layer of backfill. Thus, Cummings's rebuilding offers a number of opportunities to explore many of Kinishba's

Table 6.4. Summary of Key Architectural Characteristics and Suggestions for Future Research.

Architectural Characteristic	Kinishba: Present	Kinishba: Future
Community Layout	Layout on either side of drainage implies distinct social groups	Renewed excavations in Group II and the Outliers as described in the rows below
	Presence of large public spaces implies Mogollon cultural traditions for both units	
	Outliers vs. Core architecture imply change in occupation intensity, likely late in the occupation	
Room Construction and Community Growth Patterns	Agglomerative growth of Group I from north to south implies gradual arrival of immigrants	Analysis of exposed original wall faces and corners could facilitate a more in-depth understanding
		Renewed excavations in Group II to delineate construction units
Wall Features	Rebuilding and lack of thorough documentation render these of no utility	Analysis of exposed original wall faces could facilitate a more in-depth understanding
	Doorways recorded on Cummings' map may or may not be accurate	Renewed excavations in Group II, including detailed architectural documentation
Building Stone	Information is currently not available	Analysis of exposed original wall faces could facilitate a more in-depth understanding
		Sourcing of rock used in construction on each side of the stream channel could be helpful
Wood Use	Extant Tree-ring catalog provides information primarily on Group I (100 samples)	Renewed excavations in Group II to recover roofing materials
	Group II is represented by 6 samples	Species identification of extant samples
	Species not specified	

ancient architectural features. Although this was not Cummings's original intent, it does provide the interested scholar the opportunity to test many of the ideas described here as well as others that I have undoubtedly missed. Many of the questions posed in Table 6.4 can only be answered through renewed intensive excavations, especially in Group II. Although Cummings's desire to expose an entire room block is consistent with his visionary goals for Kinishba as an outdoor museum and monument, from a sampling perspective this singular focus on Group I was short sighted. Although a 100 percent sample of a building as large as Group I is almost unique, its meaning and scientific value for intra- and inter-site comparison is limited by the lack of exposure elsewhere at Kinishba.

The politics of doing archaeology have changed immensely since Cummings excavated Kinishba in the 1930s. Today, the conservation imperative and commitment to respect the interests and preferences of descendant and steward communities outweigh most scientific curiosity. Hence, it is unlikely that excavations in Group II will be conducted in the near term. On the other hand, this study demonstrates that there is yet much to be learned from Kinishba and Cummings's work there without breaking new ground. Although we will likely not be able to compare the two large room blocks at Kinishba in detail in the near term, we do have thoroughly sampled and well reported analogs like Grasshopper to help us fill in many of the gaps in our knowledge about Kinishba, not as a ruin, but as a once living community. For now, we have to be content with comparisons like the one undertaken here.

Chapter 7
"By their fruits ye shall know them"
The Pottery of Kinishba Revisited

Patrick D. Lyons

> "By their fruits ye shall know them," is nowhere demonstrated more forcefully than in the pottery manufactured at Kinishba. From the bushels upon bushels of fragments dug out of the ruined rooms and the fine specimens obtained with burials much can be learned of their individual tastes and skill, and of the relationship of this pueblo to others in the Southwest (Cummings 1940:77).

The first study devoted entirely to the whole vessel assemblage from Kinishba (AZ V:4:1[ASM]), a master's thesis by Margaret Murry [Shaeffer] (1937), was designed as an exploration of the effects of "foreign influences" on what was assumed to be an indigenous pottery tradition. Seventy-five years later, with the benefit of refined typologies, improved chronological control, an understanding of regional patterns in pottery production and circulation informed by compositional analyses, and theoretical and methodological frameworks developed to distinguish among the material residues of emulation, exchange, and enculturation, much can be learned by revisiting the questions at the heart of Murry's study.

In this chapter, I describe the whole and reconstructible vessel assemblage from Kinishba curated by the Arizona State Museum (ASM) and explore what can be learned from these objects regarding the site's chronology, the dynamics of the Kayenta diaspora, the dating and distribution of late Roosevelt Red Ware types, and the development of a late prehispanic Roosevelt Red Ware feasting tradition. When appropriate, I incorporate information gleaned as a result of a cursory study of the bulk excavated sherds, non-vessel ceramic objects, and surface collections from the site. I begin, however, by reviewing the history of research on Kinishba pottery, as this large and diverse group of vessels (n = 624) has influenced Southwesternists' understanding of White Mountain Red Ware, Roosevelt Red Ware, and Cibola White Ware for decades. I have included tables which include corrected (if previously published) and previously unpublished concordance data that will assist other researchers in tracking Kinishba vessels used in past studies.

PREVIOUS RESEARCH ON THE KINISHBA CERAMIC ASSEMBLAGE

The first glimpses of Kinishba's pottery were provided by Eleanor Clarke, in her 1933 master's thesis, which was posthumously published by the University of Arizona (UA) in 1935. Clarke used specimens recovered from Kinishba as examples of "Tularosa Black-on-white" (Pinedale Black-on-white), "Little Colorado Black-on-red" (Pinedale Black-on-red), "Jeddito Yellow" (Awatovi Black-on-yellow?), and "Late Gila Polychrome" (Whiteriver Polychrome – see Roosevelt Red Ware, below – and Tonto Polychrome) (Clarke 1933:46-48, 48-49, 51-52, 66-68, Plates XVIII upper, XIX, XXIII, XXXVIII, XXXIX).

Research on the pottery of Kinishba has continued in three spurts over the last century. The timing and analytical foci of different projects reflect prevailing trends in North American archaeology as a whole and in Southwestern archaeology, as well as the dynamics of the UA archaeological field school program. The initial burst of activity occurred in the 1930s, with some products published in the early 1940s. This work was very Kinishba-centric, a natural outgrowth of the then-current paradigm (a focus on building local cultural historical sequences) and the fact that the research products were largely master's theses and site reports.

There followed a twenty-year hiatus (including World War II), during which Byron Cummings was replaced by Emil Haury as Head of the Department of Archaeology (later Anthropology) and ASM Director, the UA archaeological field school was established at Forestdale (1939–1941), and the focus of field school excavations was shifted to Point of Pines (1946–1960). The second phase of research, between 1960 and 1970, reflects a move toward regional synthesis (Carlson 1961, 1970; Mauer 1970; Young 1967). Kinishba vessels were included in these studies for comparative purposes and in attempts to discern larger-scale patterns.

Another two-decade gap in work with Kinishba pottery occurred during the 1970s and 1980s, when the "new archaeology" focus on theory, method, the environment, and multidisciplinary studies likely made Kinishba an unattractive research prospect, given the coarse recovery methods employed by its excavators and the relatively sparse documentation they left behind. This period also witnessed an explosion in cultural resource management projects and a related resurgence of interest in the archaeology of the Hohokam region.

Studies of Kinishba ceramics from the early 1990s through the early 2000s continued to focus on "big picture" issues and, like those of the 1960s, incorporated Kinishba information into much larger databases. Work during this interval was a direct outgrowth of the research programs of the UA field schools at Grasshopper (1963–1992) and Silver Creek (1993–2004), where migration, aggregation, and ceramic production and circulation were explored in large part via studies of pottery style and provenance analyses (e.g., Crown 1981a; Mills Herr, Stinson, and Triadan 1999; Montgomery 1992, 1993; Montgomery and Reid 1990; Stinson 1996; Triadan 1989, 1994, 1997; Triadan et al. 2002; Van Keuren 1994, 1999; Zedeño 1991, 1994).

Research During the 1930s: The Kinishba-Centric Period

Gordon Baldwin's 1934 master's thesis, which reports the results of the 1931–1933 UA excavations at Kinishba, includes an extended discussion of the whole vessel assemblage that set the stage for Murry's later analysis. Baldwin documented an abundance of Gila and Tonto Polychrome, indicating that the former was dominant over all decorated types present. Noted by Baldwin as unusual is the fact that about half of the Gila Polychrome bowls from the site bear black-on-white painted decoration on their exteriors only and that the interiors of these vessels are slipped red (see Roosevelt Red Ware, below).

Baldwin also reported high frequencies of Little Colorado polychromes (White Mountain Red Ware; he indicated that Fourmile Polychrome was the most abundant and that St. Johns Polychrome was scarce), lesser amounts of black-on-white pottery (which he described as stylistically related to Tularosa Black-on-white), and traces of material from the Hopi Mesas. Although he did not identify it as Zuni in origin, he described and illustrated a bowl of Kechipawan Polychrome which depicts a *katsina* (Baldwin 1934:70-71, Plate XXV).

In addition, Baldwin's (1934:71) thesis includes an early description of Kinishba Polychrome, a type he later formally defined (Baldwin 1938b; also see Haury 1934:135-137; Hough 1903:294, 1930:20). He also briefly describes "Fort Apache Polychrome" (Baldwin 1934:65, Plate XXII1a, 2a; Guenther 1937:40-41). The vessel he illustrates is ASM Catalog No. 20004, which Carlson (1970:Figure 29e) later used as an example of Cedar Creek Polychrome. Other ceramic phenomena mentioned include what would later be called Kinishba Red (Wendorf 1950:42-43) and Cibicue Polychrome (Haury 1934:131-134).

Baldwin (1934:71, 108-110) assumes that most pottery found at Kinishba was locally produced. He suggests that similarities between vessels found at the site and those characteristic of other regions indicate a coming together of different cultural traditions at Kinishba. He refers to these traditions as Middle Gila (associated with what is now called Roosevelt Red Ware), Little Colorado (marked by what is now known as White Mountain Red Ware), and Upper Gila (associated with what we now call Cibola White Ware).

There are indications that Baldwin (1934:12-13, 18) considered population movement—rather than exchange or emulation—the main factor contributing to ceramic diversity at Kinishba, but he provides no explicit discussion of this topic. Instead, he often refers to undefined "influences" from adjacent regions. One important exception is his discussion of "Old Hopi pottery," in which he specifically invokes "trade" (Baldwin 1934:71). Implicit in Baldwin's analysis is the "criterion of abundance" (Bishop et al. 1982:301; Rands and Bishop 1980:20)—the notion that well-represented types are more likely to be local products and that rare types ought to be imports.

In a later publication, Baldwin (1939) is explicit about his inferences regarding local pottery production and the role that the people of Kinishba played in regional ceramic developments. He unequivocally opines that, aside from a few vessels from the Hopi Mesas, the Zuni area, and the Hohokam region, all pottery found at the site was made there. He even goes so far as to suggest that Kinishba was the cradle of Little Colorado pottery (St. Johns Black-on-red and later White Mountain Red Ware types), Roosevelt Red Ware, and the Salado phenomenon. In support of these ideas, he writes that Kinishba is, to his knowledge, the site that has yielded the most complete, unbroken sequence showing the development of these types.

Murry's (1937) master's thesis, which built on Baldwin's, specifically focuses on the use of pottery to reconstruct group origins and migrations. She argues that decoration is easily copied, whereas other traits such as vessel form more reliably reflect a potter's cultural identity (Murry 1937:2, 14, 26). She also addresses the fact that evidence of exchange can be difficult to distinguish from evidence of migration and she highlights the importance of "hybrid" vessels in establishing co-residence by different cultural groups (Murry 1937:72-74).

Southwesternists still wrestle with these basic issues today, but have made noteworthy progress due to improved theory and methods, especially ceramic compositional analysis. Unfortunately, Murry's thesis predates the rise of provenance studies and, despite the fact that she framed her investigation in a sophisticated way—attempting to analytically separate the residues of migration, exchange, and emulation—her inferences are hindered by assumptions about local production, leading to vaguely formed and sometimes contradictory ideas regarding the nature of different "influences" on and sources of "inspiration" for the potters of Kinishba.

Murry concludes that although most ceramics found at Kinishba were made there (including what we would today call Cibola White Ware, White Mountain Red Ware, Roosevelt Red Ware, Kinishba Red, and corrugated pottery), all vessels of some types and some vessels of other types are present in the assemblage as a result of exchange (Murry 1937:29, 34-35, 42, 62-65, 72, 76). Specifically, she argues that "Old Hopi" (she was referring to Kinishba Polychrome; see White Mountain Red Ware, below), Zuni glaze-paint pottery, and some specimens of Fourmile Polychrome were brought to the pueblo from other places.

Suggesting that the dominant pottery tradition of Kinishba (Roosevelt Red Ware and Kinishba Red) was indigenous to the area, she reasons that the pueblo was established by local groups, who she refers to as Middle Gila people (Murry 1937:28-30, 53, 65, 72, 75-76). Assuming local production of most of the White Mountain Red Ware from the site and inferring "Little Colorado influence" on local potters making Roosevelt Red Ware, she concludes that immigrants from adjacent areas joined the community (Murry 1937:53, 75-76). She attributes the similarities between some Kinishba pots and those of the Kayenta region, however, to "imitation" (Murry 1937:42-43).

Cummings's 1940 report on the site was the next product of this period. In discussing the pottery of Kinishba, Cummings covers much the same ground as Baldwin and Murry. He assumes local production of most types and asserts that pottery that appears to have been made on the Hopi Mesas, at Zuni, and in the Hohokam region was indeed imported (Cummings 1940:77, 89-90). He concludes that local manufacture of Roosevelt Red Ware, White Mountain Red Ware, Cibola White Ware, and Tusayan White Ware was the result of regular contact with and sharing of ideas between potters at Kinishba and those from other places, i.e., emulation.

Though the report failed to satisfy contemporaries because of a lack of theoretical focus, inferential rigor, synthesis, and detail—especially regarding artifact counts and proveniences (Martin 1941)—it remains today a critical starting point for reanalysis. The most important contribution Cummings makes toward Kinishba pottery research, from my perspective, is the set of images he presents in the monograph: 32 color plates, 16 photographs, and three drawings of vessels and sherds from the site. It was these which led me to focus on the Kinishba collection as a resource for exploring regional and temporal variability in Roosevelt Red Ware.

I should mention here that Cummings's illustration of a whole bowl of St. Johns Polychrome has been a source of confusion (1940:Plate XVIII; also see Cummings 1953:Plate IX). The caption refers to it as "a Kinishba interpretation of a St. John's [sic] type." However, this object, ASM Catalog No. 16464, is not from Kinishba; it was recovered from Turkey Hill Ruin (AZ I:14:1[ASM]). Additional drawings and photographs of non-Kinishba vessels are included as well and are identified as such by Cummings.

Baldwin's 1941 doctoral dissertation represents the final work of this period and something of a transitional piece in that it presents the results of the excavations at Kinishba in the context of a regional synthesis that compares and contrasts developments in the Upper Salt, the Upper Gila, the Middle Gila, the Little Colorado, the Kayenta region, the Chaco region, and the Verde and Mimbres valleys. The major conclusions of Baldwin's thesis and those of his 1939 *American Antiquity* article remain unchanged in the dissertation, but the author is more specific about population movement and its role in the cultural makeup of Kinishba. He hypothesizes that groups leaving the Kayenta region in the late 1200s caused population pressure in the Little Colorado River Valley, forcing Little Colorado groups to move south of the Mogollon Rim to join existing mountain communities such as Kinishba and others in the Upper Salt River drainage (Baldwin 1941:253-255, 268).

Research from 1960 to 1970: Regional Synthesis and the New Archaeology

The three studies conducted during this period are similar in that each makes use of a portion of the Kinishba whole vessel assemblage for the purpose of exploring questions pertinent on a larger scale. In the first two cases, that larger scale is the U.S. Southwest and northern Mexico. The third research project's spatial scope is more limited, but the clear focus on hypotheses and test implications related to vessel use and social organization (not to mention the use of cluster analysis), mark it as a new archaeology study.

The first regional study to make use of Kinishba pottery was Roy Carlson's (1961, 1970) dissertation. Carlson included 32 Kinishba vessels in his sample of 477 White Mountain Red Ware specimens from more than 60 sites. Twenty-four vessels from Kinishba were illustrated in his monograph, which stands as the definitive treatment of White Mountain Red Ware typology and a seminal discussion of the effects of ancient Southwestern migrations on ceramic design styles. Kinishba specimens, overall, account for nearly twenty percent of the Pinedale Polychrome, Cedar Creek Polychrome, Fourmile Polychrome, and Showlow Polychrome vessels he examined and more than twenty percent of the vessels illustrated as examples of these types (Table 7.1; all tables are at the end of this chapter).

Along similar lines, but focusing on a different regional pottery tradition, Jon Young (1967: Table 1, 1982) included 14 specimens from Kinishba in his dissertation study of 521 whole Roosevelt Red Ware vessels recovered from more than 60 sites. Young examines broad spatial patterns in Roosevelt Red Ware decoration. Vessels from Kinishba accounted for a third of his sample from the "White Mountains-Mogollon Rim" area. Young illustrates three Kinishba specimens as examples of "dual-balanced design" (bifold rotational symmetry), human effigy vessels, and the intentional creation of asymmetry ("intentional imperfections") (Table 7.2).

Michael Mauer's (1970) master's thesis, like Carlson's and Young's doctoral studies, focuses on a single ceramic phenomenon that occurs at many different sites: "Cibecue [*sic*] Polychrome." Mauer includes five vessels from Kinishba in his sample of 87 specimens recovered from eight sites (Table 7.3).

Although Mauer (1970) lumps similar vessels with corrugated exteriors under the rubric of Cibicue Polychrome (and misspells the name), I adhere to Haury's (1934:131-134) original type description and limit the use of this label to vessels with smooth exterior surfaces. Thus, corrugated vessels resembling Cibicue Polychrome should be referred to as Cibicue Painted Corrugated (Zedeño 1994:30; Hagenbuckle 2000:10-11).

Mauer's investigation differs from the others in this period in terms of the much smaller spatial range of Cibicue Polychrome compared to White Mountain Red Ware and Roosevelt Red Ware, and also in that his study focuses not only on typology, chronology, and distribution, but also on use. Based on the fact that an overwhelming majority of vessels in his sample were recovered from burials (mostly from Grasshopper Pueblo, AZ P:14:1[ASM]; two of the Kinishba specimens are known to have been recovered from mortuary contexts) and a use-wear study which showed that very few of these vessels exhibited any appreciable abrasion, Mauer concludes that Cibecue [*sic*] Polychrome (Cibicue Polychrome and Cibicue Painted Corrugated) was a "mortuary ware." Mauer also works a bit of ceramic sociology into his study, commenting on how gender-differentiated patterns in the burial assemblages he examined might reflect aspects of social organization.

Mauer (1970: Figure 6) illustrates three Kinishba vessels as examples of his "Smooth Variety" of Cibecue [*sic*] Polychrome. He employs these objects (and the other two vessels from the site) in a chronological argument regarding the relative dating of his corrugated and smooth surface varieties, erroneously suggesting that the occupation at Kinishba ended circa 1325. Like Hagenbuckle (2000:55; see also Riggs 2001:17-19), I think Mauer (1970:73-74, 90) was incorrect in asserting that Cibicue Polychrome predates Cibicue Painted Corrugated. Cibicue Painted Corrugated is present at Chodistaas (AZ P:14:24[ASM]), occupied circa 1263–1300, but Cibicue Polychrome is absent from the site. Grasshopper Pueblo (ca. 1275–1390) has yielded both types, and Canyon Creek Ruin (AZ V:2:1[ASM]), occupied circa 1327 to post-1375, is the type site for Cibicue Polychrome but lacks Cibicue Painted Corrugated. This pattern and corroborating data from sites in the Silver Creek drainage strongly suggest that Cibicue Painted Corrugated is the earlier of the two types.

Research During the 1990s and the Early 2000s: Migration, Aggregation, Style, and Sourcing

Work involving the Kinishba collection during this period was synthetic and regionally relevant but, unlike investigations of the previous period, also significantly advanced knowledge about the site and its inhabitants. The first such study was Alexander Lindsay's treatment of the origin, dating, distribution, painted design style, and typology of Tucson Polychrome. Lindsay examines all four vessels of Tucson Polychrome from Kinishba and uses two of them (ASM Catalog Nos. A-33430 and 23788) in illustrations that accompany his type description (Lindsay 1992: Figures 28.1a, 28.3a). Lindsay's efforts call attention to the type's presence at Kinishba—it had not been recognized by earlier researchers—and also highlight the many indications of immigrants from the Kayenta region (such as Tucson Polychrome, other Maverick Mountain Series types, and perforated plates) at sites where Roosevelt Red Ware was likely produced. Crown (1994:8, Table 1.1) uses 45 vessels from Kinishba in her magnum opus on Roosevelt Red Ware, which analyzes 779 whole or reconstructible specimens from 72 sites. The vessels from Kinishba comprise 40 percent of her sample from the "Mogollon Rim/Anasazi Region" category, which she employs in comparisons with other areas of the Southwest in a search for spatial patterns in manufacturing technology, vessel form, painted decoration, use, and discard context.

Crown illustrates five Kinishba vessels (Table 7.4). These specimens play a significant role in communicating her inference that Roosevelt Red Ware motifs depict, among other things, serpents, shields, and *katsinam*. She also uses a Kinishba vessel (ASM Catalog No. A-33390) as her type specimen for "Tusayan-Kayenta Style" Roosevelt Red Ware painted decoration.

In her compositional analysis, which proves that Roosevelt Red Ware production occurred in many parts of Arizona, New Mexico, and northern Mexico, Crown (1994:23, Table 3.1) uses sherds from Kinishba. Her results indicate that Roosevelt Red Ware was very likely produced at the site and that vessels made at Kinishba circulated to Point of Pines and Grasshopper. One of Crown's (1994:208-209) major conclusions, that Roosevelt Red Ware was developed by immigrants from the Kayenta region living among local host groups, casts Kinishba in a new light in terms of its relevance to understanding the Salado phenomenon.

The connections Crown discusses among migration, ethnic co-residence, and styles of painted ceramic decoration have been addressed by others using the Kinishba collection. In his master's thesis, Scott Van Keuren (1994, 1999) uses 82 whole vessels from at least 15 different sites, including eight recovered from Kinishba, to define the rules that comprise the Pinedale Black-on-white pottery painting tradition (Table 7.5). Specifically, he seeks to differentiate, based on brushstroke analysis, between Pinedale Black-on-white vessels painted by potters from the Colorado Plateau and potters from the Arizona mountains. His results indicate that Kinishba vessels exhibit microstylistic characteristics of pots produced in the Silver Creek drainage. Although the majority of the specimens in his sample have been subjected to chemical or mineralogical provenance analysis, the Kinishba vessels have not. Nonetheless, their appearance strongly suggests a Silver Creek origin. Van Keuren, in a sophisticated way, is able to eliminate from consideration the notion that local Kinishba potters emulated Pinedale Black-on-white and also the idea that immigrant potters from the Silver Creek drainage brought the tradition to the site, producing vessels according to old stylistic canons and using new raw materials. Still, without more research, it is impossible to exclude either the possibility that these vessels arrived at Kinishba as the household inventory of immigrants or that they were exchanged with the village's inhabitants.

Daniela Triadan (1994, 1997), like Van Keuren, builds upon her research with collections from Grasshopper by incorporating material from Kinishba into her analyses. She includes seven Fourmile Polychrome sherds and two samples of clay from the site in her dissertation study of the production and distribution of White Mountain Red Ware through instrumental neutron activation analysis (INAA), weak-acid inductively-coupled plasma emission spectroscopy, and petrography. Triadan suggests that most of the White Mountain Red Ware found at Kinishba, including Kinishba Polychrome, was produced north of the Mogollon Rim.

In a follow-up study reported in this volume, Triadan (also see Triadan et al. 2002) subjected 136 more sherds from Kinishba to INAA and compares the results with a much larger regional compositional database. She succeeds in demonstrating that, indeed, the great majority of the White Mountain Red Ware found at Kinishba had not been produced there. She shows that these vessels most likely were made in the Silver Creek area. Triadan also documents production of red-slipped White Mountain Red Ware (i.e., not Kinishba Polychrome) at both Kinishba and Point of Pines, and establishes that Kinishba Red was a local product at Kinishba.

The most recent study involving Kinishba pottery that predates the work reported here is Scott Van Keuren's (2001) dissertation project. Van Keuren examines regional patterns in White Mountain Red Ware painted decoration and considers what these could reveal about social interaction in ethnically diverse, "post-migration" pueblos. He includes 36 vessels from Kinishba in his sample of 832 specimens from more than 16 sites.

Van Keuren, like Triadan, approaches his study from the perspective of Grasshopper. He builds upon the methods he developed in his earlier examination of Pinedale Black-on-white vessels, employing brushstroke analysis. Van Keuren compares patterns in the execution of White Mountain Red Ware vessels made north and south of the Mogollon Rim, both in synchronic and diachronic perspective. He concludes that poorly executed copies of Fourmile Style pottery, such as Grasshopper Polychrome and Point of Pines Polychrome, reflect purposeful restriction of information flow between potters from the Colorado Plateau—who moved southward into the Mogollon highlands—and potters native to the Arizona mountains. He suggests that this may have been an unintended consequence of factionalism.

Reanalysis of Kinishba Ceramics

When I began systematically researching Kinishba pottery in 2008, I found that ASM had catalog records in its collections database relating to 622 vessels or vessel fragments and 39 additional ceramic artifacts attributed to the site. In addition to the cataloged objects, 36 boxes of bulk sherds from the 1931–1939 excavations are curated by ASM. Other sherds from Kinishba had been dispersed throughout the ASM pottery type sherd collection over the years. There are also ASM (one box) and Gila Pueblo surface collections (one box each from AZ C:4:5[GP], AZ C:4:6[GP], and AZ C:4:7[GP]) from Kinishba.

After checking each whole or reconstructible vessel against catalog cards and other documentation, I found that some database records were duplicates; some vessels had, upon returning from loans, been assigned new catalog numbers and their old numbers had remained in the system. One number was found to pertain to a non-ceramic object.

A total of 45 vessels for which ASM has catalog records are not currently available for physical reanalysis. Ten are supposed to be at ASM but are missing, 34 have been exchanged with ("permanently loaned" to) other institutions, and one, according to its catalog card, was "destroyed" after having been typed as Kinishba Red by Emil Haury. In addition, Clarke (1933:Plates XXIII and XXXIX) and Cummings (1940:78, Plates XXVIII, XXIX, and XXXI, 1953:Plate XIII upper and lower) illustrate six whole vessels for which no possible matches with ASM records could be found (fragments comprising 20 percent of one of these vessels and 30 percent of another were discovered among the bulk sherds). Finally, one catalogued vessel fragment was located that did not appear in the ASM electronic database.

Among the exchanged vessels, thirteen were part of a much larger loan to the now defunct Kinishba Museum, located adjacent to the ruin, and six went to the Arizona Capitol Museum, in Phoenix. Most of the objects loaned to the Kinishba Museum are accounted for, but the thirteen vessels discussed here have been considered missing for many years. I believe that many, if not most of these, are represented by partially reconstructible vessels found among the boxes of Kinishba sherds at ASM. As for the Arizona Capitol Museum loan, staff there have informed ASM that this material has been missing for decades.

Most of the vessels not currently at ASM can be assigned to a type, or at least a ware, based on catalog records and, in many cases, published photographs, illustrations in masters' theses, or images provided by collections databases accessible via the internet (Table 7.6). In the end, the present analysis focuses on 624 vessels and vessel fragments, including those typed using available images. Although only 39 catalog records pertaining to non-vessel ceramic objects were present in the ASM collections database, an inventory of the storage location assigned to these objects revealed 188 cataloged items. These include nearly 100 worked sherd discs (both perforated and unperforated), as well as figurines and figurine fragments, handles (including animal effigy finials), and other objects.

Results of the Reanalysis

Slightly more than sixty percent of the whole and reconstructible vessel assemblage is utility ware and nearly forty percent is painted (Table 7.7). One burned vessel is impossible to place confidently in one of these categories. Kinishba Red accounts for nearly half of the utility pottery (and almost thirty percent of the overall assemblage), with brown ware and corrugated each comprising about one quarter. In Chapter 8, Triadan discusses the significance of Kinishba Red and its abundance. Five specimens of Tularosa Fillet Rim are also present in the utility ware assemblage. More than sixty percent of the brown ware vessels in the assemblage are non-functional (from a strictly utilitarian perspective) miniatures. Indeed, most of these objects are pinch pots.

More than forty percent of the painted vessels are specimens of Roosevelt Red Ware, and White Mountain Red Ware accounts for nearly thirty percent of the decorated assemblage. Painted wares, series, and types present in smaller quantities, ranging from more than twelve percent to less than one percent, include Cibola White Ware, the Maverick Mountain Series, Cibicue Polychrome, Tusayan White Ware, McDonald Corrugated, Zuni Glaze Ware, and Jeddito Yellow Ware. Nine vessels were classified as indeterminate decorated.

The sections that follow describe in detail Kinishba's whole and reconstructible vessels. The presentation is organized by ware, except in the case of Mogollon Brown Ware, which includes both utility and painted types. Painted pottery is addressed first, and then utility pottery. Within these larger categories of painted and utility pottery, wares are discussed in descending order of frequency. As appropriate, information from cursory studies of the bulk sherds and non-vessel ceramic artifact assemblages is used to supplement whole-vessel data.

Roosevelt Red Ware

Because I have recently proposed revisions to the typology of Roosevelt Red Ware (Lyons 2004a; Lyons, Hill, and Clark 2011; Lyons and Neuzil 2006; Neuzil and Lyons 2006) and because the Kinishba assemblage includes excellent examples of newly defined types—among them, the type specimens for Whiteriver Polychrome—here I provide a discussion of my approach to Roosevelt Red Ware types and their chronology (Table 7.8). The types Pinto, Gila and Tonto Polychrome are retained, though with modifications in the usage of the latter two based on decorative configuration, i.e., the nature of interaction between red and white slips on different portions of the vessel. Bowl interior surfaces are privileged in classification, resulting in type names such as Gila Polychrome: Tonto Variety (Gila configuration interior and Tonto configuration exterior) or Tonto Polychrome: Gila Variety (Tonto configuration interior and Gila configuration exterior). Bowls with no interior painted decoration are classified based on exterior decoration and vessel form.

Though not labeled with formal variety names, Pinto Polychrome and Gila Polychrome bowls exhibiting central, circular, red-slipped areas on their interior surfaces are indentified thus: "Pinto Polychrome, red center" and "Gila

Polychrome, red center." Likewise, bowls bearing painted decoration characteristic of Gila Polychrome but lacking a banding line are identified as "Gila Polychrome, no banding line." Tonto Polychrome jars with multiple rather than single design fields (i.e., separate neck and body decorations) are informally identified here as "Tonto Polychrome (Gila neck, Tonto body)" or "Tonto Polychrome (Tonto neck, Gila body)."

Recently Defined Types

Cliff Polychrome (Lyons 2004a; Harlow 1968) occurs only in recurved bowl form and is distinguished from Gila Polychrome by the presence of dual interior design fields—one at the rim and the other on the bottom and walls—separated by a thick banding line (Figure 7.1a). Cliff Polychrome bowls may bear exterior painted decoration. Nine Mile Polychrome (Lyons and Neuzil 2006; Neuzil and Lyons 2006) is similar to Cliff Polychrome. Both occur only as recurved bowls and exhibit a banded field of black-on-white painted decoration on the interior surface, at the rim (Figure 7.1b). Nine Mile differs from Cliff in that the remainder of the interior surface of the former is slipped red and bears no painted decoration. Nine Mile Polychrome bowl exteriors usually bear Gila- or Tonto-configuration decoration.

Phoenix Polychrome (Lyons and Neuzil 2006; Neuzil and Lyons 2006) lacks black-on-white interior decoration; the entire interior is slipped red (Figure 7.1c). Only occurring in the form of recurved bowls, Phoenix Polychrome vessels exhibit either Gila- or Tonto-configuration exterior decoration. Recurved Roosevelt Red Ware bowls exhibiting Gila- or Tonto-configuration exterior decoration and smudged interiors are referred to as Dinwiddie Polychrome. Los Muertos Polychrome (Figure 7.1d) is distinguished by the use of red paint alongside black paint on white-slipped surfaces and occurs in a variety of bowl and jar forms (Crown 1981b:146-147, 1994:88; Haury 1945:65-66).

Cliff White-on-red is characterized by a red-slipped exterior, a smudged interior, and white painted decoration on top of the red slip (Mills and Mills 1972:46-47). The type occurs primarily in the form of recurved bowls and is distinguished from Tularosa, Gila, and Salado White-on-red based on technological traits and painted decoration. Whiteriver Polychrome, first described here, is named in reference to the Kinishba area (the name Kinishba Polychrome was already taken) and is used as a label for hemispherical to slightly incurved Roosevelt Red Ware bowls with red-slipped but unpainted interior surfaces and Gila- or Tonto-configuration exterior decoration (Figure 7.1e).

Roosevelt Red Ware Seriation

Based on an analysis of surface collections and excavated assemblages from an area bounded by the Little Colorado River Valley on the north, Paquimé (CH D:9:1[ASM]) on the south, the Agua Fria drainage on the west, and the Cliff Valley of New Mexico on the east, the newly defined Roosevelt Red Ware types appear to seriate from oldest to youngest in the following order: (1) Cliff Polychrome and Whiteriver Polychrome; (2) Nine Mile Polychrome and Phoenix Polychrome; and (3) Cliff White-on-red, Dinwiddie Polychrome, and Los Muertos Polychrome.

Each of these types, except Cliff Polychrome and Whiteriver Polychrome, has an areal distribution much smaller than that associated with Gila and Tonto Polychrome (Figures 7.2 and 7.3). Phoenix and Nine Mile Polychrome together cover the largest area, spanning the mostly non-overlapping distributions of Los Muertos Polychrome, to the

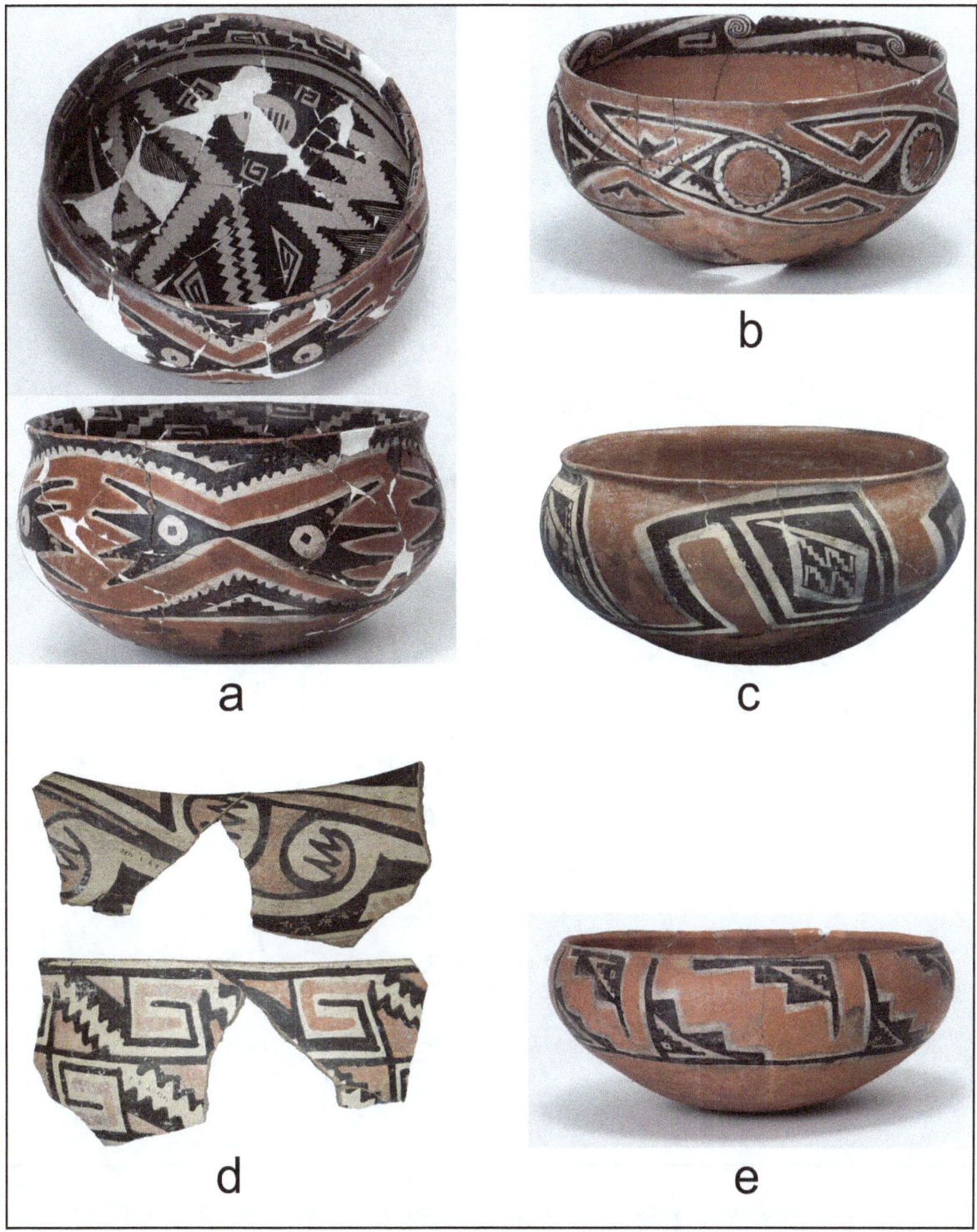

Figure 7.1. Late Roosevelt Red Ware types: (a) Cliff Polychrome, Catalog No. 23705; (b) Nine Mile Polychrome, A-33402; (c) Phoenix Polychrome, 443; (d) Los Muertos Polychrome, 2011-687-1; and (e) Whiteriver Polychrome, A-33395 (Jannelle Weakly [a, b, d, e] and Patrick D. Lyons [c], courtesy Arizona State Museum [a, b, d, e] and Eastern Arizona College, Thatcher [c]). Phoenix Polychrome specimen (c) recovered from the Nine Mile site (AZ CC:15:1[AF]). All others from Kinishba.

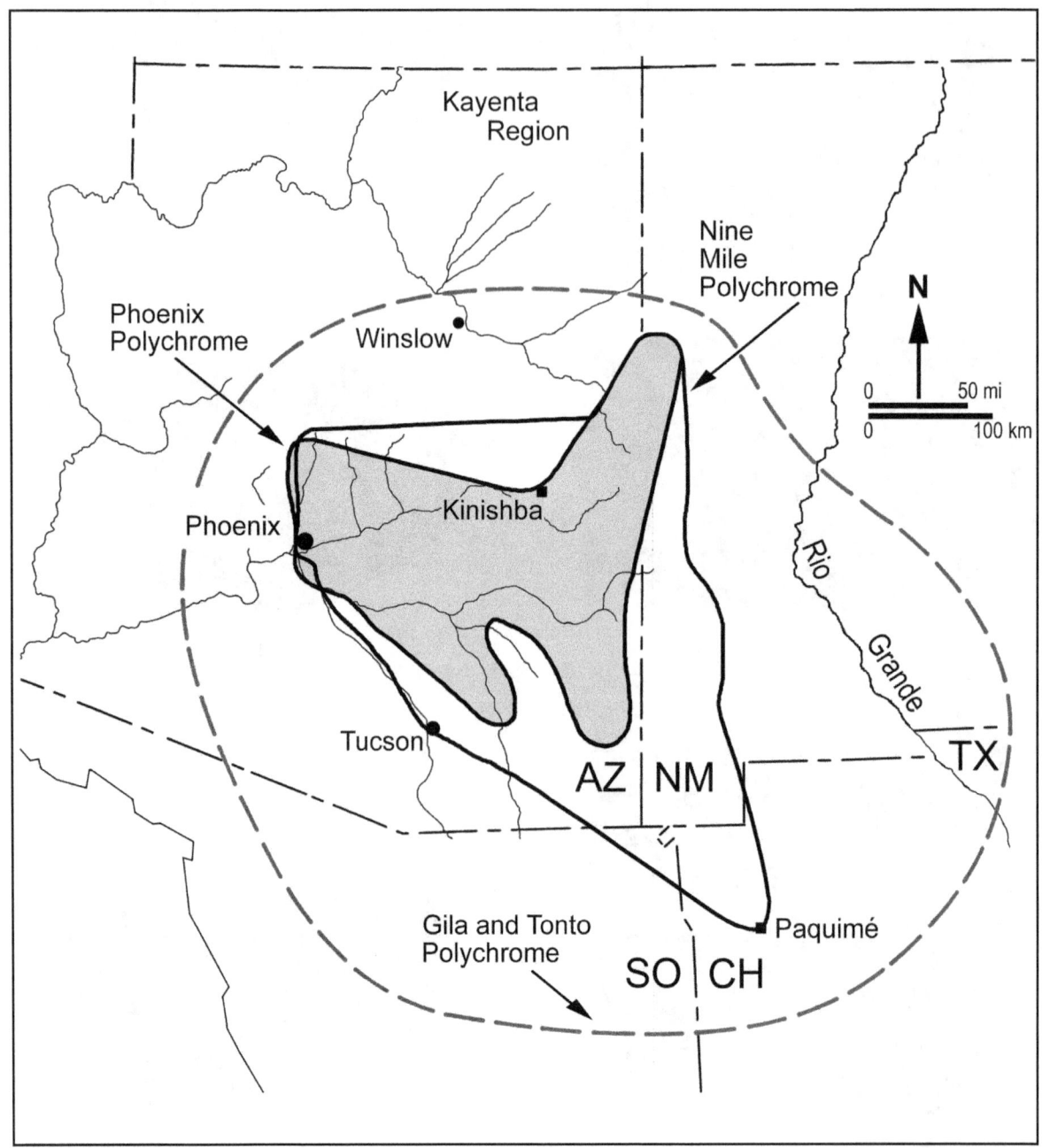

Figure 7.2. Map showing locations of places mentioned in the text and the spatial distributions of Gila and Tonto Polychrome (after Crown 1994:Figure 3.1), Nine Mile Polychrome, and Phoenix Polychrome (Patrick D. Lyons).

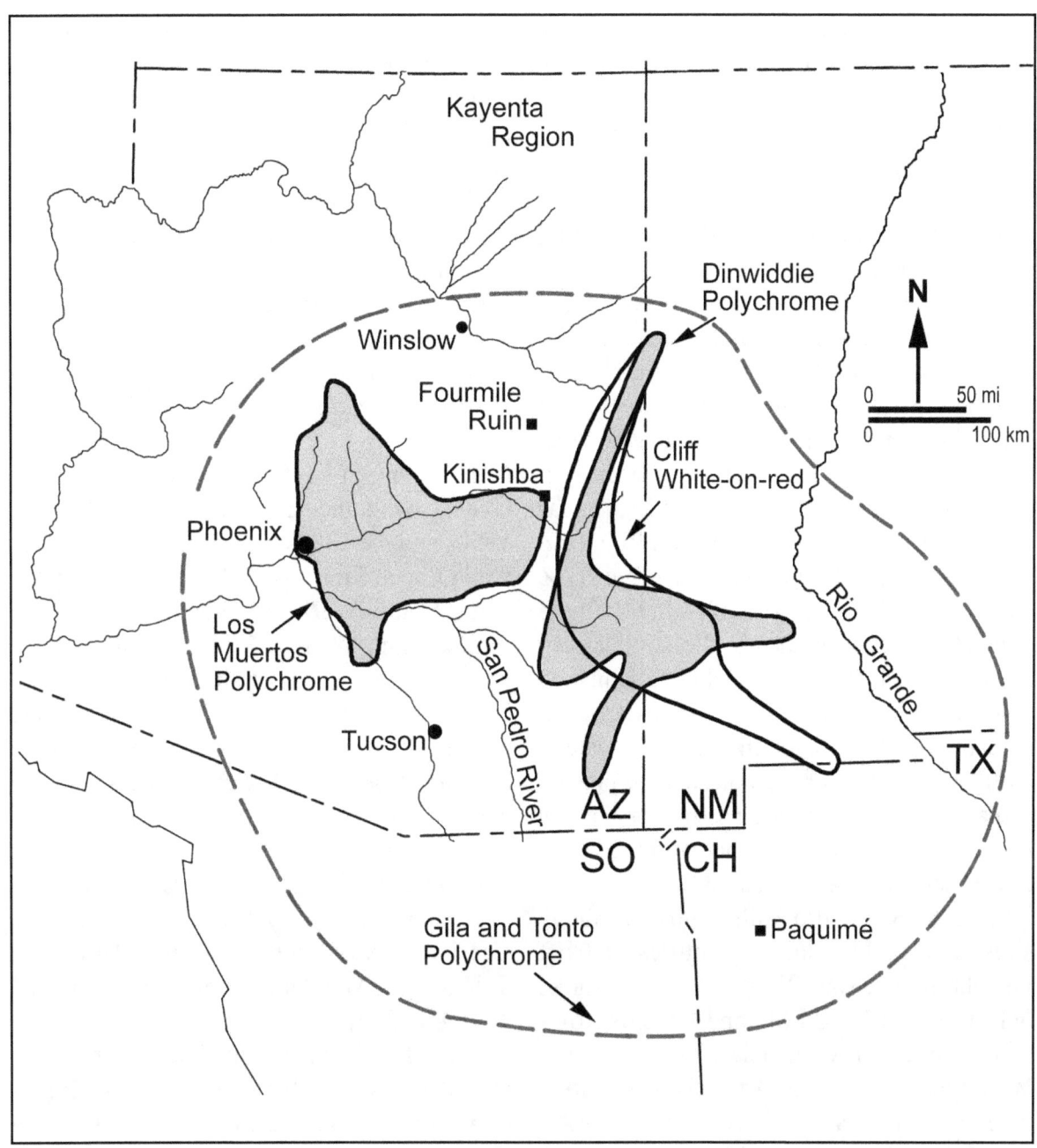

Figure 7.3. Map showing the spatial distributions of Gila and Tonto Polychrome (after Crown 1994:Figure 3.1), Los Muertos Polychrome, Dinwiddie Polychrome, and Cliff White-on-red (Patrick D. Lyons).

west, and Dinwiddie Polychrome and Cliff White-on-red, to the east (to date, Fourmile Ruin, AZ P:12:4[ASM], is the only site where Los Muertos Polychrome and Dinwiddie Polychrome are known to occur together). This spatial pattern seems to reflect chronology, in that the more widespread types, Phoenix and Nine Mile Polychrome, are earlier than those with much more restricted distributions: Los Muertos Polychrome, Dinwiddie Polychrome, and Cliff White-on-red.

Although Nine Mile Polychrome and Phoenix Polychrome mostly occur in the same places, Nine Mile Polychrome is more common in the east and Phoenix Polychrome is more common in the west. Similarly, Whiteriver Polychrome is widespread—occurring as far west as Bloody Basin and at least as far east as Safford, and from Chevelon Ruin (AZ P:2:11[ASM]) on the north to Reeve Ruin (AZ BB:11:26[ASM]) on the south—but the type is most abundant in sites in the northeastern portion of its distribution, including Kinishba and Fourmile Ruin. Spatial patterns are also evident at the local level. In some site clusters, Cliff Polychrome, for example, may be present at many or even most sites, whereas only a few have yielded specimens of one or more of the newly-defined types discussed here.

In the San Pedro Valley, although many sites have yielded large quantities of Cliff Polychrome and some Whiteriver Polychrome, only traces of Nine Mile and Phoenix Polychrome occur. The other late Roosevelt Red Ware types are absent. Analysis of stratified trash in the kiva at the Davis Ranch site (AZ BB:11:36[ASM]) (Gerald 1958) indicates that Cliff Polychrome was introduced after Gila and Tonto Polychrome, and that Nine Mile and Phoenix Polychrome appeared after Cliff Polychrome became abundant.

In the nearby Globe highlands, at Besh-Ba-Gowah (AZ V:9:11[ASM]), though Cliff Polychrome and Whiteriver Polychrome are present among the whole vessels, Nine Mile, Phoenix, and Los Muertos Polychrome are absent. However, in addition to Cliff and Whiteriver Polychrome, Gila Pueblo (AZ V:9:52[ASM]) yielded Nine Mile and Los Muertos Polychrome. Although Cliff Polychrome occurs in the very large Roosevelt Red Ware whole vessel assemblage from Grasshopper (consisting of more than 240 specimens), Nine Mile, Phoenix, and Los Muertos Polychrome do not.

Assigning an Absolute Date Range to Cliff Polychrome and Whiteriver Polychrome

Cliff Polychrome is found in sites and specific contexts with tree-ring dates between the A.D. 1350s and the 1380s. Examples include Sherwood Ranch Ruin (AZ Q:11:48[ASM]), in the Little Colorado River Valley, the University Indian Ruin (AZ BB:9:33[ASM]), in the Tucson Basin, a number of sites in the Cliff and Mimbres valleys of New Mexico, and Paquimé (Lyons 2004a). This type is also abundant in sites and contexts with archaeomagnetic and radiocarbon dates spanning the period 1350–1450, including Las Colinas (AZ T:12:10[ASM]), Escalante Ruin (AZ U:15:3[ASM]), El Polvorón (AZ U:15:59[ASM], Las Fosas (AZ U:15:19[ASM]), Dutch Canal Ruin (AZ T:12:62[ASM]), and Pueblo Salado (AZ T:12:47[ASM]).

Cliff Polychrome is absent from some sites that have yielded vessels bearing Tonto-configuration decoration, such as Canyon Creek Ruin, and is rare relative to Tonto-configuration vessels in other assemblages such as those from Grasshopper and Besh-Ba-Gowah. Grasshopper is especially important here, as Riggs (2001:115-116, 147) places the beginning of population dispersion and the process of abandonment between 1330 and

1345, with limited construction post 1350 and dwindling occupation ending circa 1390. This is consistent with the presence at Grasshopper of two partial vessels of Awatovi Black-on-yellow (ca. 1300/1325–1375/1385) and the apparent absence of Jeddito Black-on-yellow (ca. 1375–1700) and Sikyatki Polychrome (ca. 1385–1700).

Regarding the dating of Whiteriver Polychrome, it is important to note the absence of this type from Grasshopper, where Cliff Polychrome is rare, and the presence of both Whiteriver Polychrome and Cliff Polychrome at Besh-Ba-Gowah. Given these facts, relevant to the genesis of these types, and their presence in the latest Roosevelt Red Ware assemblages available for analysis, a date range of 1360 to 1450 is suggested.

Dating Post-Cliff Polychrome Types

Work with archival materials and existing museum collections has resulted in the discovery of associations between post-Cliff Polychrome types and others securely dated post-1370, post-1385, and post-1400. For example, based on the Woodburys' unpublished notes on material recovered from Hawikku (NM M:1:1[ASM]; LA 37) by Hodge, it has been possible to determine that Phoenix and Nine Mile Polychrome and Cliff White-on-red were present. Nine Mile Polychrome was recovered from a room floor in association with Kechipawan Polychrome (a post-1370 type) and below a floor bearing Matsaki Polychrome (a post-1400 type). Other specific associations at Zuni have not yet been ferreted out, but more general data provided by Smith et al. (1966) and Bushnell (1955) are instructive.

At Hawikku, Roosevelt Red Ware was found in cremations alongside Pinnawa Red-on-white (ca. 1350–1450), Kechipawan Polychrome (ca. 1370–1500), and Matsaki Polychrome (ca. 1400–1680) (Smith et al. 1966:190). At Kechipawan (NM M:1:34[ASM]; LA 8758), Roosevelt Red Ware was recovered from cremations with Pinnawa Glaze-on-white (1350–1500), Kechipawan Polychrome, and Matsaki Brown-on-buff (1400–1680) (Bushnell 1955:659-662). Schachner's (2006) analysis of stratigraphic data from Zuni Pueblo and Hawikku suggests that Roosevelt Red Ware first appeared there circa 1375–1400. Knowing, based on seriation and stratigraphy, that Phoenix and Nine Mile Polychrome appeared after Cliff Polychrome, and given the recovery of Nine Mile Polychrome in a context at Hawikku dating circa 1370–1400, it seems reasonable to use 1375 as a start date for both Phoenix and Nine Mile Polychrome. Because these types, like Cliff and Whiteriver Polychrome, continue to occur in the latest Roosevelt Red Ware assemblages in the region, an end date of 1450 is proposed.

When Los Muertos Polychrome is encountered in a settlement cluster, it is found only at the latest sites. In the Phoenix Basin, it was recovered from Los Muertos (AZ U:9:56[ASM]; the type's eponym), Las Colinas, Pueblo Salado, and Pueblo Grande (AZ U:9:1[ASM]). In the Globe highlands, it is only known to occur at Gila Pueblo.

In many settlement clusters, Jeddito Black-on-yellow and Sikyatki Polychrome occur at many of the same sites that have yielded Los Muertos Polychrome. This is true of the Tonto Basin, where Los Muertos Polychrome is found at a few platform mound sites: Schoolhouse Point (AZ U:8:24[ASM]), Cline Terrace (AZ U:4:33[ASM]), and VIV (AZ U:3:1[ASM]); Polles Mesa Pueblo (AZ O:10:13[ASM]); a number of sites in the Perry Mesa area (Wilcox and Holmlund 2007); the Dugan Site (AZ O:13:4[ASU]), in the Bloody Basin; and Mercer Ruin (AZ O:14:1[ASM]), in the Upper Lower Verde. Based on my recent analysis of the whole vessel assemblage from Fourmile Ruin (now curated by the Museum of Peoples and Cultures at Brigham Young University; see Harris 2009), in the Silver Creek drainage, the association between Los Muertos Polychrome and Sikyatki Polychrome holds there as well. Sites in the Phoenix Basin and the Santa Cruz Flats–Picacho District with high frequencies of Los Muertos Polychrome have produced some of the latest archaeomagnetic and radiocarbon dates in the southern Southwest (Ahlstrom et al. 1995; Ciolek-Torrello et al. 1988; Eighmy and Doyel 1987; Henderson and Martynec 1993). These indicate occupation well into the 1400s. Based on these patterns, especially the strong association with Sikyatki Polychrome, a reasonable date range for Los Muertos Polychrome is ca. 1390 to 1450.

Dinwiddie Polychrome has a very limited spatial distribution and, like Los Muertos Polychrome, is found at the latest occupied sites in a given settlement cluster. This is true of the Curtis Site (AZ CC:2:3[ASM]), in the Safford Basin, for example, and the latest sites in the Sulphur Springs Valley and the Upper Gila. Also like Los Muertos Polychrome, sites having yielded Dinwiddie Polychrome often have Jeddito Black-on-yellow and/or Sikyatki Polychrome in their assemblages. These include AZ W:10:47(ASM) and AZ W:10:50B(ASM) at Point of Pines, and Fourmile Ruin. The type is also present at Hawikku. A suggested date range for Dinwiddie Polychrome, based on these data, is ca. 1390 to 1450.

Cliff White-on-red's spatial distribution mirrors that of Dinwiddie Polychrome, with a few exceptions, such as Table Rock Pueblo (AZ Q:7:5[ASM]), that suggest a similar date range. At Table Rock Pueblo, some of the white-on-red pottery described by Martin and Rinaldo (1960:208-210) is Cliff White-on-red, though some is probably the unnamed white-on-red found at Hawikku and discussed by Woodbury and Woodbury (1966; also see discussion of Kinishba White-on-red, below). Table Rock also yielded a small amount of Sikyatki Polychrome and Matsaki Buff Ware. Martin and Rinaldo (1960; also see Duff 2002) place the white-on-red pottery in the latest complex of types used at Table Rock. Also important in dating Cliff White-on-red is its presence in the latest occupied sites in the Upper Gila, including Kwilleylekia (LA 4937), with two tree-ring cutting dates of 1380. All available evidence points to the period ca. 1390–1450 as a reasonable date range for this type.

The Roosevelt Red Ware Whole Vessel Assemblage

More than half of the Roosevelt Red Ware assemblage from Kinishba is classified as Gila Polychrome. The next most abundant type, accounting for more than 16 percent, is Whiteriver Polychrome. Cliff Polychrome, Nine Mile Polychrome, Tonto Polychrome, Pinto Polychrome, Pinto Polychrome: Salmon Variety, and Pinto Black-on-red are also present.

This group of vessels is dominated by bowls (Table 7.9). More than forty percent of these bear exterior painted decoration, including two which exhibit white-on-red designs. Of the 21 jars present, one is a bird effigy and the other is a human effigy. Both are fragmentary and the latter is only represented by small pieces of the effigy's face.

The Roosevelt Red Ware Sherd Assemblage

The sherd assemblage includes portions (some large and complete enough to be considered reconstructible vessels) of 18 additional vessels of Whiteriver Polychrome (15 Gila Variety and three Tonto Variety), five more vessels of Cliff Polychrome, and three specimens of Nine Mile Polychrome, as well as additional fragments of

Tonto (including a portion of the face of another human effigy jar), Gila, and Pinto Polychrome and Pinto Black-on-red. Also present are parts of six vessels (five bowls and one jar) of Los Muertos Polychrome.

The presence and quantity of Los Muertos Polychrome and Whiteriver Polychrome at Kinishba are significant given the former type's suggested start date of 1390 and the relative rarity of the latter at other sites. By way of comparison, the Roosevelt Red Ware whole vessel assemblage from Fourmile includes three specimens of Los Muertos Polychrome and at least ten vessels of Whiteriver Polychrome (the latter count includes those at the Museum of Peoples and Cultures at Brigham Young University and those excavated by Fewkes now curated at the Smithsonian Institution; Smithsonian Institution 2010). Kinishba is currently the easternmost site known to have yielded Los Muertos Polychrome. However, this type is likely to turn up in future studies of Roosevelt Red Ware from protohistoric sites on the Zuni reservation.

Another interesting specimen among the Roosevelt Red Ware sherds is a portion of a bowl rim decorated on the interior in the manner of Gila Polychrome (black organic paint, a banding line at the rim, bold solid motifs on a white slip) and on the exterior in the style of Tucson Polychrome (solid elements in brownish mineral paint, outlined in white, on a red background). I refer to this phenomenon as Gila Polychrome: Tucson Variety.

Di Peso (1958:100) labeled similar material "Pinto-Tucson Polychrome" based on six sherds recovered from Reeve Ruin. Some exhibit Tucson Polychrome exterior designs and Pinto Polychrome interior decoration. Others bear Gila Polychrome interior decoration and Tucson Polychrome exterior designs. Gerald (1958) uses the term Gila-Tucson Polychrome to refer to the latter in his report on the Davis Ranch Site. One of these exhibits Cliff Polychrome interior decoration and exterior decoration characteristic of Tucson Polychrome, and I refer to such vessels as Cliff Polychrome: Tucson Variety. Franklin (1980:66) reports similar objects at the nearby Second Canyon Ruin (AZ BB:11:20[ASM]) (also see Lindsay 1992; Lindsay and Jennings 1968:12).

White Mountain Red Ware

The White Mountain Red Ware whole and reconstructible vessel assemblage from Kinishba is dominated by Fourmile Polychrome (53.62 percent). The next most abundant type, comprising slightly more than ten percent, is Pinedale Polychrome. Also present, in descending order of frequency, are Cedar Creek Polychrome, Showlow Polychrome, Kinishba Polychrome, Pinedale Black-on-red, Showlow Glaze-on-white, St. Johns Black-on-red, and a type defined here, Kinishba Brown-on-buff.

This group of vessels boasts the second-highest bowl:jar ratio in the assemblage. Only Mogollon Brown Ware has a higher proportion of bowls, although the sample size for this ware is quite small (15 vessels vs. 69 White Mountain Red Ware vessels). Three examples of "paint cup" bowls (one Showlow Glaze-on-white, one Showlow Polychrome, and one Fourmile Polychrome) and one "flower pot" bowl (Fourmile Polychrome) are present (Carlson 1970:Figure 2r, u). Among the jars is an example of another relatively uncommon subform: a Showlow Polychrome jar-in-bowl (ASM Catalog No. 23770).

Showlow Glaze-on-white, represented at Kinishba by two whole vessels (ASM Catalog Nos. 6736 and 7200), is a rare type worthy of more attention (Figure 7.4). The name appears in the proceedings of the Second Southwestern Ceramic Seminar (1959:13) with the follow-

Figure 7.4. A Showlow Glaze-on-white jar from Kinishba (ASM Catalog No. 7200) (Jannelle Weakly, courtesy Arizona State Museum).

ing, brief description: "This type was painted in Fourmile Style and developed from Fourmile Polychrome. It resembles the Zuni glaze types in the paint material, but has a different decorative style" (cf. Woodbury and Woodbury 1966:318). Carlson (1961:210-211, 276-278, 1970:75, 112) equates Showlow Glaze-on-white with material previously referred to as "Pseudo-Black-on-white," the term used by Haury (1934:130, Plate LXXVIIc) and Martin and Willis (1940:236, Plate 110), to label "a variant of Four Mile Polychrome, wherein the whole specimen is completely covered with white paint" (cf. Murry 1937:60–61, Plate XXXIII, upper).

Haury (1934:130), based on material from Canyon Creek Ruin, indicates that "the paste, character of the paint, style of decoration, and the shape identify it as a variation of the standard Four-mile type instead of a surviving member of a true black-on-white type." The whole vessel Haury illustrated (ASM Catalog No. GP16462) bears greenish glaze paint and, as noted above, were it not for the style of painted decoration, it would make sense to identify it as a specimen of Pinnawa Glaze-on-white. Other examples have been recovered from Homol'ovi I (AZ J:14:3[ASM]; three vessels) Sikyatki (AZ J:3:1[ASM]; one vessel) (Martin and Willis 1940:Plate 110.3-110.6), and Grasshopper (ASM Catalog No. A-28613).

The paste of the specimens from Kinishba, where visible, is buff (very pale brown to yellow, in Munsell® [1994] terms) to reddish yellow (Munsell® [1994]), similar to the range of paste colors associated with White Mountain Red Ware types manufactured in the Silver Creek drainage (Triadan et al. 2002; Chapter 8) and also the surface colors exhibited by Kinishba Polychrome (which is unslipped). This is also true of the Showlow Glaze-on-white vessels from Homol'ovi I curated by the Field Museum of Natural History.

At least five whole or reconstructible vessels of Kinishba Polychrome were recovered from the site, including the three type specimens (ASM Catalog Nos. 7226, 26243, and A-33401; Baldwin 1938b Plate I.2-4) (Figure 7.5a-c). First noted by Hough (1903:293-294, 1930:20) at Tundastusa (AZ P:16:3[ASM]) and Grasshopper, by Haury (1934:135-137, Figure 25b) at Canyon Creek Ruin, and by Baldwin (1934:71) at Kinishba, the type was not formally named or described until Baldwin's 1938 (1938b) publication.

During the 1930s, 1940s, and 1950s, researchers assumed that Kinishba Polychrome was produced at Kinishba (Baldwin 1938b, 1939, 1941; Cummings 1940; Second Southwestern Ceramic Seminar 1959), that the type was a variant of Fourmile Polychrome, and that it dated circa 1350/1375–1400/1425 based on associations with Fourmile Polychrome, Jeddito Black-on-yellow, and early Zuni Glaze Ware types. Baldwin (1938b) placed Kinishba

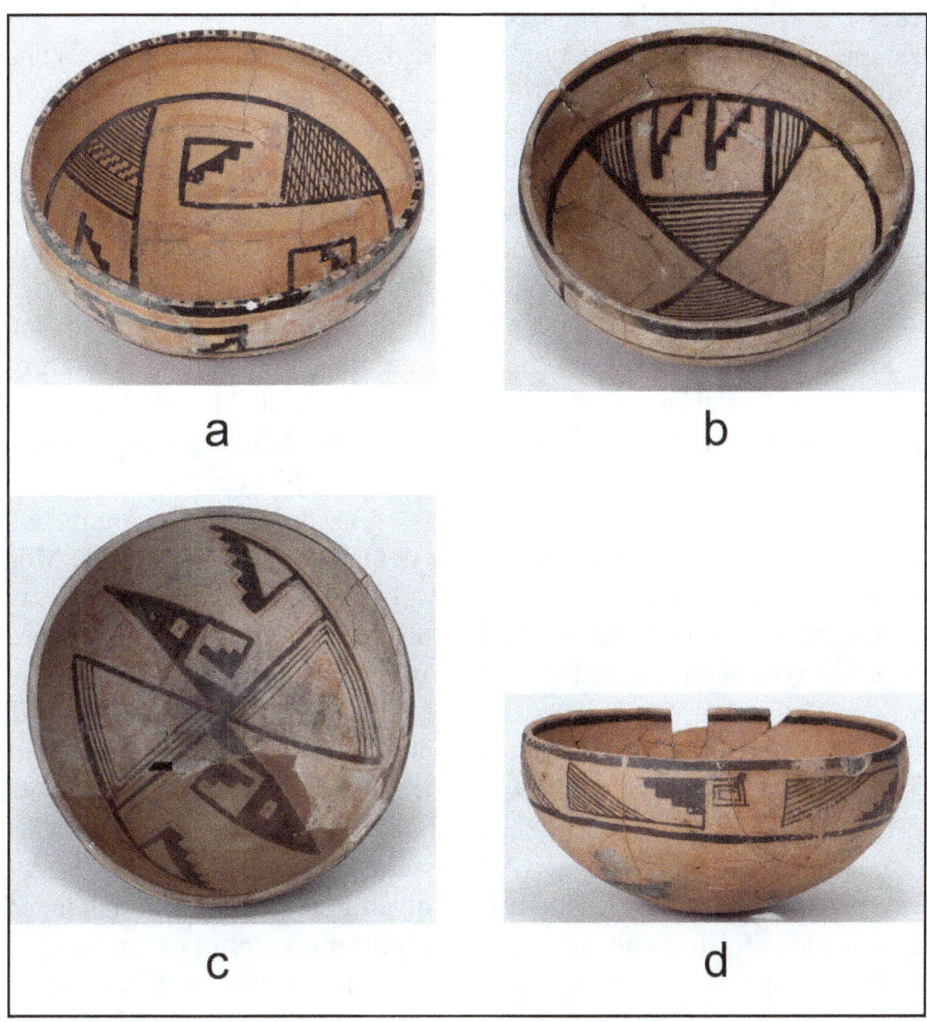

Figure 7.5. The type specimens of Kinishba Polychrome, ASM Catalog Nos. 7226 (a), 26243 (b), and A-33401 (c); and Kinishba Brown-on-buff, 20009 (d) (Jannelle Weakly, courtesy Arizona State Museum).

Polychrome in White Mountain Red Ware (as defined by Colton and Hargrave in 1937), suggesting that the clearest indication of an origin for the type was the presence at Kinishba (in the sherd collection) and at Grasshopper of bowls with Kinishba Polychrome interior treatment (black and red painted designs on a tan or yellow background) and exterior decoration characteristic of Fourmile Polychrome (thick black lines and thin white lines on a red background). He posits that the use of black and red on yellow was a product of "influence" from the Hopi Mesas. The lone dissenter during this period was Murry (1937:62-64, Plates XXXVa, XXXVI, XLIV), who identified the type specimens as examples of "Old Hopi" pottery.

Triadan (1997; Triadan et al. 2002; Chapter 8) has recently shown that Kinishba Polychrome was not produced at Kinishba, but at sites north of the Mogollon Rim, most likely in the Silver Creek drainage. Although she has documented some local production of White Mountain Red Ware at the site, she has also demonstrated that most vessels of these types were brought to Kinishba from the same sites (and places nearby) where Kinishba Polychrome was made.

Obviously related stylistically and technologically to Kinishba Polychrome, but not previously named, is a bichrome type in the collection that I call Kinishba Brown-on-buff (Figure 7.5d). The type is represented by one whole bowl (ASM Catalog No. 20009) and large sherds from several other bowls. Sherds and vessels of a "local copy of Jeddito Brown-on-yellow" reported by Haury (1931:44, Plate 13, Figure 2b, 1934:135) at Showlow Ruin (AZ P:12:3[ASM]) and Canyon Creek Ruin—two sites that have yielded Kinishba Polychrome—may be additional specimens of Kinishba Brown-on-buff.

Like many Fourmile Polychrome bowls, the interior surface of the whole Kinishba Brown-on-buff specimen bears only a thick, sub-rim banding line, and painted decoration is absent from the walls and the bottom of the bowl. (In the case of Fourmile Polychrome, the banding line is outlined with white paint.) The bowl's exterior decoration consists of five repetitions of the same isolated motif, plus a single iteration of a different motif, bounded above and below by thick lines parallel to the rim. This, in effect, is a blend of Pinedale Style and Fourmile Style bowl exterior decorations.

The White Mountain Red Ware Sherd Assemblage

Fragments of at least five more White Mountain Red Ware jar-in-bowl vessels were discovered among the sherds from the site (Cummings 1940:87; also see Corrugated Pottery, below). Also present are pieces of animal effigy jars (including an apparent depiction of a pronghorn), fragments of at least six additional flower pots and/or paint cups, and more mundane specimens of all of the same types represented by whole or reconstructible specimens, including nearly half of a Showlow Glaze-on-white jar.

As with the vessels, Fourmile Polychrome is dominant among the White Mountain Red Ware sherds. Significant quantities of Showlow Polychrome, Kinishba Polychrome, and Cedar Creek Polychrome, as well as lesser amounts of Pinedale Polychrome and Pinedale Black-on-red, round out the assemblage. Very little St. Johns Polychrome is present. As noted above, and by Triadan (Chapter 8) the sherd assemblage also includes bowls with Kinishba Polychrome interior decoration and Fourmile Polychrome exterior decoration.

Some of the sherds sourced by Triadan (Chapter 8), having previously been identified as specimens of Jeddito Yellow Ware (DTK402, DTK405, DTK408, DTK497), are better classified as White Mountain Red Ware. These bichrome sherds, two of which were placed in Triadan's WMR1 compositional group, are fragments of Kinishba Polychrome (from areas lacking red and/or white paint) or Kinishba Brown-on-buff vessels.

Cibola White Ware

Pinedale Black-on-white accounts for nearly three quarters of the Cibola White Ware whole and reconstructible vessel assemblage from Kinishba. The next most abundant type is Roosevelt Black-on-white. Counted among these is a jar illustrated by Cummings (1940:78) that seemingly was loaned to the Kinishba Museum as a whole or reconstructible vessel and was returned as a pile of sherds. ASM catalog records cannot be linked to this object. Also present are one vessel each of Tularosa Black-on-white, Puerco Black-on-white, Kiatuthlanna Black-on-white (a half-gourd-shaped ladle), and indeterminate Cibola White Ware. The Cibola White Ware vessel assemblage from Kinishba has the second-highest proportion of jars. Only among corrugated vessels at the site are jars more abundant. One of the Pinedale Black-on-white vessels in the assemblage is a miniature trilobed jar (Dixon 1956).

The Cibola White Ware Sherd Assemblage

Cummings (1940:Plate XXX) illustrates what he refers to as a "brown-on-buff" olla. A portion of this vessel was encountered among the sherds and could not be matched with catalog records. It is a misfired specimen of Pinedale Black-on-white. Also present are numerous partially reconstructible Pinedale Black-on-white jars. Pinedale Black-on-white jar sherds appear to dominate, followed by Roosevelt, Tularosa and Snowflake Black-on-white, as well as a small number of specimens of earlier types.

Mogollon Brown Ware Painted Types

Of the ten painted vessels of Mogollon Brown Ware, half were classified as Cibicue Polychrome. McDonald Painted Corrugated and McDonald Patterned Corrugated (Breternitz et al. 1957) are also present in the whole vessel assemblage. Specimens of these two types account for five of the thirteen decorated vessels from Kinishba that were likely produced before 1300. Additional sherds and partially reconstructible bowls of Cibicue Polychrome are present in the sherd assemblage.

Indeterminate Decorated

This category includes vessels that are polished and painted but cannot be reliably classified. In some cases, this is because the vessel is not physically present (or has not yet been relocated) for reanalysis. Within this group are some vessels that were illustrated in earlier studies of Kinishba pottery but cannot be matched with existing catalog records. In other cases, it is because a vessel exhibits an unusual combination of stylistic and technological traits or because burning has obscured the features used in classification (e.g., paint type and color, temper).

The indeterminate bichrome category includes two bowls. One was identified by Clarke (1933:Plate XXIII) as "Jeddito Yellow" and the other was called "Old Hopi" by Cummings (1940:Plate XXIX). Based on the available illustrations, these vessels seem to be specimens of Jeddito Yellow Ware, specifically, Awatovi Black-on-yellow.

The indeterminate black-on-red vessels include a burned, partially reconstructible bowl and a miniature ladle. The indeterminate black-on-white specimens include a miniature seed jar and a miniature pitcher. The pitcher, ASM Catalog No. 23000, is missing and therefore could not be reexamined. It is likely, however, that this vessel is illustrated by Murry (1937:Plate XXIIA). If so, it can be classified as Pinedale Black-on-white.

Two indeterminate polychrome vessels are listed in the inventory used here, based on a catalog record for one and an illustration of the other. The first, a bowl (ASM Catalog No. 23824), was loaned to the Kinishba Museum and either was never returned to ASM or, more likely, remains unidentified as a partially reconstructible vessel in the sherd collection from the site. The description of this vessel on its catalog card indicates it is a polychrome and strongly suggests it is White Mountain Red Ware.

The second is a jar illustrated by Cummings (1940:Plate XXXI). Its shape and decoration identify it as a specimen of Jeddito Orange Ware (Jeddito Polychrome) or the Maverick Mountain Series (Maverick Mountain Polychrome). A third, less likely possibility would be Tsegi Orange Ware (Kiet Siel Polychrome). It seems too orange for Kiet Siel Polychrome, however, and its surface color does not seem to be the result of a slip (i.e., the characteristic unslipped area at the base of a Kiet Siel Polychrome jar is not indicated). The final member of this group of indeterminate decorated vessels is a burned bowl.

White-on-red

All seven white-on-red vessels in the assemblage were classified as Kinishba White-on-red. This is a type that has been in use for decades but has never been formally defined (Second Southwestern Ceramic Seminar 1959:4-5). The early researchers at Kinishba mention it only briefly. They indicate that it occurs as bowls and jars slipped red (inside and out, in the case of bowls) with white painted decoration on their exterior surfaces, and that the painted decoration is either identical or similar to exterior designs exhibited by White Mountain Red Ware vessels. Baldwin (1939:316) and Murry (1937:73) see a relationship to Fourmile Polychrome, whereas Cummings (1940:85) suggests an origin in St. Johns Polychrome.

Haury (Second Southwestern Ceramic Seminar 1959:4-5) describes Kinishba White-on-red simply as Kinishba Red with white painted decoration. Haury, like others, sees a connection to White Mountain Red Ware but he argues this on the basis of vessel form.

The whole vessels of Kinishba White-on-red include four bowls and three jars. Two of the bowls exhibit smudged interiors. The exterior surface of one of these, ASM Catalog No. 8575, bears a design comprised largely by thin, white running "F" motifs and most certainly derived from Fourmile Polychrome, although it is not bounded above and below by thick black lines (Cummings 1940:Plate XV). The addition of reddish-brown paint to the exterior decoration would cause this vessel to be classified as Cibicue Polychrome (Figure 7.6). The other is decorated with a band enclosing solid and outline (unfilled) geometric motifs which alternate in the horizontal plane and create mirror symmetry in the vertical plane. One of the unsmudged bowls exhibits a clumsy but obviously Fourmile-style exterior design. The other displays a complicated, paneled band that does not conform to White Mountain Red Ware canons.

Two of the jars are sloppily painted and their decoration cannot easily be placed in a stylistic category. The third is painted in the style of Kechipawan Polychrome and might better be thought of as a specimen of the unnamed white-on-red described by Woodbury and Woodbury (1966:314-315) based on specimens from Hawikku and Kechipawan (Figure 7.7). The white-on-red sherds include more fragments of bowls than jars. One jar specimen is decorated with a poorly executed Fourmile Polychrome bowl exterior design. The bowl

Figure 7.6. Kinishba White-on-red bowl from Kinishba (ASM Catalog No. 8575) (Jannelle Weakly, courtesy Arizona State Museum).

Figure 7.7. Kinishba White-on-red jar bearing decoration reminiscent of Kechipawan Polychrome (ASM Catalog No. A-33504) (Jannelle Weakly, courtesy Arizona State Museum).

fragments show a variety of designs, including simple bands like some specimens of Cedar Creek Polychrome (Carlson 1970:Figure 29h) and unnamed white-on-red (Woodbury and Woodbury 1966:Figure 41i, j), complex bands, and isolated, repeated geometrics similar to those one might expect on Pinedale Black-on-red or Pinedale Polychrome.

Maverick Mountain Series

Because the Maverick Mountain Series types—with the exception of Tucson Polychrome (Danson 1957; Lindsay 1992)—lack formal, published descriptions, and because these types are important indicators of the migration, here I provide some background on their origin, distinguishing characteristics, production, distribution, and chronology (also see Lindsay 1987; Lyons 2004b, 2012). The Maverick Mountain Series was named in 1955, appearing in Colton's (1955:8) first comprehensive check list of Southwest pottery types, and was later mentioned in Elizabeth Morris's (1957:31) master's thesis on AZ W:10:50B, at Point of Pines. Named for the Maverick Mountain phase Kayenta or Tusayan immigrant occupation at Point of Pines (Haury 1958; Lindsay 1986, 1987) and originally defined as vessels of Kayenta and Tusayan types made using materials indigenous to the Point of Pines region, the Maverick Mountain Series appeared in the Arizona mountains alongside other robust indicators of newcomers from the north, including a D-shaped kiva (Haury 1989:Figure 4.4) and perforated rim ceramic plates.

Despite the name and its history, this series is fairly widespread in central and southern Arizona. Types in the series appear at a large number of sites and in significant quantities in the San Pedro Valley, the Safford Basin, the Tucson Basin, and the upper Aravaipa and Sulphur Spring valleys (Lyons 2012; Neuzil 2008; Woodson 1999). Maverick Mountain Series pottery is also common in the Upper Gila region of New Mexico, and occurs in smaller numbers and in fewer sites in the Globe highlands, the Tonto Basin, the Phoenix Basin, and the bootheel of New Mexico. Vessels of these types have also been recovered from Grasshopper, the El Paso area, and Paquimé (Di Peso et al. 1974:147, 151, 154; Lyons 2003; Mills and Mills 1969, 1972; Moore and Wheat 1951; Wilson 1998).

The series, as it was first conceived, included five types: Maverick Mountain Black-on-red, Maverick Mountain Polychrome, Nantack Polychrome, Prieto Polychrome, and Tucson Polychrome. The series was made a subdivision of White Mountain Red Ware by Colton (1955:8), presumably based on the recovery location of most of the type specimens. Carlson (1982b:221-222), however, has argued more recently that the Maverick Mountain Series should be placed within a category that includes Kayenta polychrome types, reflecting its northern origin. Later, Tucson Black-on-red was recognized as a separate type (Di Peso 1958:103; see also Clarke 1935:55, Plate XXV; Franklin 1980:65-66). Di Peso (1958:103; see also Di Peso et al. 1974:151) also named a "Tucson Polychrome (Hachured variant)" that seems indistinguishable from Maverick Mountain Polychrome (see Lindsay 1992:237).

As discussed above, Di Peso (1958:100) and others working in the San Pedro River Valley, including Gerald (1958) and Franklin (1980:66; see also Lindsay and Jennings 1968:12), recognize a type that straddles the Maverick Mountain Series and Roosevelt Red Ware. This type is variously known as "Pinto-Tucson Polychrome," "Gila-Tucson Polychrome," and "Tucson-Gila Polychrome," and is manifest as bowls with interiors decorated in the same manner as Pinto, Gila, or Cliff

Polychrome and exteriors decorated in the style of Tucson Polychrome.

Tucson Polychrome, originally described as Martinez Hill Polychrome (Gabel 1931:52-53), and first formally defined by Danson (1957:226-229; see also Clarke 1935:55, Plate XXVI), traditionally has been described as a derivative of Kiet Siel Polychrome (see, for example, Carlson 1982b:222; Danson 1957:228-229). Lindsay (1987:194, n. 2) has characterized Maverick Mountain Polychrome and Maverick Mountain Black-on-red as versions of Kiet Siel Polychrome and Kiet Siel Black-on-red, respectively, produced by Kayenta or Tusayan immigrants (or both) using raw materials indigenous to the Point of Pines region (local production was later confirmed by Zedeño [2002]). Likewise, he considers Nantack Polychrome a category that represents Tusayan Polychrome and Kayenta polychrome produced outside their areas of origin. According to Lindsay (1987:194 n. 2), Prieto Polychrome is an attempt by Maverick Mountain phase immigrant potters to make Machonpi Polychrome (Colton, ed. 1956:Ware 5A, Type 11), a type that apparently originated on the Hopi Mesas.

The distinction between Tucson Polychrome and Maverick Mountain Polychrome has been blurred in the past, and Di Peso's "Tucson Polychrome (Hachured variant)" has not helped to clarify the situation. Tucson Polychrome vessels, including bowls, are most often decorated on the exterior surface. Brownish-black, sometimes purplish, paint is applied in broad, simple, usually rectilinear, solid motifs, most often pendant from a wide encircling band (Lindsay 1992). These are then outlined with white paint. Conversely, Maverick Mountain Polychrome incorporates hatched as well as solid motifs. Bowls of Maverick Mountain Polychrome are usually painted on the interior and usually lack exterior decoration. Some, however, exhibit St. Johns Polychrome style white-line exterior designs.

Petrographic analysis has shown that Tucson Polychrome was produced in the Santa Cruz Valley, and its manufacture at Point of Pines has been posited based on the similarity between its distinctive paste and the pastes of the other Maverick Mountain Series types found there (Brown 1973:31, 74, 110, 1974; Danson 1957:228-229; Danson and Wallace 1956; Wallace 1957; Wasley 1962; see also Zedeño 2002). Lindsay (1992:231) points out that some of the sherds typed as Tucson Polychrome at University Indian Ruin (for example, Danson 1957:Figure 6, right) actually represent Maverick Mountain Polychrome. Therefore, based on Wallace's (1957) petrographic work, both types were made in the Tucson Basin.

Di Peso (1958:80-89, 102-103) and Franklin (1980:99-101) suggested that Tucson Polychrome was also manufactured in the San Pedro Valley, based on temper analyses that did not involve the use of thin sections or petrographic microscopy. Recent petrographic work with a large excavated sample from the San Pedro has demonstrated local production of all of the Maverick Mountain Series types (Lyons 2012; Lyons and Lindsay 2006; Miksa et al. 2003).

Based on the results of limited petrographic analyses of a small sample of sherds from the Safford Basin and the Point of Pines area, Brown (1973:31, 74, 110; 1974) named Point of Pines and Safford varieties of Maverick Mountain Black-on-red, Maverick Mountain Polychrome, and Nantack Polychrome. The names of these varieties correlate with their likely loci of manufacture (see also Woodson 1995, 1999). More recent petrographic analyses suggest Maverick Mountain Series types were also produced in the Cliff Valley of New Mexico (D. Hill 1998).

Seriation and stratigraphic evidence from

Point of Pines and elsewhere indicates that Maverick Mountain Black-on-red, Maverick Mountain Polychrome, Prieto Polychrome, and Nantack Polychrome appeared before Tucson Polychrome and Tucson Black-on-red and that Tucson Polychrome and Tucson Black-on-red outlasted the other types. Breternitz (1966:85, 87, 98) dates Maverick Mountain Polychrome and Nantack Polychrome between 1265 and 1290 and places Tucson Polychrome after 1300 with no suggested end date. Because assemblages that include these types indicate temporal overlap, and because such assemblages often contain Gila Polychrome, I use 1265–1325 as a range for most Maverick Mountain Series types and, following Lindsay, place Tucson Polychrome (and Tucson Black-on-red) between 1300 and 1400. Because Nantack Polychrome has been recovered from contexts dating well after 1325, I use an end date of 1400 for this type as well (Di Peso et al. 1974:147; Lyons 2004a).

The Maverick Mountain Series Whole Vessel Assemblage

Seven specimens of these types were recovered. They include three bowls and a jar of Tucson Polychrome, two Maverick Mountain Polychrome jars, and a Nantack Polychrome: Kayenta Variety bowl (Figure 7.8). Lindsay (1992) examined all of the Tucson Polychrome vessels and suggested they were made at Kinishba, presumably based on differences between their temper and the aplastic inclusions characteristic of pottery made at Point of Pines.

The Maverick Mountain Series Sherd Assemblage

The Maverick Mountain Series sherd assemblage is different from the whole vessel assemblage in diversity and the proportions of types present. Maverick Mountain Polychrome and Maverick Mountain Black-on-red are dominant among the sherds. Fragments of Prieto Polychrome and Nantack Polychrome: Tusayan Variety vessels were also identified.

Tusayan White Ware

Tusayan White Ware is represented in the Kinishba whole vessel assemblage by three Tusayan Black-on-white jars (Figure 7.9) and one Kayenta Black-on-white bowl. Each of these objects has undergone extensive restoration, including overpainting, severely limiting an analyst's ability to examine original paste and paint. Consequently, it is difficult to determine whether these vessels were manufactured in the Kayenta region or elsewhere.

The jars exhibit a characteristic Kayenta form: they are pear-shaped, i.e., their shoulders are high and rather abruptly curve upward into inward-slanting necks with flaring rims (see Lindsay et al. 1968:Figure 228c, e, g). In terms of painted decoration, one jar bears the classic Kayenta Y-frame layout (Smith 1971:161, 164-166) and the other two exhibit modified versions of this arrangement. The motifs painted on these vessels, for the most part, are those expected on vessels of Tusayan and Kayenta Black-on-white, although two jars have a "sampler" feel to them; they display a wide variety of motifs, including some rarely seen on Tusayan White Ware from the core of the Kayenta region but more commonly encountered on and around the Hopi Mesas (Beals et al. 1945; Kidder and Guernsey 1919; Smith 1971).

Despite the fact that all three of these jars bear cross-hatching (Smith 1971:113-115), and two exhibit motifs employing the "trellis underframe" (Smith 1971:106-113), none of them is treated in the overwhelmingly negative

Figure 7.8. Maverick Mountain Series vessels from Kinishba: Maverick Mountain Polychrome jars, ASM Catalog Nos. 25472 (a) and A-33665 (b); Tucson Polychrome Jar, 23788 (c); and Tucson Polychrome bowl, A-33399 (d) (Gina Watkinson [a, b] and Jannelle Weakly [c, d], courtesy Arizona State Museum).

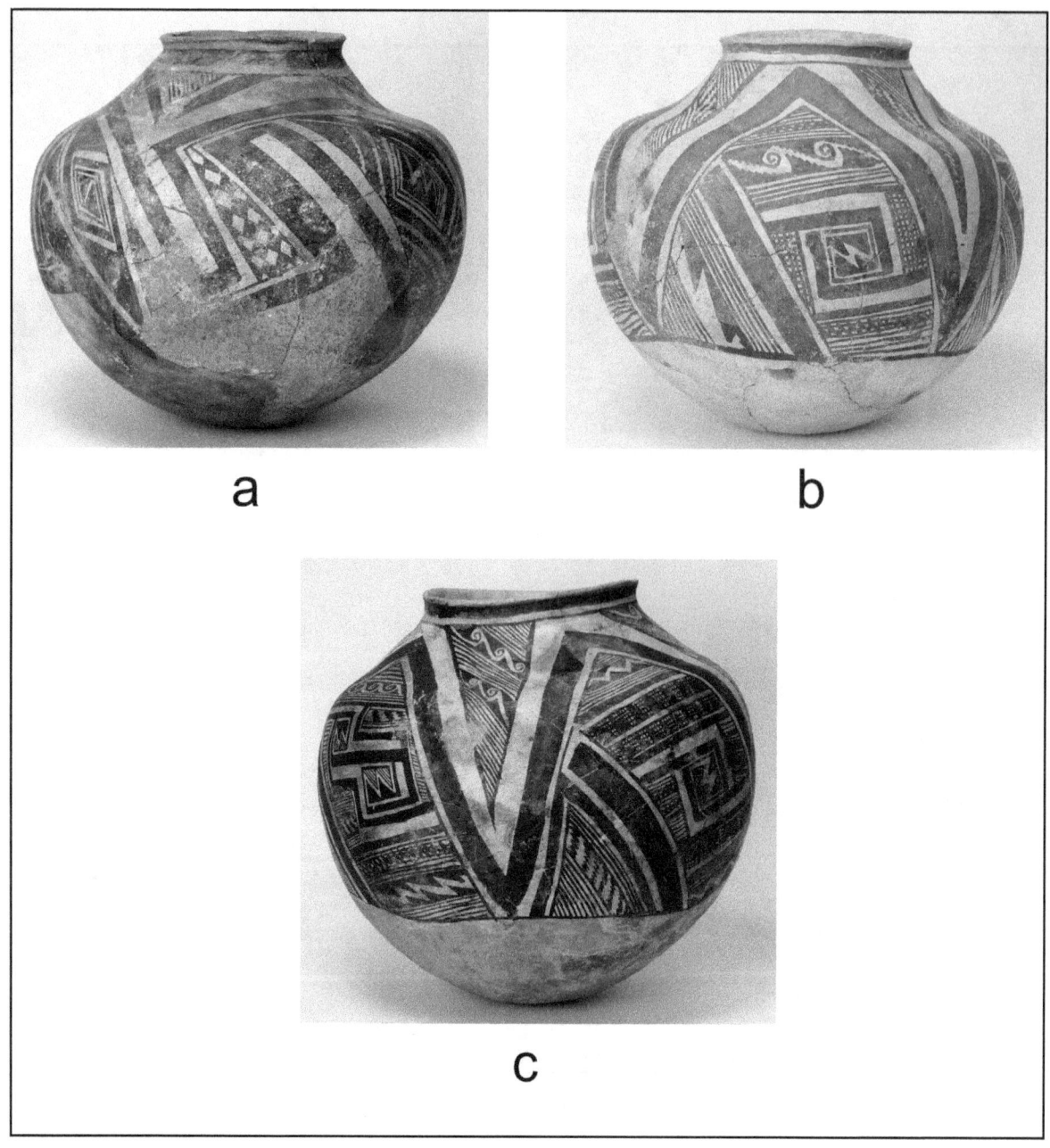

Figure 7.9. Tusayan White Ware jars from Kinishba: (a) ASM Catalog No. 7110, (b) ASM Catalog No. 7111, (c) ASM Catalog No. 7137 (Jannelle Weakly, courtesy Arizona State Museum).

(i.e., more paint than background color) manner characteristic of Kayenta Black-on-white or even many specimens of Tusayan Black-on-white. The bowl, which was decorated using a Kayenta negative offset quartered layout, is more typical in terms of motifs and negative treatment, exhibiting the "mosquito bar effect" (Colton and Hargrave 1937:218; Smith 1971:109).

The Tusayan White Ware Sherd Collection

Pieces of Kayenta Black-on-white, including a ladle fragment, and Tusayan Black-on-white vessels, among them a partial ladle, are present. The most intriguing object in this group, however, is an unpainted, nearly complete Tusayan White Ware baby figurine from a babe-in-cradle effigy (Figure 7.10a).

The babe-in-cradle effigy is a distinctive figurine form associated with the Kayenta ceramic tradition (Lyons 2003:24-25; Morss 1954:39-42). Most often, the baby is attached to a cradle which forms the handle of a ladle, although other related forms occur. Specimens have been recovered from a number of other sites identified as Kayenta or Tusayan immigrant enclaves, including Wupatki (AZ I:7:1[ASM]) (Stanislawski 1963:242-243, 246, Figure 38a, c), Homol'ovi I (AZ J:14:3[ASM]), Homol'ovi III (AZ J:14:14[ASM]), the Goat Hill Site (AZ CC:1:28[ASM]) (Woodson 1995:15, Figure 8b), and the Davis Ranch Site (Gerald 1958).

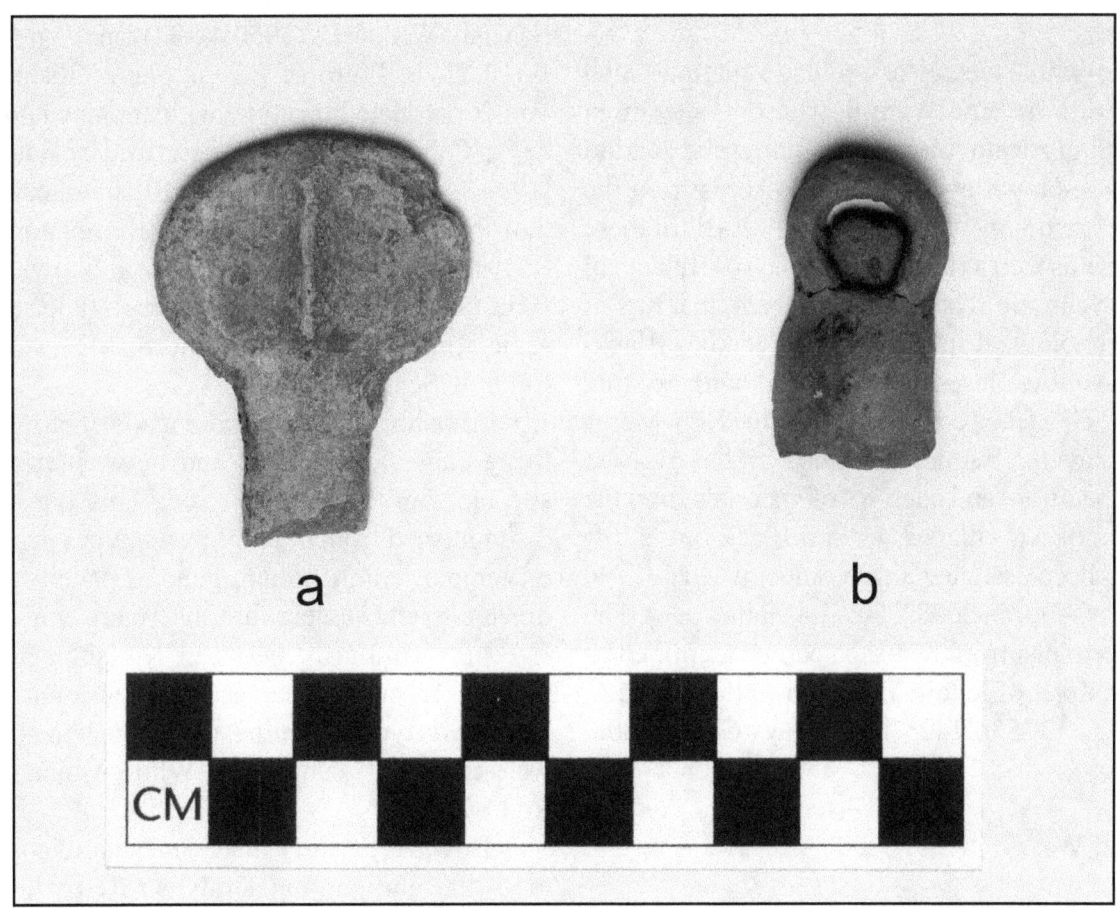

Figure 7.10. Babe-in-cradle effigy fragments from Kinishba: (a) Tusayan White Ware (ASM Catalog No. A-33749), (b) brown ware (ASM Catalog No. A-33774) (Jannelle Weakly, courtesy Arizona State Museum).

Zuni Glaze Ware

Four whole vessels of Zuni Glaze Ware, all bowls, were identified: two Heshotauthla Polychrome, one Kwakina Polychrome, and one Kechipawan Polychrome. As mentioned above, the Kechipawan Polychrome specimen, ASM Catalog No. A-33423, bears the image of a *katsina*. Among the Zuni Glaze Ware sherds, Kwakina Polychrome and Kechipawan Polychrome are most abundant (at least five additional vessels of each are represented), followed by Pinnawa Glaze-on-white (at least three vessels), and at least one additional partially reconstructible Heshotauthla Polychrome bowl.

Jeddito Yellow Ware

The whole vessel assemblage includes two Jeddito Yellow Ware bowls, one specimen each of Awatovi Black-on-yellow and Jeddito Black-on-yellow. Among the sherds from the site are fragments of additional vessels of these types as well as a single specimen of Bidahochi Polychrome. The most significant, in terms of chronological implications, is Jeddito Black-on-yellow. Based on recent work with existing tree-ring dated collections from the Hopi Mesas (excavated but not published by the Awatovi Expedition) and analyses of materials from the Homol'ovi villages, Jeddito Black-on-yellow has been assigned a date range of 1375–1700 (Hays-Gilpin 2008, 2009; LaMotta 2006). The specimens from Kinishba can be identified as examples of Jeddito Black-on-Yellow Style A, dated 1375 to 1425/1450 (Hays Gilpin 2008, 2009).

Red Ware

Three type-level categories of red ware are present among the whole vessels: Kinishba Red; Kinishba Red, Smudged; and Kinishba Red, corrugated neck. Each is described below, in descending order of frequency.

Kinishba Red

Although early researchers consistently referred to the profusion of what came to be called Kinishba Red, detailed discussions involving quantities typically indicated that corrugated pottery was more abundant (Baldwin 1934:51, 1941:94-98; Jones 1935; Mott 1936). That said, Kinishba Red is the dominant utility type in the whole vessel assemblage available for analysis (see Triadan, Chapter 8).

Despite the fact that this material had been discussed by numerous researchers during the 1930s, it lacked a formal name and type description until Wendorf's (1950:42-43) report on AZ W:10:51, at Point of Pines, was published. Wendorf equated this type with unnamed pottery at Canyon Creek Ruin, described by Haury (1934:137-138). Haury himself also indicated that the red ware informally referred to as Showlow Red, based on his work at Showlow Ruin (AZ P:12:3[ASM]), was essentially the same (Haury 1931:42; Second Southwestern Ceramic Seminar 1959:4-5).

Kinishba Red vessels are made of brown-firing clay. Jar exteriors and bowl interiors and exteriors are slipped red. This type is distinguished from other red ware types based on temper, color, polish, general paucity of fireclouds, and vessel subforms. Haury emphasized the similarity between Kinishba Red bowl forms and those of late White Mountain Red Ware types, arguing that Kinishba Red was, essentially, unpainted White Mountain Red Ware.

Bowls are nearly three times more common than jars among Kinishba Red whole vessels, suggesting that the functions of these objects may be more like those of other bowl-heavy categories such as Roosevelt Red Ware or White Mountain Red Ware rather than classes such as corrugated pottery or brown ware, which are typically dominated by jars. The whole vessel assemblage includes a half-gourd-shaped ladle, what may be a fragment of a submarine jar—a canteen form associated with the ceramic traditions of the Four Corners, the Maverick Mountain Series, and Roosevelt Red Ware (Dixon 1956)—and a unique object: a hollow, closed cylinder 9 cm long and 9.5 cm in diameter (Figure 7.11a). This artifact, ASM Catalog No. 23909, resembles a mallet head or drum that is sealed on both ends. There is a small, round, pre-firing perforation in the side of the vessel.

The Kinishba Red sherds include a number of interesting specimens, including a partial datura effigy jar, a large fragment of an animal effigy similar to Fourmile Polychrome vessels illustrated by Martin and Willis (1940:Plate 103.3, 4), bowls with incised decoration on their exteriors, a hollow ladle handle with a loop end, and a large rim sherd from a small, unusual bowl (Figure 7.11b). This bowl exhibits two circumferential ridges which are triangular in cross-section. One encircles the exterior of the vessel just below the rim and the other goes around just above the point where the wall becomes the base of the bowl. Directly above the lower ridge is a small, round, post-firing perforation.

Other Red Ware Types

Fourteen vessels, all bowls, were classified as Kinishba Red, Smudged (Wendorf 1950:43). This type is Kinishba Red with an intentionally smudged interior. "Kinishba Red, corrugated neck" is an informal variety name used here to call attention to the presence of a jar of Kinishba Red with a corrugated neck. There are other examples among the sherds from the site.

Brown Ware

The sample of brown ware available for analysis appears to have been culled from a larger group of vessels; it exhibits an unusual and unexplained ratio of miniature vessels (n = 22) and pinch-pots (n = 59) to full-size pots (n = 18), severely limiting my confidence in making comparisons across wares or sites. The pinch pots are dominated by jars, including one with incised decoration. Ladles are next most abundant, followed by bowls and objects of indeterminate form. Among the miniatures, jars again account for the majority of the sample, followed in order of decreasing frequency by bowls, ladles, and a single scoop. The miniature jars include two seed jars, a biglobular jar (which is missing and was recorded based on catalog records), a culinary shoe pot and a bird-shaped jar (Dixon 1956). The full-size vessels include 14 bowls, three jars, and one ladle.

Among the brown ware sherds and the non-vessel catalogued ceramic artifacts are three very significant objects: pieces of two perforated plates (Figure 7.12a) and a fragmentary babe-in-cradle effigy (Figure 7.10b). The latter was illustrated by Clara Lee Tanner (1976: Figure 6.13b, upper right). Perforated plates are Kayenta pottery making tools (base molds and potters' turntables) that first appeared in far northeastern Arizona by A.D. 500 and began to turn up south of the Little Colorado River after 1250 as the depopulation of the Four Corners region began (Christenson 1991, 1994; Lyons and Lindsay 2006) (Figure 7.13). The fact that these are brown ware strongly suggests they were made locally (i.e., they were not brought to the site from the Kayenta region). Locally produced perforated plates have been documented at the Homol'ovi villages, Bailey Ruin (AZ P:11:1[ASM]), Point of Pines Pueblo (AZ W:10:50[ASM]), the Goat Hill Site, and a number of sites in the San Pedro Valley and the Phoenix Basin (Lyons 2003; Lyons and

Figure 7.11. Unusual Kinishba Red vessel forms: (a) ASM Catalog No. 23909, (b) uncatalogued sherd (Jannelle Weakly [a] and Patrick D. Lyons [b], courtesy Arizona State Museum).

Figure 7.12. Perforated plate fragments from Kinishba: (a) brown ware specimens, ASM Catalog Nos. 2011-687-3 (left) and 2011-687-4 (right); and (b) Moenkopi Corrugated specimens, 2011-687-5 (left) and 2011-687-6 (right) (Jannelle Weakly, courtesy Arizona State Museum).

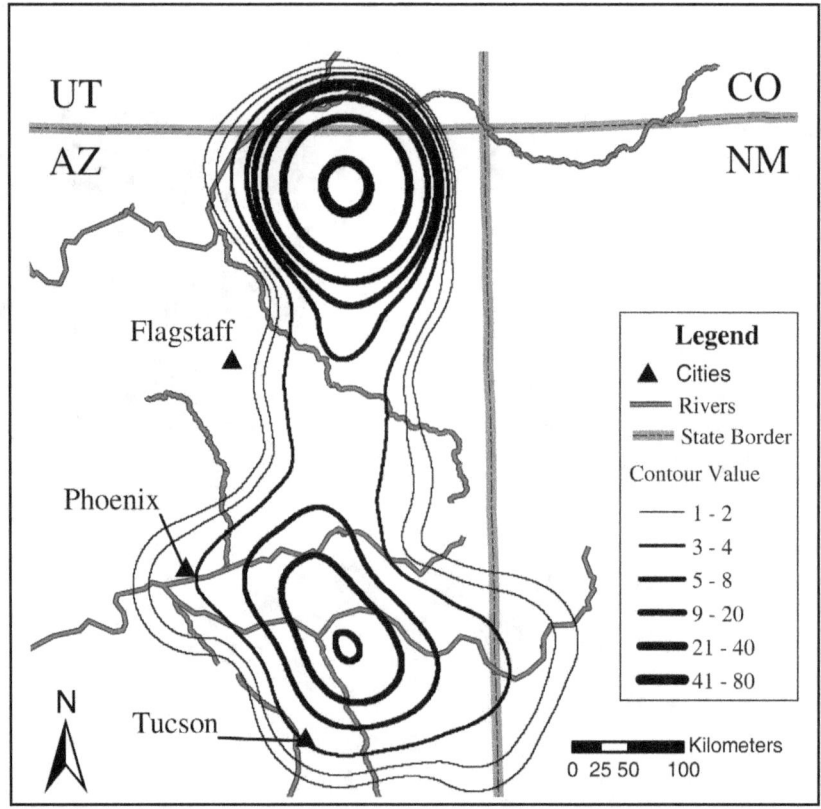

Figure 7.13. Distribution of sites that have yielded perforated plates, with contours representing numbers of sites with perforated plates per 100 km² (minimum = 1; maximum = 80) (Marina Sergeyeva).

Lindsay 2006; Stinson 1996; Woodson 1999; Zedeño, personal communication; see also Zedeño 2002).

Corrugated Pottery

Corrugated pottery was grouped into informal categories based on surface treatment (e.g., indented corrugated, indented obliterated corrugated) rather than formally named types. The dominant category, accounting for more than 40 percent, is indented flattened (partially obliterated) corrugated, followed by indented obliterated corrugated at nearly 25 percent, obliterated corrugated at nearly ten percent, and other categories comprising one to more than eight percent each.

This group of vessels is the most jar-dominant in the assemblage; jars outnumber bowls more than fourteen to one. Among them, however, are three plates ground down from large jar sherds and two modeled plates. None of these are perforated. Nonetheless, these objects were likely used in the same manner as perforated plates (Christenson 1991, 1994; Lyons and Lindsay 2006). The corrugated sherd assemblage includes two additional partially reconstructible unperforated plates and a jar-in-bowl.

Mogollon Brown Ware Utility Pottery

Unpainted Mogollon Brown Ware present at Kinishba consists of five bowls of Tularosa Fillet Rim (Gladwin and Gladwin 1934:18; Olson 1959:125-127; Rinaldo 1952:65; Wendorf 1950:121).

Wares and Types Represented in the Sherd Assemblage Only

A number of types not represented in the whole and reconstructible vessel assemblage are present among the sherds from Kinishba. These include many from the Kayenta region that help to flesh out the inference that immigrants from that area may have lived at Kinishba. Fragments of multiple vessels of Tusayan Polychrome and Kiet Siel Black-on-red (or Tusayan Black-on-red) were identified, as well as a single specimen of Tusayan Corrugated and large pieces of two Moenkopi Corrugated perforated plates (Figure 7.12b). Although no fragments of colanders—another distinctive Kayenta vessel form that helps to track ancient immigrants—were located in the material available for reanalysis, Cummings (1940:89) reports rare examples of "collander [sic] types of the north." Cummings, having worked intensively in the Kayenta region, was familiar with this form, as well as distinctions between colanders, seed jars without perforations, and perforated plates (see, e.g., Cummings 1910). Thus, I think it is a safe bet that colander sherds were recovered. Unfortunately, it is impossible to determine whether these were produced locally or in the Kayenta region. Other northern intrusives include fragments of at least two bowls of Jeddito Black-on-orange, made on the Hopi Mesas (Smith 1971), and three bowls of Homolovi Polychrome, made in the Winslow area (Lyons 2003).

Evidence of a connection between Kinishba and Point of Pines complementing the ceramic circulation events documented by Crown (1994) is present in the form of a partially reconstructible miniature jar of Prieto Indented Corrugated (Breternitz et al. 1957), a sherd of Point of Pines Punctate (Gifford 1980:113-114, Figure 91i-l; Olson 1959:101-103), and fragments of Point of Pines Polychrome (Carlson 1970:77-82).

Finally, there is a sherd of Verde Black-on-gray and a handful of sherds from the Hohokam region. The latter include specimens of Gila Butte Red-on-buff, Santa Cruz Red-on-buff, Sacaton Red-on-buff, San Carlos Red-on-brown, and Tanque Verde Red-on-brown.

CHRONOLOGY

The decorated whole vessel assemblage is dominated by specimens of types with post-1250 start dates (91.09 percent) (Tables 7.7 and 7.10). Only seven vessels (2.83 percent) are examples of painted types with pre-1300 end dates (McDonald Corrugated, McDonald Painted Corrugated, Puerco Black-on-white, and Kiatuthlanna Black-on-white), and six (2.43 percent) are of types with an end date of 1300 (St. Johns Black-on-red, Tusayan Black-on-white, Kayenta Black-on-white, and Tularosa Black-on-white). Only one fifth of the vessels in the assemblage are examples of types with pre-1275 start dates. Nearly forty percent are types that post-date 1325, ten percent post-date 1350, and three vessels (1.21 percent) are of types that postdate 1375 (Jeddito Black-on-yellow and Nine Mile Polychrome). The decorated sherd collection largely reflects the patterns exhibited by the whole vessels, although a handful of much earlier sherds are present. These and the few early vessels could be associated with earlier components at the site, or may represent heirlooms.

The available tree-ring data from the site, though lacking in cutting date clusters and provenance, are consistent with construction beginning in the late 1270s and an occupation extending into the 1370s (Bannister and Robinson 1971:28-31). Triadan and Zedeño (2004) bracket the occupation of the pueblo between 1300 and 1400. As discussed above, the sherd collection has yielded evidence of a post-1390 presence at the site consistent with Triadan and

Zedeño's proposed terminal date. Given all the available data, a date range between 1275 and 1400 for the main pueblo occupation seems reasonable.

CONCLUSION: KINISHBA POTTERY IN REGIONAL CONTEXT

As discussed above, putting the pottery of Kinishba in regional context, i.e., understanding what it can tell us regarding who lived at the site, with whom they maintained relationships, and how they purposefully expressed social identities, requires distinguishing among the residues of exchange, emulation, enculturation, and ethnicity (Carr 1995a, 1995b; Clark 2001). These processes all contribute to similarities and differences in material culture. Unfortunately, in the past, researchers addressed these questions on the basis of ill-founded assumptions about ceramic production and circulation without the benefit of provenance analyses, thereby attributing patterns to vaguely defined "influences." Compositional analyses are critical because they can identify or exclude exchange as a possibility and, in the latter case, allow researchers to focus on disentangling traces of emulation, ethnicity, and migration (Shepard 1985:336-347, Table 11; Zedeño 1994:18-21, Table 3.1).

An initial way to approach the question of who lived at Kinishba is to consider which of the dominant wares and types were made there and which of these were circulated to the site. Based on compositional analyses by Crown (1994) and Triadan and her colleagues (1994, 1997; Triadan et al. 2002), locally produced types and wares include Kinishba Red (and probably, by extension, Kinishba White-on-red) and Roosevelt Red Ware. Lindsay (1992) suggested, based on his examination of the vessels, that the Maverick Mountain Series specimens from the site were also local products. This is a fruitful avenue for future research on the collection (i.e., a prime target for sourcing via INAA), and for the purposes of this discussion, I will assume he is correct. Neither the brown ware nor the corrugated pottery from Kinishba has been subjected to compositional analysis (another obvious avenue for future work), but given what is known about contemporaneous sites in the region, it is quite likely that the people of Kinishba or nearby groups manufactured most of the utility ware recovered from the site.

Triadan and her colleagues have demonstrated that most of the White Mountain Red Ware at the site was not produced there, having circulated to Kinishba from the Silver Creek drainage. Although he did not conduct compositional analyses, Van Keuren suggests that the Pinedale Black-on-white vessels (the majority of the Cibola White Ware whole vessels recovered) at Kinishba were also made in the Silver Creek area.

In his regional provenance study of Zuni Glaze Ware, Duff (2002) concluded that production occurred only on the Zuni Reservation and in the Upper Little Colorado River Valley. I assume that the Zuni Glaze Ware found at Kinishba was not produced locally, though no specimens from the site were included in Duff's analysis. Jeddito Yellow Ware has an extremely limited production area, smaller even than that associated with Zuni Glaze Ware (Bernardini 2005; Bishop et al. 1988; Duff 2002). Thus, it is safe to assume that Jeddito Yellow Ware found at Kinishba was not made there.

Together, the wares and types just discussed account for more than 98 percent of the utility pottery, more than 90 percent of the painted pottery, and more than 95 percent of the overall Kinishba assemblage (Table 7.11). The pattern that emerges is suggestive of coresidence by two at least two distinct groups: (1)

a local, mountain population that, like others in the region, received most of its painted pottery from communities on the southern edge of the Colorado Plateau (White Mountain Red Ware and Cibola White Ware) and (2) people native to the Kayenta region who brought the pottery traditions of the Four Corners region (Maverick Mountain Series types and perhaps Tusayan White Ware; both groups of vessels should be subjected to sourcing) to Kinishba and eventually began to produce Roosevelt Red Ware.

Triadan's (Chapter 8) inference that Kinishba Red serves at Kinishba the same role that Grasshopper Polychrome serves at Grasshopper—as a locally made substitute for Fourmile Polychrome—makes sense in this context. This is consistent with Haury's observation that Kinishba Red bowls follow the forms characteristic of White Mountain Red ware types. This idea also illuminates Kinishba White-on-red, much of which seems, often clumsily, to emulate White Mountain Red Ware (especially Fourmile Polychrome) exterior decoration.

The inference that Kayenta immigrants or their descendants lived at Kinishba is supported by aspects of the sherd assemblage reported above. Arguably, there are hints of a late-1200s Kayenta assemblage consisting of Tsegi Orange Ware, Tusayan White Ware, and Tusayan Gray Ware types at the site. This may represent traces of the household inventories of families from the north who settled at Kinishba (Zedeño [2002] documented this phenomenon at Point of Pines). In addition, there are brown ware, presumably locally produced, versions of characteristic Kayenta vessel forms (perforated plates and a babe-in-cradle effigy) among the sherds and non-vessel ceramic objects (another obvious focus for future analyses).

The Kayenta Diaspora

Kinishba, of course, is not alone in having yielded clues indicating the presence of immigrants from the Kayenta region. A suite of material markers, including perforated plates, Maverick Mountain Series painted pottery, roomblock architecture, entryboxes, and kivas have been used to identify dozens of such enclaves (Di Peso 1958; Haury 1958; Lindsay 1987; Lyons 2003; Lyons and Lindsay 2006; Neuzil 2008; Woodson 1999). These are visible in nearly every major settlement cluster occupied between 1250 and 1450 in the eastern half of Arizona, bounded on the north by the Little Colorado River Valley, and on the south by the U.S./Mexico border. This pattern of spatial dispersion has led researchers to consider the utility of examining population movement from the Kayenta region, and its social consequences, in terms of the concept of diaspora (Lyons, Clark, and Hill 2011; Lyons, Hill, and Clark 2011; Mills 2011).

From an anthropological perspective, the key elements of the process of diaspora are population dispersal, preservation of identity, and a network of connections among dispersed enclaves and between these cells and the homeland (even if this homeland no longer truly exists in the same form, or is more broadly conceived than in the past) (Clifford 1994; Cohen 1997; Gilroy 1997; Hall 1990; Safran 1991, 1997, 2004; Sheffer 1986). Diasporic networks allow cooperation on a large geographical scale, moving information, goods, raw materials, and ritual specialists (Sökefeld 2002, 2004; Vertovec 1994; Wellmeier 1998).

In diaspora, a distinct group identity is often preserved through language and religion (Baumann 1995; Safran 2004). It is important to note that this identity survives through hybridity and syncretism (Clifford 1994; Gilroy 1997; Hall 1990). The process of choosing which traditions to maintain and which to discard—repeated by different groups of immigrants among different host populations—is the source of variability among diasporic cells that originated from the same homeland (Clifford 1994; Gilroy 1997; Tölölyan 1996). The ethnographic literature specifically tells us to expect the development of new ritual practices involving revival, invention, or re-invention of traditions (Parekh 1994; Sökefeld 2002, 2004; van der Veer and Vertovec 1991; Vertovec 1991, 1994). Economic specialization is also associated with diaspora (Cohen 1997). The ethnographic record shows that immigrants find niches to exploit among host populations, including specialized craft production.

Salado as the Kayenta in Diaspora

An influx of immigrants from the north was a key ingredient in the first models accounting for the dramatic changes in ceramics, architecture, and treatment of the dead that marked the shift from the pre-Classic period to the Classic period in southern Arizona—changes eventually lumped under the rubric of Salado (Gladwin 1928; Gladwin and Gladwin 1929, 1930, 1931, 1935; Hawley 1928; Schmidt 1927, 1928). By the 1930s, archaeologists had begun to infer connections between Tusayan and Kayenta ceramics, specifically, and Roosevelt Red Ware (Gladwin and Gladwin 1935; Haury 1945).

As more data have accumulated, it has become clear that many of the traits early workers insisted arrived in the Hohokam region from the north as a complex instead developed locally at different times and at different rates (e.g., Doyel 1974, 1981; Steen 1965; Wasley and Doyel 1980; Weaver 1972, 1973, 1976). In addition, many researchers have called attention to variability among "Salado" sites and components, noting that the only characteristic that ties them all together is Roosevelt Red Ware (e.g., Lindsay and Jennings 1968; Nelson and LeBlanc 1986).

Regardless of problems inherent in the original model of Salado, evidence of links between Kayenta immigrants and Roosevelt Red Ware has continued to accumulate over the last several years. Indeed, Crown (1994:203-209), who has made, by far the most significant contributions to understanding Roosevelt Red Ware, has demonstrated that these pottery types were developed by Kayenta potters. She argues, however, that production of the ware quickly spread beyond the immigrants who developed it, in the context of a regional cult.

Southwesternists have increasingly become aware of Kayenta immigrant enclaves throughout central and southern Arizona, identified on the basis of unique architectural and ceramic traits, among other indicators (Lyons 2003, 2004b; Neuzil 2008; Woodson 1999). It has also been observed, of late, that there is a consistent association, in many parts of the Southwest, between evidence of the local production of Roosevelt Red Ware, and evidence of the local manufacture of pottery types, such as the Maverick Mountain Series, and particular vessel forms, such as perforated plates (Figure 7.13), that mark the presence of Kayenta immigrants (Crown 1994:204-206; Lyons 2003, 2012). As a result, I have argued that Roosevelt Red Ware production remained closely tied to northern immigrants and their descendants rather than quickly and easily spreading to local host groups. Accordingly, I think the Salado phenomenon may best be viewed as the material residue of Kayenta groups maintaining a shared identity in diaspora (Lyons and Clark 2012; Lyons, Clark, and Hill 2011; Lyons, Hill, and Clark 2011).

The genesis of Roosevelt Red Ware, in and of itself, is evidence of the diasporic network; it represents widespread immigrant exploitation of an economic niche through craft specialization. Dispersed enclaves chose—virtually simultaneously—to shift from Maverick Mountain Series pottery to Roosevelt Red Ware and, in many cases, to exchange Roosevelt Red Ware with local host groups (Lyons 2012). The consistency of vessel forms and painted decoration, across a huge geographical expanse and over generations (Crown 1994:90), also speaks to frequent interchange among diasporic cells.

One could argue that the presence, at Grasshopper and at Point of Pines, of Roosevelt Red Ware made at Kinishba is evidence of a link forming part of the diasporic network. The same could be said of Point of Pines Punctate, Prieto Indented Corrugated, and Point of Pines Polychrome found at Kinishba (and presumably made at Point of Pines). Winslow Orange Ware (Homolovi Polychrome) could represent another such connection. Likewise, the recovery of Jeddito Orange Ware and Jeddito Yellow Ware at Kinishba could be construed as a trace of a tie between a diasporic cell and a more broadly conceived northern homeland.

The Salado Feasting Tradition

My colleagues and I have argued elsewhere that during the late 1300s, Kayenta immigrants and their descendants born in diaspora attempted to maintain widespread connections between dispersed enclaves, in part by developing a feasting tradition (Lyons and Clark 2012; Lyons, Hill, and Clark 2011). This inference is based on observed changes over time in the design of in Roosevelt Red Ware bowls. These changes have "practical" and "presentational" implications for vessel function (*sensu* Van Keuren 2004).

Practical constraints act on performance characteristics related to serving and eating, e.g., the nature of the contents the vessel will contain and the size of the group that will use the vessel. In contrast, presentational qualities relate to the vessel's ability to communicate messages. Four performance characteristics set Phoenix Polychrome, Nine Mile Polychrome, Dinwiddie Polychrome, and Cliff White-on-red apart from earlier Roosevelt Red Ware types: size, shape, decorative field (general portion of the vessel painted, such as the interior surface), and decorative focus (specific portion of the decorative field painted) (see Crown 1994:55-57). I argue that bowls of these types were designed for serving food to large groups, in public settings. Kinishba's abundant Whiteriver Polychrome, a type which also appears to have been designed with feasting in mind, suggests that suprahousehold commensalism was particularly important at this village.

Roosevelt Red Ware Bowl Size

Roosevelt Red Ware bowls became much larger through time, increasing from a mean maximum diameter of 20 cm for Gila Polychrome to an average of 35 cm for four of the five post-Cliff Polychrome types (Table 7.12). Cliff Polychrome straddles the two distributions (in fact its distribution is bimodal) and straddles Gila Polychrome and the late types chronologically speaking. These data suggest Cliff Polychrome either represents a stage in the development of the later types or that many Cliff Polychrome vessels, like specimens of the late types, were specialized feasting bowls. These differences are statistically significant (Kruskal-Wallis test statistic = 100.9489, $p < .0000$, with 2 df). Although I have not yet created a regional database for the comparison of Whiteriver Polychrome maximum diameters to those of other Roosevelt Red Ware types, the sample from Kinishba suggests that, like Cliff Polychrome, this type has a bimodal distribution. This makes sense, given its place in the seriation relative to other types, as described above.

There are many very large bowls among the Roosevelt Red Ware vessels recovered from Kinishba, including three of the five largest in the overall assemblage. One of the Whiteriver Polychrome vessels has a maximum diameter of 41 cm (the largest bowl from the site) and a Cliff Polychrome: Tonto Variety bowl has a maximum width of 40 cm (the second largest bowl in the assemblage). Tied for the third largest bowl overall is another Whiteriver Polychrome with a maximum diameter of 39 cm. One of the Nine Mile Polychrome bowls is also quite broad, measuring 36 cm in diameter at its widest point. In fact, Mills (2007:Figure 15) employs the image from the frontispiece of Cummings's (1940) report on Kinishba to illustrate the great size of some bowls found at late prehispanic sites in east-central Arizona, which she infers were used in suprahousehold feasting.

Crown (1994), using the traditional Roosevelt Red Ware typology, discerned that bowls exhibiting certain shapes became larger over time. She also found that a class of very large bowls was virtually absent from burials, suggesting that such objects were not associated with individual users—a conclusion that follows if these vessels were used for feasting.

Roosevelt Red Ware Bowl Shape

Four of the late types are defined in part by their shared form, the recurved bowl. This is the same shape exhibited by contemporaneous Rio Grande Glaze Ware and Biscuit Ware bowls which, many infer, were used as serving vessels in suprahousehold feasts (Graves and Eckert 1998; Spielmann 1998). This form is well-engineered for carrying stew (a likely feasting food) without spilling (Kidder 1915:423) and allows easy access to the contents of a container by a large number of people. These, like increased volume, are practical performance characteristics.

Decorative Field and Decorative Focus

Crown (1994:57) noted an increase over time, from eight percent to 95 percent, in exterior surface decoration on Roosevelt Red Ware bowls. I argue that the shift in decoration that defines the late types reflects presentational constraints on container design related to ritual commensalism. Because feasting vessels were used in public contexts, and because their interiors were most often obscured by their contents, painted decoration was moved to those areas of the vessel—the exterior surface and the interior surface of the rim, above the point of constriction—where participants could still observe it when the vessel was full (see Van Keuren 2004). As noted above, many Biscuit Ware bowls exhibit the same form, and from the beginning of the sequence, the interior rims of such vessels were decorated in a manner similar to that exhibited by late Roosevelt Red Ware types. Furthermore, the transition from Biscuit A to Biscuit B is marked by the addition of exterior painted decoration (Kidder and Kidder 1917).

Why Feasting?

The main goals that drive feasts are creating and sustaining relationships outside the household (see, e.g., Dietler 1996, 2001; Hayden 1996, 2001). Kayenta groups in diaspora developed the Salado feasting tradition in the context of falling regional population and overall demographic flux. In this social environment, the members of the diaspora were likely concerned about sustaining connections on a broad scale and, perhaps, maintaining viable communities.

Van Keuren (2004) asserts that historical factors underlie both the practical and the presentational qualities of artifacts used in feasting. An example of this phenomenon is the consistent association of red ware bowls and feasting in the northern Southwest (Blinman 1989; Mills 1999a; Spielmann 2004). In a sense, then, the late precontact development of feasting ritual associated with Roosevelt Red

Ware represents a (re-) invention of tradition (Hobsbawm 1983). According to Hobsbawm, such phenomena are to be expected under conditions of rapid social transformation and signify attempts to create something seemingly unchanged or unchanging during times of upheaval. Such strategies most often make deliberate claims to continuity with the past and legitimize action (Hobsbawm 1983:12; see also Connerton 1989). Many large, late vessels exhibit "classic" Kayenta motifs such as the batwing with corbel-and-hatch filler (for example, ASM Catalog No. A-33390, from Kinishba). Following Crown (1994:206-207), I suggest this phenomenon may mark a revival of northern identity (also see Mills 2011). Alternatively, or perhaps in addition to maintaining ties among diasporic cells, Salado feasts may have been designed to create political relationships among culturally diverse groups.

Comparing Feasting Traditions

A comparison of Rio Grande Glaze Ware, Biscuit Ware, and White Mountain Red Ware feasting vessels (Graves and Eckert 1998; Mills 2007; Spielmann 1998) with the Roosevelt Red Ware feasting tradition yields interesting similarities. Parallel developments in form and decoration suggest sharing of ideas and strong connections between groups in the Rio Grande and those who occupied the late precontact settlements of central and southern Arizona. Crown (1994) has interpreted these patterns in terms of a regional cult.

There is a potential point of divergence to explore as well. Rio Grande Glaze Ware feasting vessels have been described as "pieces of places"—objects imbued with the importance of their place of origin and thus appropriate for use in ritual contexts (Bradley 2000). Whereas Rio Grande Glaze Ware production was centralized, Roosevelt Red Ware was made just about everywhere. Does this mean Roosevelt Red Ware feasting vessels were not pieces of a place? Could the iconography on the late vessels—recalling the Kayenta pottery of the late 1200s—be the symbol of a reimagined homeland among groups in diaspora?

Mills (2007) links changes in White Mountain Red Ware bowl exterior decorations to the scales of ritual architecture used and the sizes of social groups participating in public performances during different periods. However, Roosevelt Red Ware feasting bowls look the same regardless of architectural context: platform mound, pueblo, compound, cliffdwelling. Thus, the scale of the social group involved is unrelated to architecture. I suggest that a regional social group was signaled, a diasporic community rather than a local community.

Looking back at Crown's (1994) study of Roosevelt Red Ware, one sees that in the process of building her explanation, she eliminated a model of Roosevelt Red Ware as a marker associated with an immigrant ethnic group. Crown may be correct about links between Roosevelt Red Ware painted decoration and a pan-Southwestern religious movement, but this notion does not exclude the diaspora model presented here or the possibility that a distinct ethnic identity was maintained among producers. Rather, we should continue to explore the relationship between diaspora, religion, and craft production. The pottery of Kinishba may have much more to tell us in this regard.

FUTURE RESEARCH

The pottery of Kinishba has been a subject of study, on and off, over a period of nearly 80 years. During this time, as archaeological theory and method have developed, important information about these artifacts has continued to accumulate, making them increasingly useful to researchers. Indeed, the Kinishba pottery assemblage is a prime example of the value of museum collections and the importance of curation, even for incompletely documented materials.

Above, I have highlighted fruitful avenues for future research, such as compositional analyses designed to test assumptions regarding local production and ceramic circulation. Such studies would assist in evaluating my inferences regarding migration, in particular, and links between Kayenta immigrants, their descendants, and Roosevelt Red Ware. Other promising foci of additional research include Kinishba White-on-red and the non-vessel ceramic artifact assemblage from Kinishba (which includes dozens of figurines, numerous shaped-sherd pottery scrapers, two unfired-clay jar-stoppers, and scores of shaped-sherd discs).

It is also important to note that many vessels, sherds, and non-vessel ceramic objects in the Kinishba collection bear contextual data, written in pencil. ASM staff recently discovered that this information was not consistently transferred to the catalog cards that then became the basis of computer records and most previous analyses. Triadan (Chapter 8) has recently explored the assemblage from the perspective of intrasite provenience, and I am hopeful that more work of this type can be done in the future.

Scaling up to Kinishba's larger local context—the group of large, Pueblo IV period, aggregated villages below the Mogollon Rim—Triadan (Chapter 8) has made useful comparisons between the archaeology of Kinishba and Grasshopper, in particular, and sometimes Point of Pines Pueblo (also see Riggs 2005). There is much to be gained by expending additional effort in this direction, and I encourage comparisons based on ceramic evidence of northern immigrants and attempts to gauge the long-term impact of coresidence at each of these, as well as other large, contemporaneous sites.

Duff (2002) has defined an "Arizona Mountains" settlement cluster in which he includes four major Pueblo IV villages, aside from Kinishba: Q Ranch Pueblo (AZ P:13:13[ASM]), Grasshopper Pueblo, Tundastusa, and Point of Pines Pueblo. He notes, however, that based on its location relative to sites in the Silver Creek drainage, Mills (1998; see also Kaldahl et al. 2004; Triadan and Zedeño 2004) places Tundastusa in the Silver Creek settlement cluster. Duff's work in the Upper Little Colorado shows that Tundastusa's placement in a site cluster may best be decided based on similarities and differences in material culture and architecture and evidence of exchange relationships, rather than distance between sites. Unfortunately, information on Q Ranch, Tundastusa, and Point of Pines Pueblo is sparse. This is especially true of ceramic data, and a necessary prerequisite to better understanding both the internal dynamics of this hypothetical cluster and its external relations would be refining the chronology of some of its constituent sites. Nonetheless, tantalizing clues abound.

In the case of Q Ranch, the Arizona Archaeological Society excavated at the site between 1989 and 2006, but to date, few data have been published or otherwise made available for comparisons. Recent ceramic analyses have resulted in the identification of Cliff Polychrome, Whiteriver Polychrome, and Los Muertos Polychrome in the assemblage (Joan Clark, personal communications and photographs 2007, 2009, 2012), indicating that Q Ranch, like Kinishba, was occupied after Grasshopper was depopulated. Sharon Urban (personal communication and photograph, 2001) reports that perforated plates have been recovered from Q Ranch, and chemical and petrographic analyses by White and Burton (1992) suggest local production of Roosevelt Red Ware occurred at the site. The presence at Q Ranch of unfired, prepared clay loaves and an unfired vessel, still in a puki (Dart 1997; see also Buck 2005) represents a rare and important opportunity to illuminate ceramic exchange relationships (the best possible way to document a local pottery compositional signature and to track circulation of vessels made at Q Ranch), and an opportunity to build on Triadan's (1997) documentation of Fourmile Polychrome recovered from Q Ranch but made at Grasshopper.

The excavated sample from Tundastusa (Hough 1903) is apparently small, dispersed, and poorly documented (Welch and Ferguson 2005:23), but Maverick Mountain Polychrome is present in the ASM surface collection from the site. Based on the Gila Pueblo and ASM surface collections, White Mountain Red Ware dominates the decorated assemblage. Roosevelt Red Ware is sparsely represented. Indeed, Roosevelt Red Ware is perhaps scarcer at this site than at any other large village in the mountains.

Point of Pines Pueblo, excavated by ASM and the UA Department of Anthropology during the 1940s and 1950s, yielded more than 700 whole or reconstructible ceramic vessels. Despite its status as the US Southwest's archetypical ancient migration case study and a touchstone for recent research on population movement and coresidence, except for Haury's (1958) classic article on the Maverick Mountain phase occupation, Point of Pines Pueblo remains a gaping hole in our knowledge of the late prehispanic occupation of the Arizona mountains. The results of work at other sites excavated as part of the Point of Pines field school have been published (Breternitz 1959; Gifford 1980; Haury 1957; Lowell 1991; Olson 1960; Smiley 1952; Wendorf 1950; Wheat 1954) or are available through master's theses (e.g., Morris 1957; Wasley 1952), and although archaeologists continue to incorporate data and artifacts from Point of Pines Pueblo into their research (e.g., E. C. Adams 1994; J. Adams 2010; Lindsay 1987; Rodrigues 2008; Stone 2000, 2002, 2003, 2005; Zedeño 2002), a synthetic report of the excavations at this particular village and their results does not exist. That said, unpublished artifact and architectural analyses conducted by Lindsay (personal communication, 2006) suggest that the Maverick Mountain phase occupation at the site was much larger than previously recognized. Possibly related is the fact that northern-style ground stone tools and technology persisted in the Point of Pines region long after the conflagration that Haury (1958) had assumed was ignited by locals in order to drive out the immigrants (J. Adams 1994, 2010).

Grasshopper Pueblo, of course, is the best documented of all the large villages in the Arizona mountains, and its excavators have long inferred co-residence by locals and northern immigrants, based on multiple lines of evidence (e.g., Ezzo 1991, 1992, 1993; Reid 1989; Reid and Whittlesey 1982, 1999; Riggs 1999, 2001; Whittlesey and Reid 2001). Even at Grasshopper, however, there are lesser-known bits of data that help to identify some immigrants more specifically as part of the Kayenta diaspora. These include the presence of perforated plates and Maverick Mountain Series pottery.

There remains much to learn about the people of Kinishba, their relationships with the inhabitants of other mountain villages, and how large-scale processes played out on the local level in east-central Arizona. One thing is clear, however, based on the discussion just presented: continued study of existing museum collections and their associated records will be central to advancing knowledge in these areas.

ACKNOWLEDGMENTS

I am grateful to Melanie Deer and Claire Barker for assisting me with the analyses reported here, and I thank Georgine Speranzo for her meticulous proofreading. Any mistakes that remain are my own.

Table 7.1. White Mountain Red Ware Vessels from Kinishba Illustrated by Carlson (1970)

Figure No.	Carlson Catalog No.	Corrected Catalog No.	Type	Form
25.f	7109		Pinedale Polychrome	Bowl
25.g	3026	23823	Kwakina Polychrome	Bowl
25.h	13723		Pinedale Polychrome	Bowl
25.i	7350		Pinedale Polychrome	Bowl
26.i	20005		Pinedale Polychrome	Bowl
29.e	20004		Cedar Creek Polychrome	Bowl
30.e	21614		Cedar Creek Polychrome	Bowl
30.h	2545	25451	Cedar Creek Polychrome	Bowl
34.b	2003	20003	Fourmile Polychrome	Bowl
34.h	7082		Fourmile Polychrome	Bowl
36.a	3012	A-33406	Fourmile Polychrome	Bowl
36.c	7135		Fourmile Polychrome	Bowl
36.d	3009	A-33405	Fourmile Polychrome	Bowl
36.e	3024	A-33419	Fourmile Polychrome	Bowl
36.f	3052	A-33397	Fourmile Polychrome	Bowl
36.g	3043	A-33463	Fourmile Polychrome	Bowl
36.h	3037	A-33664	Fourmile Polychrome	Jar
36.i	3011	A-33417	Fourmile Polychrome	Bowl
36.j	3051	A-33413	Fourmile Polychrome	Bowl
37.a	7319		Fourmile Polychrome	Bowl
39.a	23853		Showlow Polychrome	Bowl
39.d	21615		Showlow Polychrome	Bowl
39.f	3032	A-33412	Showlow Polychrome	Bowl
49, 2nd row from top, farthest left	NA	A-33413	Fourmile Polychrome	Bowl
49, 2nd row from top, farthest right	NA	A-33397	Fourmile Polychrome	Bowl
49, 3rd row from top, farthest left	NA	20004	Cedar Creek Polychrome	Bowl
54b, farthest left	NA	A-33419	Fourmile Polychrome	Bowl
54b, 3rd from left	NA	A-33417	Fourmile Polychrome	Bowl
54b, 5th from left	NA	7082	Fourmile Polychrome	Bowl
54c, 5th from left	NA	20004	Cedar Creek Polychrome	Bowl
54e, upper, 5th from left	NA	A-33403	Pinedale Polychrome	Bowl
54e, upper, 6th from left	NA	20005	Pinedale Polychrome	Bowl
54e, lower, 2nd from left	NA	7109	Pinedale Polychrome	Bowl
57	NA	25451	Cedar Creek Polychrome	Bowl
58, upper left	NA	A-33419	Fourmile Polychrome	Bowl
58, lower	NA	A-33397	Fourmile Polychrome	Bowl

Table 7.2. Roosevelt Red Ware Vessels from Kinishba Illustrated by Young (1967)

ASM Catalog No.	Type	Form	Young (1967) Figure No.
20000	Gila Polychrome	Bowl	1
23705	Cliff Polychrome: Tonto Variety	Bowl	18f
A-7370	Tonto Polychrome	Human-effigy jar	9h

Table 7.3. Cibicue Polychrome Vessels from Kinishba Studied by Mauer (1970)

ASM Catalog No.	Form	Mauer (1970) Figure No.
8550	Bowl	6, lower
8576	Bowl	
A-33427	Bowl	6, upper
A-33428	Bowl	6, center
A-33438	Jar	

Table 7.4. Roosevelt Red Ware Vessels from Kinishba Illustrated by Crown (1994)

ASM Catalog No.	Type	Form	Crown (1994) Figure No.
22374	Gila Polychrome	Bowl	9.31, left
23705	Cliff Polychrome: Tonto Variety	Bowl	9.24
A-7370	Tonto Polychrome	Human-effigy jar	8.20
A-33390	Gila Polychrome, no banding time	Bowl	5.38
A-33391	Gila Polychrome, no banding time	Bowl	9.13

Table 7.5. Pinedale Black-on-white Vessels from Kinishba Illustrated by Van Keuren (1999)

ASM Catalog No.	Form	Van Keuren (1999) Figure No.
7380	Jar	4.12l
20011	Jar	4.12k
22534*	Jar	4.12m
A-7369	Jar	4.12i
A-33443	Jar	4.12h
A-33444	Jar	4.12j
A-33445	Jar	4.13n
A-33446	Jar	4.13o

*The caption of the published image of this vessel incorrectly identifies it as A-22534.

Table 7.6. Whole or Reconstructible Vessels from Kinishba not in the Custody of the Arizona State Museum

Disposition	Catalog No.	Ware or General Category	Type	Form	Image(s)
Arizona State Capitol Museum, Phoenix	6735	Red ware	Kinishba Red	bowl	NA
	7337	White Mountain Red Ware	Fourmile Polychrome	bowl	NA
	8548	Roosevelt Red Ware	indeterminate polychrome	bowl	NA
	20061	Corrugated	Indeterminate corrugated	jar	NA
	20077	Red ware	Kinishba Red	bowl	NA
	21972	White Mountain Red Ware	Fourmile Polychrome	bowl	NA
"Destroyed"	7332	Red ware	Kinishba Red	bowl	NA
Holyoke Museum, Holyoke, Massachusetts	5856	Brown ware	plain brown	ladle	NA
	6896	Brown ware	plain brown	pinch pot, form indeterminate	NA
Instituto Etnológico Nacional, Bogotá, Colombia	8556	Cibola White Ware	Pinedale Black-on-white	pitcher	Baldwin 1934:Plate XV2b, 1941:Plate 67B; Murry 1937: Plate XIX
Kinishba Museum	7107	brown ware	plain brown	bowl	NA
	7134	corrugated	indeterminate corrugated	jar	NA
	7223	White Mountain Red Ware	Fourmile Polychrome	bowl	NA
	7225	White Mountain Red Ware	Kinishba Polychrome	bowl	NA
	7318	Roosevelt Red Ware	indeterminate polychrome	bowl	NA

Table 7.6. Whole or Reconstructible Vessels from Kinishba not in the Custody of the Arizona State Museum, cont'd

Disposition	Catalog No.	Ware or General Category	Type	Form	Image(s)
	7325	brown ware	plain brown	ladle	NA
	7330	Cibola White Ware	Black-on-white Roosevelt	jar	NA
	7334	White Mountain Red Ware	Fourmile Polychrome	jar	NA
	7335	White Mountain Red Ware	Fourmile Polychrome	jar	NA
	19994	White Mountain Red Ware	Fourmile Polychrome	jar	NA
	21611	Roosevelt Red Ware	indeterminate polychrome	bowl	NA
	23824	indeterminate decorated	indeterminate polychrome (White Mountain Red Ware?)	bowl	NA
	26016	corrugated	indeterminate corrugated	jar	NA
Missing	6732	red ware	Kinishba Red	jar	NA
	7083	brown ware	plain brown	bowl	NA
	7208	brown ware	plain brown	biglobular jar, miniature	NA
	7227	corrugated	indented flattened corrugated	jar	NA
	8535	corrugated	indented flattened corrugated	jar	NA
	8536	Roosevelt Red Ware	indeterminate polychrome	bowl	NA
	8552	red ware	Kinishba Red	bowl	NA
	19996	Roosevelt Red Ware	indeterminate polychrome	jar	NA
	23000	indeterminate decorated	indeterminate black-on-white	pitcher	NA
	A-33527	corrugated	indented flattened corrugated	jar	NA

Table 7.6. Whole or Reconstructible Vessels from Kinishba not in the Custody of the Arizona State Museum, cont'd

Disposition	Catalog No.	Ware or General Category	Type	Form	Image(s)
Musée National de Préhistoire et d'Ethnographie du Bardo, Algiers, Algeria	21612	White Mountain Red Ware	Fourmile Polychrome	bowl	Baldwin 1941:Plate 86a; Murry 1937:Plate XXXA2, XXXII
Museum of Peoples and Cultures, Brigham Young University, Provo	23723	White Mountain Red Ware	Pinedale Polychrome	bowl	Carlson 1970:Fig 25h
Peabody Museum of Archaeology and Ethnology, Harvard University	7080	red ware	Kinishba Red	bowl	Peabody Museum 2009: Catalog No. 41-47-10/23295
	7128	corrugated	indented corrugated	jar	Peabody Museum 2009: Catalog No. 41-47-10/23298
	7336	White Mountain Red Ware	Fourmile Polychrome	bowl	Peabody Museum 2009: Catalog No. 41-47-10/23194
	20043	red ware	Kinishba Red	bowl	Peabody Museum 2009: Catalog No. 41-47-10/23296
	20982	White Mountain Red Ware	Fourmile Polychrome	bowl	Peabody Museum 2009: Catalog No. 41-47-10/23300
	22378	White Mountain Red Ware	Fourmile Polychrome	jar	Peabody Museum 2009: Catalog No. 41-47-10/23306
	23688	Roosevelt Red Ware	Pinto Polychrome	bowl	Peabody Museum 2009: Catalog No. 41-47-10/23308
	23827	Roosevelt Red Ware	Whiteriver Polychrome: Tonto Variety	bowl	Peabody Museum 2009: Catalog No. 41-47-10/23311

Table 7.6. Whole or Reconstructible Vessels from Kinishba not in the Custody of the Arizona State Museum, cont'd

Disposition	Catalog No.	Ware or General Category	Type	Form	Image(s)
Whiteriver Indian School, Fort Apache Indian Reservation	8567	corrugated	indeterminate corrugated	jar	NA
University of Alaska Museum of the North, Fairbanks	23968	Roosevelt Red Ware	Whiteriver Polychrome: Gila Variety	bowl	provided to ASM 26 April, 2010 by University of Alaska Museum of the North
Unknown	unknown	indeterminate decorated (Jeddito Yellow Ware?)	indeterminate bichrome (Awatovi Black-on-yellow?)	bowl	Clarke 1933:Plate XXIII
	unknown	indeterminate decorated (Jeddito Yellow Ware?)	indeterminate bichrome (Awatovi Black-on-yellow?)	bowl	Cummings 1940:Plate XXVIII
	unknown	indeterminate decorated (Jeddito Orange Ware or Maverick Mountain Series)	Jeddito Polychrome or Maverick Mountain Polychrome	jar	Cummings 1940:Plate XXXI

Table 7.7. The Kinishba Whole and Reconstructible Vessel Assemblage by Ware (Series or General Category), Type (or Type Cluster), and Formal Variety (or Variant)

Ware, Series or General Category	Type or Type Cluster	Type; Type: Variety; or Type, Variant	N	% of Ware, Series, or General Category	% of Utility Ware	% of Painted	% of Total
red ware	Kinishba Red	Kinishba Red	160	91.43	42.55		25.64
		Kinishba Red, Smudged	14	8.00	3.72		2.24
		Kinishba Red, corrugated neck	1	0.57	0.27		0.16
Subtotal			175	100.00	46.54		28.04
brown ware			99	100.00	26.33		15.87
corrugated	indented flattened	indented flattened	42	43.30	11.17		6.73
	indented obliterated	indented obliterated	23	23.71	6.12		3.69
	obliterated	obliterated	9	9.28	2.39		1.44
	indented	indented	8	8.25	2.13		1.28
	indeterminate	indeterminate	5	5.15	1.33		0.80
	indented flattened, smudged	indented flattened, smudged	2	2.06	0.53		0.32
	zoned	zoned	2	2.06	0.53		0.32
	incised	incised	1	1.03	0.27		0.16
	indented, neck-banded	indented, neck-banded	1	1.03	0.27		0.16
	indented flattened, neck-banded	indented flattened, neck-banded	1	1.03	0.27		0.16
	obliterated punched	obliterated punched	1	1.03	0.27		0.16
	obliterated, red-slipped	obliterated, red-slipped	1	1.03	0.27		0.16
	plain	plain	1	1.03	0.27		0.16
Subtotal			97	100.00	25.80		15.54
Mogollon Brown Ware	Tularosa Fillet Rim	Tularosa Fillet Rim	5	33.33	1.33		0.80
	Cibicue Polychrome	Cibicue Polychrome	5	33.33		2.02	0.80
	McDonald Painted Corrugated	McDonald Painted Corrugated	3	20.00		1.21	0.48
	McDonald Patterned Corrugated	McDonald Patterned Corrugated	2	13.33		0.81	0.32
Subtotal			15	100.00			2.40

Table 7.7. The Kinishba Whole and Reconstructible Vessel Assemblage by Ware (Series or General Category), Type (or Type Cluster), and Formal Variety (or Variant), cont'd

Ware, Series or General Category	Type or Type Cluster	Type; Type: Variety; or Type, Variant	N	% of Ware, Series, or General Category	% of Utility Ware	% of Painted	% of Total
Roosevelt Red Ware	Gila Polychrome	Gila Polychrome	35	33.65		14.17	5.61
		Gila Polychrome: Tonto Variety	9	8.65		3.64	1.44
		Gila Polychrome, no banding line	6	5.77		2.43	0.96
		Gila Polychrome: Gila Variety	4	3.85		1.62	0.64
		Gila Polychrome, no banding line, white-on-red exterior	2	1.92		0.81	0.32
		Gila Polychrome, red center: Gila Variety	1	0.96		0.40	0.16
	Subtotal		57	54.81		23.08	9.13
	Whiteriver Polychrome	Whiteriver Polychrome: Gila Variety	12	11.54		4.86	1.92
		Whiteriver Polychrome: Tonto Variety	5	4.81		2.02	0.80
	Subtotal		17	16.35		6.88	2.72
	Pinto Polychrome	Pinto Polychrome	6	5.77		2.43	0.96
		Pinto Polychrome: Salmon Variety	3	2.88		1.21	0.48
	Subtotal		9	8.65		3.64	1.44
	indeterminate Roosevelt Red Ware polychrome	indeterminate Roosevelt Red Ware polychrome	7	6.73		2.83	1.12
	Tonto Polychrome	Tonto Polychrome	3	2.88		1.21	0.48
		Tonto Polychrome (Gila neck, Tonto body)	2	1.92		0.81	0.32
		Tonto Polychrome (Tonto neck, indeterminate body)	1	0.96		0.40	0.16
		Tonto Polychrome: Gila Variety	1	0.96		0.40	0.16
	Subtotal		7	6.73		2.83	1.12

Table 7.7. The Kinishba Whole and Reconstructible Vessel Assemblage by Ware (Series or General Category), Type (or Type Cluster), and Formal Variety (or Variant), cont'd

Ware, Series or General Category	Type or Type Cluster	Type; Type: Variety; or Type, Variant	N	% of Ware, Series, or General Category	% of Utility Ware	% of Painted	% of Total
	Cliff Polychrome	Cliff Polychrome	2	1.92		0.81	0.32
		Cliff Polychrome: Gila Variety	1	0.96		0.40	0.16
		Cliff Polychrome: Tonto Variety	1	0.96		0.40	0.16
		Subtotal	4	3.85		1.62	0.64
	Nine Mile Polychrome	Nine Mile Polychrome: Tonto Variety	2	1.92		0.81	0.32
	Pinto Black-on-red	Pinto Black-on-red	1	0.96		0.40	0.16
Subtotal			104	100.00		42.11	16.67
White Mountain Red Ware	Fourmile Polychrome	Fourmile Polychrome	37	53.62		14.98	5.93
	Pinedale Polychrome	Pinedale Polychrome	7	10.14		2.83	1.12
	Cedar Creek Polychrome	Cedar Creek Polychrome	6	8.70		2.43	0.96
	Showlow Polychrome	Showlow Polychrome	6	8.70		2.43	0.96
	Kinishba Polychrome	Kinishba Polychrome	5	7.25		2.02	0.80
	Pinedale Black-on-red	Pinedale Black-on-red	4	5.80		1.62	0.64
	Showlow Glaze-on-white	Showlow Glaze-on-white	2	2.90		0.81	0.32
	Kinishba Brown-on-buff	Kinishba Brown-on-buff	1	1.45		0.40	0.16
	St. Johns Black-on-red	St. Johns Black-on-red	1	1.45		0.40	0.16
Subtotal			69	100.00		27.94	11.06
Cibola White Ware	Pinedale Black-on-white	Pinedale Black-on-white	23	74.19		9.31	3.69
	Roosevelt Black-on-white	Roosevelt Black-on-white	4	12.90		1.62	0.64
	Kiatuthlanna Black-on-white	Kiatuthlanna Black-on-white	1	3.23		0.40	0.16
	Puerco Black-on-white	Puerco Black-on-white	1	3.23		0.40	0.16
	Tularosa Black-on-white	Tularosa Black-on-white	1	3.23		0.40	0.16
	indeterminate Cibola White Ware	indeterminate Cibola White Ware	1	3.23		0.40	0.16

Table 7.7. The Kinishba Whole and Reconstructible Vessel Assemblage by Ware (Series or General Category), Type (or Type Cluster), and Formal Variety (or Variant), cont'd

Ware, Series or General Category	Type or Type Cluster	Type; Type: Variety; or Type, Variant	N	% of Ware, Series, or General Category	% of Utility Ware	% of Painted	% of Total
indeterminate decorated	Subtotal		31	100.00		12.55	4.97
	indeterminate bichrome	indeterminate bichrome	2	22.22		0.81	0.32
	indeterminate black-on-red	indeterminate black-on-red	2	22.22		0.81	0.32
	indeterminate black-on-white	indeterminate black-on-white	2	22.22		0.81	0.32
	indeterminate polychrome	indeterminate polychrome	2	22.22		0.81	0.32
	indeterminate burned decorated	indeterminate burned decorated	1	11.11		0.40	0.16
White-on-red	Subtotal		9	100.00		3.64	1.44
	Kinishba White-on-red	Kinishba White-on-red	5	71.43		2.02	0.80
		Kinishba White-on-red, smudged	2	28.57		0.81	0.32
Maverick Mountain Series	Subtotal		7	100.00		2.83	1.12
	Tucson Polychrome	Tucson Polychrome	4	57.14		1.62	0.64
	Maverick Mountain Polychrome	Maverick Mountain Polychrome	2	28.57		0.81	0.32
	Nantack Polychrome	Nantack Polychrome: Kayenta Variety	1	14.29		0.40	0.16
Tusayan White Ware	Subtotal		7	100.00		2.83	1.12
	Tusayan Black-on-white	Tusayan Black-on-white	3	75.00		1.21	0.48
	Kayenta Black-on-white	Kayenta Black-on-white	1	25.00		0.40	0.16
Zuni Glaze Ware	Subtotal		4	100.00		1.62	0.64
	Heshotauthla Polychrome	Heshotauthla Polychrome	2	50.00		0.81	0.32
	Kechipawan Polychrome	Kechipawan Polychrome	1	25.00		0.40	0.16
	Kwakina Polychrome	Kwakina Polychrome	1	25.00		0.40	0.16
Jeddito Yellow Ware	Subtotal		4	100.00		1.62	0.64
	Awatovi Black-on-yellow	Awatovi Black-on-yellow	1	50.00		0.40	0.16
	Jeddito Black-on-yellow	Jeddito Black-on-yellow	1	50.00		0.40	0.16
indeterminate			2	100.00		0.81	0.32
	indeterminate	indeterminate	1	100.00			0.16
Grand Total			624		100.00	100.00	100.00

Table 7.8 Roosevelt Red Ware Types, Dates, Summary Descriptions, and References

Type (Date)	Summary Description	Reference(s)
Los Muertos Polychrome (1390–1450)	bowls, jars, mugs; red used as paint (alongside black paint) on white slip.	Lyons and Neuzil 2006; Neuzil and Lyons 2006
Dinwiddie Polychrome (1390–1450)	recurved bowls only; exterior: decoration like Gila or Tonto Polychrome jars, interior: smudged.	Lyons and Neuzil 2006; Neuzil and Lyons 2006
Cliff White-on-red (1390–1450)	recurved bowls only; exterior: white paint on red slip, interior: smudged.	Lyons and Neuzil 2006; Mills and Mills 1972; Neuzil and Lyons 2006
Phoenix Polychrome (1375–1450)	recurved bowls only; exterior: decoration like Gila or Tonto Polychrome jars, interior: slipped red.	Lyons and Neuzil 2006; Neuzil and Lyons 2006
Nine Mile Polychrome (1375–1450)	recurved bowls only; exterior: decoration like Gila or Tonto Polychrome jars, interior: slipped red except for band of black paint on white slip near rim.	Lyons and Neuzil 2006; Neuzil and Lyons 2006
Whiteriver Polychrome (1360–1450)	incurved and hemispherical bowls only; exterior: decoration like Gila or Tonto Polychrome jars, interior: slipped red.	this chapter
Cliff Polychrome[1,2] (1360–1450)	recurved bowls only; interior: two black-on-white design fields (one at rim and one below) separated by banding line, exterior: slipped red[3].	Harlow 1968; Lyons 2004a
Cliff Black-on-red (1360–1450)	recurved bowls only; interior: two black-on-red design fields (one at rim and one below) separated by banding line, exterior: slipped red.	Arizona State Museum Collections
Tonto Polychrome (1340–1450)	jars, bowls, mugs, ladles; bowl interior: panels or meandering ribbons of black paint on white slip surrounded by red slip, bowl exterior: slipped red[3]; jar exterior: (1) single design field comprised by panels or meandering ribbons of black paint on white slip surrounded by red slip, (2) separate design fields for neck and body, each comprised by panels or ribbons of black paint on white slip surrounded by red slip, or (3) separate design fields for neck and body: one comprised by panels or ribbons of black paint on white slip surrounded by red slip, the other consisting of horizontal band of white slip with black paint.	Colton and Hargrave 1937:90–91; Gladwin and Gladwin 1930:8–9; Haury 1945:63–80
Gila Polychrome[1,2,4] (1300–1450)	bowls, jars; bowl interior: black paint on white slip (usually wide, black, banding line at rim), bowl exterior: slipped red[3]; jar exterior: (1) single horizontal band of white slip and black paint, jar base (below black-on-white zone) slipped red, or (2) multiple, horizontal stripes of white slip and black paint separated by stripes of red slip.	Colton and Hargrave 1937:88–90; Gladwin and Gladwin 1930:6–7; Haury 1945:63–80.

Table 7.8 Roosevelt Red Ware Types, Dates, Summary Descriptions, and References, cont'd

Type (Date)	Summary Description	Reference(s)
Gila Black-on-red[5] (1300–1450)	bowls, jars; bowl interior: black paint on red slip (usually wide, black, banding line at rim), bowl exterior: slipped red; jar exterior: black paint on red slip.	Wendorf 1950:123–124
Pinto Polychrome[1,2,4] (1280–1330)	bowls only; interior: black paint on white slip (lacks wide, black, banding line at rim), exterior: slipped red.	Colton and Hargrave 1937:87–88; Gladwin and Gladwin 1930:4–5
Pinto Black-on-red[5] (1280–1330)	bowls only; interior: black paint on red slip (lacks wide, black, banding line at rim), exterior: slipped red.	Gifford 1980:36–37

Notes:
1. Includes "salmon varieties," e.g., Pinto Polychrome: Salmon Variety, Gila Polychrome: Salmon Variety (Di Peso 1958:100; Haury 1931:70–71, 1934:135; Lindsay and Jennings 1968:9; Lyons 2012). Salmon variety vessels (all bowls) exhibit a pink interior surface. Most have been slipped with a pink-firing rather than a white-firing clay, although some appear to be unslipped, i.e., the interior surface is the oxidized color of the clay used to build the vessel. In both cases, the color of the interior contrasts with the red slip applied to the exterior.
2. Includes "Tucson varieties," e.g., Gila Polychrome: Tucson Variety (also known as Pinto-Tucson Polychrome and Gila-Tucson Polychrome; see Di Peso 1958:100; Gerald 1958; Franklin 1980:66; Lindsay and Jennings 1968:12). Such vessels (all bowls) exhibit Roosevelt Red Ware technology (including black, carbon paint) and decoration on the inside and Maverick Mountain Series technology (specifically, that associated with Tucson Polychrome – solid geometric elements in brownish, mineral paint outlined in white; see Lindsay 1992) on the outside.
3. Bowl exteriors may be slipped red and lack painted decoration or, instead, may bear decoration characteristic of Gila Polychrome (e.g., Cliff Polychrome: Gila Variety) or Tonto Polychrome (e.g., Cliff Polychrome: Tonto Variety) jars.
4. Some Gila and Pinto Polychrome bowls bear banded (rather than radial) interior designs similar to those seen on the exteriors of Gila Polychrome jars. Such vessels sometimes exhibit a circular, unpainted area of red slip in the center of the design field. More rarely, black, painted decoration is applied to this area of red slip. In cases such as the latter, the vessel's layout often consists of concentric bands of black painted decoration (some on white slip and some on red slip).
5. Maverick Mountain Black-on-red is often mistakenly identified as Pinto or Gila Black-on-red.

Table 7.9. Vessel Forms Exhibited by the Kinishba Whole and Reconstructible Vessels

Ware, Series, or General Category	Type or Type Cluster	Type; Type: Variety; or Type, Variant	Bowl	Jar	Ladle	Other	Ind.	Total
red ware	Kinishba Red	Kinishba Red	117	41	1	1	0	160
		Kinishba Red, Smudged	14	0	0	0	0	14
		Kinishba Red, corrugated neck	0	1	0	0	0	1
Subtotal			131	42	1	1	0	175
brown ware corrugated	indented flattened	indented flattened	31	47	15	1	5	99
	indented obliterated	indented obliterated	2	39	0	1	0	42
	obliterated	obliterated	0	19	0	4	0	23
	indented	indented	1	8	0	0	0	9
	indeterminate	indeterminate	0	8	0	0	0	8
	indented flattened, smudged	indented flattened, smudged	1	4	0	0	0	5
	zoned	zoned	2	0	0	0	0	2
	incised	incised	0	2	0	0	0	2
	indented, neck-banded	indented, neck-banded	0	1	0	0	0	1
	Indented flattened, neck-banded	indented flattened, neck-banded	0	1	0	0	0	1
	obliterated punched	obliterated punched	0	1	0	0	0	1
	obliterated, red-slipped	obliterated, red-slipped	0	1	0	0	0	1
	plain	plain	0	1	0	0	0	1
Subtotal								
Mogollon Brown Ware	Tularosa Fillet Rim	Tularosa Fillet Rim	6	86	0	5	0	97
	Cibicue Polychrome	Cibicue Polychrome	5	0	0	0	0	5
	McDonald Painted Corrugated	McDonald Painted Corrugated	4	1	0	0	0	5
	McDonald Patterned Corrugated	McDonald Pattemed Corrugated	3	0	0	0	0	3
	Corrugated		1	1	0	0	0	2
Subtotal			13	2	0	0	0	15
Roosevelt Red Ware	Gila Polychrome	Gila Polychrome	23	12	0	0	0	35
		Gila Polychrome: Tonto Variety	9	0	0	0	0	9
		Gila Polychrome, no banding line	6	0	0	0	0	6
		Gila Polychrome: Gila Variety	4	0	0	0	0	4

Table 7.9. Vessel Forms Exhibited by the Kinishba Whole and Reconstructible Vessels, cont'd

Ware, Series, or General Category	Type or Type Cluster	Type; Type: Variety; or Type, Variant	Bowl	Jar	Ladle	Other	Ind.	Total
		Gila Polychrome, no banding line, white-on-red exterior	2	0	0	0	0	2
		Gila Polychrome, red center: Gila Variety	1	0	0	0	0	1
	Subtotal		45	12	0	0	0	57
	Whiteriver Polychrome	Whiteriver Polychrome: Gila Variety	12	0	0	0	0	12
		Whiteriver Polychrome: Tonto Variety	5	0	0	0	0	5
	Subtotal		17	0	0	0	0	17
	Pinto Polychrome	Pinto Polychrome	6	0	0	0	0	6
		Pinto Polychrome: Salmon Variety	3	0	0	0	0	3
	Subtotal		9	0	0	0	0	9
	indeterminate Roosevelt Red Ware polychrome	indeterminate Roosevelt Red Ware polychrome	4	3	0	0	0	7
	Tonto Polychrome	Tonto Polychrome	0	3	0	0	0	3
		Tonto Polychrome (Gila neck, Tonto body)	0	2	0	0	0	2
		Tonto Polychrome (Tonto neck, indeterminate body)	0	1	0	0	0	1
		Tonto Polychrome: Gila Variety	1	0	0	0	0	1
	Subtotal		1	6	0	0	0	7
	Cliff Polychrome	Cliff Polychrome	2	0	0	0	0	2
		Cliff Polychrome: Gila Variety	1	0	0	0	0	1
		Cliff Polychrome: Tonto Variety	1	0	0	0	0	1
	Subtotal		4	0	0	0	0	4
	Nine Mile Polychrome	Nine Mile Polychrome: Tonto Variety	2	0	0	0	0	2
	Pinto Black-on-red	Pinto Black-on-red	1	0	0	0	0	1
Subtotal			83	21	0	0	0	104

Table 7.9. Vessel Forms Exhibited by the Kinishba Whole and Reconstructible Vessels, cont'd

Ware, Series, or General Category	Type or Type Cluster	Type; Type: Variety; or Type, Variant	Bowl	Jar	Ladle	Other	Ind.	Total
White Mountain Red Ware	Fourmile Polychrome	Fourmile Polychrome	30	7	0	0	0	37
	Pinedale Polychrome	Pinedale Polychrome	7	0	0	0	0	7
	Cedar Creek Polychrome	Cedar Creek Polychrome	6	0	0	0	0	6
	Showlow Polychrome	Showlow Polychrome	5	1	0	0	0	6
	Kinishba Polychrome	Kinishba Polychrome	5	0	0	0	0	5
	Pinedale Black-on-red	Pinedale Black-on-red	3	1	0	0	0	4
	Showlow Glaze-on-white	Showlow Glaze-on-white	1	1	0	0	0	2
	Kinishba Brown-on-buff	Kinishba Brown-on-buff	1	0	0	0	0	1
	St. Johns Black-on-red	St. Johns Black-on-red	1	0	0	0	0	1
Subtotal			59	10	0	0	0	69
Cibola White Ware	Pinedale Black-on-white	Pinedale Black-on-white	6	16	1	0	0	23
	Roosevelt Black-on-white	Roosevelt Black-on-white	0	4	0	0	0	4
	Kiatuthlanna Black-on-white	Kiatuthlanna Black-on-white	0	0	1	0	0	1
	Puerco Black-on-white	Puerco Black-on-white	0	1	0	0	0	1
	Tularosa Black-on-white	Tularosa Black-on-white	1	0	0	0	0	1
	indeterminate Cibola White Ware	indeterminate Cibola White Ware	0	1	0	0	0	1
Subtotal			7	22	2	0	0	31
indeterminate decorated	indeterminate bichrome	indeterminate bichrome	2	0	0	0	0	2
	indeterminate black-on-red	indeterminate black-on-red	1	0	1	0	0	2
	indeterminate black-on-white	indeterminate black-on-white	0	2	0	0	0	2
	indeterminate polychrome	indeterminate polychrome	1	1	0	0	0	2
	indeterminate burned decorated	indeterminate burned decorated	1	0	0	0	0	1
Subtotal			5	3	1	0	0	9
White-on-red	Kinishba White-on-red	Kinishba White-on-red	2	3	0	0	0	5
		Kinishba White-on-red, smudged	2	0	0	0	0	2
Subtotal			4	3	0	0	0	7
Maverick Mountain Series	Tucson Polychrome	Tucson Polychrome	3	1	0	0	0	4
	Maverick Mountain Polychrome	Maverick Mountain Polychrome	0	2	0	0	0	2
	Nantack Polychrome	Nantack Polychrome: Kayenta Variety	1	0	0	0	0	1
Subtotal			4	3	0	0	0	7

Table 7.9. Vessel Forms Exhibited by the Kinishba Whole and Reconstructible Vessels, cont'd

Ware, Series, or General Category	Type or Type Cluster	Type; Type: Variety; or Type, Variant	Bowl	Jar	Ladle	Other	Ind.	Total
Tusayan White Ware	Tusayan Black-on-white	Tusayan Black-on-white	0	3	0	0	0	3
	Kayenta Black-on-white	Kayenta Black-on-white	1	0	0	0	0	1
Subtotal			1	3	0	0	0	4
Zuni Glaze Ware	Heshotauthla Polychrome	Heshotauthla Polychrome	2	0	0	0	0	2
	Kechipawan Polychrome	Kechipawan Polychrome	1	0	0	0	0	1
	Kwakina Polychrome	Kwakina Polychrome	1	0	0	0	0	1
Subtotal			4	0	0	0	0	4
Jeddito Yellow Ware	Awatovi Black-on-yellow	Awatovi Black-on-yellow	1	0	0	0	0	1
	Jeddito Black-on-yellow	Jeddito Black-on-yellow	1	0	0	0	0	1
Subtotal			2	0	0	0	0	2
indeterminate	indeterminate	indeterminate	1	0	0	0	0	1
Total			351	242	19	7	5	624

Table 7.10. Dates Assigned to Pottery Types Represented in the Kinishba Vessel or Sherd Assemblages

Ware, Series, or General Category	Type	Dates (A.D.)	Reference(s)	Vessels	Sherds
Cibola White Ware	Kiatuthlanna Black-on-white	850–930	Mills and Herr 1999:Table 8.4	X	
	Puerco Black-on-white	1030–1200	Mills and Herr 1999:Table 8.4	X	
	Snowflake Black-on-white	1100–1275	Mills and Herr 1999:Table 8.4		X
	Tularosa Black-on-white	1180–1300	Mills and Herr 1999:Table 8.4	X	X
	Pinedale Black-on-white	1270–1320	Mills and Herr 1999:Table 8.4	X	X
	Roosevelt Black-on-white	1275–1325/1350	Zedeno 1992:211	X	X
Jeddito Orange Ware	Jeddito Black-on-orange	1250–1350	Lyons 2003; Smith 1971		X
	Jeddito Polychrome	1250–1350	Lyons 2003; Smith 1971	?	
Jeddito Yellow Ware	Awatovi Black-on-yellow	1300/1325–1375/1385	Hays-Gilpin 2008, 2009	X	X
	Bidahochi Polychrome	1300/1325–1375/1385	Hays 1991		X
		1375–1425/1450	Hays-Gilpin 2008, 2009	X	
Maverick Mountain Series	Maverick Mountain Black-on-red	1265–1325	Breternitz 1966:85 (for start date)		X
	Maverick Mountain Polychrome	1265–1325	Breternitz 1966:85 (for start date)	X	X
	Prieto Polychrome	1265–1325	Breternitz 1966:85 (for start date)		X
	Nantack Polychrome: Tusayan Variety	1265–1400	Breternitz 1966:87 (for start date)		X
	Nantack Polychrome: Kayenta Variety	1265–1400	Breternitz 1966:87 (for start date)	X	
	Tucson Polychrome	1300–1400	Lindsay 1992	X	
Mogollon Brown Ware	Point of Pines Punctate	1100–1250	Olson 1959:101–103		X

Table 7.10. Dates Assigned to Pottery Types Represented in the Kinishba Vessel or Sherd Assemblages, cont'd

Ware, Series, or General Category	Type	Dates (A.D.)	Reference(s)	Vessels	Sherds
	Tularosa Fillet Rim	1100–1300	Breternitz 1966:99	X	X
	McDonald Painted Corrugated	1150–1280	Mills and Herr 1999:Table 8.4	X	
	McDonald Patterned Corrugated	1150–1280	Mills and Herr 1999:Table 8.4	X	
	Prieto Indented Corrugated	post-1300	Breternitz 1966:89		X
	Cibicue Polychrome	1330–1350	Hagenbuckle 2000:55	X	X
red ware	Kinishba Red	1300–1400	Breternitz 1966:80(for start date)	X	X
Roosevelt Red Ware	Pinto Black-on-red	1280–1330	Mills and Herr 1999:Table 8.4	X	X
	Pinto Polychrome	1280–1330	Mills and Herr 1999:Table 8.4	X	X
	Gila Polychrome	1300–1450	this chapter	X	X
	Tonto Polychrome	1340–1450	this chapter	X	X
	Cliff Polychrome	1360–1450	this chapter	X	X
	Whiteriver Polychrome	1360–1450	this chapter	X	X
	Nine Mile Polychrome	1375–1450	this chapter	X	X
	Los Muertos Polychrome	1390–1450	this chapter		X
Tsegi Orange Ware	Tusayan Polychrome	1100–1300	Ambler 1985:61–62; Breternitz 1966:100		X
	Kiet Siel Black-on-red	1200–1300	Ambler 1985:61–62		X
Tusayan Gray Ware	Tusayan Corrugated	1000–1300	Breternitz 1966:100		X
	Moenkopi Corrugated	1075–1300	Breternitz 1966:86		X
Tusayan White Ware	Tusayan Black-on-white	1200–1300	Ambler 1985:59	X	X
	Kayenta Black-on-white	1250–1300	Ambler 1985:57–59; Breternitz 1966:79	X	X
White Mountain Red Ware	St. Johns Black-on-red	1200–1300	Mills and Herr 1999:Table 8.4	X	
	St. Johns Polychrome	1200–1300	Mills and Herr 1999:Table 8.4		X
	Pinedale Black-on-red	1280–1330	Mills and Herr 1999:Table 8.4	X	X
	Pinedale Polychrome	1290–1330	Mills and Herr 1999:Table 8.4	X	X

Table 7.10. Dates Assigned to Pottery Types Represented in the Kinishba Vessel or Sherd Assemblages, cont'd

Ware, Series, or General Category	Type	Dates (A.D.)	Reference(s)	Vessels	Sherds
	Cedar Creek Polychrome	1300–1350	Mills and Herr 1999:Table 8.4	X	X
	Fourmile Polychrome	1330–1390	Mills and Herr 1999:Table 8.4	X	X
	Showlow Polychrome	1330–1390	Mills and Herr 1999:Table 8.4	X	X
	Kinishba Brown-on-buff	1330–1390	based on associations with Fourmile Polychrome	X	X
	Kinishba Polychrome	1330–1390	based on associations with Fourmile Polychrome	X	X
	Showlow Glaze-on-white	1330–1390	based on associations with Fourmile Polychrome	X	
	Point of Pines Polychrome	1390–1450	Carlson 1970:79 (adjusted back to 1390)		X
white-on-red	Kinishba White-on-red	1300–1400	Breternitz 1966:80 (for start date; based on Kinishba Red)	X	X
Winslow Orange Ware	Homolovi Polychrome	1260–1350	Lyons 2003		X
Zuni Glaze Ware	Heshotauthla Polychrome	1270–1500	Mills and Herr 1999:Table 8.4; Schachner 2006	X	X
	Kwakina Polychrome	1280–1500	Mills and Herr 1999:Table 8.4; Schachner 2006	X	X
	Kechipawan Polychrome	1370–1500	Eckert 2006; Schachner 2006; Woodbury and Woodbury 1966	X	
	Pinnawa Glaze-on-white	1350–1500	Eckert 2006; Schachner 2006; Woodbury and Woodbury 1966		X

Table 7.11. Sources of Wares and Types Recovered from Kinishba

Ware, Type, or General Category	% of Utility	% of Painted	% of Painted	Source and Reference(s)
Kinisba Red	46.54		28.04	local (Triadan, Chapter 8)
brown Ware	26.33		15.87	assumed to be local
corrugated	25.80		15.54	assumed to be local
Roosevelt Red Ware		42.11	16.67	local (Crown 1994)
White Mountain Red Ware		27.94	11.06	Silver Creek (triadan 1994, 1997; Triadan et al. 2002)
Cibola White Ware		12.55	4.97	Silver Creek (Van Keuren 1994, 1999)
Kinishba White-on-Red		2.83	1.12	local (assumed based on Kinishba Red)
Maverick Mountain Series		2.83	1.12	local (Lindsay 1992)
Zuni Glaze Ware		1.62	0.64	Zuni reservation or Upper Little Colorado (Duff 2002)
Jeddito Yellow Ware		0.81	0.32	Hopi Mesas (Bernardini 2005; Bishop et al. 1988; Duff 2002)
Total	98.67	90.69	95.35	

Table 7.12. Mean Maximum Diameter of Roosevelt Red Ware Bowls by Type

Type(s)	Mean Maximum Diameter (cm)	Standard Deviation	N
Late Types[1]	35.33	3.98	26
Cliff Polychrome	26.26	7.59	89
Gila Polychrome	20.19	5.31	290

[1]Note: Nine Mile Polychrome, Phoenix Polychrome, Dinwiddie Polychrome, and Cliff White-on-red.

Chapter 8
Compositional and Distributional Analyses of Some Fourteenth Century Ceramics from Kinishba Pueblo: Implications for Pottery Production and Migration

Daniela Triadan

Kinishba Pueblo is one of the large aggregated settlements that characterized the thirteenth and fourteenth century landscape in the mountains of east-central Arizona. During the late A.D. 1200s and the 1300s major population shifts and settlement reorganization took place on the southern Colorado Plateau and in the Mogollon mountains (e.g., Mills 1998; Reid et al. 1996). Migration of people from the northern plateau led to settlement aggregation north of the Mogollon Rim in the Silver Creek and the Upper Little Colorado River drainages in the late A.D. 1200s, where large plaza-oriented pueblos, such as Bailey and Pinedale ruins were built (Duff 2002:33-42; Mills 1998, 1999b). Settlement aggregation also started in the Point of Pines (Haury 1989; Lowell 1991) and Kinishba areas in the mountains south of the Mogllon Rim, while the Grasshopper and Q Ranch areas in the eastern part of the mountains remained lightly populated in comparison (Reid 1989). During the early 1300s populations shifted again, and most of the pueblos in the Silver Creek and Upper Little Colorado River area were depopulated, while the mountains south of the Mogollon Rim experienced massive aggregation (Reid 1989; Triadan and Zedeño 2004). Very large pueblos, such as Grasshopper, Point of Pines, and Kinishba expanded rapidly (e.g., Riggs 2001). These settlements eventually had hundreds of rooms, organized in multiple room blocks, and several enclosed plazas. They were the largest pueblos in clusters that also contained pueblos with 50 to 100 rooms and many smaller settlements (Triadan and Zedeño 2004:98-105).

A shift from predominantly black-on-white to polychrome painted pottery accompanied the aggregation. The period is also characterized by an overall increase in variability in the ceramic assemblages of these pueblos (Zedeño and Triadan 2000). Specifically, the distribution of White Mountain Red Ware seems to be linked to migration from above the Mogollon Rim into mountainous areas to the south. During the late 1200s White Mountain Red Ware occurred in high proportions in ceramic assemblages of sites in the Silver Creek area (Mills 1998, 1999c), as well as sites in the Upper Little Colorado drainage (Duff 2002). It occurred mostly as Pinedale Black-on-red and Pinedale Polychrome in the sites in these areas (Carlson 1970:47-57). After 1300, it became a dominant painted ware in the Grasshopper region as well as in other areas south of the Mogollon Rim, especially in the Kinishba and Point of Pines regions, which were previously dominated by Cibola White Ware (Haury 1989; Lowell 1991; Reid 1989; Reid et al. 1996). White Mountain Red Ware succeeded Cibola White Ware in these areas (Montgomery and Reid 1990), and Fourmile Polychrome became the most common type in many sites south of the Mogollon Rim, where its abundance on the surface helps to date those sites (Carlson 1970:65-73; Triadan 1997:97-98). Also, around 1275 White Mountain Red Ware started to occur in considerable numbers in some sites of the eastern Tonto Basin around today's Roosevelt Lake (Christenson 1995; Heidke 1995; Heidke and Stark 1995:App. D) and in sites in the Homol'ovi area (Adams 1996, 1998). The appearance of White Mountain Red Ware is interpreted as evidence for the immigration of Western Puebloan people into these areas and in the Tonto Basin it is associated with non-local, Puebloan architectural features rather than typical compound architecture (e.g., Clark 1995, 2001, 2004; Stark et al. 1995). Thus, the distribution of late thirteenth and fourteenth century White Mountain Red Ware seems to be intricately linked to the late prehistoric demographic developments in east-central Arizona.

Kinishba (together with Point of Pines and Grasshopper) is one of the key sites to understand demographic developments in the fourteenth century in east-central Arizona. Studies of the whole and reconstructible vessel assemblage, complemented by compositional analyses, provide insights into the mechanisms of migration into the mountains, as well as local preferences in ceramic styles that may reflect different interactions between local residents and immigrants. The analyses also enhance knowledge relating to the use and consumption of ceramics at Kinishba.

In this chapter I first summarize my previous research on White Mountain Red Ware. I then briefly describe the relevant ceramic types and their frequencies as whole vessels in the Arizona State Museum Kinishba collections. Next, employing Cummings's unpublished field notes and the results of the compositional analyses of Kinishba ceramics, I present a distributional analysis of whole vessels from domestic and mortuary contexts. These data are used to compare Kinishba with Grasshopper Pueblo and to discuss implications for fourteenth century population movements, regional interactions, and changes in pottery production.

PREVIOUS RESEARCH

To investigate the production, distribution, and consumption of White Mountain Red Ware and the mechanisms of its circulation, I carried out large-scale compositional studies of White Mountain Red Ware and possible local copies that eventually included ceramics from sites on the southern Colorado Plateau to the mountains south of the Mogollon Rim and the Tonto Basin. I employed both instrumental neutron activation analysis (INAA) and petrographic analysis.

In the first phase of the research I analyzed ceramics from the Grasshopper region and sites in adjacent areas south of the Mogollon Rim (Triadan 1997:27, Table 3.8). This study demonstrated that White Mountain Red Ware was imported into Grasshopper Pueblo and sites in adjacent areas during the early A.D.1300s and that this pottery could be differentiated into at least two distinct compositional groups. These nonlocal ceramics were made from light-firing, kaolinitic clays and were tempered with sherds and quartz (Triadan 1997:Plates 3 and 4, 46-49). Kaolinitic clays are not local to the Grasshopper region or the adjacent areas. The nearest outcrops occur about 40 km to the north in cretaceous shale deposits along the eastern Mogollon Rim. As mentioned, the majority of these imported ceramics were Fourmile Polychrome. Later in the occupation of Grasshopper Pueblo, diabase-tempered, brown-paste copies of Fourmile Polychrome, typed predominantly as Grasshopper Polychrome, were produced that are compositionally distinct from the imports and match clays from the pueblo (Triadan 1997:29-55, plates 5 and 6). Given the fact that, before settlement aggregation, White Mountain Red Ware was not part of the local ceramic tradition in the Grasshopper region, I have argued that the majority of the imported White Mountain Red Ware vessels were probably brought to Grasshopper by immigrants, who later started to produce local copies of these ceramics at Grasshopper Pueblo (Triadan 1997; 1998; but see Van Keuren 2001, 2006:97-102).

To address the production and circulation of White Mountain Red Ware from a supraregional perspective, and to further investigate the demographic processes that took place, in the second phase of the research I analyzed larger quantities of ceramics from Kinishba, Cedar Creek, and Point of Pines (sites south of the Mogollon Rim), as well as ceramics from sites in the Homol'ovi area along the Little Colorado River and sites in the eastern Tonto Basin. These new data were compared to and integrated with data from the Silver Creek area generated by Barbara Mills, and data from the Upper Little Colorado River generated by Andrew Duff (Triadan et al. 2002). I originally identified two compositional groups that consisted of light-paste, sherd-tempered White Mountain Red Ware imported into the mountain area south of the Mogollon Rim (Triadan 1997:46-49, Plates 3 and 4). Based on the combined data we can now define four distinct compositional groups for light-paste, sherd-tempered White Mountain Red Ware. The analysis also identified compositional groups that represent local ceramic production at Point of Pines and Kinishba (see Triadan et al. 2002:95-96) as well as two groups that represent locally produced ceramics at Grasshopper (Triadan 1997:29-35).

A good portion of the samples in the second phase of the project (n = 136) came from Kinishba Pueblo. Seven samples analyzed during the first phase brought the total number of samples from Kinishba to 143. I emphasized this site because of its similarities to Grasshopper Pueblo, incuding a generally parallel occupational trajectory (Welch 2007a:3-5; Riggs, this volume). In addition, as is the case for Grasshopper, Kinishba has provided a large collection of provenienced whole and reconstructible vessels that allow a nuanced analysis of the ceramic assemblage and its changes through time.

THE WHOLE VESSEL ASSEMBLAGE

The Kinishba whole vessel collection I originally examined at the Arizona State Museum now contains 624 whole and reconstructible vessels. Until recently the museum's records listed 503 vessels, but since 2008 additional vessels have been located in various collections and brought back to the museum. Lyons (Chapter 7 this volume) describes the whole vessel collection from Kinishba Pueblo currently housed in the museum, including the newly relocated pieces. So here I will only give a brief overview of White Mountain Red Ware, Kinishba Polychrome and Kinishba Red Plain vessels, as they are relevant to questions of White Mountain Red Ware production and distribution and its implications for sociopolitical and demographic changes in the region. I use the original museum database (n = 503) for calculations of quantities of all wares and types represented in the collection (Table 8.1; all tables are at the end of this chapter), but I analyzed all White Mountain Red Ware and Kinishba Polychrome in the collection. I also tabulated whole and reconstructible vessels excavated from different contexts and analyzed their spatial distributions using three additional sources: Cummings's original field

Table 8.1. Vessels from Kinishba in Arizona State Museum Collections[a]

Ware	No.
White Mountain Red Ware	45
Fourmile Polychrome	23
Showlow Polychrome	5
Cedar Creek Polychrome	4
Pindedale Polychrome	7
Pinedale Black-on-red	4
St. Johns Polychrome	2
Showlow Polychrome?	1
Roosevelt Red Ware	90
Tonto Polychrome	36
Gila Polychrome	45
Pinto Polychrome	9
Kinishba Polychrome	5
Zuni, indet.	1
Jeddito Yellow Ware	2
Black-on-white	28
Cibicue Polychrome	6
Maverick Mountain Polychrome	1
Tucson Polychrome	4
McDonald Painted Corrugated	4
Kinishba Red	164
Kinishba Red?	1
Salado Red	1
Corrugated/Plain	119
indet.	31
Total	503

[a]Based on the original Arizona State Museum database.

notes (Arizona State Museum Archives [ASM Arch]:A-414, A-198), Kinishba burial records (Arizona State Museum Bioarchaeology Laboratory [ASM Bio Lab]), and notes included in one of Cummings's notebooks on excavations carried out by the Shaeffers in Group VI (ASM Arch:A-414). The discrepancy between the number of vessels that are currently in the Arizona State Museum collection and the total number of whole and reconstructible vessels that were originally recovered from Kinishba is due mainly to the large number of unpainted corrugated and plain utilitarian vessels that were not curated (see below).

White Mountain Red Ware

White Mountain Red Ware vessels are characterized by a thick orange-red slip and light buff to gray to light orange pastes. The slip was produced using limonite (Haury and Hargrave 1931:26-27, 32-33, Plate 10, Figure 2) and surfaces were polished and painted. Designs were painted in black mineral paint, often a glaze (De Atley 1986; Fenn et al. 2006), and, in the case of the polychrome types, white kaolin-based paint. Vessels were tempered with light-paste sherds—often of the same ware—and quartz (Triadan 1997:46-49, Plate 4). The vast majority of vessels occur as hemispherical bowls (Carlson 1970; Triadan 1997; Van Keuren 2001). White Mountain Red Ware can be classified into a series of chronologically diagnostic types (Carlson 1970). Relevant here because they correlate with the occupation of, Kinishba Pueblo, are St. Johns Black-on-red and Polychrome (ca. A.D. 1175–1280), Pinedale Black-on-red and Polychrome (ca. 1275–1320), Cedar Creek Polychrome (ca. 1300–1350), Fourmile Polychrome (ca. 1325–1400), and Showlow Polychrome (Carlson 1970; Triadan 1997:14-15, 111-113). Showlow Polychrome (Carlson 1970:73-77) is a variant of Fourmile Polychrome and has also been used to classify Fourmile jars. Showlow Polychrome bowls have an all or partially white-slipped interior. I classify Showlow jars as Fourmile.

Fourmile Polychrome vessels are painted in Fourmile style (Figure 8.1), which represents a radical change from the earlier Pinedale style found on Pinedale Black-on-red and Polychrome and Cedar Creek Polychrome. Designs are now focused on bowl centers and are often asymmetrical and figurative, and some vessels depict masked ritual performers (Adams 1991; Hays 1991, 1994; Hays-Gilpin 2006; Van Keuren 2001).

There are 45 White Mountain Red Ware vessels in the Kinishba whole vessel collection, of which four are jars (Table 8.1). The majority are Fourmile Polychrome (n = 23), followed by Pinedale Polychrome (n = 7) and Pinedale Black-on-red (n = 4). The collection also includes Cedar Creek Polychrome (n = 4), Showlow Polychrome bowls (n = 5) and two St. Johns Polychrome bowls. A few of the vessels have orange pastes and one has a brown paste. These vessels may have been locally produced, but their exteriors and decoration are

Figure 8.1. Light-paste Fourmile Polychrome bowl, ASM A-33,397 (Daniela Triadan, courtesy Arizona State Museum).

indistinguishable from imported, light-paste vessels. Two of the sherd samples analyzed by INAA were assigned to a compositional group that represents locally produced vessels (see below). They were tempered primarily with local basalt and also contain some plagioclase and minor quantities of biotite and pyroxene minerals. This indicates that small quantities of White Mountain Red Ware ceramics were made at Kinishba, perhaps using imported slips and paints. However, in contrast to Point of Pines and Grasshopper there are no vessels that look like poorly executed local copies, such as Point of Pines Polychrome (Carlson 1970:77-82; Wendorf 1950:49), or that use carbon paint and hematite slips, such as Grasshopper Polychrome (Triadan 1997:15-16, Plate 1c and d).

Kinishba Polychrome

Kinishba Polychrome was first defined by Baldwin (1938b, 1938c). Baldwin (1938b:22) thought that it was made at Kinishba, because at that time Kinishba seemed to be the site that had the largest quantity of this type and it had whole vessels (see e.g., Cummings 1940:frontispiece). In actuality only five whole or reconstructible Kinishba Polychrome vessels were recovered from Kinishba (see Table 8.1), and it is unclear how much Kinishba Polychrome was found in discard deposits. In comparison, at Grasshopper 12 whole and reconstructible Kinishba Polychrome vessels were found on the floors of four late abandoned rooms and in three burials (Triadan 1997:Figures 4.16 and 4.24). It should be emphasized that all of these vessels were non-local.

Kinishba Polychrome vessels have a light paste, and are covered with a buff to yellowish slip (Figure 8.2). Designs are executed in black mineral paint, typically outlined in red, with some opposed black and red motifs and occasional solid red motifs and other variations. The type appears to occur only as hemispherical bowls, and most of them are fairly large. The decorative color scheme seems to invert the Fourmile Polychrome scheme and to emulate Hopi Yellow Ware, specifically Sikyatki Polychrome. Baldwin (1938b:25-26) noted this and relates Kinishba Polychrome to Fourmile Polychrome: "The new type of pottery called Kinishba Polychrome is a Pueblo IV pottery type representing an outgrowth of Four-Mile Polychrome. It has a yellowish-buff background, and is decorated in black and red. … The yellowish slip may be due to the influence of Jeddito black on yellow, but the vessel shapes, areas decorated, paste and temper and styles of design are typically Four-Mile." [Baldwin 1939:83-84]

The Kinishba assemblage also includes a few vessels that are hybrids between Fourmile Polychrome and Kinishba Polychrome (Figure 8.3). These vessels indicate that the same potters made both types of ceramics, which is also supported by the compositional data discussed below.

In general, Kinishba Polychrome occurs in low frequencies in sites along the Mogollon Rim and the mountains to the south. In

Figure 8.2. Kinishba Polychrome bowl, ASM A-33,530 (Daniela Triadan, courtesy Arizona State Museum).

Figure 8.3. Exterior (left) and interior (right) views of a sherd from a Kinishba Polychrome/Fourmile Polychrome hybrid bowl (Daniela Triadan, courtesy Arizona State Museum).

addition to the five whole and reconstructible vessels from Kinishba and 12 from Grasshopper, Haury recovered one Kinishba Polychrome bowl and some sherds from the Canyon Creek Ruin (Haury 1934:134-135, Figure 25b). The Arizona State Museum has three whole Kinishba polychrome vessels from Showlow Ruin. An inspection of the surface scatter and looter-disturbed contexts at Tundastusa Pueblo in the Forestdale Valley recorded 34 sherds (Arrighetti 2004). Van Keuren (personal communication) found two sherds at Fourmile Ruin (Table 8.2). Surface collections from the Grasshopper region and adjacent areas similarly yield low quantities of Kinishba Polychrome sherds.

Other than the 12 whole and reconstructible vessels recovered through excavations at Grasshopper Pueblo, I found no Kinishba Polychrome sherds in the systematic surface collections from the site (Triadan 1997:58). There were small numbers of sherds in the fill of some rooms at Grasshopper (Triadan 1997:Tables 4.3 and 4.4). The occurrence of some Kinishba Polychrome sherds in room fill, as well as the vessels found on room floors may indicate that Kinishba Polychrome was imported into Grasshopper sometime after the establishment of the settlement and that its production started sometime after Fourmile Polychrome was established as a type. Mills (1999c) does not report any Kinishba Polychrome sherds for the sites in the Silver Creek area she and her students inspected and partially excavated. These sites predate the Pueblo IV sites where Kinishba Polychrome was found and may support this interpretation. Although dating to the same time period as Grasshopper and Kinishba in its later occupations, no Kinishba Polychrome vessels were found at Point of Pines although there were some sherds (see below). This may indicate that the southernmost extension of Kinishba Polychrome distribution is the Salt River drainage.

Although certainly noticeable where it is found, the low frequencies of Kinishba Polychrome show that this type was neither commonly nor frequently used. Potters who were making Fourmile Polychrome may have tried to emulate Sikyatki Polychrome, which resulted in Kinishba Polychrome. Mills (2007:229) suggests on the basis of the disproportionately large size of many Kinishba Polychrome vessels that the type may have been used in communal feasting.

Kinishba Red

Kinishba Red pottery is frequently mentioned in early reports (see Baldwin 1937:2; Cummings 1940:81; Jones 1935:3; Mott 1936:3), but the formal description of Kinishba Red as a distinct type was not provided until the Point of Pines project (Wendorf 1950:42-43). Kinishba Red vessels have gray to light brown pastes, often with brown or orange edges, which indicates that the cores were insufficiently oxidized during firing (Rice 1987:88; Shepard 1985:21, 81-83). The vessels are tempered predominantly with basalt and are covered with an orange-red slip that was probably limonite-based. Many vessels show smoothing, polishing or both (Figure 8.4). The slips are similar

Table 8.2. Kinishba Polychrome Sherds Identified in Surface Collections

Site No.[a]	Site Name	No. of sherds	Type of collection
AZ P:14:15[b]	Oak Creek Pueblo	1	unsystematic, close to pothunted area
AZ P:14:25[b]	Red Canyon Tank Pueblo	6	unsystematic
AZ P:14:281[b]		1	unsystematic
AZ V:2:7[b]	Ruin's Tank Pueblo	1	unsystematic
AZ P:14:12[c]	Hilltop Pueblo	1	systematic?
AZ P:14:13[c]	Brush Mountain Pueblo	17 + 1 Kinishba/Fourmile hybrid	systematic?
AZ P:12:4[d]	Tundastusa	34	systematic, close to disturbed areas
AZ P:16:3[e]	Fourmile Ruin	2	excavations

Note:
[a] Arizona State Museum site identifier.
[b] Surface collections conducted by Triadan in 1991 (Triadan 1997:96).
[c] Surface collections conducted by David Tuggle in 1969.
[d] From 28 collection areas (Arrighetti 2004:App. B).
[e] Total sherds 2639 (Van Keuren personal communication).
I used surface collections from 33 sites from the Grasshoper region and adjacent areas (Triadan 1997:Table 3.8); only the six sites listed here had Kinishba Polychrome.

Figure 8.4. Kinishba Red bowl, ASM A-33,386 (Daniela Triadan, courtesy Arizona State Museum).

in color to White Mountain Red Ware slips, but the vessels lack painted designs. Vessels occur both as jars and hemispherical bowls with incurved rims, but bowls predominate. Most of the jars are narrow-necked and served probably as water storage jars.

There are at least 164 Kinishba Red vessels in the Arizona State Museum collection (Table 8.1) of which 127 are bowls (nine of the bowls have smudged black interiors) and 35 are jars. There is also one dipper and one unidentified object of this type.

DISTRIBUTIONS OF WHOLE AND RECONSTRUCTIBLE VESSELS

Analyses of ceramic provenience and distributional patterns within a site yield information on the differential use and deposition of pottery types and forms, but not necessarily on their provenance, or their actual locus of production. Such questions require chemical or mineralogical analyses. Discard patterns and use-life can be reconstructed by analyzing refuse deposits (R. Lightfoot 1993; Varien and Mills 1997; Schiffer 1987; Triadan 1997:58-64). Use and storage behavior may be reconstructed through de facto refuse or *in situ* artifact assemblages (Schiffer 1987; Inomata et al. 2002). At Kinishba, however, few systematic surface collections were carried out and it is unclear whether stratigraphic excavations were conducted in midden areas. Instead, most of the pottery from Kinishba comes from excavations of rooms and extramural areas aimed at uncovering occupation surfaces and burials. Because systematic sherd counts from room fills are not available, reconstructing discard patterns through refuse analysis is not possible at this time.

However, some information of how pottery was used can be gleaned from Kinishba's whole and reconstructible vessels. Although published reports (Baldwin 1938a, 1939; Cummings 1935b, 1938, 1940; Mott 1936) give little information on contexts where the whole and reconstructible vessels were found or how they were distributed across the site, Cummings's field notes and other archival material provide such information (ASM Arch:A-414; A-198; ASM Bio Lab:Kinishba burial records).

Distribution of Vessels from Room Floors and Roofs

Between 1931 and 1947 around 240 of a total of approximately 600 rooms (about 35 percent of the site), along with the Courtyard A and B were excavated at Kinishba (Table 8.3; Figure 2.2; Cummings 1940; Welch 2007a:3-5; ASM Arch:A-414:Notebooks #1 and #2, A-198: Notebook #7). Cummings lists 207 rooms in his notes, but some so-called rooms are

Table 8.3. Rooms Excavated at Kinishba Pueblo[a]

Room Block	Number of Rooms
Group I[b]	c. 200[c]
Group II	10
Group III[b]	12
Group IV	12
Group VI[b]	8
Group VIII	6?
Total	c. 242-250

Note:
[a]based on Cummings' field notes (Arizona State Museum Archives A-414 and A-198, and the Shaeffer and Schaeffer report (Chapter 3 this volume).
[b]all rooms excavated.
[c]some room numbers were given to spaces that were not rooms and some room numbers were not used.

recesses and the entryways into the room block (see Cummings 1940:2-3, plan of Group I). In comparison, at Grasshopper, 103 of a total of 447 rooms or 23 percent were excavated from 1963 to 1992 (Riggs 2001:32, Table 2.8).

The majority of the whole and reconstructible vessels from Kinishba come from room floors and roofs, with a smaller number from burials. For this analysis I took vessel counts from Cummings's field notes and room plans and notes that were associated with the Shaeffers' excavations of Group VI (ASM Arch:A-414, see also Shaeffer and Shaeffer [Chapter 3 this volume]). It should be noted that there are minor discrepancies between the numbers listed with the ASM database (Table 8.1). On the one hand some vessels in the database may not have been recorded in Cummings's notes; on the other hand not all vessels that were excavated were curated. Of a total of at least 724 whole and reconstructible vessels, 590 (possibly more) or 81.5 percent were recovered from these rooms, in contrast to 134 vessels or 18.5 percent found in burials (see Table 8.4).

Most vessels from room floors and roofs are corrugated or plain ware (n = 298 or 50.51 percent of all ceramics on floors). Corrugated storage jars predominate (Table 8.4, Figure 8.5; see also Baldwin 1937:2). Many unpainted vessels seem not to have been curated. The Arizona State Museum database lists only 119 corrugated and plain ware vessels. The next most abundant ware is Kinishba Red (n = 150, 25.42 percent), for which bowls are somewhat more common than jars. These wares are followed in frequencies by Roosevelt Red Ware, mostly Gila and Tonto Polychrome bowls (n = 67, 11.36 percent) and White Mountain Red Ware (n = 43, 7.29 percent), predominantly Fourmile Polychrome bowls. There are also a small number of Cibola White Ware ollas (n = 18, 3.05 percent), two Cibicue Polychrome vessels (0.34 percent), one Kinishba Polychrome bowl (0.17 percent), two Jeddito Yellow Ware vessels (0.34 percent), and nine indeterminate vessels (1.53 percent; Table 8.4).

The sample is heavily weighted towards Group I because this is where most room excavations occurred (see Table 8.3). Discrepancies in descriptions and numbers within the Arizona State Museum database and the unpublished field records, especially in the counts of painted vessels and types (which I assume were all curated) are likely due to ambiguities in field notes and provenience records. For instance, some descriptions in the field notes only list "polychrome bowl," without identification of the ware. On the other hand, the ASM database lists several Tucson Polychromes and one Maverick Mountain Polychrome that are not identified as such in Cummings's notes because these types were only defined after his work at Kinishba (see Table 8.1). Systematic cross-checking is needed to resolve such ambiguities.

Most of the rooms with vessels have several, and some rooms have large quantities. For example, Room 105 in Group I had 42 vessels on floors; Room 1 in Group IV had 17. As is true for Grasshopper, it is likely that rooms with reconstructible vessels on the floors were abandoned late in the pueblo's occupation (see Montgomery 1992, 1993:157-158, Figure 12.2; Reid 1973:114-118). Early abandoned rooms at Grasshopper had no *in situ* artifacts on the floors and high sherd quantities in room fills (Reid 1973:116, Triadan 1997:58-64). It is not clear what the sherd quantities in room fills at Kinishba were, but Cummings does occasionally note sherd counts or percentages by ware for rooms that do not have vessels on the floor. This suggests that those quantities might have been at least noteworthy in the overall context of excavations.

Kinishba Red bowls are by far the most common serving vessels on room floors. If those rooms, as I propose, were late in the

Table 8.4. Reconstructible and Partial Vessels on Room Floors and Roofs

Context	Brown Corr./Plain					White Mountain Red Ware				Roosevelt Red Ware				Kinishba Red Plain			
	Jars	Bowls	Plate	Total	%	Jars	Bowls	Total	%	Jars	Bowls	Total	%	Jars	Bowls	Total	%
Group I	207	18	1	226	48.29	6	32	38	8.12	16	32	57	12.18	54	65	119	25.43
Plaza A, Group I										0	1	1	100				
Group II	17	0	0	17	51.52	1	3	4	12.12	0	3	3	9.09	3	6	9	27.27
Group III	15	1	0	16	64.00	1	0	1	4.00	1	2	3	12.00	0	3	3	12.00
Group IV	3	1	0	4	44.44									0	3	3	33.33
Group VI	35	0	0	35	64.81					0	3	3	5.56	3	13	16	29.63
Total	277	20	1	298	50.51	8	35	43	7.29	17	41	67	11.36	60	90	150	25.43

Context	Black-on-White				Cibicue Poly.				Kinishba Poly				Jeditto Yellow Ware				% Indet.	Total All Types
	Jars	Bowls	Total	%	Jars	Bowls	Total	%	Jars	Bowls	Total	%	Jars	Bowls	Total	%		
Group I	17	0	17	3.63	1	1	2	0.43	0	1	1	0.21					8 1.71	468
Plaza A, Group I																		1
Group II																		33
Group III													0	2	2	8.00		25
Group IV	1	0	1	11.11													1 11.11	9
Group VI																		54
Total	18		18	3.05	1	1	2	0.43		1	1	0.17		2	2	0.34	9 1.53	590

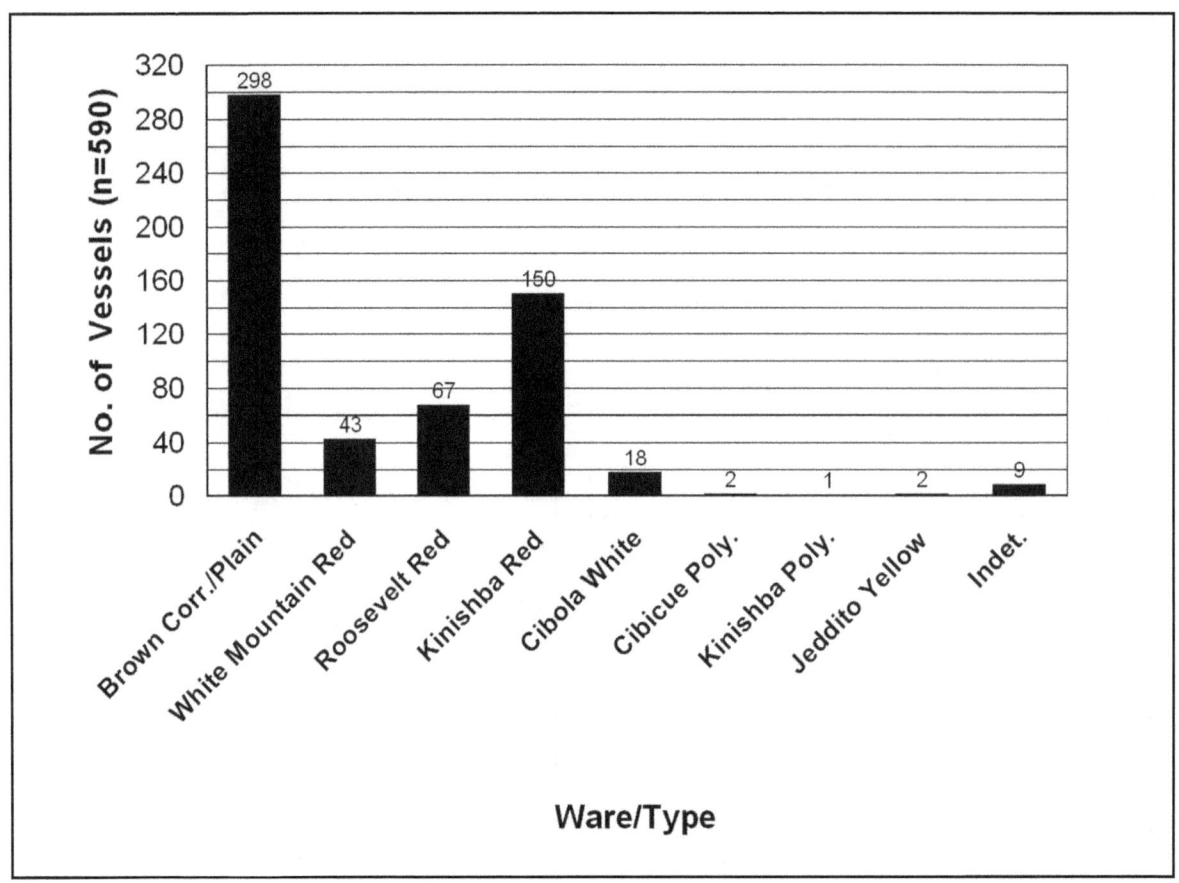

Figure 8.5. Quantity of vessels on room floors by ware or type.

occupation sequence then they would occupy a similar temporal position as Grasshopper Polychrome bowls at Grasshopper (Triadan 1997:64-65, Figure 4.7). Shaeffer and Shaeffer (Chapter 3) mention that Group IV and most parts of Group I are late in the occupation sequence because of the occurrence of Gila Polychrome and Red Plain Ware. It should be mentioned that neither Cummings nor others distinguished Gila from Tonto Polychrome, but the Arizona State Museum database lists 36 Tonto Polychrome bowls and jars out of 90 total Roosevelt Red Ware vessels (Table 8.1). Some Kinishba Red vessels were found on lower floors. This could indicate either that the room had two stories and the vessels were found on the first story floor, or that the production of Kinishba Red Polychrome started shortly after the initial aggregation and expansion of the pueblo. Interestingly, at Kinishba, Roosevelt Red Ware is the most common painted ware (Table 8.4), while at Grasshopper White Mountain Red Ware is more common on room floors, second to the locally produced Grasshopper Polychrome (Triadan 1997:64, Figure 4.7). There is little locally produced Fourmile Polychrome pottery at Kinishba. Kinishba Red appears to fill that role.

Distribution of Vessels in Burials

At Kinishba at least 266 burials and three cremations were excavated in extramural areas and rooms. The burials represent more than 266 individuals, because some of them contained multiple inhumations. Most of the burials found in rooms came from Group I. In addition one adult burial was found in Room 2 of Group II and one adult burial was found in Room 12 of Group III. Overall there were 190 burials in rooms, representing approximately 31 adults and subadults, along with 159 children (Table 8.5). This distinction is very rough, as it is not clear up to what age burials were classified as children.

A total of 76 burials were found in extramural areas, mostly Burial Grounds I, II, and III, excavated in 1931, 1932, and 1934. Burial Ground I is located directly west of Group II, Burial Ground II is slightly north of Group IV in the east bank of the eastern fork of the wash, and Burial Ground III is on the spur between the east and west fork of the wash, opposite of Group VI. Sixty-four of these burials were adults and 12 children. This brings the total burial assemblage to 95 adult and subadult burials and 171 child burials (Table 8.5).

The burial distribution shows that adults seemed to have been predominantly buried in extramural areas and children mostly under room floors. In the population of burials recovered from under room floors (n = 190), 83.7 percent are children (n = 159) and 16.3 percent are adults and subadults (n = 31). In the population from extramural areas (n = 76) the pattern is reversed: there are 84.2 percent adults (n = 64) and 15.8 percent children (n = 12) (ASM Arch:A-414, A-198; ASM Bio Lab:Kinishba burial records). The larger number of child burials in the sample overall is likely due to Cummings's decision to focus most excavations on rooms.

On the basis of the data I was able to find and tabulate from the burial records and Cummings's fieldnotes, 134 vessels were found in burials (Figure 8.6, Table 8.6). The majority of the vessels in burials are bowls (n = 71), and in this category Kinishba Red is by far the most prominent (n = 37), followed by corrugated or plain bowls (n = 15), Roosevelt Red Ware (n = 9) and White Mountain Red Ware (n = 7) (Table 8.6). By overall ware category, corrugated and plain vessels (n = 45, 33.58 percent) are present in slightly higher numbers than Kinishba Red vessels (n = 44, 32.84 percent). Jars (n = 34) are mostly small and occur mainly as corrugated or plain or Kinishba Red.

Of the 31 adult and subadult burials found in rooms, only three (9.7 percent) had vessels, a total of nine pots (Table 8.7). Many of these individuals may not have been formally interred, which might account for the low number of ceramics associated with these burials. Age and sex were not systematically recorded for these adult and subadult burials. Of the 159 child burials from rooms, 44 (27.7 percent) had pots resulting in a total of 75 vessels. There were only six or seven painted bowls among these vessels and they included three Gila or Tonto polychromes, one Pinto Polychrome, one Fourmile Polychrome, one black-on-white bowl and maybe one additional polychrome bowl. Slightly over fifty percent of the 44 child burials with ceramics had one vessel (n = 24, 54.5 percent), 10 (22.7 percent) had two vessels, nine (20.5 percent) had three vessels, and one (2.3 percent) had four vessels.

Of the 64 adult burials from extramural areas, 33 (51.6 percent) had vessels buried with them, while of the 12 child burials from these areas, only four (33.3 percent) had pots. In total there were 46 vessels associated with adults and four with children. Similar to the child burials found in rooms, the adult burials from extramural areas had few painted ceramics: the 11 polychrome vessels from these contexts include two Pinto Polychromes, one Pinedale Polychrome or Black-on-red, two Cedar Creek Polychromes, two Fourmile Polychromes, two Gila or Tonto Polychromes (including possibly a Tonto Polychrome jar), one potential Cibicue Polychrome, and one unidentified

Table 8.5. Kinishba Burials

Context	Adults					Total	Children	Total Burials
Extramural	Male	Female	prob. Male	prob. Female	Indet.			
Burial Ground I	20	15	3	2	2	42	8	50
Burial Ground II	3	7	3	2		15	1	16
Burial Ground III	1	1	1		2	5	2	7
Other	2					2	1	3
Total	26	23	7	4	4	64	12	76
In rooms						31	159	190
Total both contexts						95	171	266

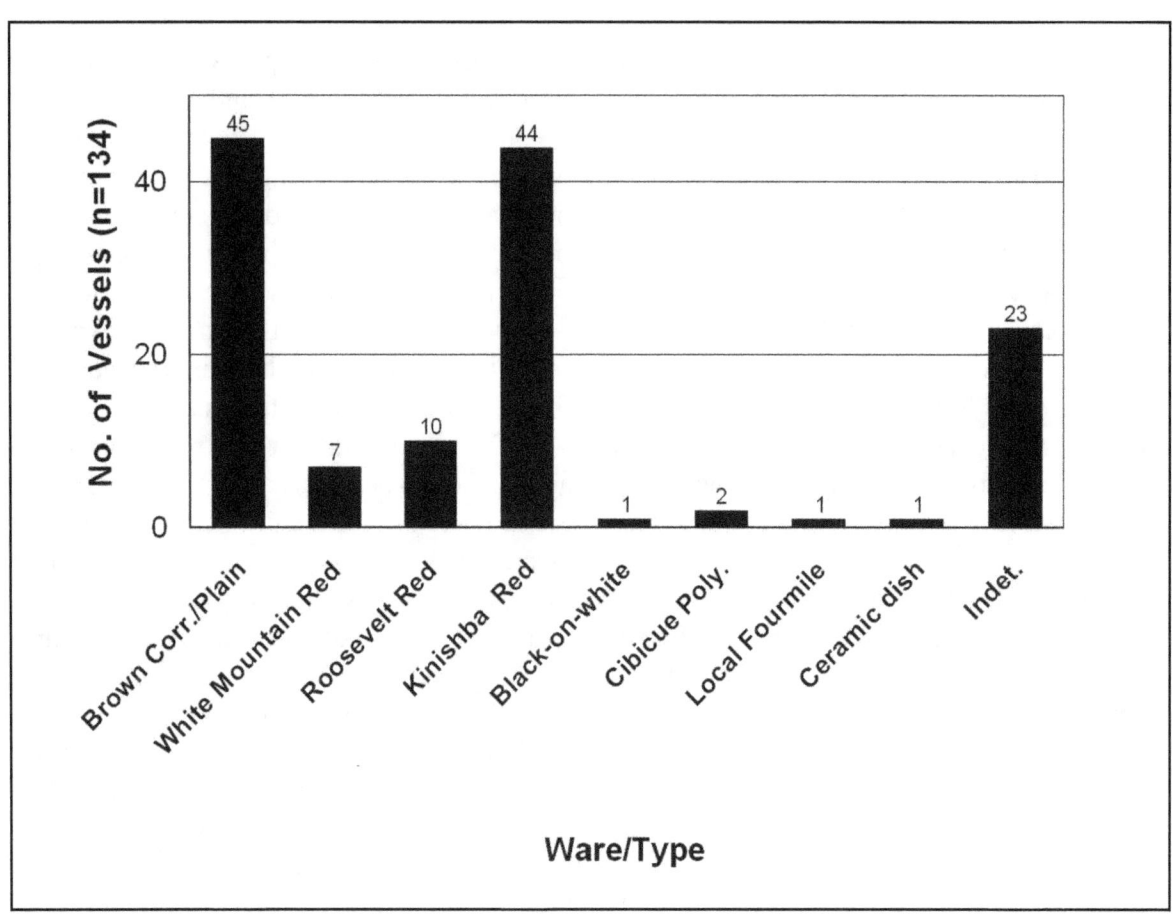

Figure 8.6. Quantity of vessels in burials by ware or type.

8: Implications for Pottery 223

Table 8.6. Vessels in Burials

Context	Brown Corr./Plain						White Mountain Red Ware				Roosevelt Red Ware				Kinishba Red Plain				
	Jars	Bowls	Plate	Indet.	Total	%	Jars	Bowls	Total	%	Jars	Bowls	Total	%	Jars	Bowls	Total	%
Burials under room floors	21	12		4	37	44.05		1	1	1.19		5	5	5.95	5	17	22	26.19
Extramural burials	4	3	1		8	16.00		6	6	12.00	1	4	5	10.00	2	20	22	44.00
Total	25	15	1	4	45	33.58		7	7	5.24	1	9	10	7.47	7	37	44	32.84

Context	Black-on-White			Cibique Poly.			Local Fourmile/ Kinishba Red			Ceramic dish			Indet.			Total all types
	Jars	Bowls	Total	%	Jars	Bowls	Total	%	Jars	Bowls	Total	%	Total	%		
Burials under room floors	1		1	1.19	1		1	1.19	1		1	1.19	1	1.19	15	17.86	84
Extramural burials				2.00		1	1	2.00							8	16.00	50
Total	1		1	1.49	1	1	2	1.49	1		1	0.75	1	0.75	23	17.16	134

Table 8.7. Burials with Vessels

Context	Adults										
	Male	With Vessels	%	Female	With Vessels	%	All Male[a]	With Vessels	%	All Female[a]	With Vessels	%	Indet.
Extramural	26	18	69.2	23	10	43.5	33	20	60.6	27	20	48.2	4
In rooms													
Total													

Context	Total Adults	With Vessels	%	Children	With Vessels	%	Total Burials	With Vessels	%
Extramural	64	33	51.6	12	4	33.3	76	37	48.7
In rooms	31	3	9.7	159	44	27.7	190	47	24.7
Total	95	36	37.9	171	48	28.1	266	84	31.6

[a] includes probable males or females.

polychrome bowl. Four of the adult burials from the extramural areas (12.1 percent) had three vessels buried with them, the maximum number found with any adult burial. The overwhelming majority of burials with vessels had one pot (n = 24, 75.8 percent), and five burials (15.2 percent) had two vessels.

In contrast to the burials found in rooms, relatively detailed burial records exist for the extramural burials. Most of the adult burials from these extramural areas have been sexed, although it is not clear how reliable these attributions are (see Table 8.7). The forms display notes and corrections that were added later, but it is not clear by whom. Walter Birkby, who used some of the Kinishba skeletal material for his dissertation, states that there were no burials records available when he was conducting his analyses (Birkby 1973:18, 46).

Based on the available information on the extramural adult burials the overall sex ratio is slightly skewed towards males, and male burials are more often associated with ceramics (Table 8.7). Of the 26 burials with individuals identified as males, 18 (69.2 percent) had ceramic vessels; of the 23 burials with individuals identified as females, 10 (43.5 percent) had vessels. If probable males and females are included, the percentages shift slightly: 20 (60.6 percent) of 33 males and 13 (48.2 percent) of 27 females had vessels. Of the four burials with three vessels, three were male and one female.

Looking at the overall pattern, ceramics occur more often in adult burials than child burials and males are more often interred with at least one pot except for the intramural adults. Cummings (1940) notes that many adult burials found in the excavated rooms seem not to have been formally interred, and the very low percentage of intramural adult burials with ceramics may reflect the informality of adult burial practices. Unfortunately his notes are not very detailed on the intramural burials.

Despite this general pattern, one child burial had the most pots (four) recorded for any burials at Kinishba. The majority of vessels found in burials are bowls and within that category the majority are Kinishba Red, although when considering both bowls and jars of different types and wares, corrugated and plain vessels are slightly more common. This pattern is somewhat different from Grasshopper, where White Mountain Red Ware is more common in burials than the locally produced Grasshopper Polychrome copies (Triadan 1997:78, Figure 4.19). Roosevelt Red Ware and White Mountain Red Ware ceramics make up only 7.47 percent and 5.24 percent of the Kinishba burial ceramics respectively.

On-site Pottery Manufacture at Kinishba

There is evidence for on-site ceramic manufacture at Kinishba, although no firing features have been documented. Several rooms had artifacts that could have been used in forming, finishing, and decorating pottery (see Triadan 1989 for pottery production evidence from Grasshopper Pueblo). Part of a floor assemblage clearly suggesting ceramic manufacture comes from Room 64 in Group I, excavated in 1934 and 1935 (ASM Arch:A-413:70:241). Among many other artifacts the room contained a basket made of yucca fiber with potting clay inside it, a small cotton bag with mineral pigments (i.e., azurite, hematite and malachite, some of which showed evidence of having been ground), a pottery smoother, and polishing stones. Clay was also found in Rooms 94 and 105 in Group I, and Rooms 48 and 54 had kaolin clay and tempering material (ASM Arch:A414). The most convincing evidence for pottery manufacture comes from Rooms 73 and 124 of Group I, where two unfired vessels were found. The vessel in Room 73 was an unfired bowl, reddish in color with "much fine sand for temper" (ASM Arch:A-414:83). This may have been an unfired Kinishba Red bowl. The vessel in Room 124 is described as an "unfired pot filled with clay, corded twilled impression on clay in pot" (ASM Arch:A-414:163). This suggests that the clay had been originally wrapped in some kind of textile. Many other rooms had mineral pigments and polishing stones, as well as bone scrapers, but it is possible that the pigments were used for decorating other objects, such as stone palettes, (see Cummings 1940:Plate XXXIV, 107) or used as body paint.

Compositional Analyses of Kinishba Ceramics

As part of my supraregional research I analyzed 143 ceramics from Kinishba Pueblo using neutron activation analysis (INAA), seven in the first phase and 136 in the second phase of the sourcing project (Triadan 1997; Triadan et al. 2002; see Table 8.8 which can be found at the end of the chapter). Thirteen of these ceramics were also analyzed petrographically (two sherds from Kinishba had been analyzed previously [Triadan 1997:Table 3.20], which brings the total to 15). The majority of the ceramics came from the excavations undertaken by Cummings, but some of the analyzed sherds also came from surface collections by Gila Pueblo and others (see proveniences in Table 8.8). Exact proveniences for the samples were not available, but it is safe to assume that the majority of samples from excavations came from rooms in Group I (see Figure 2.2).

Instrumental Neutron Activation Analysis

The ceramics were analyzed both at the then Smithsonian Center for Materials Research and Education (SCMRE) in collaboration with the reactor facilities at the National Institute for Standards and Technology (NIST) and at the Research Reactor Center of the University of Missouri (MURR). The analyses were carried out in collaboration with Dr. Ronald L. Bishop and Dr. M. James Blackman (SCMRE), and Dr. Hector Neff and Dr. Michael D. Glascock (MURR). Sample preparation, irradiation procedures, and the subsequent data analyses followed protocols established by both laboratories (Bishop and Neff 1989:63; Blackman 1986; Glascock 1992; Harbottle 1976; Sayre 1975; Triadan 1997:26-29). Principal components were first calculated on the basis of 26 elements and the whole data set, except analyzed source clays. Ellipses in the resulting figures represent a confidence interval of 90 percent for membership in the respective compositional group.

Pooling INAA data from both phases of the project and data generated by Andrew Duff and Barbara Mills resulted in a database of 772 analyzed ceramics. This unprecedented sample enables the definition of four distinct compositional groups for light-paste, sherd-tempered White Mountain Red Ware; one of those groups contains White Mountain Red Ware and Cibola White Ware exclusively from Bailey Ruin (Triadan et al. 2002). For the bivariate plots that show these compositional groups (Figures 8.7 and 8.8) principal components were calculated on the basis of 26 elements and the samples assigned to the four groups. Ellipses represent a confidence interval of 90 percent for membership in the respective compositional group. The compositional group that I originally labeled as Group 1 could be further divided into two separate groups, WMR Group 1 and WMR Group 3, a trend that was already visible in the original data set (Triadan 1997:35, 37).

Using these data as a basis, light-paste White Mountain Red Ware from Kinishba can

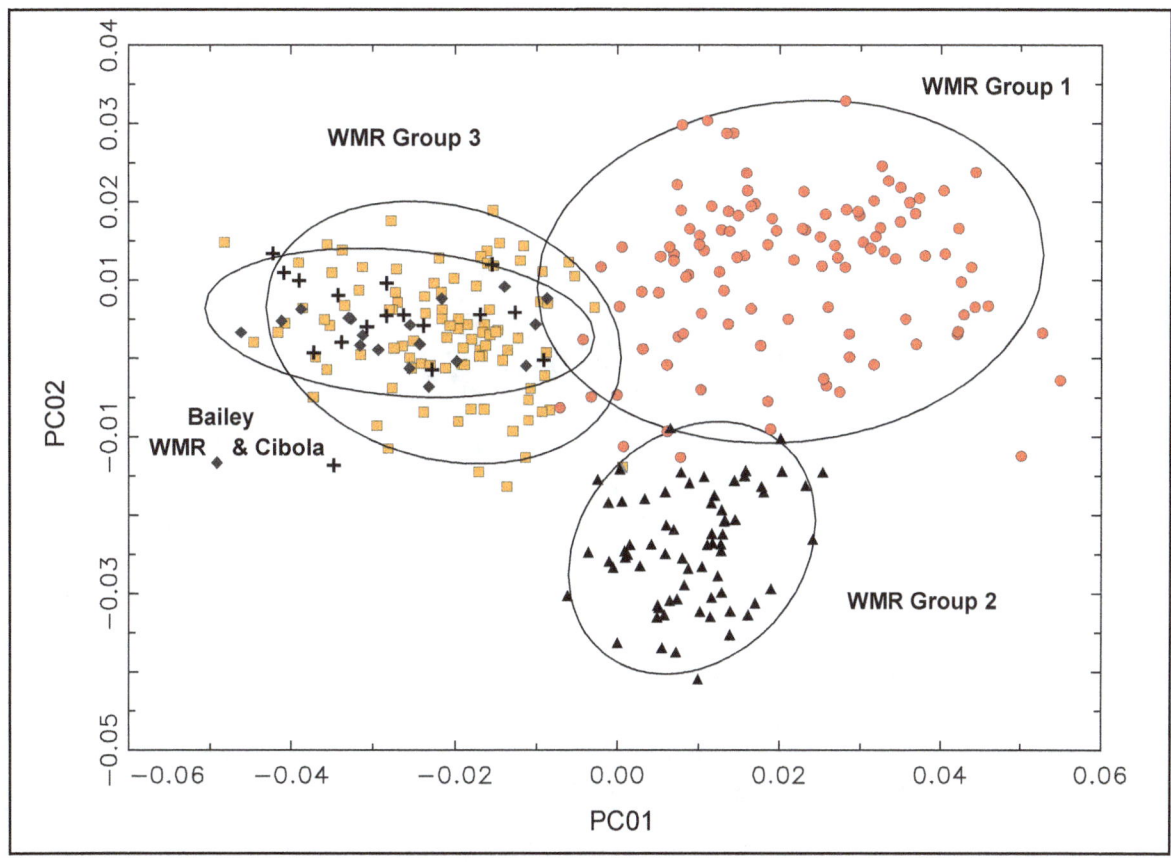

Figure 8.7. Bivariate plot of principal component scores, showing principal components 1 and 2 of the four light-paste White Mountain Red Ware groups.

be assigned to all three major White Mountain Red Ware groups (Table 8.8). These ceramics were imported into Kinishba Pueblo and appear to represent three different resource procurement zones, production loci, or both (see Bishop et al. 1982). Light-firing, kaolinitic clays weathering from Cretaceous deposits along the Mogollon Rim are the most likely source(s) (Moore 1968:72-73; Triadan et al. 2002). Interestingly, 10 of the 17 analyzed Kinishba Polychrome sherds from Kinishba fall also either into WMR Group 1 or 3 (Table 8.8), confirming that some Kinishba Polychrome was produced with the same raw materials as the imported White Mountain Red Ware.

This supports my earlier findings on Kinishba Polychrome from Grasshopper and nearby sites (Triadan 1997:32, 115-123, Appendix B). None of the seven unassigned Kinishba Polychrome sherds showed any probability of belonging to a local Kinishba group (see Figure 8.9). Three of the five Kinishba Polychrome sherds from Point of Pines that were analyzed during the second phase of the project could also be assigned to WMR Group 1. In addition, two Hopi yellow ware samples from Kinishba could be assigned to WMR Group 1, thus calling into question whether they have true yellow ware pastes. They may actually be what Lyons (Chapter 7) calls Kinishba Brown-on-buff,

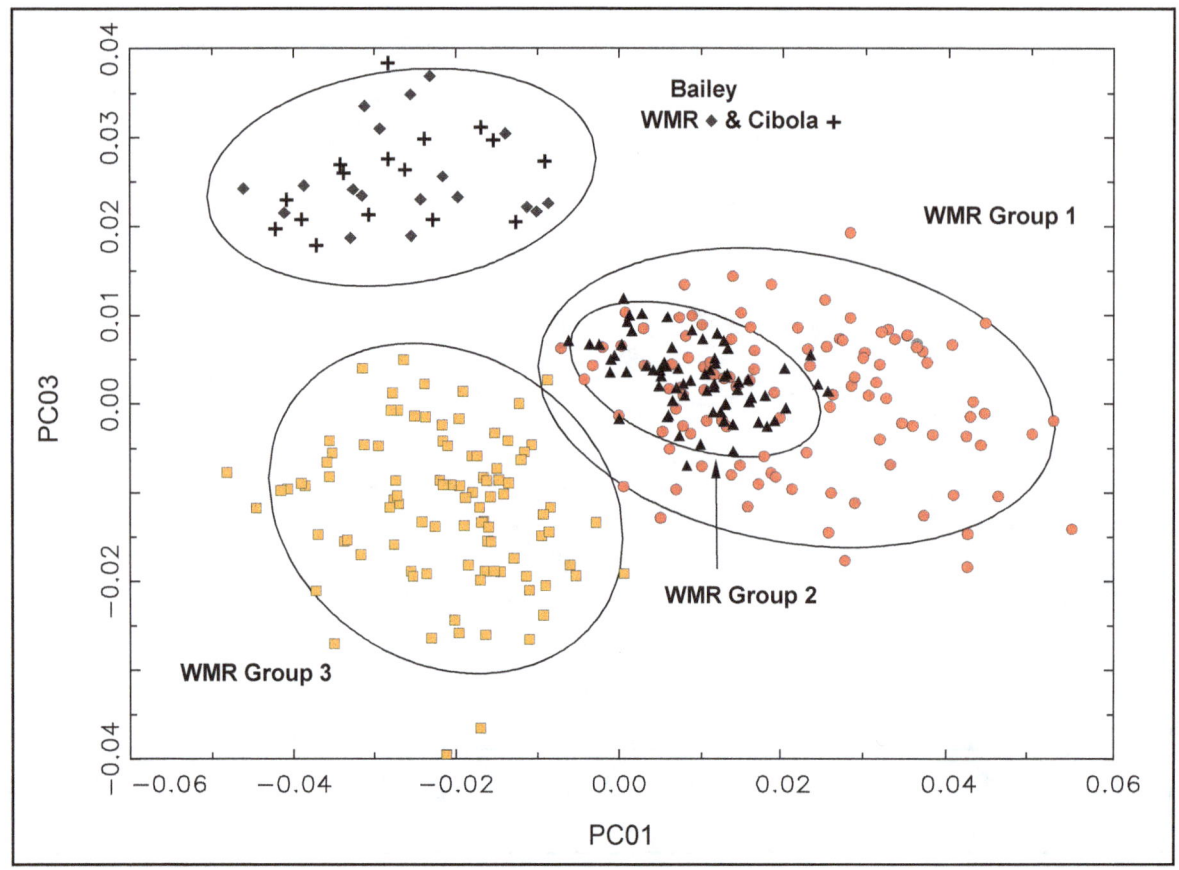

Figure 8.8. Bivariate plot of principal component scores, showing principal components 1 and 3 of the four light-paste White Mountain Red Ware groups.

attempted copies of Hopi yellow ware types, but made in the Silver Creek area.

On the other hand, Kinishba Red samples from Kinishba and Cedar Creek Pueblo, as well as two brown-paste White Mountain Red Ware sherds from Kinishba (DTK422 and DTK468, Table 8.8) form their own, distinct compositional group. The chemical compositions of these ceramics are quite distinct from those produced at Grasshopper Pueblo and Point of Pines and they were probably produced in the Kinishba area (Figure 8.9). For this illustration principal components were calculated on the basis of 26 elements and the whole data set, except analyzed source clays. As in Figures 8.7 and 8.8, ellipses represent a confidence interval of 90 percent for membership in the respective compositional group.

Petrography

Fifteen of the sampled ceramics from Kinishba were also analyzed petrographically. I selected three Kinishba Red sherds and two White Mountain Red Ware samples (DTK422 and DTK468) assigned to the compositional group local to Kinishba (see Table 8.8). With the inclusion of the other sites that were sampled, a total of 45 samples were analyzed petrographically in the second phase of the project, bringing the total number of samples for both phases to 125. Deborah Bergfeld, now at the United

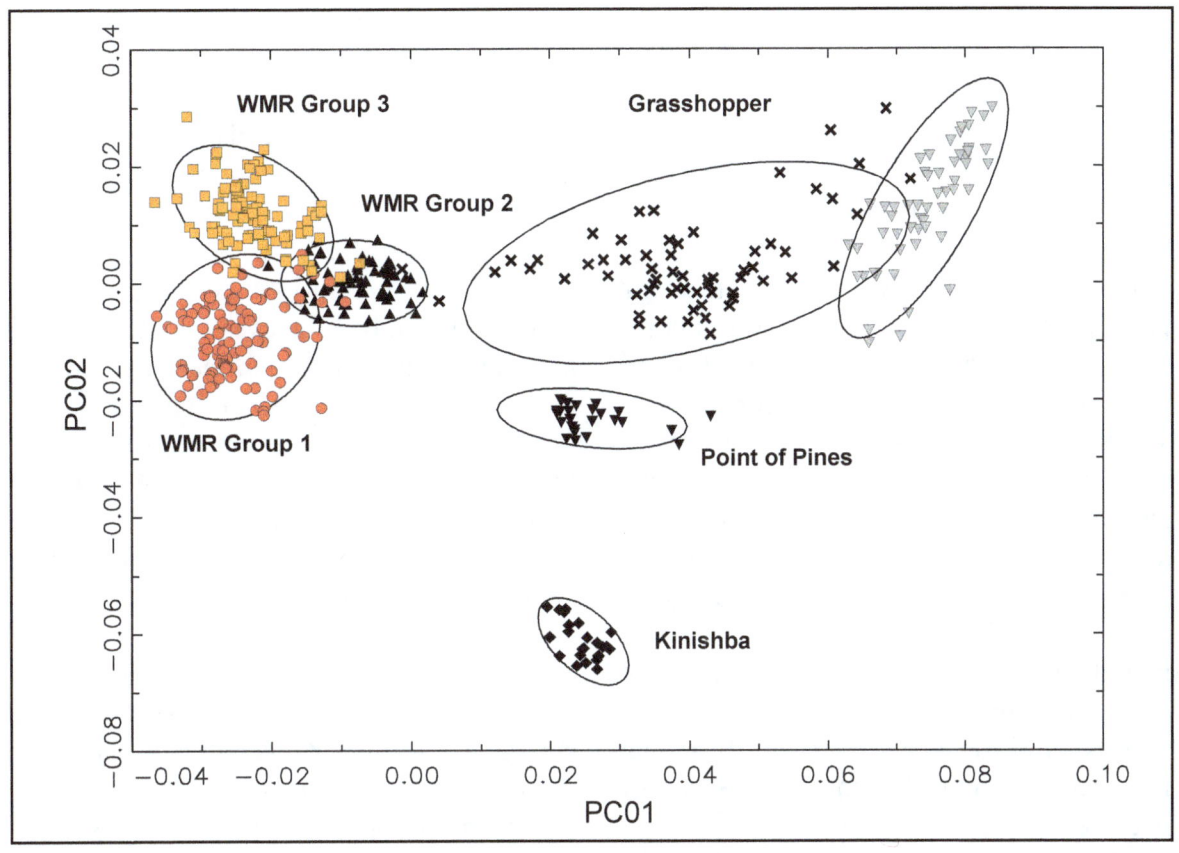

Figure 8.9. Bivariate plot of principal component scores, showing principal components 1 and 2 of the three large light-paste White Mountain Red Ware groups and groups of ceramics produced locally at Grasshopper, Point of Pines and Kinishba.

States Geological Survey in Menlo Park, carried out quantitative analysis and provided estimates of mineral quantities.

The mineralogy of the light-paste White Mountain Red Ware, imported into Kinishba, confirms earlier petrographic analyses (Triadan 1997:46-49). The ceramics are predominantly tempered with sherds and quartz in varying proportions that do not covary with the compositional groups. Most of the quartz is added as temper and thus does not represent the composition of the raw source clay. It has potentially a diluting effect on the elemental concentrations measured, but this dilution affects *all* elements equally. Accordingly, these results indicate that the three major compositional groups represent different *clay sources* used in the manufacture of light-paste White Mountain Red Ware.

The mineralogy of the samples assigned to the compositional group labeled Kinishba (Figure 8.9), confirms that both White Mountain Red Ware and Kinishba Red were produced with local materials, probably from the area around Kinishba. All sherds are tempered with basaltic rock fragments that are often porphyritic (containing visible crystals) and also contain some plagioclase, and minor quantities of biotite, and pyroxene minerals. Basalt flows along the course of the White River and its North Fork, and other andesitic to basaltic outcrops are located about 4km to the south, east and west of Kinishba Pueblo (Moore

1968:Plate 2). Interestingly, sample DTK 239 was tempered with volcanic tuff and may have been imported from Point of Pines.

Conclusions

The compositional analyses revealed that light-paste White Mountain Red Ware was imported into Kinishba Pueblo and can be associated with three raw material sources represented by WMR Groups 1 to 3. The results of the analyses are consistent with the view that these ceramics were produced at sites in the Silver Creek area north of the Mogollon Rim (Triadan et al. 2002). The large-scale settlement aggregation in the mountains south of the Mogllon Rim, including the apparently rapid expansion of Kinishba, indicates that large numbers of these vessels were brought into the pueblo by migrating groups. White Mountain Red Ware only became a dominant decorated ware in areas south of the Mogollon Rim in the early 1300s, during the time when Kinishba and other large sites were established or expanding. The fact that ceramics from Kinishba can be assigned to all three of the major compositional White Mountain Red Ware groups may indicate that people from different areas or possibly villages in the Silver Creek drainage moved to Kinishba. This in turn suggests that people moved in household units rather than whole communities, indicating that these source villages were not yet well socially and politically integrated (Triadan 2006:177-178; see also Ezzo and Price 2002:510, 513-514; Van Keuren 2001, 2006:102-103). Kinishba Red pottery and some White Mountain Red Ware were probably locally produced at Kinishba, possibly gradually replacing the White Mountain Red Ware imports.

The INAA analysis also shows that Kinishba Polychrome was produced by the same potters that made the imported, light-paste Fourmile Polychrome. This finding is supported by the chemical composition of the pastes and by occurrences of hybrid bowls with interiors decorated as Kinishba Polychrome and exteriors painted as Fourmile Polychrome (see Figure 8.3). Clearly, Kinishba polychrome was *not made at Kinishba*, but imported from the same production loci as Fourmile Polychrome, probably villages in the Silver Creek area at the southern edge of the Colorado Plateau. Given the overall small numbers of this type at all Pueblo IV sites, it seems likely that these vessels were "experimental." As noted by Baldwin (1939:83-84), Kinishba Polychrome may have been an attempt to emulate Hopi yellow ware. It should also be noted that the iconography of Fourmile Polychrome and Sityakti Polychrome is very similar and has been linked by Adams (1991, 1994) with the emergence of the Katsina cult (see also Hays 1991, 1994; Lyons, Chapter 7).

I was also able to define a compositional group that represents production at Kinishba and surrounding sites. This group contains some local, brown-paste White Mountain Red Ware copies as well as Kinishba Red vessels from Kinishba and Cedar Creek Pueblo. These ceramics are tempered with locally available basalt.

In general, Kinishba is very similar in settlement layout and occupation trajectory to Grasshopper Pueblo (Riggs 2001; Welch 2007a), although aggregation may have started earlier in the Kinishba area than in the Grasshopper region and Kinishba may have been founded earlier (see Baldwin 1935a; Triadan et al. 2002:87-90, Figures 7.3 and 7.4). With over 600 rooms, Kinishba is also somewhat larger than Grasshopper. Both pueblos have an enclosed plaza with roofed corridor access, and both have a plaza that was converted to a rectangular great kiva, then possibly returned to use as an unroofed plaza prior to depopulation (Cummings 1940; Reid and Shimada 1982:17;

Riggs 2001:107-111, Figure 3.40, Shaeffer and Shaeffer, Chapter 3 in this volume). This reconfiguration of a plaza to a great kiva suggests a shift from ritual inclusiveness for the whole community to a return to some ritual exclusiveness (Triadan 2006; see also Van Keuren 2001:267).

The overall variability of the ceramic assemblage at Kinishba is similar to Grasshopper, especially with regard to the presence of multiple painted wares and types. However, my evaluation of the whole vessel assemblage from Kinishba also reveals patterns that distinguish Kinishba.

The whole and reconstructible vessels found at Kinishba come from mortuary and domestic contexts. With regard to burials, painted vessels seem to be more common in burials from extramural areas, which are predominantly adults, but a number of children also had vessels as grave goods (Tables 8.6, 8.7). Adult men are more likely to have been buried with vessels than women or children. However, in general, painted vessels are relatively rare in burials and the most common burial goods are small plain and corrugated jars and bowls, including Kinishba Red bowls (Table 8.6). The occurrence of Kinishba Red in burials under room floors in Group I may indicate that their production started around the time of the pueblo's expansion.

Most of the vessels from Kinishba come from domestic contexts, especially room floors. As is the case at Grasshopper, it seems likely that these rooms were abandoned late in Kinishba's occupation. After brown plain and corrugated jars, which were most likely used for storage, Kinishba Red bowls are the most common pottery (Table 8.4). In contrast to Grasshopper, where Grasshopper Polychrome is most common on late abandoned room floors, followed by White Mountain Red Ware, Roosevelt Red Ware is the most common painted ware on Kinishba's room floors, followed by imported White Mountain Red Ware (Figure 8.5; Triadan 1997:Figure 4.7). There seems to be no spatial difference in the distribution of these two wares between the two major room blocks, but the sample is heavily biased toward Group I. Based on the floor assemblages, Kinishba Red pottery was probably produced until the pueblo was depopulated.

As is true for the Grasshopper assemblage, which includes all excavated food and water storage jars, the Kinishba assemblage contains a large quantity of bowls (Table 8.4). Imported, light-paste Fourmile Polychrome, as well as Kinishba Polychrome and Roosevelt Red Ware were made almost exclusively as hemispherical bowls (Carlson 1970; Crown 1994). These vessels were most likely used for serving food within households (see Cushing 1979:69, 88, 103-104 for an ethnographic example) and may also have been used on occasion in communal feasting (Mills 2007; Van Keuren 2001:168, 175, 190, 2004:193, 198). Of the 219 whole or reconstructible White Mountain Red Ware vessels from Grasshopper, 192 (87.7 percent) are bowls. For Fourmile Polychrome, the percentage of bowls is even higher: 109 of 118 (92.4 percent). Similarly, at Kinishba, of the 50 whole or reconstructible White Mountain Red Ware vessels 42 (84.0 percent) are bowls (see Tables 8.4 and 8.6).

Locally produced copies at both Grasshopper and Kinishba are also predominantly bowls. At Grasshopper these bowls were produced in the same general size range as the imports and are generally classified as Grasshopper Polychrome (see Triadan 1997:92-93, Figures 4.30 and 4.31). Imported, light-paste Fourmile bowls found at Grasshopper were originally produced so that they could be stacked within each other for easier transport, while Grasshopper Polychrome bowls do not share this "nestability" (Whittlesey 1974; Triadan 1997:92-93, Figures 4.30b and 4.31b).

Thus, the function as serving vessels for a variety of foods was maintained in the local vessels at Grasshopper, but easy transportability was no longer an important attribute.

I have argued that at Grasshopper *Fourmile style* continued to be important, because locally produced polychromes (mostly Grasshopper Polychrome) were predominantly copying Fourmile designs (but see Van Keuren 2001:192-193, 199-240, 2006:97-102). Fourmile style is a radical departure from earlier geometric design styles, and many scholars have argued that it is correlated with changes in communal ritual practices and the emergence of the katsina cult (see Adams 1991, 1994; Triadan 2006; VanKeuren 2001). Grasshopper Polychrome vessels were produced later in the occupation of the pueblo, when there might have been less back and forth movement between areas north of the Mogollon Rim and the Grasshopper region. People started to use all local raw materials to make local copies, eventually replacing the imports (Triadan 1997:93-94). Transitional hybrid vessels show that this trend started with potters using local clays for the pastes, while continuing to mix in some sherd temper and to use non-local materials for the slip and designs (Triadan 1997:Plate11, 94). In fact, a little over 50 percent of the locally produced polychromes at Grasshopper showed Fourmile designs (Triadan 1997:94). Together with the earlier, light-paste imports two-thirds of all the painted reconstructible vessels from Grasshopper were decorated in Fourmile style (Triadan 1997:94). This emphasis on Fourmile style might indicate the adoption of new ritual practices at Grasshopper as well as a continued connection between the immigrants and areas north of the Mogollon Rim (Triadan 1997:94, 106). On the other hand, the significant quantity of Roosevelt Red Ware found at Grasshopper suggests that people might also have had affiliations with other northern groups (Lyons 2003, Chapter 7).

In marked contrast to Grasshopper, at Kinishba the locally produced bowls are mostly monochrome red; there are very few local Fourmile copies. Unfortunately the Kinishba data do not at this time permit the same level of contextual and spatial analyses that I carried out with the Grasshopper whole vessel and surface discard assemblages. Even though light-paste White Mountain Red Ware was mostly imported to Kinishba during the early 1300s, it is not possible to argue with the same level of certainty that the local Kinishba Red pots then gradually replaced these vessels. It is nonetheless clear that locally produced pottery at Kinishba does not emphasize Fourmile style. As Lyons mentions (Chapter 7), Kinishba Red is similar to various red plain types, including Cliff Red and Phoenix Red—types made by the producers of Roosevelt Red Ware. The striking difference in locally produced pots at Kinishba may indicate a different ritual emphasis, different interactions of immigrant and local groups, or different origins or affinities of Kinishba's founding or in-migrating groups. It is also possible that pottery at Grasshopper was more directly linked to ritual symbolism than it was at Kinishba.

The late A.D. 1200s and 1300s were turbulent times in the mountains of Arizona. New ceramic data presented by Lyons (Chapter 7) and myself help to providea more nuanced view of the processes of migration and social and political reorganization that took place during those times (see also, Spielmann 1998, Adams and Duff 2004). Based on his reanalysis, Lyons argues that, like Point of Pines (Haury 1957), Kinishba hosted a diasporic group of Kayenta immigrants who eventually made Roosevelt Red Ware. In addition to these immigrants from farther north, groups from settlements in the Silver Creek area also moved to Kinishba, bringing with them sets of light-paste White Mountain Red Ware pots. My sourcing study indicates that these people probably moved in kin-based units from several different villages, which might also hold true for the Kayenta migrants. This finding may support Lyons' (Chapter 7) idea of dispersed Kayenta enclaves across much of east-central and southeast Arizona—people who sought to maintain distinctive identities in part through the production of Roosevelt Red Ware at their new homes. It should be emphasized that the late thirteenth century settlements in the Silver Creek area were already an amalgam of different groups, including probably some people from the Kayenta region, based on the presence of perforated plates (Mills 1998, 1999a,c). In fact it is quite possible that Pinto Polychrome, the earliest Roosevelt Red Ware type was invented in this area when those immigrants met people who made Pinedale Black-on-white and Pinedale Black-on-red. Both White Mountain Red Ware and Cibola White Ware were made at Bailey Ruin using the same clay source and temper (Triadan et al. 2002). Pinto Polychrome was also made there, but probably with different clays and organic paint (Mills et al. 1999), which indicates a difference in pottery technology, including the firing regime, from those other two wares. Thus there were probably waves of different immigrant groups who started to coreside (see also Ezzo and Price 2002:513; McClelland 2003) and in some cases their interactions may have lead to some form of integration and cooperation. The new and rapidly spreading Pinedale style may have been the material expression of this.

With regard to Kayenta groups at Grasshopper, the situation is more ambiguous. There are significant quantities of Roosevelt Red Ware in surface deposits, in burials and on room floors. In the burials Roosevelt Red Ware quantities are higher (approximately 30 percent) than White Mountain Red Ware (approximately 20 percent). However, White Mountain Red Ware is more prevalent than Roosevelt Red Ware in the surface and room floor assemblages, although in the floor assemblage that difference is not very great (Triadan 1997:58-78, Figures 4.2, 4.7,4.19). Yet some key material indicators for the presence of Kayenta migrants are less frequent. There are no babe-in-cradle figurines, and both perforated plates and Maverick Mountain types appear to be less common than at Kinishba. More studies are needed to address this matter, research that migh profitably begin with the reanalysis of decorated sherds identified as indeterminant types in the early years of Grasshooper excavation. Lyons (personal communication, 2012) has confirmed that at least some of these sherds represent Maverick Mountain types.

Along similar lines, more work is needed to assess how much of the Roosevelt Red Ware was made at Grasshopper. Zedeño (1994:95-99) has shown that Pinto Polychrome was both imported and made at Chodistaas, a late thirteenth century 18-room pueblo in the vicinity of Grasshopper. INAA established that many Pinto vessels were made with local clays, and petrography identified two distinct temper recipes. Zedeño argues immigrants brought vessels to the settlement from the Mogollon Rim area and either that these immigrants later used local temper technology to produce pots or that local residents learned to make Pinto Polychrome by direct contact with the immigrants. Thus the situation at Grasshopper may have been somewhat different from Kinishba in that groups associated with Roosevelt Red Ware may already have resided for a time with people in the Silver Creek area before moving farther south (see e.g, Ezzo and Price 2002:516).

Even though there are broad similarities between Kinishba, Grasshopper, and Point Pines there are also notable differences, which indicate that the 1300s were a time of social and political experimentation. Each of the three pueblos experienced rapid aggregations and expansions linked to the influx of immigrant groups. Each pueblo was built around large, open plazas, which indicates a shift towards more inclusive rituals in which the whole diverse community participated (Adams 1991; Mills 2007). These ritual practices seem to have been aimed in part at integrating these new, large and diverse communities. It is particularly interesting, as confirmed by the Shaeffers' work in Kinishba's Group I (Chapter 4), that occupants of each of the three pueblos eventually roofed at least one plaza and converted it into a great kiva. This may indicate a return to older, more exclusive or esoteric ritual practices in which great kivas remained a community focus but could also prevent access to one or more segments of the community (Triadan 2006). Finally, all three sites ceased to support substantial populations by around A.D. 1400.

On the other hand, the differences in the ceramic assemblages may indicate different constellations of people or alliances and different social and political dynamics in these villages. The emphasis at Grasshopper on Fourmile style may indicate especially strong connections with home communities in the Silver Creek area, where new rituals that may have involved the first katsinas were probably developed (Adams 1991). It is possible a large number of people came from that area and may have critically influenced community rituals. From a ceramic perspective, Kinishba may be more similar to Point of Pines. The greater emphasis at Kinishba on Roosevelt Red Ware and unpainted red bowls may indicate a different ritual focus at that pueblo. It may also signify that more Kayenta-derived people were living there than immigrants from the Silver Creek area.

The inhabitants of these three pueblos were grappling with challenges inherent in these new, aggregated, multi-ethnic and probably also multi-liguistic communities. They seem to have come up with communal ritual practices that varied from community to community around the common theme of integrating diverse groups. A possible sign that either things did not go smoothly or that there was movement or communication among the three pueblos is the conversion of the plazas into great kivas. Some part of the community, perhaps the immigrant latecomers, may eventually have been excluded from aspects of some rituals (Triadan 2006). Van Keuren (2001) interprets some of his ceramic data as evidence for factionalism in thsese large villages. The depopulation of all three pueblos following relatively short occupations suggests that integrative efforts ultimately did not work. In the end, the only pueblos that continued to be occupied until the Spanish entrada were the ones at Hopi and Zuñi.

Acknowledgments

My research was supported by a Materials Analysis Postdoctoral Fellowship of the then Smithsonian Center for Materials Research and Education (SCMRE) of the Smithsonian Institution, which facilitated the INAA analysis. Ronald Bishop and James Blackman provided much appreciated guidance for this project, and Deborah Bergfeld again expertly analyzed my thin sections. I would like to thank Michael Jacobs and Arthur Vokes of the Arizona State Museum for their help in accessing the museum's collections to document relevant whole vessels and in the sampling of the sherds for the analysis, and Alan Ferg of the Arizona State Museum Archives for his help in finding archival information on Kinishba. Charles Adams and Jeffery Clark generously provided samples from Homol'ovi and the Tonto Basin. The collaboration of Andrew Duff and Barbara Mills led to the pooling of our respective compositional data, which resulted in an exceptional supraregional database for east-central Arizona. Barbara Mills, Scott Van

Keuren, and Michael Jacobs also provided data on the occurrence of Kinishba Polychrome in sites in the Silver Creek region. Discussions with Patrick Lyons on the evolution of certain ceramic styles and the distribution of late thirteenth and fourteenth century painted ceramics helped to shape my interpretations. Last but not least I would like to thank John Welch for taking up the brave task of "squeezing the Kinishba lemon" and inviting me to contribute to this volume.

Table 8.8. Kinishba Ceramic Samples Analyzed by INAA and Petrography

Sample ID[a]	Institution[b]	Type[c]	INAA Group	Form	Paste	Temper	Site	Provenience	ASM Box No.	Comments
DTP238*	GFS	Fourmile Poly.	WMR2	bowl	Brown		AZ:V:4:1	1979 W>Draw		
DTP239*	GFS	Fourmile Poly.		bowl	very dark gray to black		AZ:V:4:1	1979 W>Draw		
DTP240	GFS	Fourmile Poly.	WMR2	bowl	gray-brown,coarse		AZ:V:4:1	1979 W>Draw		
DTP241	GFS	Fourmile Poly.		bowl	orange-brown		AZ:V:4:1	1979 W>Draw		
DTP242	GFS	Fourmile Poly.	WMR2	bowl	orange,dark gray core		AZ:V:4:1	1979 W>Draw		
DTP243	GFS	Fourmile Poly.	WMR2	bowl	gray-brown,orange edges		AZ:V:4:1	1979 W>Draw		
DTP244	GFS	Fourmile Poly.		bowl	gray-brown,orange edges		AZ:V:4:1			
DTK401	ASM	Hopi Yellow Ware		bowl	light buff		AZ:V:4:1		9	
DTK402	ASM	Jeddito Black-on-yellow		bowl	dark gray, buff edges		AZ:V:4:1		9	
DTK403	ASM	Hopi Yellow Ware, Black-on-orange		bowl	light orange		AZ:V:4:1		9	
DTK404	ASM	Jeddito Black-on-yellow		bowl	light buff (not YW paste)		AZ:V:4:1		9	
DTK405	ASM	Jeddito Black-on-yellow	WMR1	bowl	light gray, buff edges		AZ:V:4:1		9	
DTK406	ASM	int.Kinishba Poly., ext. Fourmile Poly.		bowl	Buff		AZ:V:4:1		11	
DTK407	ASM	int.Kinishba Poly., ext. Fourmile Poly.		bowl	Buff		AZ:V:4:1		11	
DTK408	ASM	Yellow Ware (copy?)	WMR1	bowl	Buff		AZ:V:4:1		12	
DTK409	ASM	Showlow Poly.		bowl	buff/gray		AZ:V:4:1		13	
DTK410	ASM	Showlow Poly.		bowl	very light gray		AZ:V:4:1		13	
DTK411	ASM	Showlow Poly.	WMR1	bowl	gray, orange edges, local?		AZ:V:4:1		13	
DTK412	ASM	Showlow/Fourmile Poly.		jar	White		AZ:V:4:1		13	
DTK413	ASM	Showlow/Fourmile Poly.		jar	dark gray,buff edges		AZ:V:4:1		13	
DTK414	ASM	Showlow/Fourmile Poly.		jar	dark gray,orange edges		AZ:V:4:1		13	
DTK415*	ASM	Showlow/Fourmile Poly.	WMR2	jar	Gray		AZ:V:4:1		13	
DTK416*	ASM	Showlow/Fourmile Poly.	WMR3	jar	White		AZ:V:4:1		13	
DTK417	ASM	Cedar Creek/Fourmile Poly.	WMR1	jar	light gray,buff edges		AZ:V:4:1		13	

Table 8.8. Kinishba Ceramic Samples Analyzed by INAA and Petrography, cont'd

Sample ID[a]	Institution[b]	Type[c]	INAA Group	Form	Paste	Temper	Site	Provenience	ASM Box No.	Comments
DTK418	ASM	Showlow/Fourmile Poly.	WMR1	jar	light gray/buff		AZ:V:4:1		13	
DTK419*	ASM	Cedar Creek Poly.	WMR1	bowl	very light gray		AZ:V:4:1		18	
DTK420	ASM	Cedar Creek Poly.	WMR1	bowl	gray/buff		AZ:V:4:1		18	
DTK421	ASM	Cedar Creek Poly.		bowl	gray,brown edges		AZ:V:4:1		18	
DTK422*	ASM	Pinedale/Cedar Creek Poly.	Kinishba	bowl	brown, local?	micaceous	AZ:V:4:1	"195"	18	P.V.;from R195?
DTK423	ASM	Kinishba Poly.		bowl	very dark gray		AZ:V:4:1		19	
DTK424	ASM	Kinishba Poly.		bowl	very light gray, thick wall		AZ:V:4:1		19	P.V.
DTK425	ASM	Kinishba Poly.		bowl	Buff		AZ:V:4:1		19	
DTK426	ASM	Kinishba Poly.	WMR1	bowl	Buff		AZ:V:4:1		19	
DTK427	ASM	Kinishba Poly.		bowl	very dark gray		AZ:V:4:1		19	
DTK428	ASM	Kinishba Poly.	WMR1	bowl	Gray		AZ:V:4:1		19	
DTK429	ASM	Kinishba Poly.	WMR3	bowl	very light gray, buff edges		AZ:V:4:1		19	
DTK430	ASM	Kinishba Poly.	WMR1	bowl	gray, buff edges		AZ:V:4:1		19	
DTK431	ASM	Kinishba Poly.	WMR3	bowl	Buff		AZ:V:4:1		19	
DTK432*	ASM	Kinishba Poly.	WMR3	bowl	light gray, buff edges		AZ:V:4:1		19	
DTK433*	ASM	Kinishba Poly.	WMR1	bowl	gray/buff		AZ:V:4:1		19	
DTK434	ASM	Kinishba Poly.	WMR3	bowl	dark gray, buff edges		AZ:V:4:1		19	P.V.
DTK435	ASM	Kinishba Poly.	WMR3	bowl	very light gray, buff edges		AZ:V:4:1		19	
DTK436	ASM	Kinishba Poly.		bowl	dark gray, buff edges		AZ:V:4:1		19	
DTK437	ASM	Kinishba Poly.		bowl	dark gray/buff, thick wall, burned		AZ:V:4:1		19	
DTK438	ASM	Kinishba Poly.		bowl	light gray, buff edges		AZ:V:4:1		19	
DTK439	ASM	Kinishba Poly.	WMR3	bowl	gray, buff edges		AZ:V:4:1		19	P.V.
DTK440	ASM	Cedar Creek Poly.		bowl	light gray		AZ:V:4:1		20	P.V.
DTK441	ASM	Cedar Creek Poly.		bowl	Gray		AZ:V:4:1		20	
DTK442	ASM	Cedar Creek Poly.	WMR2	bowl	gray, orange edges		AZ:V:4:1		20	
DTK443	ASM	Fourmile Poly.		jar	Orange		AZ:V:4:1	"189"	21	P.V.;from R189?

8: Implications for Pottery   237

238 Triadan

Table 8.8. Kinishba Ceramic Samples Analyzed by INAA and Petrography, cont'd

Sample ID[a]	Institution[b]	Type[c]	INAA Group	Form	Paste	Temper	Site	Provenience	ASM Box No.	Comments
DTK444	ASM	Showlow/Fourmile Poly.	WMR3	jar	White		AZ:V:4:1	"143"	23	P.V.;crude design, from R143?
DTK445	ASM	Cedar Creek Poly.	WMR1	bowl	dark gray,buff edges		AZ:V:4:1		24	
DTK446	ASM	Cedar Creek Poly.	WMR1	bowl	light gray		AZ:V:4:1		24	
DTK447	ASM	Cedar Creek Poly.	WMR1	bowl	light gray,orange edges		AZ:V:4:1		24	
DTK448	ASM	Cedar Creek Poly.	WMR1	bowl	light gray,orange edges		AZ:V:4:1		24	
DTK449	ASM	Cedar Creek Poly.	WMR1	bowl	very light gray,orange edges		AZ:V:4:1		24	
DTK450	ASM	Fourmile Poly.		bowl	White		AZ:V:4:1		24	
DTK451	ASM	Cedar Creek/Fourmile Poly.	WMR2	bowl	dark gray,orange edges		AZ:V:4:1		24	
DTK452	ASM	Cedar Creek Poly.	WMR1	bowl	very dark gray,orange edges		AZ:V:4:1		24	
DTK453	ASM	Fourmile Poly.		bowl	White		AZ:V:4:1		24	
DTK454	ASM	Cedar Creek Poly.		bowl	dark gray		AZ:V:4:1		24	
DTK455	ASM	Cedar Creek/Fourmile Poly.	WMR1	bowl	Gray		AZ:V:4:1		24	
DTK456	ASM	Cedar Creek Poly.	WMR1	bowl	dark gray		AZ:V:4:1		24	
DTK457	ASM	Cedar Creek Poly.	WMR1	bowl	very light gray	large inclusions	AZ:V:4:1		24	
DTK458*	ASM	Cedar Creek/Fourmile Poly.	WMR2	bowl	light gray,orange edges		AZ:V:4:1		24	
DTK459	ASM	Cedar Creek Poly.		bowl	light gray		AZ:V:4:1		24	
DTK460	ASM	Cedar Creek Poly.		bowl	orange/gray		AZ:V:4:1		24	
DTK461	ASM	Cedar Creek/Fourmile Poly.		bowl	Orange		AZ:V:4:1		24	
DTK462	ASM	Cedar Creek Poly.	WMR1	bowl	light orange		AZ:V:4:1		24	
DTK463*	ASM	Fourmile Poly.	WMR3	bowl	White		AZ:V:4:1		24	
DTK464	ASM	Cedar Creek Poly.		bowl	Gray		AZ:V:4:1	"R199"	24	P.V.;prob. from R199
DTK465	ASM	Cedar Creek Poly.	WMR1	bowl	Buff		AZ:V:4:1		24	

Table 8.8. Kinishba Ceramic Samples Analyzed by INAA and Petrography, cont'd

Sample ID[a]	Institution[b]	Type[c]	INAA Group	Form	Paste	Temper	Site	Provenience	ASM Box No.	Comments
DTK466	ASM	Fourmile Poly.		bowl	Gray		AZ:V:4:1		25	
DTK467	ASM	Cedar Creek Poly.	WMR1	bowl	very dark gray		AZ:V:4:1		25	bad slip
DTK468*	ASM	Pinedale/Cedar Creek Black-on-red?	Kinishba	bowl	orange/brown	micaceous	AZ:V:4:1		26	
DTK469	ASM	Kinishba Red	Kinishba	bowl	gray, orange edges	micaceous	AZ:V:4:1		31	
DTK470	ASM	Kinishba Red	Kinishba	bowl	light gray	micaceous	AZ:V:4:1		31	
DTK471*	ASM	Kinishba Red	Kinishba	bowl	light gray	micaceous	AZ:V:4:1		31	
DTK472	ASM	Kinishba Red	Kinishba	jar	Gray	quartzite?	AZ:V:4:1		31	
DTK473	ASM	Kinishba Red	Kinishba	bowl	gray, brown edges	micaceous	AZ:V:4:1		31	
DTK474*	ASM	Kinishba Red	Kinishba	bowl	Gray	micaceous, quartzite?	AZ:V:4:1		31	
DTK475	ASM	Kinishba Red		bowl	very dark gray		AZ:V:4:1		31	
DTK476	ASM	Kinishba Red	Kinishba	jar	gray, brown edges	micaceous	AZ:V:4:1		31	
DTK477	ASM	Kinishba Red		bowl	light brown	quartzite	AZ:V:4:1		32	
DTK478	ASM	Kinishba Red	Kinishba	bowl	light brown		AZ:V:4:1		32	
DTK479	ASM	Kinishba Red	Kinishba	jar	light brown	micaceous, quartzite	AZ:V:4:1		32	
DTK480*	ASM	Kinishba Red	Kinishba	bowl	Gray	micaceous	AZ:V:4:1		32	
DTK481	ASM	Kinishba Red	Kinishba	bowl	Gray	micaceous	AZ:V:4:1		32	
DTK482	ASM	Kinishba Red		bowl	brown, int. smudged	micaceous	AZ:V:4:1		32	
DTK483	ASM	Fourmile Poly.	WMR1	bowl	Gray		AZ:V:4:1		34	crude interior design
DTK484	ASM	Fourmile Poly.		bowl	gray, brown deges, local?	micaceous	AZ:V:4:1		34	
DTK485	ASM	Cedar Creek/Fourmile Poly.		bowl	gray, orange edges		AZ:V:4:1		35	
DTK486	ASM	Cedar Creek/Fourmile Poly.		bowl	Orange		AZ:V:4:1		35	
DTK487	ASM	Cedar Creek/Fourmile Poly.		bowl	White		AZ:V:4:1		35	
DTK488	ASM	Pinedale Poly.	WMR1	bowl	gray, buff edges		AZ:V:4:1		35	
DTK489	ASM	Fourmile Poly.	WMR3	jar	light gray, white edges		AZ:V:4:1		35	

240 Triadan

Table 8.8. Kinishba Ceramic Samples Analyzed by INAA and Petrography, cont'd

Sample ID[a]	Institution[b]	Type[c]	INAA Group	Form	Paste	Temper	Site	Provenience	ASM Box No.	Comments
DTK490	ASM	Fourmile Poly.	WMR3	jar	White		AZ:V:4:1		35	
DTK491	ASM	Fourmile Poly.		bowl	very light gray		AZ:V:4:1		35	slip very dark
DTK492	ASM	Fourmile Poly.	WMR3	jar	White		AZ:V:4:1		35	
DTK493	ASM	Fourmile Poly.		jar	White		AZ:V:4:1		35	
DTK494	ASM	Fourmile Poly.		bowl	Buff		AZ:V:4:1		35	
DTK495	ASM	Fourmile Poly.	WMR3	jar	White		AZ:V:4:1	"R148(?)"	35	from R148?
DTK496	ASM	Fourmile Poly.	WMR3	jar	Buff		AZ:V:4:1		35	
DTK497	ASM	Jeddito Black-on-yellow?		bowl	gray,buff edges (not YW paste)		AZ:V:4:1	surface coll.		
DTK498	ASM	Fourmile Poly.	WMR3	bowl	White		AZ:V:4:1	surface coll.		
DTK499	ASM	Fourmile Poly.	WMR3	bowl	White		AZ:V:4:1	surface coll.		
DTK500	ASM	Fourmile Poly.		jar	very light gray		AZ:V:4:1	surface coll.		
DTK501	ASM	Fourmile Poly.		jar	Gray		AZ:V:4:1	surface coll.		
DTK502	ASM	Fourmile Poly.	WMR3	bowl	White		AZ:V:4:1	surface coll.		
DTK503	ASM	Fourmile Poly.		jar	light gray		AZ:V:4:1	surface coll.		
DTK504	ASM	Fourmile Poly.		bowl	gray,orange edges		AZ:V:4:1	surface coll.		
DTK505	ASM	Fourmile Poly.	WMR3	bowl	light buff		AZ:V:4:1	surface coll.		
DTK506	ASM	Fourmile Poly.		bowl	very light gray,buff edges		AZ:V:4:1	surface coll.		
DTK507	ASM	Fourmile Poly.	WMR3	bowl	gray,white edges		AZ:V:4:1	surface coll.		
DTK508	ASM	Cedar Creek Poly.	WMR1	bowl	Gray		AZ:V:4:1	surface coll.		
DTK509*	ASM	Fourmile Poly.		bowl	gray,white edges		AZ:V:4:1	surface coll.		
DTK510	ASM	Fourmile Poly.	WMR3	bowl	very light gray		AZ:V:4:1	surface coll.		
DTK511	ASM	Fourmile Poly.		jar	light gray		AZ:V:4:1	surface coll.		
DTK512	ASM	Cedar Creek Poly.	WMR1	bowl	Gray		AZ:V:4:1	surface coll.		
DTK513	ASM	Fourmile Poly.		bowl	Buff		AZ:V:4:1	AZ:C:4:5(GP)		
DTK514	ASM	Cedar Creek Poly.		bowl	gray,orange edges		AZ:V:4:1	AZ:C:4:5(GP)		
DTK515	ASM	Showlow Poly.	WMR1	bowl	very dark gray, buff edges		AZ:V:4:1	AZ:C:4:5(GP)		
DTK516	ASM	Fourmile Poly.	WMR1	bowl	very dark gray,burned		AZ:V:4:1	AZ:C:4:5(GP)		

Table 8.8. Kinishba Ceramic Samples Analyzed by INAA and Petrography, cont'd

Sample ID[a]	Institution[b]	Type[c]	INAA Group	Form	Paste	Temper	Site	Provenience	ASM Box No.	Comments
DTK517	ASM	Cedar Creek/ Fourmile Poly.	WMR1	bowl	dark gray,buff edges		AZ:V:4:1	AZ:C:4:5(GP)		
DTK518	ASM	Fourmile Poly.		bowl	gray,orange edges		AZ:V:4:1	AZ:C:4:5(GP)		
DTK519	ASM	Showlow/ Fourmile Poly.	WMR2	jar	light gray		AZ:V:4:1	AZ:C:4:5(GP)		
DTK520	ASM	Fourmile Poly.	WMR3	bowl	light gray		AZ:V:4:1	AZ:C:4:6(GP)		
DTK521	ASM	Fourmile Poly.	WMR3	bowl	light gray		AZ:V:4:1	AZ:C:4:6(GP)		
DTK522	ASM	Fourmile Poly.		bowl	gray, coarse		AZ:V:4:1	AZ:C:4:6(GP)		
DTK523	ASM	Fourmile Poly.	WMR3	bowl	very light gray		AZ:V:4:1	AZ:C:4:6(GP)		
DTK524	ASM	Fourmile Poly.	WMR3	bowl	Gray		AZ:V:4:1	AZ:C:4:6(GP)		
DTK525	ASM	Fourmile Poly.	WMR2	bowl	light gray		AZ:V:4:1	AZ:C:4:6(GP)		
DTK526	ASM	Fourmile Poly.	WMR3	bowl	White		AZ:V:4:1	AZ:C:4:6(GP)		surf spalled
DTK527	ASM	Fourmile Poly.	WMR1	bowl	very dark gray,orange edges		AZ:V:4:1	AZ:C:4:6(GP)		
DTK528	ASM	Cedar Creek/ Fourmile Poly.	WMR2	bowl	light gray,orange edges		AZ:V:4:1	AZ:C:4:6(GP)		
DTK529	ASM	Fourmile Poly.	WMR1	bowl	gray,orange edges		AZ:V:4:1	AZ:C:4:6(GP)		
DTK530	ASM	Fourmile Poly.	WMR3	bowl	White		AZ:V:4:1	AZ:C:4:6(GP)		
DTK531	ASM	Pinedale Poly.	WMR2	bowl	Orange		AZ:V:4:1	AZ:C:4:6(GP)		
DTK532	ASM	Cedar Creek/ Fourmile Poly.	WMR1	bowl	light gray		AZ:V:4:1	AZ:C:4:6(GP)		
DTK533	ASM	Pinedale/ Cedar Creek Poly.	WMR1	bowl	very dark gray		AZ:V:4:1	AZ:C:4:6(GP)		
DTK534	ASM	Pinedale/ Cedar Creek Poly.		bowl	gray,orange edges		AZ:V:4:1	AZ:C:4:6(GP)		
DTK535	ASM	Cedar Creek/ Fourmile Poly.		bowl	Buff		AZ:V:4:1	AZ:C:4:6(GP)		
DTK536	ASM	Pinedale? Cedar Creek Poly.	WMR2	bowl	dark gray/orange		AZ:V:4:1	AZ:C:4:6(GP)		

a DTP238-244 were analyzed during the first phase of the project. Samples with * were also analyzed by petrography.
b ASM = Arizona State Museum, GFS = Grasshopper Field School.
c White Mountain Red Ware polychrome jars painted in Fourmile style were typed as Showlow/Fourmile Polychrome.

Chapter 9
The Kinishba Boundary Survey

John R. Welch, Nicholas C. Laluk, and Mark T. Altaha

Studies of *settlement patterns*—spatial distributions of sites—and *settlement systems*—defined as landscapes having economic, political, and spiritual functions and meanings—have been important in archaeology since the mid 1900s (Kowalewski 2008; Vogt and Leventhal 1983). Other chapters in this volume frame Kinishba Ruins in terms of its various systemic roles as a pueblo successor to pit house villages, as a ceramic production locus and a node in fourteenth century exchange networks, and as an ancestral Zuni and Hopi community. This chapter looks beyond Kinishba's immediate boundaries to examine the site in intra- and inter-regional context. Our premise is that information concerning Kinishba's nearest neighboring sites contributes to understanding, interpreting, and managing Kinishba as a once-vital and still-honored community, as part of an ancient settlement cluster, and as a national historic landmark conserved for its cultural, educational, and research values.

Our capabilities to address questions concerning the types, frequencies, and intensities of relations between Kinishba and nearby sites are limited. Applicable constraints fall into two categories. First and most generally, constraints imposed by archaeological method and theory limit the inferences that can be made about settlement systems on the basis of settlement patterns. Second and more specifically, detailed data for ancient settlement around Kinishba derive primarily from a single systematic site identification survey conducted in the summer of 2004 by White Mountain Apache tribal archaeologists Mark Altaha and Nicholas Laluk. Directed by Welch, the survey was instigated in part by a boundary assessment grant provided to the White Mountain Apache Tribe Historic Preservation Office by the National Historic Landmarks (NHL) program of the U.S. National Park Service. The project's two proximal goals were to inventory archaeological sites within a one-mile radius of Kinishba's main ruins groups and to improve archaeological knowledge of more far-flung terrain through judgmental reconnaissance inspections. We targeted the one-mile radius to advance the twin mandates to gather information needed to assess the designated NHL boundary and to obtain data parallel with and comparable to the results of the one-mile radius site inventory conducted around the ruins of Grasshopper Pueblo (see Longacre et al. 1982; Reid 1978, 1989). With these mandates in mind, we re-located and improved the documentation for previously recorded sites, identified and recorded additional sites, and compiled basic information on other large residential sites within about 10 miles of Kinishba. The survey and follow-up analyses, although obviously limited, boost the quantity and quality of evidence bearing on Kinishba's ancient land use and available for interpreting the NHL to visitors.

The primary research application for the

results from the one-mile radius survey and more extensive reconnaissance involves assessing settlement around Kinishba in relation to settlement in other regions, especially around Grasshopper Pueblo (Reid 1978, 1989; Reid and Whittlesey 1999; Tuggle 1970; Tuggle et al. 1984; Triadan and Zedeño 2004). Accordingly, data presentation and discussion in this chapter center on one question: What can be learned about Kinishba's settlement system by comparing the small amount of settlement pattern information from the Kinishba region to the larger body of more completely analyzed settlement data from the Grasshopper region? Several subsidiary questions follow: How similar or different to the Grasshopper pattern is settlement around Kinishba? What do variations in the two patterns indicate about how the two systems emerged and changed through time? How might future analyses of Kinishba settlement patterns or interregional comparisons complement and advance investigations grounded in the more intensive studies of Grasshopper settlement pattern and system? What are the analytic advantages and limitations of thinking in terms of regional settlement clusters centered on the largest pueblos along both sides of the Mongollon Rim, especially as residents of these clusters may have cooperated and conflicted with one another and people having ties to settlements or settlement clusters in other regions?

This chapter reports the results of our boundary survey and compares settlement pattern and system around Kinishba with what we know from intensive study of the Grasshopper region. As noted in previous chapters, parallels between Kinishba and Grasshopper center on several unmistakable similarities. Both sites include at least 500 rooms. Both were built within the largest expanses of arable bottomlands in their respective regions. Both sites are situated near the heads of drainages and are bisected by spring-fed stream channels that supported surface flows year-round through the early 1900s. Both sites consist of massive, plaza-focused ruins groups (also known as "room blocks") surrounded by a number of smaller, generally low-walled ruins groups (also known as "outliers"). Even though the two sites share temporal and cultural affinities in general, the ceramic and architectural indications are that Kinishba was occupied somewhat earlier as well as later, and that the community participated in exchange networks that were greater in number, more extensive, or both (Lyons Chapter 7; Triadan Chapter 8). To this list we add that both sites seem to have been built up rapidly and largely by immigrants from regions north of the Mogollon Rim. As we await more and better settlement pattern data from Kinishba and adjacent areas, this list of similarities and contrasts provides a point of departure for considering what we think we now know, respectively, about Grasshopper and Kinishba settlement.

Prior to presenting and interpreting evidence for regional settlement, a few comments are in order concerning data sources and qualities. Most of the data come from FAIRsite, the site files maintained by the White Mountain Apache Tribe Historic Preservation Office at Fort Apache (Welch 2000). FAIRsite is the most complete repository of settlement pattern information for the White Mountain Apache Tribe's lands and the only site records system that includes unique identifiers and information compendia for all of the sites discussed here, notably including the sites recorded during the 2004 survey around Kinishba. The column headings for the data tables reflect our primary interests in clarifying site identity (including FAIRsite number and site name, where appropriate) and in comparing estimated site sizes (as indicated by the number of rooms) and topographic locations. Our simple, mostly descriptive site categories enable assessment of differences and similarities between the

Grasshopper and Kinishba data sets. Most or all of the sites with Mogollon Pueblo affinities (referred to by some authors as Ancestral Pueblo, see Riggs 2005) represent Canyon Creek Phase occupations (A.D. 1325–1400), as indicated by the dominance in the painted ceramic assemblages of White Mountain Redwares, especially Four Mile Polychrome.

Grasshopper Settlement

Previous studies of Grasshopper settlement have aptly described the region's biophysical and sociopolitical settings, so the emphasis here is on those aspects of research and settlement history necessary to facilitate comparisons with Kinishba. Riggs (Chapter 6) discusses the structural similarities—including room size, function, and community layout—that further suggest Grasshopper and Kinishba were established and developed through time as something akin to "twin" village farming communities. Welch (1996) reviews the research emphases of the sequence of archaeological site surveys around Grasshopper that began in 1969 (Tuggle 1970) and continued into the 1980s. Over the course of about 12 field seasons, Grasshopper survey crews inspected terrain within one-, two-, and three-mile radii around the main pueblo, as well as distant reaches of the Grasshopper Plateau and adjacent landforms. Systematic survey data are not available beyond Kinishba's one-mile radius. Accordingly, Tables 9.1 and 9.2 list the sites located within one mile of Grasshopper and Kinishba, respectively.

The Grasshopper radius surveys are complemented by systematic inventory survey tracts across more than 200 square miles of the Grasshopper region, as well as by judgmental topographic transects conducted along the steep-sided ridges and rugged cliffs that dominate the margins of the Grasshopper Plateau south and west of the main ruin. These surveys, along with the archaeological site inventory of the north-south power transmission line corridor through the Q Ranch region west of Grasshopper and Canyon Creek, documented hundreds of sites ranging from chipped-stone and ceramic scatters to field house sites, refuge sites, and multi-household pueblo ruins located on various landforms and in cliff alcoves (Reid 1982; Reid et al. 1982; Figure 9.1; see also Lange 2006).

The results of Grasshopper settlement studies join other chapters in this volume by using Grasshopper as an interpretive basis for building inferences and suggesting follow-up research concerning Kinishba's settlement. Tuggle (1970) provides the pottery-based seriation essential to assigning sites to time periods and moving from settlement pattern description to settlement system interpretation. Longacre and Reid (1971) outline a strategy to build on Tuggle's foundations and boost understanding of changes in Grasshopper settlement and land use through time.

Although many avenues for Grasshopper region settlement research remain to be more fully explored, some findings are particularly relevant to Kinishba. At the intra-site scale, Reid (Chapter 11) and Reid and Whittlesey (1999:63-66) describe the 10 small room groups, generally built after about 1325, that surround Grasshopper's three primary room blocks and form part of Grasshopper's main pueblo complex. Fewer details are available for the smaller room groups at Kinishba, but similar patterns exist. Cummings' (1940) descriptions and the results of Shaeffers' excavations (Chapter 4) are consistent with the view that the smaller room groups represent households that emerged or arrived into circumstances in which the main room blocks were completely occupied, thus obliging them to build or take up residence in less structurally substantial and more spatially peripheral quarters. Riggs'

Table 9.1 Sites within One Mile of Grasshopper Ruin

FAIRsite	Type	Cultural Affinity	Landform
18009	Fieldhouse	Pueblo	Bottomland
18011	Ceramic/chipped-stone scatter	Pueblo	Slope
18012	Ceramic/chipped-stone scatter	Pueblo	Bottomland
18129	Fieldhouse	Pueblo	Slope
18160	Fieldhouse	Pueblo	Bottomland
18161	Ceramic/chipped-stone scatter	Pueblo	Bottomland
18162	Check dam	Pueblo	Slope
18163	Brush structures – "wickiup"	Apache	Slope
18164	Fieldhouse	Pueblo	Hilltop / Ridge crest
18165	Fieldhouse	Pueblo	Bottomland
18166	Fieldhouse	Pueblo	Slope
18167	Ceramic/chipped-stone scatter	Pueblo	Hilltop / Ridge crest
18168	Ceramic/chipped-stone scatter	Pueblo	Bottomland
18169	Ceramic/chipped-stone scatter	Pueblo	Hilltop / Ridge crest
18170	Fieldhouse	Pueblo	Slope
18173	Ceramic/chipped-stone scatter	Pueblo	Bottomland
18180	Ceramic/chipped-stone scatter	Pueblo	Hilltop / Ridge crest
18189	Fieldhouse	Pueblo	Hilltop / Ridge crest
18190	Ceramic/chipped-stone scatter	Pueblo	Bottomland
18192	Pueblo (*Chodistaas*)	Pueblo	Hilltop / Ridge crest
19085	Fieldhouse	Pueblo	Bottomland
19086	Ceramic/chipped-stone scatter	Pueblo	Slope
19087	Ceramic/chipped-stone scatter	Pueblo	Hilltop / Ridge crest
19092	Fieldhouse	Pueblo	Hilltop / Ridge crest
19093	Fieldhouse	Pueblo	Hilltop / Ridge crest
19107	Fieldhouse	Pueblo	Slope
19108	Ceramic chipped-stone scatter	Pueblo	Hilltop / Ridge crest
19109	Ceramic chipped-stone scatter	Pueblo	Bottomland
19110	Ceramic chipped-stone scatter	Pueblo	Bottomland
19111	Ceramic chipped-stone scatter	Pueblo	Hilltop / Ridge crest
19112	Ceramic chipped-stone scatter	Pueblo	Hilltop / Ridge crest
19113	Ceramic chipped-stone scatter	Pueblo	Bottomland
19114	Fieldhouse	Pueblo	Bottomland
19116	Fieldhouse (rock alignment)	Pueblo	Slope
19117	Ceramic chipped-stone scatter	Pueblo	Bottomland
19118	Ceramic chipped-stone scatter	Pueblo	Bottomland
19120	Fieldhouse	Pueblo	Bottomland
19122	Pueblo (Grasshopper Spring)	Pueblo	Slope
19135	Ceramic chipped-stone scatter	Pueblo	Slope
19136	Fieldhouse	Pueblo	Slope
19137	Ceramic chipped-stone scatter	Pueblo	Hilltop / Ridge crest
19143	Ceramic chipped-stone scatter	Pueblo	Bottomland
19250	Martinez Ranch	Pueblo & Apache	Slope

Table 9.2 Sites within One Mile of Kinishba Ruin

FAIRsite	Site Type	Cultural Affinity	Landform
46004	Field house	Pueblo	Bottomland
46010	Campsite	Apache	Bottomland
46016	Field house	Pueblo	Bottomland
46017	Field border	Pueblo	Bottomland
46094	Corn field	Apache	Bottomland
46104	Ceramic and chipped-stone scatter with brush structure	Apache-Pueblo	Bottomland
46126	Campsite	Apache-Pueblo	Bottomland
46127	Fieldhouse	Apache-Pueblo	Bottomland
46128	Ceramic and chipped-stone scatter	Pueblo	Hilltop / Ridge crest
46129	Ceramic, chipped-stone, and groundstone scatter	Pueblo	Hilltop / Ridge crest
46130	Campsite	Apache	Slope
46131	2-3 room pueblo	Pueblo	Bottomland
46132	Historical-period dump	Apache	Bottomland
46133	Grave and Petroglyph	Pueblo? -Indeterminate	Slope
46135	Ceramic and chipped-stone scatter with stone cairn	Pueblo	Hilltop / Ridge crest
46136	Ceramic and chipped-stone scatter	Pueblo	Bottomland

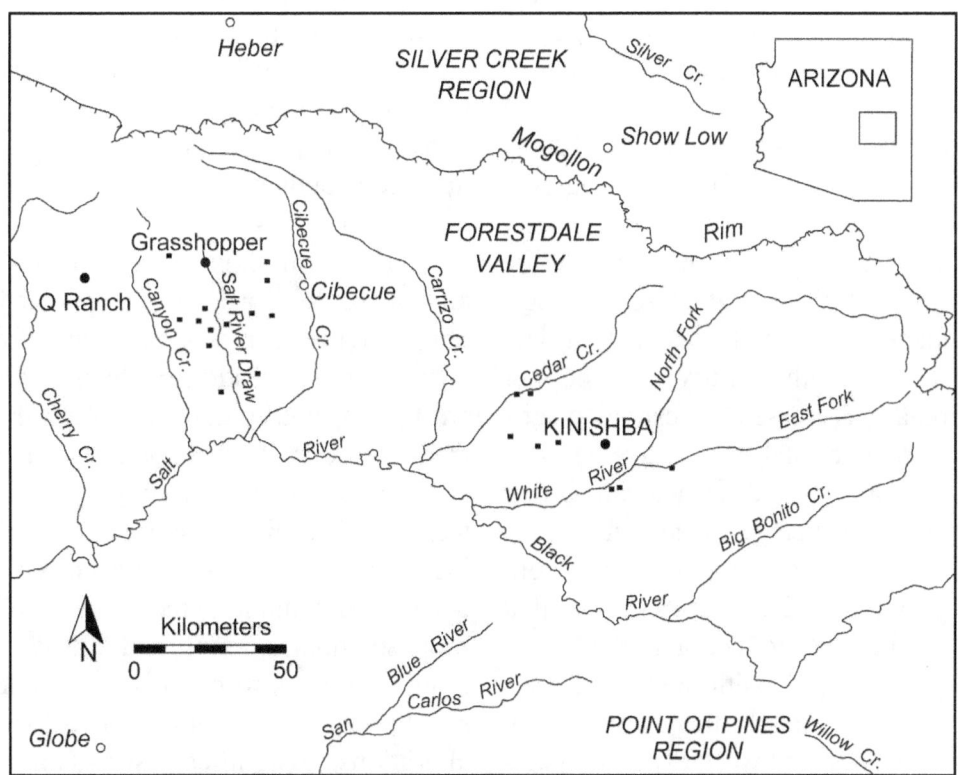

Figure 9.1. The Kinishba and Grasshopper regions, including schematic locations for all large Pueblo sites located within about 10 miles of Grasshopper and Kinishba.

(2001:142-145) analyses of Grasshopper's architectural development present evidence for slower growth in the smaller room groups as a possible indication of households unable to establish themselves in the main room blocks. Riggs suggests that these households, spatially and perhaps socially peripheral, were more likely to opt, sooner or later, to relocate themselves away from the main pueblos, in satellite settlements being established around both Grasshopper and, as discussed below, Kinishba.

Tuggle et al. (1984), Reid (1989), Triadan and Zedeño (2004), and Welch (1996) discuss Grasshopper Pueblo as the hub in a regional settlement cluster. This inferred system featured large residential sites (i.e., satellite pueblos of 25 or more rooms, Table 9.3; depicted schematically in Figure 9.1) as well as low-walled, one- to three-room structures referred to as field houses. Both types of sites are predominantly located within or adjacent to the region's best agricultural soils (Tuggle et al. 1984). Reid (1989) reviews developments in Grasshopper region settlement, describing immigration into the region in the later 1200s, followed by population expansion and aggregation at Grasshopper Pueblo by 1300 and then, after about 1330, dispersion into the satellite pueblos. Welch (1996) synthesizes ecological, settlement, and social organization data to suggest fourteenth century Grasshopper region populations crossed a threshold to agricultural dependence and would have had few intra-regional options aside from locating their residences and organizing their communities to optimize chances for success in dry land corn farming. Tuggle and Reid (2001) argue that uncertainties in food production in the Grasshopper region, coupled with the rise of large and possibly expansionist settlement systems in regions to the south and west, explain aspects of the circa 1330 shift in the Grasshopper settlement pattern. This shift includes not only the establishment and rapid expansion of the satellite pueblos, but an apparent reorientation in settlement emphasis toward the Grasshopper Plateau's western flank, as evidenced by the dozens of residential and fortified sites on precipitous landforms or other tactically advantageous positions along that flank (see also Welch 2001; Triadan and Zedeño 2004). Whether due to external threats of violent conflict, to tensions embedded in social commitments to dry land corn farming in the Mogollon Rim region's marginal agricultural setting (i.e., due to thin soils and variable climate), or to other factors, the Grasshopper region seems to have been largely depopulated by about 1400.

Kinishba Settlement

Despite the Kinishba region's generally gentler terrain and the site's location near paved roads and modern amenities, limited personnel and finances have prevented systematic site recordation in the Kinishba region on anything like the scale of the Grasshopper surveys. No systematic, research-driven archaeological survey had been conducted around Kinishba prior to our work in 2004.

On the other hand, the growing body of ancient settlement information that is available provides a reasonable basis for initial comparisons. In addition to our 2004 field work, Kinishba settlement pattern data come from two sources: (1) explorations and casual site recordings by Cummings (1940) and his teams; and (2) diverse, compliance-driven site identification surveys conducted across many decades. Beginning in the 1960s, planning for proposed homes, roads, and utilities began to require surveys to comply with federal and tribal rules for designing projects to minimize alterations to significant sites (for example, Ciolek-Torello and Halbirt Chapter 5; McKenna and Rice 1980). Unlike the Grasshopper

Table 9.3 Pueblos with 25 or More Rooms in the Grasshopper Region

FAIRsite	Site Name	Rooms	Miles from Grasshopper	Landform
18033	Hilltop	65	2.5	Hilltop / Ridge crest
18103	Oak Creek	35	5.25	Hilltop / Ridge crest
18130	Brush Mountain	150	5	Hilltop / Ridge crest
18146	Sam Canyon	31	4.5	Hilltop / Ridge crest
18146	Red Rock House	30	4	Cliff alcove
19174	Red Canyon	45	4	Hilltop / Ridge crest
29057	Canyon Butte	65	11	Bottomland
29083	Canyon Creek	120	7.5	Cliff alcove
30037	Blue House Mountain	140	6.25	Slope
30063	Ruins Tank	100	11	Hilltop / Ridge crest
30072	Spotted Mountain	85	6.5	Hilltop / Ridge crest
30094	Black Mountain	70	8	Hilltop / Ridge crest

surveys, pre-2004 site identification efforts in the Kinishba region lack common research orientations and are seldom larger than minimally required to assess impacts from specific land disturbance proposals.

As a means to facilitate comparison with the Grasshopper data, our 2004 surveys had two emphases. First, our two-person crew systematically inspected terrain within a one-mile radius of Kinishba. Second, we conducted reconnaissance and site re-documentation within about 10 miles of Kinishba. Because less research has thus far focused on Kinishba's biophysical setting and settlement patterns compared to Grasshopper's, strictly parallel comparisons are possible only for the results of the one-mile radius surveys; comparisons of the settlement patterns beyond the one-mile perimeter are less systematic and more constrained and speculative. The following two sections compare settlement within the Grasshopper and Kinishba regions at two spatial scales. The first of these presents data from our one-mile perimeter boundary surveys around Kinishba. The subsequent section compares data relating to known pueblo sites of at least 25 rooms within reasonable pedestrian reach (i.e., about 10 miles) of Kinishba and Grasshopper.

Sites Within a One-mile Perimeter of Grasshopper and Kinishba

Our inventory of sites within a one-mile radius of the Kinishba perimeter fence (Table 9.2) re-identified six sites and documented 10 new sites (46126–46136). Figure 9.2 depicts the 16 sites within the one-mile radius as well as 13 other sites beyond the one-mile radius. Sites in the Kinishba vicinity include the same general types of sites found around Grasshopper, plus a greater number and variety of reservation-period Apache sites—five as opposed to two within a mile of Grasshopper. Three of these five sites contain a mixture of Mogollon Pueblo and reservation period Apache materials, including ceramic and chipped-stone concentrations, grinding stones, metal cooking pots, metal cans, and fragments of glass and metal containers. These occurrences are not surpris-

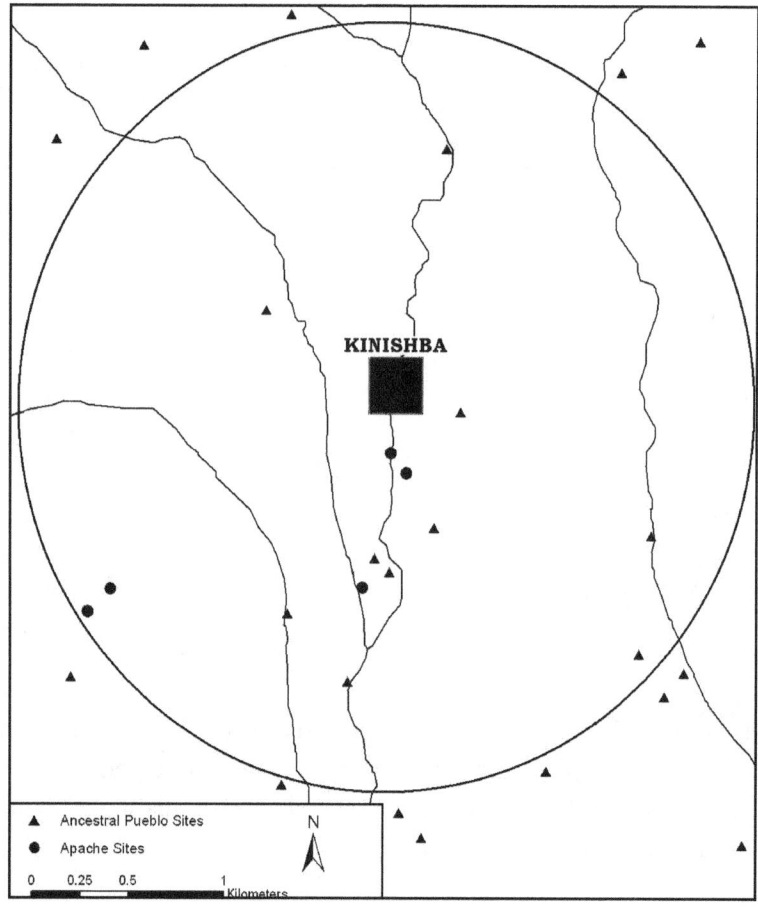

Figure 9.2. Sites in the Kinishba vicinity.

ing given Kinishba's proximity to the community of Canyon Day, a sprawling, discontinuous cluster of structures and features traceable to ephemeral Apache camps that became rooted in place due to U.S. government requirements for regular headcounts of Apache populations at and through nearby Fort Apache (McKenna and Rice 1980; Welch and Brauchli 2010; Welch 2010).

The expansive arable lands extending from Kinishba southward are well suited for agriculture. Cummings (1940:3) notes that meadows surrounding Kinishba were "covered with the corn fields of the Apache.... this land produces one good crop of corn or beans or anything else that grows in a temperate climate on a good dry-land farm." The Apache Agriculture Enterprise, a small-scale, tribally owned producer of alfalfa, grain and orchard crops, is located about three miles south of Kinishba. In contrast, the area around Grasshopper hosted a small trading post (circa 1910s–1930s), the headquarters for a livestock association (1940s–1960s), and a cowboy camp (1940s–present). The Grasshopper vicinity has been only occasionally utilized by Apache farmers. It may be that farming activities tend to leave behind more distinct, site-like archaeological indicators than ranching. In any case, the most important determinant of the number of Apache sites is probably that Grasshopper field crews in the 1970s and early 1980s were less intrigued with or focused upon twentieth century artifacts and features than our team, and seldom recorded historical period sites that lacked abundant artifacts, structures or structural remnants. Interests in Apache archaeology by Grasshopper researchers played an important role in launching ethoarchaeology (Longacre and Ayres 1968), and Graves' (1982) collaborations with Basso's (1996) Cibecue Apache place names project produced an excellent framework for follow-up research. Nonetheless, substantive archaeological contributions to understanding Western Apache history and pre-reservation lifeways have been few, far between, and generally limited (see Herr et al. 2009; Welch 1997; Welch and Ferguson 2007).

Given Kinishba's setting in the midst of a broad valley, it is not surprising to note the general clustering of sites along stream channels, primarily the large, typically dry, wash which bisects Kinishba's east and west room blocks (Figure 9.2). Kinishba's setting in relation to major landforms, and generally lower topographic diversity within one mile, probably also account for the bottomland locations of 11 of the 16 sites (69 percent) and only three (19 percent) on hilltops or ridge crests within a mile of Kinishba (Table 9.2). Within a mile of Grasshopper, 17 of the 43 sites (39 percent) are located in bottomlands and 13 (30 percent) occupy the tops of landforms. The gentle arable basin surrounding Kinishba to the north, east, and south makes visual monitoring from Kinishba possible for most areas within the one-mile radius.

As for Apache occupations, the basin is strewn with evidence of modern landscape uses and alterations, including the above-noted fields and other agriculture-related features, such as fences, wells, pipelines, livestock trails, and two-track access roads. Apache collection and re-use of Mogollon Pueblo surface materials has likely occurred since shortly after depopulations at both Kinishba and Grasshopper, adding to the challenges of making inferences about ancient behavior on the basis of items observed on the surface since the 1930s (Herr et al. 2009; Welch and Ferguson 2007). Various isolated ancient and historical period artifact occurrences were observed during the 2004 survey. Because these could not be reliably linked to features or other artifacts, they were not documented as sites.

Most of the sites in the Kinishba vicinity occur south of the main pueblo (14 of 16 within the one-mile radius; 22 of the 29 total sites depicted in Figure 9.2). Of the seven sites located north of the pueblo, four exhibit dense ceramic and chipped-stone scatters. Only two of the sites south of Kinishba have dense ceramic scatters, a finding that may indicate a preference for living to the north and farming to the south of the pueblo. Excluding the sites with unambiguous indications of Apache use, general patterns of site type distributions are similar at Kinishba and Grasshopper. Of Grasshopper's 43 one-mile radius sites 22 (51 percent) are artifact scatters and 16 (37 percent) are field houses; at Kinishba 5 (31 percent) are scatters and 4 (25 percent) are field houses.

Graves et al. (1982:112) observe that, "perhaps the most important resource available to the inhabitants of Grasshopper was the expanse of alluvial bottomland suitable for cultivation, extending over four square km immediately south of the pueblo." The area of the arable land around Kinishba approaches 40 square km. Also unlike Grasshopper, the area within a mile of Kinishba does not include various small residential sites. The largest site near Kinishba is a two to three room pueblo with a surface artifact scatter suggesting full-time or sustained fourteenth century occupation. This seems to be the best, and possibly the only candidate for the sorts of small pueblos and field houses that occur along Salt River Draw, and mostly to the south of Grasshopper itself.

Sites with 25 or more Rooms

FAIRsite records include 19 Mogollon Pueblo sites consisting of 25 or more rooms and located within about 10 miles of either Grasshopper or Kinishba (Tables 9.3 and 9.4). We selected the 25-room and approx. 10 mile cutoffs to maintain general parallels to previous analyses (especially Reid 1989). We think seperations of greater than about 10 miles render one-day, round-trip travel between settlements less likely. We think people using similar objects and living in similar residences within a day's round-trip walk are more likely to have been participants in the Grasshopper and Kinishba settlement systems discussed here. Although it appears that some of the large sites in the Kinishba cluster were occupied earlier—i.e., by the middle of the Pinedale Phase (1250–1325)—each of these 20 sites were occupied intensively during the Canyon Creek Phase (1325–1400). All are located close to tabular sedimentary bedrock, and standing timber; all or most seem to have been built around a discrete, spring-fed source of domestic water; all except the cliff dwellings in the Grasshopper region (18146, 29083) were built in or adjacent to near arable land suitable for dry farming under favorable precipitation and temperature regimes. Farmers living at the East Fork site (47002) likely irrigated at least some of their fields.

The 12 sites consisting of more than 25 rooms in the Grasshopper region (Table 9.3; Figure 9.1) range from 2.5 to 11 miles from Grasshopper. The original site map for the largest site in this class (18130, 150 rooms) depicts possible garden plots at the north end of the site. The Kinishba region also includes a single, second-largest site, 45001, with a possible curvilinear great kiva or other architectural features not identified elsewhere in the region. The two largest cliff dwellings in the Grasshopper region are not directly associated with expanses of arable lands, but both are perched just above spring-fed canyons that may have been terraced or otherwise altered to support intensively irrigated and cultivated gardens similar to those maintained at most Hopi villages (Vasquez and Jenkins 1994). Regardless, the density of Canyon Creek Phase ceramics at both of these cliff dwellings, and at most of the 25 smaller cliff dwellings located south and southwest of Grasshopper, indicates household or multi-household occupations contemporaneous with other large, post-1325 pueblos in the region. Although agriculturalists, the cliff dwellers probably exploited the full spectrum of plant and animal foods accessible in and via the canyons they occupied (Reid 1989; Tuggle and Reid 2001). The four small cliff dwellings in the Kinishba region (probably fewer than 30 rooms combined) occupy alcoves in canyons walls along agriculturally favorable reaches of Cedar Creek and East Fork. The stretches of these streams drain much larger watersheds than the precipitous, plateau-edge canyons that host the Grasshopper region alcove sites. On the other hand, the Kinishba region does not include vertical exposures of Dripping Spring quartzite or other formations that produce south-facing alcoves and otherwise support the masonry construction characteristic of most of the American Southwest's cliff dwellings.

Excluding the two major (that is, containing greater than 25 rooms) cliff dwellings in the Grasshopper cluster (18146 and 29083 in Table 9.3), the landform settings of the large sites in each cluster are generally similar. One of the Grasshopper cluster's 10 multi-household pueblos (10 percent) occupies bottomlands and eight (80 percent) occupy hilltops or ridge crests. Two of the eight members (25 percent) of the Kinishba cluster are located in bottomlands; five (63 percent) occupy the tops of landforms.

Discussion and Conclusions

Despite the limitations of our survey results and comparative analyses, the settlement data highlight at least four issues bearing on Kinishba settlement systems and subject to partial assessment using available evidence for thirteenth and fourteenth century residential and non-residential land uses. We discuss these overlapping issues bundled in the four following sections—site visibility and agricultural intensification, boundary validity, social centrality and agricultural ecology, and interregional tension.

Site Visibility and Agricultural Intensification

The most striking contrast between the Kinishba and Grasshopper settlement patterns appears to be the lower density of sites in the Kinishba vicinity. This distinction, especially apparent within the one-mile radius, seems anomalous given that (1) Kinishba was probably occupied longer and more intensively than Grasshopper; and (2) more Apache sites have been recorded around Kinishba. Alternative explanations for the site density differential are that (a) land use by participants in the Kinishba and Grasshopper settlement systems varied significantly; (b) land use was the same, but site preservation and visibility varied; or (c) both land uses and the formation of the surface archaeological records varied enough to account for the observed difference in site density.

A full explanation for the smaller number of sites immediately surrounding Kinishba is probably beyond the limits of the evidence in hand, but some differences between the regions' hydro-geological contexts warrant consideration. Kinishba's broad basin is dominated by precipitous, basalt-capped sedimentary sidewalls that separate it from adjacent landforms. The stream channel that divides Kinishba's principal room blocks, like those that run parallel to it on their short run (generally less than 10 km) to White River, drain dissected, south-facing sandstone and limestone slopes. These uplands are vegetated, often sparsely, by piñon-juniper-scrub oak woodlands fringed on the south by chaparral. Wildfires and violent monsoonal and convectional storms result in episodic sediment relocations off these uplands and valley walls and into the basin. As one indicator of exceptionally high aggradation rates and magnitudes, rains in the wake of the 2003 Kinishba Fire resulted in sediment redepositions as deep as 1 m across broad areas of the Kinishba basin, causing occasional road closures through 2006 (Nickens 2006). It is unlikely that similarly large and intensive wildfires ravaged the Kinishba region prior to the introductions, in the late 1800s, of large herds of livestock and, in the mid 1900s, of systematic fire suppression (Welch 2012). Nevertheless, regular introductions of sediments from the uplands have undoubtedly affected site visibilities.

The view of the Kinishba basin as a dynamic depositional context also speaks to the issue of agricultural intensification. Sediment relocations from upper reaches of watersheds into the Kinishba basin would have contributed to soil fertility and renewal. Our 2004 survey found little in terms of the boulder alignments and field houses used as indicators of intensified agricultural practices in the Point of Pines regions and to a lesser extent around Grasshopper (Tuggle et al. 1984; Welch 1996; Woodbury 1961). Evidence for agricultural intensification, which is not particularly strong in the Grasshopper region, is even weaker around Kinishba. Available evidence cannot rule out the possibility that many sites—including field houses and boulder alignments used for agricultural terraces and check dams—have been lost to erosion or buried by gradual or episodic deposition. On the other hand, field houses and other alignments have not been observed in stream channel cutbanks or road cuts around Kinishba. We recommend further study of indications that land in the Kinishba basin may have been more fertile and abundant than lands around Grasshopper, Q Ranch, Point of Pines, etc., and that Kinishba's lower elevation (at 5250 feet above sea level, about 700 feet lower than Grasshopper) translates in most years into a longer frost-free growing season. These differences may have obviated the need for intensification. We think it is likely that alignment and field house features (i.e., physical capital) were unnecessary, or at least less necessary to support farming in Kinishba's gentle basin. Finally, the generally low densities of thirteenth and fourteenth century sites around Kinishba suggests steady rather than spiking increases in labor investment (i.e., human capital) in food production.

On the broader, regional level, our confidence in the available data as a valid representation of Kinishba's fourteenth century settlement pattern is similarly reserved. Kinishba is the only fourteenth century site below the Mogollon Rim between Grasshopper and Point of Pines to have been studied beyond occasional reconnaissance (Triadan and Zedeño 2004). Given the scale of the landscapes considered here and the likely mobility of their occupants prior to community-scale migrations and reservation establishments, a one-mile radius survey is little more than a good start. We have, individually and collectively, spent many days walking the Kinishba region's stream terraces, parklands and ridge crests. While we doubt the existence of undocumented pueblos larger than about 25 rooms, the lack of systematic regional survey is a persistent nag. The Cedar Creek and Carrizo Creek watersheds, in particular, contain several larger sites, none of which has been mapped in accord with twenty-first century standards. Both Cedar Creek and East Fork warrant especially careful attention. Were the villages along these perennial streams part of the Kinishba system or did one or both operate as distinctive settlement systems at one or more periods in time? In other words, despite the many similarities between Grasshopper and Kinishba on intra-site and regional scales, as well as our efforts to create roughly parallel data sets, analytic and interpretive challenges will constrain interpretations pending further research.

National Historic Landmark Boundary Validity

Despite the lack of certainty regarding site visibility, available evidence supports the validity, of the officially designated boundary for Kinishba Ruins NHL. The perimeter fence present in 2012 follows the same lines as the Kinishba property's first fence, erected by 1939 (see Cummings 1940). In 1958, the land within the same fenced enclosure was proposed for transfer to National Park Service management as Kinishba National Monument (Welch 2007a). This generally square enclosure (about 36.5 acres) encompasses the meaningfully interrelated structures and features that constitute Kinishba. The enclosure fence features two gates, including the main visitor entryway, which includes a cattle guard and since 2003 a lock to discourage unauthorized livestock and vehicle access.

The fenced area encompasses the structural and archaeological features immediately associated with the late Mogollon Pueblo occupation and the structures Cummings investigated and interpreted. The boundary fence also encloses (1) the spring that likely served as the primary attraction and domestic water source for the village's builders and occupants; (2) the bedrock exposures quarried to exhaustion by Kinishba's builders; and (3) reasonably representative sections of the juniper woodlands, ponderosa pine stringers, and fertile flatlands that contributed to the locality's attractiveness to corn-farming pueblo dwellers. The NHL-designated acreage does not include "buffer zones" or other areas not contributing to Kinishba's national significance.

Social Centrality and Agricultural Sustainability

By *social centrality* we refer to the degree to which Kinishba and Grasshopper served as hubs or centers in their respective settlement systems. As used here, *agricultural sustainability* refers to settlement pattern indications of concern with obtaining food, especially reliable yields from the dry-farmed corn fields that undoubtedly fed most of the people most of the time at Kinishba and Grasshopper. In part because previous analyses of Grasshopper region settlement have justifiably emphasized arable land as a determinant of large pueblo locations, these two issues are so closely interrelated that separate discussions are impractical. Instead, we examine these issues at a regional scale before zooming in to discuss factors affecting site location.

As previously noted, Kinishba and Grasshopper are the largest sites in the largest expanses of arable lands in the sub-Mogollon Rim region extending from Cherry Creek in the west to the Point of Pines and Blue River site clusters in the east (Triadan and Zedeño 2004; Welch Chapter 2). Grasshopper researchers described and assessed the significance of the spatial distribution of agricultural opportunity in the Grasshopper region. Graves et al. (1982:114) suggest rapid population growth and aggregation at Grasshopper exceeded the capacity for community self governance as well as farmland availability. Whether on their own initiative or due to guidance from Grasshopper residents, newcomers—and possibly some of Grasshopper's occupants—founded new villages, mostly to the south, mostly adjacent to patches of arable soils not contiguous to the farmlands nearest to Grasshopper. and mostly after 1325. This development seems to have coincided with the rehabilitation and roofing of Grasshopper's Plaza 3 to create a large, rectangular great kiva (Reid and Whittlesey 1999:125, 156-157).

Reid's (1989) approach to understanding changes in Grasshopper settlement through time are grounded in the observations that (1) the three small (less than 20 rooms) sites occupied prior to about 1290 were all burned to the ground as a prelude to aggregation at Grasshopper Pueblo; (2) the large (more than 25 rooms) sites founded after about 1325 filled village farming community "niches" available in the Grasshopper vicinity; and (3) immigrants into the Grasshopper region from the 1290s to the 1320s came from various northerly (i.e., Colorado Plateau) and west-southwesterly (i.e., Sonoran desert) areas outside of the Mogollon Rim region (see also Tuggle and Reid 2001; Tuggle et al. 1984).

Each of these elements of Reid's interpretation merits discussion in relation to the information available from the Kinishba region, including the improved documentation for the creation of a great kiva in the plaza of Kinishba's Group I (Shaeffer and Shaeffer Chapter 4). Regarding site burning, we are unaware of evidence pertaining to the possibility of a destructive campaign against thirteenth century residential sites prior to aggregation at Kinishba. On the other hand, evidence from Kinishba suggests parallel occurrences of immigrant diversity. Triadan's and Lyons' contributions to this volume (chapters 7 and 8) provide evidence that Kinishba and Grasshopper participated in different suites of ceramic exchange networks and that these networks likely reflect both the source regions and evolving social networks of at least some of the groups who built, occupied and sustained the big pueblos. It may also be useful to note that cultural heritage damage assessment surveys conducted in the Carrizo Creek watersheds in the wake of the 2002 Rodeo-Chediski Fire identified and documented at least four large residential pueblo sites dating to the 1100s and 1200s (Gregory n.d.; see Mills et al. 2008). Gregory's (n.d.) findings indicate the need to review prevailing interpretations of low population densities south of the Mogollon Rim prior to colonization(s) in the late 1200s. Beyond this, the limited quantities and qualities of survey, excavation, and burial records leave us without more to say about ethnic co-residence in the Kinishba region.

Slightly more information is available to assess the prospects for regional settlement pattern expansion as a result of population dispersion from Kinishba and niche filling. Reid's inferences regarding Grasshopper settlement are based in part on evidence for a size hierarchy in the Grasshopper region's large, post-1325 pueblos: there are four sites with 30–45 rooms (a sort of 'basal pueblo' for this period and region), four sites roughly twice that size (65–85 rooms), and four sites about four times the size (100–150 rooms) of the basal pueblos. Some form of hierarchy may also be evident in the Kinishba data (Table 9.4), but the sample seems too small and the room count and chronometric estimates too uncertain to offer more conclusive suggestions.

Comparative data on the satellite pueblos' locations with respect to farmland contiguity and watershed locations may be relevant to understanding how niches were defined and filled in the two regions. Arable lands around Grasshopper Pueblo and across the Grasshopper region occur in parkland patches, large and small, mostly along the main stem and tributaries of Salt River Draw. Farmlands around Kinishba occupy an expansive, colluvium-filled basin that is today dissected by numerous, generally shallow and gentle gullies. But the area within 10 miles of Kinishba includes other watersheds that feature arable lands as well as satellite pueblos. Only two of Grasshopper's surface pueblo ruins lie outside of the lands drained by Salt River Draw (18103 and 30094); seven of Kinishba's eight satellite pueblos are found in adjacent watersheds. These seven sites share with the Grasshopper satellites an apparent orientation toward arable lands non-contiguous with the farmlands surrounding the main pueblo (i.e., Kinishba). Moreover, four of Kinishba's eight satellites are located along active perennial streams with large areas of irrigable alluvium, an option less available in the Grasshopper region west of Cibecue Creek.

In terms of factors affecting specific locations chosen for pueblo building, Kinishba and Grasshopper both occupy the apical, spring-fed position within their respective landforms. But, the landforms themselves are different from one another and from those present in adjacent regions. Kinishba lies about 300 m lower in elevation than Grasshopper, toward the northern edge of a large, southerly draining basin. Grasshopper occupies the head of the central drainage (Salt River Draw) for a distinctive, south-sloping plateau, more precisely, a cuesta. Whether intentional or otherwise, the founders of both Kinishba and Grasshopper chose the most northerly, highest elevation spring surrounded by the largest expanses of arable land within about 100 km. Other sites in the Mogollon Rim region are located in places with water, land, and the raw materials for pueblo construction, but the extent of the available farmlands and the optimization of elevation within the arable landform both define the Grasshopper and Kinishba locations (as they do Q Ranch and Tundastusa, among others).

In this sense we think it may be useful to examine Tuggle and Reid's (2001:95) conclusion that "Grasshopper Pueblo is not located where it should be," as well as their sugges-

Table 9.4 Pueblos with 25 or More Rooms in the Kinishba Region

FAIRsite	Site Name	Rooms	Miles from Kinishba	Landform
33001	Water Tanks	45	8.5	Hilltop / Ridge crest
45001	Amos Wash	200	5	Bottomland
45002	R-14 Ranch	50	9	Hilltop / Ridge crest
45010	Geronimo Pass	35	4.5	Hilltop / Ridge crest
46001	Canyon Day School	25	3.5	Hilltop / Ridge crest
46096	Site not named	30	4	Hilltop / Ridge crest
46097	Amos Spring	60	3.5	Hilltop / Ridge crest
47100	East Fork	60?	5	Bottomland

tion that Grasshopper populations would have aggregated in the more fertile Cibecue Valley were it not for security concerns. Our questions center, first, on timing. Aside from fundamental preferences for aggregated residential units, security concerns are not evident in settlement pattern data until about 1325.

Setting aside concerns about interregional conflict, additional questions relate to founding group preferences for site and farming locations. From several vantages Grasshopper was located precisely where it should have been. Tuggle and Reid's conclusion that it was not appears to discount the influence of established preferences—on the part of the corn-farming founders of Grasshopper, Kinishba, Point of Pines, Q Ranch, Tundastusa, and (possibly) other pueblos—for locating primary settlements to optimize a delicate balance among temperature, precipitation, and topographic profiles. Tuggle (1970:35) correctly observes that the Cibecue Valley floodplain, located on the eastern edge of the Grasshopper region, slightly more than 10 miles from Grasshopper Pueblo, is the most intensively cultivated area on the western half of the White Mountain Apache Tribe's lands. He also acknowledges that fields along Cibecue Creek, like those along the bottoms of valleys across the Mogollon Rim region, are susceptible to destructive floods. It seems likely that Grasshopper's founders were aware of opportunities for irrigation and that both this factor and, at least initially, security concerns were less influential than establishing unequivocal control over a reliable spring and a vast expanse of previously un- or under-cultivated land suitable for dry farming.

From these perspectives on regional settlement, niche-filling in both regions may well have operated to direct population dispersions to farmlands not-contiguous with those under cultivation by the occupants of the principal pueblos. At Kinishba, this led to more major pueblos located outside of the Kinishba drainage basin. Both regions appear to be internally united by the presence of a single, especially large pueblo and the post-1325 presence, at both Grasshopper and Kinishba but nowhere else in the region, of a great kiva.

At least one additional difference between the two regions deserves mention. Settlement data from the Kinishba region do not seem to indicate the sort of partial return, after 1350, to a more dispersed settlement pattern (Reid 1989). We think the fact that agricultural lands in Kinishba's immediate vicinity are more abundant and more contiguous may explain the smaller number of satellite pueblos compared to the Grasshopper region.

Interregional Tensions

Our discussion of interregional tensions refers to settlement pattern indications of concerns with extra-regional populations in general and raiding or war parties in particular. Welch (1996:157) suggests that the "fortress-like" physiography of the Grasshopper Plateau—along with the area's fertile, generally well-watered soils, numerous springs, and abundant game—attracted immigrants.... [who] may have selected an aggregated community form due to previous experience or a real or imagined security threat." Both Welch (1996, 2001) and Tuggle and Reid (2001) go on to describe the extensive Grasshopper region settlement evidence for concerns with personal and collective security. It is not much of an exaggeration to claim that every suitable prominence in the Grasshopper region is fortified and that every major access route onto the Grasshopper Plateau from the south and west is monitored by fourteenth century lookouts, guarded by a satellite pueblo, or both. Tuggle and Reid (2001:99) rightly observe that, "large pueblos are defensive by nature," but beginning in the 1320s, Grasshopper residents decided to complement their 'strength in numbers' strategy with aggressive investments in establishing tactical advantages over known or anticipated invaders. This was done through site placement in relation to landforms and landform-defined travel corridors as well as by the construction of perimeter walls, breastworks, maze gateways, and various other features (Welch 2001; see Lange 2006). Actual evidence of inter-group violence dating to the Grasshopper region in the 1300s has not surfaced. It is nonetheless clear that many decisions made about where to locate sites and how to build them reflect concerns—substantial, persistent, and widespread—with protecting the occupants of Grasshopper and other pueblos along Salt River Draw.

Data limitations aside, settlement data from the Kinishba region include compelling indications of parallel concerns. One site recorded during the 2004 survey, but outside the one-mile radius, is located on a high ridge north of Kinishba. The commanding view of the Kinishba basin suggests the site may have served as a lookout. Farther afield from Kinishba, but within a five mile radius, there are two unmistakably fortified lookouts (too small for inclusion in Table 9.4) and three satellite pueblos (45002, 45010, 46001) located to optimize tactical advantages. Each of these five sites is located on a prominent landform. Three of the other major pueblo sites—33001, 46096, 46097—are located on landforms overlook, constrict or otherwise dominate obvious travel routes connecting the Kinishba region. The final evidence supporting parallels between Kinishba settlement and security concerns in the Grasshopper region is that every one of the sites just mentioned is located to the south or west of Kinishba. To the extent that real or perceived security threats had a real or perceived source, for the people of both the Kinishba and the Grasshopper settlement systems the threat lay to the southwest. It is possible that threats were linked, directly or indirectly, to fourteenth century conflicts and systemic collapses in the Tonto and Salt-Gila basins (see Lange 2006; Lyons et al. 2008; Wilcox 2005; Wilcox et al. 2001a,b).

RESEARCH AND MANAGEMENT RECOMMENDATIONS

Changing environmental conditions, recent land uses, and previous settlement pattern analyses have all affected our perceptions and interpretations of Kinishba's local and regional settlement. Setting aside these issues—along with general parallels in site types, locations, layouts, construction or composition, and distributions—the comparison undertaken here has highlighted questions that may warrant follow-up studies: Why is site density in the Kinishba region lower than it is in the Grasshopper region? Are the observed settlement pattern similarities confined to the Grasshopper and Kinishba regions or more widely distributed in adjacent regions—Q Ranch, Point of Pines, Cibecue-Carrizo, Silver Creek, etc.?

In particular, is arable land contiguity a significant determinant of the size and distribution of large pueblo sites in adjacent regions? Are large pueblo sites in thirteenth century settlement patterns associated with antecedent or source populations located to the north and northeast? Are large pueblo sites in later fourteenth and fifteenth century settlement patterns associated with successor or destination populations located around Hopi, Zuni, or elsewhere?

The following recommendations for study and action arise from these questions and our optimism that the demand for additional information will ultimately overcome the current lack of opportunities and support for settlement pattern research. First, we see the need for additional, more detailed and incisive comparisons of Kinishba and Grasshopper settlement systems, regional alliances, and agricultural and exchange economies. Such work would provide higher resolution information on population distributions, land uses, and cultural histories. Specific activities to address these needs might involve extending site inventory surveys beyond Kinishba's one-mile boundary and more systematic searches for Kinishba satellites, perhaps based in part on digital site location modeling.

Second, we recommend settlement investigations along and east of Cibecue Creek, especially including the identification and mapping of the large pueblos in the Carrizo Creek watershed that separates the Grasshopper and Kinishba region (Welch 1996:89). Along these lines, it would be useful to systematically revisit all of the large pueblos along the southern edge of the Mogollon Rim, in the Kinishba region and areas to the east and west, to systematically map and record the features and diagnostic artifacts at each site. Until this is accomplished, uncertainties will accompany inferences relating to the temporal and spatial boundaries and constituents of the Kinishba settlement system.

Third, in addition to data creation, better data management is needed. Although FAIRsite is the unique source for all settlement data for White Mountain Apache lands, the data available for even large pueblos is generally uneven, often distributed among organizations and researchers, and sometimes incorrect. With this in mind, acting on behalf of the White Mountain Apache Tribe Historic Preservation Office, Altaha and Welch have initiated a collaboration with Archaeology Southwest, Digital Antiquity and the Digital Archaeological Record (tDAR) to develop a data base and a protocol for digitizing and securely archiving all FAIRsite records. Among the ultimate goals of this pilot project is to integrate information on the major pueblos in the Kinishba and adjacent regions into the database supporting the Southwest Social Networks project, an initiative examining relationships among the major, precontact settlements of the Southwest between A.D. 1200 and 1550 (Hill et al. 2004; Mills and Clark 2009).

Fourth, with or without coordination with the Southwest Social Networks project, the archaeological record of the Kinishba region and adjacent portions of the White Mountain Apache Tribe's lands merit careful consideration as regards the colonization, population displacements, aggregations, and interregional tensions characteristic of the period from about 1200 to 1400. Effective investigations of these issues on appropriate spatial scales will likely require use of geographic information science (GIS) tools. Analyses of least-cost travel corridors linking the Grasshopper and Kinishba regions from the southwest, and of the inter-visibility of fortified and refuge sites along these corridors could be effectively and efficiently supported by GIS applications (see Scheiber and Finley 2011). As with all settlement research, however, the essential first ingredients in GIS studies are high quality data on site sizes and locations, including regional digital elevation models.

Last but not least, follow-up research should continue to support and receive support from the inter-tribal collaborations that have enabled the most important and innovative aspects of regional archaeological research on White Mountain Apache lands since the last season of the Grasshopper field school in 1992. Representatives of the Apache, Hopi, and Zuni tribes have been involved in the planning and implementation of all of the work done at Kinishba since 1992 (Mills et al 2008; Welch and Ferguson 2007). Discussions with these elders and cultural specialists have enhanced our understanding of the meanings of "community" and "region." For example, consultant guidance has redirected our attention to cairns, glyphs, and other subtle on-the-ground indicators of travel routes, cultural affinities, and settlement system boundaries, significantly increasing the possibilities that these will be identified in future site inventory surveys.

In sum, we think community, management, and research benefits are likely to accrue from further regional comparison of spatial dimensions of social, economic, and political organization and security. We look forward to leading or participating in the realization of these benefits and to learning more about the people who made Kinishba and the surrounding areas their home.

Chapter 10
Apache, Hopi, and Zuni Perspectives on Kinishba History and Stewardship

John R. Welch and T. J. Ferguson

As an Ancestral Mogollon Pueblo village on Apache land, and as a publicly accessible monument to an early experiment in community-based heritage tourism, Kinishba embodies multiple values, interests and expectations among affiliated tribes, visitors, archaeologists, and stakeholders in regional economic development and cultural perpetuation. In 2003 and 2004, as part of an effort to balance the relative wealth of archaeological data with Pueblo and Apache oral traditions and site conservation perspectives, the White Mountain Tribe worked with the Hopi Tribe, Pueblo of Zuni, and the Western Apache Repatriation Working Group to complete a geography-based cultural affiliation study of its lands (Figure 10.1). The project built upon archaeological data by collecting cultural and historical information from duly designated representatives of American Indian tribes to identify past social groups that occupied White Mountain Apache lands and to connect those groups to living descendants. Project participants shifted the focus from artifacts and archaeological cultures to oral traditions and other forms of knowledge linking geographies, memories, rituals and important sites to one another and to social groups past and present. Project results provide foundations for intertribal repatriation processes and for enhanced management and conservation policy and practice at Kinishba and elsewhere. The diverse cultural principles and values that guide Kinishba's stewardship are expressed both in what is present (for example, structural forms, masonry styles and interpretive materials that visitors can see) and what has been left out (for example, intrusive and industrial traces of excavation and rebuilding that have been removed in order to improve visitor satisfaction). Both inclusions and omissions can be expected to influence the site's interpretation, as well as its physical treatment as an ancestral Hopi and Zuni village and multi-tribal sacred site.

This chapter bridges Kinishba's past and future by discussing links between the site and ongoing intertribal programs in cultural heritage conservation, interpretation and repatriation. Using archaeological knowledge of Kinishba and the Mogollon Rim region as a point of departure, we examine the meanings and values Kinishba has for American Indians. As individuals representing their ancestors and tribes, the Apaches, Hopis and Zunis we worked with care about and share in the histories, management activities, and still-unfolding destinies of Kinishba. Tribal perspectives, coupled with professional policy and practice in masonry ruins preservation and interpretation, are guiding Kinishba's management and public use in the early twenty-first century.

Each of this chapter's five main sections pursues a distinct purpose. The first section situates Kinishba in the broader context of intertribal cultural heritage protection, repre-

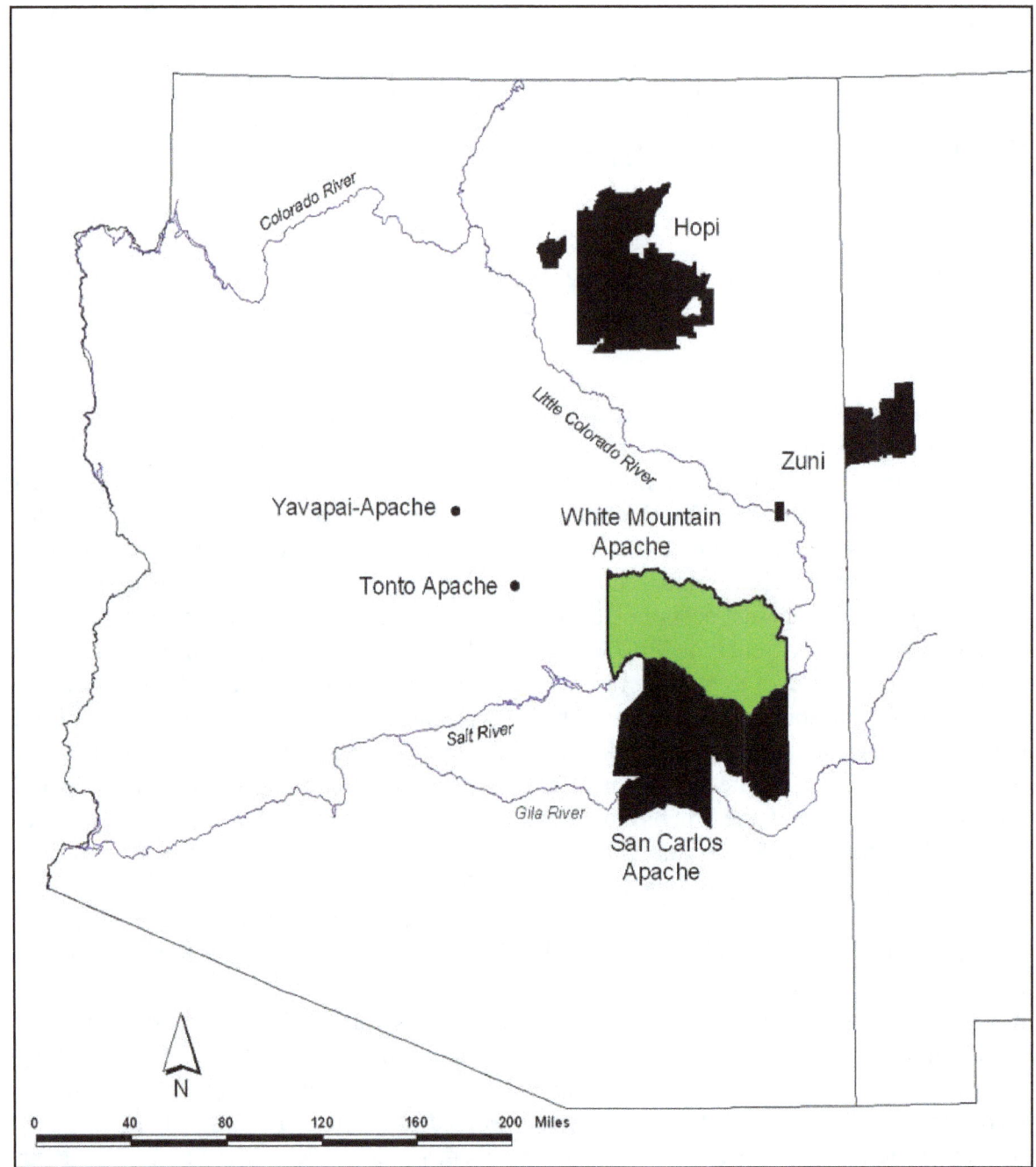

Figure 10.1. White Mountain Apache, San Carlos Apache, Hopi, and Zuni tribal lands in eastern Arizona.

sentation, and reclamation, including repatriations conducted under the aegis of the Native American Graves Protection and Repatriation Act (NAGPRA, 25 USC 3001 and following). Sections two through four summarize pertinent findings from the geography-based cultural affiliation study of White Mountain Apache lands, devoting detailed attention to Hopi, Zuni, and Apache perspectives on Kinishba (Welch and Ferguson 2005, 2007).

Section five discusses the implications of the cultural affiliation study, focusing on Kinishba as a case study in the translation of traditional wisdom and culturally appropriate landscape- and site-level management principles into site management policy and practice.

WHITE MOUNTAIN APACHE TRIBE HERITAGE STEWARDSHIP AND REPATRIATION

Kinishba has been close to the center of a long struggle between American Indians and non-Indians over cultural heritage in the uplands of eastern Arizona. Understanding Kinishba's current appearance and treatment as a ruin requires a foray into how Apaches and non-Apaches have negotiated conflicts over the values and uses of heritage sites, objects, and human remains.

Since the beginning of sustained contacts between Apaches and non-Indians in 1870, White Mountain Apache lands, encompassing a rich legacy of more than 2,500 heritage sites, have been removed from exclusive Apache control. Apache lands were then used, and often devalued, via varied extractive enterprises (for example, livestock and timber production, mining, archaeology), before being quietly returned to Apache jurisdiction. Most of these resource extractions have been pursued under the cover of "opportunity" for the White Mountain Apaches, but Apaches have realized few sustained benefits. Apache suspicions concerning non-Indian schemes for improving their welfare are both longstanding and likely to continue (Welch 1997, 2008, 2009; Welch and Riley 2001).

To protect tangible cultural heritage, especially archaeological sites and artifacts, Apaches have repeatedly translated concerns with the misappropriation of their geographical and cultural birthrights into concerted resistance, including many repatriation initiatives.

In the earliest recorded instance of this type of initiative, Apaches in 1880 responded to the looting of Geronimo's Cave, a burial and storage site used by both Pueblo and Apache people (Figure 10.2). Local Apache men confronted Army officials at Fort Apache, demanding the immediate return of human remains and cultural items (Barnes 1941:115-116). The soldiers acceded to these repatriation demands, presumably because they knew of Apache cultural norms for respecting the deceased. These cultural norms entailed avoidance of the dead and their belongings in deed and word by all except specially trained cultural practitioners.

The Army yielded to Apache cultural mandates in 1880, but the cave and innumerable other places and objects of historical and cultural importance to the Apaches subsequently became targets for digging and collecting. In 1901, as part of the Chicago Field Museum's McCormick expedition, curator George A. Dorsey (1903) wrote to Charles L. Owen, dispatching him to amass Navajo and Apache materials: "I need say no more than that they are among the most interesting Indians of our country, that they are extremely conservative and as a consequence have preserved in an exceedingly pure form a great many rites and ceremonies, all of great importance and all carrying with them an extensive amount of ceremonial paraphernalia, a good representation of which I shall expect Mr. Owen to collect" (Dorsey 1901). Less than a month later, Owen was removing materials from Geronimo's Cave and elsewhere (Hoerig 2010).

Owen's aggressive collecting focused in part on items that Apache cultural specialists identify, using the terms legislatively defined in NAGPRA, as sacred objects and objects of cultural patrimony. Owen's ability to obtain large numbers of uniquely significant objects led the Field Museum to send him back to Apache lands in 1903 to continue his collecting. In a brief note to Dorsey following his

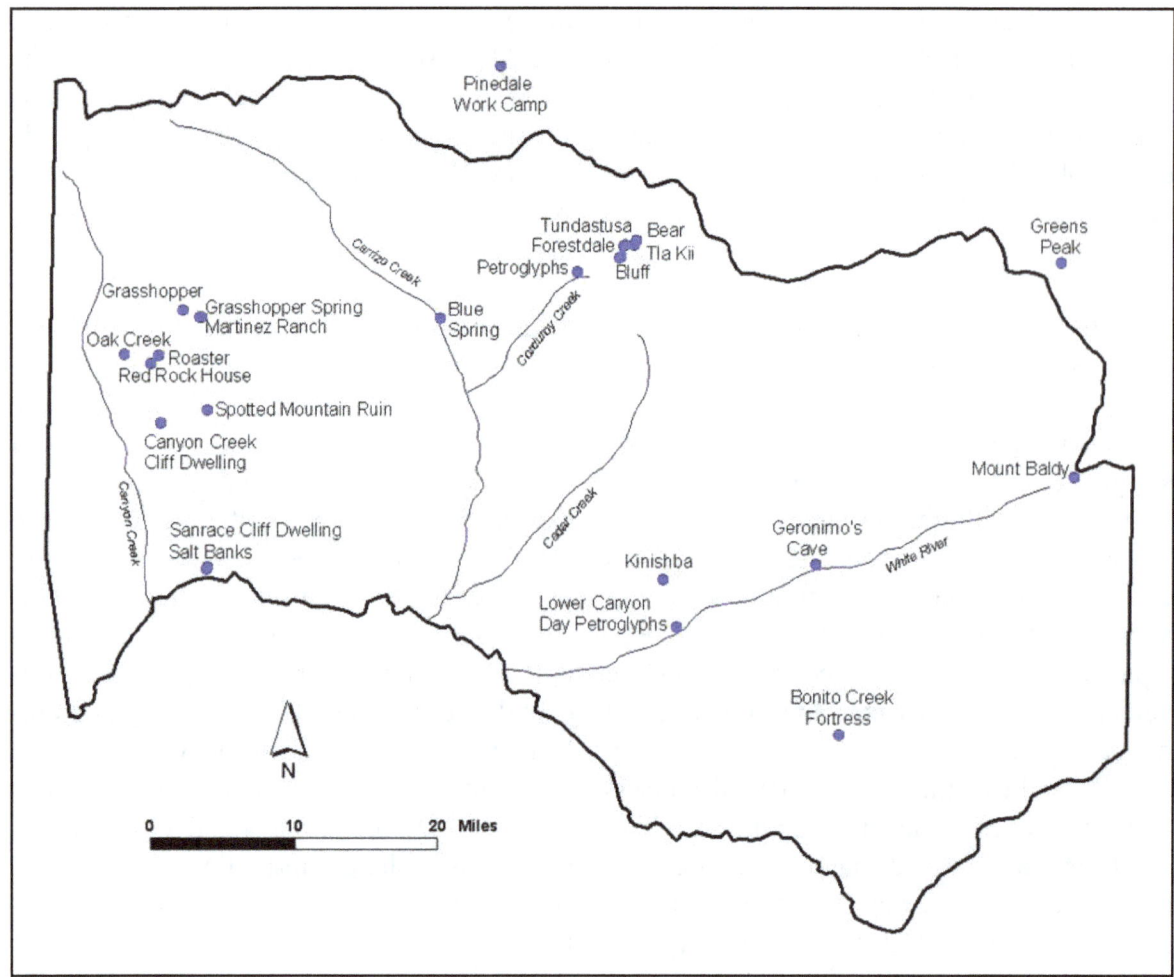

Figure 10.2. Locations for fieldwork completed for the cultural affiliation project, White Mountain Apache Tribe lands.

return to eastern Arizona, Owen (1903) states, "Find conditions very much changed ... Owner of one of the Medicine Shirts I bought in 1901 has been sick ever since and I fear that fact will hurt my business not a little. However, yesterday I succeeded in landing another Medicine shirt at a cost of $55.00. Have also gotten symbolism.... Had to pay for it of course. Money must not stand in the way of getting things now. Conditions are getting worse very rapidly.... Will scour the Res before leaving it. Hastily" (emphases in original).

Owen's communications, and comparable documentation from other collectors, explicitly refer to Apache resistance to and despair over museum collecting, as well as to the extreme poverty and coercive pressures exerted by non-Apaches to compel Apache participation in unbalanced transactions (Reagan 1930:302-306). So thorough was Owen in "getting things," that no other museum perceived promise in mounting a major effort targeting White Mountain Apache ritual items. Museums interested in such ritual "specimens" bartered with Field Museum; others turned to collecting opportunities presented by archaeological excavations.

Apaches also resisted authorized archaeological collecting. Even during the depths of the Great Depression, Byron Cummings found it difficult to recruit Apaches to work at Kinishba (Welch 2007a). The local manager of the Indian Emergency Conservation Work program wrote to Cummings on June 18, 1935, "We have not had any success in persuading Apaches to go to work on your project.... I believe they consider those ruins as 'Chindi'." Eventually, however, social and economic forces in the form of coercive race relations, national drives for assimilation, and the poverty characteristic of life in Arizona's Apache country, overwhelmed Apache reluctance (for a picture of prevailing social conditions, see Watt and Basso 2004). Although the project went forward, Apache suspicions concerning Cummings and his digging persist in local memory through the pejorative term *bini'dayiłsołe*, meaning "they blow in their faces" (referring to excavators' exhalations to clear loose sediments from human remains).

Cummings and the other duly permitted research-oriented, collectors who followed Owen were not the only impediments to Apache stewardship of heritage sites (see Welch and Ferguson 2007:Table 1). Looters from communities neighboring Apache lands and beyond operated almost at will on the Tribe's lands into the 1960s, when tribal pressure obliged federal authorities to make a few arrests. The first meaningful attempt to curb the use of Indian lands as collectors' playgrounds came in 1979 with the passage of the Archaeological Resources Protection Act (ARPA). But ARPA did not protect materials less than 100 years old or provide for the return of objects removed without moral or legal authority.

Apache concerns over proper care for the human remains, funerary items, and artifacts removed from their lands continued without a constructive outlet until NAGPRA became federal law in 1990. More than 1,400 sets of human remains now in Arizona State Museum collections were excavated or collected from White Mountain Apache Tribe lands. These human remains represent both formal burials with relatively complete skeletons, and isolated human bones gathered during excavations or surveys. Arizona State Museum collection records document thousands of associated funerary objects from the Tribe's lands, including ceramics, lithics, projectile points, bone artifacts, grinding tools, shell, minerals, and textiles.

At Kinishba, Cummings's excavations (1931–1939) removed 195 sets of human remains from Group I, including 26 adults and 169 children. An additional 74 adult burials were uncovered outside of room blocks, including 21 burials on the east side of the drainage and 53 burials southwest of Group II. Three cremations were also found at Kinishba. Two were associated with cremation pits and one with a small, corrugated jar. Cummings (1940:94-103) reports a total of 272 human remains. The Arizona State Museum database lists 144 human remains, including 66 skeletons (Birkby 1973:8; Shipman 1982:78). Some of the human remains documented in excavations at Kinishba were apparently not brought to the State Museum.

Funerary objects were found with 73 of the 169 children buried in the room block and about half of the adults (Cummings 1940:102). These objects include ceramic vessels, bone implements, jewelry, and stone tools. It is likely that there are additional unassociated funerary objects in the Kinishba collections at the State Museum. Ongoing consultations with the affected tribes are expected to include diligent efforts to reassemble all items interred with all the individuals excavated under Cummings's direction.

The White Mountain Apache Tribe recognizes that Hopi and Zuni ancestors occupied the ancient pueblos located on its lands and collaborates with the Hopi Tribe and Pueblo of Zuni on stewardship and repatriation. The White Mountain Apache Tribe also collaborates on heritage issues with the other federally recognized tribes of the Western Apache, or Ndee, cultural tradition—the San Carlos Apache Tribe, Yavapai-Apache Nation, and Tonto Apache Tribe.

NAGPRA Mandates and Repatriation Realities

Kinishba offers a case study in changing conceptions of appropriate use and treatment of heritage sites, and especially in the reassertion of control over heritage sites by descendant and steward communities. Guided by cultural principles, the White Mountain Apache today act as caretakers for thousands of heritage sites, working to facilitate NAGPRA processes relating to their 1.67 million acre reservation (Figure 10.1, 10.2). White Mountain Apache stewardship principles include longstanding mandates to avoid and protect all places associated with all ancestors, as well as emergent demands to restore community connections to lands, sites, objects and traditions disrupted by collections and excavations. Current needs also place emphasis on creating opportunities by training tribal member personnel and otherwise building capacity in tribal institutions.

NAGPRA is a principal instrument in the tribe's stewardship toolkit. In passing NAGPRA, Congress explicitly protected Native American graves and ensured descendants' rights to provide culturally appropriate care for ancestors. Under NAGPRA, lineal descendants and culturally affiliated tribes can seek repatriation and reburial of ancestral human remains, associated and unassociated funerary offerings, sacred objects, and objects of cultural patrimony from federally funded museums.

Cultural affiliation is central to NAGPRA, and is defined as "a relationship of shared group identity which can be reasonably traced historically or prehistorically between a present day Indian tribe or Native Hawaiian organization and an identifiable earlier group" (25 USC 3001). The cultural affiliation criteria codified in NAGPRA's regulations (43 CFR 10.10.14.c) require that the present-day Indian tribe be federally recognized and that the existence of the earlier identifiable group be documented by establishing its cultural characteristics, its distinct patterns of manufacturing and distributing material culture, or its distinctiveness as a biological population. Cultural affiliation determinations require evidence that the present-day Indian tribe has been identified from the past to the present as descending from the earlier group. Such determinations require overall evaluations of evidence, and are not to be ruled out solely because of gaps in the record or a lack of scientific certainty. Specifically, cultural affiliation is to be established by the preponderance of ten classes of evidence: geography, kinship, biology, archaeology, anthropology, linguistics, folklore, oral tradition, history, and other relevant information or expert opinion. NAGPRA recognizes archaeology as only one of the ten sources of information and perspective on cultural heritage. NAGPRA obliges archaeologists and museum professionals to approach archaeological data as just one means for assessing values and meanings of places, objects, and traditions.

The human remains, associated and unassociated funerary objects, sacred objects, and objects of cultural patrimony collected from Kinishba and other sites on White Mountain Apache Tribe lands, and either curated in museums or involved in transactions, are subject to NAGPRA. NAGPRA's Section 5 mandates that federal agencies and any museums having possession or control over Native American human remains and associated funerary objects compile an inventory of these items and identity the geographical and cultural affiliation of each item wherever possible (25 USC 3003). NAGPRA further requires federal agencies and museums to consult with tribal government officials and traditional religious leaders in completing these inventories by November 16, 1995. Agencies and museums must then file a *Notice of Inventory Completion* that identifies Native American human remains or associated funerary objects and the circumstances of their acquisition. The *Notice* must also identify the human remains or associated funerary objects that are identifiable as to tribal origin, and the remains and associated objects not clearly identifiable as being culturally affiliated with an identifiable Indian tribe but which are reasonably believed to be remains or objects culturally affiliated with an Indian tribe.

Section 6 of NAGPRA mandates that federal agencies and museums with possession or control over Native American unassociated funerary objects (and sacred objects and objects of cultural patrimony) prepare a written summary of these objects (25 USC 3004). Unassociated funerary objects are burial offerings separated from the human remains they were associated with. In lieu of an object-by-object inventory, the summary must document the scope of the collection, the kinds of objects and their geographical source, the means and period of acquisition, and the cultural affiliation or affiliations, where this is ascertainable. NAGPRA requires federal agencies and museums to complete the summaries on or before November 16, 1993, and thereafter consult with tribal government officials and traditional religious leaders.

Culturally affiliated tribes and land-holding tribes (referred to in this chapter as "steward communities") both have important roles in NAGPRA. As a land-holding tribe, the White Mountain Apache Tribe asserts ownership of collections from its trust lands. The Bureau of Indian Affairs, however, controls the collections by virtue of its role as the tribal trustee designated by the United States and, after 1935, as the federal agency issuing permits authorizing the archaeological removal and curation of heritage collections (see Horn 1988). The Bureau has legal and fiscal responsibilities for collections under its control, including duties to insure that NAGPRA inventories and summaries are prepared and submitted. Although the Bureau of Indian Affairs has not completed NAGPRA inventories and summaries for collections from archaeological sites on White Mountain Apache Tribe lands, collaborations among tribes, the Arizona State Museum, and the Bureau of Indian Affairs made it possible for initial repatriations of ancestral Hopi and Zuni human remains and funerary objects to begin in the summer of 2011.

The full story of how this came to pass is beyond the scope of this chapter, but references to key developments here and in other parts of the chapter enhance understanding Kinishba's cultural, historical, and current significance. Following NAGPRA's passage, consultations began on matters relating to Kinishba cultural affiliation and the disposition of human remains and other materials excavated from Kinishba and other sites on White Mountain Apache lands. By 1993, the White Mountain Apache Tribe initiated government-to-government discussions about heritage stewardship with neighboring tribes, including the Fort McDowell Indian Community, Hopi Tribe, Navajo Nation, Pueblo of Acoma, Pueblo of Laguna, Pueblo of Zuni, San Carlos Apache Tribe, Tonto Apache Tribe, and Yavapai-Apache Nation. The Arizona State Museum conducted consultations with the Western Apache, Hopi and Zuni tribes, and the Bureau of Indian Affairs. Tribal participants in the consultations consistently agreed on the need for repatriation claims and processes to be grounded in Apache and Pueblo cultural principles, as well as NAGPRA (Fort Apache Scout 1993a; Lupe 1993a, 1994, 1995). As discussed in the next section, these principles are embodied in the cultural affiliation project's research processes and recommendations, and specifically included in Kinishba's management program.

PUTTING PATRIA BACK INTO REPATRIATION: PROJECT METHODS

The White Mountain Apache Tribe pursued the cultural affiliation project to balance archaeological and anthropological scholarship with community-based knowledge and perspective. There are numerous scholarly works pertaining to Kinishba, including two dissertations, four master's theses, one book, twelve research-based monographs, and fifteen book chapters and journal articles (Welch 2007c). These works provide lines of evidence pertinent to cultural affiliation—including archaeology, anthropology, and biology—that have dominated discourse relating to regional cultural and settlement history (see Gregory and Wilcox 2007).

For these reasons, and because the archaeological and anthropological literature is more widely accessible than Native American stories and memories, the cultural affiliation project focused on documentation of oral traditions linking present-day tribes to past identifiable groups. The project sought to put "patria"—native country or homeland—back into repatriation and to embrace the importance of connections among history, land, memory, and social identity as understood by the cultural representatives of the Hopi, Zuni, and Western Apache tribes. Marvin Lalo, a Hopi cultural advisor, explained, "Our history is oral, verbal between generations. Our oral traditions are in songs—some are a mystery to us. When we go out to visit sites, sometimes we can identify names." History and land are inseparable.

Study methods distilled to traveling over the land, visiting ancestral sites, and facilitating sharing by Hopi, Zuni, and Apache cultural advisors of their inherited knowledge in relation to field observations. The research process brought forward information and perspectives relevant to the cultural affiliation and stewardship of Kinishba and other sites on Apache lands. Zuni tribal member Eldrick Seoutewa explained that oral tradition is abstract until you visit an area and realize your ancestors were there: "You confirm what you see on the basis of the relationship between oral tradition and physical evidence.... Land brings up memory of place." Mr. Seoutewa noted that Zuni oral traditions include plants that do not occur on their current reservation, such as *mek'yaba metda:we* ("big-earred cactus with fruit coming off the side"), a variety of prickly pear. The Zunis saw *mek'yaba metda:we* on White Mountain Apache lands, thus helping to situate oral traditions in a geographical frame of reference. In this and other ways, the project gave particular attention to categories of NAGPRA evidence less common in the region's anthropological studies, especially geography, oral tradition, and traditional history.

With tribal authorizations and external funding in place by early 2003, the project began with an intertribal meeting to refine the preliminary research design. This was followed by six sessions of fieldwork encompassing just over 100 person days. Fieldwork involved teams of between three and 17 tribal cultural advisors visiting Kinishba and 25 other heritage sites on and adjacent to White Mountain Apache lands (Figure 10.2). At Kinishba and Forestdale, where the University of Arizona Archaeological Field School was in the process of restoring and stabilizing site damage, visits included opportunities for members of tribal teams to discuss their views with field school participants (Mills et al. 2008; see also Mills 2000, 2005). The final project phase prior to report preparation involved review sessions with the Hopi Cultural Resources

Advisory Task Team and the Zuni Cultural Resources Advisory Team on their respective reservations.

San Carlos tribal members participating in the project meetings included Jeanette Cassa and Vernelda Grant. Seth Pilsk, a non-Indian employee of the San Carlos Apache Tribe, also participated. Yavapai-Apache tribal members who participated in fieldwork included Rozella Hines, Vincent Randall, and Elizabeth Rocha. White Mountain Apache tribal members who participated in meetings and fieldwork included Bernadette Adley-Santa Maria, Mark Altaha, Paul Declay, Levi DeHose, Shaunna Ethelbah, Doreen Gatewood, Gregg Henry, Cornelia Hoffman, Beverly Malone, Ramon Riley, and Ann Skidmore. Karl Hoerig, a non-Indian employed by the tribal museum, also participated in the fieldwork. Ben Numvumsa, a member of the Hopi Tribe and the Superintendent of the Fort Apache Agency of the Bureau of Indian Affairs, participated in project planning and contributed views on Hopi history in a discussion with University of Arizona field school participants (Mills 2000, 2005; Mills et al. 2008).

Zuni tribal members participating in project fieldwork and review meetings included John Bowannie, Leland Kaamasee, Davis Nieto, Eldrick Seoutewa, Octavius Seowtewa, and Perry Tsadiasi. Hopi tribal members participating in fieldwork and meetings included Alban Mooya, Allen Talayumptewa, Bradley Balenquah, Clay Hamilton, Russell Honie, Frank Honahnie, ValJean Joshevama, Wilton Kooyahoema, Leigh Kuwanwisiwma, Marvin Lalo, Lee Wayne Lomayestewa, Floyd Lomakuyvaya, Garrin Mansfield, Harlan Nakala, Gilbert Naseyowma, Lewis Numkena, Jr., Owen Numkena, Joel Nicholas, Garrett Pochoema, Harold Polingyumptewa, Lannell Poseyesva, Raleigh Puhuyaoma, Morgan Saufkie, Martin Talayumptewa, and Dalton Taylor. Non-Indian Hopi tribal employees participating in the project included Greg Glassco and Terry Morgart.

Hopi Cultural Affiliation with Kinishba

Hopis collectively refer to clan ancestors as *hisatsinom* ("Ancient People"). Hopi ancestors are not identified in Hopi history in a manner that coincides directly with archaeologically established social or cultural identity. Instead, Hopi ancestors belonged to clans and religious societies that occupied Kinishba and other sites archaeologists classify as Mogollon, Anasazi, Ancestral Pueblo or Western Pueblo.

The Hopi Tribe has formally claimed cultural affiliation with the Ancestral Pueblo residents of White Mountain Apache Tribe lands. A 1994 resolution of the Hopi Tribal Council (Hopi Tribe 1994) states that the Hopi Tribe "declares its formal cultural affinity and affiliation with the Hisatsinom (Anasazi), Fremont, Mogollon, Sinaguan, Salado, Mimbres, Hohokam and Cohonino cultural groups." To understand this claim in the geographical context of Kinishba and the legal context of NAGPRA, Hopi participants identified specific clans as the identifiable groups through which the Hopi Tribe traces its relationship to the ancient occupants of White Mountain Apache lands.

Matrilineal clans, organized into phratries, are cornerstones of Hopi social organization (Eggan 1950:61-89). When the Hopi emerged into the (current) Fourth Way of Life, they entered into a spiritual covenant with the owner of the world, *Máasaw*, to migrate until they reached their destiny at Tuuwanasavi, the earth center near Third Mesa. According to Marvin Lalo, *Máasaw* told the Hopi, "Go and walk the earth, look at my land." *Ang kuktota*, literally, "along there, make footprints," was among the instructions given by *Maásaw*. Hopi ancestors were told to live in place for a time, to grow food, to raise their children, and then continue their journey.

The historical metaphor of "footprints" includes the ruins of former settlements, and the pottery, stone tools, petroglyphs, and other artifacts left behind as offerings. As Floyd Lomakuyvaya noted while visiting White Mountain Apache lands, migration traditions and footprints constitute Hopi records of the past and thus evidence of cultural affiliation. Hopi advisors identified many footprints of clan ancestors on Apache lands. Architectural styles, village plans, plazas, kivas, petroglyphs and pictographs, functional and stylistic affinities in pottery, grinding tools, other artifacts, and grave sites all signal historical links between the Hisatsinom and their descendants, members of today's Hopi Tribe. For Hopis, these footprints are proof of ancestral migration and land stewardship (Kuwanwisiwma and Ferguson 2004).

Migration traditions for Hopi clans that traveled from the south refer to Sakwtala, Place of the Green Plants, a verdant paradise of plants and blossoms that lay between deserts. Leigh Kuwanwisiwma suggests this place name encompasses the Mogollon Rim region, including White Mountain Apache lands. Hopi migration included three travel corridors relevant to the study area. The Fire clan and several other clans followed a western route up the Colorado River.

Other clans, including Water and Bow, took a middle route up the Santa Cruz and San Pedro Rivers to Tavanki (Snaketown) and Nasavi (Casa Grande) on the Gila River, and then northward. A third set of clans, including the Parrot and Katsina clans, took an eastern route that extended northward through the Mimbres region and lower Rio Grande, eventually leading to the occupation of sites like Kwayvi (Place of the Eagle, aka Casa Malpais) in the upper Little Colorado River area northeast of White Mountain Apache lands.

Some Hopis also refer to eastern part of White Mountain Apache lands as Pavanqatsi because the abundance of grasslands, rivers, and forests is a paradise for *qatsi*, life.

The histories of clans associated with the middle route are relevant to Hopi cultural affiliation with the people of Kinishba and other ancient villages on Apache lands. Oral traditions of the Bear, Bearstrap, Bluebird and Spider clans describe the area around Grasshopper, on the western part of White Mountain Apache lands. The Greasewood and Bow clans have traditions about Kinishba, in the middle of the reservation. The Crane, Sparrowhawk, Squash, Gray Eagle, Eagle, and Sand clans have traditions in the area around Casa Malpais and Springerville, and thus with the reservation's northeastern reaches.

In Hopi history the ancient villages on White Mountain Apache lands were occupied between the collapse of Palatkwapi (the fabled "Red-Walled City of the South") and the gathering of clans on the Hopi Mesas. The Palatkwapi collapse followed a period of moral disintegration that culminated in a destructive flood, an event that provided an opportunity for common people who had been subjugated by the Bow Clan's ritual leaders to free themselves.

The people fled, migrating northward. The Bow clan followed, seeking to recapture the commoners. During this period of strife, many clans are said to have lived in defensive sites, suggesting one explanation for the cliff dwellings and fortresses common across the central Arizona uplands (Welch 2001). When the clans arrived at the Hopi Mesas, they determined to live together peacefully and without coercive leaders, core tenets of Hopi philosophy.

The aggregation processes evidenced at Kinishba and comparable large pueblos in the region (see Mills 1998; Reid and Whittlesey 1999; Riggs 2001, 2005) are familiar to Hopis. Hopi traditions recount the piecemeal arrival of clans, who were required to prove themselves before admission into a Hopi village. Although today's Hopi are a "tribe," each Hopi clan's distinctive identity reflects its particular migration experiences. For example, the Eagle, Crane, and Sparrowhawk clans resided for a time at Kwayvi (Casa Malpais) and other sites, where they lived with Zuni people belonging to the same clan. Centuries later, a group of Zuni from Halona (Zuni Pueblo) lived at the Hopi village of Orayvi on Third Mesa. Some of these Zuni intermarried with Hopis and stayed, while others decided to return to Halona. The co-residence of Hopi and Zuni clans along the middle route on and near White Mountain Apache lands gives the two tribes a shared history and cultural affiliation.

While not conclusive in and of themselves, parallels between Hopi oral history and archaeological reconstructions of social processes support Hopi cultural affiliation with the occupants of Kinishba and other Mogollon Pueblo sites. Burial practices documented at Kinishba and Grasshopper, including burying children within rooms, are similar to the mortuary practices of Hopi and Zuni (Reid and Whittlesey 1999:142; compare to Parsons 1939:71 and Bunzel 1932a:483). At Kinishba, these similarities led Cummings (1940:95) to conclude that "here once lived the ancestors of the Hopi."

Such findings raise research questions pertinent to NAGPRA (see Clark 1967:126; Fenton 1998:169-170). In using Hopi as an analogue for Grasshopper Pueblo, Reid and Whittlesey (1999:14, 71) note that analogy is not the same as affirmation of historical connections between past and present-day groups. Nonetheless, at least some anthropological theories about Kinishba's "sister" site of Grasshopper based on Hopi and Zuni models are concordant with archaeological findings (Griffin 1969:169, 173).

Specific features at Kinishba also indicate links to Hopi traditions. The plaza in the reconstructed Group I has two entrances. Leigh Kuwanwisiwma says the number of plaza entrances relates to clan migration timing. Plazas occupied prior to the coming together of clans at the Hopi Mesas should have fewer than four entrances. Two plaza entrances mean the clan has completed two directional migrations. Today all Hopi villages have plazas with four entrances, symbolizing offerings made to all four directions and the completion of migrations.

Hopis view these and other elements of plaza architecture at Kinishba as evidence that the site was occupied during the course of Hopi clan migrations. Benches, such as the one along Kinishba's Group I plaza perimeter, and subterranean rooms, such as the one adjacent to the Kinishba plaza, are common in Hopi plazas (see Chapter 4). Additionally, a *pahoki* or shrine is present in the Kinishba plaza (Figure 10.3). This shrine was used in 1941 by Hopi dancers, who participated in the opening ceremonies for the reconstructed site (Cummings 1940). The shrine was maintained for many years by Bill Dalton, a Hopi man married to an Apache woman and living close to Fort Apache. Titus Lamson, a member of the Hotvela Greasewood clan, deposited prayer feathers at the shrine during pilgrimages made as late as the 1990s, when Mr. Lamson was more than 90 years old. Leigh Kuwanwisiwma observed prayer feathers at the collapsing shrine in 1992. During fieldwork in 2003, Leigh Kuwanwisiwma and Lee Wayne Lomayestewa found willow fragments from Hopi prayer sticks. The shrine confirms Kinishba as a sacred site for Hopis.

Hopis have place names for several landforms near Kinishba. One of these is Muntsotsokpi (The Place of the Water Going Over), a waterfall located above the site, where cattails and reeds once grew (Figure 10.4). According to Hopi traditions, these riparian plants were collected for ritual use when the

Figure 10.3. Hopi research team stands around the remains of the shrine in the Kinishba plaza, showing the size of the area deserving protection (June 24, 2004, T. J. Ferguson).

Figure 10.4. Leigh Kuwanwisiwma and John Welch discuss Muntsotsokpi, as Lee Wayne Lomayestewa and Ramon Riley inspect the dry waterfall (May 12, 2003, T. J. Ferguson).

village was occupied. Hopi traditions describe pictographs of hand prints near the stream at Muntsotsokpi.

Another place is Mongtsomo (Owl Hill). Owen Numkena said the One Horn Society at Musangnuvi, on Second Mesa, has traditional knowledge of Mongtsomo. This distinctive landform highlights the horizon west of Kinishba (Figure 10.5). People from the Hopi villages of Songòopavi and Musangnuvi, including Smiley Humeyumptewa and Philip Kuwanyama, continue to use Mongtsomo. Mr. Numkena said he had visited Kinishba and seen the hill, thus experiencing the history his uncles passed on to him.

Marvin Lalo, Floyd Lomakuyvaya and Owen Numkena explained that Kinishba's room blocks, plazas, plaza entries, and kiva, along with the clan signs (petroglyphs) at Lower Canyon Day, downstream from Kinishba, are all evidence of a shared identity between the Hopi Tribe today and the ancient occupants of Ma'öp'ovi and the other Puebloan sites on White Mountain Apache lands. ValJean Joshevama said, "our songs in our Hopi way give us a connection to those places. Through songs we remember the places where the Hopi went to."

Mr. Lalo noted that Zuni and Hopi have different traditions but share history in the same ancestral sites. Although the details of Hopi and Zuni traditions differ, the underlying history is similar.

In contrast, Hopi traditions do not recount occupying the Mogollon Rim region together with Apaches. Historically, Hopis had limited contact with Apaches, some of which involved conflict. Wilton Kooyahoema noted that Hopis visited and traded with Western Apache, and that some Hopis refer to the area around Kinishba as Yotsi'sivay (Apache Stream). While standing at the Hopi shrine in the Kinishba plaza, Morgan Saufkie discussed a place called Tuwki, in the Hopi Buttes area. At this place, Apaches and Hopis from First Mesa met and became friends, trading buckskins

Figure 10.5. Mongtsomo (Owl Point) on the horizon west of Kinishba. Kinishba's standing walls are visible in the middle distance (June 24, 2004, T. J. Ferguson).

for Hopi crafts. They took turns dancing but did not sleep because of mutual suspicions. After the friendship dances, Hopis began to visit and trade with Apaches, providing Hopi people with an opportunity to reestablish their relationship with Kinishba and other ancestral sites. A friendship song is still sung at Hopi to commemorate the dances at Tuwki. Mr. Saufkie sang a segment of this song during fieldwork, noting that when Hopis sing this song, they "make it straight," with a smooth melody with no drops in the song. Mr. Saufkie said that Hopis from First Mesa have several songs sung with Apache words using Hopi inflections.

Hopi advisors left religious offerings at the places they visited during the cultural affiliation study to honor their ancestors and recognize the spiritual importance these places have for their relatives living in villages on the Hopi Mesas. Leigh Kuwanwisiwma noted that Hopis place religious offerings at springs and rivers, and that these water sources are alive and important because they sustained both the ancestors and people today. Hopis pray that it will always be thus.

ZUNI CULTURAL AFFILIATION WITH KINISHBA

Documented claims for Zuni cultural affiliation with sites on White Mountain Apache lands date to at least 1883, when the Governor of Zuni Pueblo told Adolph Bandelier that ruins near Fort Apache have Zuni origins (Lange and Riley 1970:69). In 1995, the Pueblo of Zuni claimed cultural affiliation with the Ancestral Pueblo residents of White Mountain Apache Lands (Eriacho 1995; Pueblo of Zuni 1995). The Pueblo of Zuni also filed a specific claim of affiliation to human remains from Ancestral Pueblo sites near Grasshopper (Eriacho 1997).

During the cultural affiliation project, Zuni advisors talked about the *Ino:de:kwe,* or "Ancient Ones," and the *A:łashshina:we*, "the keepers of the roads," beneficent ancient protectors of human life identified with land and rain (Bunzel 1932a:510). The *Ino:de:kwe* and *A:łashshina:we* are the past ancestral groups the Zunis identify as having lived at Kinishba and neighboring sites. The *Ino:de:kwe* and *A:łashshina:we* do not correspond directly with archaeologically defined cultures, and Zuni advisors are less concerned with archaeological terminology than with identifying their ancestral sites and migration routes from physical evidence and oral teachings. "All we have is petroglyphs, pottery, and villages that tie into those areas," Octavius Seowtewa explained, "Architecture and shrines are like a book, and they tie the Zuni to the area of the Fort Apache Indian Reservation."

Zuni ancestors brought religious societies and clans with them when they settled at Zuni Pueblo and nearby sites. Zuni social and religious organization integrates Zuni kin and clan groups through ceremonial activities (Kroeber 1917:148-165). The Zuni socio-religious system is comprised of four interlocking components, including 14 matrilineal clans, six kiva groups, 12 curing societies, and the Rain and Bow Priesthoods (Ladd 1979:482-485). Clans and kiva groups are organized in the Kachina (Kokko) Society. Kinship structures the social relations that connect Zuni people to one another and shared histories (Eggan 1950:177-198). An annual ceremonial cycle operated by the clans and religious groups follows the agricultural seasons (Washburn 1995:34-37). Octavius Seowtewa noted that the spiral found at petroglyph panels on White Mountain Apache lands is associated with the Galaxy Society, as are the stars observed at the Lower Canyon Day and Corduroy Creek panels, located southeast and northwest of Kinishba, respectively. Zuni advisors think the recurrence of imagery in ancient petroglyphs and today's Zuni religious iconography signals important relationships between Zuni people and ancestral lands and migration routes.

Zuni ancestral territory incorporates an extensive geographical area and considerable time depth associated with a long period during which the Zuni people migrated from their place of emergence to Zuni Pueblo (Bunzel 1932a, 1932b, 1932c; Cushing 1896; Ferguson and Hart 1985:21; Parsons 1923; Stevenson 1904:73-88). After emerging in the Grand Canyon, the Zunis began a slow migration up the Little Colorado Valley, traveling as a tribe and stopping at sacred springs. At each stop they built a village and grew corn before continuing. Along the way one group of Zunis left the main body and migrated south, never to return. Two other groups, comprised of members of the Sword Swallower and Big Fire religious societies, split off and traveled to the Rio Grande Valley before heading west and rejoining the main body of the tribe that had settled in the "Middle Place," the Zuni River Valley.

Zuni clans were named not long before they arrived at the "Middle Place." Clan naming occurred at Hantłbinkya, located near what is now the Arizona-New Mexico borderline. The narratives of Zuni migration are thus retained primarily in the prayers of Zuni religious societies rather than clans. The ancient sites on White Mountain Apache lands were actively occupied before Zuni clans were named, so the group with which Zunis share identity is the collective body of the *Ino:de:kwe*. Oral traditions that describe and explain Zuni migration through central Arizona are not associated with a specific religious society or group but with the Zuni people as a whole. Zuni advisors explained that oral traditions provide an outline of history rather than an inventory of ancestral sites. As Davis Nieto said, "We were one people until we split and separated."

Zuni migration traditions are more than literal history because they include essential spiritual information. As one Zuni religious leader pointed out after providing a list of the places referenced in his origin account, "These are the places that are discussed as a trail, but it is a religious idea, or religious trail that is recited in the prayer and not an actual path" (Ferguson and Hart 1985:21). In addition to ancestral sites located along the route described in prayers, Zuni cultural advisors say there are many other ancestral villages in a much larger geographical area.

Translating Zuni words into English can be difficult, but Eldrick Seoutewa provided the term for ancestral sites occupied during the migration as *heshoda ułapna*, "houses all around." Cliff dwellings are called *heshoda'ułtha*, "ancient houses against a cliff." Octavius Seowtewa explained that the migration traditions describe different types of houses built using locally available materials. The sequence of occupation related in Zuni migration traditions includes pit houses, pueblos, cliff dwellings and, finally, the construction of large pueblos. According to Octavius Seowtewa, Zuni narratives describe constant movement, with different groups of people reoccupying sites over time. Zunis think their ancestral lands were never "abandoned." People would come back, rebuild walls, live for a time, then move on, leaving objects behind to welcome newcomers or those who returned. The Zunis have continuing cultural and spiritual attachments to the ancestors and the sites where they resided in the ancient past.

In summarizing the relationship between Zuni migration narratives and cultural affiliations to Apache lands, Octavius Seowtewa explained, "Our ancestors…roamed the Southwest, as far as California. Now we go out and see sites and that solidifies the migration and the history of different routes to the Middle Place." He said important themes in the migration traditions include hardship and struggle. Visiting archaeological sites and petroglyphs provides tangible reflections of the routes traveled and the many hardships endured to reach the Middle Place. Mr. Seowtewa concluded "These places need to be protected—they are our living history."

Although Zuni traditions do not recount occupation of the area when it was inhabited by Apaches, Zuni stories recall post-emigration use of the White Mountains for hunting, gathering, and religious purposes. Zuni advisors say their forebears returned on pilgrimages, a claim substantiated by religious offerings found at shrines on mountain tops and at springs, including Green's Peak, Mount Baldy, and other sites visible from Kinishba (Greenwood and White 1970; Morris 1982). These religious offerings include ceramics, beads, sherd disks, stone and ceramic effigies, projectile points, and turquoise mosaic fragments. The ceramics at the shrines include types made when Zuni ancestors occupied pueblos on Apache lands in the 1300s and 1400s, as well as later types made when Zuni people were living in the Zuni River Valley.

Zuni ancestral sites are associated with ongoing religious practices. As Octavius Seowtewa noted, "All the sites are important because our ancestors were out there, and whenever they stopped, they had a place to worship." He notes that although shrines are harder for archaeologists to find than middens, he knows there are shrines at and near ancestral villages. Eldrick Seoutewa added that springs are also important and described how high peaks are used to pray for rain and in other spiritual activities. Although the direct personal use of these peaks is limited to a few religious leaders charged with conducting ritual activities, the landforms are important areas for the health and well-being of the entire tribe. Most of the high points in the northeastern part of White Mountain Apache lands have Zuni names, clear indications of the cultural importance of shrine areas.

Leaving ritual offerings at ancestral sites is a longstanding Zuni custom. Visiting ancestral ruins is similar to visiting other sacred spots where religious inspiration is sought. Eldrick Seoutewa explained, "When you see a site, you leave an offering." During the cultural affiliation project, Zuni advisors left ritual offerings at almost all of the sites they visited.

Zuni advisors affirm cultural affiliation between the Pueblo of Zuni and the ancient occupants of White Mountain Apache lands. The pueblo architecture, shrines, ceramics, and petroglyphs found on the land are interpreted as evidence in support of their oral traditions and cultural knowledge. Zuni advisors also link the cremations found at Kinishba and other archaeological sites on Apache lands to Zuni mortuary practices at the ancestral village of Hawikku located on the Zuni Reservation. They think this provides a historical connection between Zuni people and the ancient occupants of the White Mountain Apache lands.

In discussing cultural affiliation, Octavius Seowtewa observed, "We didn't have to justify claims of affiliation to other people until NAGPRA came around. We just knew they were our ancestors." Regarding shared cultural affiliation, Eldrick Seoutewa explained, "different tribes were within the same area, and are thus related." For this reason, the Zunis do not claim an exclusive cultural affiliation; they recognize the Hopi Tribe shares cultural affiliation. Octavius Seowtewa commented, "We are of the same people; we need to work together."

Zuni cultural advisors understand it will take years to implement NAGPRA and rebury all ancestors removed from Kinishba and other sites on White Mountain Apache lands. In noting Zuni appreciation for cooperation and assistance from the White Mountain Apache people and Tribe, Eldrick Seoutewa said, "Our ancestors were there in the past, but we can't say it's our land, because someone else owns it. We need permission to use it."

Apache Perspectives on Kinishba Cultural Affiliation

Western Apache cultural precepts and perspectives on the past are at the heart of the approach taken in the cultural affiliation project. Apaches conceive of the past as a well-worn path or trail (*'intin*) that was traveled by the ancestors. As Basso (1996:31) explains,

> Beyond the memories of living persons, this path is no longer visible—the path has disappeared—and thus is unavailable for direct consultation and study. For this reason, the past must be constructed—which is to say, imagined—with the aid of historical materials, sometimes called 'footprints' or 'tracks' (*biké' goz'ąą́*), that have survived into the present. These materials come in various forms, including Apache place-names, Apache stories and songs, and different kinds of relics found at locations throughout Apache country…what matters most to Apaches is *where* events occurred, not when, and what they serve to reveal about the development and character of Apache social life…temporal considerations …are given secondary importance."

In contrast to the Hopi and Zuni assessments, in which two tribes with similar cultural traditions identified specific links to Kinishba and other pueblo sites on White Mountain Apache lands, the Apache assessment traced geographical ties for Apache bands and clans. Western Apache (Ndee) identity is distinct from the Hopi, known to the Apache as Tse ká kiné ("Houses on the Rocks") and the Zuni, known as Nast'ishē ("Thick Eyebrows"). Most Apache elders and cultural specialists agree that Ancestral Pueblo people migrated away long ago and made their way to Hopi and Zuni.

Many Apaches also assert that their people have lived in their homeland, including all lands within the Fort Apache Reservation, since time immemorial. In 1883, Adolph Bandelier reported that the Apache chiefs "protested they had no [migration] traditions, that they had always lived here. They feigned absolute ignorance in regard to the ruins" (Lange and Riley 1970:89). Some Apaches think their ancestors may have lived in or near ancient villages, engaging in trade and intermarriage with pueblo occupants (Fort Apache Scout 1993b; Lupe 1993b). Albert Reagan wrote that an "old medicineman" told him that the Apache people came from the cold north, and that when they arrived in this land, they found people living in cliffs, in caves, and in mud and stone houses and villages. The original inhabitants and the Apaches fought one another, and the Apaches overtook the cliff-dwellers and drove them south toward the oceans (Reagan 1930:288; see also Goodwin 1994:49). It may be possible to eventually reconcile these perspectives, perhaps through studies of how Apache origin narratives and conceptualizations of the past embody spiritual teachings, histories and interests in protecting against further land losses.

Apache advisors Bernadette Adley-Santa Maria and Ramon Riley said that cultural borrowing between Apaches and Pueblos is evident in similarities in religious masks, headdresses, color symbolism, dances, rituals, and origin stories. Ramon Riley explained that Apache people show the highest form of respect for ancient sites through avoidance. The primary exception to this rule is the collection from ruins of black, red, and white stones and beads for use in religious activities, like the Sunrise Ceremony. As an indication of the esteem Apache religious practitioners have for the ancient village sites and their people, colored stones and beads from these sites are ground with corn and pollen and used in blessings.

For a suite of conceptual and historical

reasons, information about the ancient Western Apache is scarce (Welch 1997). Almost all of the archaeological literature pertaining to Apache lands relates to Pueblo rather than Apache cultural traditions. Jeanette Cassa pointed out that Apache people were adept at minimizing the traces they left on the land, a practice consistent both with deeply seated cultural mandates to live in harmony with creation and with the need, especially during the last half of the 1800s, to avoid detection wherever possible.

A hiatus in the active occupation of the White Mountain Apache lands follows the emigration of Pueblo people. Gregory (1981:257, 264) thinks that initial Apache use of what is now their land occurred after A.D. 1600. Apache artifacts and structures occasionally overlie Ancestral Pueblo materials, but never vice-versa. The earliest Apache archaeological remains in the region, dating ca. 1640 to 1700, occur at Plymouth Landing, an archaeological site along State Route 260 to the north of the White Mountain Apache lands (Herr et al. 2009).

Western Apache kinship, place names, and oral traditions provide guidance for and complements to archaeological studies. Apaches have historically traceable identities shared with two main past—and present—identifiable groups: bands and clans. Vincent Randall and Elizabeth Rocha explain that Apache clans and geography are inseparable. Apaches are tied to their clan origin place and band territory, which form much of their core social identity. Marriage, whether through familial arrangements or raiding, provided a primary means for consolidating territorial control by bands as well as distributing social relationships across the landscape. Links between groups and lands are sustained in part through "mental maps" and place names that integrate memories, kinship, landmarks, food distributions across seasons and landscapes, and residential and farming localities. Most clan names derive from the names for their places of origin, as identified in clan oral traditions. Although few of these places remain occupied in the twenty first century, most Western Apache retain their clan identities, traced matrilineally. Apache clan stories reveal strong links among migration routes and the springs, streams and events associated with farmsteads that served as "hubs for clusters of extended family households (Buskirk 1986; McGuire 1980). The federal government divided Western Apaches into four different tribes and curtailed their access to most of their lands, but Apache band and clan relations endure as bases for a distinctive cultural tradition. Most adult members of a given Western Apache tribe recognize kinship with members of other Apache tribes. Bonds to lands, family, and history cut across Apache reservation borders.

Employing geography as the study framework, the cultural affiliation project contributed to knowledge and understanding of Apache use of Kinishba, both prior to and following the establishment of the Fort Apache Indian Reservation. Apache knowledge and anthropological evidence emphasize three classes of associations between Kinishba and Apaches: clan and band connections to land, historical sites in the Kinishba vicinity, and individual participants in the mid-century excavation and reconstruction projects.

Kinishba is located within the territory that Goodwin (1942) associates with the Western White Mountain Band, one of five bands with ancestral territories within the White Mountain Apache's reservation (Figure 10.6, Table 10.1). Historically, these bands were territorial organizations of differing size and organization (Goodwin 1942:6-7). Western Apache bands exhibit differences in linguistic dialects and religious and social practices. Vincent Randall pointed out that, possibly because of the heavier snowfalls in the Oak

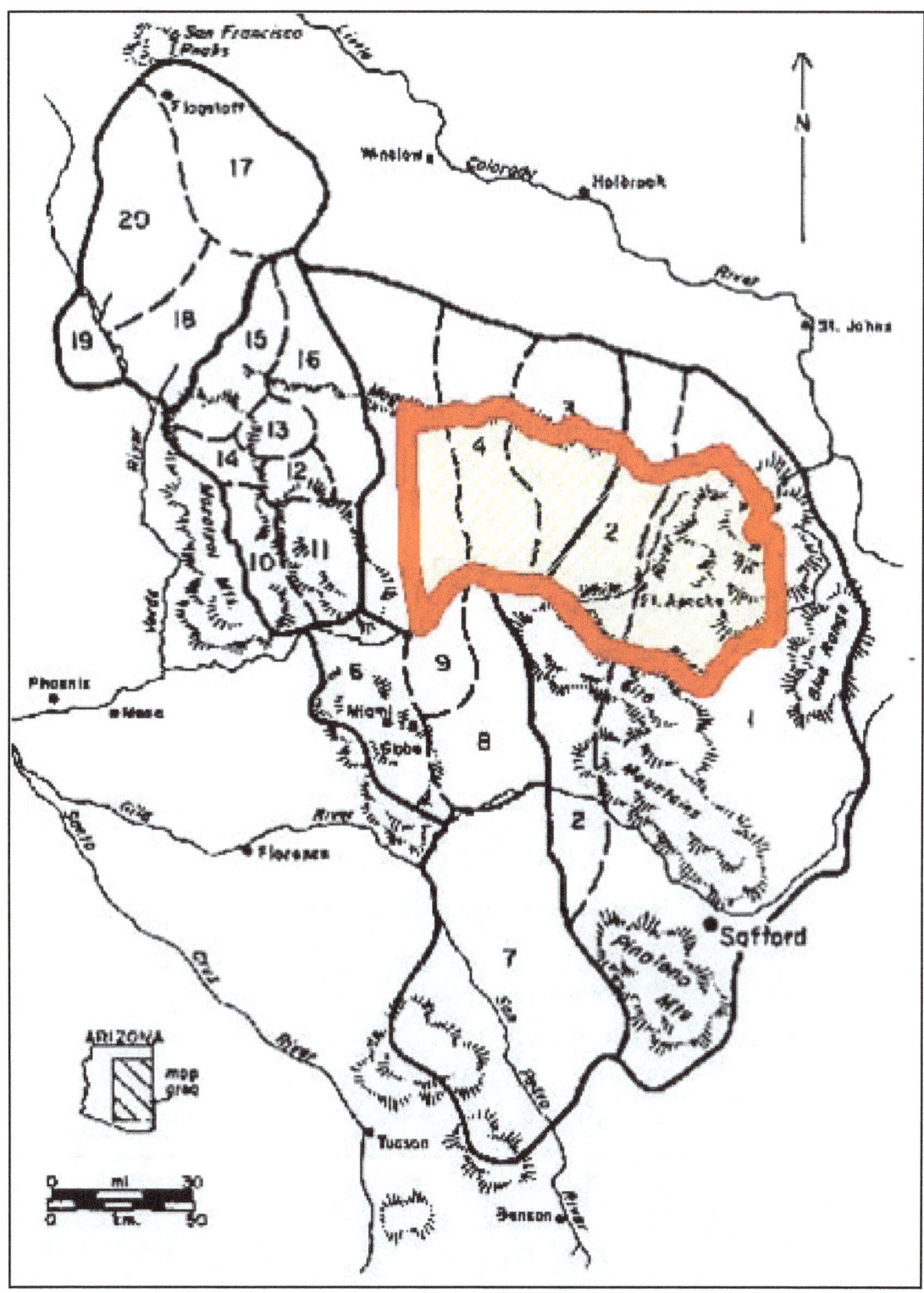

Figure 10.6. White Mountain Apache tribal lands superimposed on the distribution of Western Apache groups and bands circa 1850 (After Goodwin 1942:4-5) See Table 10.1 for listing of bands corresponding to numbers shown on this map.

Table 10.1. Western Apache groups, with constituent bands numbered to connect to territories in Figure 10.6

White Mountain
    1. Eastern White Mountain Band
    2. Western White Mountain Band

Cibecue
    3. Carrizo Band
    4. Cibecue Band
    5. Canyon Creek Band

San Carlos
    6. Pinal Band
    7. Arivaipa Band
    8. San Carlos Band
    9. Apache Peaks Band

Southern Tonto
    10. Mazatzal Band
    11. First Semi-band, Southern Tonto
    12. Second Semi-band, Southern Tonto
    13. Third Semi-band, Southern Tonto
    14. Fourth Semi-band, Southern Tonto
    15. Fifth Semi-band, Southern Tonto
    16. Sixth Semi-band, Southern Tonto

Northern Tonto
    17. Mormon Lake Band
    18. Fossil Creek Band
    19. Bald Mountain Band
    20. Oak Creek Band

Creek and Cibecue areas, the "eastern Apache" made wickiups more pointed than the more clearly domed structures made by Diłzhé'e (Tonto Bands).

The Western White Mountain band was known as Łq•nbà•há (many go to war), a name derived from raiding expeditions the band made to obtain horses (Goodwin 1942:15-16). People in this band lived mainly on Cedar Creek and along White River below the East and North Fork confluence (Fort Apache). Their principal farming sites were on at Canyon Day and Bear Springs on Cedar Creek. Their hunting and gathering territory ranged as far north as Snowflake, and as far south as the foot of the Natanes Rim, Turnbull Mountain, and the Galliuro Mountains.

The social significance of Apache clans stems in part from the networks of kinship obligations created by the mandate to marry outside of one's own clan and closely related clans. Apache clans are matrilineages that, at least in the past, were localized within band groupings, especially in the White Mountain bands (Goodwin 1942:8, 97-101). Vincent Randall pointed out that the ability to move safely across large areas helped dispersed foragers-farmers find mates. The alliances formed between affinal relatives both facilitated travel and provided protection. Apaches continue to rely upon matrilineal clan relatives to guide them through tough times. "It is having relatives that makes you feel comfortable when you travel," Mr. Randall said.

The migration of Apache clans from their origin places, as depicted in Figure 10.7, suggests complex geographical and social relations. The migration map also offers initial guidance in identifying groups to participate in NAGPRA consultations regarding objects from known locations and place-focused stewardship. At least 21 Apache clans have geographical associations with White Mountain Apache tribal lands. Two of these, the Biszaha ("adobe cut bank people," shown as "21" on Figure 10.7) and the Iyahaiyé ("mesquite plants grow in this place people"), appear to be traceable to farming areas near Bear Springs, just northeast of Kinishba (Goodwin 1942:152, 610; Beverly Malone, personal communication, 2005). Goodwin (1942:610) describes the Biszaha as one of the largest White Mountain Apache clans and notes associations with black corn, the Tséyidn (a clan with origins along the Little Colorado River), and residential groupings, circa 1935, near Cedar Creek, Canyon Day, and East Fork. Cornelia Hoffmann recalls that one of Goodwin's principal consultants, John Rope, was Iyahaiyé, but little information is available otherwise. Goodwin (1942:610) says that dry conditions in 1864 forced Apaches to move away from the Bear Springs farm site.

Members of these and other clans associated with the Apache towns of Cedar Creek and Canyon Day were the primary sources for the workers Cummings and the Shaeffers drafted into service in support of excavation and construction activities. As noted above, Apaches were reluctant to work in excavations in general and burials in particular. Friends and University of Arizona students provided the labor for Cummings's summer fieldwork seasons from 1931 to 1934. In 1935, however, when Civilian Conservation Corps-Indian Division (CCC-ID) funds became available, Cummings saw the opportunity to advance his vision of an open-air monument and museum of Indian civilization (Welch 2007a). Cummings tasked Apache crews with rebuilding the rooms excavated in prior years and many other labors.

CCC-ID payroll records indicate that at least 26 Apaches worked at Kinishba in 1935, 24 in 1936, and 23 in 1937 (Welch 2007a:Table 2). Recently retired from the University of Arizona, Cummings obtained a CCC position as "foreman, grade 7," thus providing him with a modest salary of $1,680. In 1938, Cummings started the project season in April and stayed

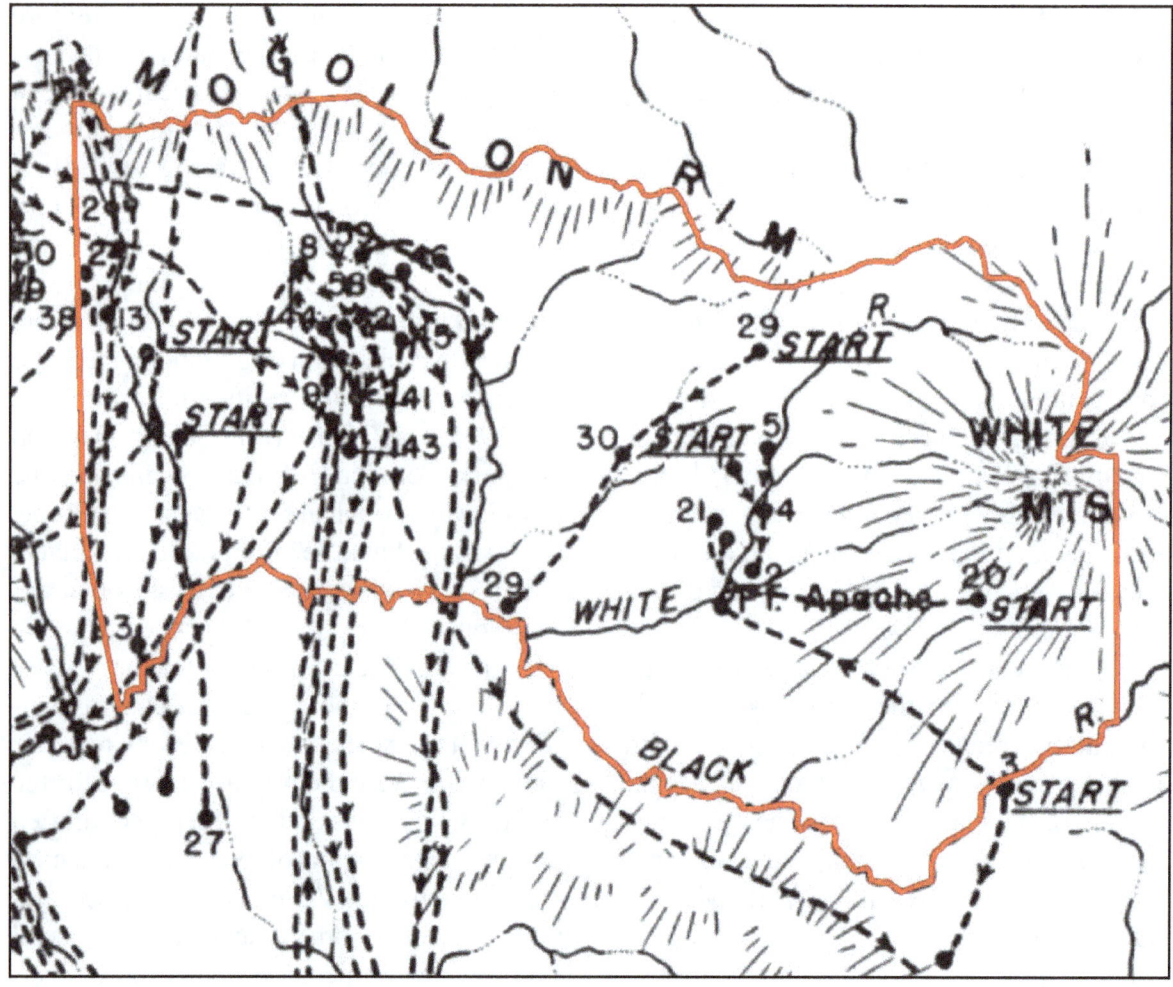

Figure 10.7. Migrations of Apache clans, superimposed with White Mountain Apache tribal lands. Kinishba is located just south of "21" (After Goodwin 1942:Map 6).

through much of the fall, leading students and about 50 Apaches in excavating 40 rooms, rebuilding about 20 of them, and beginning construction of the Kinishba Museum. In 1939, Cummings used the final season of CCC funding to run crews of students and at least 27 Apaches from March through October, completing the excavation of the remainder of Group I (about 20 rooms), the construction of the museum and custodian's quarters, and the rebuilding of 92 ground floor rooms and 48 second-storey rooms. Altogether, over 100 Apache men worked with Cummings. Some, including Ira Declay, Chester Holden, David Kane, and Turner Thompson, spent five or more seasons at the site, forming close associations with the project, Cummings and the Shaeffers (Welch 2007a:Table 2, 2007b).

There are only occasional indications of Apache involvement with Kinishba in the 1940s, and few records have been found of the many Apaches who worked with the Shaeffers, circa 1950, when the roof of the rebuilt pueblo was repaired and a new drainage system was installed (see Chapter 2). Although it has not been possible to make personal contact with any Apaches who worked at Kinishba, many descendants of these men recall stories of the Kinishba project and regard the site as a source of justifiable pride in their forebears' accomplishments. As discussed in the next section of this chapter, the affinities that Cummings and the Shaeffers constructed (literally) between local Apaches and Kinishba are less important to NAGPRA processes than to land management and heritage site stewardship more generally.

Translating Wisdom into Policy and Practice

The cultural affiliation project provides general support and specific guidance to restore and perpetuate connections between people, land, places, oral traditions and religious practices. As these connections were documented, they were also translated, wherever possible, into recommendations for stewardship policies and practices.

At Kinishba, discussions relating to cultural affiliation occurred in the context of a site that has been used and managed since the 1930s for archaeological research and what we today call "heritage tourism." The intertribal and interagency partnerships necessary to progress through repatriation processes have also played important roles in incorporating Kinishba National Historic Landmark into the Fort Apache Historic Park and addressing the site's stewardship needs. Deliberations among the White Mountain Apache Tribe and its partners before, during and after the cultural affiliation project have yielded general guidance on stewardship and repatriation. The discussions have also identified Kinishba-specific recommendations that constitute multi-cultural mandates for respecting and protecting Kinishba's most sensitive elements. This also includes consensus preferences for on-site reburial of human remains and funerary objects. The next section describes and discusses the advisors' recommendations, giving particular attention to issues and concerns bearing on Kinishba's management and interpretation.

General Stewardship Recommendations

The White Mountain Apache Tribe continues to develop cultural and environmental heritage stewardship policies that sustain and balance links among existing resource conditions, community and cultural values, and intrinsic ecosystem processes (Welch 2000; Welch et al. 2009). Landscapes provide powerful research and management frameworks for identifying, understanding, representing, restoring and reinvigorating connections among communities, stewardship policy and practice, and heritage sites, objects and traditions (Ferguson and Anyon 2001; Welch 2009, 2012). Landscapes and their relationships to human groups that resided in or used the areas at different times direct scholars and managers to community interests, values and perspectives relating to resource protection and appropriate treatment of minerals, water, plants, wildlife and cultural heritage. Landscapes are pertinent to repatriation because geography is one of the ten lines of evidence NAGPRA mandates be considered in determining cultural affiliation. NAGPRA provides an important context for learning about human-land relations and developing widely shared, culturally appropriate management recommendations.

Hopi references to the verdant lands of the White Mountain Apache as pavapastuskwa (inspiring land) and other favorable terms connote the blessings of abundant rain and running streams. Water provides the basis for all life and is of particular interest to arid region farmers, including all groups having cultural affinities with White Mountain Apache lands. The ancient petroglyphs and pictographs that grace

White Mountain Apache lands include images of snakes, tadpoles, frogs, and birds, symbols associated with specific Zuni medicine societies, as well as water sources more generally. Viewing these petroglyphs, Eldrick Seoutewa explained, "When you see the real animals, it's a blessing." Mr. Seoutewa further described how high peaks are used to pray for rain and for performing spiritual activities.

Water thus emerged from the project as the most prominent theme connecting sites, teachings, and stewardship. From the advisors' perspectives, so many water sources and related habitats have already been degraded through overgrazing and other short-sighted actions that restoration is required to maintain ecosystems and cultural vitality. In response to these findings, the White Mountain Apache Tribe increased the protection of all water sources through their universal inclusion in the FAIRsite heritage resource inventory.

As part of Zuni, Apache and Hopi spiritual mandates to foster and maintain balance and to evince respect, representatives of the three cultural traditions made frequent offerings wherever knowledge was transferred or collections of plant materials were made. Zuni advisor Eldrick Seoutewa explained, "When you see a site, you leave an offering." Octavius Seowtewa noted that you don't look for these signs for material gain, saying "they tell if it's going to be a good year for the people." The implications or guidance for stewardship are to "listen" closely to places and their constituents (i.e., plants, animals, water sources, etc.) and to give, spiritually, in proportion to what is sought or obtained as a means of maintaining balance. Hopi and Apache project participant agreed on the need and value of seeking to harmonize taking and giving.

Archaeologists, collectors, and resource managers have not always maintained this balance, sometimes taking more than they left, ignoring or downplaying the spiritual dimension of interactions with people, places and pasts, or otherwise acting disrespectfully. Historical and ongoing connections between distant lands and Indigenous communities provide a basis for Zuni, Hopi, and Apache criticism of the archaeological concept of "abandonment." As Octavius Seowtewa, explained, the Zuni people have not "abandoned" their ancestors or their sites; the places remain important and are cared for deeply. When the Zuni visit areas mentioned in migration traditions, they recall the sacred prayers that describe the buttes, peaks, and waterways. Eldrick Seoutewa commented that, "When we walk these sites, we see the knowledge of our ancestors was right.' He added, "Our ancestors are still there—these sites are not abandoned. We enter their habitation. It feels good to make the connection to what my uncles told us….our ancestors were out there, and whenever they stopped, they had a place to worship." When the Zunis visit ancestral sites, they seek indications of ancient shrines and refresh spiritual connections through ceremonial offerings. "We have respect for entering sites," he said. Perry Tsadiasi added that "The sites are in our prayers—our ways are to do individual offerings for the migrating ancestors."

When Welch asked Hopi representatives about the management of trees and other native vegetation growing in and around the Kinishba plaza, Leigh Kuwanwisiwma explained that the village had life, and that when people left, the village was retired. Titus Lamson, a Hopi living on White Mountain Apache lands, maintained the shrine in the Kinishba plaza until recently (Welch 2007a), but the reconstruction and stabilization of *kiikiqö* (ancestral villages) is not part of the Hopi way. Trees, however, are a natural part of the environment of ruins, and it is thus appropriate to allow the trees to express life.

Apache concerns with the archaeological concept of abandonment center more on sacred sites and ceremonial objects than on ancestral residential areas. Through prayers and the respectful avoidance of sacred places and objects, including those retired as the final phase of ceremonial use, Apaches maintain connections to lands, sites, objects and cultural traditions. Archaeologists, collectors and land managers are slowly coming to recognize that Apache use of sacred sites and ceremonial objects is actively maintained through avoidance of direct physical contacts (Welch 1997, 2009). Apaches offer prayers to and through sacred sites from their homes and sweat lodges, but also visit sacred sites still under Apache control. Disrespect to or desecration of Apache sacred sites can interfere with prayers and harm those who depend upon the sites, as well as those responsible for the disrespect. For ceremonial objects put away on the land, the disturbance of their resting places or use of the places or objects for any other purpose brings a premature and potentially counteractive or dangerous end to the ceremony. The message for collectors, archaeologists and land managers is that neither sites nor objects should be considered abandoned without consultations with recent regional occupants and the groups having or sharing cultural affiliation with the landscape.

Repatriation Policy and Action Recommendations

The cultural affiliation assessment supports and substantiates the determinations previously made by the Arizona State Museum that Hopi and Zuni are culturally affiliated with the human remains and funerary objects removed from ancient masonry village sites on White Mountain Apache lands. Hopi, Zuni, and Apache tribal officials agree that these human remains and funerary objects require respectful reburial. Although the past identifiable groups that Hopis and Zunis claim affiliation with are referred to using different terms than those applied by archaeologists, anthropological and tribal views concerning cultural affiliation are consistent.

The repatriation and reburial of Ancestral Mogollon Pueblo human remains collected from White Mountain Apache lands will continue to be an expensive and time-consuming project. Political, logistical and financial issues remain incompletely resolved, but continued intertribal collaboration is essential. The Zuni and Hopi must rely on the White Mountain Apache Tribe to provide the secure reburial site and to respect the sanctity of the reburial proceedings. The White Mountain Apache Tribe must rely on Zuni and Hopi, the culturally affiliated tribes, to submit repatriation claims. The Zuni and Apache must rely on Hopi to take the leading roles in reburials using appropriate ritual protocols. Project participants recognize it will take years to implement NAGPRA and rebury the ancestors on White Mountain Apache lands, and that the legal mandate to determine cultural affiliation is one of the reasons why the NAGPRA process takes so long. Mr. Seowtewa concluded that "Hopefully we can rebury our ancestors; they didn't ask to be taken out."

Even as the Hopi and Zuni tribes assert their claims of cultural affiliation, they recognize that Western Apache are now the stewards for many of their ancestors' graves and villages. Mr. Seowtewa said, "They are our ancestors, but we can't bring them onto our land. They need to be reburied where they came from." Although there was not a "reburial ceremony" prior to NAGPRA, members of the Hopi Cultural Resource Advisory Task Team are now charged with reburying ancestors in a culturally appropriate manner. Hopi and Zuni advisors agree that the cycle of life and death for the excavated individuals has been broken and requires restoration. In Hopi culture, graves are not revisited—you allow people to travel in the earth back to the womb, with a release of the spirit that returns in another life form, as clouds and life-giving moisture.

Among the issues remaining is who will fund the effort. Hopi cultural advisor Bradley Balenquah voiced the consensus view that it is the financial responsibility of the federal government, as well as the institutions that sponsored the collecting in the first place, to pay for reburial. Hopi advisor Michael Lomayaktewa asserted that because the National Science Foundation and the University of Arizona were both involved in funding the excavation of human remains they each have financial and moral obligations to assist with repatriation. The Bureau of Indian Affairs claims legal control over the collections and NAGPRA proceedings but is still in the process of meeting NAGPRA mandates to complete inventories and summaries, to account for all funerary objects, to physically re-associate human remains with their burial offerings, and to work with the tribes to repatriate all eligible remains and objects. The Arizona State Museum and the Bureau of Indian Affairs reinvigorated consultations among Hopi, Zuni, and White Mountain Apache tribal representatives in 2009, and all parties are collaborating toward consensus goals.

Tribal representatives agree on the need for cooperation to work through the administrative and logistical arrangements, beginning with the smaller groups of human remains recovered from the surface of looted ruins and proceeding to the larger groups of remains with hundreds and thousands of associated funerary objects. Recommendations from the participants in the cultural affiliation project are guiding the repatriation and reburial of Ancestral Pueblo human remains and funerary objects removed from White Mountain Apache lands. These recommendations include:

> Bureau of Indian Affairs, National Science Foundation and the University of Arizona should fund the Arizona State Museum to re-assemble human remains and their funerary objects in preparation for reburial.

> All human remains and funerary objects should be reburied as close as possible to where they were found.

> Institutions and individuals involved in any disrespectful or unauthorized collections or excavations of human remains or cultural items should seek atonement through apologies to the affected descendents and through material and spiritual support for the repatriation efforts.

Kinishba Stewardship Recommendations

The Zuni, Hopi and Apache advisors' consensus guidance for Kinishba preservation and development espouses the following four principles:

> minimize disturbance to all ancient remains and architecture;

> maximize opportunities for Apache, Zuni, and Hopi control over, participation in, and benefits from stewardship decisions and development directions;

> minimize the presence of intrusive and industrial elements associated with Cummings's rebuilding; maximize peaceful and respectful visitation to and interpretation of Kinishba as a resting place, sacred site, and community important in multiple Native cultural and oral traditions.

Hopi advisor Raleigh Puhuyaoma explained that the shrine is "rooted" in Kinishba and should not be removed. After discussion, the consensus of the Hopi research team visiting the site in 2004 was that the shrine should be fenced to keep people from walking over it (Figure 10.3). The White Mountain Apache Tribe has placed dirt on top of the shrine to protect it, and will fence the area.

Leigh Kuwanwisiwma explained that Hopis are farmers, so the farm fields associated with Kinishba are considered important parts of the site. Because petroglyph panels close by and within the valley are important markers of Hopi clans, these need study to interpret and manage the site.

Conclusion: Reclaiming Kinishba

With support from the White Mountain Apache Tribe's Council, ongoing intertribal consultations, and financial and technical assistance from the *Save America's Treasures* program administered by the National Park Service and the *Arizona Heritage Fund* administered by Arizona State Parks, the Tribe's Heritage Program and the Fort Apache Heritage Foundation have worked to revitalize Cummings's vision while restoring an indigenous sense of place. Through tribal member training in ruins preservation and the installation of culturally sensitive interpretive signs, trails, and other visitor amenities, Apaches and their advisors have made Kinishba a safe and respectful place to experience the Ancestral Pueblo legacy on Apache lands and to explore stewardship opportunities appropriate to local economic and cultural realities. This emphasis on stewardship based on applications of authentic Apache, Hopi, and Zuni perspectives—and on the representation of these perspectives to visitors through multi-lingual signs and other interpretive media—is resulting in decreased vandalism and deepened visitor experiences.

Beyond collecting information and making specific recommendations, the cultural affiliation project has reaffirmed the enduring cultural truth that elders and cultural specialists are crucial sources of guidance in challenging circumstances. Through this project they interpreted diverse cultural elements deriving from and reaffirming the importance of resilient and regenerative stewardship. Cultural memories live, revive and reverberate through contacts with land, sites, objects and the keepers of knowledge and wisdom. Not only do these persistent memories and feelings contradict many aspects of the archaeological and western legal concepts of site and object abandonment, they also suggest that echoes from this project and similar efforts will assist future generations in carrying forward the best and most useful elements of the Apache, Hopi, and Zuni cultural traditions.

The cultural advisors made clear that as these recommendations are honored, and as repatriation proceeds, spiritual balance will be restored to the White Mountain Apache lands, and the world will be a better place.

Acknowledgments

A NAGPRA Documentation grant administered by the National Park Service and awarded to the White Mountain Apache Tribe Historic Preservation Office supported the cultural affiliation project. Welch presented an initial draft of the paper that evolved into this chapter at the meeting of the Society for Applied Anthropology, Vancouver, British Columbia, March 28, 2006. The authors are forever grateful for the opportunity to serve as the recipients and compilers of Apache, Zuni, and Hopi knowledge and wisdom.

Chapter 11
Encounters with Kinishba: A Grasshopper Perspective

J. Jefferson Reid

Kinishba Pueblo played an iconic role throughout most of the thirty years of Grasshopper field school instruction. Conversely, most of what we can say about Kinishba's past must be viewed through the prism of what is known about Grasshopper. The investigation of large, late prehistoric pueblos by University of Arizona archaeological field schools began at Kinishba, moved to Point of Pines (1946-1960) on the San Carlos Reservation, and then to Grasshopper (1963-1992) back on the Fort Apache Reservation. All three field schools and their research programs owe much to the participation of Western Apache, whose knowledge of landscapes and lore as well as skilled labor contributed to this understanding. Grasshopper is the best known of these three pueblos; Point of Pines a distant second; and Kinishba the least well known. The present volume goes a long way toward giving voice to an important pueblo place. Byron Cummings took a very personal interest in the Kinishba project, so I, too, approach these encounters from that same highly personal perspective. A major objective of these concluding comments, therefore, is for me to underscore the long-term significance of Grasshopper research.

KINISHBA: CLASSROOM AND SHOWROOM

Kinishba was Cummings's largest archaeological project, begun in 1931, his seventieth year (Welch 2007a,b). He left seventeen years later in 1948 after extensive excavations, reconstructions, and construction of a museum and living quarters for a caretaker (Bostwick 2006; Chapter 2:Figure 2.3).

I have known Grasshopper more than twice as long as Cummings knew Kinishba. A Grasshopper perspective, therefore, is broad in time and space. It is the view from the Grasshopper region, Grasshopper Pueblo and surrounding smaller pueblos. It is also the view of the field school staff and students, who came to these Apache mountain places from across the nation and many distant parts of the world (Reid and Whittlesey 1999, 2005). The editor and most of the authors in this volume are Grasshopper alumni—Welch, Riggs, Triadan, Ciolek-Torello, and I were field school staff who completed doctoral dissertations on Grasshopper topics, and Ferguson was on the staff for many years. My personal perspective is not unique.

My initial encounter with Kinishba was in 1970 on a one-day field trip out of Grasshopper. It had become routine to take students and staff to Fort Apache, picnic on the grass at General Crook's cabin, and then go to Kinishba to walk around the ruined west unit. Kinishba was seen as a companion pueblo to Grasshopper with room blocks on both sides of an arroyo and occupied at the same time during the 1300s

(Reid and Whittlesey 1997:162-163). Kinishba was instructive in demonstrating the collapse of a large, surface pueblo to contrast with the cliff dwellings of Canyon Creek and Red Rock House in the Grasshopper region. Kinishba also provided an excellent example of pueblo reconstruction for those students new to the Native American Southwest. Kinishba was not only a good excuse to get out of camp but also an instructive example of pueblo architecture and the processes of a reconstructed pueblo slowly becoming once again a rubble pile of rock. This was before the concept of formation processes of the archaeological record had been fully formalized (Schiffer 1975, 1976). The Kinishba field trip continued intermittently until the field school closed in 1992, principally because excavation at the large Grasshopper Pueblo had shifted to smaller sites like the eighteen-room Chodistaas and Grasshopper Spring pueblos. The large, crumbling Kinishba ruin had less heuristic value than in earlier times.

To position these personal comments, consider the field school in 1970. Throughout Grasshopper field school's 30-year history, students were isolated in camp for eight, then later for six weeks. No students' cars were allowed, and in the early years only staff went in to Show Low for groceries every two weeks (see Reid and Whittlesey 2005). The potential for cabin fever was partially relieved through one-day field trips to sites in the Grasshopper region and to those farther afield at Kinishba and Forestdale.

It was also 1970 that Canyon Creek cliff dwelling was rediscovered. Bill Longacre had invited Emil Haury to Grasshopper to lead the field school to the cliff dwelling that Haury had excavated in the summer of 1932 and had not visited since (Haury 1934). In 1932, Haury and crew had ridden in from the west with Slim Ellison's pack horses, starting at the Rock House, crossing Canyon Creek, and approaching the cliff dwelling from below. Haury was sixty-six in the summer of 1970 and no doubt disinclined to wander aimlessly in the rough country of the Grasshopper Plateau, so he hired a plane to fly him over the area to pinpoint the site's location and plot the best route in. I recall the plane flying low over camp one morning, but we had no idea until later who it was. Haury selected a route that used back roads down Salt River Draw to get us to the western edge of the plateau, and then we had to wind our way through the rough chaparral growth down to the ruin. And, of course, it was spectacular. From 1970 until the end of the field school, Canyon Creek became a regular field-trip excursion and the subject of ongoing research.

Canyon Creek cliff dwelling augmented our view of Kinishba in that it was original, not reconstructed, and thus we could easily comprehend the extent of wall height essential for a second-story room. This basic fact of mountain pueblo architecture would play an important role in our initial, archival-based evaluation of Kinishba architecture, especially our argument that the original Group I was primarily or exclusively one story in height (Reid and Whittlesey 1989).

Canyon Creek is also a critical chronometric datum for determining the timing and rate of events of the 1300s throughout the area below the Mogollon Rim. This goes back to Haury's work there in 1932, which was part of a Gila Pueblo Archaeological Foundation project to support the efficacy of A. E. Douglass's tree-ring dating technique (Haury and Hargrave 1931). It was only three years earlier in 1929 that A. E. Douglass had "bridged the gap" at Show Low, Arizona (Haury 1962). Not everyone was convinced of the viability of tree-ring dating (Nash 1999). After 1970, Canyon Creek cliff dwelling joined Red Rock

House as the major contributors to the absolute dating of pueblo ruins and associated pottery types in the region below the Mogollon Rim (Reynolds 1981).

Canyon Creek securely dated the period from A.D. 1325 to 1350s, and Red Rock House, though unexcavated, provided tree-ring dates from 1350 to 1370s, which, along with noncutting dates from Grasshopper Pueblo, placed an estimated date for the abandonment of the Grasshopper Plateau at around A.D. 1400. Subsequent excavation at Chodistaas Pueblo and Grasshopper Spring Pueblo would document the architectural and ceramic history of the region during the Great Drought from A.D. 1275 to 1300.

Chodistaas and Canyon Creek provide cutting dates to bracket the major expansion at Grasshopper and to date with precision never before possible the highly variable ceramic assemblages of the 1300s throughout the circum-Mogollon Rim region (Mills and Herr 1999; Lyons, Chapter 7). No other excavations below or above the Mogollon Rim—not Kinishba, Point of Pines, or Bailey pueblos—had provided this high level of chronometric precision. The Show Low Ruin, object of the 1929 Third Beam Expedition (Haury 1931), had produced more dates in the 1300s, but the lack of adequate provenience information renders them useless except to say that the pueblo was inhabited in the 1300s, a fact known to Douglass, Colton, Hargrave, and Haury in 1929. In this regard, it is instructive to note that not one tree-ring date exists for Point of Pines in the 1300s, when it is absolutely beyond question that its major occupation was during that century. Grasshopper region research, therefore, provides the only reliable, well-provenienced absolute dating for Kinishba and the circum-Mogollon Rim.

It is difficult to chronicle how many times the field school and I visited Kinishba and Fort Apache. But it was Kinishba that was of greatest interest because it provided an almost living example of the kind of pueblo village that we were dealing with at Grasshopper. I have 35-mm slides dated 1976, and John Welch and I have determined that the field school went there in 1984, when we also visited the work at East Fork (Ciolek-Torello and Halbirt, Chapter 5).

My closest encounter came in 1989 when Stephanie Whittlesey and I undertook a contract with the National Park Service to do an archival survey of Kinishba-related documents and an evaluation of Cummings's reconstruction of the pueblo. We investigated all the known repositories of Kinishba material to discover that the records were exceedingly spare. The treasure trove of documents from the Schaeffers requires a reevaluation of what is interpretable from the archives (Welch, Shaeffer and Shaeffer, Triadan, all this volume). Whittlesey and I used Grasshopper architecture as a template with which to measure Cummings's reconstruction and concluded our report with evaluations based on our personal experience (Reid and Whittlesey 1989). It is now possible to do a far more complete analysis using the synthetic work by Riggs (2001, this volume) on the architecture of Grasshopper Pueblo. Riggs's architectural analysis of Grasshopper will not be duplicated in this century.

In 1992, after the field school at Grasshopper had ended, I sought to extend my archival knowledge of Kinishba by an on-site analysis and evaluation of the historical accuracy and structural integrity of the reconstruction through the Challenge Cost-Share Program of the National Park Service. The proposal was not selected for funding, and my personal encounters with Kinishba came to an abrupt end. Grasshopper research, as this volume so amply demonstrates, continues to assist in the interpretation of Kinishba, and, thereby, continues to underscore the significance of Kinishba as "a monument to Native civilization" (Welch 2007a).

A Framework For Future Critiques

In place of an evaluation of individual chapters, I offer general comments on the nature of contemporary archaeological theory, method, and discourse interspersed with reference to chapters in this volume. Like the different archaeologies of Grasshopper research documented in Reid and Whittlesey (2005), I have extensive experience in three prominent paradigms—culture history, processual archaeology, and behavorial archaeology. It is from this vantage that I offer the following generalizations.

Culture historians were much given to discovering new taxonomic units and applying new labels, which, during the 1930s, were essential to establishing the metalanguage necessary for scholarly communication. The McKern Midwest Taxonomic System is the classic example of organizing material cultural complexes, and the *Handbook of Northern Arizona Pottery Types* by Colton and Hargrave (1937) is the paragon of ceramic systemization. Naming new phases and pottery or projectile point types was the end product of the culture historian's goal of "filling in the gaps" in the time-space matrix. This simple procedure enabled archaeologist to achieve research closure as well as to establish labels that other archaeologists would be compelled to reference in the higher narrative level of cross-cultural or temporal comparison. The multitude of pottery types proposed for Kinishba falls squarely within this cultural historical tradition and deserves close scrutiny in terms of their taxonomic utility at the next level of analysis (Lyons, this volume).

A contemporary irony exists in that behavioral archaeologists have been criticized for creating jargon-laden concepts, whereas the proliferation of phase names and pottery types, though semantically similar, is rarely seen in the same light.

Other lexical inconsistencies lurk in the background of archaeological discourse. One of these is the legitimate call to write plainly for the general reader (see Jameson 1997; Little 2002) and then proceed to shift the language away from established nouns or embed the description of simple behaviors in dense, convoluted prose understandable only to learned members of the discipline. Almost all of postprocessual discourse falls within this latter category of obfuscation These objectives are mutually exclusive.

On a related note, I am no fan, for example, of abandoning the concept of abandonment (Welch and Ferguson, Chapter 10). Our book *Grasshopper Pueblo, A Story of Archaeology and Ancient Life* (Reid and Whittlesey 1999) was written for a general audience, especially the Cibecue Apache, and all royalties are assigned to the White Mountain Apache Tribe. In that book we discuss room abandonment processes and the reasons of abandoning the Grasshopper Plateau and the Arizona mountains by 1400.

Furthermore, I am uncomfortable with the pervasive trend elsewhere to homogenize our efforts to maintain Mogollon distinctiveness with the Ancestral Pueblo label. This trend is discussed in Reid and Whittlesey (2010:150; see Whittlesey, Reid, and Lekson 2010).

This is an appropriate place to mention Jim Shaeffer's "seldom-cited dissertation." Completed in 1954 at Columbia University, the year after Joe Ben Wheat's dissertation, it examined the same data and arrived at the opposite conclusion. Whereas Wheat substantiated Haury's concept of a Mogollon culture separate from Basketmaker-Pueblo, Shaeffer concluded that Mogollon was not a separate culture, but simply a regional variant of a broad pueblo pattern. Wheat's work was widely distributed by 1955 and brought to a conclusion the Mogollon controversy, thus relegating countervailing arguments within the culture history paradigm to obscurity (see Reid and Whittlesey 2010).

A third linguistic problem follows observations made years ago by Manners and Kaplan (1968) that anthropologists in general, and I would add archaeologists, tend to confuse vocabulary with theory or, rather, they offer a term and a definition as theory:

> "…anthropologists use the term theory in a great variety of ways—almost whimsically—sometimes as a synonym for a concept, or a synonym for an inductive generalization or for a model…, sometimes merely to lend tone or dignity to the obvious" (Manners and Kaplan 1968:1).

It is not uncommon that a traditional concept may be rebranded with a new label. For example, the culture historians firmly believed that pottery could equal people. Processual archaeologists vehemently denied this simplistic equation, yet today we have returned to the position of the culture historians. I would place diaspora within this category of relabeling a traditional interpretive tool—pottery equals people (see Lyons this volume; also Ciolek-Torello and Halbirt Chapter 5).

W. W. Taylor (1972) spoke of "Old Wine in New Skins," but Manners and Kaplan (1968:11) provide an anthropologically specific illustration of this phenomenon: "Those who have no memory of the history of anthropology are doomed to repeat it. Among the consequences of this failure is that theory-building in cultural anthropology comes to resemble slash-and-burn agriculture as Anthony Wallace has recently noted: 'After cultivating a field for a while, the natives move on to a new one and let the bush take over; then they return, slash and burn and raise crops in the old field again' (1966:1254)."

As at Grasshopper, a culture historical foundation must be created and critiqued and past behaviors must be reconstructed before reliable explanations can be presented. Building on the work presented in this volume should speed efforts to achieve the explanatory level in the past life of Kinishba.

ARCHAEOLOGY AND THE WHITE MOUNTAIN APACHE

Thirty years of Grasshopper research stands also as a monument to Apache tribal wisdom and leadership during a critical period of political, economic, and social transition. In the spring of 1973, when I was acting director of the field school at the time to renew the excavation permit and lease, the tribal chairman came to the University of Arizona to meet with Raymond Thompson in his office. Thompson was then Head of the Department of Anthropology and Director of the Arizona State Museum, the same positions held by Byron Cummings. When I became permanent director in the spring of 1979, a transition had taken place. It was necessary to appear before the Tribal Council in Whiteriver to request a formal resolution to operate the field school, and that request and resolution was renewed annually until the field school ended in 1992. Ronnie Lupe was Tribal Chairman in 1979 and throughout most of the final years of the field school. He played a major role in supporting the research. The Apache role in Grasshopper research is well illustrated in our book *Thirty Years into Yesterday, A History of Archaeology at Grasshopper Pueblo* (Reid and Whittlesey 2005). It is best summed up in a quotation from that book.

"Another important intellectual influence on Grasshopper research might be labeled for convenience a form of postprocessualism, as long as we clearly distinguish the unique source. Our inquiry into ideology and the ritual character of Grasshopper life owes nothing to the writings of Foucault, Derrida, or Lacan and everything to the words and deeds of Tessays, Cromwells, and Quays—Cibecue Apache people who lived and worked with us at Grasshopper" (Reid and Whittlesey 2005:192). To them and to many other White Mountain Apache, we owe a debt of gratitude that may in part be fulfilled by a Grasshopper perspective on Kinishba.

I conclude this brief reflection with optimism for Kinisba's future. With this volume Kinishba's past achieves a level of fact and interpretation that makes it eligible for close scrutiny, scholarly critique, and comparison to other large, late communities of east-central Arizona and beyond. Kinishba now has a strong voice in the collaborative effort to explain the Pueblo past.

References Cited

Adams, E. Charles
    1983   The Architectural Analog to Hopi Social Organization and Room Use, and Implications for Prehistoric Northern Southwestern Culture. *American Antiquity* 48:44-61.

    1991   *The Origin and Development of the Pueblo Katsina Cult*. University of Arizona Press, Tucson.

    1994   The Katsina Cult. In *Kachinas in the Pueblo World*, edited by Polly Schaafsma, pp. 35-46. University of New Mexico Press, Albuquerque.

    1996   The Pueblo III-Pueblo IV Transition in the Hopi Area, Arizona. In *The Prehistoric Pueblo World A.D. 1150–1350*, edited by M. A. Adler, pp. 48-58. University of Arizona Press, Tucson.

    1998   Late Prehistory in the Middle Little Colorado River Area, a Regional Perspective. In *Migration and Reorganization: The Pueblo IV Period in the American Southwest*, edited by Katherine A. Spielmann, pp. 65-80. Anthropological Research Papers No. 51. Arizona State University Press, Tempe.

Adams, E. Charles, and Andrew I. Duff (editors)
    2004   *The Protohistoric Pueblo World, A.D. 1275–1600*. University of Arizona, Tucson.

Adams, Jenny L.
    1994   The Development of Prehistoric Grinding Technology in the Point of Pines Area, East-Central Arizona. Ph.D. dissertation, Department of Anthropology, University of Arizona Tucson. ProQuest, Ann Arbor.

    2010   Engendering Households Through Technological Identity. In *Engendering Households in the Prehistoric Southwest*, edited by Barbara J. Roth, pp. 208-228. University of Arizona Press, Tucson.

Adler, Michael A., and Richard H. Wilshusen
    1990   Large-scale Integrative Facilities in Tribal Societies: Cross-cultural and Southwestern US Examples. *World Archaeology* 22(2):133-146.

Ahlstrom, Richard V. N., Mark L. Chenault, M. Zyniecki, and David H. Greenwald
    1995   Chronology, Compound Growth, and Demography. In *The Sky Harbor Project, Early Desert Farming and Irrigation Settlements: Archaeological Investigations in the Phoenix Sky Harbor Center, Volume 3: Pueblo Salado*, edited by David H. Greenwald, Mark L. Chenault, and Dawn M. Greenwald, pp. 369-381. SWCA Anthropological Research Paper No. 4. SWCA, Inc. Environmental Consultants, Flagstaff.

Ambler, J. Richard
    1985   Northern Kayenta Ceramic Chronology. In *Archaeological Investigations Near Rainbow City, Navajo Mountain, Utah*, edited by Phil R. Geib, J. Richard Ambler, and Martha M. Callahan, pp. 28-68. Northern Arizona University Archaeological Report No. 576. Northern Arizona University, Flagstaff.

Anyon, Roger
    1984   *Mogollon Settlement Patterns and Communal Architecture*. Master's Thesis, Department of Anthropology, University of New Mexico, Albuquerque.

Anyon, Roger and Steven A. LeBlanc
    1980   The Evolution of Mogollon-Mimbres Communal Structure. *The Kiva* 45(3):253-277.

Arrighetti, Kathryn M. L.
  2004 Typology and Chronology of Tundastusa Ceramic Assemblages. In *Report for the White Mountain Apache Tribe*, prepared by Barbara J. Mills. Unpublished report on file, School of Anthropology, University of Arizona, Tucson.

Baldwin, Gordon Cortis
  1934 The Prehistoric Pueblo of Kinishba. Unpublished Master's thesis, College of Letters, Arts and Sciences, University of Arizona, Tucson.

  1935a Dates from Kinishba Pueblo. *Tree-Ring Bulletin* 1(4):30.

  1935b Ring Record of the Great Drought (1276-1299) in Eastern Arizona. *Tree-Ring Bulletin* 2(2):11-12.

  1937 The Pottery of Kinishba. *The Kiva* 3(1):1-4.

  1938a Excavations at Kinishba Pueblo, Arizona. *American Antiquity* 4(1):11-21.

  1938b A New Pottery Type from Eastern Arizona. *Southwestern Lore* 4(2):21-26.

  1938c New Pottery Type from Eastern Arizona: Summary. *New Mexico Anthropologist* 2:83-94.

  1939 The Material Culture of Kinishba. *American Antiquity* 4(4):314-327.

  1941 The Archaeology of the Upper Salt River Valley, Arizona: Its Sequence and Interrelationships. Unpublished Ph.D. dissertation, Department of Anthropology, University of Southern California, Los Angeles.

Bandelier, Adolph F.
  1890-1892 Final Report of Investigations among the Indians of the Southwestern United States Carried on Mainly in the Years from 1880 to 1885, Part I-II. *Papers of the Archaeological Institute of America, American Series* II-IV. John Wilson and Son, Cambridge.

Bannister, Bryant, and William J. Robinson
  1971 Tree-Ring Dates from Arizona U-W: Gila-Salt Rivers Area. Laboratory of Tree-Ring Research, University of Arizona, Tucson.

Bannister, Bryant, Elizabeth A. M. Gell, and John W. Hannah
  1966 Tree-Ring Dates from Arizona N-Q, Verde, Showlow, St. Johns Area. Laboratory of Tree-Ring Research, University of Arizona, Tucson.

Barnes, Will C.
  1941 *Apaches and Longhorns*. The Ward Ritchee Press, Los Angeles.

Basso, Keith H.
  1996 *Wisdom Sits in Places: Landscape and Language Among the Western Apache*. University of New Mexico Press, Albuquerque.

Baumann, Martin
  1995 Conceptualizing Diaspora: The Preservation of Religious Identity in Foreign Parts, Exemplified by Hindu Communities Outside India. *Temenos* 31:19-35.

Baxter, Laura, Kate J. Baird, Lisa C. Pedicino, and Karriaunna Scotti
  1997 The Dendrochronology of the Reconstruction of Kinishba. *Tree-Ring Bulletin* 54:11-21.

Beals, Ralph L., George W. Brainerd, and Watson Smith
  1945 *Archaeological Studies in Northeast Arizona.* University of California Publications in American Archaeology and Ethnology 44(1). University of California Press, Berkeley and Los Angeles.

Berg, Gregory E., Eric Bushèe, and David E. Doyel
  2003 Trends in Mortuary Practices at the SR 88-Wheatfields Sites. In *Human Remains and Mortuary Patterns*, edited by David E. Doyel and Teresa L. Hoffman, pp. 239-284. Settlement History along Pinal Creek in the Globe Highlands, Arizona, vol. 2. Cultural Resources Report No. 112. Archaeological Consulting Services, Tempe, Arizona.

Bernard, H. Russell
  2006 *Research Methods in Anthropology: Qualitative and Quantitative Approaches* (Forth Edition). AltaMira Press, Lanham, MD.

Bernardini, Wesley
  2005 *Hopi Oral Tradition and the Archaeology of Identity.* University of Arizona Press, Tucson.

Birkby, Walter H.
  1973 Discontinuous morphological traits of the skull as population markers in the prehistoric Southwest. Unpublished Ph.D. dissertation, Department of Anthropology, University of Arizona, Tucson.

  1982 Biosocial Interpretations from Cranial Nonmetric Traits of the Grasshopper Pueblo Skeletal Remains. In *Multidisciplinary Research at Grasshopper Pueblo, Arizona*, edited by William A. Longacre, Sally J. Holbrook, and Michael W. Graves, pp. 36-41. Anthropological Papers 40. University of Arizona Press, Tucson.

Bishop, Ronald L., and Hector Neff
  1989 Ceramic Compositional Analysis in Archaeological Perspective. In *Archaeological Chemistry IV*, edited by R. O. Allen, pp. 57-86. Advances in Chemistry Series 220. American Chemical Society, Washington D.C.

Bishop, Ronald L., Robert L. Rands, and George R. Holley
  1982 Ceramic Compositional Analysis in Archaeological Perspective. In *Advances in Archaeological Method and Theory*, vol. 5, edited by Michael B. Schiffer, pp. 275-330. Academic Press, New York.

Bishop, Ronald L., Veletta Canouts, Suzanne P. De Atley, Alfred Qöyawayma, and C. W. Aikins
  1988 The Formation of Ceramic Analytical Groups: Hopi Pottery Production and Exchange, A.C. 1300-1600. *Journal of Field Archaeology* 15(3):317-337.

Blackman, M. James
  1986 Precision in Routine I.N.A.A. over a Two-year Period at NBSR. In *NBSR Reactor Summary of Activities July 1986 through June 1986*, edited by F. Shorten, pp.122-126.

Blinman, Eric
  1989 Potluck in the Protokiva: Ceramics and Ceremonialism in Pueblo I Villages. In *The Architecture of Social Integration in Prehistoric Pueblos*, edited by Michelle Hegmon and William D. Lipe, pp. 113-124. Occasional Papers of the Crown Canyon Archaeological Center No. 1. Crown Canyon Archaeological Center, Cortez.

Bostwick, Todd W.
  2006 *Byron Cummings: Dean of Southwestern Archaeology.* University of Arizona Press, Tucson.

Bradley, Richard
  2000 *An Archaeology of Natural Places.* Routledge, London.

Breternitz, David A.
　1959　*Excavations at Nantack Village, Point of Pines, Arizona.* Anthropological Papers No. 1. University of Arizona Press, Tucson.

　1960　*Excavations at Three Sites in the Verde Valley, Arizona.* Bulletin No. 34. Museum of Northern Arizona, Flagstaff.

　1966　*An Appraisal of Tree-Ring Dated Pottery in the Southwest.* Anthropological Papers of the University of Arizona No. 10. University of Arizona Press, Tucson.

Breternitz, David A., James C. Gifford, and Alan P. Olson
　1957　Point of Pines Phase Sequence and Utility Pottery Type Revisions. *American Antiquity* 22(4):412-416.

Britton, Jim
　n.d.　Prehistoric Sites—Q Ranch Pueblo. Arizona Archaeological Society. http://www.azarchsoc.org/Resources/Documents/QRanch%20Prehistoric%20Site.pdf, accessed 5 January 2012.

Brown, Jeffrey L.
　1973　The Origin and Nature of Salado: Evidence from the Safford Valley, Arizona. Unpublished Ph.D Dissertation, Department of Anthropology, University of Arizona, Tucson.

　1974　Pueblo Viejo Salado Sites and Their Relationship to Western Pueblo Culture. *The Artifact* 12(2).

Brown. David E., and Charles H. Lowe
　1980　Biotic Communities of the Southwest. 1:1,000,000 scale map. Forest Service General Technical Report RM-78.

Buck, Stephen H.
　2005　Q-Ranch: A Historical and Archaeological Treasure. *Old Pueblo Archaeology* 43:1-2, 6-7.

Bullard, William R., Jr.
　1962　*The Cerro Colorado Site and Pithouse Architecture in the Southwestern United States Prior to A.D. 900.* Papers of the Peabody Museum of Archaeology and Ethnology, Harvard University 44(2), Cambridge.

Bunzel, Ruth L.
　1932a　Zuni Ceremonialism. In *Forty-Seventh Annual Report of the Bureau of American Ethnology, 1929-1930*, pp. 467-544. Smithsonian Institution, Washington, D.C.

　1932b　Zuni Origin Myths. In *Forty-Seventh Annual Report of the Bureau of American Ethnology, 1929-1930*, pp. 545-609. Smithsonian Institution, Washington, D.C.

　1932c　Zuni Ritual Poetry. In *Forty-Seventh Annual Report of the Bureau of American Ethnology, 1929-1930*, pp. 611-835. Smithsonian Institution, Washington, D.C.

Bushnell, G. H. S.
　1955　Some Pueblo IV Pottery Types From Kechipauan, New Mexico, U.S.A. In *Anais do XXXI Congresso Internacional de Americanistas, São Paulo, 23 a 28 de Agôsto de 1954, vol. 2*, compiled by Herbert Baldus, pp. 657-665. Editora Anhembi, São Paulo.

Buskirk, Winfred
　1986　*The Western Apache.* University of Oklahoma Press, Norman.

Cameron, Catherine M.
1999 *Hopi Dwellings: Architecture at Orayvi*. University of Arizona Press, Tucson.

Carlson, Roy L.
1961 White Mountain Red Ware: A Stylistic Tradition in the Prehistoric Pottery of East Central Arizona. Unpublished Ph.D. dissertation, Department of Anthropology, University of Arizona, Tucson.

1970 *White Mountain Redware: A Pottery Tradition of East-Central Arizona and Western New Mexico*. Anthropological Papers of the University of Arizona No. 19. University of Arizona Press, Tucson.

1982 The Polychrome Complexes. In *Southwestern Ceramics: A Comparative Review*, edited by Albert H. Schroeder, pp. 201-234. Arizona Archaeologist No. 15. Arizona Archaeological Society, Phoenix.

Carr, Christopher
1995a Building a Unified Middle-Range Theory of Artifact Design: Historical Perspectives and Tactics. In *Style, Society, and Person: Archaeological and Ethnological Perspectives*, edited by Christopher Carr and Jill E. Neitzel, pp. 151-170. Plenum Press, New York.

1995b A Unified Middle-Range Theory of Artifact Design. In *Style, Society, and Person: Archaeological and Ethnological Perspectives*, edited by Christopher Carr and Jill E. Neitzel, pp. 171-258. Plenum Press, New York.

Chenhall, Robert G.
1972 Random Sampling in an Archaeological Survey. Unpublished Ph.D. dissertation, Department of Anthropology, Arizona State University, Tempe.

Christenson, Andrew L.
1991 Identifying Pukis or Potters' Turntables at Anasazi Sites. *Pottery Southwest* 18(1):1-6.

1994 Perforated and Unperforated Plates as Tools for Pottery Manufacture. In *Function and Technology of Anasazi Ceramics from Black Mesa, Arizona*, edited by Marion F. Smith, Jr., pp. 55-65. Center for Archaeological Investigations Occasional Paper No. 15. Southern Illinois University at Carbondale.

1995 Non-Buffware Decorated Ceramics and Mean Ceramic Dating. In *The Roosevelt Community Development Study: Ceramic Chronology, Technology, and Economics*, Vol.2, edited by James M. Heidke and Miriam T. Stark, pp.85-132. Anthropological Papers 14. Center for Desert Archaeology, Tucson.

Ciolek-Torrello, Richard
1996 Domestic Group Composition and Platform Mounds in Two Nonriverine Hohokam Communities. In *People Who Lived in Big Houses: Archaeological Perspectives on Large Domestic Structures*, edited by Gary Coupland and E.B. Banning, pp. 47-69. Monographs in World Archaeology No, 27. Prehistory Press, Madison, Wisconsin.

1998a Prehistoric Settlement and Demography in the Lower Verde Region. In *Vanishing River: Landscapes and Lives of the Lower Verde Valley: The Lower Verde Archaeological Project: Overview, Synthesis, and Conclusions*, edited by Stephanie M. Whittlesey, Richard Ciolek-Torrello, and Jeffrey H. Altschul, pp. 531-595. SRI Press, Tucson.

1998b Sites of the Early Formative Period. In *Early Farmers of the Sonoran Desert: Archaeological Investigations at the Houghton Road Site, Tucson, Arizona*, edited by Richard Ciolek-Torrello, pp. 229-255. Technical Series 72. Statistical Research, Tucson.

Ciolek-Torrello, Richard
    2012   Hohokam Household Organization, Sedentism, and Irrigation in the Sonoran Desert, Arizona. In *Ancient Households of the Americas*, edited by John G. Douglass and Nancy Gonlin, pp. 221-268. University of Colorado Press, Boulder.

Ciolek-Torrello, Richard and Carl D. Halbirt
    1982   Technical Proposal for Archaeological Data Recovery Program at Site AZ V:4:6 (ASU), Confluence of Kinishba Wash and White River, Fort Apache Indian Reservation, Arizona. Submitted by Museum of Northern Arizona to White Mountain Apache Tribe. Ms. on file, Museum of Northern Arizona, Flagstaff.

Ciolek-Torrello, Richard, and J. Jefferson Reid
    1974   Change in Household Size at Grasshopper. *The Kiva* 40(1-2):39-47.

Ciolek-Torrello, Richard, Martha M. Callahan, and David H. Greenwald (editors)
    1988   *Hohokam Settlement Along the Slopes of the Picacho Mountains: The Brady Wash Sites*. Museum of Northern Arizona Research Paper No. 35(2). Museum of Northern Arizona, Flagstaff.

Ciolek-Torrello, Richard, Edgar K. Huber, and Robert B. Neily
    1999   *Investigations at Sunset Mesa Ruin: Archaeology at the Confluence of the Santa Cruz and Rillito Rivers, Tucson, Arizona* (with Edgar K. Huber and Robert B. Neily, editors). Technical Series 66. Statistical Research, Tucson.

Ciolek-Torrello, Richard, Eric E. Klucas and Rein Vanderpot
    2009   Summary and Conclusions: A Final Look at the Sycamore Creek Project. In *The State Route 87 - Sycamore Creek Project, Vol. 3. From the Desert to the Mountains: Archaeology of the Transition Zone*, pp. 315-331. Technical Series 73. Statistical Research, Inc., Tucson.

Ciolek-Torrello, Richard, Eric E. Klucas, and Stephanie M. Whittlesey
    2000   Hohokam Households, Settlement Structure, and Economy in the Lower Verde Valley. In *The Hohokam Village Revisited*, edited by David E. Doyel, Suzanne K. Fish, and Paul R. Fish, pp. 65-100. American Association for the Advancement of Science, Southwestern and Rocky Mountain Division, Fort Collins, Colorado.

Clark, Geoffrey A.
    1967   A Preliminary Analysis of Burial Clusters at the Grasshopper Site, East-Central Arizona. Unpublished Master's thesis, Department of Anthropology, University of Arizona, Tucson.

Clark, Jeffery J.
    1995   The Role of Migration in Social Change. In *The Roosevelt Development Study: New Perspectives on Tonto Basin Prehistory*, edited by Mark D. Elson, Miriam T. Stark, and David A. Gregory, pp. 369-384. Anthropological Papers No. 15. Center for Desert Archaeology, Tucson.

    2001   *Tracking Prehistoric Migrations: Pueblo Settlers Among the Tonto Basin Hohokam*. Anthropological Papers of the University of Arizona No. 65. The University of Arizona Press, Tucson.

    2004   Tracking Cultural Affiliation. In *Identity, Feasting, and the Archaeology of the Greater Southwest*, edited by Barbara J. Mills, pp. 42-73. University Press of Colorado, Boulder.

Clarke, Eleanor P.
    1933   Designs on the Prehistoric Pottery of Arizona. Unpublished Master's thesis, College of Letters, Arts and Sciences, University of Arizona, Tucson.

    1935   *Designs on the Prehistoric Pottery of Arizona*. University of Arizona Bulletin Vol. 6(4). Social Science Bulletin No. 9. University of Arizona, Tucson.

Clifford, James
   1994   Diasporas. *Cultural Anthropology* 9(3):302-338.

Cohen, Robin
   1997   *Global Diasporas: An Introduction*. University of Washington Press, Seattle.

Colton, Harold S.
   1955   *Check List of Southwestern Pottery Types*. Museum of Northern Arizona Ceramic Series No. 2. Northern Arizona Society of Science and Art, Flagstaff.

Colton, Harold S. (editor)
   1956   *Pottery Types of the Southwest*. Museum of Northern Arizona Ceramic Series No. 3C. Northern Arizona Society of Science and Art, Flagstaff.

Colton, Harold S., and Lyndon L. Hargrave
   1937   *Handbook of Northern Arizona Pottery Wares*. Museum of Northern Arizona Bulletin No. 11. Northern Arizona Society of Science and Art, Flagstaff.

Colwell-Chanthaphonh, Chip
   2005   The Incorporation of the Native American Past: Cultural Extermination, Archaeological Protection, and the Antiquities Act of 1906. *International Journal of Cultural Property* 12:375-391.

Connerton, Paul
   1989   *How Societies Remember*. Cambridge University Press, Cambridge.

Cosgrove, C.B.
   1932   *The Swartz Ruin, a Typical Mimbres Site in Southwest New Mexico*. Peabody Museum of Archaeology and Ethnology, Vol. XV, Cambridge, Massachusetts.

Creel, Darrell
   1989   A Primary Cremation at the NAN Ranch Ruin, with Comparative Data on Other Cremations in the Mimbres Area, New Mexico. *Journal of Field Archaeology* 16(3): 309-329.

Crown, Patricia L.
   1981a   Variability in Ceramic Manufacture at the Chodistaas Site, East-Central Arizona. PhD dissertation, Department of Anthropology, University of Arizona, Tucson. Proquest, Ann Arbor

   1981b   Analysis of the Las Colinas Ceramics. In *The 1968 Excavations at Mound 8, Las Colinas Ruins Group, Phoenix, Arizona*, edited by Laurens C. Hammack and Alan P. Sullivan, III, pp. 87-169. Arizona State Museum Archaeological Series No. 154. Arizona State Museum, Tucson.

   1994   *Ceramics and Ideology: Salado Polychrome Pottery*. University of New Mexico Press, Albuquerque.

Cummings, Byron S.
   1910   *The Ancient Inhabitants of the San Juan Valley*. University of Utah Bulletin Vol. 3(3, part 2). University of Utah, Salt Lake City.

   1931   Kinishba Ruin near Fort Apache, Arizona: A Preliminary Report on the First Season's Work, July 20 - Sept. 1. Arizona State Museum Archives, A-143.

   1932   Kinixba—the Brown House: Report of Progress on the Excavations Conducted in the Summer of 1932. Arizona State Museum Archives, A-413.

   1933   Archaeological Fieldwork in North America during 1932. *American Anthropologist* 35(3):486.

Cummings, Byron S., cont'd
- 1934 Report: Kinishba Ruin near Fort Apache, Arizona, Season of 1934. Arizona State Museum Archives, A-413.

- 1935a Archaeological Field Work in North America during 1934: Arizona. *American Antiquity* 1(1):50.

- 1935b Progress of the Excavation at Kinishba. *Kiva* 1(3):1-4.

- 1935c Report: Kinishba Ruins near Fort Apache, Arizona, October 19, 1935. Arizona State Museum Archives, A-143.

- 1938 Kinishba: The Brown House. *Kiva* 4(1):1-3.

- 1940 *Kinishba: A Prehistoric Pueblo of the Great Pueblo Period.* Hohokam Museums Association and the University of Arizona, Tucson.

- 1952 *Indians I Have Known.* Arizona Silhouettes, Tucson.

- 1953 *First Inhabitants of Arizona and the Southwest.* Cummings Publication Council, Tucson.

Cummings, Jeane and Malcom B. Cummings
- n.d. Nantani Yazzi, The Little Captain or The Dean of Kinishba. Manuscript biography on file, Special Collections and Archives, Cline Library, Northern Arizona University.

Cushing, Frank H.
- 1896 *Outlines of Zuni Creation Myths.* Thirteenth Annual Report of the Bureau of American Ethnology for the years 1891-1892, pp. 321-447. Washington, D.C: Smithsonian Institution.

- 1979 My Adventures at Zuñi. In *Zuñi: Selected Writings by Frank Hamilton Cushing*, edited by Jesse Green, pp. 46-134. University of Nebraska Press, Lincoln.

Danson, Edward B.
- 1957 Appendix G: Pottery Type Descriptions. In *Excavations 1940, at University Indian Ruin*, by Julian D. Hayden, pp. 219-231. Southwestern Monuments Association Technical Series Vol. 5. Gila Pueblo, Globe.

Danson, Edward B., and Roberts M. Wallace
- 1956 A Petrographic Study of Gila Polychrome. *American Antiquity* 22:180-183.

Dart, Allen
- 1997 Fabulous Finds Made at Q-Ranch Pueblo. *Old Pueblo Archaeology* 10:1, 5-7.

De Atley, Suzanne P.
- 1986 Mix and Match: Traditions of Glaze Paint Preparation at Four Mile Ruin, Arizona. In *Technology and Style*, edited by W. David Kingery and Esther Lense, pp. 297-329. Ceramics and technology, Vol. 2. American Ceramic Society, Columbus, Ohio.

Dietler, Michael
- 1996 Feasts and Commensal Politics in the Political Economy: Food, Power, and Status in Prehistoric Europe. In *Food and the Status Quest: An Interdisciplinary Perspective*, edited by Polly Wiessner and Wulf Schiefenhövel, pp. 87-125. Berghahn Books, Providence.

- 2001 Theorizing the Feast: Rituals of Consumption, Commensal Politics and Power in African Contexts. In *Feasts: Archaeological and Ethnographic Perspectives on Food, Politics, and Power*, edited by Michael Dietler and Brian Hayden, pp. 65-114. Smithsonian Institution Press, Washington, D.C.

Di Peso, Charles C.
  1958 *The Reeve Ruin of Southeastern Arizona: A Study of a Prehistoric Western Pueblo Migration into the Middle San Pedro Valley*. The Amerind Foundation No. 8. The Amerind Foundation, Inc., Dragoon.

Di Peso, Charles C., John B. Rinaldo, and Gloria J. Fenner
  1974 *Casas Grandes: A Fallen Trading Center of the Gran Chichimeca, vol. 8*. The Amerind Foundation No. 9. Amerind Foundation, Dragoon, and Northland Press, Flagstaff.

Dixon, Keith A.
  1956 The Archaeological Significance of Certain Unusual Pottery Shapes of the Prehistoric Southwest. Unpublished Ph.D. dissertation, Department of Anthropology, University of California, Los Angeles.

Dorsey, George A.
  1901 April 5 memo to the Field Museum Director, F.J.V. Skiff. On file White Mountain Apache Tribe Historic Preservation Office, Fort Apache.

  1903 *Indians of the Southwest*. Atchison, Topeka, and Santa Fe Railway System.

Doyel, David E.
  1974 *Excavations in the Escalante Ruin Group, Southern Arizona*. Arizona State Museum Archaeological Series No. 37. Arizona State Museum, University of Arizona, Tucson.

  1981 *Late Hohokam Prehistory in Southern Arizona*. Contributions to Archaeology 2. Gila Press, Scottsdale.

  1991 Hohokam Cultural Evolution in the Phoenix Basin. In *Exploring the Hohokam: Prehistoric Desert Peoples of the American Southwest*, edited by George J. Gumerman, pp. 231-278. Amerind Foundation New World Studies No. 1. University of New Mexico Press, Albuquerque.

Doyel, David E., and Joseph S. Crary
  1996 Regional Dynamics in the Lower Verde Area. In *The Bartlett Reservoir Cultural Resources Survey*, edited by Teresa L. Hoffman, pp. 85-109. Cultural Resources Report No. 92. Report submitted to Bureau of Reclamation, Phoenix Area Office. Archaeological Consulting Services, Tempe.

Duff, Andrew I. L.
  2002 *Western Pueblo Identities: Regional Interaction, Migration, and Transformation*. University of Arizona Press, Tucson.

Eckert, Suzanne L.
  2006 The Production and Distribution of Glaze-Painted Pottery in the Pueblo Southwest. In *The Social Life of Pots: Glaze Wares and Cultural Dynamics in the Southwest, AD 1250-1680*, edited by Judith A. Habicht-Mauche, Suzanne L. Eckert, and Deborah L. Huntley, pp. 34-59. University of Arizona Press, Tucson.

Eggan, Fred
  1950 *Social Organization of the Western Pueblos*. University of Chicago Press, Chicago.

Eighmy, Jeffrey L., and David E. Doyel
  1987 A Reanalysis of First Reported Archaeomagnetic Dates from the Hohokam Area, Southern Arizona. *Journal of Field Archaeology* 14(3):331-342.

Elson, Mark D.
  1992 Settlement, Subsistence, and Cultural Affiliation Within the Upper Tonto Basin. In *The Rye Creek Project: Archaeology in the Upper Tonto Basin, Volume 3: Synthesis and Conclusions*, edited by Mark D. Elson and Douglas B. Craig, pp. 119-153. Anthropological Papers No. 11. Center for Desert Archaeology, Tucson.

Elson, Mark D., and Michael Lindeman
- 1994 The Eagle Ridge Site, AZ V:5:104/1045 (ASM/TNF). In *Introduction and Small Sites*, by Mark D. Elson and Deborah L. Swartz, pp. 23-116. The Roosevelt Community Development Study. Anthropological Papers No. 13, Vol. 1. Center for Desert Archaeology, Tucson.

Eriacho, Donald
- 1995 Pueblo of Zuni Statement of Cultural Affiliation with Prehistoric and Historic Cultures, 11 July 1995. On file Repatriation Program, Arizona State Museum, Tucson.

- 1997 7 November letter from Governor of the Pueblo of Zuni, to Raymond Thompson, Director of the Arizona State Museum. On file Repatriation Program, Arizona State Museum, Tucson.

Ezzo, Joseph A.
- 1991 Dietary Change at Grasshopper Pueblo: The Evidence from Bone Chemistry Analysis. Ph.D. dissertation, Department of Anthropology, University of Wisconsin, Madison. ProQuest, Ann Arbor.

- 1992 Dietary Change and Variability at Grasshopper Pueblo, Arizona. *Journal of Anthropological Archaeology* 11:219 289.

- 1993 *Human Adaptation at Grasshopper Pueblo, Arizona: Social and Ecological Perspectives*. International Monographs in Prehistory, Archaeological Series 4, Ann Arbor.

- 1994 Paleonutrition at Grasshopper Pueblo, Arizona. In *The Diet and Health of Prehistoric Americans, Center for Archaeological Investigations Occasional Paper 22*, edited by K. D. Sobolik, pp. 265 279. Southern Illinois University, Carbondale.

Ezzo, Joseph A., Clark M. Johnson, and T. Douglas Price
- 1997 Analytical Perspectives on Prehistoric Migration: A Case Study from East-Central Arizona. *Journal of Archaeological Science* 24:447-466.

Ezzo, Joseph A., and T. Douglas Price
- 2002 Migration, Regional Reorganization, and Spatial Group Composition at Grasshopper Pueblo, Arizona. *Journal of Archaeological Science* 29:499-520.

Fagan, Brian
- 1995 The Arrogant Archaeologist. In *Archaeological Ethics*, edited by Karen Vitelli, pp. 238-243. Alta Mira Press, Walnut Creek.

Fenn, Thomas R., Barbara J. Mills, and Maren Hopkins
- 2006 The Social Contexts of Glaze Paint Ceramic Production and Consumption in the Silver Creek Area. In The *Social Life of Pots*, edited by Judith A, Habicht-Mauche and Suzanne L. Eckert, and Deborah L. Huntley, pp. 60-85. University of Arizona Press, Tucson.

Fenton, Todd William
- 1998 Dental Conditions at Grasshopper Pueblo: Evidence for Dietary Change and Increased Stress. Unpublished Ph.D. dissertation, Department of Anthropology, University of Arizona, Tucson.

Ferguson, T. J.
- 1996 Native Americans and the Practice of Archaeology. *Annual Review of Anthropology* 25:63-79.

Ferguson, T. J., and Roger Anyon
- 2001 Hopi and Zuni Cultural Landscapes: Implications of History and Scale for Cultural Resources Management. In *Native Peoples of the Southwest, Negotiating Land, Water, and Ethnicities*, edited by Laurie Weinstein, pp. 99-122. Bergin and Garvey, Westport, Connecticut.

Ferguson, T. J., and E. Richard Hart
  1985 *A Zuni Atlas*. University of Oklahoma Press, Norman.

Fish, Paul R., and Suzanne K. Fish
  1977 *Verde Valley Archaeology: Review and Perspective*. Research Paper No. 8. Museum of Northern Arizona, Flagstaff.

  1984 Directions in Verde Valley Archaeology. In *Research Issues in the Prehistory of Central Arizona: The Central Arizona Water Canal Study*, Vol. I, edited by G.E. Rice and R. Most, pp. 41-54. Office of Cultural Resource Management, Arizona State University, Tempe.

Fish, Paul R., Peter J. Pilles, Jr,, and Suzanne K. Fish
  1980 Colonies, Traders, and Traits: The Hohokam in the North. In *Current Issues in Hohokam Prehistory: Proceedings of a Symposium*, edited by D.E. Doyel and F. Plog, pp. 151-175. Anthropological Research Papers No. 23, Arizona State University, Tempe.

Fort Apache Scout
  1993a 'Hopis Claim Ancient Kinship to Apache Land.' *Fort Apache Scout* 32(7):1, 8.

  1993b 'Who Says Apaches Haven't Been Here Forever?' *Fort Apache Scout* 32(7):9.

Franklin, Hayward Hoskins
  1980 *Excavations at Second Canyon Ruin, San Pedro Valley, Arizona*. Arizona State Museum Contribution to Highway Salvage Archaeology No. 60. Arizona State Museum, University of Arizona, Tucson.

Gabel, Norman
  1931 Martinez Hill Ruins: An Example of Prehistoric Culture of the Middle Gila. Unpublished Master's thesis, College of Letters, Arts, and Sciences, University of Arizona, Tucson.

Garraty, Christopher P., Mitchell A. Keur, Joseph T. Hefner, Lorrie Lincoln-Babb, and Penny Dufoe Minturn
  2010 Human Remains and Mortuary Practices at the Mescal Wash Site. Manuscript on file at Statistical Research, Inc. Tucson, Arizona.

Geib, Phil R., and Bruce B. Huckell
  1994 Evidence of Late Preceramic Agriculture at Cibecue, East central Arizona. *Kiva* 59:433 454.

Gerald, M. Virginia
  1957 Two Great Kivas at Point of Pines Ruin. Unpublished M.A. thesis, Department of Anthropology, University of Arizona, Tucson.

Gerald, Rex E.
  1958 Davis Ranch Site (ARIZ:BB:11:7[AF]). Manuscript on file, Amerind Foundation, Dragoon.

Giddens, Anthony
  1979 *Central Problems in Social Theory: Action, Structure, and Contradiction in Social Analysis*. Macmillan, London.

Gifford, James C.
  1980 *Archaeological Explorations in Caves of the Point of Pines Region, Arizona*. Anthropological Papers of the University of Arizona No. 36. University of Arizona Press, Tucson.

Gilroy, Paul
  1997 Diaspora and the Detours of Identity. In *Identity and Difference*, edited by Kathryn Woodward, pp. 299-343. Sage, London.

Gladwin, Harold S.
　1928　*Excavations at Casa Grande, Arizona, February 12 - May 1, 1927*. Southwest Museum Papers No. 2. Southwest Museum, Los Angeles.

Gladwin, Winifred, and Harold S. Gladwin
　1929　*The Red-on-buff Culture of the Gila Basin*. Medallion Papers No. 3. Pasadena.

　1930　*Some Southwestern Pottery Types: Series I*. Medallion Papers No. 8. Gila Pueblo, Globe, Arizona.

　1931　*Some Southwestern Pottery Types: Series II*. Medallion Papers No. 10. Gila Pueblo, Globe, Arizona.

　1934　*A Method for the Designation of Cultures and Their Variations*. Medallion Papers No. 15. Gila Pueblo, Globe, Arizona.

　1935　*The Eastern Range of the Red-on-buff Culture*. Medallion Papers No. 16. Gila Pueblo, Globe, Arizona.

Glascock, Michael D.
　1992　Characterization of Archaeological Ceramics at MURR by Neutron Activation Analysis and Multivariate Statistics. In *Chemical Characterization of Ceramic Pastes in Archaeology*, edited by H. Neff, pp. 11-26. Monographs in World Archaeology No. 7. Prehistory Press, Madison, Wisconsin.

Goldstein, Lynne
　2001　Ancient Southwest Mortuary Practices: Perspectives from Outside the Southwest. In *Ancient Burial Practices in the American Southwest*, edited by Douglas R. Mitchell and Judy L. Brunson-Hadley, pp. 249-253. University of New Mexico Press, Albuquerque.

Goodwin, Grenville
　1942　*The Social Organization of the Western Apache*. University of Chicago Press, Chicago.

　1994　*Myths and Tales of the White Mountain Apache*. Originally published 1939, University of Arizona Press, Tucson.

Graves, Michael W.
　1982　Apache Adaptation to the Mountains. In *Cholla Project Archaeology, Volume 3: The Q Ranch Region*, edited by J. Jefferson Reid, pp. 193-215. Arizona State Museum Archaeological Series 161. Tucson.

Graves, Michael W., Sally J. Holbrook, and William A. Longacre
　1982　Aggregation and Abandonment at Grasshopper Pueblo: Evolutionary Trends in the Late Prehistory of East-Central Arizona. In *Multidisciplinary Research at Grasshopper Pueblo, Arizona*, edited by W.A. Longacre, S.J. Holbrook and M.W. Graves, pp. 110-121. Anthropological Papers of the University of Arizona, University of Arizona Press, Tucson.

Graves, William M., and Suzanne L. Eckert
　1998　Decorated Ceramic Distributions and Ideological Developments in the Northern and Central Rio Grande Valley, New Mexico. In *Migration and Reorganization: The Pueblo IV Period in the American Southwest*, edited by Katherine A. Spielmann, pp. 263-283. Arizona State University Anthropological Research Papers No. 51. Arizona State University, Tempe.

Greenwald, David and Richard Ciolek-Torrello
　1987　Picacho Pass Site, NA18,030. In *The Picacho Area Sites*, edited by Richard Ciolek-Torrello, pp. 130-216. Hohokam Settlement along the Slopes of the Picacho Mountains: Tucson Aqueduct Project, vol. 3. Research Paper 35. Museum of Northern Arizona, Flagstaff.

Greenwood, N. H., and C. W. White
  1970   Mogollon Ritual, A Spatial Configuration of a Non-Village Pattern. *Archaeology* 25(4):298-301.

Gregory, David A.
  n.d.   Field notes and site descriptions for cultural heritage damage assessment surveys conducted as part of the Burned Area Emergency Rehabilitation program for the 2002 Rodeo-Chediski Fire. White Mountain Apache Tribe Historic Preservation Office, Fort Apache, Arizona.

  1981   Western Apache Archaeology: Problems and Approaches. In *The Protohistoric Period in the North American Southwest*, AD 1450 - 1700, edited by David R. Wilcox and W. Bruce Masse, pp. 257-274. Arizona State University, Anthropological Papers No. 24. Tempe.

  1995   Prehistoric Settlement Patterns in the Eastern Tonto Basin. In *The Roosevelt Community Development Study, New Perspectives on Tonto Basin Prehistory*, edited by M. D. Elson, M. T. Stark, and D. A. Gregory, pp. 127-184. Anthropological Papers No. 15. Center for Desert Archaeology, Tucson.

  2004   Plan view map of Kinishba Museum ruins. On file, White Mountain Apache Tribe Historic Preservation Office, Fort Apache, Arizona.

Gregory, David A., and David R. Wilcox (editors)
  2007   *Zuni Origins: Toward a New Synthesis of Southwestern Archaeology*. University of Arizona Press, Tucson.

Griffin, P. Bion
  1969   Late Mogollon Readaptation in East Central Arizona. Ph.D. dissertation, Department of Anthropology, University of Arizona, Tucson.

Guenther, Linda Young
  1937   Gila Polychromes: The Origin and Development of Polychrome Pottery in the Gila River Drainage Area. Unpublished Master's thesis, Department of Archaeology, University of Arizona, Tucson.

Haas, Jonathan
  1971   The Ushklish Ruin: A Preliminary Report on Excavation of a Colonial Hohokam Period Site in the Lower Tonto Basin, Central Arizona. Ms. on file, Arizona State Museum, University of Arizona, Tucson.

Hagenbuckle, Kristin A.
  2000   Ritual and the Individual: An Analysis of Cibicue Painted Corrugated Pottery from Grasshopper Pueblo, Arizona. Master's thesis, Department of Anthropology, University of Arizona, Tucson. Proquest, Ann Arbor.

Halbirt, Carl D.
  1983   Final Research Design for an Archaeological Data Recovery Program for Two Mogollon Sites at the Confluence of Kinishba Wash and White River, Fort Apache Indian Reservation, Arizona, Ms. on file, Museum of Northern Arizona, Flagstaff.

  1984   Bo bi laa Village: A Forestdale Phase Mogollon Pit House Site Near Fort Apache, Arizona. Paper presented at the Third Mogollon Conference, Las Cruces, New Mexico.

Halbirt, Carl D., and Richard Ciolek-Torrello
  1985   Changing Interactions in the Northern Mogollon Region Prior to A.D. 1000. Paper presented at the 50th Annual Meeting of the Society for American Archaeology, Denver.

Halbirt, Carl D., and Steven G. Dosh
  1986   The Late Mogollon Pit House Occupation of the White River Region, Gila and Navajo Counties, Arizona. Draft Final Report on file, Museum of Northern Arizona, Flagstaff.

Hall, Edward T.
　1968　Proxemics. *Current Anthropology* 9:83-103.

Hall, Stuart
　1990　Cultural Identity and Diaspora. In *Identity: Community, Culture, Difference*, edited by Jonathan Rutherford, pp. 222-237. Lawrence and Wishart, London.

Harbottle, Garman
　1976　Activation Analysis in Archaeology. *Radiochemistry, Specialist Periodical Reports* 3:33-72.

Harlow, Francis H.
　1968　Fourteenth Century Painted Pottery from near Cliff, New Mexico. Manuscript on file, Office of Archaeological Studies, Museum of New Mexico, Santa Fe.

Harris, Rachel M.
　2009　Collecting, Protecting, and Sharing the Past: The History of the Terrence and Jean Reidhead Collection. Unpublished Undergraduate honors thesis, Department of Anthropology, Brigham Young University, Provo.

Hartman, Dana
　1986　Human Remains from the Pit House Villages. In *The Late Mogollon Pit House Occupation of the White River Region, Gila and Navajo Counties, Arizona*, edited by C. D. Halbirt and S. G. Dosh, pp. 247-265. Draft Final Report on file, Museum of Northern Arizona, Flagstaff.

Haury, Emil W.
　1930　A Sequence of Decorated Redware from the Silver Creek Drainage. *Museum of Northern Arizona, Museum Notes*, Vol. 2, No. 11, Flagstaff, Ariz.

　1931　Showlow and Pinedale Ruins. In *Recently Dated Pueblo Ruins in Arizona*, by Emil Haury W. and Lyndon L. Hargrave, pp. 4-79. Smithsonian Miscellaneous Collections Vol. 82(11). Smithsonian Institution, Washington, D.C.

　1932　*Roosevelt:9:6, A Hohokam Site of the Colonial Period*. Medallion Papers 9, Gila Pueblo, Globe, Arizona.

　1934　*The Canyon Creek Ruin and the Cliff Dwellings of the Sierra Ancha*. Medallion Papers No. 14. Gila Pueblo, Globe, Arizona.

　1936　*The Mogollon Culture of Southwestern New Mexico*. Medallion Papers 20, Globe, Arizona.

　1940　*Excavations in the Forestdale Valley, East-Central Arizona*. Social Sciences Bulletin 12. University of Arizona Bulletin 11(4). Tucson.

　1945　*The Excavation of Los Muertos and Neighboring Ruins in the Salt River Valley, Southern Arizona, Based on the Work of the Hemenway Southwestern Archaeological Expedition of 1887-1888*. Papers of the Peabody Museum of American Archaeology and Ethnology Vol. 24(1). Harvard University, Cambridge.

　1950　A Sequence of Great Kivas in the Forestdale Valley, Arizona. In *For the Dean*, edited By Erik K. Reed and Dale S. King, pp. 29-39. Hohokam Museum Association and Southwestern Monuments Association. Tucson and Santa Fe.

　1957　An Alluvial Site on the San Carlos Indian Reservation, Arizona. *American Antiquity* 23(1): 2-27.

　1958　Evidence at Point of Pines for a Prehistoric Migration from Northern Arizona. In *Migrations in New*

World Culture History, edited by Raymond H. Thompson, pp. 1-8. University of Arizona Bulletin 29(2); Social Science Bulletin 27. University of Arizona Press, Tucson.

1962   HH-39: Recollections of a Dramatic Moment in Southwestern Archaeology. *Tree-Ring Bulletin* 24(3-4):ll-14.

1976   *The Hohokam: Desert Farmers and Craftsmen, Excavations at Snaketown*, 1964-1965. The University of Arizona Press, Tucson.

1985   *Mogollon Culture in the Forestdale Valley, East-Central Arizona*. The University of Arizona Press, Tucson.

1986   Correspondence with Richard Woodbury. Shaeffer papers, Kinishba files, Arizona State Museum Archives, University of Arizona, Tucson.

1989   *Point of Pines, Arizona: A History of the University of Arizona Archaeological Field School*. University of Arizona Anthropological Papers No. 50. University of Arizona Press, Tucson.

Haury, Emil W., and E.B. Sayles
1947   *An Early Pit House Village of the Mogollon Culture, Forestdale Valley, Arizona*. University of Arizona Bulletin 18(4). Social Science Bulletin 16, Tucson.

Haury, Emil W., and Lyndon L. Hargrave
1931   *Recently Dated Pueblo Ruins in Arizona*. Smithsonian Miscellaneous Collections 82(11).

Hammack, Laurens C.
1969   Highway Salvage Archaeology in the Forestdale Valley, Arizona. *The Kiva* 34(2-3):58-89.

Hawley, Florence M.
1928   Pottery and Culture Relations in the Middle Gila. Unpublished Master's thesis, College of Letters, Arts and Sciences, University of Arizona, Tucson.

Hayden, Brian
1996   Feasting in Prehistoric and Traditional Societies. In *Food and the Status Quest: An Interdisciplinary Perspective*, edited by Polly Wiessner and Wulf Schiefenhövel, pp. 127-147. Berghahn Books, Providence.

2001   Fabulous Feasts: A Prolegomenon to the Importance of Feasting. In *Feasts: Archaeological and Ethnographic Perspectives on Food, Politics, and Power*, edited by Michael Dietler and Brian Hayden, pp. 23-64. Smithsonian Institution Press, Washington, D.C.

Hays, Kelley Ann
1991   Ceramics. In *Homol'ovi II: Archaeology of An Ancestral Hopi Village, Arizona*, edited by E. Charles Adams and Kelley Ann Hays, pp. 23-48. Anthropological Papers of the University of Arizona No. 55. University of Arizona Press, Tucson.

1994   Kachina Depictions on Prehistoric Pueblo Pottery. In *Kachinas in the Pueblo World*, edited by Polly Schafsmaa, pp. 47-62. University of New Mexico Press, Albuquerque.

Hays-Gilpin, Kelley Ann
2006   Icons and Ethnicity: Hopi Painted Pottery and Murals. In *Religion in the Prehispanic Southwest*, edited by C. S. VanPool, T. L. VanPool, and D. A. Phillips, Jr., pp. 67-80. AltaMira Press, Lanham, Maryland.

2008   Sikyatki Style: Origins, Iconography, Cross-media Comparisons, and Organization of Production. Paper presented at the Amerind Foundation Advanced Seminar of Jeddito Yellow Ware. Amerind Foundation, Dragoon.

Hays-Gilpin, Kelley Ann (compiler)
   2009   Notes of the Museum of Northern Arizona Southwestern Ceramic Seminar on Jeddito Yellow Ware. Manuscript on file, Museum of Northern Arizona, Flagstaff.

Heidke, James M.
   1995   Overview of the Ceramic Collection. In *The Roosevelt Community Development Study: Ceramic Chronology, Technology, and Economics*, Vol.2, edited by James M. Heidke and Miriam T. Stark, pp.6-18. Anthropological Papers No. 14. Center for Desert Archaeology, Tucson.

Heidke, James M. and Miriam T. Stark (editors)
   1995   *The Roosevelt Community Development Study: Ceramic Chronology, Technology, and Economics*, Vol.2. Anthropological Papers No. 14. Center for Desert Archaeology, Tucson.

Henderson, T. Kathleen, and Richard J. Martynec (editors)
   1993   *Classic Period Occupation on the Santa Cruz Flats: The Santa Cruz Flats Archaeological Project*. Northland Research, Inc., Flagstaff.

Herr, Sarah A.
   2001   *Beyond Chaco: Great Kiva Communities on the Mogollon Rim Frontier*. Anthropological Papers of the University of Arizona 66. University of Arizona Press, Tucson.

Herr, Sarah A., Elizabeth M. Perry, and Scott Van Keuren
   1999   Excavations at Three Great Kiva Sites. In *Living on the Edge of the Rim: Excavations and Analysis of the Silver Creek Archaeological Research Project 1993-1998*, edited by B. J. Mills, S. A. Herr, and S. Van Keuren, pp. 53-115. Archaeological Series No. 192, Vol. 1. Arizona State Museum, University of Arizona, Tucson.

Herr, Sarah A., Chris North, and J. Scott Wood
   2009   Scouting for Apache Archaeology in the Sub-Mogollon Rim Region. *Kiva* 75(1):35-62.

Hill, J. Brett Hill, Jeffery J. Clark, William H. Doelle, Patrick D. Lyons
   2004   Prehistoric Demography in the Southwest: Migration, Coalescence, and Hohokam Population Decline. *American Antiquity* 69:689-716.

Hill, David V.
   1998   Petrographic Analysis for Ceramics from the Ormand Site. In *The Ormand Village: Final Report on the 1965-1966 Excavation*, by Laurel T. Wallace, pp. 287-290. Archaeology Notes No. 229. Office of Archaeological Studies, Museum of New Mexico, Santa Fe.

Hill, James N.
   1970   Broken K Pueblo: Prehistoric Social Organization in the American Southwest. *Anthropological Papers of the University of Arizona* No. 18. University of Arizona Press, Tucson.

Hillier, Bill and Julienne Hanson
   1984   *The Social Logic of Space*. Cambridge University Press, London.

Hinkes, Madeleine Joyce
   1983   *Skeletal Evidence of Stress in Subadults: Trying to Come of Age at Grasshopper Pueblo*. Ph.D. dissertation, Department of Anthropology, University of Arizona, Tucson.

Hobsbawm, Eric
   1983   Introduction: Inventing Traditions. In *The Invention of Tradition*, edited by Eric Hobsbawm and Terence Ranger, pp. 1-14. Cambridge University Press, Cambridge.

Hoerig, Karl A.
    2010   From Third Person to First: A Call for Reciprocity Among Non-Native and Native Museums. *Museum Anthropology* 33(1):62-74.

Hoffman, C. Marshall
    1992   Archaeological Data Recovery Investigations at the Diamond Creek Site, AZ W:1:18 (ASM), White Mountain Apache Tribal Lands, Arizona. Prepared for the U.S. Indian Health Services, Whiteriver, Arizona, by Archaeological Research Services, Inc., Tempe, Arizona.

Hohmann, John W.
    2004   The Archaeology of Q-Ranch Pueblo. Paper Presented at the 13th Mogollon Archaeology Conference, Silver City, NM, September 30-October 2, 2004.

Hopi Tribe
    1994   Hopi Tribal Council Resolution H-70-94. The Hopi Tribe, Kykotsmovi, Arizona. On file Cultural Preservation Office, Kykotsmovi, Arizona.

Horn, William
    1988   April 22 memo from Assistant Secretary of the Interior for Fish, Wildlife and Parks. On file White Mountain Apache Tribe Historic Preservation Office, Fort Apache.

Hough, Walter
    1903   Archeological Field Work in Northeastern Arizona: The Museum-Gates Expedition of 1901. In *Annual Report of the U.S. National Museum for 1901*, pp. 279-358. Government Printing Office, Washington, D.C.

    1907   *Antiquities of the Upper Gila and Salt River Valleys in Arizona and New Mexico*. Bulletin 35, Bureau of American Ethnology. Smithsonian Institution, Washington, D.C.

    1923   Pit Dwellings and Square Kivas of the Upper San Francisco Ruins. *El Palacio* 15(1). Santa Fe, New Mexico.

    1930   Exploration of Ruins in the White Mountain Apache Indian Reservation, Arizona. *Proceedings of the United States National Museum* Vol. 78(13):1-21. Smithsonian Institution, Washington, D.C.

Howard, Jerry B.
    1985   Courtyard Groups and Domestic Cycling: A Hypothetical Model of Growth. In *Proceedings of the 1983 Hohokam Symposium*, pt. 1, edited by Alfred E. Dittert, Jr. and Donald E. Dove, pp. 311-326. Occasional Paper No. 2. Arizona Archaeological Society, Phoenix.

Huntington, Frederick W.
    1986   Household and Community Organization. In *Archaeological Investigations at the West Branch Site: Early and Middle Rincon Occupation in the Southern Tucson Basin*, by F. W. Huntington, pp. 79-125. Anthropological Papers No. 5. Institute for American -Research, Tucson.

Inomata, Takeshi, Daniela Triadan, Erick Ponciano, Estela Pinto, Richard E. Terry, and Markus Eberl
    2002   Domestic and Political Lives of Classic Maya Elites: The Excavation of Rapidly Abandoned Structures at Aguateca, Guatemala. *Latin American Antiquity* 13(3):305-330.

Jameson, James H.
    1997   Presenting Archaeology to the Public: Digging for Truths. AltaMira Press, Walnut Creek, CA.

Jones, David
    1935   Progress of the Excavation at Kinishba. *The Kiva* 1(3):1-4.

Kaldahl, Eric J., Scott Van Keuren, and Barbara J. Mills
    2004   Migration, Factionalism, and the Trajectories of Pueblo IV Period Clusters in the Mogollon Rim Region. In *The Protohistoric Pueblo World, A.D. 1275-1600*, edited by E. Charles Adams and Andrew I. Duff, pp. 85-107. University of Arizona Press, Tucson.

Keller, Donald R.
    1984   Archaeological Survey of 1.4 mi of Sewer Trunk Line Alignment, Fort Apache, Navajo County, Arizona. Ms. on file, Museum of Northern Arizona, Flagstaff.

Kent, Susan (editor)
    1990   *Domestic Architecture and the Use of Space: An Interdisciplinary Cross-Cultural Study*. Cambridge University Press, Cambridge.

Kessell, William B.
    1974   The Battle of Cibecue and Its Aftermath: A White Mountain Apache's Account. *Ethnohistory* 21(2): 123-134.

Kidder, Alfred V.
    1915   *Pottery of the Pajarito Plateau and of Some Adjacent Regions in New Mexico*. Memoirs of the American Anthropological Association 2(6):407-462.

    1927   The Southwestern Archaeological Conference. *Science* 66:489 491.

Kidder, M. A., and Alfred V. Kidder
    1917   Notes on the Pottery of Pecos. *American Anthropologist* 19(3):325-360.

Kidder, Alfred V., and Samuel J. Guernsey
    1919   *Archeological Explorations in Northeastern Arizona*. Bureau of American Ethnology Bulletin 65. Government Printing Office, Washington D.C.

Kingsolver, Barbara
    1990   *Animal Dreams*. Harper Collins, New York.

Klucas, Eric E., Richard Ciolek-Torrello, and Charles R. Riggs
    1998   Site Structure and Domestic Organization. In *Vanishing River: Landscapes and Lives of the Lower Verde Valley: The Lower Verde Archaeological Project: Overview, Synthesis, and Conclusions*, edited by Stephanie M. Whittlesey, Richard Ciolek-Torrello, and Jeffrey H. Altschul, pp. 491-530. SRI Press, Tucson.

Kroeber, A. L.
    1917   *Zuni Kin and Clan*. Anthropological Papers of the American Museum of Natural History 18(2):39-205.

Kowalewski, Stephen A.
    2008   Regional Settlement Pattern Studies. *Journal of Archaeological Research* 16:225-285.

Kuwanwisiwma, Leigh, and T. J. Ferguson
    2004   *Ang Kuktota*, Hopi Ancestral Sites and Cultural Landscapes (with Leigh J. Kuwanwisiwma). *Expedition* 46(2):24-29.

Ladd, Edmund
    1979   Zuni Social and Political Organization. In *Handbook of the North American Indians, Vol. 9*. Alfonso Ortiz, ed., pp. 482-491. Washington: Smithsonian Institution.

Laluk, Nicholas, and Mark Altaha
  2004 Kinishba Boundary Study Cultural Heritage Resource Survey. Report prepared for National Park Service. On File, White Mountain Apache Tribe Historic Preservation Office, Fort Apache, Arizona.

LaMotta, Vincent M.
  2006 Zooarchaeology and Chronology of Homol'ovi I and Other Pueblo IV Period Sites in the Central Little Colorado River Valley, Northern Arizona. Ph.D. dissertation, Department of Anthropology, University of Arizona, Tucson. Proquest, Ann Arbor.

Lange, Richard C.
  1982 Steatite: An Analysis and Assessment of Form and Distribution. In *Cholla Project Archaeology, Volume 1: Introduction and Special Studies*, edited by J. J. Reid, pp. 167-192. Arizona State Museum Archaeological Series No. 161. University of Arizona, Tucson.

Lange, Richard C. (editor)
  2006 *Echoes in the Canyons: The Archaeology of the Southeastern Sierra Ancha, Central Arizona.* Arizona State Museum Archaeological Series No.198. Arizona State Museum, Tucson.

Lange, Charles H., Carroll L. Riley
  1970 *The Southwestern Journals of Adolph F. Bandelier, 1883-1884.* University of New Mexico Press, Albuquerque,

Lemonnier, Pierre
  1986 The study of material culture today: Toward an anthropology of technical systems. *Journal of Anthropological Archaeology* 5:147-186.

Lemonnier, Pierre (editor)
  1993 *Technological Choices: Transformations in Material Culture since the Neolithic.* Routledge, London.

Lightfoot, Kent G.
  1984 The Duncan Project: A Study of the Occupation Duration and Settlement Pattern of an Early Mogollon Pithouse Village. Anthropological Field Studies No. 6. Office of Cultural Resource Management, Department of Anthropology, Arizona State University.

Lightfoot, Ricky R.
  1993 Abandonment Processes in Prehistoric Pueblos. In *Abandonment of Settlements and Regions: Ethnoarchaeological and Archaeological Approaches*, edited by Catherine M. Cameron and Steve A. Tomka, pp. 165-177. Cambridge University Press, Cambridge.

Lindsay, Alexander J., Jr.
  1986 Late 13th-Century Pit House and Pueblo Occupations at the Point of Pines Ruin, Arizona. Paper presented at the 51st Annual Meeting of the Society for American Archaeology, New Orleans.

  1987 Anasazi Population Movements to Southeastern Arizona. *American Archaeology* 6(3):190-198.

  1992 Tucson Polychrome: History, Dating, Distribution and Design. In *Proceedings of the Second Salado Conference*, edited by Richard C. Lange and Stephen Germick, pp. 230-237. Arizona Archaeological Society, Phoenix.

Lindsay, Alexander J., Jr., J. Richard Ambler, Mary Anne Stein, and Philip M. Hobler
  1968 *Survey and Excavations North and East of Navajo Mountain, Utah, 1959-1962.* Museum of Northern Arizona Bulletin No. 45. Glen Canyon Series No. 8. Northern Arizona Society of Science and Art, Inc., Flagstaff.

Lindsay, Alexander J., Jr., and Calvin H. Jennings (compilers)
　1968　*Salado Red Ware Conference: Ninth Southwestern Ceramic Seminar, October 13-14, 1967*. Museum of Northern Arizona Ceramic Series No. 4. Northern Arizona Society of Science and Art, Flagstaff.

Lipe, William D.
　1974　A Conservation Model for American Archaeology. *Kiva* 39:213-245.

Little, Barbara J.
　2002　*Public Benefits of Archaeology*. University Press of Florida, Gainesville.

Longacre, William A.
　1975　Population Dynamics at the Grasshopper Pueblo, Arizona. In *Population Studies in Archaeology and Biological Anthropology: A Symposium*, edited by A.C. Swedland, pp. 71-74. Memoir 30, Society for American Archaeology.

Longacre, William A., and James Ayres
　1968　Archaeological Lessons from an Apache Wickiup. In *New Perspectives in Archaeology*, edited by Sally R. Binford and Louis R. Binford, pp. 151-159. Aldine Press, Chicago.

Longacre, William A., Sally J. Holbrook, Michael W. Graves (editors)
　1982　*Multidisciplinary Research at Grasshopper Pueblo, Arizona*. Anthropological Papers of the University of Arizona, University of Arizona Press, Tucson.

Longacre, William A., and J. Jefferson Reid
　1971　Research Strategy for Locational Analysis: An Outline. In *The Distribution of Prehistoric Population Aggregates*, edited by George J. Gumerman, pp. 103-110. Prescott College Anthropological Reports No. 1, Prescott, Arizona.

　1976　*Arizona's Natural Environment: Landscapes and Habitats*. University of Arizona Press, Tucson.

Lowell, Julie C.
　1991　*Prehistoric Households at Turkey Creek, Arizona*. Anthropological Papers of the University of Arizona No. 54. University of Arizona Press, Tucson.

Lupe, Ronnie
　1993a　'Chairman's Corner: A View of these Ancient Apache Artifacts Brought me in Touch with My Apacheness', *Fort Apache Scout*, 29 October 1993.

　1993b　15 April letter to Lynn Teague, Arizona State Museum, University of Arizona. On file Repatriation Program, Arizona State Museum, Tucson.

　1994　16 March letter to Raymond H. Thompson, Director, Arizona State Museum, University of Arizona. On file Repatriation Program, Arizona State Museum, Tucson.

　1995　2 June Letter to Raymond H. Thompson, Director, Arizona State Museum, University of Arizona. On file Repatriation Program, Arizona State Museum, Tucson.

Lynott, Mark J., and Alison Wylie (editors)
　1995　*Ethics in American Archaeology: Challenges for the 1990s*. Society for American Archaeology, Washington, D.C.

Lyons, Patrick D.
　2003　*Ancestral Hopi Migrations*. Anthropological Papers of the University of Arizona No. 68. University of Arizona Press, Tucson.

2004a Cliff Polychrome. *Kiva* 69(4):361-400.

2004b Ceramics. In *Ancient Farmers of the Safford Basin: Archaeology of the U.S. 70 Safford-to-Thatcher Project*, edited by Jeffery J. Clark, pp. 95-126. Anthropological Papers No. 39. Center for Desert Archaeology, Tucson.

2012 Ceramic Typology, Chronology, Production, and Circulation. In *Migrants and Mounds: Classic Period Archaeology of the Lower San Pedro Valley*, edited by Jeffery J. Clark and Patrick D. Lyons. pp. 211-308 Anthropological Papers No. 45. Center for Desert Archaeology, Tucson.

Lyons, Patrick D., and Jeffery J. Clark
2012 A Community of Practice in Diaspora: The Rise and Demise of Roosevelt Red Ware. In *Potters and Communities of Practice: Glaze Paint and Polychrome Pottery in the American Southwest A.D. 1200–1700*, edited by Linda S. Cordell and Judith Habicht-Mauche, pp.19-33. University of Arizona Press, Tucson.

Lyons, Patrick D., Jeffery J. Clark, and J. Brett Hill
2011 Ancient Social Boundaries Inscribed on the Landscape of the Lower San Pedro Valley. In *Contemporary Archaeologies of the Southwest*, edited by William H. Walker and Kathryn Venzor, pp. 175-196. University Press of Colorado, Boulder.

Lyons, Patrick D., J. Brett Hill, and Jeffery J. Clark
2008 Demography, Agricultural Potential, and Identity among Ancient Immigrants. In *The Social Construction of Communities: Agency, Structure, and Identity in the Prehispanic Southwest*, edited by Mark Varien and James M. Potter, pp. 191-213. AltaMira Press, Lanham, MD.

2011 Irrigation Communities and Communities in Diaspora. In *Movement, Connectivity, and Landscape Change in the Ancient Southwest*, edited by Margaret C. Nelson and Colleen Strawhacker, pp. 375-401. University Press of Colorado, Boulder.

Lyons, Patrick D., and Alexander J. Lindsay, Jr.
2006 Perforated Plates and the Salado Phenomenon. *Kiva* 72:5-54.

Lyons, Patrick D., and Anna A. Neuzil
2006 Research on the Mills Collection. *Archaeology Southwest* 20(2):17.

Mabry, Jonathan B.
1998 *Paleoindian and Archaic Sites in Arizona*. State Historic Preservation Office, Arizona State Parks, Phoenix.

Manners, Robert A., and David Kaplan
1968 *Theory in Anthropology: A Source-book*. Aldine Publishing Company, Chicago.

Martin, Paul S.
1940 The SU Site: Excavations at a Mogollon Village, Western New Mexico, 1939. *Fieldiana: Anthropology* 32(1):1-97.

1941 Review of *Kinishba: a Prehistoric Pueblo of the Great Pueblo Period* by Byron Cummings. *American Anthropologist* 43(4):653-654.

1943 The SU Site: Excavations at a Mogollon Village, Western New Mexico, Second Season, 1941. *Fieldiana: Anthropology* 32(2):99-271.

Martin, Paul S., William A. Longacre and James N. Hill
 1967 Chapters in the Prehistory of Eastern Arizona, III. *Fieldiana: Anthropology* 57(1):1-178.

Martin, Paul S., and John B. Rinaldo
 1947 The SU Site: Excavations at a Mogollon Village, Western New Mexico, Third Season, 1946. *Fieldiana: Anthropology* 32(3):273-382.

 1950 Sites of the Reserve Phase, Pine Lawn Valley, Western New Mexico. *Fieldiana: Anthropology* 38(3):403-577.

 1960 Table Rock Pueblo, Arizona. *Fieldiana: Anthropology* 51(2):128-298.

Martin, Paul S., John B. Rinaldo, and Ernst Antevs
 1949 Cochise and Mogollon Sites: Pine Lawn Valley, Western New Mexico. *Fieldiana: Anthropology* 38(1):1-234.

Martin, Paul S., John B. Rinaldo and William A. Longacre
 1961 Mineral Creek Site and Hooper Ranch Pueblo, Eastern Arizona. *Fieldiana: Anthropology* 52:1-181.

Martin, Paul S., George I. Quimby and Donald Collier
 1947 *Indians Before Columbus*. University of Chicago Press, Chicago.

Martin, Paul S. and Elizabeth S. Willis
 1940 *Anasazi Painted Pottery in Field Museum of Natural History*. Anthropology Memoirs Vol. 5. Field Museum of Natural History, Chicago.

Mauer, Michael David
 1970 Cibecue Polychrome, A Fourteenth Century Ceramic Type from East-Central Arizona. Unpublished Master's thesis, Department of Anthropology, University of Arizona, Tucson.

McClelland, John A.
 2003 Refining the Resolution of Biological Distance Studies Based on the Analysis of Dental Morphology: Detecting Subpopulations at Grasshopper Pueblo. Ph.D. dissertation, Department of Anthropology, University of Arizona, Tucson.

McGuire, Randall H.
 1977 *The Copper Canyon-McGuireville Project: Archaeological Investigations in the Middle Verde Valley, Arizona*. Contribution to Highway Salvage Archaeology in Arizona No. 45. Arizona State Museum, University of Arizona, Tucson.

McGuire, Thomas R.
 1980 *Mixed Bloods, Apaches, and Cattle Barons: Documents for a History of the Livestock Economy on the White Mountain Reservation, Arizona*. Arizona State Museum, Archaeological Series No. 142. Tucson.

McKenna, Jeanette A., and Glen E. Rice
 1980 An Archaeological Survey of the Whiteriver Wastewater Treatment Facility, Whiteriver, Arizona. Manuscript on file, Office of Cultural Resource Management, Arizona State University, Tempe.

Miksa, Elizabeth J., Sergio F. Castro-Reino, and Carlos P. Lavayen
 2003 An Actualistic Sand Petrofacies Model for the San Pedro Valley, Arizona, with Application to Classic Period Ceramics. Ms. on file, Center for Desert Archaeology, Tucson.

Mills, Barbara J.
   1998   Migration and Pueblo IV Community Reorganization in the Silver Creek Area, East-Central Arizona. In *Migration and Reorganization: The Pueblo IV Period in the American Southwest*, edited by Katherine A. Spielman, pp. 65-80. Anthropological Research Papers No. 51, Arizona State University, Tempe.

   1999a   Ceramics and the Social Contexts of Food Consumption in the Northern Southwest. In *Pottery and People: A Dynamic Interaction*, edited by James M. Skibo and Gary M. Feinman, pp. 99-114. University of Utah Press, Salt Lake City.

   1999b   The Reorganization of Silver Creek Communities from the 11th to 14th Centuries. In *Living on the Edge of the Rim: Excavations and Analysis of the Silver Creek Archaeological Research Project 1993-1998*, edited by Barbara J. Mills, Sarah A. Herr, and Scott Van Keuren, pp. 505-511. Archaeological Series No. 192. Arizona State Museum, Tucson.

   1999c   Ceramic Ware and Type Systematics. In *Living on the Edge of the Rim: Excavations and Analysis of the Silver Creek Archaeological Research Project 1993-1998*, edited by Barbara J. Mills, Sarah A. Herr, and Scott Van Keuren, pp. 243-268. Archaeological Series No. 192. Arizona State Museum, Tucson.

   2000   The Archaeological Field School in the 1990s: Collaboration in Research and Training. In *Working Together: Native Americans and Archaeologists*, edited by Kurt E. Dongoske, Mark Aldenderfer, and Karen Doehner, pp. 121-128. Society for American Archaeology, Washington, D.C.

   2005   Curricular Matters: The Impact of Archaeological Field Schools on Southwest Archaeology. In *Southwest Archaeology in the Twentieth Century*, edited by Linda S. Cordell and Don D. Fowler, pp. 60-80. University of Utah Press, Salt Lake City.

   2007   Performing the Feast: Visual Display and Suprahousehold Commensalism in the Puebloan Southwest. *American Antiquity* 72(2):210-239.

   2011   Themes and Models for Understanding Migration in the Southwest. In *Movement, Connectivity, and Landscape Change in the Ancient Southwest*, edited by Margaret C. Nelson and Colleen Strawhacker, pp. 345-359. University Press of Colorado, Boulder.

Mills, Barbara J., Mark Altaha, John R. Welch, and T. J. Ferguson
   2008   Field Schools Without Trowels: Teaching Archaeological Ethics and Heritage Preservation in a Collaborative Context. In *Collaborating at the Trowel's Edge: Teaching and Learning in Indigenous Archaeology*, edited by Stephen W. Silliman, pp. 25-49. University of Arizona Press, Tucson.

Mills, Barbara J., and Jeffrey Clark
   2009   "Southwest Social Networks in Late Prehistory." Archaeology Southwest, Tucson. http://www.archaeologysouthwest.org/what-we-do/investigations/salado/networks/, accessed November 4, 2012.

Mills, Barbara J., and Sarah A. Herr
   1999   Chronology of the Mogollon Rim Region. In *Living on the Edge of the Rim: Excavations and Analysis of the Silver Creek Archaeological Research Project 1993-1998*, edited by Barbara J. Mills, Sarah A. Herr, and Scott Van Keuren, pp. 269-293. Arizona State Museum Archaeological Series No. 192. Arizona State Museum, University of Arizona, Tucson.

Mills, Barbara J., Sarah A. Herr, Eric J. Kaldahl, Joanne M. Newcomb, Charles R. Riggs, and Ruth Van Dyke
   1999   Excavations at Pottery Hill. In *Living on the Edge of the Rim: Excavations and Analysis of the Silver Creek Archaeological Research Project 1993-1998*, edited by B. J. Mills, S. A. Herr, and S. Van Keuren, pp. 117-148. Archaeological Series No. 192, Vol. 1. Arizona State Museum, University of Arizona, Tucson.

Mills, Barbara J., Sarah A. Herr, and Scott Van Keuren (editors)
　1999　*Living on the Edge of the Rim: Excavations and Analysis of the Silver Creek Archaeological Research Project 1993-1998.* Arizona State Museum Archaeological Series No. 192. Arizona State Museum, University of Arizona, Tucson.

Mills, Barbara J., Sarah A. Herr, Susan L. Stinson, and Daniela Triadan
　1999　Ceramic Production and Distribution in the Silver Creek Area. In *Living on the Edge of the Rim: Excavations and Analysis of the Silver Creek Archaeological Research Project, 1993-1998*, edited by B. J. Mills, S. A. Herr, and S. Van Keuren, pp. 295-324. Arizona State Museum Archaeological Series No. 192. University of Arizona, Tucson.

Mills, Barbara J., Scott Van Keuren, Susan L. Stinson, William M. Graves, III, Eric J. Kaldahl, and Joanne M. Newcomb
　1999　Excavations at Bailey Ruin. In *Living on the Edge of the Rim: Excavations and Analysis of the Silver Creek Archaeological Research Project 1993-1998*, edited by B. J. Mills, S. A. Herr, and S. Van Keuren, pp. 149-242. Archaeological Series No. 192, Vol. 1. Arizona State Museum, University of Arizona, Tucson.

Mills, Jack P., and Vera M. Mills
　1969　*The Kuykendall Site: A Prehistoric Salado Village in Southeastern Arizona.* Special Report No. 6. El Paso Archaeological Society, El Paso.

　1972　The Dinwiddie Site: A Prehistoric Salado Ruin on Duck Creek, Western New Mexico. *The Artifact* 10(2):i-50. El Paso Archaeological Society, Inc., El Paso, Texas.

Mindeleff, Cosmos
　1900　*Localization of Tusayan Clans.* 19th Annual Report of the Bureau of American Ethnology for the Years 1897-1898, Pt. 2, pp. 635-653. Washington, D.C.

Mindeleff, Victor
　1891　A Study of Pueblo Architecture: Tusayan and Cibola. In *Eighth Annual Report of the Bureau of American Ethnology 1886-1887*, pp. 13-228. Government Printing Office, Washington, D.C.

Mitchell, Douglas R., Penny Dufoe Minturn, Deirde J. Hungerford, and Michael S. Foster
　1994　The Pueblo Grande Burials: A Descriptive Summary. In *Feature Descriptions, Chronology, and Site Structure*, edited by Douglas R. Mitchell, pp. 107-156. The Pueblo Grande Project, vol. 2. Publications in Archaeology No. 20. Soil Systems, Phoenix.

Montgomery, Barbara Klie
　1992　Understanding the Formation of the Archaeological Record: Ceramic Variability at Chodistaas Pueblo, Arizona. PhD Dissertation, Department of Anthropology, University of Arizona, Tucson. Proquest, Ann Arbor.

　1993　Ceramic Analysis as a Tool for Discovering Processes of Pueblo Abandonment. In *Abandonment of Settlements and Regions: Ethnoarchaeological and Archaeological Approaches*, edited by Catherine M. Cameron and Steve A. Tomka, pp. 157-164. Cambridge University Press, Cambridge.

Montgomery, Barbara Klie, and J. Jefferson Reid
　1990　An Instance of Rapid Ceramic Change in the American Southwest. *American Antiquity* 55(1):88-97.

Moore, Mrs. Glenn E. (Marilyn), and Mrs. Joe Ben (Frances I.) Wheat
　1951　An Archeological Cache from the Hueco Basin, Texas. *Bulletin of the Texas Archeological and Paleontological Society* 22:144-163.

Moore, Richard T.
    1968   *Mineral Deposits of the Fort Apache Indian Reservation*. Bulletin No. 177. Arizona Bureau of Mines, Tucson.

Morris, Donald H.
    1970   Walnut Creek Village: A Ninth-Century Hohokam-Anasazi Settlement in the Mountains of Central Arizona. *American Antiquity* 35:49-61.

Morris, Elizabeth Ann
    1957   Stratigraphic Evidence for a Cultural Continuum at the Point of Pines Ruin. Unpublished MA Thesis, Department of Anthropology, University of Arizona, Tucson.

    1982   High Altitude Sites in the Mogollon Rim Area of Arizona and New Mexico. Ms. on file at Zuni Heritage and Historic Preservation Office, Zuni, New Mexico.

Morss, Noel
    1954   *Clay Figurines of the American Southwest with a Description of the New Pillings Find in Northeastern Utah and a Comparison with Certain Other North American Figurines*. Papers of the Peabody Museum of American Archaeology and Ethnology Vol. 49(1). Harvard University, Cambridge.

Motsinger, Thomas N.
    1993   Mortuary Features at La Ciudad de Los Hornos. In *In the Shadow of South Mountain: the Pre-Classic Hohokam of La Ciudad de Los Hornos, 1991-1992 Excavations*, edited by M. L. Chenhault, R. V. N. Ahlstrom, and Thomas N. Motsinger, pp. 215-227. Archaeological Report No. 93-30. SWCA Environmental Consultants, Tucson.

Mott, Dorothy Challis
    1936   Progress of the Excavation at Kinishba. *The Kiva* 2(1):1-4.

Munsell® Color
    1994   *Munsell Soil Color Charts*. Revised edition. Macbeth Division of Kollmorgen Instruments Corporation, New Windsor, New York.

Murry, Margaret W.
    1937   The Development of Form and Design in the Pottery at Kinishba. Unpublished Master's thesis, Department of Archaeology, University of Arizona, Tucson.

Nash, Stephen E.
    1999   *Time, Trees, and Prehistory: Tree-ring dating and the development of North American archaeology, 1914-1950*. University of Utah Press, Salt Lake City.

Neely, James A.
    1974   The Prehistoric Lunt and Stove Canyon Sites, Point of Pines, Arizona. Unpublished Ph.D. dissertation. Department of Anthropology, University of Arizona, Tucson.

Nelson, Ben A., and Steven A. LeBlanc
    1986   *Short-Term Sedentism in the American Southwest: The Mimbres Valley Salado*. Maxwell Museum of Anthropology and University of New Mexico Press, Albuquerque.

Nesbitt, Paul Homer
    1938   *Starkweather Ruin: A Mogollon-Pueblo Site in the Upper Gila Area of New Mexico; and Affiliative Aspects of the Mogollon Culture Publications in Anthropology 6*. Logan Museum, Beloit, Wisconsin.

Neuzil, Anna A.
    2008   *In the Aftermath of Migration: Renegotiating Ancient Identity in Southeastern Arizona.* Anthropological Papers of the University of Arizona No. 73. University of Arizona Press, Tucson.

Neuzil, Anna A., and Patrick D. Lyons
    2006   *An Analysis of Whole Vessels from the Mills Collection Curated at Eastern Arizona College, Thatcher, Arizona.* Technical Report No. 2005-001. Center for Desert Archaeology, Tucson.

Nicholas, George P., J.R. Welch, and Eldon C. Yellowhorn
    2007   Collaborative Encounters. In *Archaeological Practice: Engaging Descendant Communities*, edited by Chip Colwell-Chanthaphonh and T. J. Ferguson, pp. 273-298. AltaMira Press, Walnut Creek, California.

Nickens, Paul R.
    2006   Implementation of Site Protection Features at the National Historic Landmark Kinishba Ruins, Fort Apache Historic Park, Arizona. Report prepared for the White Mountain Apache Tribe, on file, White Mountain Apache Tribe Historic Preservation Office, Fort Apache, Arizona.

Olson, Alan P.
    1959   An Evaluation of the Phase Concept in Southwestern Archaeology: As Applied to the Eleventh and Twelfth Century Occupations at Point of Pines, East-Central Arizona. Unpublished Ph.D. dissertation, Department of Anthropology, University of Arizona, Tucson, Arizona.

    1960   The Dry Prong Site, East-Central Arizona. *American Antiquity* 26(2):185-204.

Oppelt, Norman T.
    2008   *List of Southwestern Pottery Types and Wares with Dates and References to Descriptions and Illustrations.* Norman T. Oppelt, Greeley, Colorado.

Owen, Charles L.
    1903   May 3 memo to George Dorsey. On file White Mountain Apache Tribe Historic Preservation Office, Fort Apache.

Parekh, Bhikhu
    1994   Some Reflections on the Hindu Diaspora. *New Community* 20(4):603-620

Parsons, Elsie Clews
    1923   The Origin Myth of Zuni. *Journal of American Folk-Lore* 36:135-162.

    1939   *Pueblo Indian Religion.* 2 vols. Bison Books edition, 1996. University of Nebraska Press, Lincoln.

Peabody Museum of Archaeology and Ethnology at Harvard University
    2009   Collections Online. Electronic document, http://140.247.102.177/col/default.cfm, accessed February 5, 2010.

Pilles, Peter J., Jr.
    1976   Sinagua and Salado Similarities as Seen from the Verde Valley. *The Kiva* 42:113-124.

Price, T. Douglas, Clark M. Johnson, Joseph A. Ezzo, Jonathan Ericson, and James H. Burton
    1994   Residential Mobility in the Prehistoric Southwest United States: A Preliminary Study using Strontium Isotope Analysis. *Journal of Archaeological Science* 21:315-330.

Pueblo Chieftain
    2004   Obituary for Margaret Whiting Murry (Shaeffer) Dowd, 16 October. Pueblo, Colorado.

Pueblo of Zuni
1995 Pueblo of Zuni Statement of Cultural Affiliation with Prehistoric and Historic Cultures, July 11, 1995. Zuni, NM: Pueblo of Zuni.

Rands, Robert L., and Ronald L. Bishop
1980 Resource Procurement Zones and Patterns of Ceramic Exchange in the Palenque Region, Mexico. In *Models and Methods in Regional Exchange*, edited by Robert E. Fry, pp. 19-46. Society for American Archaeology Papers No. 1. Society for American Archaeology, Washington D.C.

Reagan, Albert B.
1930 Archaeological Notes on the Fort Apache Region, Arizona. *Transactions of the Kansas Academy of Science* 33:111-132. Manhattan, Kansas.

Reed, Erik K.
1942 Special Report (Supplementary) on Kinishba, Arizona. On file, Kinishba NHL records, National Park Service, Santa Fe.

1946 The Distinctive Features and Distribution of San Juan Anasazi Culture. *Southwestern Journal of Anthropology* 2:295-305.

1948 The Western Pueblo Archaeological Complex. *El Palacio* 55(1):9-15.

Reid, J. Jefferson
1973 Growth and Response to Stress at Grasshopper Pueblo, Arizona. Ph.D. Dissertation, University of Arizona, Tucson. University Microfilms, Ann Arbor.

1978 Response to Stress at Grasshopper Pueblo, Arizona. In *Discovering Past Behavior: Experiments in the Archaeology of the American Southwest*, edited by Paul F. Grebinger, pp. 195 213. Gordon and Breach, London.

1989 A Grasshopper Perspective on the Mogollon of the Arizona Mountains. In *Dynamics of Southwest Prehistory*, edited by L S. Cordell and G. J. Gumerman, pp. 65-97. Smithsonian Institution Press, Washington.

2001 Late Mogollon. In *Encyclopedia of Prehistory, Volume 6: North America*, edited by Peter N. Peregrine and Melvin Ember, pp. 287-290. Klumer Academic/Plenum, New York.

Reid, J. Jefferson (editor)
1982 *Cholla Project Archaeology, Volume 3: The Q Ranch Region*. Archaeological Series No.161. Arizona State Museum, Cultural Resource Management Division, Tucson.

Reid, J. Jefferson, and Izumi Shimada
1982 Pueblo Growth at Grasshopper: Methods and Models. In *Multidisciplinary Research at Grasshopper Pueblo, Arizona*. Anthropological Papers of the University of Arizona No. 40, edited by William A. Longacre, Sally J. Holbrook, and Michael W. Graves, pp. 12 18. University of Arizona Press, Tucson.

Reid, J. Jefferson, H. David Tuggle and Barbara J. Klie
1982 Chapter 4: The Q-Ranch Sites. In *Cholla Project Archaeology, Volume 3: The Q-Ranch Region*, edited by J. Jefferson Reid, pp. 33-122. Arizona State Museum Cultural Resource Management Division Archaeological Series No. 161, Arizona State Museum, Tucson.

Reid, J. Jefferson, John R. Welch, Barbara K. Montgomery, and Maria Nieves Zedeño
1996 A Demographic Overview of the Late Pueblo III Period in the Mountains of East-Central Arizona. In *The Prehistoric Pueblo World, A.D. 1150 - 1350*, edited by Michael A. Adler, pp. 73 85. University of Arizona Press, Tucson.

Reid, J. Jefferson, and Stephanie M. Whittlesey
　1982　Households at Grasshopper Pueblo. *American Behavioral Scientist* 25:687 703.

　1989　Byron Cummings' Architectural Reconstruction of Kinishba: An Archival Analysis. Report prepared for the National Park Service, Western Regional Office, San Francisco.

　1997　*The Archaeology of Ancient Arizona*. University of Arizona Press, Tucson.

　1999　*Grasshopper Pueblo: A Story of Archaeology and Ancient Life*. University of Arizona Press, Tucson.

　2005　*Thirty Years into Yesterday: A History of Archaeology at Grasshopper Pueblo*. University of Arizona Press, Tucson.

　2010　*Prehistory, Personality, and Place: Emil W. Haury and the Mogollon Controversy*. University of Arizona Press, Tucson.

Reynolds, William
　1981　The Ethnoarchaeology of Pueblo Architecture. Unpublished doctoral dissertation, Department of Anthropology, Arizona State University, Tempe.

Rice, Prudence M.
　1987　Pottery Analysis: A Sourcebook. University of Chicago Press, Chicago.

Riggs, Charles R., Jr.
　1999　The Architecture of Grasshopper Pueblo: Dynamics of Form, Function, and Use of Space in a Prehistoric Community. Ph.D. dissertation, Department of Anthropology, University of Arizona, Tucson. ProQuest, Ann Arbor.

　2001　*The Architecture of Grasshopper Pueblo*. University of Utah Press, Salt Lake City.

　2005　Late Ancestral Pueblo or Mogollon Pueblo? An Architectural Perspective on Identity. *Kiva* 70:323-348.

　2007　Architecture and Identity at Grasshopper Pueblo, Arizona. *Journal of Anthropological Research* 63:489-513.

Rinaldo, John B.
　1952　Pottery. In *Mogollon Cultural Continuity and Change: The Stratigraphic Analysis of Tularosa and Cordova Caves*, by P. S. Martin, J. B. Rinaldo, E. Bluhm, H. C. Cutler, and R. Grange, Jr., pp. 51-101. *Fieldiana: Anthropology* Vol. 40.

Rinaldo, John B.
　1964　Notes on the Origin of Historic Zuni Culture. *The Kiva* 29:86-98.

Roberts, Frank H.H., Jr.
　1929　*Shabik'eshohee Village*. Bureau of American Ethnology, Bull. 92, Washington, D.C.

　1931　*The Ruins at Kiatuthianna*. Bureau of American Ethnology, Bull. 100, Washington, D.C.

　1932　*The Village of the Great Kivas on the Zuni Reservation*. Bureau of American Ethnology, Bull. III, Washington, D.C.

　1939　*Archaeological Remains in the Whitewater District, Eastern Arizona*. Bureau of American Ethnology Bull. 121, Washington, D.C.

Rodrigues, Teresa
   2008   Social Change and Skeletal Trauma in the Point of Pines Region (~AD 400-1450) of the American Southwest. Ph.D. dissertation, School of Human Evolution and Social Change, Arizona State University, Tempe. ProQuest, Ann Arbor.

Roos, Christopher Izaak
   2008   Fire, Climate, and Social-Ecological Systems in the Ancient Southwest: Alluvial Geoarchaeology and Applied Historical Ecology. Ph.D. dissertation, University of Arizona. University Microforms International, Ann Arbor, Michigan.

Sackett, James R.
   1990   Style and Ethnicity in Archaeology: The Case for Isochrestism. In *The Uses of Style in Archaeology*, edited by M.W. Conkey and C.A. Hastorf, pp. 32-43. Cambridge University Press, Cambridge, England.

Safran, William
   1991   Diasporas in Modern Societies: Myths of Homeland and Return. *Diaspora* 1(1):83-99.

   1997   Comparing Diasporas: A Review Essay. *Diaspora* 8(3):255-291.

   2004   Deconstructing and Comparing Diasporas. In *Diaspora, Identity and Religion: New Directions in Theory and Research*, edited by Waltraud Kokot, Kachig Tölölyan, and Carolin Alfonso, pp. 9-29. Routledge, London.

Sayre, Edward V.
   1975   Brookhaven Procedures for Statistical Analyses of Multivariate Archaeometric Data. Unpublisehd Brookhaven National Laboratory Report BNL-23128. Brookhaven National Laboratory, New York.

Schachner, Gregson
   2006   The Decline of Zuni Glaze Ware Production in the Tumultuous Fifteenth Century. In *The Social Life of Pots: Glaze Wares and Cultural Dynamics in the Southwest, A.D. 1250-1680*, edited by Judith A. Habicht-Mauche, Suzanne L. Eckert, and Deborah L. Huntley, pp. 124-141. University of Arizona Pres, Tucson.

Scheiber, Laura L., and Juson Bird Finley
   2011   Mobility as Resistance: Colonialism among Nomadic Hunter-Gatherers in the American West. In *Hunter-Gatherer Archaeology as Historical Process*, edited by Sassaman, Kenneth E., Donald H. Holly, Jr., pp. 176-183. University of Arizona Press, Tucson.

Schiffer, Michael B.
   1975   Behavioral Chain Analysis: Activities, Organization, and the Use of Space. In Chapters in the Prehistory of Eastern Arizona, IV, by Paul S. Martin, Ezra B. W. Zubrow, Daniel C. Bowman, David A. Gregory, John A. Hanson, Michael B. Schiffer, and David R. Wilcox, pp. 103-119. *Fieldiana: Anthropology*, Vol. 65. Field Museum of Natural History, Chicago.

   1976   *Behavioral Archaeology*. Academic Press, New York.

   1987   *Formation Processes of the Archaeological Record*. University of New Mexico Press, Albuquerque.

Schmidt, Erich F.
   1927   A Stratigraphic Study in the Gila-Salt Region, Arizona. *Proceedings of the National Academy of Sciences of the United States of America* 13(5):291-298.

   1928   *Time-Relations of Prehistoric Pottery Types in Southern Arizona*. Anthropological Papers of the American Museum of Natural History Vol. 30(5). American Museum of Natural History, New York.

Schrader, Robert F
    1983   *The Indian Arts and Crafts Board: An Aspect of New Deal Indian Policy*. University of New Mexico Press, Albuquerque.

Schroeder, Albert H.
    1953   The Problem of Hohokam, Sinagua and Salado Relations in Southern Arizona. *Plateau* 26(2):75-83.

    1957   The Hakataya Cultural Tradition. *American Antiquity* 23:176-178.

    1960   *The Hohokam, Sinagua, and Hakataya*. Archives in Archaeology No. 5. Society for American Archaeology, Menasha, and University of Wisconsin Press, Madison.

Second Southwestern Ceramic Seminar
    1959   *Second Southwestern Ceramic Seminar: White Mountain Red Ware and Shiwanna Red Ware*. Museum of Northern Arizona, Flagstaff.

Sellers, William D. and Richard H. Hill
    1974   *Arizona Climate: 1931-1972*. The University of Arizona Press, Tucson.

Shaeffer, James B.
    1949   The Area of the Great Kiva, Group I, Kinishba Ruins. Manuscript report on excavations, on file, Shaeffer papers, Arizona State Museum Archives, University of Arizona, Tucson.

    1951   Group VI, A Small House Unit at Kinishba Ruins. Manuscript report on excavations, on file, Shaeffer papers, Arizona State Museum Archives, University of Arizona, Tucson.

    1954   The Mogollon Complex: Its Cultural Role and Historical Development in the American Southwest. Unpublished PhD. dissertation, Columbia University, New York City.

    1960   *Salvage Archaeology in Oklahoma*, 2 volumes. Oklahoma Archaeological Salvage Project, Norman.

    1963   The Stuhr Museum of the Prairie Pioneer. *Plains Anthropologist* 8(21):207-209.

Shaeffer, Margaret M., and James B. Shaeffer
    1956   *Kinishba...A Classic Site of the Western Pueblos*. U.S. Department of the Interior, Bureau of Indian Affairs, Printing Department, Chilocco Indian Agricultural School, Oklahoma.

Sheffer, Gabriel
    1986   A New Field of Study: Modern Diasporas in International Politics. In *Modern Diasporas in International Politics*, edited by Gabriel Sheffer, pp. 1-15. Croom Helm, London.

Shepard, Anna O.
    1985   *Ceramics for the Archaeologist*. Reprinted. Braun-Brumfield, Ann Arbor. Originally published 1956, Carnegie Institution Publication No. 609. The Carnegie Institution, Washington, D.C.

Shipman, Jeffrey H.
    1982   *Biological Relationships among Prehistoric Western Pueblo Indian Groups based on Metric and Discrete Traits of the Skeleton*. Doctoral dissertation, Department of Anthropology, University of Arizona, Tucson.

Smiley, Terah L.
    1951   A Summary of Tree-Ring Dates from some Southwestern Archaeological Sites. *University of Arizona Bulletin* Vol. 22, Laboratory of Tree-Ring Research bulletin, No. 5. Tucson.

1952 *Four Late Prehistoric Kivas at Point of Pines, Arizona.* Social Science Bulletin, No. 21. University of Arizona Press, Tucson.

Smith, Watson
1971 *Painted Ceramics of the Western Mound at Awatovi.* Papers of the Peabody Museum of Archaeology and Ethnology Volume 38. Harvard University, Cambridge.

Smith, Watson, Richard B. Woodbury, and Nathalie F. S. Woodbury
1966 *The Excavation of Hawikuh by Frederick Webb Hodge: Report of the Hendricks-Hodge Expedition, 1917-1923.* Contributions from the Museum of the American Indian Heye Foundation Vol. 20. Museum of the American Indian, New York.

Smithsonian Institution
2010 National Museum of Natural History Department of Anthropology, Detailed Search of the Anthropology Collections. Electronic document, http://collections.nmnh.si.edu/anth/pages/nmnh/anth/DtlQuery.php, accessed October 30, 2009.

Sökefeld, Martin
2002 Alevi Dedes in the German Diaspora: The Transformation of a Religious Institution. *Zeitschrift für Ethnologie* 127(2):163-186.

2004 Religion of Culture?: Concepts of Identity in the Alevi Diaspora. In *Diaspora, Identity and Religion: New Directions in Theory and Research,* edited by Waltraud Kokot, Kachig Tölölyan, and Carolin Alfonso, pp. 133-155. Routledge, London.

Spielmann, Katherine A.
1998 Ritual Influences on the Development of Rio Grande Glaze A Ceramics. In *Migration and Reorganization: The Pueblo IV Period in the American Southwest,* edited by Katherine A. Spielmann, pp. 253-261. Arizona State University Anthropological Research Papers No. 51. Arizona State University, Tempe.

2004 Communal Feasting, Ceramics, and Exchange. In *Identity, Feasting, and the Archaeology of the Greater Southwest,* edited by Barbara J. Mills, pp. 210-232. University Press of Colorado, Boulder.

Spielmann, Katherine A. (editor)
1998 *Migration and Reorganization: The Pueblo IV period in the American Southwest.* Anthropological Research Paper 51. Arizona State University, Tempe.

Spier, Leslie
1919 Ruins in the White Mountains, Arizona. *Anthropological Papers of the American Museum of Natural History* Vol. 18, Part 5. New York.

Stafford, C. Russell, and Glen E. Rice (editors)
1980 *Studies in the Prehistory of the Forestdale Region, Arizona.* Anthropological Field Studies Number 1, Office of Cultural Resources Management, Arizona State University, Tempe.

Stanislawski, Michael B.
1963 *Wupatki Pueblo: A Study in Cultural Fusion and Change in Sinagua and Hopi Prehistory.* PhD dissertation, Department of Anthropology, University of Arizona, Tucson. ProQuest, Ann Arbor.

Stark Miriam T., Mark D. Elson, and Jeffery J. Clark
1995 The Causes and Consequences of Migration in the 13th century Tonto Basin. *Journal of Anthropological Archaeology* 14:212-246.

Steadman, Sharon
    1996   Recent Research in the Archaeology of Architecture: Beyond the Foundations. *Journal of Anthropological Research* 4:51-93.

Steen, Charlie R.
    1965   Excavations in Compound A, Casa Grande National Monument, 1963. *The Kiva* 31(2):59-82.

Stevenson, Matilda C.
    1904   *The Zuni Indians: Their Mythology, Esoteric Fraternities, and Ceremonies*. Twenty-Third Annual Report of the Bureau of American Ethnology, 1901-1902, pp. 13-604. Washington, D.C.

Stinson, Susan Lynne
    1996   Roosevelt Red Ware and the Organization of Ceramic Production in the Silver Creek Drainage. Master's thesis, Department of Anthropology, University of Arizona. Proquest, Ann Arbor.

Stone, Tammy
    2000   Prehistoric Community Integration in the Point of Pines Region of Arizona. *Journal of Field Archaeology* 27(2):197-208.

    2002   Kiva Diversity in the Point of Pines Region of Arizona. *Kiva* 67(4):385-411.

    2003   Social Identity and Ethnic Interaction in the Western Pueblos of the American Southwest. *Journal of Archaeological Method and Theory* 10(1):31-67.

    2005   Late Period Pithouses in the Point of Pines Region of Arizona. *Kiva* 70(3):273-292.

Swartz, Deborah L.
    1992   The Deer Creek Site: AZ O:15:52 (ASM). In *Introduction and Site Descriptions*, by Mark Elson and Douglas B. Craig, pp. 93-164. The Rye Creek Project: Archaeology in the Upper Tonto Basin. Anthropological Papers No. 11, Vol. 1. Center for Desert Archaeology, Tucson.

Tanner, Clara Lee
    1976   *Prehistoric Southwestern Craft Arts*. University of Arizona Press, Tucson.

Taylor, Walter W.
    1972   Old Wine and New Skins: A Contemporary Parable. In *Contemporary Archaeology*, edited by M. Leone, pp. 28-33. Southern Illinois University Press, Carbondale.

Thompson, Raymond H.
    2005   Anthropology at the University of Arizona, 1893-2005. *Journal of the Southwest* 47:327-374.
    Thompson, Raymond H., and William A. Longacre

    1966   The University of Arizona Archaeological Field School at Grasshopper, East-Central Arizona. *The Kiva* 31(4):255-275

Tölölyan, Kachig
    1996   Rethinking Diaspora(s): Stateless Power in the Transnational Moment. *Diaspora* 5(1):3-36.

Triadan, Daniela
    1989   Defining Local Ceramic Production at Grasshopper Pueblo, Arizona. Unpublished Master's thesis, Freie Universität, Berlin, Germany.

    1994   White Mountain Redware: Expensive Trade Goods or Local Commodity? A Study of the Production,

Distribution and Function of White Mountain Redware During the 14th Century in the Grasshopper Region, East-central Arizona. Ph.D. dissertation, Freie Universität Berlin, Germany. Proquest, Ann Arbor.

1997 *Ceramic Commodities and Common Containers: Production and Distribution of White Mountain Red Ware in the Grasshopper Region, Arizona.* Anthropological Papers of the University of Arizona No. 61. University of Arizona Press, Tucson.

1998 Socio-Demographic Implications of Pueblo IV Ceramic Production and Circulation: Sourcing White Mountain Redware from the Grasshopper Region. In *Migration and Reorganization: The Pueblo IV Period in the American Southwest*, edited by Katherine A. Spielman, pp. 233-249. Anthropological Research Papers 51, Arizona State University, Tempe.

2006 Dancing Gods: Ritual, Performance, and Political Organization in the Prehistoric Southwest. In *Archaeology of Performance: Theaters of Power, Community, and Politics*, edited by T. Inomata and L. S. Coben, pp. 159-186. Altamira Press, Landham, Maryland.

Triadan, Daniela, Barbara J. Mills, and Andrew I. Duff
2002 From Compositional to Anthropological: Fourteenth-Century Red Ware Circulation and Its Implications for Pueblo Reorganization. In *Ceramic Production and Circulation in the Greater Southwest: Source Determination by INAA and Complementary Mineralogical Investigations*, edited by Donna M. Glowacki and Hector Neff, pp. 85-97. Monograph 44, The Cotsen Institute of Archaeology, University of California, Los Angeles.

Triadan, Daniela, and María Nieves Zedeño
2004 The Political Geography and Territoriality of 14th-Century Settlements in the Mogollon Highlands of East-Central Arizona. In *The Protohistoric Pueblo World, A.D. 1275-1600*, edited by E. Charles Adams and Andrew I. Duff, pp. 95-107. University of Arizona Press, Tucson.

Tuggle, H. David
1970 Prehistoric Community Relationships in East Central Arizona. Ph.D. dissertation, Department of Anthropology, University of Arizona, Tucson.

Tuggle, H. David, and J. Jefferson Reid
2001 Conflict and Defense in the Grasshopper Region of East-Central Arizona. In *Deadly Landscapes: Case Studies in Prehistoric Southwestern Warfare*, edited by G. E. Rice and S. A. LeBlanc, pp. 85-107. University of Utah Press, Salt Lake City.

Tuggle, H. David, J. Jefferson Reid, and Robert C. Cole
1984 Fourteenth Century Mogollon Agriculture in the Grasshopper Region of Arizona. In *Prehistoric Agricultural Strategies in the Southwest*, edited by Suzanne K. Fish and Paul R. Fish, pp. 101-110. University of Utah Press, Salt Lake City.

Trouillot, Michel-Rolph
1995 *Silencing the Past: Power and the Production of History.* Beacon Press, Boston.

U.S. Department of Agriculture
1941 *Climate and Man: Yearbook of Agriculture 1941.* United States Government Printing Office, Washington, D.C.

Vanderpot, Rein, Eric Eugene Klucas, and Richard Ciolek-Torrello (editors)
1999 *From the Desert to the Mountains. Archaeology of the Transition Zone. The State Route 87-Sycamore Creek Project, Volume 1: Prehistoric Sites.* Technical Series No. 73. Statistical Research, Tucson.

Vanderpot, Rein, Steven D. Shelly, and Su Benaron
1994 AZ U:8:225/1580 Riser Site. In *Prehistoric Rural Settlements in the Tonto Basin, edited by Richard*

Ciolek-Torrello, Steven D. Shelley, and Su Benaron, pp. 292-344. *The Roosevelt Rural Sites Study, Vol. 2, pt. 1*. Technical Series No. 28. Statistical Research, Tucson.

van der Veer, Peter, and Steven Vertovec
    1991   Brahmanism Abroad: On Caribbean Hinduism as an Ethnic Religion. *Ethnology* 30(2):149-166.

Van Keuren, Scott
    1994   Design Structure Variation in Cibola White Ware Vessels from Grasshopper and Chodistaas Pueblos, Arizona. Unpublished Master's thesis, Department of Anthropology, University of Arizona, Tucson.

    1999   *Ceramic Design Structure and the Organization of Cibola White Ware Production in the Grasshopper Region, Arizona*. Arizona State Museum Archaeological Series No. 191. Arizona State Museum, University of Arizona, Tucson.

    2001   Ceramic Style and the Reorganization of Fourteenth Century Pueblo Communities in East-Central Arizona. Ph.D. dissertation, Department of Anthropology, University of Arizona, Tucson. Proquest, Ann Arbor.

    2004   Crafting Feasts in the American Southwest. In *Identity, Feasting, and the Archaeology of the Greater Southwest*, edited by Barbara J. Mills, pp. 192-209. University Press of Colorado, Boulder.

    2006   Decorating Glaze-Painted Pottery in East-Central Arizona. In *The Social Life of Pots*, edited by Judith A, Habicht-Mauche and Suzanne L. Eckert, and Deborah L. Huntley, pp. 60-85. University of Arizona Press, Tucson.

Varien, Mark D., and Barbara J. Mills
    1997   Accumulations Research: Problems and Prospects for Estimating Site Occupation Span. *Journal of Archaeological Method and Theory* 4:141-191.

Vasquez, Miguel, and Leigh Jenkins
    1994   Reciprocity and Sustainability: Terrace Restoration on Third Mesa. *Practicing Anthropology* 16(2):14-17.

Vertovec, Steven
    1991   Inventing Religious Tradition: Yagnas and Hindu Renewal in Trinidad. In *Religion, Tradition, and Renewal*, edited by Armin W. Geertz and Jeppe Sinding Jensen, pp. 79-97. Aarhus University Press, Aarhus.

    1994   "Official" and "Popular" Hinduism in Diaspora: Historical and Contemporary Trends in Surinam, Trinidad and Guyana. *Contributions to Indian Sociology* 28(1):123-147.

Vitelli, Karen D., and Chip Colwell-Chanthaphonh
    2006   *Archaeological Ethics*. AltaMira Press, Walnut Creek, California.

Vogt, Evon Z., and Richard M. Leventhal, Editors
    1983   *Prehistoric Settlement Patterns: Essays in Honor of Gordon R. Willey*. University of New Mexico Press, Albuquerque.

Voss, Barbara L.
    2012   Curation as Research. A Case Study in Orphaned and Underreported Archaeological Collections. *Archaeological Dialogues* 19(2):145-169.

Wallace, Roberts M.
    1957   Petrographic Analysis of Pottery from University Indian Ruin. In *Excavations, 1940, at the University Indian Ruin, Tucson, Arizona*, by J. D. Hayden, pp. 209-219. Technical Series No. 5. Southwestern Monuments Association, Globe, Arizona.

Washburn, Dorothy K.
   1995   *Living In Balance: The Universe of the Hopi, Zuni, Navajo, and Apache.* Philadelphia: The University Museum University of Pennsylvania.

Wasley, William W.
   1952   The Late Pueblo Occupation at Point of Pines, East-Central Arizona. Unpublished Master's thesis, Department of Anthropology, University of Arizona, Tucson.

   1962   A Ceremonial Cave on Bonita Creek, Arizona. *American Antiquity* 27:380-394.

Wasley, William W., and David E. Doyel
   1980   Classic Period Hohokam. *The Kiva* 45(4):337-352.

Watt, Eva Tulene, with Keith H. Basso
   2004   *Don't Let the Sun Step Over You.* University of Arizona Press, Tucson.

Weaver, Donald E., Jr.
   1972   A Cultural-Ecological Model for the Classic Hohokam Period in the Lower Salt River Valley, Arizona. *The Kiva* 38(1):43-52.

   1973   Excavations at Pueblo del Monte and the Classic Period Hohokam Problem. *The Kiva* 39(1):75-87.

   1976   Salado Influences in the Lower Salt River Valley. *The Kiva* 42(1):17-26.

Welch, John R.
   1996   The Archaeological Measures and Social Implications of Agricultural Commitment. Ph.D. dissertation, University of Arizona, Tucson. University Microfilms, Ann Arbor.

   1997   White Eyes' Lies and the Battle for Dzil Nchaa Si An. *American Indian Quarterly* 27(1):75-109

   2000   The White Mountain Apache Tribe Heritage Program: Origins, Operations, and Challenges. In *Working Together: Native Americans and Archaeologists*, edited by Kurt E. Dongoske, Mark Aldenderfer, and Karen Doehner, pp. 67-83. Society for American Archaeology, Washington, DC.

   2001   Ancient Masonry Fortresses of the Upper Salt River. In *The Archaeology of Ancient Tactical Sites*, edited by John R. Welch and Todd Bostwick, pp. 77-96. The Arizona Archaeologist No. 32, Arizona Archaeological Society, Phoenix

   2007a   'A Monument to Native Civilization': Byron Cummings' Still-Unfolding Vision for Kinishba Ruins. *Journal of the Southwest* 49(1):1-94

   2007b   The White Mountain Apache Photographs of Chuck Abbott and Esther Henderson. *Journal of the Southwest* 49(1):95-116

   2007c   Kinishba Bibliography. *Journal of the Southwest* 49(1):117-127.

   2008   Places, Displacements, Histories and Memories at a Frontier Icon in Indian Country. In *Monuments, Landscapes, and Cultural Memory*, edited by Patricia E. Rubertone, pp. 101-134. World Archaeological Congress and Left Coast Press, Walnut Creek, California.

   2009   Reconstructing the Ndee (Western Apache) Homeland. In *The Archaeology of Meaningful Places*, edited by Brenda Bowser and M. Nieves Zedeño, pp. 149-162. University of Utah Press, Salt Lake City

   2010   National Historic Landmark Nomination for Fort Apache and Theodore Roosevelt School. Historic Sites Review Board, National Park Service, Washington, D.C.

Welch, John R., cont'd
   2012   Effects of Fire on Intangible Cultural Resources: Moving Toward a Landscape Approach. In *Wildland Fire in Ecosystems: Effects of Fire on Cultural Resources and Archaeology*, edited by Ryan, K.C., Jones, A.T., and Koerner, C. H., pp. 157-170, RMRS-GTR-42-vol. 3. U.S. Department of Agriculture, Forest Service, Rocky Mountain Research Station, Ft. Collins, CO.

Welch, John R., Mark K. Altaha, Karl A. Hoerig and Ramon Riley
   2009   Best Cultural Heritage Stewardship Practices by and for the White Mountain Apache Tribe. *Conservation and Management of Archaeological Sites* 11(2):148-160

Welch, John R., and Todd Bostwick (editors)
   2001   *The Archaeology of Ancient Tactical Sites*. The Arizona Archaeologist No. 32, Arizona Archaeological Society, Phoenix.

Welch, John R., and Robert C. Brauchli
   2010   "Subject to the Right of the Secretary of the Interior:" The White Mountain Apache Reclamation of the Fort Apache and Theodore Roosevelt School Historic District. *Wicazo Sa Review* 25(1):47-73.

Welch, J.R., and T. J. Ferguson
   2005   *Cultural Affiliation Assessment of White Mountain Apache Tribal Lands (Fort Apache Indian Reservation)*. Historic Preservation Office, Heritage Program, White Mountain Apache Tribe, Fort Apache.

   2007   Putting Patria into Repatriation: Cultural Affiliations of White Mountain Apache Tribe Lands. *Journal of Social Archaeology* 7:171-198.

Welch, John R., Dana Lepofsky, Megan Caldwell, Georgia Combes, and Craig Rust
   2011   Treasure Bearers: Personal Foundations for Effective Leadership in Northern Coast Salish Heritage Stewardship. *Heritage and Society* 4(1):83-114.

Welch, John R., and Ramon Riley
   2001   Reclaiming Land and Spirit in the Western Apache Homeland. *American Indian Quarterly* 25(1):5-12.

Wellmeier, Nancy J.
   1998   *Ritual, Identity, and the Mayan Diaspora*. Garland, New York.

Wendorf, Fred
   1950   *A Report on the Excavation of a Small Ruin Near Point of Pines, East Central Arizona*. University of Arizona Bulletin Vol. 21(3). Social Science Bulletin No. 19. University of Arizona Press, Tucson.

Wheat, Jo Ben
   1954   *Crooked Ridge Village* (Arizona W:10:15). Social Science Bulletin 24. Bulletin 21(3). University of Arizona, Tucson.

   1955   *Mogollon Culture Prior to A.D. 1000*. Memoir No. 10, Society for American Archaeology, Menasha, and Memoir No. 82, American Anthropological Association, Menasha.1955.

White, Diane E., and James Burton
   1992   Pinto Polychrome: A Clue to the Origin of the Salado Polychromes. In *Proceedings of the Second Salado Conference, Globe, AZ 1992*, edited by Richard C. Lange and Stephen Germick, pp. 216-222. Occasional Paper. Arizona Archaeological Society, Phoenix.

Whittlesey, Stephanie M.
   1974   Identification of Imported Ceramics Through Functional Analysis of Attributes. *Kiva* 40(1-2):101-112.

Whittlesey, Stephanie, M., Richard Ciolek-Torrello, and J. Jefferson Reid
  2000 Salado: The View from the Arizona Mountains. In *Salado*, edited by Jeffrey S. Dean, pp. 241-261. Amerind Foundation Publication, University of New Mexico Press, Albuquerque.

Whittlesey, Stephanie M., and J. Jefferson Reid
  2001 Mortuary Ritual and Organizational Inferences at Grasshopper Pueblo, Arizona. In *Ancient Burial Practices in the American Southwest: Archaeology, Physical Anthropology, and Native American Perspectives*, edited by J. L. Brunson-Hadley and D. R. Mitchell, pp. 68-96. University of New Mexico Press, Albuquerque.

Whittlesey, Stephanie M., J. Jefferson Reid, and Stephen H. Lekson
  2010 Introduction. *Kiva* 76:123-140

Wilcox, David R.
  1979 The Hohokam Regional System. In *An Archaeological Test of Sites in the Gila Butte-Santan Region, South-Central Arizona*, edited by Glen E. Rice, David Wilcox, Kevin Rafferty, and James Schoenwetter, pp. 77-116. Technical Paper No. 3. Anthropological Research Papers No. 18. Office of Cultural Resource Management, Department of Anthropology, Arizona State University, Tempe.

  2005 Perry Mesa and its World. *Plateau: The Land and People of the Colorado Plateau* 2(1):24-35.

Wilcox, David R., and James Holmlund
  2007 *The Archaeology of Perry Mesa and its World*. Bilby Research Center Occasional Papers No. 3. Northern Arizona University, Flagstaff.

Wilcox, David R., Thomas R. McGuire, and Charles Sternberg
  1981 *Snaketown Revisited: A Partial Cultural Resource Survey, Analysis of Site Structure and an Ethnohistoric Study of the Proposed Hohokam-Pima National Monument*. Archaeological Series No. 155. Cultural Resources Management Division, Arizona State Museum, University of Arizona, Tucson.

Wilcox, David R., Gerald Robertson Jr., and J. Scott Wood
  2001a Antecedents to Perry Mesa: Early Pueblo III Defensive Refuge Systems in West-Central Arizona. In *Deadly Landscapes: Case Studies in Prehistoric Southwestern Warfare*, edited by Glen Rice and Steven LeBlanc, pp. 109-140. University of Utah Press, Salt Lake City.

  2001b Organized for War: The Perry Mesa Settlement System and Its Central Arizona Neighbors. In *Deadly Landscapes: Case Studies in Prehistoric Southwestern Warfare*, edited by Glen E. Rice and Steven LeBlanc, pp. 141-194. University of Utah Press, Salt Lake City.

Wilk Richard R. and William L. Rathje
  1982 Household Archaeology. *American Behavioral Scientist* 25:617-639.

Wilson, C. Dean
  1998 Ormand Ceramic Analysis: Part I. Methodology and Categories. In *The Ormand Village: Final Report on the 1965-1966 Excavation*, by Laurel T. Wallace, pp. 195-251. Archaeology Notes No. 229. Office of Archaeological Studies, Museum of New Mexico, Santa Fe.

Woodbury, Richard B.
  1961 *Prehistoric Agriculture at Point of Pines, Arizona*. Memoirs of the Society for American Archaeology No. 17, University of Utah Press

Woodbury, Richard B., and Nathalie F. S. Woodbury
  1966 Decorated Pottery of the Zuni Area. In The *Excavation of Hawikuh by Frederick Webb Hodge: Report of the Hendricks-Hodge Expedition, 1917-1923*, by Watson Smith, Richard B. Woodbury, and Nathalie F.

S. Woodbury, pp. 302-336. Contributions from the Museum of the American Indian Heye Foundation Vol. 20. Museum of the American Indian, New York.

Woodson, M. Kyle
   1995   The Goat Hill Site: A Western Anasazi Pueblo in the Safford Valley of Southeastern Arizona. Unpublished Master's thesis, Department of Anthropology, University of Texas, Austin.

   1999   Migrations in Late Anasazi Prehistory: The Evidence from the Goat Hill Site. Kiva 65(1):63-84.

Young, Jon Nathan
   1967   The Salado Culture in Southwestern Prehistory. Unpublished Ph.D. dissertation, Department of Anthropology, University of Arizona, Tucson.

Zedeño, María Nieves
   1991   Refining Inferences of Ceramic Circulation: A Stylistic, Technological, and Compositional Analysis of Whole Vessels from Chodistaas, Arizona. Unpublished Ph.D. dissertation, Southern Methodist University, Dallas.

   1992   Roosevelt Black-on-white Revisited: The Grasshopper Perspective. In *Proceedings of the Second Salado Conference*, edited by Richard C. Lange and Stephen Germick, pp. 206-211. Arizona Archaeological Society, Phoenix.

   1994   *Sourcing Prehistoric Ceramics at Chodistaas Pueblo, Arizona: The Circulation of People and Pots in the Grasshopper Region.* Anthropological Papers of the University of Arizona No. 58. University of Arizona Press, Tucson.

   2002   Artifact Design, Composition, and Context: Updating the Analysis of Ceramic Circulation at Point of Pines, Arizona. In *Ceramic Production and Circulation in the Greater Southwest: Source Determination by INAA and Complementary Mineralogical Investigations*, edited by Donna M. Glowacki and Hector Neff, pp. 74-84. Monograph 44, The Cotsen Institute of Archaeology, University of California, Los Angeles.

Zedeño, M. Nieves, and Daniela Triadan
   2000   Ceramic Evidence for Community Reorganization and Change in East-central Arizona. *Kiva* 65(3):215-233.

Zimmerman, Larry J
   2006   Liberating Archaeology, Liberation Archaeologies, and WAC. *Archaeologies* 2:85-95.

www.ingramcontent.com/pod-product-compliance
Lightning Source LLC
Chambersburg PA
CBHW081328230426
43667CB00018B/2862